Proceedings

23rd Annual Conference on Local Computer Networks

LCN '98

The 23rd Annual Conference on Local Computer Networks

The Conference on the Leading Edge of Practical Computer Networking

Proceedings

23rd Annual Conference on Local Computer Networks

LCN '98

October 11-14, 1998
Lowell, Massachusetts

Sponsored by
IEEE Computer Society Technical Committee on Computer Communications

IEEE COMPUTER SOCIETY

Los Alamitos, California

Washington • Brussels • Tokyo

IEEE Computer Society Order Number PR08810
ISBN 0-8186-8810-6
ISBN 0-8186-8818-1 (microfiche)
ISSN 0742-1303
IEEE Order Plan Catalog Number 98TB100260

Additional copies may be ordered from:

IEEE Computer Society
Customer Service Center
10662 Los Vaqueros Circle
P.O. Box 3014
Los Alamitos, CA 90720-1314
Tel: + 1-714-821-8380
Fax: + 1-714-821-4641
E-mail: cs.books@computer.org

IEEE Service Center
445 Hoes Lane
P.O. Box 1331
Piscataway, NJ 08855-1331
Tel: + 1-732-981-1393
Fax: + 1-732-981-9667
mis.custserv@computer.org

IEEE Computer Society
Asia/Pacific Office
Watanabe Building,
1-4-2 Minami-Aoyama
Minato-ku, Tokyo 107-0062 JAPAN
Tel: + 81-3-3408-3118
Fax: + 81-3-3408-3553
tokyo.ofc@computer.org

Editorial production by Kristine Kelly

Cover art production by Joseph Daigle / Studio Productions

Printed in the United States of America by The Printing House

IEEE COMPUTER SOCIETY

IEEE

Table of Contents

Message from the General Chair

Welcome to LCN '98, the 23rd Annual Conference on Computer Networks. Each year the LCN presents papers, panels and tutorials from academia and industry focusing on practical solutions to fundamental problems in computer networking. Our audience comprises vendor and user technologists, academic researchers and network managers.

This year we offer two paper tracks each with five sessions, four Expert Panel discussions, a luncheon presentation, and a keynote presentation from Dr. David Clark of MIT.

Thank you for joining us at LCN'98 in Boston, Massachusetts. Speaking for the entire Organizing and Program Committees, may your experiences at LCN '98 be personally and professionally rewarding.

Ellis S. Nolley
General Chair, LCN '98

Message from the Program Chairs

LCN '98 broke with tradition and is held in Lowell, Massachusetts, a town within the greater Boston area and rich in its own history. Lowell is widely considered the birthplace of the American Industrial Revolution. Textile mills took advantage of the steep drop in the Merrimack river, cutting channels to divert the water to drive the turbines.

As we meet in Lowell and watch the water flow through these channels, we can't help but see similarities between the flow of water and the flow of information. Each were the seminal factor in a revolution, first the Industrial Revolution, and then the Information Revolution. Local networks enabled people sitting miles apart to work together as though they were sitting right next to each other. Confederacies of local networks formed the wider Internet, just as town after town formed industrial dependencies.

Today we no longer use the power of water to drive factories, and in local networking, we are moving more from copper to fiber and wireless. Looking back over the 23 years of LCN's existence, you can trace the history of networks and see larger patterns in the LCN technical programs. This year we see much emphasis on communications quality and on new communications media, namely wireless. Our expectation is that LCN will continue to track the evolution of local communications to include personal local area networks (see David Clark's Keynote Abstract), smart spaces, and ubiquitous integrated services.

We, the Program Chairs, would like to thank the members of the Program Committee for their hard work in reviewing the papers. Their comments to us helped form the program, and their comments to the authors helped raise the quality of the papers. We would also like to thank Simon Lam of IEEE/ACM Transactions on Networking for allowing us to channel several papers to him for fast track consideration for TON. We also selected for the first time a Best Paper, "Improving Network Simulation with Feedback" by Kathleen M. Nichols. She's to be congratulated.

We hope you enjoy this year's technical program, and look forward to carrying on the evolution of the information revolution.

Tim Strayer, BBN Technologies
Frank Huebner-Szabo de Bucs, AT&T Labs
Program Committee Co-chairs, LCN '98

Conference Committee

General Chair
Ellis Nolley, *Strategic Growth*

Tutorial Chair
Gary Kessler, *Hill Associates*

Panel Chairs
Kanti Prasad, *University of Massachusetts, Lowell*
Bhumip Khasnabish, *GTE Labs*

Standing Committee
Howard Salwen, *Proteon*
Joe Bumblis, *Seagate Technologies*
Harvey Freeman, *HAF Consulting*

Local Arrangements Chair
Kanti Prasad, *University of Massachusetts, Lowell*

Program Chairs
Tim Strayer, *BBN Techologies*
Frank Huebner-Szabo de Bucs, *AT&T Labs*

Program Committee
J. William Atwood, *Concordia University, Canada*
Mohammed Atiquzzaman, *University of Dayton*
Bikram Bakshi, *Intel Corporation*
Milind M. Buddhikot, *Washington University*
Torsten Braun, *University of Berne, Switzerland*
Jose' Carlos Brustoloni, *Lucent / Bell Labs*
Bert Dempsey, *University of North Carolina at Chapel Hill*
Cathy Fulton, *Schlumberger APC-Research*
Maurice Gagnaire, *Ecole Nationale Superieure des Telecommunications, France*
Patrick S. Gonia, *Honeywell Technology Center*
Markus Hofmann, *University of Karlsruhe, Germany*
Alden Jackson, *BBN Technologies*
Anura Jayasumana, *Colorado State University*
Chao-Ju Jennifer Hou, *The Ohio State University*
Gary Kessler, *Hill Associates*
Khalid M. Khalil, *Bellcore*
Sridhar Komandur, *Ascend Communications*
P. Krishna, *Digital Corporation*
Bruce Mah, *Sandia National Laboratories*
Peter Martini, *University of Bonn, Germany*
Magda Mourad, *IBM T.J. Watson Research Center*
Kanti Prasad, *UMASS Lowell*
Parameswaran (Parmesh) Ramanathan, *University of Wisconsin-Madison*
Ravi Sankar, *University of South Florida*
Dimitrios N. Serpanos, *University of Crete, Greece*
Burkhard Stiller, *Swiss Federal Institute of Technology*
Ahmed N. Tantawy, *IBM Corporation*
Rose Tsang, *Sandia National Laboratories*
Vijay Varadharajan, *University of Western Sydney Nepean, Australia*
Alfred C. Weaver, *University of Virginia*
Maria C. Yuang, *National Chiao Tung University*
Martina Zitterbart, *TU Braunschweig, Germany*

LCN '98 would like to thank the following for their support

AT&T

Keynote Address

"Wiring up the user: Are we done yet?"

David Clark
MIT Laboratory for Computer Science

Abstract

It might seem that the Local Area Net is a done deal. If 10 mb/s is not fast enough, just make it 100 or 1000 mb/s. In fact, the broad set of issues in hooking up the user are unsolved, difficult, and pressing.

Traditional LANs work well in the corporate world, but how about the home? The issues there are not higher bandwidth, but working over existing wiring, costing little, and requiring no management or attention. And the wiring internal to the home is not the biggest issue. Why is broadband access to the home and small business so slow to emerge? Answering that question requires us to broaden our horizons to look at issues of economics.

The most profound change that is coming is the end of the PC era. While the PC is not about to vanish, its primacy as a consumer computing paradigm is certainly going to be challenged. As computers become cheaper, and are embedded in more and more objects, the network will be the basis by which people communicates with essentially all the devices that surround them. This network will exploit wireless technology, will demand even lower cost elements, but must at the same time have a level of reliability and invisibility consistent with consumer appliances.

Finally, once we have ubiquitous access to the user, we must wire up the user himself. We must hook the eyeglass display to the wrist display to the input device to the router on the belt. What seems like geek experiments today will become commonplace in the future, and if the future seems to get here slowly, we must not underestimate the potential for eventual change. Local area networks are the infrastructure that will make all of these changes happen, and the infrastructure is necessary for the higher level applications to emerge. Our job is cut out for us.

Paper Session 1
Track A: Wireless

Session Chair: Anura P. Jayasumana
Colorado State University

EFR: A Retransmit Scheme for TCP in Wireless LANs*

Yosuke Tamura †, Yoshito Tobe ‡, and Hideyuki Tokuda II

† Graduate School of Media and Governance,
‡ Keio Research Institute at SFC,
II Faculty of Environmental Information,
Keio University, 5322 Endo Fujisawa, Kanagawa, 252-8520, JAPAN
{*tamura, tobe, hxt*}*@sfc.keio.ac.jp*

Abstract

In this paper, we propose a new, efficient, fast retransmission scheme for wireless LANs. Wireless LANs are becoming popular and providing an efficient protocol over a wireless link is important. In our experiments with 2.4 GHz WaveLAN, the poor TCP performance observed was attributed to frequent expiration of the retransmission timer. To avoid unnecessary expiration of the retransmission timer, we propose a scheme in which fast retransmission is performed efficiently. The proposed modification only affects a TCP sender, and our version of TCP with the change is interoperable with existing TCP implementations. The change is especially effective in wireless LAN environments, where we have demonstrated significant improvements in throughput, 10 - 15%, via experiments with 2.4 GHz WaveLAN.

1. Introduction

Transmission Control Protocol (TCP) [16] has been widely used in computer networks to achieve reliable communication. Many popular applications such as web browsing, File Transfer Protocol (FTP) [17], and telnet [18] use TCP as the transport protocol. Recent emergence of wireless local area network (LAN) technology enables these applications to be used in wireless environments as well. Wireless networking, using AT&T's WaveLAN, has recently been introduced in our university campus, with a resulting change in computer usage. When many students access the wireless network simultaneously, interference among mobile hosts sharing a wireless link causes significant performance degradation when using existing TCP implementations. To minimize the performance degradation of TCP over wireless LANs, a more efficient TCP algorithm and its implementation are needed.

Efficient TCP operation over wireless links is also an important consideration for *ad-hoc networks* [8, 15]. In ad-hoc networks, multiple mobile hosts share the same wireless link, which leads to a higher data loss rate due to interference, multi-path phasing, and collision. Efficient TCP implementations suited to wireless LANs are also beneficial in ad-hoc networks. As we migrate to a more mobile world, we need to determine how we can enhance current TCP implementations over wireless links in a more general sense.

Ever since the release of BSD version 4.3, TCP implementations include sophisticated congestion control schemes such as *fast retransmit* and *fast recovery* [10]. In addition, many schemes have been introduced to improve TCP performance. For example, *selective acknowledgment* (SACK) [11] and an improved version of this mechanism, *forward acknowledgment* (FACK) [14], have been proposed. These performance improvement schemes have been tuned for wired links [4], and although some studies have examined TCP performance over collections of links, including wireless ones [3], we are not aware of any studies that address TCP performance improvements for a single wireless link.

Balakrishnan *et al.* [4] compared various schemes that proposed improvements to TCP performance over wireless links and concluded that the SMART scheme [12], a modification of the basic SACK approach that combines Go-Back-N, outperforms other schemes. A major drawback of the various SACK schemes is the need to modify the TCP software at both the sender and the receiver. Interoperability with existing schemes is thus not possible.

In this paper, we first present results of a study of the dynamics of TCP windowed flow control in a

*This research is conducted under the fund of Information-technology Promotion Agency, Japan(IPA).

0-8186-8810-6/98 $10.00 © 1998 IEEE

wireless LAN which identifies frequent expiration of the retransmission timer as a major cause of reduced throughput. We then analyze the cause of the expiration. Since retransmission is essential to provide data reliability, we seek a way of reducing the number of timer expirations. In many cases, timer expiration at the sender occurs because the sender waits for a fixed number of duplicate acknowledgments (ACKs) from the receiver before retransmitting data; the problem is that the receiver does not send as many duplicate ACKs as the sender expects. This situation always occurs when the window size of the TCP sender is small, ranging from 1 to 4. We call such windows "tiny windows." Often, retransmission timeouts can be avoided for tiny windows; those timeouts that unnecessarily occur are referred to as "wasted timeouts." Based on this observation, we propose the following *efficient fast retransmit* (EFR) scheme: (1) The sender dynamically estimates the maximum number of duplicate ACKs that it expects to receive. (2) When the sender receives this many ACKs, it immediately fast retransmits.

The work presented in this paper proposes a modification to TCP called *efficient fast retransmit* (EFR) that improves the performance of TCP over a wireless LAN by more efficiently performing fast retransmission. Our scheme interoperates with existing TCP implementations. Evaluation of this scheme was performed using the wireless LAN. Results show that EFR improves TCP throughput by 10 - 15% in a WaveLAN environment.

The remainder of the paper is organized as follows. Section 2 addresses issues in TCP congestion control in wireless LAN environments. Section 3 describes related work. Observations of actual TCP behavior in our experimental testbed are presented in Section 4, leading to a discussion of our proposed scheme and its implementation in Section 5. Section 6 presents an evaluation of our scheme. Discussions and future work are presented in Section 7, and we conclude in Section 8.

2. Basic Behaviors in TCP Retransmission

In this section, we briefly review TCP-Reno's retransmission algorithms and observe the basic behavior of TCP. This forms the basis of discussions in the following sections.

Let us assume that a TCP sender transmits a sequence of segments, segment i ($i = 1, 2, 3, \ldots$), to a TCP receiver. When segment k is lost and the receiver receives segment $(k+1)$, the receiver sends an ACK requesting segment k. When the receiver receives the following segments, segment $(k+2)$, $(k+3)$,..., it also sends an ACK requesting segment k. These ACKs are called duplicate ACKs. The sender initiates retransmission of segment k when either of the following conditions is satisfied. (1) The number of received duplicate ACKs reaches the threshold value for determining the loss of a segment. (2) The number of received duplicate ACKs does not reach the threshold value and the retransmission timer expires.

2.1. Retransmission Timer

The retransmission timeout in non-congestion networks can cause an unnecessary degradation of TCP performance. When the TCP sender transmits a segment, the retransmission timer is set. If the segment is not acknowledged, TCP will retransmit the segment. The value of this timer is calculated dynamically, based on the round-trip time measured by the sender. The retransmission timer is bounded to a value between 1 and 64 seconds. Reno's round-trip time and variance estimates are calculated using a coarse-grained timer (around 500 ms), assuming that the round-trip time (RTT) estimate is not accurate. If the retransmission timer expires, TCP uses the Slow-Start algorithm [10]; the TCP sender starts with a congestion window of one segment and increases the congestion window exponentially[1].

2.2. Fast Retransmit and Fast Recovery

Based on duplicate ACKs, the fast retransmit algorithm enables earlier detection of missing segments. Since the sender does not know whether a duplicate ACK is caused by a lost segment or merely a reordering of segments, it waits for three consecutive duplicate ACKs to be received [19]. When the sender receives three consecutive duplicate ACKs, it initiates retransmission. The fast recovery is a mechanism which enables the sender to go into congestion avoidance mode instead of slow start mode after the fast retransmit.

These schemes have improved TCP performance since the sender can retransmit the lost segments without waiting for a retransmission timeout. The waiting time for a retransmission timeout is very long for TCP in the order of seconds.

3. Related Work

This section describes the previous work on TCP performance improvements over wireless links. We also

[1] It is not exactly exponential because the receiver may delay its ACKs, typically sending one ACK for every two segments that it receives

state the difference between our goals and these works.

As described in the previous section, reducing the occurrence of the retransmission timer's timeouts improves TCP performance. The NewReno [9] TCP is an approach that changes the fast retransmit algorithm that eliminates Reno's waiting for the retransmission timer's timeout when multiple segments are lost within a single window. As described in [9], loss of multiple segments prohibits invoking fast retransmit of the second lost segment. The NewReno TCP solves this problem by modifying the fast retransmit algorithm.

TCP Vegas [1, 6] also seeks to eliminate unnecessary expiration of the retransmission timer. In TCP Vegas, a fine-grained timer is introduced to calculate RTT more precisely. When a single duplicate ACK is returned to the sender, the sender retransmits a segment without waiting for the three duplicate ACKs if the calculated RTT is greater than the timeout value.

The TCP receiver with SACK options [11] can inform the sender which segments have been correctly received, when it holds non-contiguous segments. A simulation-based study [7] investigated the robustness of SACK under several types of segment loss. An advanced version of SACKs is FACK [14] which uses the additional information provided by the SACK option to keep an explicit measurement of the amount of segment outstanding in the network, and then uses this information to improve congestion control.

Indirect TCP(I-TCP) [3] and Snoop [5] Protocols use split-connections. The key idea behind these protocols is to split one TCP connection into multiple pieces in wired and wireless links. Congestion control at the wireless link is performed differently from the control at the wired link. Thus, these protocols aim to improve the performance of the overall TCP connection.

Our goals in designing this scheme were achieving interoperability between the existing TCP implementation and improving TCP over a single wireless LAN. In this respect, the objectives of I-TCP and Snoop Protocol are different from ours. Although SACKs and related algorithms improve TCP performance, they require cooperation between the sender and the receiver.

The objectives of NewReno and Vegas are similar to ours. Although NewReno focuses on loss of multiple segments, we are seeking a scheme that solves wasted timeouts for the loss of a single segment too. Vegas may improve TCP performance over a wireless LAN, but we are seeking a scheme that does not introduce an extra timer. We compare our scheme with Vegas in Section 7. Like NewReno, we are looking at behavioral problems of TCP with an actual wireless LAN and create algorithms to solve the problems.

4. TCP Behaviors in Wireless Networks

In this section, we examine behavior of the TCP sequence number at a sender in the experiments with 2.4GHz AT&T WaveLAN and investigate the cause of retransmission.

4.1. Experimental Methodology

Figure 1 shows the experimental environment which is used throughout the experiments in this paper. In Figure 1, Host CH, connected to a wired 10BASE-T Ethernet, is an IBM PC-AT compatible computer with 200-MHz Pentium Pro and 32-MByte RAMs. Hosts MH1-MH4 are Toshiba Dynabook SSR-590 with 90-MHz Pentium and 16-MByte RAMs equipped with a PC-Card of 2 Mbps WaveLAN. Hosts MH1-MH4 communicate with Host CH via WavePOINT. The round-trip delay between Hosts MH1-MH4 and Host CH measured with ping program is about 6 ms. In our lab, the segment loss rate in transferring data between a single MH and CH with no other network traffic is maintained at approximately 3.0×10^{-4}. We maintained the loss rate to measure performance under a typical environment without any electromagnetical interference.

FreeBSD 2.2.1-Release which includes TCP-Reno, the current standard TCP implementation, is installed in all hosts. All the experiments noted in this paper use 1440-byte segment size, and the maximum window size for a connection is set to 35 segments.

We measure the throughput at the sender in the unit of 10^3 bit per second (kbps). To compare our scheme with TCP-Reno, we use the same setup in all hosts. In addition, all information regarding the segment transmissions on the Ethernet and WaveLAN are recorded for analysis using both tcpdump[13] and a Toyo Technica's LAN protocol analyzer "Network-General Sniffer". We have modified the TCP source code to obtain information of TCP Control Block (TCB).

4.2. Overhead of TCP Retransmission

In Figure 1, Hosts MH1-MH3 continue to transmit data to Host CH through TCP sockets, to provide a sharing link environment common in LANs. Throughout the experiment, MH1-MH3 are the senders, and CH is the receiver. We investigated the behavior of the TCP connection between Host MH1 and CH by conducting ftp for a 1Mbyte data under this environment.

In Figure 2-5, we show the dynamics of only one host, MH1, since all hosts have the same state. The measured transition of sequence numbers is shown in Figure 2. In this figure one can see a frequent gap of time where the growth of the sequence number ceases.

The gaps are caused by the expiration of either the retransmission timer, or the fast retransmit.

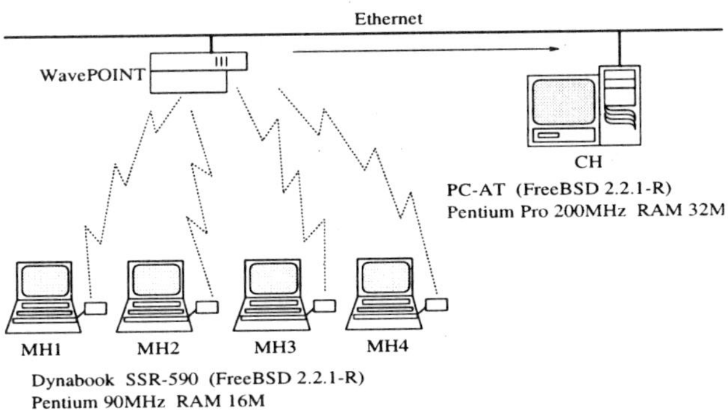

Figure 1. Our Evaluation Environment

Figure 3 shows the magnified portion of Figure 2 where retransmission occurs due to timer expiration. We can observe that the sender receives only one ACK corresponding to a lost segment, which results in the timer expiration after approximately 2 sec. Each timer expiration ceases transmission for approximately 2 sec. and all ceased periods noticeable in Figure 2 are due to the timer expiration.

Figure 4 shows the magnified portion where retransmission occurs due to the fast retransmit. The fast retransmit invokes the *tcp_output()* function immediately after the sender receives the third duplicate ACK. Transmission of other segments is prioritized over the fast retransmit, but the overhead associated with this fast retransmit is only 0.2 sec. which proves to be substantially smaller than that with the timer expiration.

The difference in overhead between the two is closely related to the retransmit timeout value (RTO) and the number of the timer expiration. The RTO is set to the average RTT plus 4 times its variance. Since the statistics of RTT are measured in 500 ms clock ticks, the typical RTO is set to 2 sec.

4.3. Causes of Retransmission

Let us further investigate what occurs when the retransmission timer expires. Figure 5 shows an enlarged portion where the retransmission timer expires due to TCP's tiny window. In Figure 5, a segment corresponding to sequence number 650,000 is lost. We call this segment k. The segments corresponding to sequence number 651,440, 652,800, and 654,320 will be expressed as segments $(k+1)$, $(k+2)$, and $(k+3)$, respectively. In the figure, ACKs of segments $(k+1)$ and $(k+2)$ are returned to the sender, while ACK of segment k is not returned. Hence, segment k is lost. The ACK of segment $(k+2)$ becomes the first duplicate ACK. Since segment $(k+3)$ is not transmitted

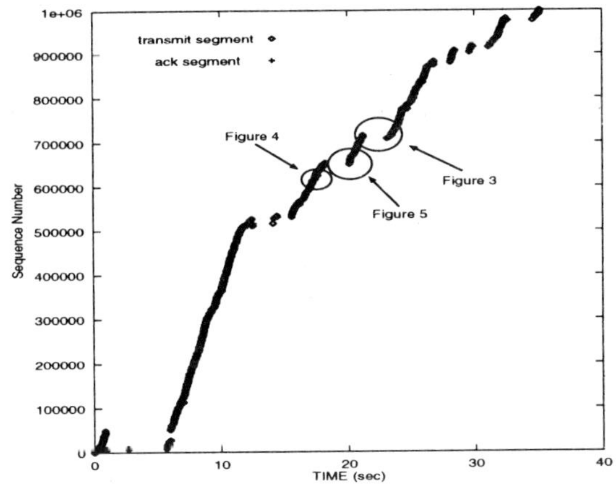

Figure 2. A 1-Mbyte transfer in a wireless environment with 3 hosts (Sequence Number versus Time)

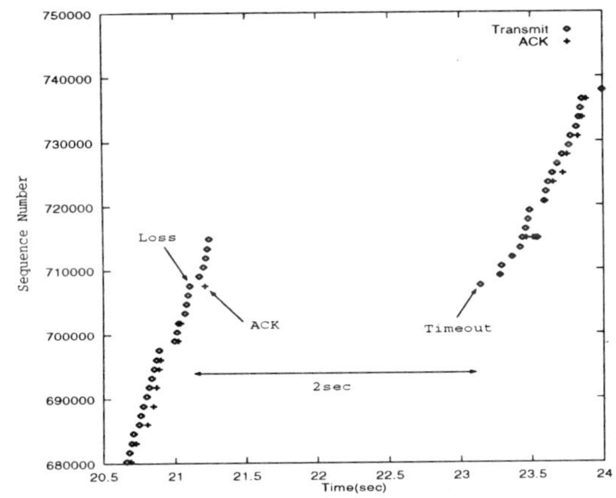

Figure 3. The retransmission timeout occurs because the sender does not receive any duplicate ACKs

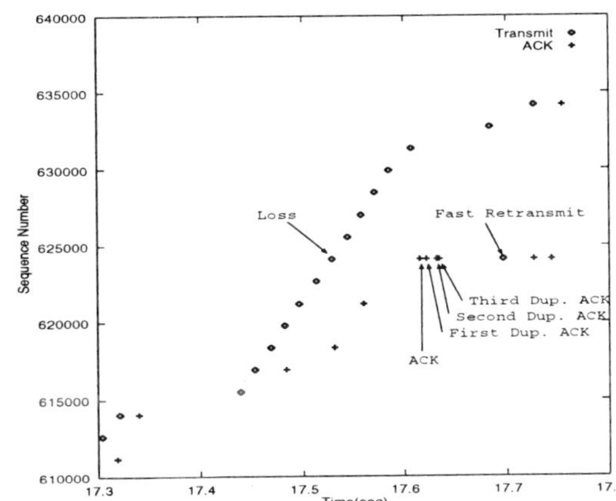

Figure 4. The fast retransmit is performed after the sender receives the third duplicate ACK

from the sender because the window size is presumed to be 3, the sender cannot receive the ACK of segment $(k+3)$. Therefore both the sender and the receiver cease transmission that causes the expiration of the retransmission timer. Whenever the window size ranges from 1 to 4, the fast retransmit is never invoked and the expiration of the retransmission timer always happens. If the fast retransmit is performed whenever the sender receives a duplicate ACK of a lost segment, several benefits to the TCP connection will occur; (1) Retransmission of the lost segment with the fast retransmit starts 1.5 seconds earlier than that without the fast retransmit. (2) Unnecessary congestion control is avoided. (3) The throughput is improved by the fast recovery.

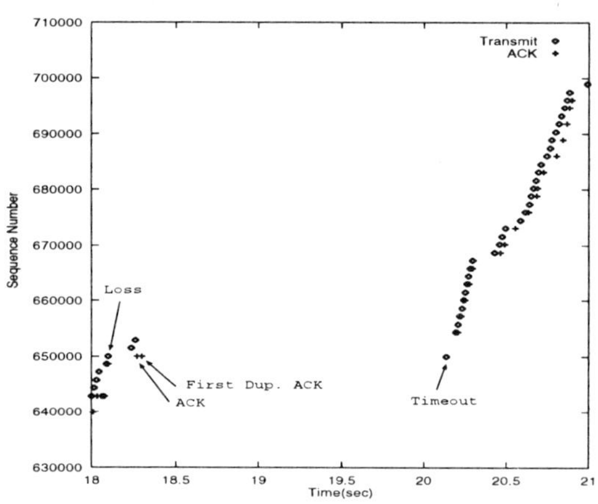

Figure 5. The retransmission timeout occurs because the sender receives only one duplicate ACK

4.4. Trace of Windows

Next, we traced the behavior of the sender window. In Figure 1, Hosts MH1-MH3 continue to transmit data to Host CH through TCP sockets. Figures 6, 8, and 10 show the acquired behavior of sequence number of MH1-MH3. Although only behavior of sequence number at one host is presented in Figure 2, we can see the gaps are similarly seen in all hosts in these figures.

Here, we let *snd_cur* denote the window size. The value of *snd_cur* corresponds to the minimum of *cwnd*, a congestion window, and *snd_wnd*, the receiver's advertised window. Figures 7, 9, and 11 illustrate transition of *snd_cur* for three Hosts, MH1-MH3. The vertical line is expressed in units of 1440 bytes, one segment. Bars are drawn when transmission is done and the value of *snd_cur* is zero when the transmission is not performed. The areas where the value of *snd_cur* is equal to or less than 4 segments are shaded in these figures. The area represents where TCP has a tiny window, and a possible wasted timeout.

As seen in Figures 7, 9, and 11, *snd_cur* increases as ACKs are successfully returned to Hosts MH1-MH3, but once they fail in receiving ACKs, it is decreased to a small number within the shaded area, The value of *snd_cur* remains less than four segments. To make a comparison with a wired LAN, Hosts MH1-MH3 transmit data to Host CH continuously through TCP sockets with 10BASE-T. Figure 12 shows the behavior of *snd_cur* in the wired LAN. Since the values are drawn with bars, most of the *snd_cur* is 17280 bytes. Unlike wireless LAN, the value of *snd_cur* is mostly outside the area. Remaining in the area results in unavailability of receiving three consecutive duplicate ACKs and trigger of wasted timeout. Wasted timeout is likely to occur more in wireless LAN.

5. Efficient Fast Retransmit Scheme

In this section, we propose a modification to the fast retransmit algorithm that comes bundled with current TCP implementations. The fast retransmit algorithm retransmits a segment after a fixed number of duplicate ACKs (three) for the same segment are received. In contrast, our modified algorithm, called EFR (Efficient Fast Retransmit), dynamically calculates *tcprexmtthresh*, the number of consecutive duplicate ACKs that trigger fast retransmit.

We also consider the timing of acknowledgments and the issue of false fast retransmit.

5.1. EFR Overview

The goals of EFR are to be interoperable with existing TCP implementations and to prevent wasted timeouts from occurring. To meet these goals, EFR requires changing only a TCP sender. The sender avoids waiting for duplicate ACKs that the receiver will never transmit and initiates retransmission before the retransmission timer expires.

In EFR, when the sender receives the first duplicate ACK, it calculates *tcprexmtthresh*, the maximum number of duplicate ACKs it can receive before retransmitting the lost segment corresponding to the duplicate ACKs. When the number of duplicate ACKs received at the sender reaches this threshold, the sender retransmits the lost segment. The value of *tcprexmtthresh* is determined based on the window size.

Figure 13 compares period of time before a retransmission occurs between TCP-Reno and EFR when the

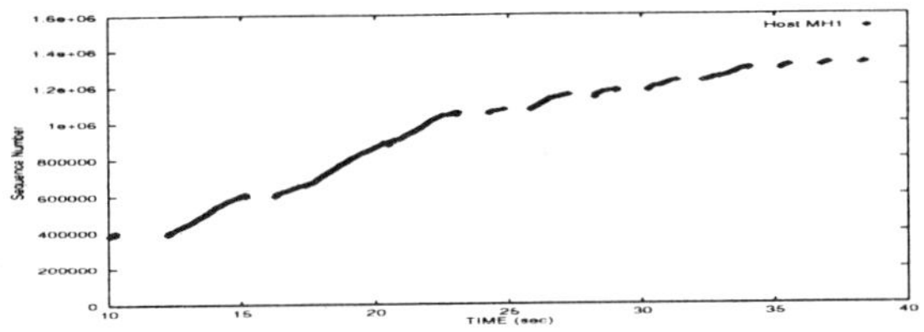

Figure 6. Sequence number at MH1

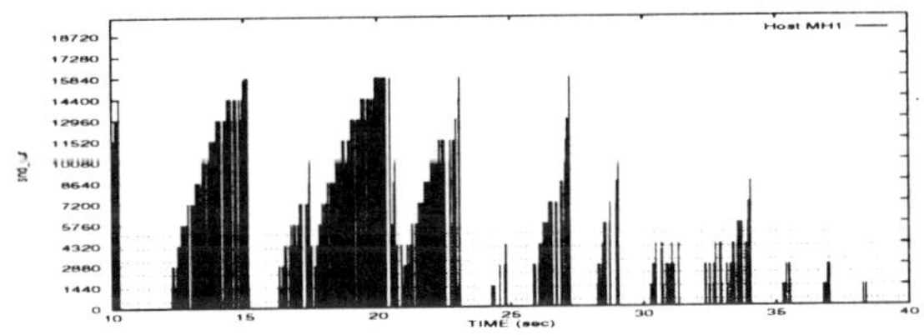

Figure 7. snd_cur at MH1 (wireless LAN)

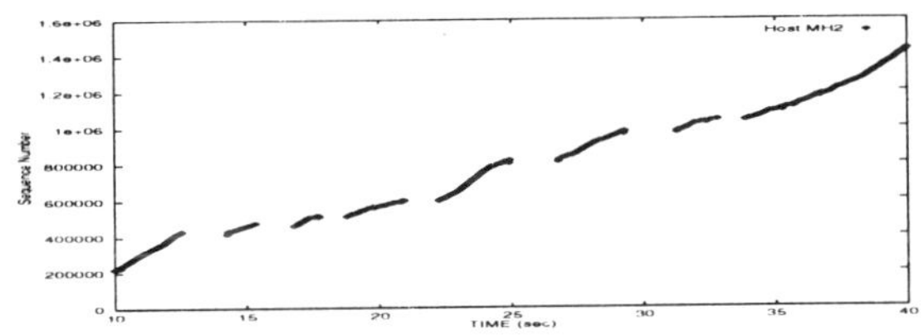

Figure 8. Sequence number at MH2

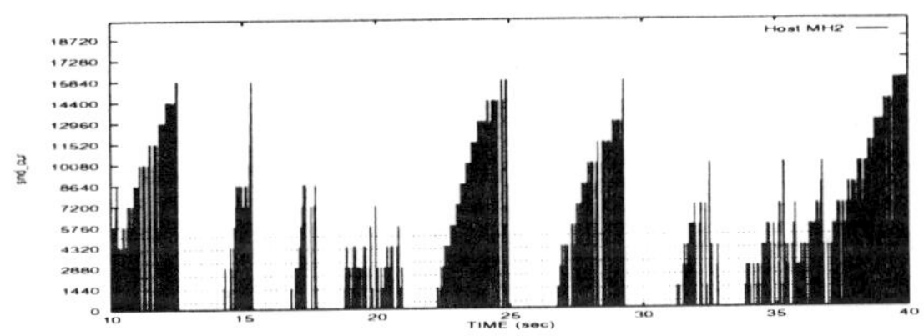

Figure 9. snd_cur at MH2 (wireless LAN)

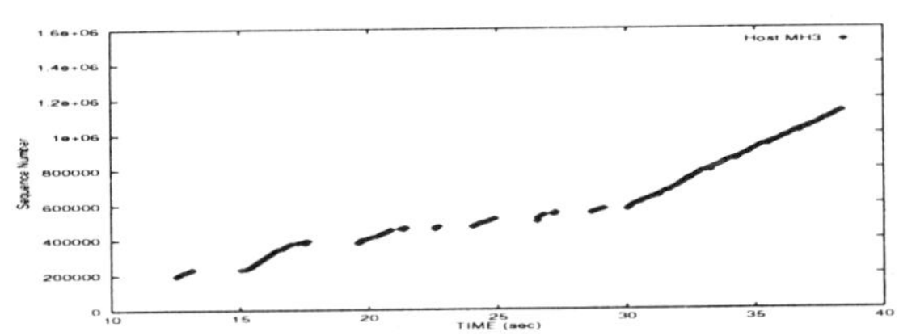

Figure 10. Sequence number at MH3

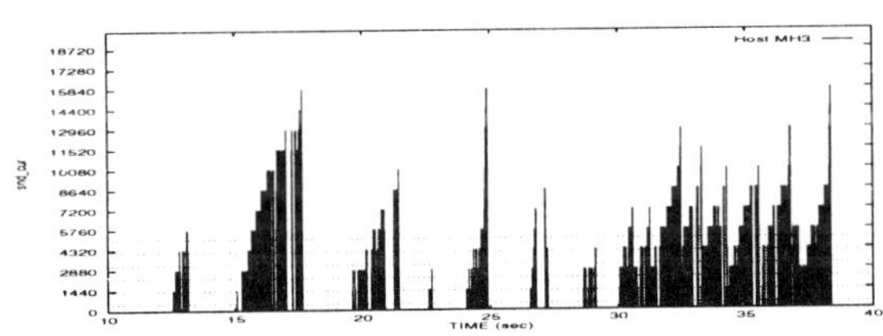

Figure 11. snd_cur at MH3 (wireless LAN)

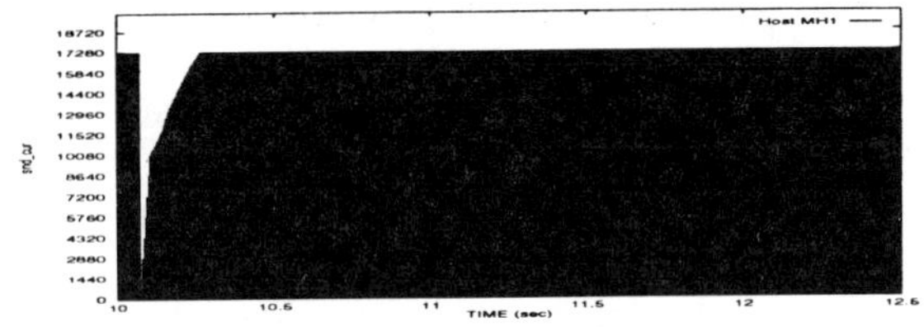

Figure 12. snd_cur at MH1 (wired LAN)

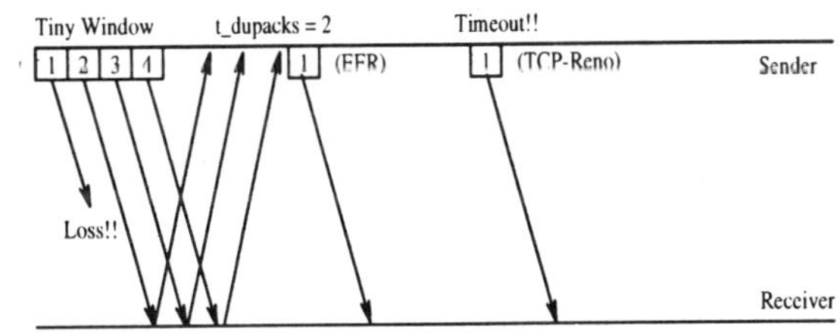

Figure 13. Period of time before a retransmission occurs when TCP has a tiny window

value of *snd_cur* is four; TCP has a tiny window. In the figure, *t_dupacks* is the number of received duplicate ACKs. In EFR, the sender performs the fast retransmit when it receives the second duplicate ACK, while in TCP-Reno the sender waits until the retransmission timer expires (on the order of seconds) before retransmitting the lost segments. Note that EFR retransmits the lost segment without waiting for the retransmission timer to expire.

5.2. Issue in False Fast Retransmit

TCP operates on top of the Internet Protocol (IP), which does not guarantee reliable packet delivery. In some cases, when segments arrive out of sequence at a receiver, a false fast retransmit may occur. Despite no actual congestion, the fast retransmit algorithm may mistakenly force the sender into congestion avoidance mode. When the TCP sender has a large current window, these false fast retransmissions significantly degrade TCP performance. As *tcprexmtthresh* becomes smaller, the probability of falsely invoking fast retransmit increases. We therefore dictate the policy that *tcprexmtthresh* should not be fixed at one or two.

In our scheme, however, EFR is triggered only when TCP has a tiny current window. In this case, even if false fast retransmit occurs and TCP enters congestion avoidance mode, TCP performance is not substantially affected.

5.3. Consideration of Acknowledgments

TCP does not always send an ACK immediately on receipt of a segment. Instead, normal acknowledgements occur when either a 200 ms ACK timer expires or the window at the receiver has increased by two segments. On the other hand, a receiver sends a duplicate ACK immediately upon receipt of out-of-order segments. We should note here that an ACK of segment $(k-1)$ may not be transmitted to the sender when segment k is lost and the ACK of segment $(k+1)$ is transmitted to the sender.

EFR counts duplicate ACKs to trigger retransmissions. However, it is not always possible to distinguish between the first ACK and subsequent duplicate ACKs. Consider the following example. As shown in Figure 13, assume that segment 0 is transmitted before segment 1 and suppose that segment 1 is lost. If the ACK of segment 0 is not received by the sender, then the ACK of segment 2 corresponds to the first ACK received by the sender. Then, the ACK of segment 3 becomes the first duplicate ACK. On the other hand, if the ACK of segment 0 is received by the sender, the ACK of segment 2 becomes the first duplicate ACK because the ACK of segment 0 has already requested segment 1. In either case, when the send window is four segments, the sender can send up to segment 4. Therefore the number of duplicate ACKs is 2 and 3, respectively. If we set the threshold value of duplicate ACKs to 2, a false fast retransmit can occur. But if we set the threshold value of duplicate ACKs to 3, wasted timeouts can occur. In designing EFR, we assume that the ACK of segment 0 is not received by the sender because the cost of a false fast retransmit is less than that of wasted timeouts when TCP has a tiny window.

5.4. Implementation of EFR

In this section, we describe our implementation of EFR in detail, using the FreeBSD TCP-Reno source code as our initial starting point. The EFR algorithm is only added to the fast retransmit part of the TCP source code. We add two variables to TCB: *snd_cur* and *tcprexmtthresh*. The variable *tcprexmtthresh* represents the threshold value used to trigger fast retransmit; it is implemented as a global variable. A default value of *tcprexmtthresh* is fixed at three in the FreeBSD TCP-Reno implementation. In EFR however, a separate *tcprexmtthresh* is maintained per connection and dynamically changed, based on the value of *snd_cur*.

Figure 14 presents the EFR algorithm. Each time a TCP sender receives a duplicate ACK, it executes a portion of the EFR algorithm. If the received duplicate ACK is the first for a segment, the minimum of

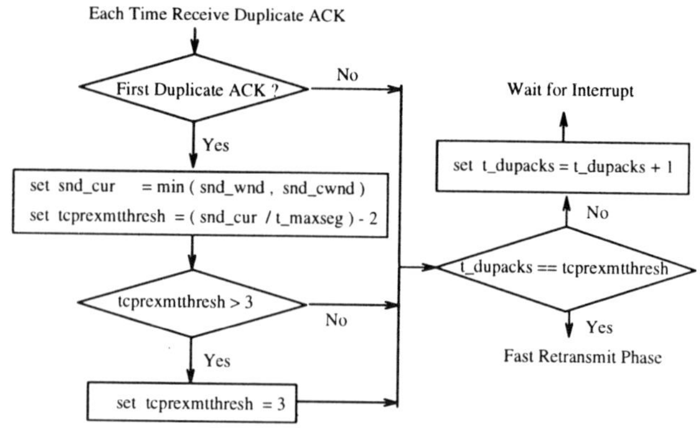

Figure 14. EFR algorithm

snd_wnd and *snd_cwnd* is saved into *snd_cur*. To estimate the number of segments, *snd_cur* is divided by *t_maxseg*, the maximum segment size. We set *tcprexmtthresh* to (*snd_cur* / *t_maxseg*) - 2. Recall that our proposed modification only invokes the fast retransmit to recover lost segments when the sender has a tiny window. If *tcprexmtthresh* is more than three, EFR sets this variable to three. Note that we do not claim that the smaller value of *tcprexmtthresh* is desirable, but we need to adjust *tcprexmtthresh* to a more reasonable value when the send window is tiny.

6. Performance Results

In this section, we present the performance of EFR. The experimental environment, which is shown in Figure 1, is described in section 4 in detail. We have compared EFR with TCP-Reno under multiple access environments.

6.1. Retransmission Characteristics

To examine how the number of timeouts is reduced by EFR, we transmitted 10-Mbyte using a UNIX socket-type client-server program. The number of hosts was varied from 2 to 4 by averaging the results of 50 trials in consideration of statistical fluctuations.

Figures 15 shows the number of retransmitted segments. Regardless of the number of hosts, the number of retransmitted segments caused by a timeout was reduced by approximately 10% with EFR.

To investigate timeouts further, let $N_{dup}(i)$ represent the number of each occurrence that the number of duplicate ACKs is i. When i is greater than 3, the occurrence is counted in $N_{dup}(3)$. The value of $N_{dup}(3)$ can be positive because the fast retransmitted segment and the following segments may be lost.

The values of $N_{dup}(i)$ $(i = 0, 1, 2, 3)$ are shown in Figure 16. When the number of hosts is 2, $N_{dup}(1)$ and $N_{dup}(2)$ are both reduced with EFR from 12 to 8, and from 30 to 7, respectively. It is presumed that this is because wasted timeouts are removed with EFR. The reduction of $N_{dup}(1)$ and $N_{dup}(2)$ results in the reduction of the number of timeouts. The values of $N_{dup}(1)$ and $N_{dup}(2)$ are not zero because there are cases when *tcprexmtthresh* is 2 and the sender receives only one duplicate ACK, and when *tcprexmtthresh* is 3 and the sender receives either one or two duplicate ACKs. These cases occur when segments following a lost segment or a duplicate ACK are lost. The value of $N_{dup}(0)$ cannot be reduced because the number of duplicate ACKs is zero when a burst of segments is lost. The value of $N_{dup}(3)$ is counted, for instance, when the segment of the fast retransmit is lost. The timeouts at which the number of duplicate ACKs is more than or equal to three are not wasted timeouts. EFR does not remove such timeouts.

The following point should also be noted. The addition of the number of timeouts and fast retransmit is with EFR. If EFR were to simply change some timeouts to the fast retransmit, the added value would remain the same. A possible explanation for this is that the possibility of segment loss with collision increases with transmission. If the overhead of the timeout is much larger than that of the fast retransmit, reduction of the total loss time is expected. The total loss time of a TCP connection is calculated as follows,

$$T_{loss} = N_{out} \times T_{out} + N_{fast} \times T_{fast},$$

where T_{loss}, T_{out}, T_{fast}, N_{out}, and N_{fast} are the total loss time, the consumed time for timeout, the consumed time for the fast retransmit, the number of timeout, and the number of the fast retransmit, respectively. An evaluation of effectiveness needs to be carried out with the throughput of TCP connections described in the following section. Although we only present a case using two hosts, the same arguments are valid for other cases as well.

6.2. Throughput Measurements

Figure 17 shows the total aggregate throughput through each pair of TCP connections using either EFR and TCP-Reno. The values shown in the figure are obtained by averaging results fifty times. Since a segment loss causes transmission to be interrupted and causes additional messages to be sent, the 2 Mbps bandwidth of WaveLAN is not fully utilized. Yet, EFR contributes to enhancing the effective usage of bandwidth.

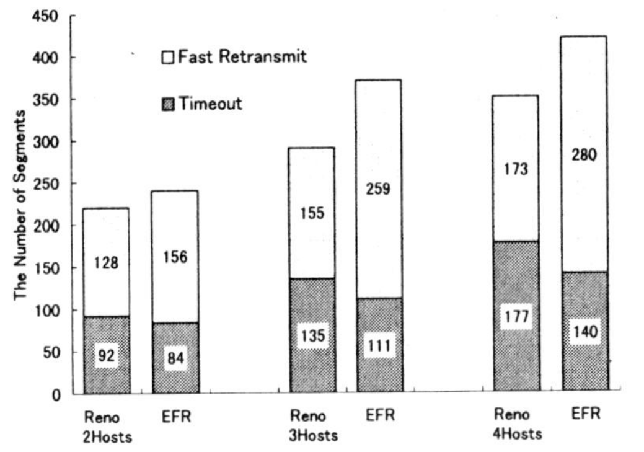

Figure 15. Number of retransmitted segments (TCP-Reno vs. EFR)

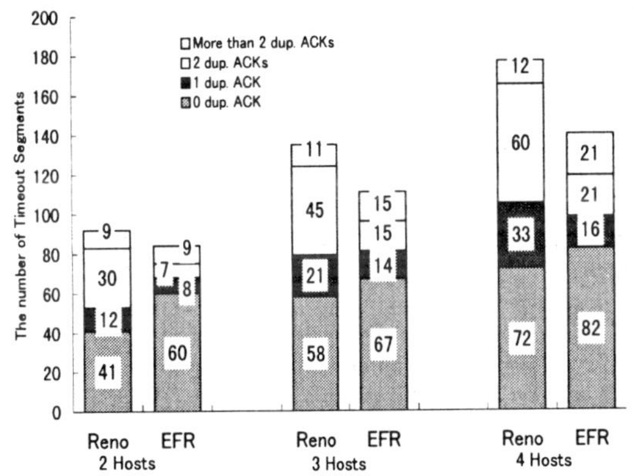

Figure 16. Number of duplicate ACKs when the retransmission timer expires(TCP-Reno vs. EFR)

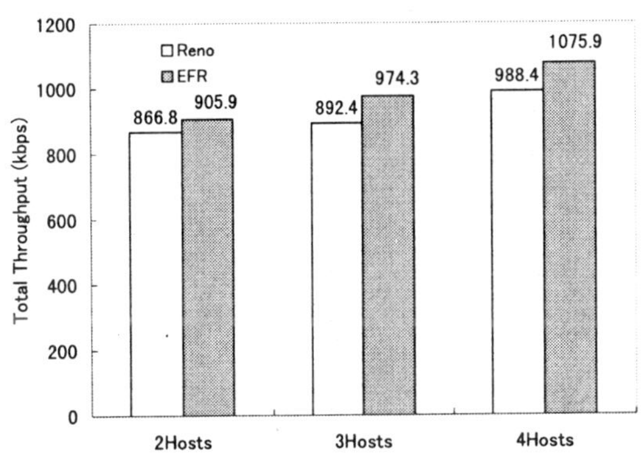

Figure 17. Total Throughput of all hosts

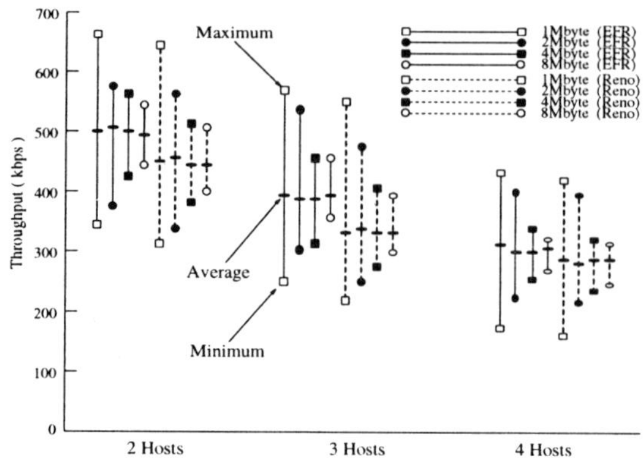

Figure 18. Comparison of throughput

Figure 18 shows throughput with 1 Mbytes, 2 Mbytes, 4 Mbytes, and 8 Mbytes of data. It was obtained by averaging results fifty times. The bars indicate the averaged values and the straight lines associated with the bars show the range of measured values. As the data size decreases, the variance of the throughput spreads over wider range. These figures indicate that EFR has higher performance than TCP-Reno under a multiple hosts environment. In the case of 8 Mbyte data transfer with three and four hosts, the throughputs with EFR are 14.4 % and 12.2 % higher than that with TCP-Reno, respectively. These results demonstrate that EFR attains better performance than TCP-Reno in a shared wireless link with multiple hosts.

7. Discussions and Future Works

In this section, we compare EFR with TCP Vegas and discuss applicability of EFR to various types of networks. At the end of this section, we address our future works.

7.1. EFR vs. Other Schemes

EFR and TCP Vegas's retransmission approach are similar in that both attempt to reduce wasted timeouts. They differ in their mechanisms. EFR is based on the send window, *snd_cur*, while TCP Vegas uses RTT estimation with its fine-grained timer. Unlike RTT, the send window does not depend on the amount of traffic. Therefore we can eliminate wasted timeouts easily with EFR.

Initial Lager Windows can also reduce wasted timeout. Allman *et al.* [2] evaluates the effect on TCP performance of changing the initial window (IW) size. It also shows that using an initial window of 4 segments, IW=4, provides a better chance for good loss recovery compared to 2 and 3 segment initial windows. However, according to our experiments in the case when multiple wireless hosts transmit segments aggressively, the value of an initial window of 4 is too large for TCP to avoid network congestion. Therefore we believe that EFR is more adaptable for network traffic than IW=4.

7.2. EFR Performance

We have only investigated EFR over wireless links because our motivation was in improvements in a wireless LAN in this paper. EFR is designed, however, to enhance TCP throughput when the current window size is small and the TCP sender cannot push enough segments to receive three duplicate ACKs. In wired networks, the same situation may happen, for instance, at the beginning of slow-start mode after the expiration of the retransmission timer or the establishment of a TCP connection. Therefore EFR can be also used to improve such situation in wired networks.

7.3. Wired LAN Environments

A wired LAN has a lower error rate and a smaller round-trip delay compared with a wireless LAN. Unlike Carrier Sense Multiple Access with Collision Avoidance (CSMA/CA) used in a wireless LAN, Carrier Sense Multiple Access with Collision Detection (CSMA/CD) deployed in a wired Ethernet supports detection of collision and retransmission of collided frames at the link layer with limitation in the number of retries. Therefore the multiple access over wired Ethernet does not induce TCP segment loss as seriously as that over a wireless link except a case where retransmission at the link layer fails frequently in overloaded traffic. Thus, the size of the congestion window increases smoothly and the window size is so large that EFR algorithm is not operated in the wired LAN. As a result, EFR offers almost the same performance as a TCP-Reno's fast retransmit with some exceptions with segment retransmission at the beginning of slow-start mode after the expiration of the retransmission timer or the establishment of a TCP connection.

We emphasize that EFR offers performance not worse than TCP-Reno even in wired LANs because an algorithm cannot be accepted when the performance is improved in a domain and deteriorates in another with it.

7.4. WAN Environments

TCP connections in WAN environments, such as these for access to World Wide Web servers, may not be able to transfer data smoothly due to packet losses over the connections with a long delay. In this case, for instance, Web server's TCP window is kept small due to congestion control. In addition, RTO becomes long. Therefore, EFR can be performed in WAN Environments when TCP waits for non-existing duplicate ACKs.

Congestion in routers leads to bursty segment losses. Since EFR does not work in the multiple losses within single window, EFR is not an obstacle to congestion control which will bring about a network collapse.

7.5. Future Works

Although we have evaluated our algorithm in an experimental system, evaluation in a larger real wireless environment remains for our future work.

Evaluation of extensive feasibility of our algorithm to long delay networks which include end-to-end wired link is also our future work.

We are planning to further evaluate EFR scheme combined with NewReno to investigate improvements in the occurrence of multiple segments loss. Evaluation of such a combined scheme in our operating wireless network should be done based on various mobile applications.

8. Summary

We proposed a new, Efficient Fast Retransmit (EFR) scheme for improving TCP performance over wireless LANs. Since TCP is becoming popular over wireless as well as wired LANs, TCP should run efficiently also on lossy wireless multiple access networks.

EFR is based on the clever determination of the timing of the fast retransmit. It allows a TCP sender to adjust the timing of retransmission dynamically depending on the current window size; the TCP sender is able to avoid a duplicate ACK which the receiver never transmits and initiate retransmission before the retransmission timer expires. EFR is compatible with existing TCP implementations.

We implemented our proposed algorithm on FreeBSD-2.2.1R. Evaluation with multiple hosts under 2.4 GHz WaveLAN as is common in actual environments demonstrated significant improvements in throughput, 10-15%, compared with TCP-Reno.

Acknowledgment

The authors are grateful to members of the MKng/R3 Project for valuable comments and criticisms, especially Hiroshi Inamura supplied ideas for extending this research.

We thank Kevin Fall, Ion Stoica, and the anonymous LCN reviewers for several comments and suggestions that helped improve the quality of this paper. Our special thanks to Yasunori Matsui, Richard Buskens, and Stephen Chou, who gave us valuable comments and suggestions on a draft of this paper.

References

[1] J. S. Ahn, P. B. Danzig, Z. Liu, and L. Yan. Evaluation of TCP Vegas: Emulation and Experiment. In *Proceedings of ACM SIGCOMM '95, Oct. 1995.*

[2] M. Allman, C. Hayes, and S. Ostermann. An Evaluation of TCP with Larger Initial Windows. *Computer Communication Review, vol.28, no.3, July, 1998.*

[3] A. Bakre and B. R. Badrinath. I-TCP: Indirect TCP for Mobile Hosts. In *Proceedings of ICDCS '95, May. 1995.*

[4] H. Balakrishnan, V.N. Padmanabhan, S. Seshan, and R.H. Katz. A Comparison of Mechanisms for Improving TCP Performance over Wireless Links. In *Proceedings of ACM SIGCOMM '96, Aug. 1996.*

[5] H. Balakrishnan, S. Seshan, and R.H. Katz. Improving TCP/IP Performance over Wireless Networks. In *Proceedings of ACM MOBICOM '95, Nov. 1995.*

[6] L. S. Brakmo, S. W. O'Malley, and L. L. Peterson. TCP Vegas: New Techniques for Congestion Detection and Avoidance. In *Proceedings of ACM SIGCOMM '94, May. 1994.*

[7] K. Fall and S. Floyd. Simulation-based Comparisons of Taho, Reno, and SACK TCP. *Computer Communication Review, vol.26, no.3, pp.5-21, July 1996.*

[8] T. D. Hodes, R. H. Katz, E. S. Schreiber, and L. Rowe. Composable Ad-hoc Mobile Services for Universal Interaction. In *Proceedings of ACM MOBICOM '97, Sep. 1997.*

[9] J. C. Hoe. Improving the Start-up Behavior of a Congestion Control Scheme for TCP. In *Proceedings of ACM SIGCOMM '96 Aug. 1996.*

[10] V. Jacobson. Congestion Avoidance and Control. In *Proceedings of ACM SIGCOMM '88 Aug. 1988.*

[11] V. Jacobson and R. Braden. TCP Extensions for Long-Delay Paths. *Network Working Group, Request for Comments: 1072 Oct. 1988.*

[12] S. Keshav and S.P. Morgan. SMART Retransmission: Performance with Overload and Random Losses. *http://www.cs.att.com/netlib/att/cs/home/keshav/papers/smart.ps.Z, 1996.*

[13] S. McCanne and V. Jacobson. The BSD Packet Filter: A New Architecture for User-Level Packet Capture. In *Proceedings of Winter '93 USENIX Conference, Jan. 1993.*

[14] M. Mathis and J. Mahdavi. Forward Acknowledgment: Refinding TCP Congestion Control. In *Proceedings of ACM SIGCOMM '96, Aug. 1996.*

[15] V. D. Park and M. S. Corson. A Highly Adaptive Distributed Routing Algorithm for Mobile Wireless Networks. In *Proceedings of INFOCOM '97 Apr. 1997.*

[16] J. Postel. Transmission control protocol. *Network Working Group, Request for Comments: 793, Sep. 1981.*

[17] J. Postel and J. Reynolds. FILE TRANSFER PROTOCOL(FTP). *Network Working Group, Request for Comments: 765, Sep. 1985.*

[18] J. Postel and J. Reynolds. TELNET PROTOCOL SPECIFICATION. *Network Working Group, Request for Comments: 854, Sep. 1983.*

[19] W. R. Stevens. TCP/IP Illustrated, Volume1 The Protocols(p.312). *Addison-Wesley Publishing Company. 1994.*

Effect of Hidden Terminals on the Performance of IEEE 802.11 MAC Protocol

Sumit Khurana, Anurag Kahol, Anura P. Jayasumana
Colorado State University
Ft. Collins, Colorado, U.S.A.
{khurana, kahol}@CS.ColoState.EDU, jayasuma@ENGR.ColoState.EDU

Abstract

The hidden terminal problem is unique to wireless networks and as of now, there is very limited understanding about it's effects on network performance. Results are presented from a simulation study of the IEEE 802.11 MAC protocol when operating in the presence of hidden terminals. We also propose a framework for modeling hidden terminals which can handle complex scenarios of both mobility and static obstructions. Our simulations indicate that hidden terminals can have a very detrimental effect on the performance of the IEEE 802.11 MAC protocol. Although throughput is acceptable when about 10 percent of station pairs are hidden, packet delay can increase by an order of magnitude. Performance of the protocol drops sharply when the number of hidden pairs exceeds 10 percent.

1. Introduction

Wireless Networking is one of the fastest growing areas in the network industry today. Wireless Local Area Networks(WLANs) are gaining special interest as they provide flexibility of location along with low infrastructural and maintenance costs. Of late only proprietary solutions for WLANs were available, but with the adoption of the IEEE 802.11 MAC and physical layer standards, WLANs are expected to become more ubiquitous.

Wireless communications are inherently error prone and introduce greater concerns for security and human safety. Wireless links are less reliable, more susceptible to fading and interference and have a limited bandwidth due to scarcity of the radio spectrum. Communicating hosts can be mobile, and maintaining connectivity without loss of performance is a challenge. Several new issues must be considered in WLAN MACs [2] which are not important in their wired counterparts:

1. A station cannot transmit and sense the channel at the same time. This is because the receiver is overwhelmed by the transmitting power of it's own transmitter. Hence MAC protocols like CSMA/CD, which were applicable for wired networks, cannot be used.

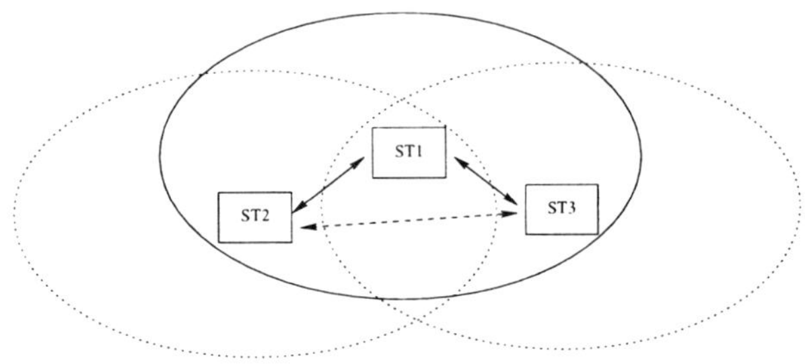

Figure 1. Hidden terminal problem

2. Due to signal fading and attenuation, transmission of a station may not be heard by another, ie. it is *hidden* from the first station. As shown in figure 1, ST1 can communicate with both ST2 and ST3 but ST2 and ST3 are hidden from each other. Thus two stations hidden from each other have a different view of the channel state (busy or idle). Collisions can result if two stations hidden from each other, both believing the channel to be idle, try to simultaneously transmit to a common destination.

3. Maximum channel utilization can be achieved by allowing multiple users to contend for the same channel, but this results in degradation of Quality of Service (QOS). With the advent of multimedia applications, there can be strict QOS requirements for data. In wired networks QOS can be supported by providing more bandwidth, but this is not possible in WLANs as the radio spectrum is limited. Thus support for QOS at the MAC layer becomes necessary.

In this paper we present simulation based results for the performance of the IEEE 802.11 MAC protocol operating

0-8186-8810-6/98 $10.00 © 1998 IEEE

in the ad-hoc (DCF) mode, in the presence of hidden terminals. We propose a structured scheme for modeling hidden terminals in a WLAN. While the DCF operation of IEEE 802.11 has been studied by several researchers [1] [3] [4] [7], they have either ignored the effect of hidden terminals or proposed trivial ways of modeling them. We model the geographical area of a WLAN as a mesh of hexagons and evaluate hidden terminals caused by both mobility and static obstructions. Our simulations show, that throughput is acceptable when the number of hidden pairs is less than 10%, but can fall sharply with an increase in the number of hidden terminals. The blocking probability increases with an increase in the number of hidden terminals but the average packet delay is the worst affected and increases by an order of magnitude, even under moderate hidden terminal conditions. The use of the RTS/CTS mechanism results in an improvement in both throughput and delay with best results obtained when RTS/CTS is used for each frame, regardless of it's length.

The rest of the paper is organized as follows. In Section 2 we give an overview of the IEEE 802.11 WLAN specification for MAC. In Section 3 we present our hidden terminal model which is followed by the simulation model in Section 4. In Section 5 we present results of our simulation and close the paper with a conclusion in Section 6.

2. IEEE 802.11 MAC Protocol

The IEEE 802.11 WLAN has a hierarchical architecture with the fundamental building block known as the Basic Service Set (BSS). A set of stations residing in a certain geographical area (known as the Basic Service Area(BSA)), communicating with each other using the same coordination function (DCF or PCF) form a BSS. All transmissions by stations in a BSS are broadcasts, and should conceptually be heard by all other stations in the BSS.

Three different types of frames are supported: management, control and data. The management frames are used for timing and synchronization, and authentication and deauthentication. Control frames include positive acknowledgments. Data frames handed down from the LLC to the MAC may be fragmented if they exceed a threshold value *Fragmentation_threshold*. Each fragment MPDU formed from the fragmented MSDU, other than the last, is of length *Fragmentation_threshold*. In Point Coordination (PCF) mode polling occurs with a point coordinator determining which station has the right to transmit. In the Distributed Coordination Function (DCF) mode, a BSS operates as an ad-hoc network in which any station can communicate with any other station in the BSA without the intervention of a centralized access point (AP) by contending for a shared channel. All stations have equal priorities and hence an equal chance of getting the channel.

The DCF is based on Carrier Sense Multiple Access with Collision Avoidance (CSMA/CA). As stated earlier, Collision Detection (CSMA/CD) cannot be used because a station cannot transmit and listen to the channel at the same time. This increases the cost of a collision in the system because a station cannot detect collisions until it has transmitted the entire frame. There is also a greater vulnerability to collisions due to the presence of hidden terminals in the system as two stations hidden from each other may concurrently try to send data to another station which is not hidden from either of them. Hence various mechanisms incorporated into the protocol to either avoid collisions, or to minimize the penalty on system performance when a collision does occur are :

1. The time at which a station can start transmission is slotted. This ensures that a collision takes place only when two stations start transmission in the same time slot. In order to avoid simultaneous transmissions, each station executes an exponential back-off procedure whenever it has a frame to send and senses the channel to be idle.

2. Positive acknowledgments are implemented along with a timeout mechanism. Acknowledgment frames enable a station to determine whether it's transmission was successful or not, since it cannot detect a collision otherwise.

3. The protocol implements a concept of Virtual Carrier Sensing in which a frame carries the transmission duration of succeeding frames, in it's header. Each unfragmented data frame carries the duration of it's acknowledgment in it's header. Fragment MPDUs carry the time that succeeding fragments will take to transmit. All stations listening to a frame set their Network Allocation Vector(NAV), equal to the duration value. Stations start contending for the channel only after their NAV elapses and they physically sense the channel to be idle. This ensures that stations do not contend for the channel while a transmission is in progress.

4. There is a high penalty for collisions between long data frames. As a station cannot hear collisions, it continues the transmission of a frame even when there are simultaneous transmissions. This results in wastage of bandwidth. To overcome this problem, control frames namely Request to Send (RTS) and Clear to Send (CTS) have been introduced. If the length of a data frame is greater than a preset RTS Threshold, the station sends an RTS, reserving the channel for the following data frame by setting it's duration field to the time it would take to transmit the long data frame. All stations hearing the sender set their NAVs to this value and the destination responds with a CTS, which again

carries the duration information. All stations hearing the destination again set their NAVs and once this pair has been exchanged, the stations are assured of having no collisions. Since all stations set their NAVs both for the RTS and CTS frames, it helps combat the hidden terminal problem as it is likely that a station will hear the CTS even if it is hidden from the station sending the RTS or vice versa and will not try to transmit during the period

5. Frames have a prioritized access to the channel. Highest priority is given to acknowledgment, CTS and Fragment frames, which wait only for a Short Inter Frame Space(SIFS) duration before accessing the channel. Other frames like Data and RTS have to wait for a DFS-IFS(DIFS) interval to access the channel. This also provides a randomization effect to avoid collisions.

3. Hidden Terminal Model

We consider an ad-hoc network of independent stations capable of communicating with every other station in the BSS. The model for hidden terminals is based on the following observations

1. Stations in a wireless LAN can change their location. Due to it's mobility a station may move out of the transmission range of another station, causing the pair to be hidden from each other. The number of stations a given station is hidden from varies over time and at any given time it can hear only the stations in it's vicinity.
2. Hidden terminals can also be caused by static obstructions, which prevent signals of one station from reaching the other.

We base our modeling of hidden terminals on groups as proposed in [6].

- Consider a symmetric matrix **H**.

$$H_{ij} = \left\{ \begin{array}{ll} 1 & \text{station i is hidden from station j} \\ 0 & \text{otherwise} \end{array} \right\}$$

$$H_{ij} = H_{ji}$$

- All stations that can hear exactly the same subset of stations constitute a *group*. Stations with identical rows or columns in **H** form a group. Also, if station i cannot hear station j, station j also cannot hear station i. This would be the case when all stations have the same transmission power and the cause of their being hidden is also isodirectional.
- Two groups able to hear transmissions from each other are said to be *dependent*.
- A *hearing graph* can be constructed based on dependencies between groups. Each node in the graph represents a group and there exists an edge between two nodes if they are *dependent*.

We extend this model to include the following.

- The geographical area of a WLAN and its vicinity are modeled as a mesh of hexagonal cells.
- Stations occupy cells and the number of stations in a hexagonal cell varies over time. In our simulations we populate cells with stations according to a probability distribution.
- All stations in a given hexagonal cell form a *group* as they can hear exactly the same subset of stations. Here the assumption is that each cell is small enough to approximate the location of each station to the center of the hexagon.
- Different scenarios under which hidden terminals can occur are modeled by assigning dependencies between groups. When hidden terminals caused only by the transmission range of stations and their mobility are considered, dependencies can be assigned on the basis of distance between cells. When static obstructions in the geographical layout of the WLAN are considered as the cause of hidden terminals, dependencies can be assigned by analyzing which locations are hidden from each other due to obstructions. More complex interactions taking both the mobility of stations and the geographical layout into account, can also be similarly modeled.

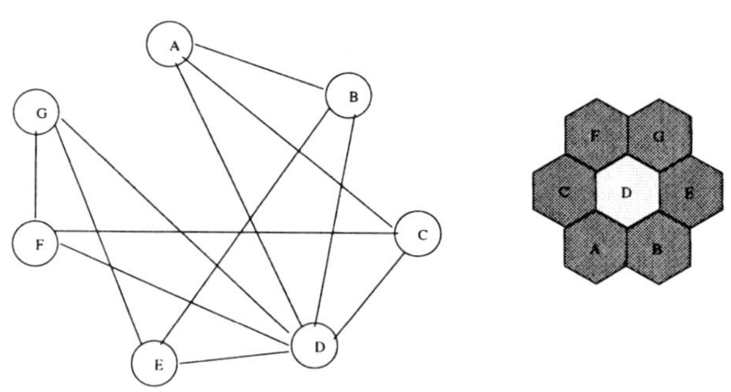

Figure 2. Groups: Hearing graph and hexagonal cells for $d = 1$

- When assigning dependencies based on distance, a station in a given cell is assumed to be able to communicate with stations in neighboring cells within a radius of d cells from it's cell (Figure 2 shows dependencies between groups with $d = 1$). The value of d would depend on the granularity at which the region is divided into hexagons and the transmission range of each station. By increasing the number of cells representing a given region, better approximations for the location of a station can be obtained. The value of d will have to be correspondingly increased when more cells represent a given area.

- When a geographical layout is considered, dependencies between cells are defined according to the location of the static obstructions.

Next, we show how the concept of geographical hexagonal areas can be used to model hidden terminals caused by both mobility of stations (section 3.1), as well as obstructions (section 3.2).

3.1. Dynamic Location Model

In this section we consider hidden terminals caused by mobility of stations. Our model is based on associates a *location probability* with each station. We make the following assumptions:

- Stations are most likely to be located in their BSA but occasionally move out. They are more likely to be near the BSA, rather than far from it. The probability of their being at a distance n from the center of their BSA (in hexagonal units), decreases as n increases, tending to zero, as n approaches infinity.
- This probability does not vary with time. Every *Reassignment_Time* seconds we reassign the geographical location of each station based on this probability. Thus a station belongs to different cells (groups) at different times.
- Besides other stations in the same group as it, a station can also hear stations in the neighboring six hexagonal cells but none outside that region i.e d is assumed to be one.
- Each station has the same location probability.

We can view our model as composed of ring of hexagons (numbered from 1 to ∞) around the central hexagon constituting the BSA (numbered 0)(figure 3). The nth ring of hexagons around the BSA has $6n$ cells. We assume that within a given ring a station is equiprobable to be in any of the cells. Thus the probabilities of a station being in a hexagon in ring n, around the BSA (location probability) is assigned as follows.

$$p_n = \frac{\alpha(1-\alpha)^n}{6n}; n \geq 1$$

A station is in the BSA with probability

$$p_0 = \alpha$$

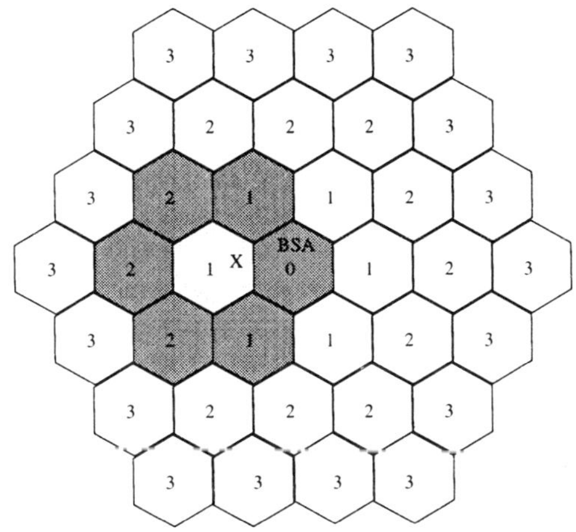

Figure 3. Dynamic Location Model: Shaded portion shows locations which are within hearing range of a station in cell X

α is a measure of the likelihood of a station remaining in it's BSA. By varying the value of α the average number of stations hidden from each other at any given time changes. An estimate of the average number of pairs hidden from each other based on the value of α can be obtained as follows.
Let N be the number of stations.
Let X_n be the average number of stations at a cell in level n

$$X_n = \sum_{i=0}^{N} i p_n^i (1-p_n)^{N-i}$$

Let Y_n be the number of stations that can be heard by a cell at level n.

$$Y_n = 3X_n + 3X_{n+1} + X_{n-1} \; ; \; n \geq 1$$

$$Y_0 = X_0 + 6X_1$$

Thus at a cell at level n, each of X_n stations is hidden from $(N - Y_n)$ other stations. Moreover there are $6n$ cells at each level. Thus, average number of hidden pairs is

$$\frac{\sum_{n=1}^{\infty} X_n(N - Y_n).6n + (N - Y_0)X_0}{2}$$

Figure 4 gives a plot of alpha versus the percentage of hidden terminals. By varying the value of α we model different mobility scenarios. By measuring the throughput, average delay and blocking probability for each case we obtain a measure of the performance of the IEEE 802.11 protocol.

3.2. Wall Model

In this model we consider hidden terminals caused by static obstructions neglecting the effect of mobility. We assign stations to geographical areas, only once at the start of

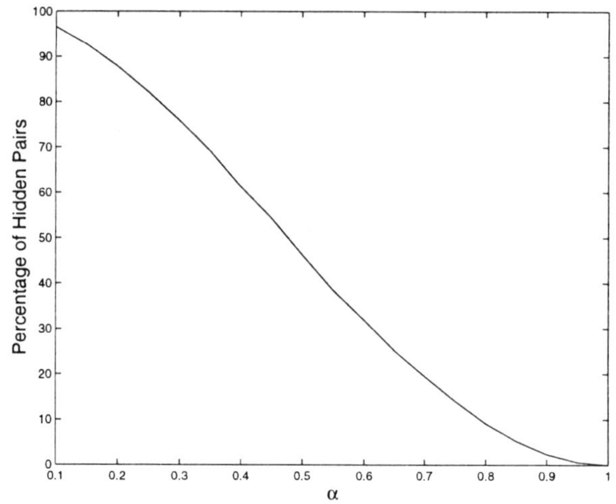

Figure 4. Relationship between α and the percentage of hidden terminals

the simulation. Their position does not change with time. Stations in a given hexagonal region can hear stations in the same cell and those in other cells that have an unobstructed path between them. Figure 5 gives an example of such a scenario and also gives the associated hearing graph. Note that here we have used a geometric granularity much smaller than that for the model in the previous section. The model in fact can be extended to cover both conditions simultaneously.

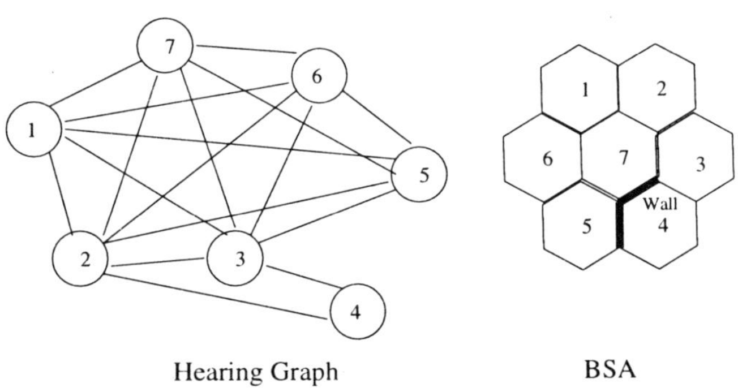

Figure 5. Modeling hidden terminals due to static obstructions

4. Simulation Model

Two separate models have been considered for fixed and mobile stations as explained above. The following assumptions have been made in both cases in order to simplify the models :

- The effect of bit errors in the channel has been neglected. This is necessitated because our objective is to study how the performance of the network deteriorates in presence of hidden terminals. The addition of bit errors complicates the interpretation.
- We assume that no station operates in the "power saving" mode. This implies that a station will respond immediately after the receipt of a frame with some kind of acknowledgment.

The arrival of packets to the MAC from higher layers has been modeled as a Poisson process. The rate of arrival of packets at each station is assumed to be the same. The packet lengths have been modeled as a truncated geometric distribution with a maximum length of 2312 octets. A finite buffer is maintained by each station and all packets that exceed the capacity are dropped. A sender selects the destination for a message with equal probability for all stations. In case of a collision, retransmission takes place and stations execute the random back-off procedure. The number of retransmissions of a packet is limited by a Retry_Limit.

An ongoing transmission can be corrupted only when another station within the hearing range of either the sender or the receiver, and not hidden from either, starts a simultaneous transmission. Thus it is possible for two simultaneous transmissions to go on if the senders and receivers in the two transmissions belong to *groups* not *dependent* on each other. This condition is also termed as the capture effect and has been implemented in our simulations.

We assume that the physical layer uses Direct Sequence Spread Spectrum (DSSS). This entails addition of a DSSS header and DSSS preamble to each packet and adds to the protocol overhead.

4.1. SES Implementation

The simulation was carried out using SES/Workbench, [5] a simulation and modeling tool. SES uses an object oriented approach, defining a set of nodes and transactions to model system behavior. Different nodes have different functionality, e.g. a blocking node to block transactions till a condition is satisfied, a delay node to delay the transaction for a specific simulation time interval etc. Transactions follow a predefined path between nodes, executing specific code at each node. A graphical interface provides an easy way to put simulation objects together. Our implementation has different modules to model the sending of frames, receiving of frames and the wireless channel. Each of these is dimensioned on the number of stations in the system. Thus by actually tracing a path that a frame takes from the sender to the receiver, the implementation of the protocol was greatly simplified. However, the use of SES had the disadvantage of large binaries and slow execution times.

4.2. Simulation parameters

Values for system parameters were taken as defined in table 1, unless otherwise specified.

Parameter	Default Value
Data Stations	40
Average MSDU Length	1000 octets
Channel Rate	1Mbps
RTS_Threshold	250 octets
Fragmentation_Threshold	800 octets
Retry_Limit	7
DSSS preamble	144 bits
DSSS header	48 bits
Station Buffer Size	300 frames
Slot_Time	$20\mu s$
SIFS_Time	$10\mu s$
DIFS_Time	$50\mu s$
Propagation_Delay	$5\mu s$
Reassignment_Time	5s
Offered Load	0.65Mbps

Table 1. Simulation Parameters

5. Simulation Results

In this section we present simulation results for the dynamic location model under various hidden terminal conditions. We also give results for the wall model explained in section 3.2.

Effect of hidden terminals on the protocol can be explained as follows :

- When there are no hidden terminals, the time window for a collision is equal to the *slot time* plus the propagation delay of the first packet. This is because a station that has data to transmit, executes an exponential backoff in which it checks the state of the channel after each *slot time* duration. If another station starts transmission, then the information about channel status can be at most *slot time* plus the propagation delay duration old. Any transmission started within this duration would result in a collision.

- In the presence of hidden terminals, the collision window can be much larger. When a packet is being transmitted without the exchange of the RTS/CTS control frames, a station hidden from the sender but in vicinity of the receiver can cause a collision by transmitting anytime during the entire transmission duration of the frame. By exchanging the RTS/CTS pair, this window can be reduced to the transmission delay of RTS (refer to section 2(4)), but it is still much larger than the ideal case.

A larger contention window results in more collisions which in turn has a detrimental effect on system performance.

5.1. Dynamic Location Model

Here we present results for the model explained in section 3.1. All graphs have been plotted for different values of α and the relationship between α and the number of hidden terminals is given in Figure 4.

5.1.1. Effect of Hidden Terminals on Throughput

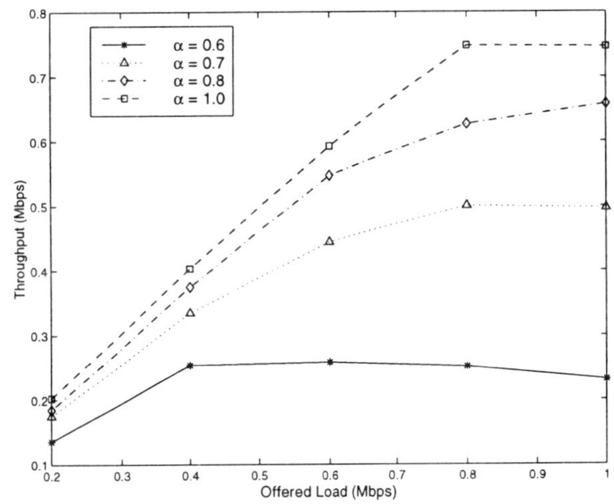

Figure 6. Effect of hidden terminals on throughput

Offered load is defined as the average number of bits per second passed down to the MAC sublayer at the source. Throughput is the average number of bits per second passed up from the MAC sublayer at the destination.

Figure 6 shows the aggregate throughput in Mbps versus offered load in Mbps for various numbers of hidden terminal pairs in the system. When all stations can hear each other ($\alpha = 1$), system throughput saturates at approximately 75 percent. However, when approximately 30 percent of stations pairs are hidden ($\alpha = 0.6$), throughput can drop to as low as 22 percent. The throughput actually becomes slightly lesser with increasing load because at higher arrival rates, chances of simultaneous transmissions become higher. A system with $\alpha = 0.8$, on an average can see about 10 percent hidden stations and the protocol performs acceptably under these conditions with a maximum throughput of 65 percent.

5.1.2. Effect of Hidden Terminals on Delay

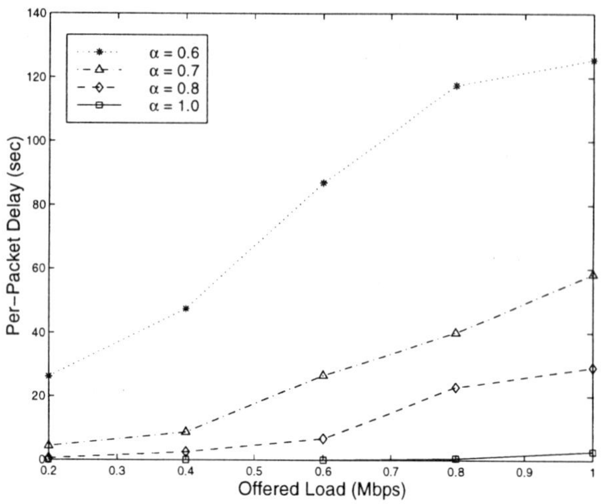

Figure 7. Effect of hidden terminals on delay

Presence of hidden terminals has a pronounced effect on the average packet delay in the system. Delay is defined as the difference between the time at which a frame is accepted by the sender's MAC sublayer and the time at which it receives an acknowledgment from the receiver's MAC. Figure 7 shows the average delay in seconds versus offered load in Mbps, for different number of hidden terminal pairs. The average delay increases by about an order of magnitude even under conditions of moderate load and 10 percent hidden stations. The performance becomes much worse as the load increases.

5.1.3. The Effect of Hidden Terminals on Blocking Probability

Blocking probability is defined as the fraction of packets dropped from the system after experiencing *Retry_Limit* number of collisions. Figure 8 shows blocking probability versus the number of hidden pairs at an offered system load of 0.65 Mbps. The blocking probability increases steadily with a increase in the number of hidden terminals and can reach about 13% when approximately 30% of station pairs are hidden.

5.1.4. The Effect of RTS on Delay

As explained in section 2(4), the RTS/CTS mechanism is used to reduce the chances of collisions in the presence of hidden terminals. In figure 9, average delay in seconds is plotted against RTS_Threshold for a number of hidden terminal pairs. Minimum delays are achieved when the RTS_Threshold is zero, ie. the RTS/CTS pair is exchanged for all packets. Delays can increase by more than two orders

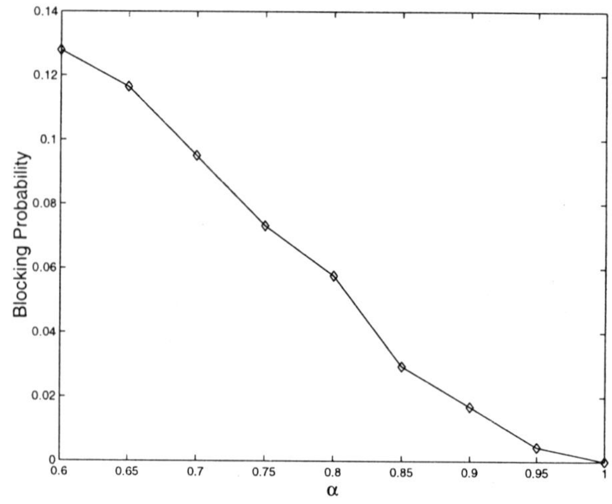

Figure 8. Effect of hidden terminals on blocking probability

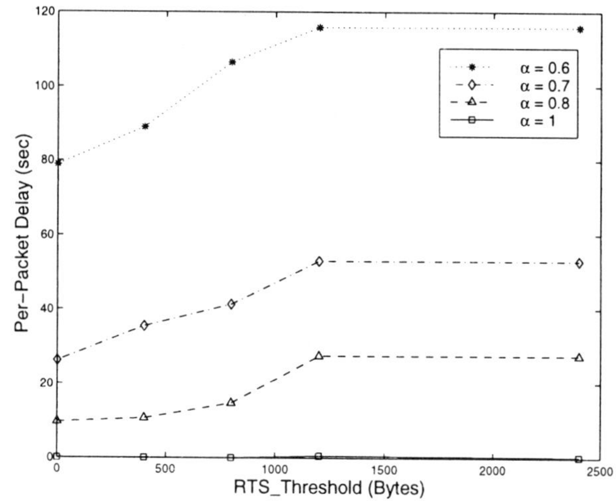

Figure 9. Effect of RTS on delay

of magnitude when RTS/CTS is never used (RTS_Threshold = 2400). The curves even out after RTS_Threshold is about 1100 because the average MSDU length for the experiment was taken as 1000 bytes. Experiments with lower average MSDU lengths, yield similar results.

5.1.5. The Effect of RTS on Throughput

Figure 10 shows the throughput against RTS_Threshold, for various numbers of hidden terminal pairs (α). As expected, the throughput for a given value of α decreases with an increase in RTS_Threshold. The maximum achievable throughput also decreases with an increase in the number of hidden terminals. Also, of importance is the shape of the curves for different values of α. When there are a large

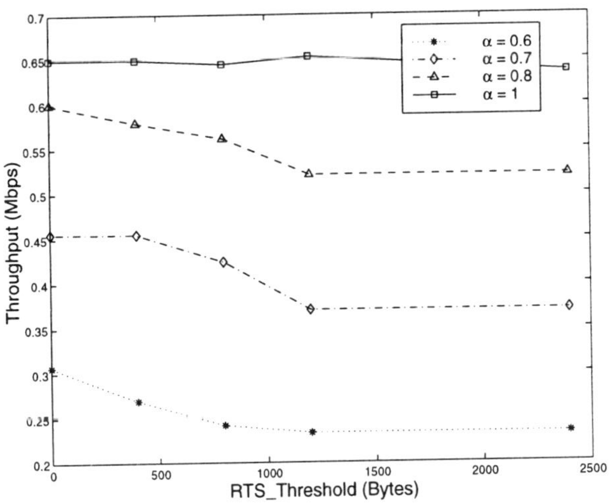

Figure 10. Effect of RTS on throughput

number of hidden terminals (α = 0.6), throughput drops much more sharply for a small increase in RTS_Threshold.

5.2. Wall Model

Simulation results are presented for the the example layout shown in figure 5. We used the following simulation parameters :

- Each cell has 6 stations
- Each station generates the same load, with an aggregated offered load of 0.6 Mbps
- Stations remain static for the entire simulation run. The H matrix also remains constant for the entire duration of the simulation.

As shown in figure 5, stations in cells 2 and 3 can hear all other stations. Stations in cell 4 are hidden from all other stations, except stations in cells 2,3 and 4.

5.2.1. Effect on Throughput

In Figure 11, throughput is represented as a percentage of the offered load aggregated over all stations in a cell. A 100% throughput means that stations in a cell were able to transmit all generated frames. Stations in cells 2 and 3 can hear all stations, and hence get a 100% throughput, but stations in cell 4 which are hidden from all others except those in 2 and 3 get almost 0% throughput. Although the rest of the cells are hidden only from 4, they have a substantial decrease in throughput and can manage to get only about 20% of their frames through.

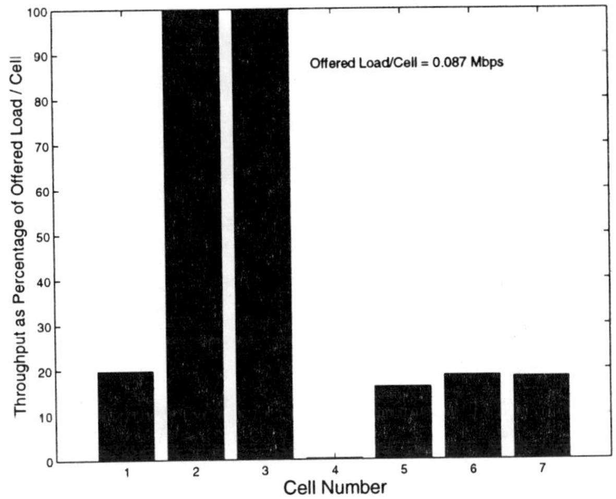

Figure 11. Wall model : Effect on throughput

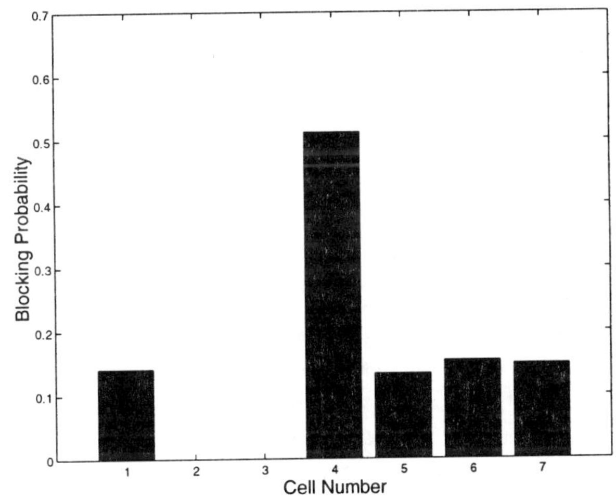

Figure 12. Wall model : Effect on blocking probability

5.2.2. Effect on Blocking Probability

As shown in figure 12, stations in cell 4 have a very high blocking probability, as they are hidden from most other stations. Stations in cells 2 and 3 experience no blocks while rest of the stations have about 15% of their packets blocked.

5.2.3. Effect on Delay

Figure 13 shows the average packet delay experienced by stations in each cell. Stations in cell 4 have a low delay because most of their frames are directed towards hidden stations. These are blocked, and hence do not contribute towards average delay. Stations in cells 5,6,7 and 8 experience delays of more than an order of magnitude as compared to

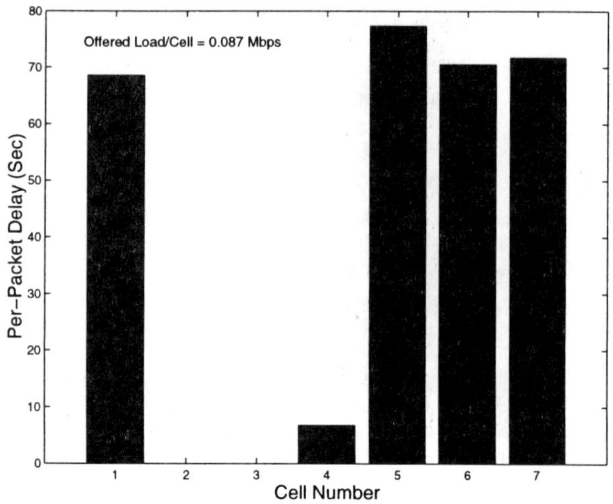

Figure 13. Wall model : Effect on delay

stations in cells 2 and 3 which are within the hearing range of all other stations.

6. Conclusion

In this paper we have studied the performance of the IEEE 802.11 MAC protocol in the presence of hidden terminals. For this we have proposed a general model for modeling hidden terminals in a WLAN.

Our simulations show that the performance of the IEEE 802.11 protocol deteriorates in the presence of hidden terminals. While the throughput is acceptable when less than 10 percent of station pairs are hidden, the average per frame delay increases by as much as an order of magnitude.

Given other system parameters, the system throughput, average packet delay and blocking probability is dependent only on the percentage of station pairs hidden from each other. The average delay, throughput and blocking probability seen by a particular station is not uniform and varies greatly depending on the number of stations hidden from it.

The RTS/ CTS mechanism used in the protocol helps improve it's performance. In the presence of hidden terminals best throughput and average delay are obtained when RTS/ CTS is used before the transmission of each frame regardless of the frame length.

Our modeling of hidden terminals is general enough to be able to model complex scenarios of mobility and static layouts. In this paper we have considered two simple scenarios. Although other intricate models may depict more realistic scenarios, we expect their effect on protocol performance to be similar as it is a function of the number of hidden terminals, rather than their cause.

References

[1] F. Cali, M. Conti, and E. Gregori. IEEE 802.11 Wireless LAN: Capacity Analysis and Protocol Enhancement. In *Proceedings of IEEE INFOCOM '98*, 1998.

[2] K. Chen. Medium Access Control of Wireless LANs for Mobile Computing. *IEEE Network*, 8(5):50–63, Sept. 1994.

[3] H. S. Chhaya and S. Gupta. Throughput and Fairness Properties of Asynchronous Data Transfer Methods in the IEEE 802.11 MAC Protocol. In *Proceedings of the Sixth International Symposium on Personal, Indoor and Mobile Radio Communications*, 1995.

[4] B. P. Crow, I. Widjaja, J. G. Kim, and P. T. Sakai. IEEE 802.11 Wireless Local Area Networks. *IEEE Communications Magazine*, Sept. 1997.

[5] Scientific and Engineering Software Inc., Austin, TX. *SES Workbench Creating Models*.

[6] F. A. Tobagi and L. Kleinrock. Packet Switching in Radio Channels: Part II - The Hidden Terminal Problem in Carrier Sense Multiple-Access and the Busy-Tone Solution. *IEEE Transactions on Communications*, COM-23(12):1417–1433, Dec. 1975.

[7] J. Weinmiller, M. Schlager, A. Festag, and A. Wolisz. Performance Study of Access Control in Wireless LANs - IEEE 802.11 DFWMAC and ETSI RES 10 HIPERLAN. *Mobile Networks and Applications*, 2(1):55–67, June 1997.

A NEW AUTHENTICATION PROTOCOL FOR GSM NETWORKS

Khalid Al-Tawil   Ali Akrami   Habib Youssef
Department of Computer Engineering
King Fahd University of Petroleum and Minerals
Dhahran – 31261, Saudi Arabia
e-mail: {khalid,akrami,Youssef}@ccse.kfupm.edu.sa

Abstract

Mobile communication is one of the fastest growing sectors of the telecommunication industry. Mobile users can make and receive calls while they are moving independent of time, location and network access. The Global System for Mobile communication (GSM) is a Pan-European digital cellular mobile system supporting widespread roaming and personal communication services (PCS) in a worldwide wireless communication network. However, wireless mobile systems are more vulnerable to fraudulent access and eavesdropping. Although the authentication process in GSM is giving a reasonable security level, it is overloading the network with significant signaling traffic and increasing the call set up time. The signaling load and the authentication delay are of particular importance and become the subject of widespread research interest. In this paper, we will study and analyze the GSM privacy and authentication protocols, and propose new authentication protocol with less signaling traffic and better call set up time, that can be used in GSM networks.

Keywords: Mobile communication, GSM, Authentication, Authentication delay, Security.

1 Introduction

The Global System for Mobile communication (GSM), is an European digital cellular system standard providing a broad spectrum of communication capabilities and supporting personal and terminal mobility through a worldwide Personal Communication System (PCS) [10, 15]. Personal mobility is provided through the insertion of a small smart card called subscriber identity module (SIM) allowing its holder to make and receive calls independent of both the network point of attachment and the specific terminal. This means that the services to which a user has subscribed are available even if he moves to other network areas or changes his terminals. However, wireless transmission is vulnerable to relatively easy interception such as fraudulent call attempts and intrusion or listening-in by third party. For these reasons, a secure mobile communication system is needed. In GSM networks, two requirements have been considered: privacy and authentication. Privacy involves ensuring that an eavesdropper cannot intercept the conversations of the parties, and authentication involves ensuring that the service is not obtained fraudulently in order to avoid usage charges [1, 2]. GSM network can be subdivided into two major

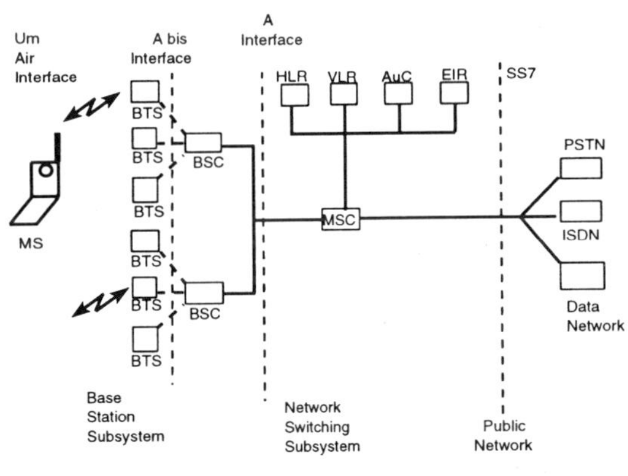

Figure 1: GSM System Architecture

subsystems: the radio part and the switching part as shown in Figure 1.

1. The radio subsystem or the Base Station Subsystem (BSS) provides and manages radio transmission paths between mobile stations (MS) and the Mobile Switching Center (MSC).

2. The Network and Switching Subsystem (NSS). The NSS manages the switching functions through the Mobile Switching Center (MSC) and provides an external access to several customer databases. The MSC is the core of the NSS subsystem that

0-8186-8810-6/98 $10.00

handles all the switching functions needed for all mobiles users within its geographical area.

In the NSS, we find four basic customers databases:

- The Home Location Register (HLR): contains the permanent subscriber parameters and features for a group of subscribers within a given network.
- The Visited Location Register (VLR): a dynamic data base, whose entries move with subscribers, containing information for all users within one or more location area (group of cells).
- The Authentication Center (AuC): a strongly protected database which contains all the authentication and encryption information, needed by the HLR and VLR, for every mobile user.
- The Equipment Identity Register (EIR): used to prevent the use of stolen or fraudulent MS equipments.

In this paper, a new GSM authentication protocol is presented. We present and analyze the conventional GSM authentication protocol in Section 2 and 3 respectively. Our new GSM authentication protocol is presented and analyzed in Section 4. In Section 5 we compare the two protocols. Section 6 concludes this paper.

2 GSM Authentication Protocols

Authentication involves both identification and verification of mobile users. Identification is the process where an entity presents its identity, while verification is the process where the identity is checked [11]. The authentication process is carried out through the challenge/response mechanism which consists of asking a question that only the right user equipment (SIM) may answer. The returned answer computed internally in the user SIM card, will be compared in the authentication center. More precisely, a random number RAND is sent and the expected answer, called the signed result (SRES), is returned. The 128-bit RAND is generated locally by HLR/AuC and then combined with the User's secret K_i through the (A3) algorithm to get the 32-bit SRES. Each time a mobile station is authenticated, the network and the MS has to compute the ciphering key (K_c) which is used for ciphering and deciphering of transmitted data. The ciphering key K_c computation is basically similar to the SRES, using the A8 algorithm. The mobile station is continuously listening to the location area identity (LAI) being transmitted on the broadcast channel, comparing the new LAI received with the last LAI (stored in the SIM [7]. Whenever the received LAI is different than the old LAI stored in its SIM cards, the MS proceeds with a new registration. The registration starts first with getting access to the Stand-alone Dedicated Control Channel (SDCCH) over which the BTS and the MS communicate to each other, then the authentication process has to be carried out as follows:

- *Step 1*: the MS transmits the registration request (location update) to the base station over the SDCCH. The BTS forwards the registration request to the MSC, which informs the corresponding VLR about this request. The registration request includes the temporary mobile subscriber identity (TMSI) and LAI.
- *Step 2*: once the new VLR receives the TMSI, it sends a request to the HLR asking for the authentication parameters for that MS.
- *Step 3*: the HLR forwards this request to the AuC.
- *Step 4*: the AuC computes SRES and K_c by applying the MS's secret key K_i and a RAND number to the A3 and A8 algorithms, then sends the authentication triplet (RAND, SRES, and K_c) to the VLR through the HLR.
- *Step 5*: the VLR sends the RAND to the MS through the MSC, and asks the MS to compute the SRES and sends it back.
- *Step 6*: the MS computes the SRES and the K_c locally using that RAND number and the K_i through the A3 and A8 algorithms, then sends SRES back to the VLR and keeps K_c for later use.
- *Step 7*: the VLR once receives the SRES from the MS, compares it with the SRES provided from the AuC. If the two are equal, the MS passes the authentication process.

The authentication process is summarized in Figure 2 and Figure 3. The privacy of users is achieved by ciphering the traffic between the user's terminal and the radio base station to prevent eavesdropping and protecting the exchange of the signaling messages. The ciphering key K_c is used to cipher and decipher transmitted data, by applying an exclusive OR operation between the radio burst and a ciphering sequence using a specific ciphering algorithm A5 as shown in Figure 4. The secrecy of K_i is the cornerstone on which all the security mechanism is based.

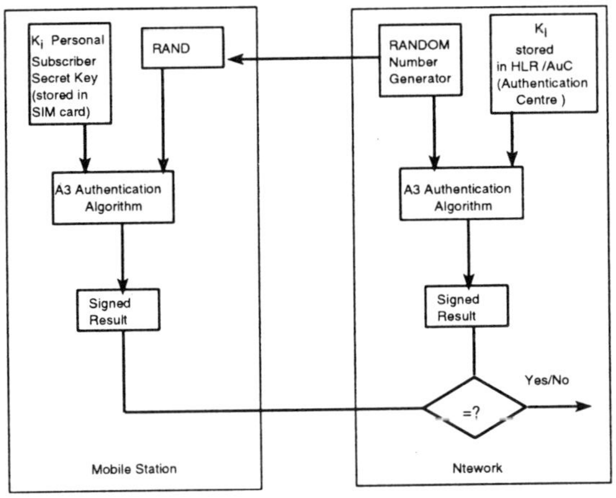

Figure 2: GSM privacy and authentication

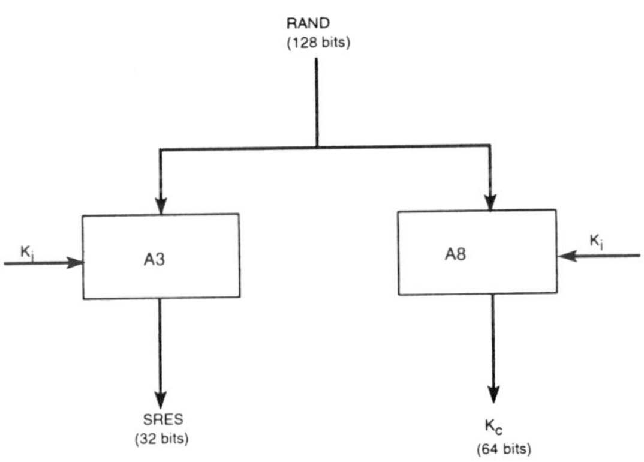

Figure 3: GSM privacy and authentication Results Generation

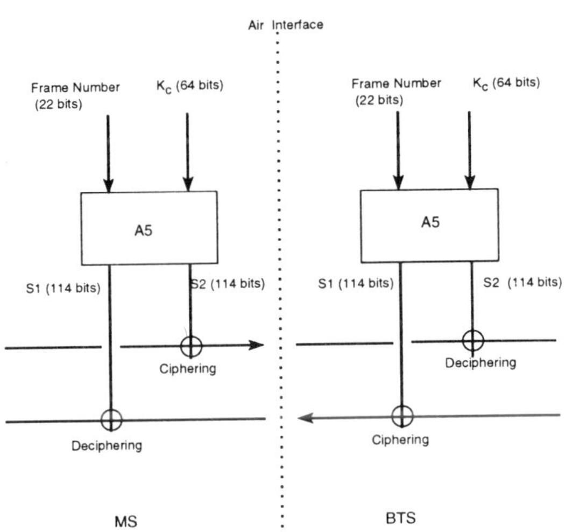

Figure 4: GSM ciphering and deciphering process

3 Analysis of GSM Authentication Protocols

When users move from one location area to another, the MS has to register in the new location area and implicitly deregister from the old one. The authentication process is triggered on every registration, call attempts (originating or terminating) and with service changes (a network option). While this mechanism is giving a reasonable level of security, it is generating a large amount of signaling, increasing the call setup time.

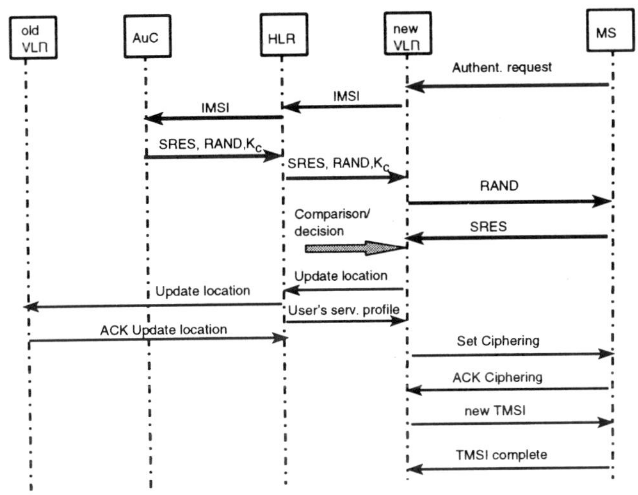

Figure 5: GSM challenge/response signaling flow

In our analysis, we concentrate on the signaling load generated by these protocols and the delay that might add to the whole call setup time [9, 13]. A widely used terminal/user mobility model is the fluid flow mobility model described in [12]. This model assumes that mobile users carrying terminals are moving at an average velocity of v, their direction of movement is uniformly distributed over $[0, 2\pi]$, mobile users are uniformly populated with the density ρ, and the registration area boundary is of length L. In [13], it has been shown that the rate of registration area crossing, R, is given by:

$$R = \frac{\rho \times v \times L}{\pi}$$

The above model is used with the following assumptions taken from a real GSM environment to analyze the traffic involved in the authentication process:

- One HLR for the whole network service area (SA), and each location area is served with one VLR
- 64 registration areas (64 VLRs).
- Square registration area size $(8.65km)^2 = 66.60$ sq km.

- Border length L = 34.6 km.
- Mean call origination rate = mean call termination rate = 2.6/hr/user.
- Total number of MS users =764,000.
- Mean density of MS = ρ = 267/sq km.
- Average speed of MS, v = 6.3 km/hr.

The traffic due to registration is generated by MS moving into a new registration area (RA). In the steady state, the rate at which users move into a RA is equal to the rate at which MS move out of that RA. Since every registration area is handled by one VLR, the rate of registration area crossing, R, is given by:

$$R_{Reg.,RA} = \frac{267x34.6x6.3}{3600\pi} = 5.14/s$$

Similarly, $R_{dereg.,VLR}$ is 5.14/s. This must also be equal to the number of deregistrations (registration cancellations). Thus the total number of registration messages per second arriving at the HLR is equal to:

$$R_{reg.,HLR} = R_{reg,VLR} \times \text{ total number of registration areas}$$
$$= 5.14 \times 64/s = 329/s$$

Therefore we have 5.14/s and 329/s authentication requests per each VLR and HLR respectively. Now we compute the total number of authentication requests due to call origination (CO) and call termination (CT) for the entire serving area (SA).

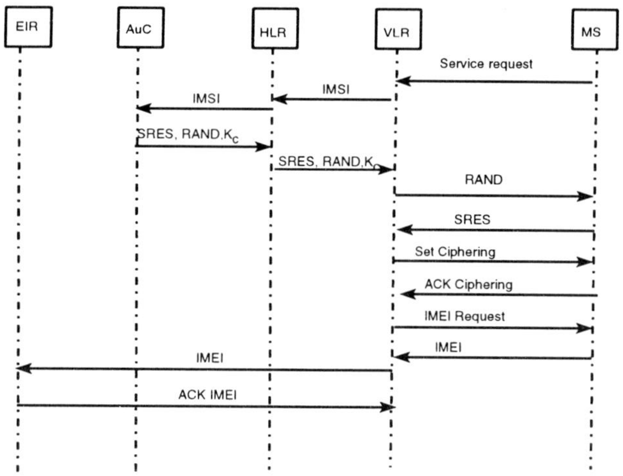

Figure 6: GSM call origination authentication signaling messages

The total number of call originating per serving area is equal to:

$$R_{callOrig./SA} = \frac{2.6x764,000}{3600} = 551.7/s.$$

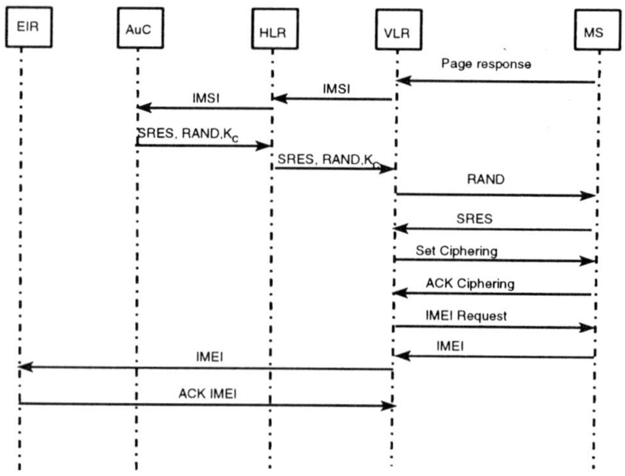

Figure 7: GSM call termination authentication signaling messages

Similarly, the total number of call terminating will be equal to 551.7/s. Thus the number of calls originating per RA is equal to:

$$R_{callOrig./RA} = \frac{551.7}{64} = 8.62/s.$$

and the number of calls terminating/delivered per RA is 8.62/s. Table 1 summarizes the total authentication request rate per VLR and HLR for each type of activity as computed above.

Table 1: Authentication request rate.

	VLR/sec	HLR/sec
Registration	5.14	329
Call Termination	8.62	551.7
Call Origination	8.62	551.7
Total/network	22.38	1432.4

Using the signaling messages flow between network data bases (registers) as illustrated in Figure 5, Figure 6, and Figure 7, we find the number of signaling messages per authentication request for the registration, call origination and call termination activities as illustrated in Table 2. Table 3 shows the total signaling messages generated per VLR and HLR for each type of activity. For the registration, for example, there are 5.14 authentication requests per second for the VLR and 329 for the HLR. For each authentication request, there are 5 messages processed by the VLR and 4 by the HLR as shown in Figure 5. The total signaling message/s for the registration activity for VLR and HLR will be as follows:

VLR: 5.14 X 5 = 25.7 signaling messages/s
HLR: 329 x 4 = 1316 signaling messages/s

Table 2: Signaling messages per Authentication request

Activity	Auc	HLR	VLR	Old VLR
Registration	2	4	5	1
Call Origination	2	4	5	0
Call Termination	2	4	5	0

Table 3: Total signaling messages: GSM

	VLR	HLR
Registration	25.7	1316
Call Origination	43.1	2206.8
Call Termination	43.1	2206.8
Total	111.9	5729.6

The authentication delay is defined as the time interval from the instant the user starts the authentication process until the network takes the final decision (acceptance or rejection) of the user [5]. In GSM, radio interface signaling transactions and user information are transferred on dedicated channels. These channels could be used among several users employing combined random access and reservation techniques. The random access procedure is based on a slotted-ALOHA concept [8]. Figure 8 depicts the messages involved in authentication delay.

Let us assume that the time delay due to network data bases (DB) message exchange, is TDB and it is the same between all of them, and the time between MS and BTS is assumed to be TRF (Radio frequency), using Figure 8 the authentication delay (TAd) for the GSM conventional protocol can be computed as:

$$TAd = 4TDB + TRF$$

From the equation above we can see that the authentication delay is linearly dependent on the TRF.

4 Proposed Authentication Protocol for GSM Networks

The term protocol for data communication procedure is a kind of agreement for the exchange of information in a distributed system [4]. Authentication

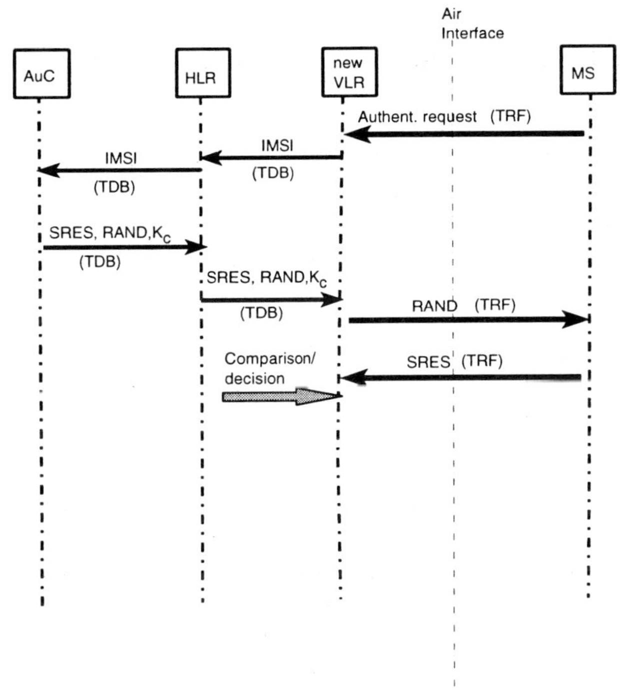

Figure 8: Signaling messages flow for GSM Authentication delay

protocols are the basis of security in many distributed systems, and in particular in wireless communication systems. The analysis of this protocol has shown an important signaling load generated due to the challenge response mechanism used. In addition to that, the process is giving a considerable delay, called the authentication delay, making the call setup time longer. The GSM protocol is based on challenge response mechanism [3] which consists of sending a RAND number to the MS and challenge it for answering with the same signed result SRES already computed in the AuC using the subscriber secret key K_i. Several signaling messages have to be exchanged between different network elements. We propose a new efficient authentication approach, using "mobile user events counter" (COUNTM) used basically in GSM networks for statistics. This counter is stored in the network (HLR) and it can be added in the mobile user SIM card. The counter is changing upon any activity such as registration, call terminating, call originating and SIM attach/detach. In the devised scheme, a random number RANDM (64 bits) is generated locally by the MS to compute a pre-authentication result AUTHR. The AUTHR is the output of A3 algorithm when RANDG and K_i are used as inputs. The counter (COUNTM) concatenated to the RANDM form the global random number called RANDG (128 bits).

4.1 Proposed Authentication Scheme

We are interested in reducing the authentication delay and the network signaling overhead by reducing the number of messages which lead to decreasing the call setup time without compromising GSM security. As for every network access (registration, call attempts) the MS sends a channel request over the Random Access Channel (RACH), the base station receives the request message, and allocates a SDCCH that will be used by the MS to communicate with the network. The proposed scheme is as follows:

- *Step 1*: the MS transmits the registration request (location update) to the base station over the SDCCH. The BTS forwards the registration request to the MSC, which informs the corresponding VLR about this request. The registration request includes the TMSI, LAI, RANDM and the AUTHR which is the output of A3 algorithm when K_i and the RANDG are applied as inputs.
- *Step 2*: once the new VLR receives the TMSI, it sends a request to the HLR asking for the verification of the AUTHR of that MS.
- *Step 3*: the HLR adds the MS's COUNTM to the request, then forwards it to the AuC.
- *Step 4*: the AuC produces the RANDG, then computes the AUTHR and K_c by applying the MS's secret K_i and the RANDG number to the A3 and A8 algorithms respectively, and finally compares the two AUTHRs. If the two are equal, the MS passes the authentication process.

The RANDM is generated locally from the MS, and it is sent to the network to be used in the AuC. The COUNTM is an event log counter used in the network and in the MS, where all activities are recorded. After each activity the counter's value is changing and a RANDM is generated to prepare the AUTHR to be used for the next authentication request. Figure 9 and Figure 10 show the proposed protocol, and Figure 11 depicts the corresponding signaling message flow.

4.2 Security Correctness of the proposed scheme

The proposed protocol preserves the same security level achieved by the original GSM authentication protocol. In order to show this, we use a comparison

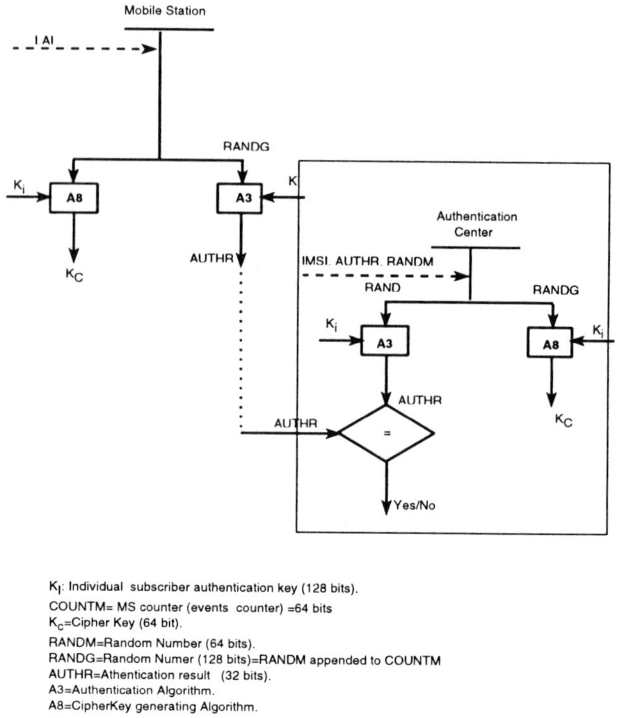

Figure 9: Proposed authentication protocol

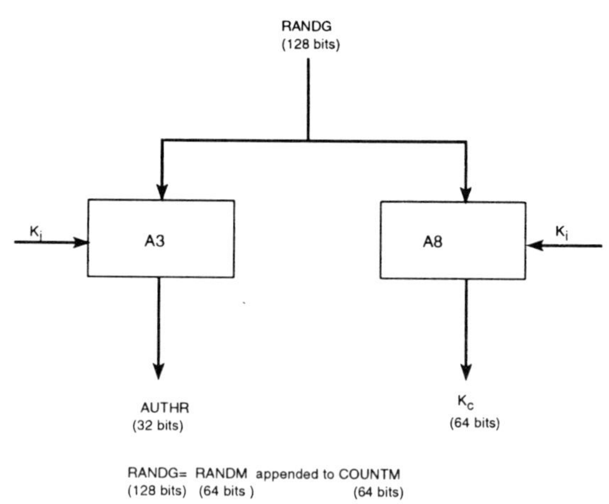

Figure 10: AUTHR and K_c generation for the proposed scheme

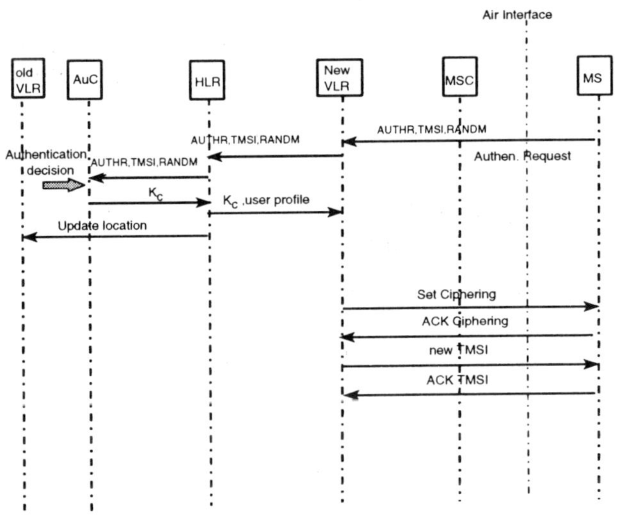

Figure 11: Signaling messages flow for the proposed scheme

methodology between the two approaches. In GSM approach, the authentication protocol consists of the following steps:

1. The MS sends its identity to the network with a service request.
2. The VLR/network identifies the MS and prepare the security triplet (RAND, SRES, K_c).
3. The VLR sends a RAND to MS and asks for the SRES computed using that RAND.
4. The MS sends back the SRES computed in the SIM. The VLR compares the SRES coming from the SIM card to the SRES computed in AuC.

For the proposed scheme:

1. The MS prepare an AUTHR computed locally in the SIM using a RANDG, user's secret key, then sends the service request, the user identity, the RANDM to the network.
2. The network identifies and verifies that the AUTHR coming from the MS is the same as the AUTHR computed locally in the AuC.

So we can see from the steps listed above that the idea of GSM authentication is based on comparing an entity called SRES computed in two different places, the AuC and SIM, using the same input parameters RAND and K_i through A3 algorithm. In our devised scheme the same idea is preserved, the protocol consist of computing an AUTHR in two different places, the AuC and SIM, using the input parameters RANDG and K_i. The RANDG now consists of a COUNTM and a normal random number RANDM. In GSM, SRES and RAND are used as public parameters while K_i and K_c are used as private parameters that are never transmitted on the air. For our scheme, we have AUTHR, RANDM, as public parameters, and K_i, K_c are also maintained as private parameters. In GSM, RAND is used to compute SRES, but in our case, RANDM, is used as a part of the RANDG which is used to compute AUTHR. The security aspect in our scheme is enhanced by using the counter COUNTM, which is not transmitted on the air. The counter is modified for every activity such as registration, successful call attempt, and SIM attach/detach. Without the counter, an intruder will not benefit from collecting the RANDM and AUTHR from the air. In both schemes the secrecy of K_i is still the cornerstone on which all the security mechanism is based.

4.3 Signaling load of the proposed scheme

The term signaling refers to the set of actions required to set up a connection between hosts across the network under software control [6]. Actions here are messages sent from different GSM entities. Using the same model and analysis used in analyzing GSM protocol, we find that the number of messages is clearly less than the conventional GSM protocol. In Table 4, we find the number of signaling message per authentication request for each database register (AuC, VLR and HLR) using the rate of authentication requests per second for each type of activity (registration, call termination and origination), Table 5 summarizes the total number of messages per authentication request for each VLR and HLR.

Table 4: Signaling messages per authentication request

Activity	AuC	HLR	VLR	old VLR
Registration	1	2	2	1
Call Origination	1	2	2	0
Call Termination	1	2	2	0

4.4 Authentication Delay of the Proposed Scheme

The authentication delay of the proposed scheme is computed using the same assumptions used with GSM

Table 5: Total signaling messages: Proposed scheme

	VLR	HLR
Registration	10.28	658
Call Origination	17.24	1103.4
Call Termination	17.24	1103.4
Total	45.76	2866.72

protocol. Let us assume that network databases message exchanges, produce a delay of TDB and it is the same between all of them, and the time that the message takes from MS to BTS is denoted by TRF. From Figure 12, the authentication delay TAd can be computed as:

$$\text{TAd} = 1\text{TRF} + 2\text{DB}.$$

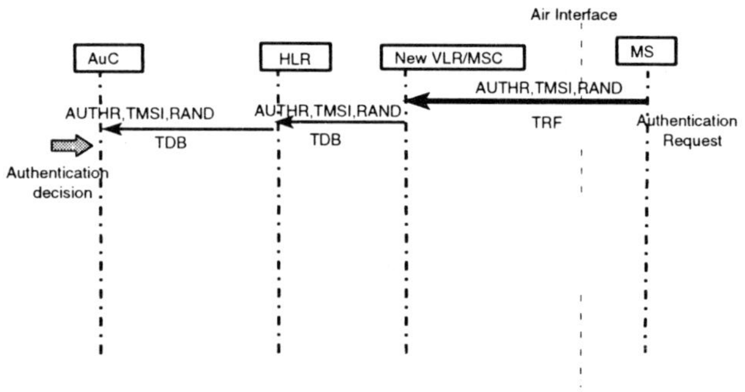

Figure 12: Signaling message flow for the Authentication delay

4.5 RAND number generation

In GSM approach, the RAND number is generated upon user authentication request, and it is used individually only once. In the proposed scheme, a RANDM number generated by the MS is concatenated to the mobile user's event counter (COUNTM) to form a global random number RANDG. Using the secret key and RANDG, the AUTHR is computed. RANDM is the one sent to the network. Generating RANDM from MS means an extra load (hardware) is added to the mobile equipment (ME). Both the battery life and the cost will be affected accordingly by this additional function implemented in the ME. However, the extra load added due to RANDM generation will not be high compared to the load generated by the A3 and A8 algorithms.

4.6 Bandwidth Requirement

In our proposed scheme we are using the following authentication parameters:

- The RANDM number is 64 bits.
- The size of AUTHR is 32 bits.
- LAI is 40 bits.
- Service Request (location update request/call attempt) is 8 bits.
- Temporary mobile subscriber identity TMSI is 32 bits.

The messages sent from the MS to the network (BST or VLR) for authentication will be of the following size: RANDM + AUTHR + LAI + SerReq. + TMSI = 64 + 32 + 40 +8 + 32 =191 bits (24 bytes). It has been shown in Section 3 that there are 5.14 authentication requests/s, due to registration and 8.62 authentication requests/s due to call attempts for each VLR. Thus for the registration activity, the bandwidth used between MS and BTS will be equal to 191x5.14=957 bits/s (119 bytes/s), and 191x 8.62 =1630 bits/s (204 bytes/s) for either call origination or call termination.
For the original GSM protocol, the following parameters are used:

- The RAND number is 64 bits.
- The size of SRES is 32 bits.
- LAI is 40 bits.
- Service Request (location update request/call attempt) is 8 bits.
- Temporary mobile subscriber identity TMSI is 32 bits.

The messages sent in the air from/to the network are the service request (8 bits), RAND (128 bits), and SRES (32 bits). Thus the maximum bandwidth will be 128 bits x 5.14=657 bits/s (83 bytes/s) for registration, and 128 bits x 8.62=1104 bits/s =138 bytes/s for call origination or termination. In both cases the bandwidth needed is still considered to be much lower than the GSM capacity.

5 Comparison and Discussion

The merit of our proposed scheme can be evaluated with respect to many criteria. The first criterion is security where authentication and privacy are preserved. The MS is still authenticated using the secret key and the authentication result is computed first in the MS SIM card then it is send to the authentication center AuC for verification and validation. The second criterion is the important reduction in the signaling messages between the various network elements.

Table 6: Total Network traffic (signaling messages/s)

	GSM	Prop. Scheme	% Improvement
VLR	111.9	45.76	50
HLR	5729.6	2864.8	50
Total	5841.5	2909.56	50

Table 6 outlines the difference between the GSM approach and our scheme in terms of total network traffic. The VLR has 111.9 signaling messages per second in the GSM protocol and 45.76 in our proposed scheme. The HLR is handling around 5729 signaling message per second when the GSM approach is used and 2864 messages per second when our scheme is used. The percentage of improvement is more than 50 percent. Varying the MS mobility rate (the speed of movement), we can see in Table 7 that the proposed scheme is maintaining the same level of improvement in terms of total network signaling which is around 50 percent compared to the conventional GSM approach. The third determinant factor in our analysis is the authentication delay which is normally added to the pre-selection or post-selection delay perceived by the user. As a consequence of that, the update of the old VLR will be only after the authentication decision has been taken. If a MS receives a call during that transition time, the network will page it in the area covered by the old VLR, but that MS has already moved to a new location area, therefore the paging request will be lost and the call will be aborted. The proposed scheme is clearly causing less delay than GSM protocol as shown in Figure 13.

The fourth advantage of the proposed scheme is the structure itself which is a very important issue in this analysis study. In the GSM challenge response mechanism, the process is based on challenging the MS after preparing the authentication triplet (SRES, RAND, K_c) in the authentication center. Then the VLR has to send the RAND number to the SIM of that MS and

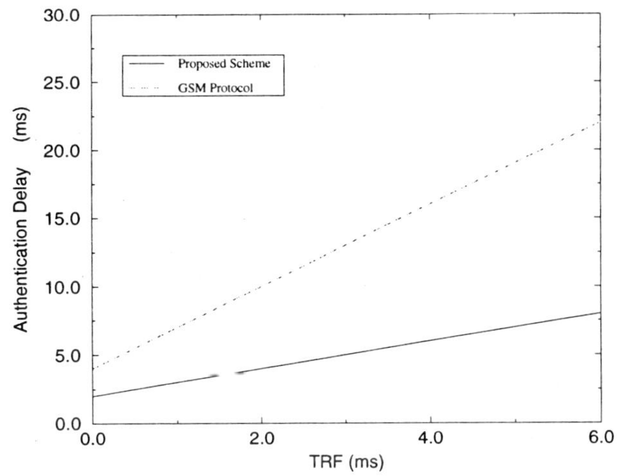

Figure 13: Authentication delay: comparison GSM and Proposed scheme

waits for the response (SRES), and upon comparison the authentication decision is taken. Our design concept is based on the general form of the authentication definition. So, instead of the long process described in the GSM conventional scheme, our idea starts from preparing the authentication result in the MS, then sending it to the AuC for verification and validation in three messages only. Using a counter in the computation of the AUTHR makes the possibility of security breaches more complicated. However, synchronizing the counter value between the MS and the HLR will introduce a problem that needs to be addressed. We are currently working in resolving this issue. Another advantage of the proposed scheme is that updating (deregistration) the old VLR is faster than the GSM approach.

6 Conclusion

In this paper we have studied and analyzed the GSM privacy and authentication protocols and the relevant signaling traffic generated. The signaling overhead and the delay incurred in accessing the service (delay in user authentication and data base registers) are key traffic performance parameters for mobile communication networks. This delay is basically due to the protocol architecture which is based on the challenge response mechanism. A new approach has been proposed for authenticating users in their home domain. The proposed scheme outperform the GSM authentication process in terms of number of signaling messages and authentication delay.

Table 7: Network Signaling Traffic with Different Mobility Rate

Mobility Rate (R)		GSM Protocol			Proposed Scheme		
Speed(V)	R	VLR	HLR	Tot. Sig.	VLR	HLR	Tot. Sig.
2	1.64	94.4	4833.4	4927.8	38.08	2311.76	2349.5
4	3.28	102.6	5253.2	5335.8	41.36	2628.64	2670
6.3	5.14	111.9	5729.6	5841.5	45.76	2866.8	2912.56
10	8.2	127.2	6512.8	6640	50.88	3488.8	3539.68
15	12.3	147.7	7562.4	7710.1	59.08	3783.2	3842.28

References

[1] Michael J.Beller, Li-Fung Chang,and Yacov Yacobi, "Privacy and Authentication on a Portable Communications System," *IEEE Journal on Selected Areas in Communications*, vol. 11, no. 6, pp. 821-829, Aug. 1993.

[2] Dan Brown, "Techniques For Privacy and Authentication in Personal Communication systems," *IEEE Personal Communications*, vol. 2, no. 4, pp. 6-10, Aug. 1995.

[3] Giovanna D'Aria, Flavio Muratore, and Valerio Palestini, "Simulation and Performance of the Pan-European Land Mobile Radio System," *IEEE Transaction on Vehicular Technology*, vol. 41, no. 2, pp. 177-189, May 1992.

[4] Gerard J. Holzman, "Design and Validation of Computer Protocols," *Prentice Hall*, 1991.

[5] Chih-Lin I, Gregory P. Pollini and Richard D. Gitlin, " PCS Mobility Management Using the Reverse Virtual Call Setup Algorithm," *IEEE/ACM Transactions on Networking*, vol.5, no.1, pp. 13-23, Feb. 1997.

[6] Jay Jayapalan and Mike Burke, "Cellular Data Services Architecture and Signaling," *IEEE Personal Communications*, Second Quarter, pp. 44-55, 1994.

[7] Mikko Laitinen and Jari Rantala, "Integration of intelligent network services into future GSM Networks," *IEEE Communication Magazine*, pp. 76-85, June 1995.

[8] Thomas F. La Porta, Malathi Veeraraghavan, Philip A. Treventi, and Ramachandran Ramjee, "Distributed Call Processing for Personal Communications Services," *IEEE Communication Magazine*, pp. 66-75, June. 1995.

[9] Thomas F. La Porta, Malathi Veeraraghavan, and Richard W. Buskens, "Comparison of Signaling Loads for PCS Systems," *IEEE/ACM Transactions on Networking*, vol.4, no.6, pp. 840-855, Dec. 1996.

[10] Yi-Bing Lin, "No Wires attached," *IEEE Potentials*, pp. 28-33, Oct./Nov. 1995.

[11] Refik Molva, Didier Samfat and Gene Tsudik, "An Authentication Protocol For Mobile Users," *IEE Colloquium on Security and Cryptography Applications to Radio System*, London, UK, June 1994.

[12] R.Thomas, H. Gilbert, and G. Mazziotto, "Influence of the Mobile station on the Performance of the Radio Mobile Cellular Network," *Proc. 3rd Nordic Seminar*, Paper 9.4, Copenhagen, Danmark, Sept. 1988.

[13] Gregory P. Pollini, Kathleen S. Meier-hellstern, and David J. Goodman, "Signaling Traffic Volume Generated by Mobile and Personal Communications," *IEEE Communications Magazine*, pp. 60-65, June 1995.

[14] Gregory P. Pollini, and David J. Goodman, "Signaling System Performance Evaluation for Personal Communications," *IEEE Transactions on Vehicular Tecnology*, vol. 45, no. 1, pp. 131-138, Feb. 1996.

[15] Moe Rahnema, "Overview of the GSM system and protocol Architecture," *IEEE Communication Magazine*, pp. 92-100, April 1993, .

QoS Routing in Ad Hoc Wireless Networks†

Chunhung Richard Lin

Dept. of Computer Science and Information Engineering, National Chung Cheng University, TAIWAN
Email: chlin@cs.ccu.edu.tw

Abstract

The emergence of nomadic applications have recently generated a lot of interest in wireless network infrastructures which support multimedia services. In this paper, we propose a bandwidth routing algorithm for multimedia support in a multihop wireless network. This network can be interconnected to wired networks (e.g. ATM or Internet) or stand alone. Our bandwidth routing includes bandwidth calculation and reservation schemes. Under such a routing algorithm, we can derive a route to satisfy bandwidth requirement for QoS constraint. At a source node, the bandwidth information can be used to decide to accept a new call or not immediately. This is specially important to carry out a fast handoff when interconnecting to an ATM backbone infrastructure. It enables an efficient call admission control. The simulation results show that the bandwidth routing algorithm is very useful in extending the ATM virtual circuit service to the wireless network. Different types of QoS traffic can be integrated in such a dynamic radio network with high performance.

1. INTRODUCTION

Personal communications and mobile computing require a wireless network infrastructure which is fast deployable, possibly multihop, and capable of multimedia service support. The wireless network is often connected to a wired network (e.g. ATM or Internet) so that the ATM or Internet multimedia connection can be extended to the mobile users. There are several contributions which have already appeared in the wireless extensions of the wired ATM networks [1, 15]. Most of them focus on the cellular architecture for wireless PCN (Personal Communication Networks) supported by ATM backbone infrastructures. In this architecture, all mobile hosts in a communication cell can reach a base station in one hop. A TDMA scheme is generally used in the wireless extension for bandwidth reservation for the mobile host to base station connections.

In parallel with (and separately from) the single hop cellular model, another type of model, based on radio to radio multihopping, bas been evolving to serve a growing number of applications which rely on a fast deployable, multihop, wireless infrastructure [3]. The classic examples are battlefield communications, (in the civilian sector) disaster recovery (fire, earthquake), and search and rescue. A recent addition to this set is the "ad hoc" personal communications network, which could be rapidly deployed on a campus, for example, to support collaborative computing and to access to the Internet during special events (concerts, festivals, etc.). Multihopping through wireless repeaters strategically located on campus permits to reduce battery power and to increase network capacity (via spatial reuse). Interestingly, the multihop requirement may also arise in cellular networks. For example, if a base station fails, a mobile node may not be able to access the wired network in a single hop [12].

The problem of interconnecting of the multihop wireless network to wired backbone acquires QoS guarantee not only over a single hop, but also over an entire wireless multihop path. The QoS parameters are required to be propagated within the network. In order to extend the ATM VC (Virtual Circuit) into the wireless network, or to carry out fast handoff between ATM gateways (base stations), the bandwidth information in the wireless network is very important. If a source node has the bandwidth information of a path to an intended destination, then it can decide a new VC with QoS requirements to be accepted or not immediately. This is specially important in the handoff.

In the broadband multimedia ad hoc network, the bandwidth problem is a very important issue. Mobility and radio properties make the QoS in such a network more difficult than in a cellular network. The bandwidth calculation and reservation are the first step for further control in such an environment. Due to mobility, the bandwidth information is changed dynamically. Thus, to maintain the QoS of a connection is more difficult. In this paper, we propose an algorithm for bandwidth calculation and reservation based on the distance vector routing algorithm for multimedia support in a multihop wireless network. We consider different QoS traffic to evaluate the system performance. The paper is organized as follows. Section 2

† This work was in part supported by the National Science Council, Taiwan, R.O.C., under Contract NSC-87-2213-E-194-036 "The Design of a Seamless Multimedia Wireless Network".

0-8186-8810-6/98 $10.00 © 1998 IEEE

presents the algorithm of bandwidth calculation and reservation. In section 3, there are some simulation experiments to be done to evaluate the system performance. Section 4 concludes the paper.

2. BANDWIDTH RESERVATION

Multimedia applications such as digital audio and video have much more stringent QoS requirements than traditional datagram applications. For a network to deliver QoS guarantees, it must reserve and control resources. A major challenge in multihop, multimedia networks is the ability to account for resources so that bandwidth reservations (in a deterministic or statistical sense) can be placed on them. We note that in cellular (single hop) networks such accountability is made easy by the fact that all stations learn of each other's requirements, either directly, or through a control station (e.g. base station in cellular systems). However, this solution can not be extended to the multihop environment. To set up a connection with QoS constraint, routing is the first step. The routing protocol first finds a path with sufficient resources. Then, the resource allocation protocol makes the reservations along the path.

We only consider "bandwidth" as the QoS (thus omitting Signal to Interference Ratio, SIR, packet loss rate, etc.). This is because bandwidth guarantee is the most critical requirement for real time applications. "Bandwidth" in time-slotted network systems is measured in terms of number of "free" slots. The goal of the bandwidth routing algorithm is to find a shortest path such that the available bandwidth on the path is above the minimum requirement. To compute the "bandwidth" constrained shortest path, we not only have to know the available bandwidth on each link along the path, but also have to determine the scheduling of free slots. Though some algorithms were proposed to solve this QoS routing problem, unfortunately they may only work in some special environments [2, 4, 10].

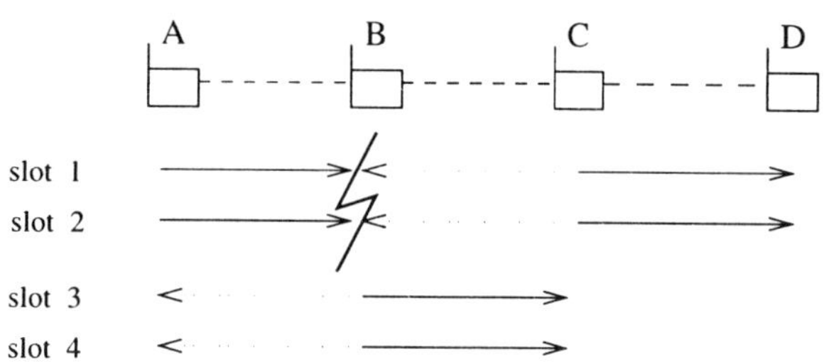

Figure 1: Hidden terminal problem

2.1. TDMA over CDMA

Consider the example of a radio network shown in Figure 1 which uses TDMA for data transmission. The mobile host A wants to transfer data to the mobile host D. All slots in the TDMA frame are assumed to be free. Suppose that A reserves slot 1 and 2 for transmitting data to B, and B uses slot 3 and 4 to forward packets to C. Because A and C are hidden to each other, C may want to send packets by using slot 1 and 2 to D. Thus there will exist a collision at B (because B may receive packets from A and C simultaneously).

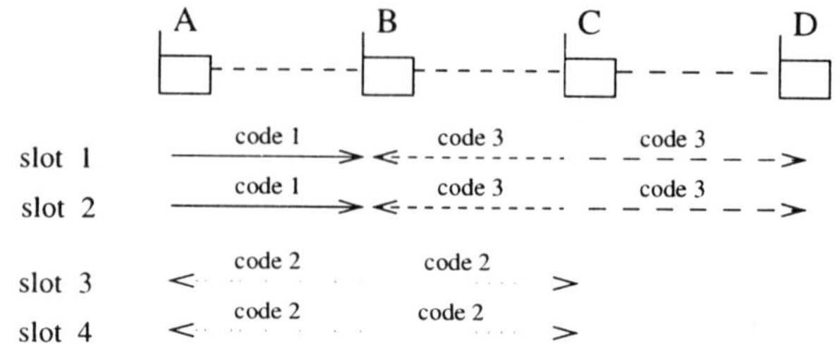

Figure 2: TDMA over CDMA

CDMA can be used to solve this problem (all spreading codes are assumed orthogonal to each other). For example, consider the same topology in Figure 1. Figure 2 shows that when B uses slot 3, 4 to transmit packets to C, we can assign a code (code 2) to node B which is different from the code (code 1) used by A. That is, we use transmitter-based code assignment [11] to assign a code to each transmitter for data transmission. A spreading code can be reused if two nodes have hop distance great than 2 [6]. In Figure 2, C can use the same slots (1 and 2) as A to send packets to D encoded by a different code (code 3) without any collision at B. It is notable that this case is assumed only one session through A, B, C and D.

In the network, each real-time connection will be assigned a VC. The VC is an end-to-end path along which slots have been reserved. As we shall later see, the path and slots of a VC may change dynamically during the lifetime of a connection due to mobility. Each node schedules each of its slots to transmit either datagram or VC traffic. Since real time traffic (which is carried on a VC) needs guaranteed bandwidth during its active period, each node has to reserve its own slots to the VC at connection setup time.

The information of available bandwidth between two nodes is critical. It is used to select the route which satisfies the QoS requirement. In addition, it is also used to decide whether a new connection is allowed to into the network. As we mentioned, the topology is changed dynamically. Although the end-to-end bandwidth converges to the correct answer, it may do so slowly. Therefore, the "current bandwidth" kept in a node may not react the "real bandwidth" because of hop-by-hop propagation delay. If the current bandwidth is less than the real bandwidth (i.e. "underestimated"), we may miss some feasible paths and the system utilization is low. Otherwise (i.e. "overestimated"), the call setup along a selected path may fail at some link because of the lack of enough bandwidth. The system then has to backtrack to free all reserved slots and choose another route. Obviously, the system performance will be bad. However, no matter which case (i.e. underestimated or overestimated) occurs, the performance of the system will be better than the one without bandwidth information. If having the bandwidth information at the beginning of a call setup, we can avoid the failure of the setup at some intermediate node of a given route. We will show this result later.

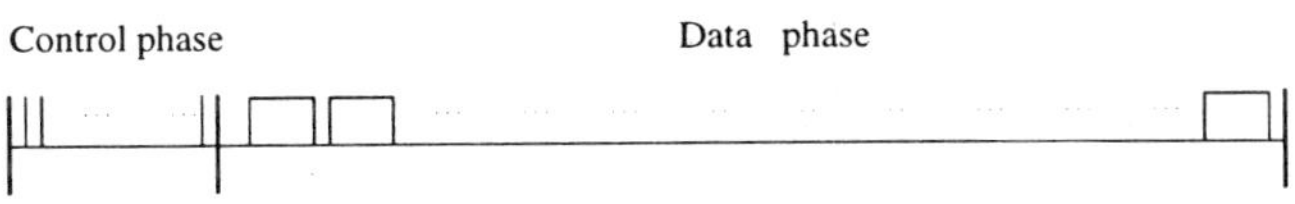

Figure 3: Frame structure

2.2. Bandwidth Calculation

Our bandwidth calculation and reservation are used over the loop-free DSDV (Destination Sequenced Distance Vector) routing algorithm [14]. The MAC (Medium Access Control) layer is implemented using a time slotted frame. Namely, time is divided into slots which are grouped into frames. Each frame is divided into two phases, control phase and data phase. The size of each slot in control phase is much smaller than the one in data phase. The frame structure is shown in Figure 3. Every node in the network is assigned a slot in control phase (i.e. pure TDMA) to transmit control information to reserve slots in data phase. Only adjacent nodes can hear this reservation packet. Because of multihop (i.e. reservation packets heard by each node may be different), the free slots recorded at every node may be different. We define the set of the common free slots between two adjacent nodes to be the *link bandwidth*. Consider the example shown in Figure 4 in which C wants to compute the bandwidth to A. We assume the next hop is B. If B can compute the available bandwidth to A, then C can use this information and the link bandwidth to B to compute the bandwidth to A.

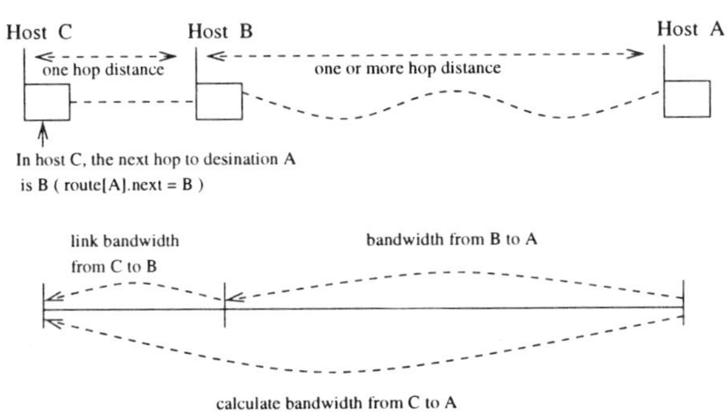

Figure 4: Bandwidth information calculation overview

We define the *path bandwidth* between two nodes, which are not necessary to be adjacent, to be the set of available slots between them. If two nodes are adjacent, the path bandwidth is the link bandwidth. Consider the example in Figure 4 and assume A and B are of one hop distance. If C has free slots $\{1, 3, 4\}$, and B has free slots $\{1, 2, 3\}$. The *link bandwidth* between C and B is $\{1, 3\}$. We can easily find that $link\_BW(A, B) = free\_slot(A) \cap free\_slot(B)$. $free\_slot(X)$ is defined to be the slots, which are not used by any host to receive or to send packets, from the point of view at node X. We can employ link bandwidth to compute path bandwidth. From the path bandwidth, we can know if there exits a QoS route between a given source-destination pair. We will use the following 4 cases as examples to show how to calculate the path bandwidth.

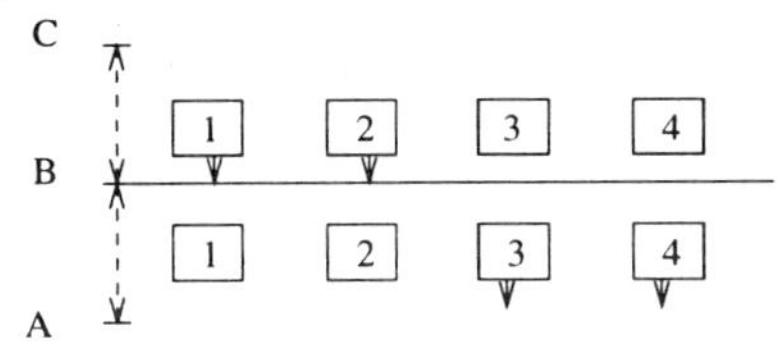

Figure 5: Equal case

Case 1: Assume the link bandwidth of both (A, B) and (B, C) are $\{1, 2, 3, 4\}$ as in Figure 5. If C uses slot 1, 2 to send packets to B, then B can only use slot 3, 4 to forward packets to A. This is because B can not be in transmitting mode and listening mode simultaneously. So the path bandwidth from C to A can be $\{1, 2\}$ and its size is 2. In this case, 4 free slots can only contribute 2 slots for path bandwidth.

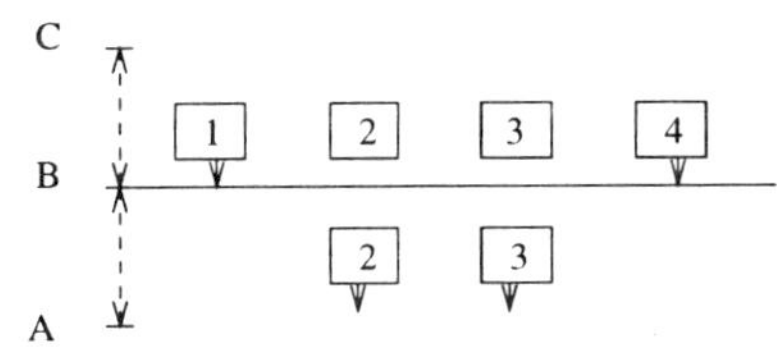

Figure 6: Containing case

Case 2: Assume link_BW(A, B) = $\{2, 3\}$ and link_BW(B, C) = $\{1, 2, 3, 4\}$ as in Figure 6. Namely, link_BW(A, B) $\subset$ link_BW(B, C). If C uses slot 2, then B can not use slot 2 any more. So in this case, C should use slots in link_BW(B, C) − link_BW(A, B) = $\{1, 4\}$ first to maximize system utilization. Therefore if C uses slot 1, 4, then B can use slot 2, 3. So the path bandwidth from C to A can be $\{1, 4\}$ and its size is 2.

Case 3: If link_BW(A, B) $\cap$ link_BW(B, C) = $\emptyset$, no conflict will occur. Figure 7 shows the example. C can choose either slot 3 or 4 and B chooses slot 2. The path bandwidth from C to A can be $\{3\}$ and its size is 1.

Case 4: This is a general case as shown in Figure 8. Follow the slot assignment policy in case 2. We assign slot 9

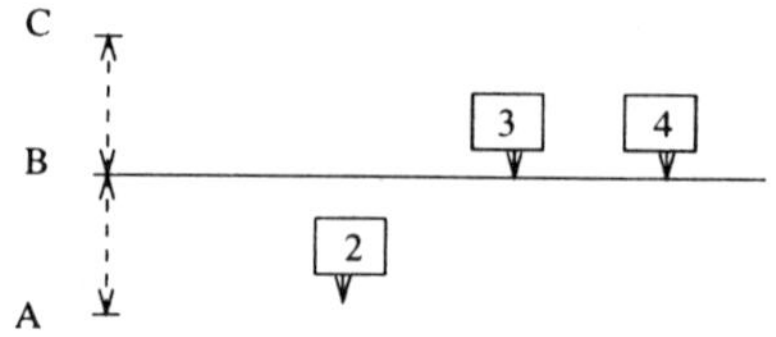

Figure 7: Exclusive case

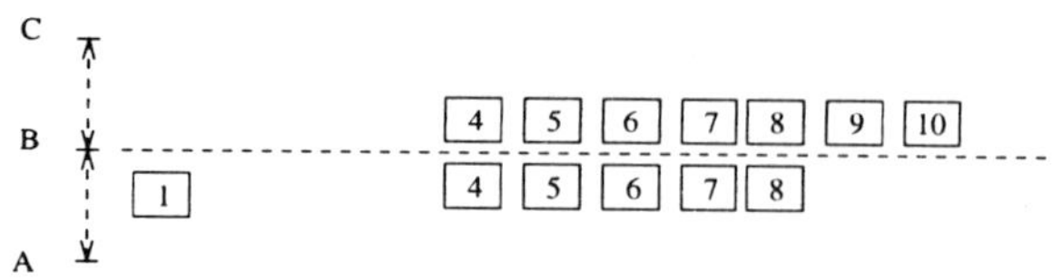

Figure 8: General case

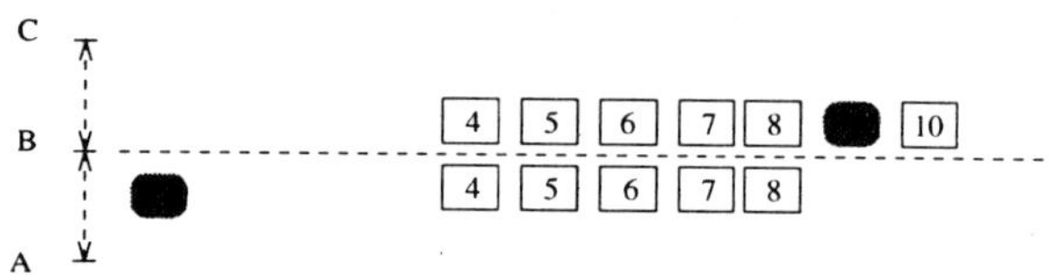

Figure 9: Step 1 bandwidth information calculation in Host C

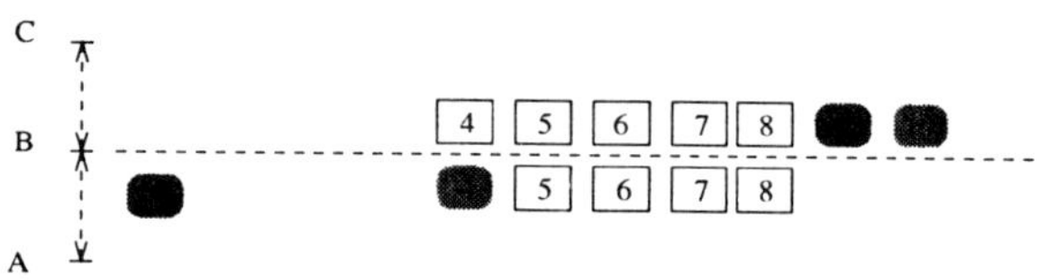

Figure 10: Step 2 bandwidth information calculation in Host C

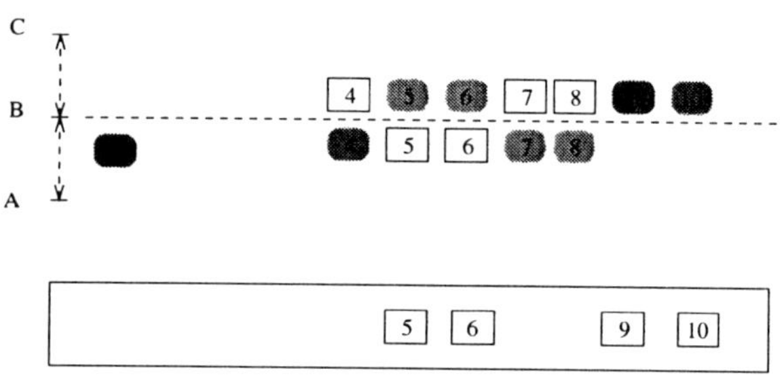

Figure 11: Final result of bandwidth information in Host C

to C and slot 1 to B first. Figure 9 shows the slots left. Next, we assign slot 10 to C and slot 4 to B. Figure 10 shows only slots {5, 6, 7, 8} left (slot 4 can not be used by C any more since B is in transmitting mode). This is the same situation as in case 1. So C can be assigned slot 5, 6 and B is assigned slot 7, 8 as shown in Figure 11. Here we let the *path_BW(C, A)* be {5, 6, 9, 10}. That is, C uses slots {5, 6, 9, 10} to send packets to B, and B uses {1, 4, 7, 8} to forward packets to A. The size of path bandwidth from C to A is 4.

The last case is the general case. In fact, it covers the above three cases. Our assignment policy is to consider the slots not in link_BW(B,C) ∩ link_BW(A,B) first until one of the special cases (i.e. case 1-3) occurs. Slot

Path Bandwidth Calculation Algorithm:

```
when receive routing table from neighbor:
(bandwidth information is embedded in the routing table)

for all host i do
{
  if (i==sender)
  {
    link_BW = free_slots & free_slots of sender;
    route[sender].bandwidth = link_BW;
  }
  else if (route[i].next == sender)
  {
    common_BW = link_BW & route[i].bandwidth of sender;
    common_BW_size  = size(common_BW);
    difference_BW1  = size(link_BW ^ common_BW);
    difference_BW2  = size(route[i].bandwidth of sender ^ common_BW);

    if (difference_BW1 <= difference_BW2)
    {
      route[i].bandwidth_size = difference_BW1;
      remain_BW_size  = difference_BW2-difference_BW1;
    }
    else /* difference_BW1 > difference_BW2 */
    {
      route[i].bandwidth_size = difference_BW2;
      remain_BW_size = difference_BW1-difference_BW2;
    }

    if (remain_BW_size > 0  &&  common_BW_size > 0)
    {
      if (common_BW_size <= remain_BW_size)
        route[i].bandwidth_size = route[i].bandwidth_size + common_BW_size;
      else /* comm_BW_size> remain_BW_size */
      {
        rout[i].bandwidth_size = route[i].bandwidth_size + remain_BW_size;
        common_BW_size = floor((common_BW_size - remain_BW_size)/2);

        if (common_BW_size > 0)
          route[i].bandwidth_size=route[i].bandwidth_size + common_BW_size;
      }
    }
  }
}
```

Figure 12: Path bandwidth calculation algorithm

assignment problem can be reduced to the graph coloring problem which is a NP complete problem. We use the heuristic approach to assign slots as discussed in case 4. The detail of the bandwidth calculation algorithm is shown in Figure 12. Compared with [10], this algorithm is simple and efficient. In this algorithm, we only record the size of the path bandwidth. This value is useful to choose a QoS path. Thus the system can immediately decide to admit a new connection to be set up or not at the beginning of connection request. Actually, it reduces the possibility of the failure of the call setup. To further generalize case 4, in Figure 4, if the hop distance between A and B is more than 1, C still can compute *path_BW(C, A)* from the information *link_BW(C, B)* and *path_BW(B, A)* by using the algorithm in Figure 12.

2.3. Slot Assignment

We have already described how to calculate path bandwidth. In this section, we will discuss how to do the slot assignment. The algorithm in Figure 12 only calculates the size of path bandwidth. However, it does not tell us how to assign the available slots efficiently. We use the example in Figure 8 to describe how to do the slot assignment.

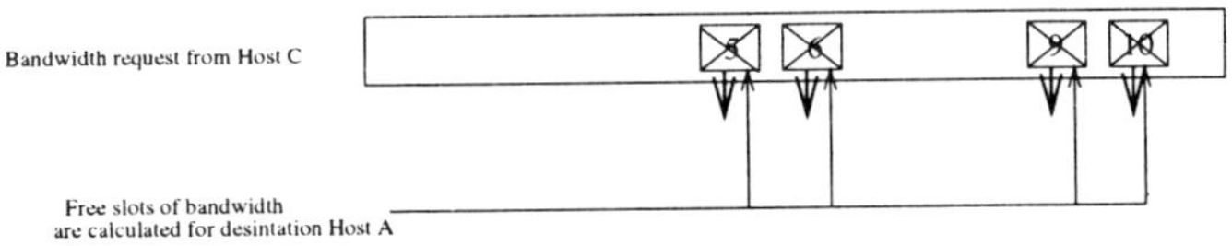

Figure 13: Bandwidth information in Host C

Source node: According to the bandwidth calculation algorithm, $path\_BW(C, A) = \{5, 6, 9, 10\}$ as shown in Figure 11. Thus, the caller C can reserve all of these slots. When $\{5, 6, 9, 10\}$ are reserved, we must remove these slots from the path bandwidth of the other destinations. For example, if $path\_BW(C, E)$ also contains slot 5, 6, 10 and the size of the path bandwidth is 5, then C must remove slot 5, 6, 10 away and the size becomes 2 ($5 - 3 = 2$). Figure 13 shows slots $\{5, 6, 9, 10\}$ are reserved and then marked.

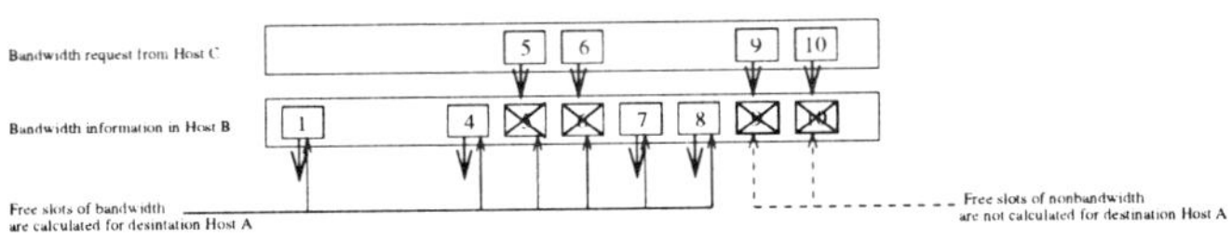

Figure 14: Bandwidth information in intermediate Host B

Intermediate nodes: $path\_BW(B, A) = \{1, 4, 5, 6, 7, 8\}$. When B receives the reservation packet from C, it must check if its slots $\{5, 6, 9, 10\}$ are free. If so, then it can receive data packets from C. Notice that B must remove these slots from the path bandwidth of each destination nodes. In addition, B must check if there are free slots which can be used for forwarding packets to next hop (i.e. A). In this case, slots $\{1, 4, 7, 8\}$ are available. Thus B reserves them (shown in Figure 14). In the meantime, B must delete these slots from each path bandwidth. If any one slot in $\{5, 6, 9, 10\}$ is busy or if no enough free slots (4 slots in this case) to forward the packets, this reservation will fail. At this time, B must reject the reservation request. Because C has already reserved slots $\{5, 6, 9, 10\}$, B needs to send a control packet, say *RESET*, to C to ask to free these slots.

Destination node: When the destination A receives the reservation packet from previous hop (i.e. B), it only reserves slots $\{1, 4, 7, 8\}$ for receiving data packets from B as shown in Figure 15. Each path bandwidth must delete these slots. Like intermediate nodes, if A finds any one slot in $\{1, 4, 7, 8\}$ is not free, it must send RESET hop-by-hop backward to ask to free those reserved slots.

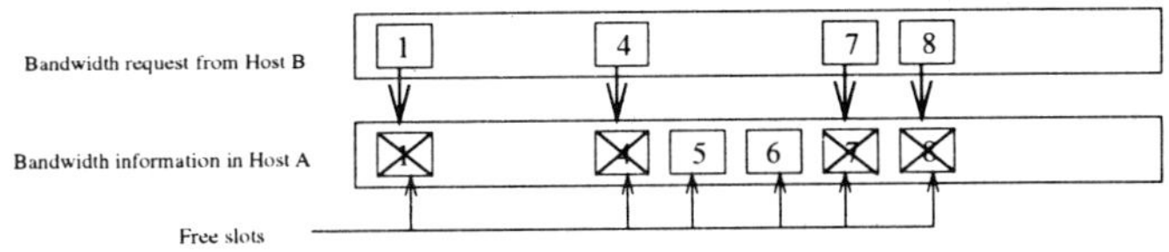

Figure 15: Bandwidth information in destination Host A

```
Part 1: Source node (issuing a call request)

if (available bandwidth < request bandwidth)
  return;
else
{
  mark all needed free slots;
  remove these needed slots from every path bandwidth;
  send the reservation packet;
}

Part 2: Intermediate nodes and destination node

if (I am the destination)
{
  check if slots which are used to receive packets are free;
  if TRUE
  {
    remove these needed slots from every path bandwidth;
    send REPLY to the source;
  }
  else
    send RESET along the path back to the source to free
    all reserved bandwidth;
}
else /* I am the intermediate node */
{
  /*incoming bandwidth check*/
  check if slots which are used to receive packets are free;
  if TRUE
  {
    /*outgoing bandwidth check*/
    check if bandwidth to destination is enough;
    if TRUE
    {
        remove all needed slots for incoming and outgoing
        from the available slots;
        forward the reservation packet to the next hop;
    }
    else
        send RESET along the path back to the source to free
        all reserved bandwidth;
  }
  else
    send RESET along the path back to the source to free all
    reserved bandwidth;
}
```

Figure 16: Reservation algorithm

In the above example, we discuss how to reserve the bandwidth. When every host receives a reservation packet, it must check if the slots which the sender will use for transmitting packets are free, and find if there are free slots which can be reserved for forwarding packets. If both are satisfied, the reservation can be passed to the next hop. Finally, the destination sends *REPLY* back to the source to acknowledge having set up the connection. The reservation algorithm is shown in Figure 16. In the algorithm, when the call setup fails, it is necessary to free all reserved slots along the path backward to the source. This operation is very important since the bandwidth in the wireless network is quite limited. A topological change may make it impossible to send either a REPLY or a RESET back along the path that has been established so far. Thus if an intermediate node does not receive a REPLY by a predefined time, the reserved slots will be freed automatically.

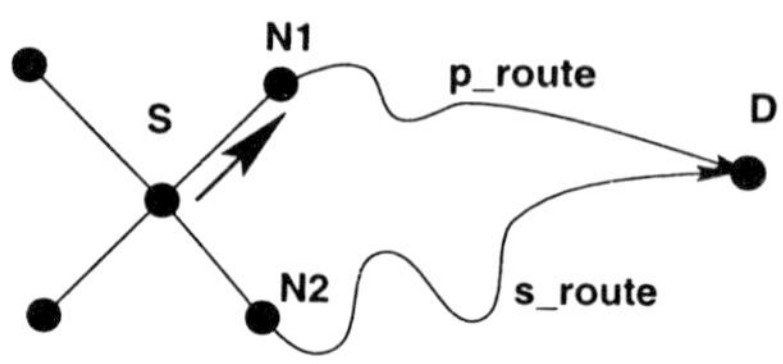

Figure 17: Standby routing

2.4. Rerouting When Path Broken

During the active period of a connection, a topological change may destroy the VC. The connection control must re-route or re-establish the VC over a new path. Therefore, it is important for a routing scheme to support alternative paths in a mobile environment. In such an environment, routing optimality is of secondary importance. The routing protocol must be capable of finding new routes quickly when a topological change destroys existing routes. To this end, we propose to maintain secondary paths which can be used immediately when the primary path fails [13]. In Figure 17, each node uses the primary route (i.e. the DSDV route) to route its packets. When the first link (s, N1) on the path fails, the secondary path (s, N2) becomes the primary path, and another standby path (s, N3) will be computed, as shown in Figure 18. It is worth emphasizing that these routes must use different immediate successors to avoid failing simultaneously.

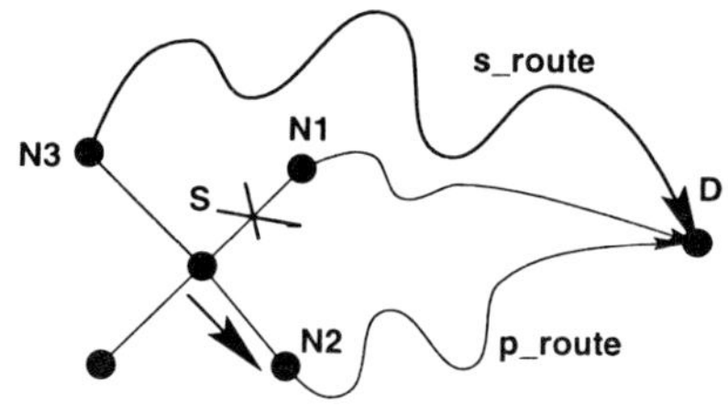

Figure 18: The primary route fails and the standby route becomes the primary route. Another standby route is constructed.

The secondary (standby) route is easily computed using the DSDV algorithm. Referring to Figure 17, each neighbor of node S periodically informs S of its distance to destination D. The neighbor with shortest distance yields the primary route. The runner up yields the secondary route. This scheme guarantees that the first link is different for the two paths. Furthermore, the standby route computation requires no extra table, message exchange or computation overhead. Like the DSDV (or primary) route, we must compute bandwidth information from all neighbors to decide the standby routes. The algorithm in Figure 19 is to maintain the routing table (two alternative routes in the algorithm, i.e. *next*2 and *next*3). The "*next*" in the algorithm means the primary route.

Routing Table Maintenance Algorithm

```
When receiving a routing table from a neighbor:
for all i
{
 if (i != sender &&
   sender routing table[i].next != myself &&
   my routing table[i].next != sender &&
   my routing table[i].next != sender routing table[i].next)
 {
   if (sender != my routing table[i].next3)
   {
     calculate bandwidth to destination host i using
     the same algorithm in DSDV.

     if (calculate_BW > bandwidth from original next2)
     {
       new next2 = sender;
       update next2 bandwidth information;
     }
   }

   if (sender != my routing table[i].next &&
      sender != my routing table[i].next2)
   {
     calculate bandwidth to destination host i
     using the same algorithm in DSDV.

     if (calculate_BW > bandwidth from original next3)
     {
       new next3 = sender;
       update next3 bandwidth information;
     }
   }
 }
}
```

Figure 19: The standby routing algorithm

When a host generates a new call, it uses the algorithm in Figure 20 to construct the path. In the algorithm, we will choose the route which satisfy the QoS requirement in order of precedence "next", "next2", and "next3". The chosen route will be the primary route. The "next" entry in the routing table may be changed depending on QoS requirement. After choosing the primary route, the source node will send out a call setup message to "next". When receiving the message, a node will run the protocol in Figure 21 to reserve bandwidth for the new call. When a topological change destroys the primary route as in Figure 18, node *s* will try to rebuild a new path immediately using either next2 or next3 if the QoS is satisfied. Thus a new route from the broken node will be built by sending call setup message hop-by-hop to the destination.

Construct a QoS path

```
if (bandwidth of next > required bandwidth)
{
  update bandwidth information of next;
  send this call;
}
else if (bandwidth of next2 > required bandwidth)
{
  copy next2 bandwidth to next bandwidth;
  copy next2 to be next;
  update next2 bandwidth information;
  send this call as using the original DSDV method;
}
else if (bandwidth of next3 > request bandwidth)
{
  copy next3 bandwidth to next bandwidth;
  copy next3 to be next;
  update next3 bandwidth information;
  send this call as using the original DSDV method;
}
```

Figure 20: Construct a QoS path for a new call

Bandwidth reservation in the intermediate node

```
if (sender using first next for path building)
  the same action as original DSDV;
else
{  /* sender initial this call by next2 or next3 */

  if (bandwidth calculated from next > request bandwidth)
  {
    reserve bandwidth using next;
    forward this call setup message to next;
  }
  else if (bandwidth calculated from next2 > request bandwidth)
  {
    copy next2 bandwidth to be next bandwidth;
    copy next2 to be next;
    reserve bandwidth;
    forward this call setup message as original DSDV method;
  }
  else if (bandwidth calculated from next3 > request bandwidth)
  {
    copy next3 bandwidth to be next bandwidth;
    copy next3 to be next;
    reserve bandwidth;
    forward this call setup message as original DSDV method;
  }
  else /* no bandwidth */
    backward "RESET" message to clean existing path bandwidth
    in other hosts reserved for this path;
```

Figure 21: Bandwidth reservation in the intermediate nodes

3. PERFORMANCE

The environment which we consider consists of 20 mobile hosts roaming uniformly in a 1000 × 1000 feet square area. Each node moves randomly at uniform speed. Radio transmission range is 400 feet. That is, two nodes can hear each other if their distance is within the transmission range. Data rate is 2 Mbps. In Figure 3, the data slot in data phase is 5 ms, and the control slot in control phase is 0.1 ms (both including overhead). We assume there are 16 data slots in data phase. So the frame length is 20*0.1 + 16*5 = 82 ms. Since the number of data slots is less than the number of nodes, nodes need to compete for these data slots. The source-destination pair of a call is randomly chosen and their distance must be more than 1. Once the call request is accepted on a link, a transmission window (i.e. data slots) is reserved (on that link) automatically for all the subsequent packets in the connection. The window is released when either the session is finished or the *RESET* packet is received (Figure 16). Conceptually, this scheme is an extension of PRMA (Packet Reservation Multiple Access) [9] to the multihop environment.

There are three levels of QoS for the offered traffic. QoS_1, QoS_2, and QoS_4 need one, two, and four data slots in a frame respectively. The total simulation time is 10^6 ms and the calls are only generated in the first 10^5 ms. A new call is generated every cycle (82 ms). Each call duration is 3 minutes. The interarrival time of packets within a QoS_1 session is exponential distribution with 100 ms average. Similarly, the mean values of the interarrival time for QoS_2 and QoS_4 are 100/2 ms and 100/4 ms respectively. The maximal delay of a data packet within a node is assumed to be 4 frame length (328 ms). If a packet stays in a node more than the time, it will be dropped.

In the first experiment, we consider the effect of variable mobility on incomplete connection ratio. A call may not be completed due to the mobility. We define the incomplete ratio to be the percentage of calls to be stopped. Here only one link on a path is broken, a call will be stopped. From the result, we can see the probability of a connection which needs to be re-routed during the active period. Figure 22 illustrates the result. The curve QoS_i means QoS is uniform for all traffic. Hybrid QoS means different QoS traffic in the system. We can find that high mobility causes paths to be broken frequently. When mobility is 20 feet/sec, about 1/2 connections need to be re-routed.

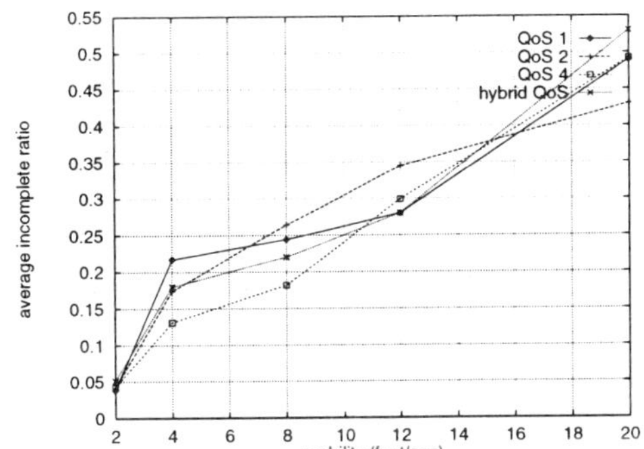

Figure 22: Incomplete ratio of different QoS

The second experiment is to find the average throughput. The simulation results in Figure 23 show the throughput of each connection decreases as the mobility increases. From Figure 23, we can also find when the QoS is high, the average throughput is high, too. This is because we allocate more slots for high QoS call, and we get more throughput from per call. In addition, the throughput of hybrid traffic is similar to QoS_2 traffic.

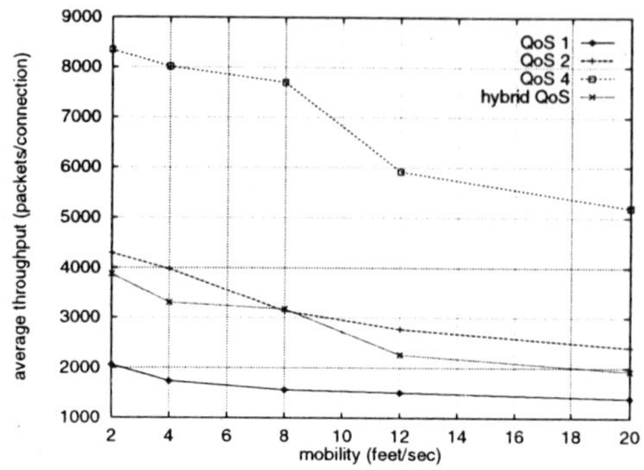

Figure 23: Average throughput of different QoS

The average hop delay is shown in Figure 24. Since path length is not the same for all VCs, we show the hop delay instead of end-to-end delay. Because of bandwidth reservation, the delay is stable. For example, the QoS_1 VC has a stable hop delay about 95 ms which is close to the frame length (82 ms). QoS_2 and QoS_4 also have stable delay 66 ms and 53 ms respectively. When the QoS level is higher (i.e. more slots are allocated per frame), the packets will have a chance to be transmitted sooner. So the delay is lower. Mobility doesn't affect the delay. Figure 25 shows the total number of VCs of different QoS traffic can be supported by the current system bandwidth (16 data slots). There is about 35 connections of QoS_1 traffic simultaneously in the system.

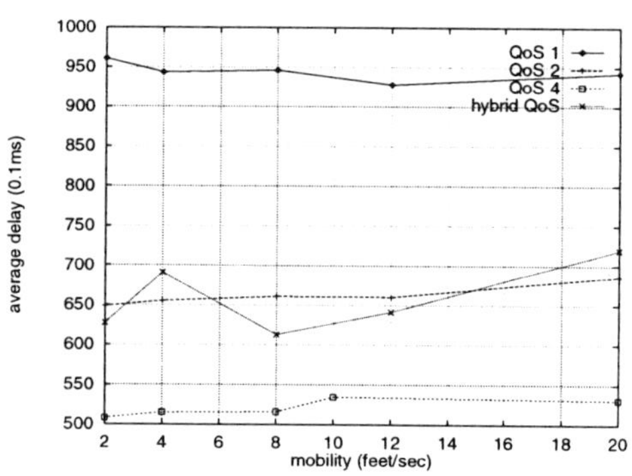

Figure 24: Average hop delay

Figure 26 reports the packet loss for varying mobility. The maximal delay of a packet within a node is assumed to be limited to four frame length (328 ms). If a packet stays in a node more than 328 ms, it will be dropped. Packets is served in FIFO order. Figure 26 appears that the packet loss is about 5% (QoS_1) or less (1% for QoS_2, QoS_4, and hybrid QoS). This performance is quite well. The mobility does not affect this result too much. For the traffic with high QoS level, the packet loss is small because more bandwidth is allocated. Namely, the high QoS traffic gets better service.

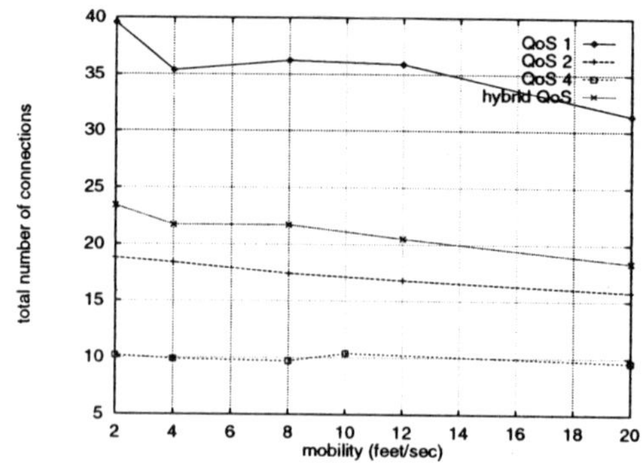

Figure 25: The total number of connections

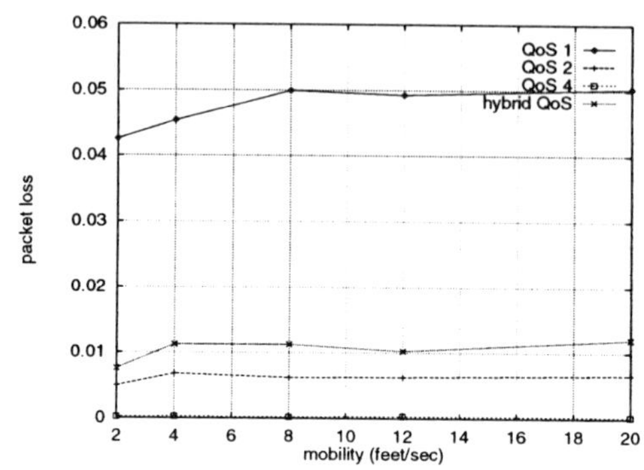

Figure 26: Packet loss per host

The following set of experiments is to assess the improvement introduced by the "standby" routing feature, i.e. the availability of an alternate route in case the preferred route fails. This feature is of critical importance when stations are mobile. In the experiments, the total simulation time is 10^8 ms. A new call is generated every two cycles (2 * 82 ms). If no data packet is sent over the reserved slots for 10 cycles (10 * 82 ms), the reserved slots will be released. There are 4 experiments to be run. In the first one, we evaluate the successful ratio for each route from source to destination. Figure 27 shows the result. Each node is considered to run the algorithm in Figure 20 to setup a new call. For example, at 20 feet/sec mobility, 98% calls which use *next* (primary route) at source node can setup the QoS VC successfully, and 2% will fail because of outdated bandwidth information. Because of mobility which causes the topological change, the bandwidth information is changed dynamically. If a node does not receive the newest bandwidth information, then the QoS VC setup may fail in an intermediate node because of lack of bandwidth. However, in Figure 27, since there are standby routes in each node, no matter which route is selected at the source, we have high probability (more than 90% for "next", and about 75% for "next3") to construct the VC successfully. It is notable that the moving speed does not affects the successful probability too much.

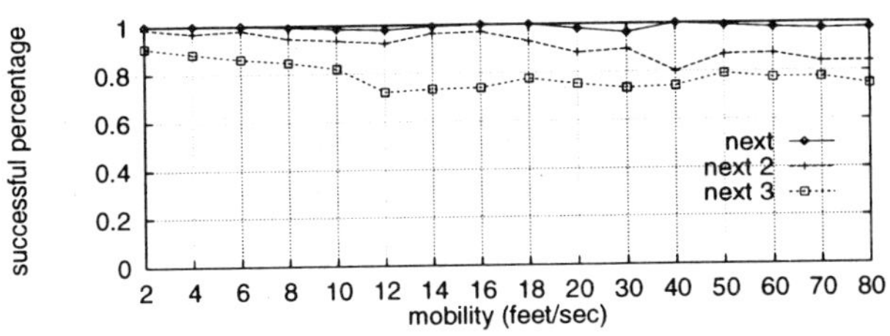

Figure 27: The reliability of different routes for QoS requirement

For a given VC of a call, it may be constructed by different route at source. Figure 28 shows that near 40%-50% VCs are setup by the primary route (i.e. "next"). Interestingly, "next2" has the similar percentage as the primary route. From this figure, we can find the standby route is quite useful. The primary route is the shortest path calculated by DSDV algorithm. However, if all source-destination pairs only consider the shortest path, there will be some hot spots which lack enough bandwidth. Once a call setup request is passing through those nodes, it will be denied. Thus there is only 40%-50% VCs over the primary route. Because of the existence of standby routes, the real-time traffic load will be evenly distributed among the network avoiding hot spots. We can find there is only about 10% VCs using *next*3. That means if *next*2 does not have enough bandwidth, it has small probability for *next*3 to have enough bandwidth. Actually at this time, the system is saturated.

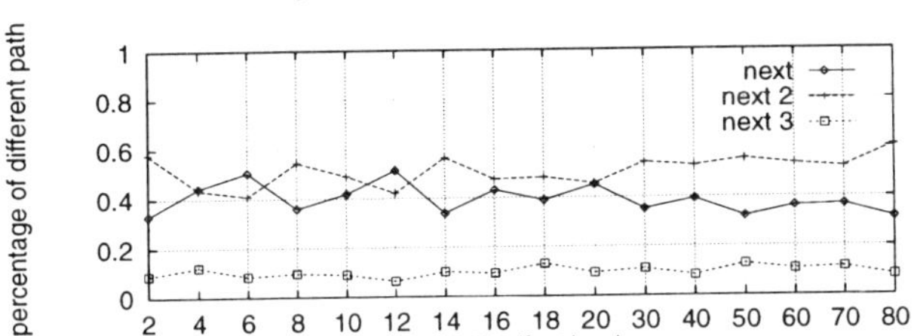

Figure 28: Route selection at source for a given VC

When a link of a VC is broken, the new VC can be constructed from the "breakpoint" (like node *s* in Figure 18) if there exists enough bandwidth in a standby route. In case of no bandwidth in any standby route, After timeout, a new VC will be reconstructed from the source node. All reserved bandwidth by the old VC will be released. In Figure 29, at mobility 20 feet/sec for example, there is a probability of 0.3 for *next*2 (0.21 for *next*3) having enough bandwidth to destination at the breakpoint. Figure 30 shows the probability that the breakpoint selects different routes (i.e. *next*2 or *next*3) and finally a new QoS VC is really setup. The *next*2 path can have a probability of more than 0.9 to setup a new VC in low mobility. In high mobility, the probability can be still retained more than 0.8.

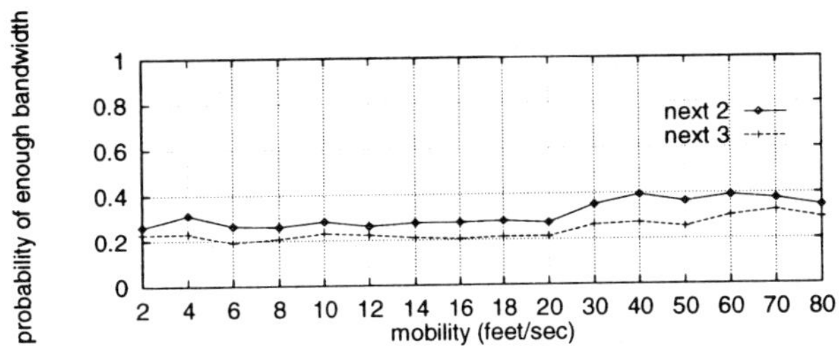

Figure 29: Probability of the breakpoint having QoS alternative routes

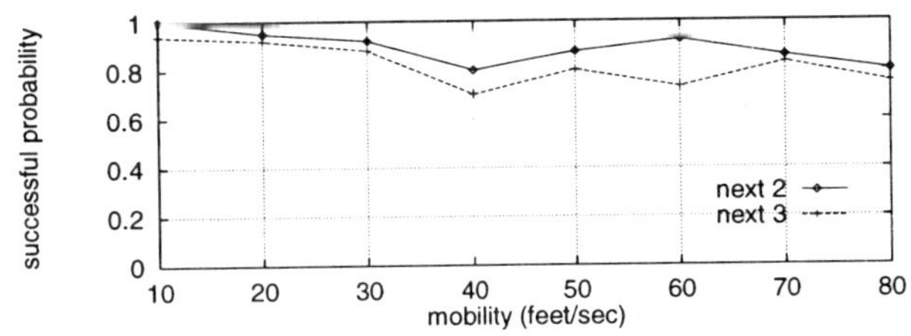

Figure 30: The performance of the standby routing at the breakpoint

The bandwidth calculation algorithm in Figure 12 is very useful. It can provide the information about whether a given route has enough bandwidth before the call setup begins. If we only use the distance vector routing algorithm (i.e. DSDV) and the reservation algorithm (Figure 16), then a new call may be blocked in an intermediate node which is saturated. No source can construct a VC which passes through the saturated node, until one of the VCs over the node ends its transmission and bandwidth becomes available.

Mobile nodes exchanges bandwidth information periodically. It is propagated hop by hop. Thus it cannot reach all nodes immediately. In the following experiment, we compare the DSDV algorithm with and without bandwidth information (both cases use the reservation algorithm in Figure 16). In addition, we consider the case in which bandwidth information shows that there is no bandwidth. However, the new call can be set up by DSDV. That is, the bandwidth is "underestimated" (the current bandwidth is less than the real bandwidth). The simulation results in Figure 31 report that the system with bandwidth information obviously has much better performance. This information provides the source node to decide if call setup will be started. In addition, this information is seldom "underestimated" by our algorithm. That is, the "reliability" of the information is quite high. Thus it is very useful in admission control. Figure 31 also shows the impact of mobility on the call setup failure is limited.

mobility	with bandwidth information	bandwidth info under-estimate	without bandwidth information
2 feet / sec	1.9	0.2	650
4 feet / sec	2.1	0.3	667
8 feet / sec	2.1	0.3	661
12 feet / sec	2.6	0.3	656
20 feet / sec	2.8	0.5	686

Figure 31: The average number of call blocking of "DSDV + reservation algorithm"

4. CONCLUSIONS

In this paper, we propose a novel bandwidth routing scheme which contains bandwidth calculation and reservation for wireless networks. It can apply to two important scenarios: multimedia ad hoc wireless networks and multihop extension wireless ATM networks. Specially, the bandwidth information can be used to assist in the handoff of the mobile host between two ATM base stations. Furthermore, it enables more effective call admission control. In the case of ATM interconnection, ATM virtual circuit service can be extended to the wireless networks with possible renegotiation of QoS parameters at the gateways (base stations). In the simulation experiments, traffic with different QoS level is considered. Simulation results show the performance of the bandwidth routing is well. It is specially useful in admission control. Furthermore, "standby" routing enhances performance in the mobile environment. Finally, the comparison between "DSDV + reservation algorithm" with and without bandwidth calculation illustrates the importance of bandwidth routing to call admission control.

REFERENCES

[1] A. Acampora, "Wireless ATM: A Perspective on Issues and Prospects", *IEEE Personal Communications*, pp. 8-17, August 1996.

[2] I.F. Akyildiz, W. Yen, and B. Yener, "A New Hierarchical Routing Protocol for Dynamic Multihop Wireless Networks", *Proceedings of IEEE INFOCOM'97*, 1997.

[3] A. Alwan, R. Bagrodia, N. Bambos, M. Gerla, L. Kleinrock, J. Short and J. Villasenor, "Adaptive Mobile Multimedia Networks", *IEEE Personal Communications*, pp. 34-51, April 1996.

[4] V.D. Park and M.S. Corson, "A Highly Adaptive Distributed Routing Algorithm for Mobile Wireless Network", *Proceedings of IEEE INFOCOM'97*, 1997.

[5] R. Bagrodia and W. Liao, "Maisie: A Language for the Design of Efficient Discrete-Event Simulations", *IEEE Transaction on Software Engineering*, pp.225-238, 1994.

[6] I. Chlamtac and S.S. Pinter, "Distributed Nodes Organization Algorithm for Channel Access in a Multihop Dynamic Radio Network", *IEEE Transactions on Computers*, Vol. c-36, No. 6, pp. 728-737, 1987.

[7] M. Gerla and J.T.-C. Tsai, "Multicluster, Mobile, Multimedia Radio Network", *ACM-Baltzer Journal of Wireless Networks*, Vol. 1, No. 3, pp. 255-265, 1995.

[8] M. Gerla, "Routing and Flow Control in ISDN's", *ICCC'86*, pp. 643-647, 1986.

[9] D. Goodman and R.A. Valenzuela, K.T. Gayliard and B. Ramamurthi, "Packet Reservation Multiple Access for Local Wireless Communications", *IEEE Transactions on Communications*, pp. 885-890, Aug. 1989.

[10] Y.-C. Hsu and T.-C. Tsai, "Bandwidth Routing in Multihop Packet Radio Environment", *Proceedings of the 3rd International Mobile Computing Workshop*, March 1997.

[11] L. Hu, "Distributed Code Assignments for CDMA Packet Radio Networks", *IEEE/ACM Transactions on Networking*, pp. 668-677, Dec. 1993.

[12] C.R. Lin and M. Gerla, "Adaptive Clustering for Mobile Wireless Networks", *IEEE Journal on Selected Areas in Communications*, pp. 1265-1275, September 1997.

[13] C.R. Lin and M. Gerla, "Real-time Support in Multihop Wireless Networks", to appear in *ACM-Baltzer Journal of Wireless Networks*.

[14] C.E. Perkins and P. Bhagwat, "Highly Dynamic Destination-Sequenced Distance-Vector Routing (DSDV) for Mobile Computers", *Proceedings of ACM SIGCOMM '94*, pp. 234-244, 1994.

[15] D. Raychaudhuri, "Wireless ATM Networks: Architecture, System Design and Prototyping", *IEEE Personal Communications*, pp. 42-49, August 1996.

Track B: Congestion Control

Session Chair: Peter Martini
University of Bonn

New Techniques for Regulating TCP Flow over Heterogeneous Networks

Paolo Narváez Kai-Yeung Siu *

Abstract

We study a typical network environment where TCP traffic is generated from a source connected to a LAN (e.g. Ethernet) aggregated through an IP edge router to an access network (e.g. ATM, frame relay). Congestion at the edge router occurs when the bandwidth available in the access network cannot support the aggregated traffic generated from the LAN. This paper presents a novel approach to reduce router congestion and improve TCP performance. In particular, we propose new techniques that regulate TCP acknowledgments at the edge router without changing existing TCP implementations at the end systems. Our techniques minimize buffer requirement at network edges while maximizing throughput. Analytical and simulation results are presented in this paper to substantiate our claims.

1. Introduction

Most Internet data applications today use TCP as the transport layer protocol. Since the Internet is becoming increasingly heterogeneous, most TCP traffic traverses a wide range of networks with different bandwidth characteristics. Currently, TCP traffic is typically generated from a source connected to a LAN (e.g. Ethernet) aggregated through an IP edge router to an access network that uses a different link layer technology such as ATM. Congestion at the edge router occurs when the bandwidth available in the access network cannot support the aggregated traffic generated from the LAN.

While TCP handles network congestion and resulting packet loss quite effectively with its end-to-end window flow control mechanism, recent research [2] has shown that its throughput can be improved if intermediate routers can detect incipient congestion and explicitly inform the TCP source to throttle its data rate before any packet loss occurs. Such throughput improvement is particularly significant in a high latency network environment [2]. However, while the access network may have its own traffic control mechanism, its effect terminates at edge routers and, consequently, cannot improve the end-to-end performance perceived by TCP applications. In fact, when different flow control mechanisms are employed simultaneously, in some cases TCP throughput can actually be reduced [8].

In our earlier work [6], we present a scheme that regulates TCP traffic at an ingress router attached to an ATM subnetwork that employs an available bit rate (ABR) service. The ABR service assumes a congestion control mechanism at the ATM layer in which a source receives feedback from the network to transmit data at an explicit rate (ER), which corresponds to the bandwidth available for a particular connection and is computed based on the network congestion level. It is shown in [8] that ABR flow control relieves network congestion inside the ATM subnetwork at the expense of congestion at the edge routers. Moreover, in many cases, TCP throughput actually degrades when the ABR flow control is used [8]. With our scheme presented in [6], an edge router controls the data rate of a TCP source by regulating its returned acknowledgments based on the ABR explicit rate, effectively extending ABR flow control to the TCP source. This method is called the *acknowledgment bucket scheme* because of its functional similarity to the leaky bucket scheme commonly employed in regulating the transmission rate of a source.

The original acknowledgment bucket scheme works under the assumptions that 1) the TCP version is known and 2) an ABR explicit rate command is available at the network edge. Under these conditions, it is possible to guarantee that the packet buffer at the network edge will always be empty at steady state.

In this paper, we generalize the acknowledgment bucket scheme to handle more general network environ-

*P. Narváez and K.-Y. Siu are with the d'Arbeloff Laboratory for Information Systems & Technology, Rm. 3-449C, Massachusetts Institute of Technology, Cambridge, MA 02139. Email: pnarvaez@list.mit.edu, siu@list.mit.edu ments regardless of the underlying link layer technologies. Our new results provide significant improvement over our previous results [6] in several ways. First, the new schemes presented here do not assume explicit knowledge about the available bandwidth inside the subnetwork. Second, our new schemes can be implemented without having to simulate the TCP source behavior, leading to drastic reduction in implementation complexity. Third, our new schemes can be applied to an aggregation of multiple TCP flows using only a FIFO queue, while achieving fairness in throughput among the flows.

We will present different variations of a basic scheme that minimizes the edge buffer requirement while achieving maximum throughput. Each variation is derived based on different assumptions made on the amount of information available and the computational complexity involved.

The rest of the paper is organized as follows. The next section describes the network model and the assumptions used. To help understand the new schemes to be discussed in subsequent sections, in Section 3 we describe some related work and our previous work in more detail. We then present in Section 4 the basic scheme and some theoretical performance bounds on the queue size and the throughput. A key step in the basic scheme makes use of an estimate of the *effective queue* size (to be defined in Section 4) at the network edge. Different ways of estimating the effective queue size yield different schemes. In Section 5, we present a scheme where the effective queue size can be estimated quite accurately with knowledge of the TCP implementation version. Then, in Section 6, we present three different schemes where such knowledge is not assumed. Section 7 describes how the schemes presented can be applied to handle aggregate TCP traffic rather than on a per-connection basis. Section 8 presents simulation results illustrating the performance of our schemes and matching the theoretical results. Concluding remarks are given in Section 9. All proofs are omitted from this paper and can be obtained from [7].

2. Network model

The network model addressed in this paper assumes that TCP traffic originates in some local area network (LAN) and is aggregated through an edge router to an access network where bandwidth is more limited and delay is larger than the LAN. For convenience, we will refer to the access network as the *bandwidth constrained* (BC) network.

Figure 1 illustrates the basic network model. We have a TCP source sending data from the LAN to the

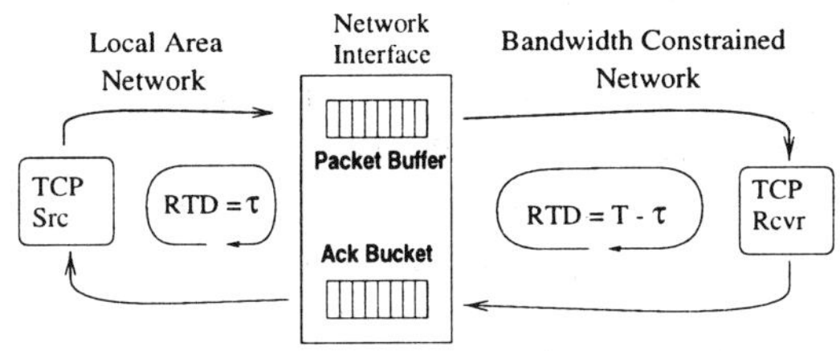

Figure 1. General model.

BC network. The network edge receives TCP packets from the LAN, buffers them if necessary, and then transmits them to the BC network. When a TCP receiver gets its packets, it returns acknowledgments for the packets to its source. On the way back, the acknowledgments pass by the network edge which can withhold them for some time in the acknowledgment bucket.

We assume that the LAN has sufficiently large bandwidth and does not impose any restrictions on how fast data packets and acknowledgments can flow between the TCP source and the network edge. On the other hand, the BC network imposes constraints on the bandwidth available from the network edge to a TCP receiver. In other words, the limited bandwidth in the BC network constrains how fast the packet buffer at the network edge can be drained. The available bandwidth or available rate $r(t)$ for a TCP connection is the rate at which the edge can transmit the packets in its buffer to the BC network. Our proposed schemes do not assume explicit knowledge about the available rate for any TCP connection.

The objective of our schemes is to maximize TCP throughput, while minimizing the buffer requirement at the network edge. The round-trip delay (RTD) time in the LAN is denoted by τ and that of the whole network is denoted by T. Though these two parameters can vary with time, we assume they have upper bounds, which are denoted by τ_{max} and T_{max}, respectively.

3. Previous work

The ideas of delaying acknowledgments to improve TCP throughput have been independently developed by others recently [1, 3]. The work in [1] focuses on the wireless TCP environment. The problem of TCP over ATM is also addressed in [3]. Both of these works propose heuristics in delaying TCP acknowledgments without analysis. Our previous work [6] involves both simulation and analytical results.

To understand our new schemes, it is helpful to first review our previous work [6]. Our original acknowledgment bucket scheme assumes the network model in

Figure 1 where the BC network uses an ATM ABR service and the round trip delay time in the LAN is negligible. The scheme also makes use of the following assumptions: 1) the TCP version is known and 2) an ABR explicit rate command is available at the network edge. Because TCP is a deterministic protocol, the network edge can determine precisely how it should release acknowledgments in such a way that the TCP source will comply with ABR's command when the acknowledgments arrive at the source. There are two components at the network edge which perform this function: the TCP observer and the rate translator.

The TCP observer simulates the flow control dynamics of the TCP source. The observer keeps track of some essential TCP states, such as the congestion window size and the phase of operation (i.e., slow start, congestion avoidance). Whenever an acknowledgment is released at the network edge, the TCP observer updates its states as if the TCP source had already received the acknowledgment. The TCP observer then correctly predicts the behavior of the TCP source and knows exactly what the effect of the released acknowledgment will be.

The rate translator transforms ABR's explicit rate command into an appropriately timed sequence of acknowledgments. The translator on the one hand keeps track of all the data U that has been requested by the network edge through previously released acknowledgments. This information is obtained from the TCP observer. On the other hand, it keeps track of all the data R that the ATM subnetwork has requested so far through its ABR explicit rate command. Whenever $R > U$, the translator releases an acknowledgment, leading to an increase in U. Therefore, R and U are maintained as close to each other as possible, which then ensures that the TCP source rate complies with ABR's explicit rate command. This original acknowledgment bucket scheme is capable of maintaining the packet buffer at the network edge virtually empty while maximizing throughput.

There is some additional implementation complexity of the scheme when an acknowledgment is piggy-backed in another data packet traversing in the backward direction. In this case, the network edge first extracts the sequence number of the acknowledgment from the packet. Then, it writes into the acknowledgment field the same sequence number as the last released ack. The recomputed packet with the data portion remaining intact is then forwarded to the source. Because this packet carries no new acknowledgment, it will not trigger the source to send more packets; because the packet is not empty, it will not cause a fast retransmit. When the network edge wants to release the acknowledgment, it simply creates an empty packet that contains the appropriate new acknowledgment information and sends it to the source.

4. Basic scheme

Whereas the original scheme assumes that the desired source rate is known through an explicit rate command from the BC network, we do not make such an assumption in our new schemes. The basic scheme and its variations presented here will make use of the queue length to determine the desired source rate. We shall later show performance bounds in terms of maximum queue length and guaranteed throughput for each of our new schemes. The new basic scheme withholds the acknowledgments in the same way as the original scheme in our previous work.

It is easy to describe our new basic scheme using the notion of the *effective queue* size $q^*(t)$ at the network edge, which is the sum of the actual queue size $q(t)$ and the total amount of data that has been requested through acknowledgment release but has not yet arrived at the network edge. We will refer to the latter (the amount of data requested but not received) as the *residual* queue size $q_{res}(t)$. More formally, these notions can be defined as follows.

Definition 1 The *residual* queue size at time t, $q_{res}(t)$, is the total amount of data contained in the packets in transit between the source and the edge at time t plus the total amount of data that will be transmitted by the source after time t triggered by the acknowledgments that are in transit between the edge and the source at time t.

Definition 2 The *effective* queue size at time t is the sum of the actual queue size $q(t)$ and the residual queue size $q_{res}(t)$ at time t, i.e., $q^*(t) = q(t) + q_{res}(t)$.

Since the round trip delay of the LAN is time varying and the exact TCP source behavior might not be known, the effective queue size cannot be always determined precisely. We shall present various ways of estimating the effective queue size. Each method of estimation will yield a different algorithm. For the moment, we will assume that there is some algorithm that gives an estimate $q^*_{est}(t)$ of the effective queue size with an estimation error bounded as follows:

$$\alpha q^*(t) \leq q^*_{est} \leq \beta q^*(t) \ . \qquad (1)$$

where $0 < \alpha \leq 1 \leq \beta$ are constants.

The basic scheme operates by first setting a queue threshold Q_{th} at the network edge to be some positive constant. Whenever the effective queue estimate $q^*_{est}(t)$ is smaller than the threshold Q_{th}, an acknowledgment is released. The operation of the basic scheme is described as follows:

The Basic Scheme

```
while # acks > 0
    {
    UPDATE q*_est(t)
    if (Q_th > q*_est(t))
        Release An Acknowledgment
    }
```

The basic scheme aims to maintain the effective queue size to be close to but smaller than the predetermined queue threshold. The reason for using the effective queue size rather than the actual queue size is to eliminate possible instability caused by the link delays. Furthermore, introducing the effective queue allows us to prove performance bounds in terms of Q_{th} and the maximum round trip delay in the LAN.

The following theorem gives a worst-case upper bound on the actual queue size with our basic scheme in terms of the error bound in estimating the effective queue size. Informally, the theorem implies that a constant-factor lower bound on the estimate of the effective queue size will yield an actual queue size that is no larger than the queue threshold by the same factor. The proofs of this and the following theorems are contained in [7].

Theorem 1 Suppose the error in estimating the effective queue size is bounded below as follows: $q^*_{est}(t) \geq \alpha q^*(t)$ $(0 < \alpha \leq 1)$ whenever $q^*(t) \geq Q_{th}/\alpha$, and TCP source timer retransmission does not occur. Then the basic scheme guarantees that the actual queue size $q(t)$ at the network edge is at most $\max\{q^*(0), Q_{th}/\alpha + s\}$, where s is the size of a TCP packet.

Before deriving the worst-case bounds for throughput at the network edge using our basic scheme, we first give a definition of throughput over a time interval and introduce the notion of a guaranteed rate.

Definition 3 The throughput of a connection at the network edge at time t over a period T is the total amount of data that is transmitted from the queue at the network edge during the interval of time between $t-T$ to t divided by T:

$$Th(t,T) = \frac{1}{T}\sum(\text{packets serviced at } t') \times \text{packet size},$$
$$\text{where } t - T \leq t' < t\ . \tag{2}$$

Definition 4 Let $r(t)$ be the available bandwidth in the BC network. Given a persistent TCP source, the *guaranteed rate* of the TCP connection at the edge router is the highest R such that its throughput $Th(t,T)$ satisfies the following inequality:

$$\forall t \text{ and } T > 0, \tag{3}$$
$$Th(t,T) \geq \frac{1}{T}\left[\int_{t-T}^{t} \min(r(t),R)dt - R \times \tau_{max}\right] .$$

Note that the guaranteed rate R is defined with respect to a persistent TCP source. It can be interpreted as the minimum amount of the available bandwidth $r(t)$ that a TCP source can utilize at any time. In other words, if the available rate during some interval of time Δt is some constant r_1, we know that the queue will service at least $[\min(R,r_1)\Delta t - R \times \tau_{max}]$ more data by the end of the interval Δt. The $(R \times \tau_{max})$ term is included to account for the lack of data being serviced during the initial round-trip delay. Note that the long-time averaged throughput reduces to the long-time average of $min(R, r(t))$.

The following theorem gives a worst-case bound on the guaranteed rate in terms of the queue threshold Q_{th} and the maximum round trip delay in the LAN.

Theorem 2 Suppose the error in estimating the effective queue size is bounded above as follows: $q^*_{est}(t) \leq \beta(q^*(t) + \pi(t))$ $(\beta \geq 1)$. Then, whenever the acknowledgment bucket is non-empty, the basic scheme achieves a guaranteed rate of at least $R = Q_{th}/(\beta\tau_{max})$.

In the next sections, we will describe various ways in which the effective queue size can be estimated. Each estimate will be used in conjunction with the basic scheme to yield a different algorithm. The theorems established in this section will be used to derive performance bounds for each one of the algorithms.

5. With knowledge of TCP version

When the TCP version is known, the effective queue size can be estimated quite accurately. The estimation makes use of the TCP observer [6] and keeps account of the actual queue size and the amount of data being received at the network edge from the source. Let $U(t)$ denote the total amount of data that has been requested by the network edge through acknowledgment release up to time t. $U(t)$ can be computed precisely using the TCP observer. Let $I(t)$ denote the total amount of data received at the network edge from the source by time t. The estimate of the residual queue size can be obtained by computing the difference of the two. The estimate of the effective queue size is then obtained by adding to the residual queue estimate the actual queue size $q(t)$.

In our first scheme the estimated residual size and effective queue size are respectively:

Scheme 1

$$q_{res}^{est1}(t) = U(t) - I(t) \ , \tag{4}$$

$$q_{est1}^{*}(t) = q(t) + q_{res}^{est1}(t) \ . \tag{5}$$

As long as there is no error in the TCP observer, the above estimate of the effective queue size is exact, i.e, $q_{est1}^{*}(t) = q^{*}(t)$. Using Theorems 1 and 2, the following performance bounds can be derived for Scheme 1:

- The maximum actual queue size is: $q(t) \leq Q_{th}$,
- The guaranteed rate is: $R \geq Q_{th}/\tau_{max}$.

Note that in most cases, the maximum delay τ_{max} of the LAN is orders of magnitude less than the delay of the entire connection. Therefore, for a given guaranteed rate R, the amount of buffer $R \times \tau_{max}$ that this scheme requires is much less than the case when no mechanism is implemented at the network edge. In the latter case, if the same guaranteed rate R is desired, it is easy to show that the TCP connection could use up to $R \times T$ amount of buffer in the worst case.

6. Without knowledge of TCP version

In practice, it may not be feasible for the edge router to know the TCP version used by each source. The next scheme we present will only assume that the TCP source will send either one or two packets after receiving a new acknowledgment. (All existing versions of TCP behave in this way.) It is no longer possible to predict exactly how many packets the source will send.

Though it is no longer possible to have an exact estimate of the effective queue, a reasonable estimate is attainable. The actual queue size can still be measured directly. However, the residual queue can no longer be obtained by simply keeping account of the total amount of data requested $U(t)$ and data received $I(t)$ because of the uncertainty in computing $U(t)$; otherwise, the accumulated error in $U(t)$ will cause the error in estimating the effective queue size to be unbounded.

We next describe three different ways in which the residual queue size $q_{res}(t)$ can be estimated. The three schemes are described in order of decreasing computational complexity.

6.1. Scheme 2: one timer with per-packet state

One way of estimating the residual queue is by using knowledge of the round trip delay in the local network. With such knowledge the controller at the network edge can count how many acknowledgments are released over the time interval of τ_{max} (maximum round-trip delay in the LAN). The new estimate of the residual queue size and the effective queue size are respectively:

Scheme 2

$$q_{res}^{est2}(t) = \sum_{t'} (\#\ \textit{acks released at time } t') \times \textit{packet size},$$
$$\textit{where } t - \tau_{max} \leq t' < t \ , \tag{6}$$

$$q_{est2}^{*}(t) = q(t) + q_{res}^{est2}(t) \ . \tag{7}$$

The above computation can be performed by using a timer and a register to hold the timestamp $\hat{t} + \tau_{\max}$ for each released acknowledgment at time $\hat{t}$. The estimate $q_{res}^{est2}(t)$ is then equal to all registers with timestamps larger than t. Those registers with timestamps smaller than the current time can be used to hold the new timestamps for future released acknowledgments.

Unlike Scheme 1, this scheme cannot estimate the residual queue size and effective queue size precisely. However, the error in the estimate can be bounded as follows (in the case of persistent sources):

Lemma 1

$$q_{est2}^{*}(t) \geq \frac{1}{2} q^{*}(t) \ , \tag{8}$$

$$q_{est2}^{*}(t) \leq q^{*}(t) + \pi(t) \ . \tag{9}$$

Incorporating this estimate of effective queue size into the basic scheme, i.e., an acknowledgment is released from the network edge to the source only if $q_{est2}^{*}(t) < Q_{th}$, we obtain the following performance bounds for Scheme 2 (in the case of persistent sources) using Theorems 1 and 2.

- The maximum actual queue size is: $q(t) \leq 2Q_{th}$,
- The guaranteed rate is: $R \geq Q_{th}/\tau_{max}$.

Compared with Scheme 1, we see that Scheme 2 achieves the same lower bound on the guaranteed rate but twice the upper bound on the actual queue size when the sources are persistent. We can interpret the extra Q_{th} in the queue bound as caused by the lack of knowledge on the TCP source behavior. Note also that from the above argument, $q_{res}^{est2}(t) \leq Q_{th}$ for all time t. Thus, the number of registers needed to compute $q_{res}^{est2}(t)$ is no more than Q_{th}/packet size.

6.2. Scheme 3: one timer with limited number of states

In Scheme 2, we want to count the number of acknowledgments released during a time interval of $\tau_{\max}$ precisely and, consequently, we use one register to keep track of the timestamp for each such acknowledgment. To further reduce implementation complexity, we now present a scheme that uses similar ideas as in Scheme 2 but uses only a fixed number $N > 1$ of registers with one timer. The key idea in this Scheme 3 is to estimate the residual queue size by approximating the number of acknowledgments released over a time interval of $\tau_{\max}$.

In Scheme 3, each of the N states, denoted by $d[n]$ for $n = 1, ..., N$, holds the number of acknowledgments that are released by the network edge during some consecutive time interval of duration τ_{max}/N, with $n = N$ corresponding to the current time interval. When an acknowledgment is released, the value of the first state $d[N]$ is incremented by one. At the beginning of each time interval τ_{max}/N, the value of each state is passed to the state of the previous time interval ($d[n-1] \leftarrow d[n]$, for $1 < n \leq N$) and $d[N]$ is reset to zero. The residual and effective queue size estimates in this scheme are as follows:

Scheme 3

$$q_{res}^{est3}(t) = \sum_{n=1}^{N} d[n] \times \textit{packet size}\ , \tag{10}$$

$$q_{est3}^{*}(t) = q(t) + q_{res}^{est3}(t)\ . \tag{11}$$

Note that the above estimate of the residual queue size at time t is an underestimate of the packet size times the number of acknowledgments released between time $t - \tau_{\max}$ and t, i.e.,

$$\sum_{n=1}^{N} d[n] \leq \sum \#\ \text{acks released at}\ t' \tag{12}$$
$$\text{where}\ t - \tau_{max} \leq t' < t\ .$$

The error bounds on the estimate of the effective queue size are (in the case of persistent sources):

Lemma 2

$$q_{est3}^{*}(t) \geq \frac{1}{4} q^{*}(t) \quad \text{when}\ q^{*}(t) \geq 4Q_{th}\ , \tag{13}$$

$$q_{est3}^{*}(t) \leq q^{*}(t) + \pi(t)\ . \tag{14}$$

Once again, by using Theorems 1 and 2, the following performance bounds can be derived for Scheme 3 (in the case of persistent sources):

- The maximum actual queue size is: $q(t) \leq 4Q_{th}$,
- The guaranteed rate is: $R \geq Q_{th}/\tau_{max}$.

In the worst case, using a larger N in Scheme 3 will not bring a better bound than a smaller N. However, in most cases, a larger N will give us a better performance. A larger N means that the approximation to the number of acknowledgments released over a time interval $\tau_{\max}$ becomes more accurate, thus bringing the performance bounds of Scheme 3 closer to Scheme 2.

6.3. Scheme 4: without knowledge of delay

In some cases, the maximum LAN round trip delay $\tau_{\max}$ is not known or cannot be bounded. To deal with these cases, we now present a scheme that does not make use of knowledge about $\tau_{\max}$. In this scheme, the estimate of the residual queue size $q_{res}^{est4}(t)$ is computed by incrementing $q_{res}^{est4}(t)$ by one when an acknowledgment is released and decrementing it by one when a packet arrives at the network edge. This technique will tend to underestimate the residual queue. We limit the residual queue estimate error by preventing $q_{res}^{est}(t)$ from becoming negative.

Scheme 4

If an acknowledgment is released:

$$q_{res}^{est4}(t) \leftarrow q_{res}^{est4}(t) + 1$$

If a packet is received:

$$q_{res}^{est4}(t) \leftarrow q_{res}^{est4}(t) - 1$$

$$\textit{If}\ q_{res}^{est4}(t) < 0, \quad q_{res}^{est4}(t) \leftarrow 0$$

$$q_{est4}^{*} = q(t) + q_{res}^{est4}(t)\ . \tag{15}$$

Since every acknowledgment triggers the release of at least one packet from the source, this estimation technique always guarantees the bound $q_{res}^{est4}(t) \leq q_{res}(t)$. Using Theorem 2 we can prove that the guaranteed rate is $R \geq Q_{th}/\tau_{max}$ (we assume $\tau_{\max}$ is finite though it is unknown). However, there is no constant-factor lower bound for $q_{res}^{est4}(t)$ with respect to $q_{res}(t)$. In fact, it is not hard to construct a worst-case scenario in which $q_{res}^{est4}(t) = 0$ and $q_{res}(t)$ is unbounded. In summary, for Scheme 4,

- The worst case queue size is unbounded,
- The guaranteed rate is: $R \geq Q_{th}/\tau_{max}$.

This scheme shows how some throughput guarantee is still possible even when there is no knowledge of the LAN round-trip time. However, because of the 1) uncertainty in the TCP source model, and 2) the lack of any knowledge of the round-trip delay time, the worst-case queue size is unbounded. In fact, it is not hard to show that no other scheme under these two conditions can ensure both a queue bound and a non-zero guaranteed rate.

The idea of counting the packets arriving at the network edge can also be applied to Schemes 2 and 3, which rely on the knowledge of $\tau_{\max}$. Under the original schemes 2 and 3, a temporarily idle TCP source can keep receiving acknowledgments as long as the acknowledgment bucket is non-empty. The improved schemes will be more robust and will reduce the burstiness of traffic due to non-greedy sources. The basic idea is to allow the residual queue size to be reduced only when some packet has been previously received at the network edge. Thus, when the TCP source becomes active again, it will not send a big burst of packets to the network edge.

Specifically, we use a register *perms* that increments by one every time a packet arrives at the edge router. The value of *perms* is never allowed to be higher than the estimate of the residual queue. When the residual queue size needs to be decremented in schemes 2 and 3, this operation will be delayed until *perms* is greater than zero. When this is true, *perms* and the residual queue can be decremented by the same amount as long as *perms* is nonnegative.

In Table 1, we summarize the performance parameters of each of the four schemes. The variables q_{wc} and R_{wc} are the maximum queue size and the minimum guaranteed rate respectively under worst-case scenarios.

Static Threshold Q_{th}	Queue Bound q_{wc}	Guaranteed Rate R_{wc}	Ratio R_{wc}/q_{wc}
Scheme 1	Q_{th}	Q_{th}/τ_{max}	$1/\tau_{max}$
Scheme 2	2 Q_{th}	Q_{th}/τ_{max}	$1/2\tau_{max}$
Scheme 3	4 Q_{th}	Q_{th}/τ_{max}	$1/4\tau_{max}$
Scheme 4	unbounded	Q_{th}/τ_{max}	0

Table 1. Performance bounds.

7. Aggregate traffic

Our discussion so far has been focused on regulating the traffic of only one TCP connection. In the case of Schemes 2-4, it is quite simple to apply them to regulate aggregate traffic.

In the scenario we are considering, all the different TCP flows are merged into one FIFO queue. The objective is to minimize the total FIFO queue size while maximizing the total throughput. This can be achieved by treating all the packets for all the connections in the same way. The actual queue size is the total number of packets in the FIFO queue; the residual queue size is the sum of all the packets and acknowledgments that are in transit. The algorithms are used in the same way except that all the packets are considered collectively.

There is only one modification that the algorithms require. In order to ensure fairness among the different connections, the acknowledgments for each TCP connection are kept in separate buckets and are released in a round-robin fashion. In other words, when the scheme commands to release an acknowledgment from the network edge, it looks for the next nonempty bucket and releases an acknowledgment from that bucket. In this fashion we can achieve similar performance bounds for the cumulative queue and throughput, while treating all the connections fairly.

8. Simulation results

In this section, we will present simulation results performed with OPNET to illustrate the performance of our schemes. In the first set of simulations, we evaluate the performance of a single TCP connection with steady bandwidth and persistent sources. These simple results serve to illustrate the dynamics of the different schemes. In the second set of simulations, we present a more realistic example, where ten TCP connections share the same bandwidth constrained network. The simulations also involve time-varying bandwidth and bursty sources.

8.1. Single connection

In the first set of simulations, we have a single TCP connection traversing via an edge router over a bandwidth constrained (BC) wide area network (see Figure 1 in Section 1). The delay between the TCP source and the edge router is 2 milliseconds. The BC network itself has a (one-way) propagation delay of 50 milliseconds.

The edge router connecting the TCP source's LAN to the WAN has an available output bandwidth of 256 KB/sec. We assume that all packets are of size 1 KB. In this set of simulations, the TCP source is assumed to be persistent, i.e., it always has data to send. The window size advertised by the TCP receiver *swindow* is of size 128 KB, which is larger than the product of the round-trip delay and the available bandwidth. The initial slow start threshold *ssthresh* is 64 KB. The edge router has an unlimited buffer. Every packet transmitted from the source arrives at the destination, except that we discard packet 1000 before it gets to the destination. We are interested in understanding how our schemes behave when there is packet loss.

This scenario is simulated using schemes 1, 2, and 4 described earlier in this paper; scheme 3 is omitted since it is an implementation approximation to scheme 2 and is expected to perform similarly. At the edge router, the queue threshold Q_{th} is set to 5 packets. Figures 2–3 show how the queue size, bucket size, and congestion window size evolve with time for each of the schemes.

Figure 2 illustrates how the congestion window *cwnd* and the queue size at the edge router behave when no acknowledgments are withheld at all. The queue size grows quite rapidly, filling the gap between the bandwidth-delay product and the congestion window size. The maximum bandwidth delay product is roughly $256 \times 0.1 \approx 26$ packets. When the window size becomes larger than this, the queue starts building up at the same rate as the window. After the retransmission of packet 1000 takes place, the same phenomenon occurs again.

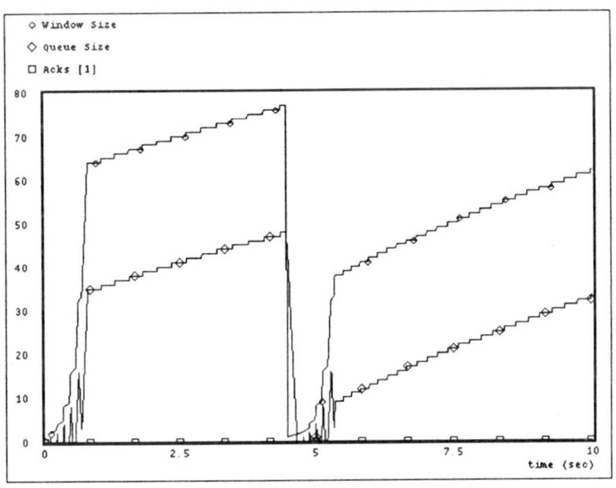

Figure 2. Without withholding acks.

Figures 3 shows what happens under the same scenario, but when acknowledgment release is regulated by scheme 4 (the traces produced from the other schemes are practically identical). This time, it is the acknowledgment bucket size (the number of acknowledgments retained at the edge router) which follows the window size as it grows. The acknowledgment bucket serves to fill the gap between the congestion window size and the bandwidth-delay product. However, the queue size always remains at very low levels. The peak queue sizes are 4, 5, and 6 packets for schemes 1, 2, and 4 respectively. Since the queue threshold Q_{th} is 5 packets, these results confirm our theoretical bounds.

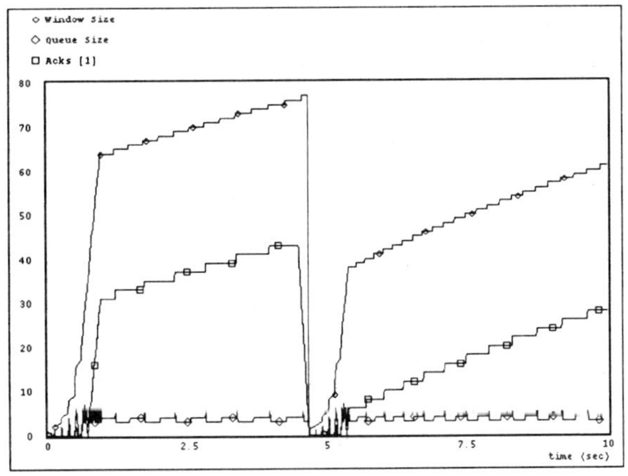

Figure 3. Using scheme 4.

8.2. Multiple sources

The previous set of simulations illustrated the dynamics of our schemes. In the second set of simulations, there are 10 TCP source connected to the edge router. The delays are still the same: 50 milliseconds for the bandwidth constrained WAN and 2 milliseconds for the LAN. The edge router now has a maximum available bandwidth of 1024 packets/sec. As in the first set of simulations, each packet has a size of 1KB, the window advertised by the receiver is 128 KB, and the initial slow start threshold is 64 KB for each connection. The packets from different TCP connections are buffered in a FIFO queue at the edge router; the total buffer size is limited to 50 packets. When the buffer is full, arriving packets are discarded.

Since we have multiple sources, we use the aggregate version of the algorithms described in Section 7, where the acknowledgments are released in a round-robin fashion. This represents considerable saving in computation (particularly for Scheme 4) since only one effective queue needs to be considered. The aggregate queue threshold Q_{th} is set to 20 packets. We also modify slightly Scheme 2 as described at the end of Subsection 6.3 so that it will stop releasing acks when the source becomes idle.

In our simulations, during some intervals the sources can become bursty. When this happens, the sources will be periodically shut off for 0.1 seconds and then will send as much data as possible (constrained by the TCP windowing scheme) for the next 0.1 second. This time period is chosen so that it is approximately the same as the network round-trip delay.

During some other intervals of time, the bandwidth available at the edge router becomes time-varying.

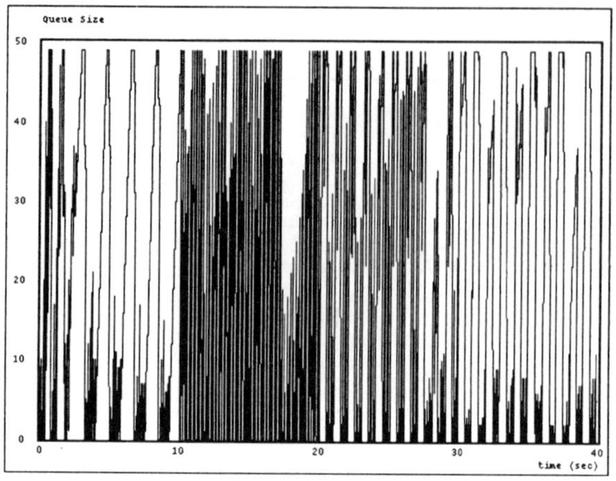

Figure 4. Queue size with a limited buffer.

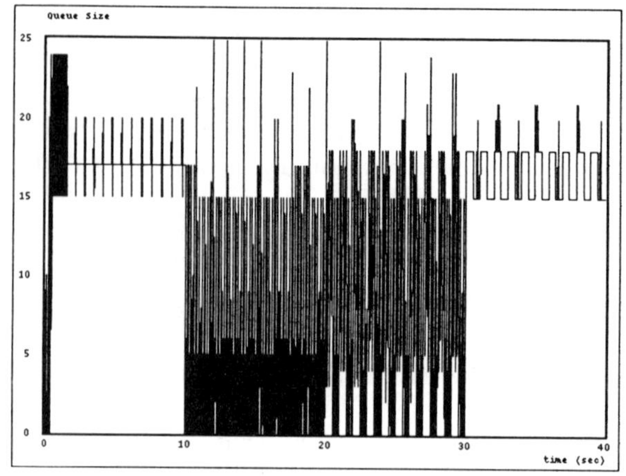

Figure 5. Queue size using scheme 4.

When this happens, the available bandwidth periodically drops to 256 KB/sec for 0.5 second and then recovers to 1024 KB/sec for the next 0.5 second.

The simulation is performed during 40 seconds. During the first interval of 10 seconds, the available bandwidth is steady (1024 KB/sec) and the sources are non-bursty. During the next 10-second interval, the available bandwidth is still steady, but the sources are now bursty. In the third 10-second interval, the available bandwidth is fluctuating and the sources are bursty. Finally, during the last 10-second interval, the bandwidth is still fluctuating, but the sources become persistent (non-bursty).

Figure 4 shows what happens to the queue size (cumulative queue for all the connections) when no acknowledgment is withheld. The buffer often exceeds its limit of 50 packets and overflows. The queue is empty at other times and the BC network is underutilized.

Figure 5 shows the packet queue sizes at the edge router when scheme 4 is used. The queue sizes for the other schemes are practically identical. The packet queue size for scheme 1 never exceeds the queue threshold of 20 packets (as theoretically predicted). For scheme 2, the queue sometimes reaches the size of 23 packets, while for scheme 4, the queue reaches up to the size of 25. Even when slow start takes place with bursty source conditions and varying available bandwidth, the observed packet queue sizes never exceeds the limit of 50 packets. From the figure, we also observe that during the intervals where the sources are persistent (0 to 10 sec and 30 to 40 sec), the packet queue is always non-empty. As predicted, the throughput is maximized when the sources are persistent.

Figure 6 shows the sequence number of the current packet being transmitted for each of the ten sources when no acknowledgment is withheld and the buffer is limited to 50 packets. The results indicate that there is a certain degree of unfairness in throughput among the different TCP connections. Figure 7 presents the result when the aggregate scheme 4 is used. It is clear that the scheme achieves much better throughput while achieving almost perfect fairness. The other acknowledgment bucket schemes also exhibit the same fairness property.

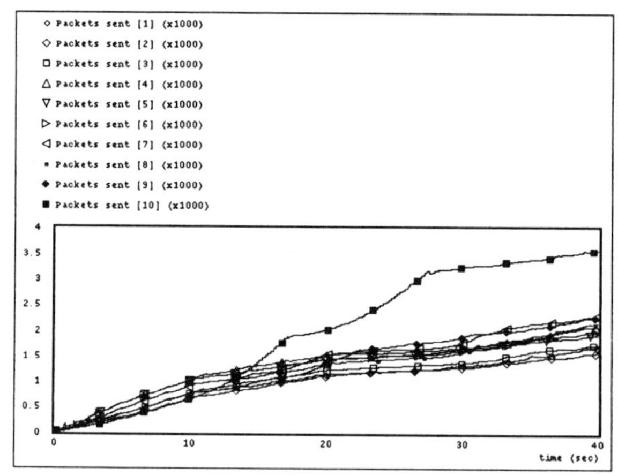

Figure 6. Individual source rates without acknowledgment withholding.

Finally, Table 2 summarizes the goodput for each acknowledgment withholding scheme as well as for regular TCP traffic with a limited (at 50 packets) buffer. Each entry contains the the sum of the maximum contiguous sequence numbers that have been successfully received at the destinations. The entry is expressed as a percentage of the goodput achieved by a regular TCP connection with an infinite buffer. The goodputs of our scheme are maximized when the sources are persistent, but is somewhat suboptimal when the sources become bursty. On the other hand, regular TCP traffic without acknowledgment withholding and limited buffer always lags behind our schemes.

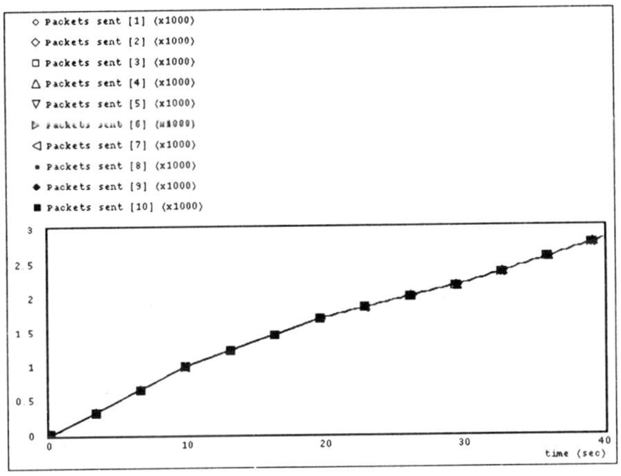

Figure 7. Individual source rates using scheme 4.

	Persistent Sources Steady Bwdth	Bursty Sources Steady Bwdth	Bursty Sources Varying Bwdth	Persistent Sources Varying Bwdth
Regular TCP	82%	59%	51%	60%
Scheme 1	100%	68%	75%	100%
Scheme 2	100%	69%	76%	100%
Scheme 4	100%	69%	76%	100%

Table 2. Goodputs of each scheme in the multi-source scenario.

When no acknowledgment is withheld, the packets are continuously dropped from the limited packet buffer and need to be retransmitted. In our acknowledgment withholding schemes, no packets are dropped at the buffer and no retransmission needs to take place. Note that the regular TCP goodput is worse even with a larger buffer (50 packets) compared with our acknowledgment withholding schemes with a smaller buffer (fewer than 20 packets). The improvement in goodput of the acknowledgment withholding schemes is particularly significant for cases where the router available bandwidth is fluctuating. This is mainly because the feedback loop in our schemes is so much faster (in this case 4 milliseconds rather than more than 100 milliseconds) and effective: the TCP source rate is directly controlled to adapt to the available bandwidth, rather than progressively adjusted through TCP window flow control, which relies on packet drop as indication of network congestion.

9. Conclusion

We have presented a variety of schemes that resolve congestion of TCP traffic at network edges by regulating the flow of returned acknowledgments to the sources. While the flow control mechanism of TCP relies on packet drop as indication of congestion, our schemes implemented at edge routers can improve TCP throughput by avoiding buffer overflow and resulting packet loss. Our schemes also minimize the buffer requirements of edge routers. Each of these schemes has different implementation complexities and tradeoffs in terms of queue bound and throughput.

References

[1] V. Chim and V. Leung "End-to-end acknowledgments for indirect TCP over wireless Internetworks," Proceedings of Pacific Rim Conference on Communications, Computers and Signal Processing, Aug. 1997, pp. 774-777.

[2] S. Floyd, "TCP and Explicit Congestion Notification," Computer Communication Review, Vol. 24, Number 5, October 1994.

[3] A. Koike, "TCP flow control with ACR information," ATM Forum contributions 97-0758R1.

[4] A. Kolarov and G. Ramamurthy, "A Control Theoretic Approach to the Design of Closed Loop Rate Based Flow Control for High Speed ATM Networks," to appear in IEEE INFOCOMM '97.

[5] S. Mascolo, D. Cavendish, and M. Gerla, "ATM Rate Based Congestion Control using a Smith Predictor: an EPRCA Implementation," IEEE INFOCOMM '96.

[6] P. Narváez and K.-Y. Siu, "An Acknowledgment Bucket Scheme to Regulate TCP Flow over ATM," Proceedings of IEEE Globecom, November 1997.

[7] P. Narváez and K.-Y. Siu, "New Techniques for Regulating TCP Flow over Heterogeneous Networks," Technical Report, May 1998, http://list.mit.edu/~pnarvaez/papers/paper5-tech.ps

[8] N. Yin and S. Jagannath. End-to-End Traffic Management in IP/ATM Internetworks *ATM Forum Contribution 96-1406*, October 1996.

Smooth Slow-Start: Refining TCP slow-start for Large-Bandwidth with Long-Delay Networks

Yoshifumi Nishida
Keio University
Graduate School of Media and Governance
nishida@sfc.wide.ad.jp

Abstract

Transmission Control Protocol (TCP) adopts some techniques that use network resource efficiently by estimating the characteristic and condition of network.

Slow-start algorithm is the primary technique for effective resource usage.

The goal of slow-start is to establish TCP connection in optimum state for network path quickly unless giving an excessive load to the network.

However, in the large-bandwidth with long-delay links such as satellite links, slow-start algorithm does not work properly and causes substantial performance degradation.

In this paper, we describe the problem of current slow-start algorithm in large-bandwidth with long-delay networks. We propose new slow-start algorithm that can increase network transfer performance for large bandwidth with long delay networks. We also implemented this algorithm on a network simulator for evaluation and resulted over 60% efficiency compared to a normal slow start algorithm.

1. Introduction

TCP is a flexible communication protocol enabling low speed communication links such as telephone lines to a high speed links such as FDDI or an ATM network.

This TCP's flexibility is established by 'self clocking' method which takes advantage of acknowledgement segment. Self clocking is designed based on the following concepts.

1. Performance of the data transfer rate is determined by the slowest bottleneck bandwidth path along the communication path.

   Data transfer rate can not exceed the bandwidth of its communication media. Therefore, the maximum transfer rate matches the allowable bandwidth of the slowest link on the communication path.

2. When packets are transmitted continuously from a high-speed link enter into a slow link, the interval of the packets is expanded.

   For example, the transfer of a 1024 byte packet costs 0.08 seconds in the 1Mbps link. But in the 100kbps link, cost takes 0.8 seconds. Therefore, when packets which are transmitted with no interval enter into 100Kbps link from 1Mbps link, the interval of packets is expanded to 0.8 seconds.

3. The transmission interval of acknowledge segments is equal to the receiving interval of transmitted data segments from sender.

   The acknowledgement segments are transmitted at the moment of the receipts of sender's segments. Therefore, the interval of the acknowledgement segments is almost equal to the sender's segment which was expanded through bottleneck link.

4. Using acknowledgement segment as a trigger of transmitting segment enables to attain optimum transfer rate for communication path.

   The arrival interval of the acknowledgement segments matches the interval of the sender's segments which was expanded through the bottleneck link. This interval is optimum for the bottleneck link and also optimum for the whole communication path.

   Therefore if acknowledgement segment is used as a trigger of transmitting segment, the transmit interval will match the bandwidth of the bottleneck link and will become optimal for communication path.

The main goal of TCP is to make communication status approach to self clocking status. But under the TCP/IP architecture, it is difficult to estimate the allowable bandwidth of bottleneck link along communication path. When segments are transmitted at the rate that are far higher than allowable bandwidth of the bottleneck link, buffer overflow at intermediate router will occur. When segments are transmitted at the rate that are far lower than allowable bandwidth of the bottleneck link, the interval of acknowledgement segment is not varied. In this case, self-clocking does not work and this results in poor transmission performance.

To solve this problem, Slow-start algorithm was devised [1] [2].

Slow-start algorithm adds 'congestion window' parameter to TCP's sliding window scheme. TCP cannot inject more than 'congestion window' segments of unacknowledged data into the network. By controlling congestion window, TCP adapts transfer rate to communication path. Slow-start has two data transfer phases, slow-start and congestion avoidance. Two phases have different congestion window control algorithm.

TCP enters in slow-start phase when new communication is started or when TCP increases traffic again after the congestion period. In the slow-start phase, TCP initializes congestion window to 1 segment. For each ACK received, TCP increases the value of congestion window by 1 segment. Therefore congestion window is doubled in every 1 round trip time. Doubled congestion window soon exceed the capacity of bottleneck link and it causes congestion and segment losses.

When TCP detects the segment loss by duplicate ack or timeout, it decreases congestion window to avoid congestion collapse. The algorithm that decreases congestion window slightly varied from implementation of TCP[1][5]. When TCP decides that congestion period comes to an end, TCP increase the congestion window again. If increased window size reaches half of the window size when congestion was detected, TCP moves to the congestion avoidance phase from slow-start phase.

In the congestion avoidance phase, TCP increases congestion windows at the graceful rate by 1 segment in every 1 round trip time.

The goal of slow-start algorithm is to establish TCP connection into to self-clocking condition as quickly as possible. By using slow-start algorithm, TCP can approach to the best window size roughly in slow-start phase and approach to more precisely in congestion avoidance phase.

Slow-Start algorithm is suitable in short delay networks or small bandwidth networks. However in large bandwidth with long delay link such as the satellite link, slow-start maintains poor transmit performance.

The next section explains problem of slow-start algorithm in large bandwidth with long delay networks.

2. Problem of Slow-Start algorithm

To analyze TCP's dynamics in large bandwidth with long delay network, We used ns network simulator [4] developed by LBL.

First, slow-start algorithm in short delay network is analyzed. Figure 1 shows the network configuration of the analysis.

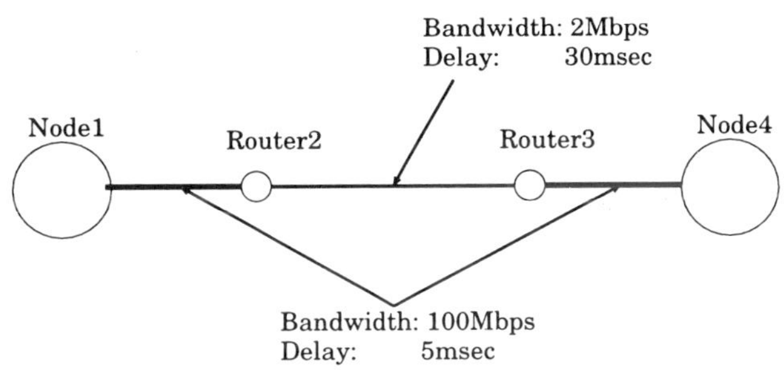

Figure 1. network configuration

In figure 1, node 1, 4 are connected by 10Mbps link. The propagation delay of 10Mbps link is set to 5msec. The link between router 2 and 3 is a bottleneck link. This bottleneck link has 2Mbps bandwidth and 30msec propagation delay. The queue size of router is set to 6.

In this configuration, node 1 sends data to node 4 over TCP. We use TCP reno[5] among various TCP algorithms. Figure 2 describes the variation of window size and its transfer period.

We see from figure 2 that during 0 sec to 0.5 sec, window size is increased exponentially by slow-start phase algorithm. And after the segment loss is occurred, from 2.0 sec, window size is increased linearly by congestion avoidance phase algorithm.

The performance of TCP is calculated by window size and round trip time as follows.

$$Throughput(byte/sec) = \frac{Window\,Size(bytes)}{Round\,Trip\,Time(sec)}$$

Therefore, the optimum window size for specific bandwidth can be calculated by following formula:

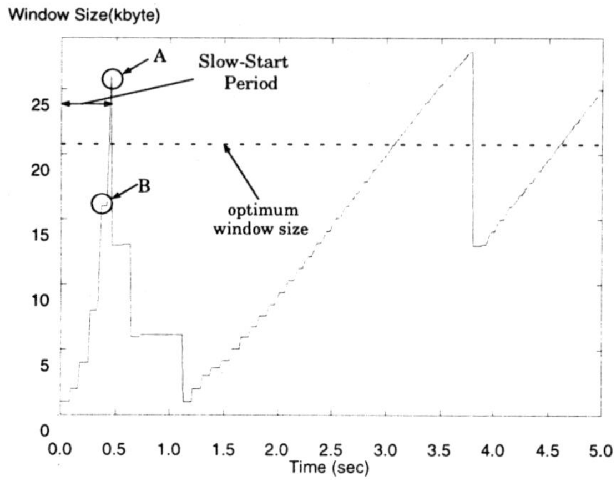

Figure 2. variation of window size

$$Windowsize \;=\; Allowable\,Bandwidth\,of\;Path \times Round\,Trip\,Time$$

If there is no other traffic on the network path, transmit rate from node1 to node 2 is equal to 2Mbps of the bottleneck link's bandwidth. As the round trip time is 0.08 sec, the optimum window size for network is given by:

$$\frac{2048000(bps)}{8(bit/byte)} \times 0.08(sec) = 20480(byte)$$

As seen in figure 2, the maximum window size in slow-start phase is 28000 byte (in the circled region A) and the window size that is 1 round trip time previous to the maximum is 16000 byte (in the circled region B).

The optimum window size is 20480 byte. This is between 28000 byte and 16000 byte, thus slow-start works fine in this case.

When the propagation delay of the bottleneck link is increased from 30msec to 240msec, round trip time for network path becomes 500msec, thus optimum window size is 128Kbyte.

Figure 3 shows the result of data transfer from node1 to node2. As seen in figure 3, slow-start phase finished in 3.5 sec. The maximum window size in slow-start phase is 25Kbyte which is far lower than 128Kbyte. This miss behavior of slow-start leads to long congestion avoidance phase and causes severe performance degradation.

To analyze this degradation, we compute transfer rate in every 2 msec. The result is shown in figure 4. As seen in figure 4, 4.4Mbps burst data transfer that

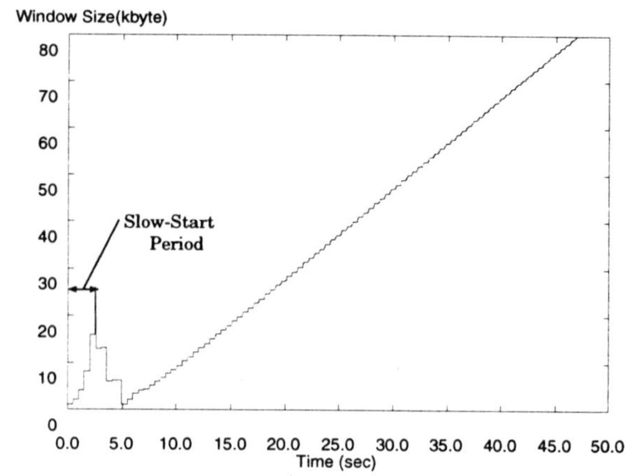

Figure 3. variation of window size in long delay networks

far exceed bottleneck link's bandwidth is occurred at the time 2.0 sec and 2.5 sec.

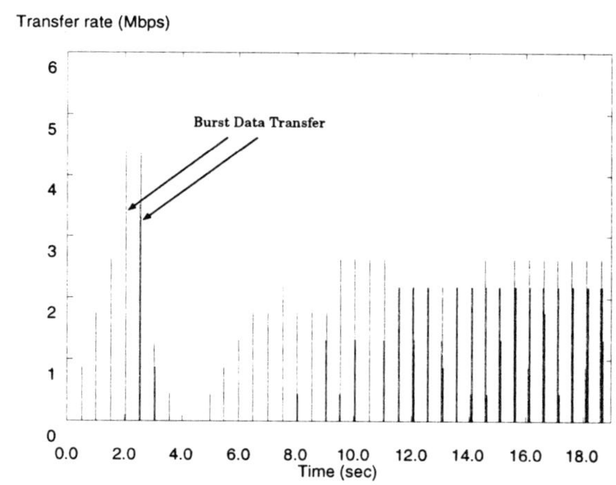

Figure 4. variation of transfer rate

The reason for bursty data transfer can be described by figure 5

Figure 5 shows the reached time of the sequence number of packet. We see that sequence number is bursty increased at every 0.5sec. This is the result that all segments in the congestion window are injected in around 0.1 sec, while window size is increased at every 0.5 sec. Therefore, while the average transfer rate of 1 round trip time is lower than allowable bandwidth, burst data transfer is occurred in short interval. This burst data transfer causes congestion. In short-delay

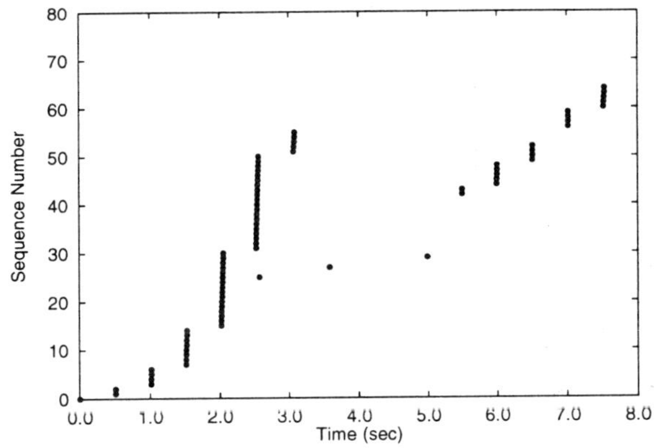

Figure 5. variation of sequence number

networks, the optimum window size is small and there is no significant difference between round trip time and actual data transfer time. Thus, burst data transfer is not occurred in short-delay networks.

But in long-delay networks, slow-start leads to burst data transfer and causes congestion with far lower window size than optimum window size. This leads to short slow-start phase and long congestion avoidance phase. In this situation, arrival to self-clocking status is delayed and it results in severe performance degradation.

3. Smooth Slow Start

3.1 Requirement for controlling interval of data transfer

To avoid burst data transfer in long-delay network, controlling interval of data transfer is required.

If TCP is in self-clocking status, to control interval of data transfer may destroy the status. However when TCP is in slow-start phase, TCP connection does not establish self-clocking status yet. Therefore, to control interval of data transfer in slow-start phase does not destroy essence of TCP.

But the method to control interval of data transfer is expected to satisfy the following requirement.

- Does not affect TCP performance
  To avoid burst data transfer, expansion of data transmit period is required. However if interval is expanded too much, all segments in congestion window are not transmitted in its round trip time. This leads to collapse of slow-start timing. In this case, slow-start may not work correctly.

- Easy algorithm to implement on existing operating systems
  To control interval of data transfer, we need to use interrupt timer provided by operating system. However, frequent use of timer interrupt loads operating system. This results in performance degradation. Most current implementation of TCP use coarse 200 msec and 500 msec timers [3]. To use these timer to control interval of data transfer makes this method suitable to existing systems and makes implementation easier.

- Adapt to fluctuation of round trip time
  The round trip time fluctuate frequently in large area networks. For flexible control of data transfer interval, adaptation of round trip time fluctuation is required.

3.2 Design of smooth slow start

Based on these requirement, we designed smooth slow start algorithm to reduce burst data transfer in slow-start phase.

Figure 6 shows example of smooth slow-start algorithm proposed in this paper. This figure compares smooth slow-start with existing slow-start (we call this normal slow-start) in the networks which has 250 msec propagation delay.

Left side of figure 6 shows the behavior of normal slow-start. As seen in figure, the number of transmitted segment is doubled in every 500 msec. The right side of figure shows behavior of smooth slow-start. As seen in figure, compared with normal slow-start, smooth slow-start reduces burst segment transfer. Furthermore, despite interval of segment transfer is expanded, the number of transmitted segment in 1 round trip time is no difference compared to normal slow-start.

The next section explains behavior of smooth slow start in detail.

3.2.1 Controlling data transfer by timer interrupt

Most existing TCP implementation use 200msec and 500msec timer interrupt. Smooth slow start uses 200msec timer interrupt to control data transfer. This design simplifies implementation.

Using normal slow-start algorithm , when sender receives an acknowledge segment,sender increases congestion windows by 1 segment. As a result, two segments are transmitted bursty. With smooth slow-start implementation, when sender receives an acknowledge segment, sender's TCP decides whether interval of data transfer should be expanded. If TCP decides to expand

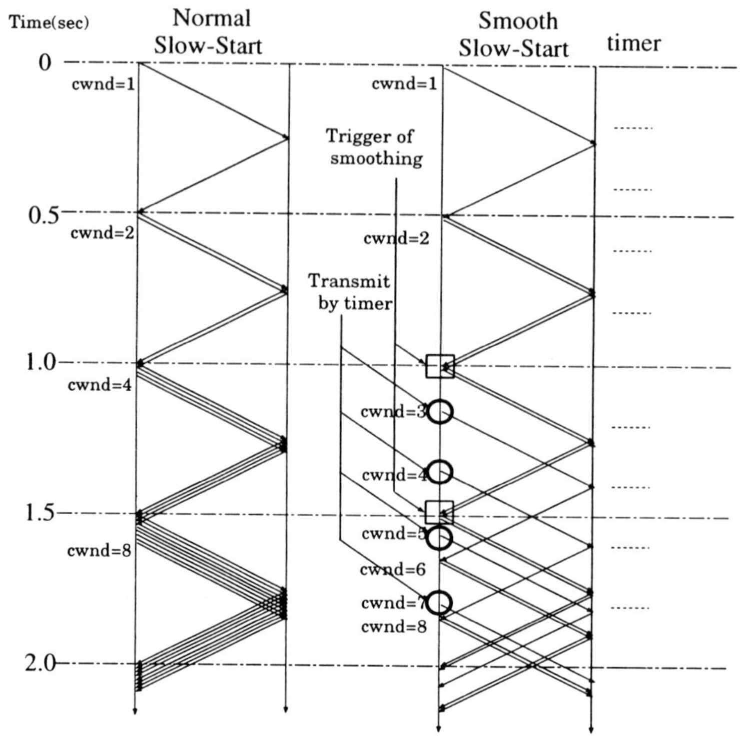

Figure 6. example of smooth slow-start

interval, TCP only sets flag to increase congestion window but does not increase actually. As a result, only one segment is transmitted when acknowledge segment is received by sender.

Timer interrupt routine which is invoked in every 200msec checks the flag to increment congestion window. If flag is set, TCP increase congestion window and invoke segment transfer routine. To avoid burst data transfer by timer interrupt, the number of transmitted segments in one timer interrupt is restricted to 1.

As shown above, by using timer interrupt, interval of two transmitted segments can be expanded. In right side of figure 6, segment transfer by timer interrupt is established at time 1.2 sec, 1.6sec and 1.8sec (circled region).

3.2.2 Decision of delay segment transfer

When acknowledgment for the segments delayed by timer is received and if TCP decides to delay to increase congestion window by this acknowledgement, the delay of data transfer may become too large. This leads to collapse of slow-start algorithm.

Thus, to delay segment transfer is limited only head of burst data transfer. Current design of smooth slow start allows only two segments delay in 1 round trip time. Furthermore when congestion window is less than two, delayed transmission is not allowed. Therefore, the two segments in head of RTT are never delayed and these segments are trigger of smoothing(squared region).

In figure 6, delayed transmission is determined at the time acknowledgement for segment 4,5 and segment 7,9 is received.

3.2.3 Adapt to fluctuation of round trip time

Figure 7 shows behavior of slow-start when round trip time fluctuates suddenly. The left side of the figure shows normal slow-start's behavior and the right side of the figure shows smooth slow-start's.

As seen in figure 7, round trip time is varied at the time 1.5sec from 500msec to 200msec. Using normal slow-start method, data transfer becomes bursty, thus fluctuation of round trip time does not affect too much. When smooth slow-start method is used, TCP does not increase congestion window at the time 1.5sec but sets flag to increase congestion window. This flag leads to transmit segment at the time 1.6sec and 1.8sec. But

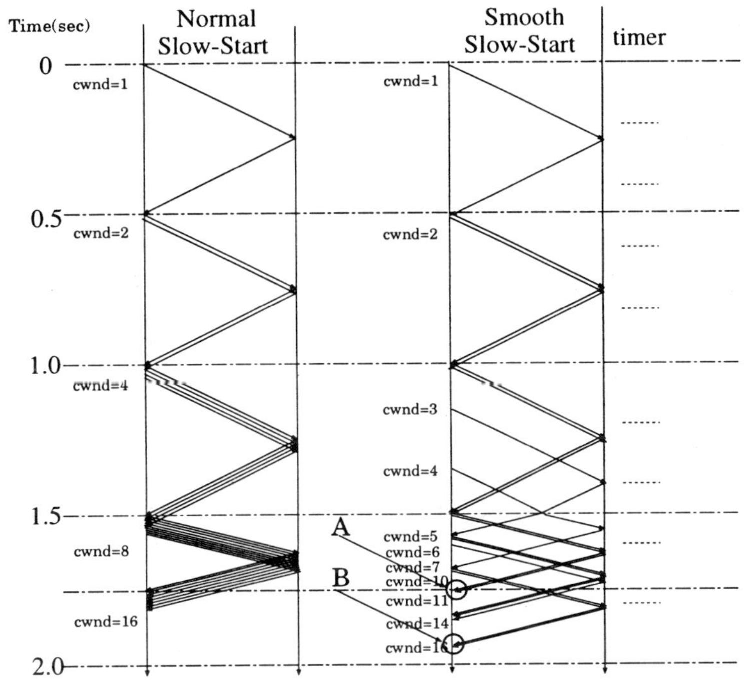

Figure 7. slow-start behavior when RTT is varied

round trip time fluctuates at the time 1.5sec, thus acknowledgement for the trigger segment of delay transfer is received at the time 1.75sec (circled region A), before timer interrupt occurs at the time 1.8sec.

When acknowledgement for trigger segment is received before delayed transmission by timer occurs, smooth slow-start increase congestion window by 2 more segments for 1 unsent delayed segment. Smooth slow-start regard unsent delayed segments as already transmitted and acknowledged.

In this example, smooth slow-start increase congestion window by 3, since there is 1 unsent segment at the time circled region A in the figure. Thus the size of congestion window is varied from 7 to 10.

By this operation, the size of congestion window in next round trip is equal to its of normal slow-start. In this example, the size of congestion window is set to 16 at the time 1.9sec (circled region B) which is same size of normal slow-start.

As a result, chance of 1 segment transfer is lost. But this does not destroy essence of slow-start algorithm. To lose the chance of 1 segment data transfer does not affect much whole performance of data transfer.

3.2.4 Recovery from multiple packet loss

In slow-start phase, congestion windows is increased exponentially, and multiple packet loss within one window of data will occur in most case. J.Hoe pointed out that during the recovery of multiple packet loss, a large ACK may trigger burst transmission [8]. By using smooth slow-start, TCP can attain larger window size. But larger window size makes this problem more remarkable. To solve this problem, Hoe suggested to limit the number of segments which TCP can inject into the network successively.

To reduce this burst transmission, we use timer interrupt. When TCP finds burst data transmission after the slow-start phase, TCP divides data transmission to some parts according to round trip time. For example, When RTT is 700msec, 200msec timer interrupt is invoked 3 times. In this case, times of divided data transmission is set to 4(= 3+1), and number of segment which is injected in one burst transmission is set to quarter of window. More elegant algorithm to solve this problem is need to study as future work. There are many researches that argue for recovery from multiple packet loss [6][7][8][9]. We also plan to combine the techniques from these researches.

3.3 Simulation result

To analyze effect of smooth slow start, we implemented this algorithm on ns simulator. Our implementation is based on TCP reno module in ns.

3.3.1 Simulation in large bandwidth with long-delay network

The network configuration used in this simulation is same as figure 1. The bandwidth of bottleneck link is set to 2Mbps, the queue size of router is set to 6 segment and the propagation delay is set to 240msec. In this configuration, node 1 sends data to node 4 over TCP.

Figure 8 shows the variation of sequence number by smooth slow-start algorithm. Compared to Figure 9, we see that the interval of segment transfer is dispersed and burst data transfer is reduced. This leads to attain large size of congestion window and improve performance of data transfer. Using normal slow-start, congestion occurs due to burst data transfer at the time 3.0sec.

Figure 10 shows zoomed-in view of circled region in figure 8. As seen in this figure, intermittent data transfer occurs around the time 9.5sec (circled region). This is the effect of division of burst transfer described in 3.2.4. Figure 11 shows the result that does not divide burst transfer. In this case, burst data transfer causes segment losses and leads to poor performance.

Figure 12 shows sequence number variations of two slow-start algorithm during 20 seconds of data transfer. The black dots shows smooth slow-start and the white dots shows normal slow-start. As seen in this figure, smooth slow-start sends 760 segments in 20 seconds, while normal slow-start sends only 450 segments. Over 60% improvement of transmit performance is maintained in this simulation.

Figure 13 shows variation of window size when node1 sends data to node4. The x-axis shows passage time and y-axis shows window size.

The solid line shows smooth slow-start and the dashed line shows normal slow-start. As seen in this figure, using smooth slow-start congestion does not occur until at the point window size of 75Kbyte, while in case of slow-start congestion occur at the point window size of 25Kbyte . Smooth slow-start makes 300% improvement of maximum window size in slow-start phase. This window size is closer to optimum window size of 128Kbyte than normal slow-start.

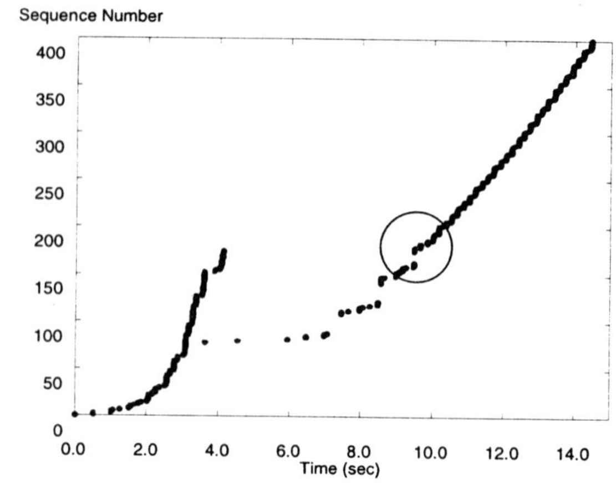

Figure 8. sequence number variation by smooth slow start in large bandwidth network

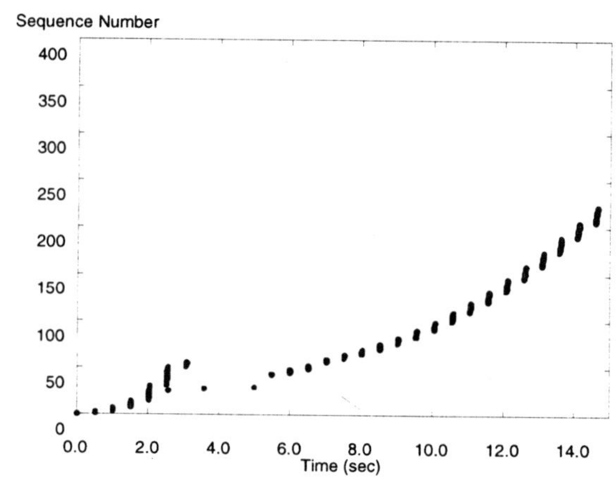

Figure 9. sequence number variation by normal slow start in large bandwidth network

3.3.2 Simulation in small bandwidth with long-delay network

Smooth slow-start algorithm is suitable for large bandwidth with long-delay networks. But it is difficult to estimate allowable bandwidth of communication path in large area networks. Thus, whether to apply smooth slow-start algorithm depends on only round trip time and smooth slow-start may be applied to small bandwidth with long-delay network. Therefore, analysis of smooth slow-start behavior in small bandwidth with long-delay network is required.

The network configuration used in this simulation is the same configuration described in figure 1. The bandwidth of bottleneck link is set to 64Kbps, queue

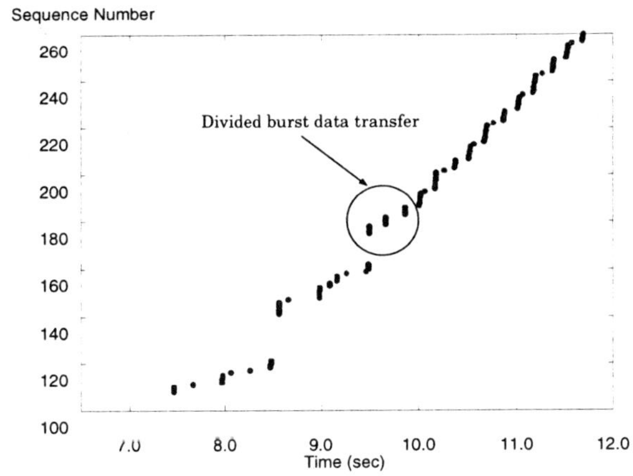

Figure 10. zoomed-in view of circled region in figure 8

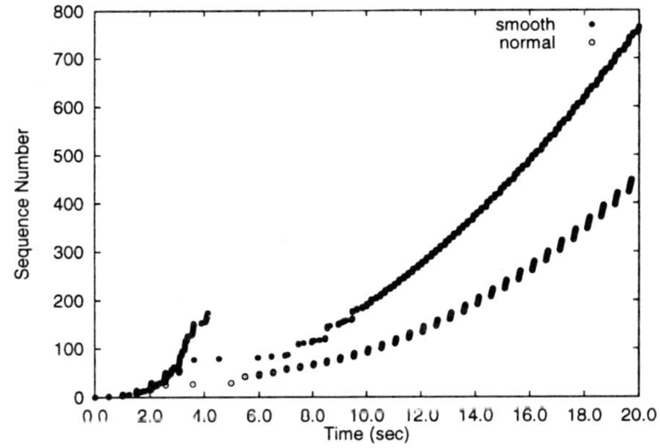

Figure 12. comparison of the variation of sequence number

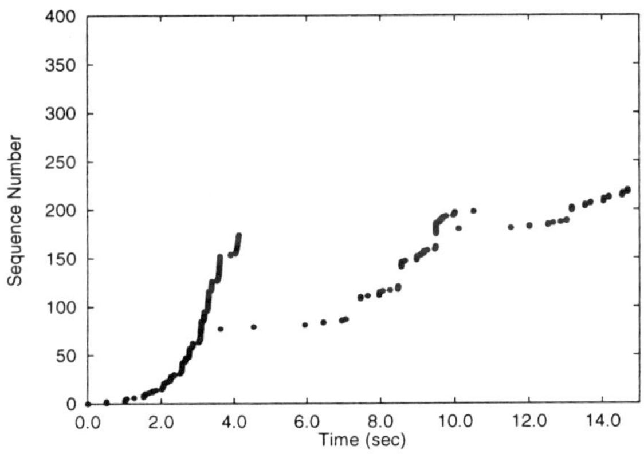

Figure 11. sequence number variation by smooth slow start without division of burst data transfer

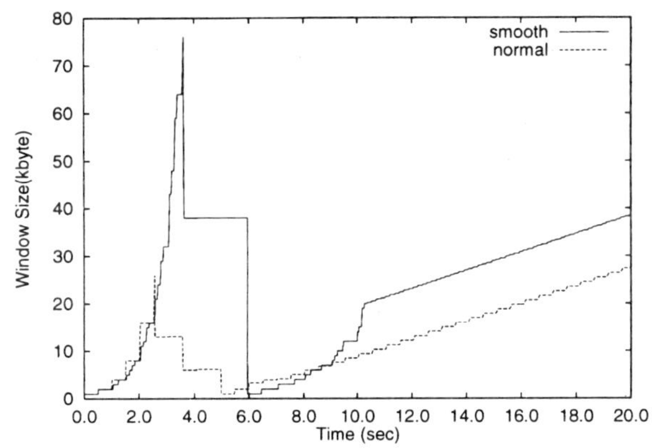

Figure 13. comparison of the variation of window size

size of router is set to 6 segment and propagation delay is set to 240msec. Figure 14 shows variation of window size. The solid line shows smooth slow-start and the dashed line shows normal slow-start. As seen in this figure, there is no significant difference between two algorithms. Figure 15 shows variation of sequence number by smooth slow-start and figure 16 shows variation of sequence number by normal slow-start. As seen in these figures, no significant difference between two algorithms can be showed.

In small bandwidth with long-delay networks, the window size that causes congestion is small, thus data transfer does not become bursty. In this case, smooth slow-start does not improve performance of data transfer but does not degrade either. Therefore, we can say that to apply smooth slow-start to small bandwidth with long-delay networks does not cause problems.

4. Conclusion

In this paper, we analyzed the performance degradation of slow-start in large bandwidth with long delay networks. We presented smooth slow-start algorithm to solve this degradation. Smooth slow-start only disperse burst segment transmission. It does not have any aggressive transmission strategy, and does not destroy essence of TCP. Tested in simulations, this technique reduces arrival time of optimum window size and over 60% improvement of transmit performance in large bandwidth networks.

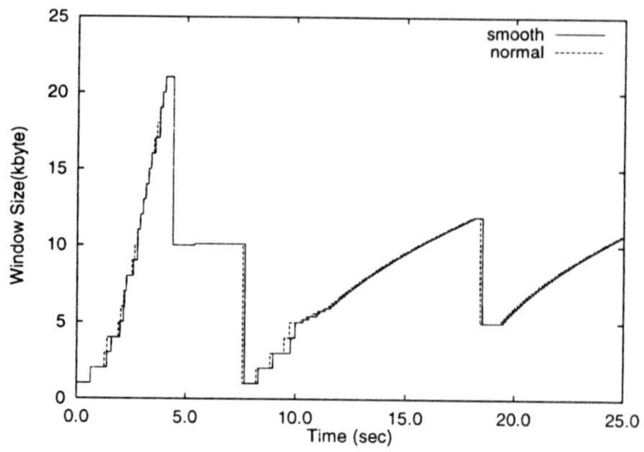

Figure 14. comparison of the variation of window size

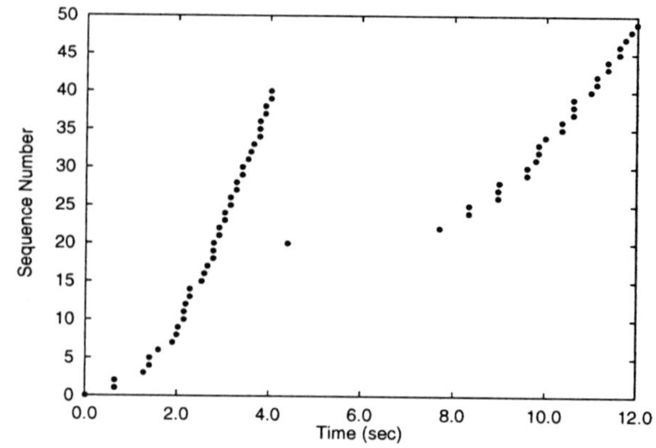

Figure 15. variation of sequence number by smooth slow-start in small-bandwidth network

Although smooth slow-start is suitable for large bandwidth and long-delay networks, smooth slow-start does not degrade transmit performance in small bandwidth networks.

The design of smooth slow-start is simple and is easy to implement this algorithm on existing operating systems. More analysis of algorithm and extensive experiment over simulation and real internet are being conducted.

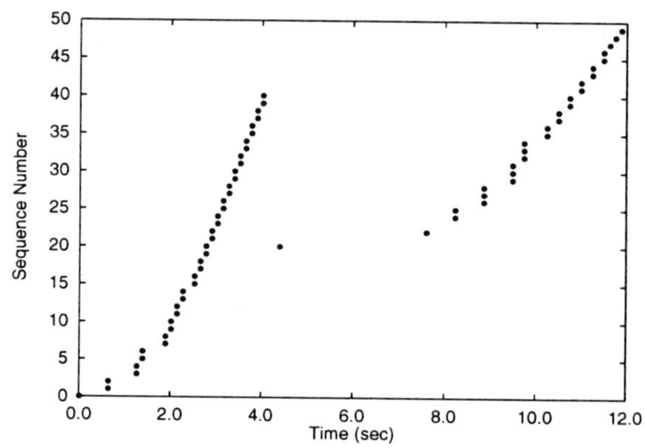

Figure 16. variation of sequence number by normal slow-start in small-bandwidth network

5. Acknowledgement

The author would like to thank Jun Murai for generous help with this work. The author also thanks Hiroyuki Kusumoto for his detailed and helpful comments and suggestions on this paper. Finally, the author would like to thank Kenjiro Cho and Osamu Nakamura and Susumu Sano and members of WIDE project for their helpful comments on early draft of this paper.

References

[1] Van Jacobson. Congestion Avoidance and Control *Proceedings of ACM SIGCOMM '88*, August 1988.

[2] W. Richard Stevens. TCP Slow Start, Congestion Avoidance, Fast Retransmit, and Fast Recovery Algorithms *RFC2001*, January 1997.

[3] W. Richard Stevens. TCP/IP Illustrated, Volume 1 The Protocols *Addision-Wesley Publishing Company*, 1995.

[4] Sally Floyd. Simulator Test. *Technical report*, July 1995.

[5] Van Jacobson. Berkeley TCP evolution from 4.3-tahoe to 4.3-reno *Proceedings of 18th IETF*, page 365 1990.

[6] L. Brakmo and L. Peterson. Performance Problems in BSD4.4 TCP *Computer Communication Review Vol 25*, pages 69-86, October 1995

[7] Sally Floyd. TCP and successive fast retransmits ftp://ftp.ee.lbl.gov/papers/fastretrans.ps, October 1994.

[8] Janey C. Hoe. Improving the Start-up Behavior of a Congestion Control Scheme for TCP *Proceedings of ACM SIGCOMM '96*, August 1996.

[9] M. Mathis, J. Mahdavi. Forward acknowledgment: Refining TCP congestion control *Proceeding of ACM SIGCOMM '96*, August 1994.

ABR Service in ATM Networks: Performance Comparison between Adaptive Stochastic and ERICA Flow Control Schemes with Guaranteed Minimum Cell Rate

Slobodan S. Petrovic (IEEE Student Member)
Department of Electrical Engineering J03, University of Sydney, Sydney, NSW 2006, Australia
Email: ssp@ee.usyd.edu.au Fax: +61.2. 9351.3847, Phone: +61.2.9351.2842

Abstract

Two explicit rate-based flow control schemes for congestion avoidance in ATM networks: Explicit Rate Indication for Congestion Avoidance (ERICA) and a proposed Adaptive Stochastic (AS), are compared under heavy load conditions. Neither of the schemes dictates a particular switch architecture. The requirements tested include: utilization, queuing delay, delay variance and queue size. A simple network topology involves an ATM switching node which is modeled as a single server queuing system fed by a number of highly bursty traffic sources. Neither packet discarding, nor packet retransmission mechanisms are included. The controllable sources' allowed cell rates (ACR) have been dynamically shaped by the explicit feedback messages from the switch.. The results of a simulation study are presented which suggest that AS scheme can provide for higher priority traffic considerably shorter queuing delay, delay variance and average queue size, particularly on shorter links, with slightly lower utilization.

1 Introduction

It is now widely assumed that the future ATM networks will be dominated by bursty traffic [7]. Regarding the traffic control policies for ATM networks, the preventive congestion control implemented by a conjunction of connection admission control (CAC) and usage parameter control (UPC) is not preferred. Unpredictable statistical fluctuations and burstiness of traffic sources make it difficult to guarantee quality of service and high utilization of the network resources using source traffic parameters declared by the users, such as average rate and burst duration. Gains due to statistical resource utilization come at risk of potential congestion when many applications compete for network resources. Proper congestion control must be in place to ensure that the network resources can be shared in a fair manner and that performance objectives can be maintained. Traffic management in ATM networks should be, therefore, accomplished in a reactive, rather than in a preventive manner. A number of congestion control schemes for ATM networks have been developed [1] - [10]. By experimenting with ERICA and a few other congestion control schemes it was noticed that queuing delay, queuing delay variance and queue sizes in the ATM switch output buffer are relatively high. Hence there is a need for a scheme able to remarkably improve quality of service (QoS) for the delay sensitive traffic by reducing its queuing delay and queuing delay variance. That was a motivation for doing this work.

The remainder of the paper is organized as follows: in Section 2 the assumed network structure and how it operates is described; in Section 3 the design of AS control scheme is presented in more details while ERICA scheme is only briefly outlined; in Section 4 the simulation model and obtained results are reported and in Section 5 conclusion remarks are made.

2 Assumed network structure

It is assumed that two types of traffic share the ATM network resources. The first type consists of Variable Bit Rate (VBR) traffic which is delay sensitive i.e. which has stringent delay requirements and is not subjected to any control and hence is uncontrollable. The second type of traffic requires good loss performance, but agrees to have its bit rate controlled when necessary, thus accepting the possibility of longer mean delays during periods of high demand, i.e. cell loss is avoided at the expense of delay and hence is controllable. All delay insensitive, or Best Effort, i.e. Available Bit Rate (ABR) traffic can join this category which is designed for normal data traffic such as file transfer and email. In

0-8186-8810-6/98 $10.00 © 1998 IEEE

these experiments delay sensitive traffic was given a higher priority. The ACRs of the ABR traffic sources take the values being conveyed by the feedback messages which are carried from the switch to the sources' terminals through backward Resource Management (RM) cells. Each source could also be a switch acting as a virtual source and generating RM cells periodically as if it was a source. The switch acts as a virtual destination and returns all RM cells received from the source as if the switch was the destination. In this study RM cells are "in-rate" since they are counted toward the ACR, what means that the total rate of data and RM cells should not exceed the ACR of the source. During idle periods a source does not generate RM cells. A RM cell is always sent as the first cell after an idle period for the source. In the compared schemes each individual lower priority (controllable) traffic virtual connection (VC) is guaranteed by the network only a minimum bandwidth of a minimum cell rate (MCR). However, it is allowed to dynamically share the available resources left over from the higher priority (uncontrollable) traffic i.e. the lower priority traffic grabs whatever remains of the network resources (bandwidth and buffer space) after the higher priority traffic is served. Thus the ABR capacity is not fixed, but varies according to the VBR load. Switch complexity does not depend on the number of VCs since there is no per VC queuing. In the switch, output buffering is used, which means that the queuing happens at the output port. The cells of both traffic classes are treated here, in the switch output buffer, by equal priority and are served with first-in-first-out (FIFO) discipline. The same service discipline applies also to all sources' queues. In order to support the feedback control schemes a simple CAC policy ensures that the peak cell rate of the total higher priority (VBR) traffic is within the ATM switch server capacity in every moment and that the long term mean rate of all the traffic (higher and lower priority together) is within the ATM switch server capacity. Both AS and ERICA schemes operate at the ATM switch output queuing point.

3 Description of the compared algorithms

3.1 Adaptive Stochastic (AS) Scheme

The traffic flowing from the sources to the ATM switch is assumed to be a process which takes place in random environment. The design of the control algorithm has been based upon input-output model of the process which allows analysis over the transfer function and realization of the control algorithm with minimal a priori knowledge about the dynamics and parameters of the process. The transfer function is defined as

$$y(k)u^{-1}(k) = B(z^{-1})A^{-1}(z^{-1})$$

where z^{-1} is delay operator meaning

$$z^{-1}y(k) = y(k-1), \qquad z^{-1}u(k) = u(k-1)$$

and integer k is the control interval's time index. Since the process is modeled here as the first order linear dynamical system,

$$A(z^{-1}) = 1 + a(k)z^{-1}, \qquad B(z^{-1}) = b(k)z^{-1},$$

it is described by the stochastic difference equation

$$y(k+1) = -a(k)y(k) + b(k)u(k).$$

y(k) is the output equal to instantaneous queue length minus the reference level (threshold). The scalar u(k) is the control input generated by the algorithm. It is a function of the queue size measurement and is used for identification of parameters and for attaining the desired system response. u(k) determines the ACRs of the ABR sources with the goal to maintain the ATM switch output buffer occupancy as close as possible to a certain reference level. u(k) is partitioned among active ABR sources accordingly. ABR sources seen by the switch as inactive are allocated MCR only. An active ABR source's ACR is then formed as the sum of the source's long term mean cell rate and its share of u(k). In proportion to its absolute value, a negative u(k) reduces and a positive u(k) increases the ABR sources' ACRs. Hence, the ACRs fluctuations are dictated by u(k) but can not go below the MCR (agreed during the connection setup) or above the link rate. The unknown parameters are a(k) and b(k). Their actual values are random and time varying. The uncertainty in b(k) corresponds to uncertainty in the system gain while the uncertainty in a(k) corresponds to uncertainty in the system time constant. Not knowing a(k) exactly is equivalent to not knowing the pole location of the system function. Since the system is operating in a stochastic environment, both y(k) and u(k) are random sequences. The objective of the problem is to find in each control interval the optimal control input that minimizes the scalar real-valued cost functional i.e. the performance criterion

$$J(u) = E\{qy^2(k+1) + ru^2(k) + qy^2(k)\} \qquad k = 0, 1, \ldots$$

where E denotes expected value. q and r are positive scalars (weighting factors). As the only information about the process comes from the observation of the queue size, since the queue size is the only directly measurable quantity at the switch, the optimal control policy can be interpreted as follows: at the end of the k-th control interval an optimal control input $u^o(k|k)$ (superscript o stands for optimal) is generated, based on the queue length measurement. k on the left side of | denotes the control input's time index and k on the right side of | means that the measurement of the queue length was taken during the control interval k. The next control input $u^o(k+1|k+1)$ is again computed, but based on the information about the queue size available at the control interval k + 1. Thus, the optimal deterministic control shall be recomputed after new information becomes available at each control interval. The switch gives only one feedback value in a single control interval which is equal to the round-trip delay because there is little point in sending further control feedbacks to the sources until previous feedback has had time to take effect. The overall adaptive controller can be viewed as combined of an identifier and a zero-memory controller in the feedback loop. The former is the learning device where the estimates of the parameters are generated in real time and can be designed independently of the controller objectives. The later computes the on-line optimal control for a deterministic system and is parameter adaptive. Accordingly, as this adaptive control problem involves nonlinear parameter estimation, the extended Kalman filter is used to generate the approximate conditional means and the associated error covariances of the unknown parameters. This approach led to the design of a simple proportional controller that has the desired adaptive properties. The closed loop feedback optimal control is given by

$$u^o(k|k) = -g(k)y(k) \qquad k = 0, 1, \ldots$$

The adaptive feedback gain g(k) depends not only on parameters a(k) and b(k) estimates ($a^{est}(k|k)$ and $b^{est}(k|k)$ resp.), but also on conditional error covariances

$$e_a(k|k) = a^{est}(k|k) - a(k) \quad \text{and} \quad e_b(k|k) = b^{est}(k|k) - b(k),$$

i.e. it is modulated by the current parameters uncertainty (vectors and matrices are denoted in bold letters, superscript T stands for 'transposed')

$$g(k) = -\{[R(k|k) + \mathbf{b}^T(k|k)\mathbf{Q}\mathbf{b}(k|k)]^{-1}\mathbf{b}^T(k|k)\mathbf{Q}\mathbf{\Phi}(k|k) + R^{-1}(k|k)\mathbf{d}^T(k+1|k)\}[1, 0, 0]^T$$

where $\mathbf{b}^T(k|k) = [b^{est}(k|k), S_{bb}(k|k), S_{ab}(k|k)]$,

$$\mathbf{d}^T(k+1|k) = [qS_{ab}(k|k), qa^{est}(k|k), 0],$$

$$\mathbf{\Phi}(k|k) = \mathbf{F}(k|k) - \mathbf{b}(k|k)R^{-1}(k|k)\mathbf{d}^T(k+1|k),$$

$$\mathbf{F}(k|k) = \begin{bmatrix} a^{est}(k|k) & 0 & 0 \\ S_{ab}(k|k) & a^{est}(k|k) & 0 \\ S_{aa}(k|k) & 0 & a^{est}(k|k) \end{bmatrix},$$

$$S_{aa}(k|k) = e_a^2(k|k), \qquad S_{bb}(k|k) = e_b^2(k|k),$$

$$S_{ab}(k|k) = S_{ba}(k|k) = e_a(k|k)e_b(k|k),$$

$$R(k|k) = r + qS_{bb}(k|k), \qquad \mathbf{Q} = \begin{bmatrix} q & 0 & 0 \\ 0 & 0 & 0 \\ 0 & 0 & 0 \end{bmatrix}.$$

The parameters estimates are generated via the equations

$$\mathbf{p}^{est}(i+1|i+1) = \mathbf{p}^{est}(i|i) + \mathbf{G}(i+1)[y(i+1) - \mathbf{c}^T(i)\mathbf{p}^{est}(i|i)],$$

$$\mathbf{p}^{est,T}(i|i) = [a^{est}(i|i), b^{est}(i|i)], \qquad \mathbf{c}^T(i) = [-y(i), u(i)].$$

The filter gain matrix $\mathbf{G}(i+1)$ satisfies the relation

$$\mathbf{G}(i+1) = \mathbf{S}(i|i)\mathbf{c}(i)[\mathbf{c}^T(i)\mathbf{S}(i|i)\mathbf{c}(i)]^{-1} \quad i = 0, 1, \ldots, k-1$$

$$\mathbf{S}(i+1|i+1) = [\mathbf{S}(i|i) - \mathbf{G}(i+1)\mathbf{c}^T(i)\mathbf{S}(i|i)] / ff,$$

$$\mathbf{S}(i|i) = \begin{bmatrix} S_{aa}(i|i) & S_{ab}(i|i) \\ S_{ba}(i|i) & S_{bb}(i|i) \end{bmatrix},$$

with the initial estimates given by

$$\mathbf{p}^{est,T}(0|0) = [a_0, b_0], \qquad \mathbf{S}(0|0) = \begin{bmatrix} S_{a0} & 0 \\ 0 & S_{b0} \end{bmatrix}.$$

The AS control algorithm expresses its dual nature by simultaneously performing two functions: perpetual parameters estimation i.e. "learning" and process control. The forgetting factor 'ff' allows the controller's capacity for adaptation on changes in the system parameters to be preserved, by preventing error covariance matrices to become approximately equal to zero. Estimating of parameters could continue only if the matrices are different from zero, i.e. if some level of parameters uncertainty remained. Owing to the forgetting factor, the identification of parameters even if they for some time remain constant, will never be completed. Fortunately, the exact identification of the unknown parameters is not necessary for good control. Through the parameters uncertainty the controller expresses its "cautiousness".

3.2 Explicit Rate Indication for Congestion Avoidance (ERICA) Scheme

This algorithm calculates two quantities: fair share and the connection's (VC's) share. The switch periodically monitors the load on each link and determines a load factor z, the available capacity and the number of currently active VCs. It computes a load factor

z = ABR Input Rate/ABR Capacity

ERICA measures the required quantities over an interval called the switch averaging interval and uses the measured quantities to calculate the feedback in the next averaging interval. The above steps are executed at the end of the switch averaging interval. Utilizing the load factor z, the VC share is calculated as

VCShare = CCR/z

where CCR is the current cell rate derived from the forward RM cell received, or measured independently by the switch. In order to achieve fairness, this algorithm allows connections to increase their rates to a fair share during underload. The fair share is calculated by the following formula:

FairShare = ABR Capacity/Number of Active Sources

The number of active sources is obtained by marking a bit in the VC table whenever a cell is seen on each VC. The bits are counted at the end of each averaging interval and cleared at the beginning of each interval. Upon reception of a backward RM cell, its Explicit Rate (ER) field which indicates the rate that the network can support at the particular instant in time, is marked down as follows:

ER = min{ER, max(FairShare, VCShare)}.

ERICA gives at most one feedback value per source during any averaging interval.

4 Simulation model and results

Both congestion control algorithms were tested and compared on the same network simulation model (Fig. 1), with the same MCR. Each source S generates cells that are queued in its buffer waiting there for transmission by the transmitter T. Each of the transmitters T independently removes cells from its source queue and transmits them to the receiver R. R is a point of congestion somewhere in the network, e.g. an output buffer on an ATM switch. There is a transmission delay between each transmitter transmitting a cell and the cell being received at the receiver. The transmission delay represents the combination of the propagation delay and the switching delay from the source to the point of congestion. For simplicity all the sources are equidistant to the ATM switch and hence the propagation delay is the same between the ATM switch and all the sources. AS scheme's control interval as well as ERICA scheme's averaging interval were equal to the round trip delay, i.e. the control rate was matched to the feedback rate. This illustrates a fundamental principle in control theory, which says that the system is unstable when the control is faster than feedback. But the system is unresponsive if the control is slower than feedback. The performance of the algorithms was examined over source - switch distances (link lengths): 1 km, 10 km, 100 km and 1000 km, with corresponding control/averaging intervals 10 μsec, 100 μsec, 1 msec and 10 msec resp. (1 km implies 5 μsec propagation delay). The schemes were not tested and compared on distances longer than 1000 km where the round trip delays can be very large and performances of the schemes consequently would deteriorate. This problem could be fixed by segmenting the feedback loop in smaller pieces and letting the switches act as "virtual source" and/or "virtual destination". Large buffers are assumed and the effect of cell losses is not modeled. The terminals are connected to the switch

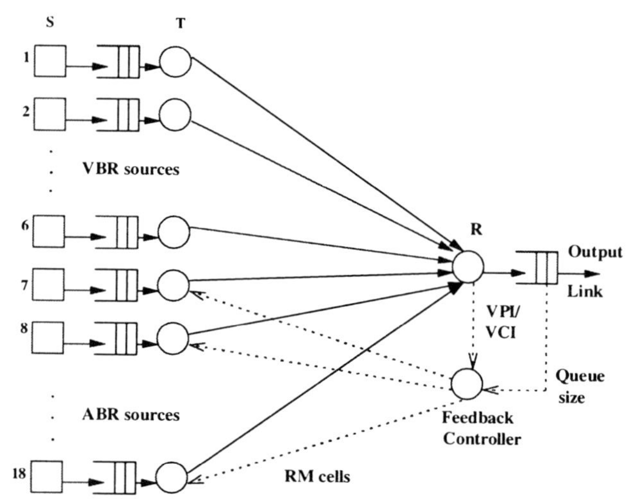

Figure 1: The simulation model

through links running at 155 Mbps (155 Mbps = 365566 cells/s). The switch receives traffic from terminals that are attached to its input ports. All input ports have traffic flowing to a common output port operating at 155 Mbps. The input to the ATM switch is a superposition of streams from 18 (12 ABR and 6 VBR) different ON/OFF sources, also referred to as Interrupted Bernoulli Process (IBP), which alternate active periods, transmitting at their peak cell rate (PCR) and idle periods, transmitting at zero bit rate. Both periods of burst and silence are exponentially distributed with constant average lengths during a simulation. Each burst in average contained 100 cells. The switch server rate was assumed to have a fixed ratio with respect to the long term mean arrival rate. As AS scheme has been primarily designed for ATM LANs where ideal value of the switch target utilization parameter was determined to be 0.95 [10], ABR traffic sources were given 60% and VBR traffic sources 35% bandwidth. In order to have more than a million cells generated, a simulation run time was 3 seconds. The higher priority (VBR) traffic was generated by the sources 1, 2, 3, 4, 5, 6 with PCR 50 Mbps, 40 Mbps, 30 Mbps, 20 Mbps, 10 Mbps, 5 Mbps resp., totally 155 Mbps , therefore equal to the switch server rate and with source utilizations 0.4, 0.5, 0.2, 0.2, 0.3, 0.25 resp.. The lower priority (ABR) traffic was generated by the sources 7, 8, ..., 18 with PCR 155 Mbps each, what means that each ABR traffic source was capable of filling the entire server capacity of the switch. The ABR traffic sources' utilization was 0.10 for sources 7 and 13, 0.08 for sources 8 and 14, 0.05 for sources 9 and 15, 0.04 for sources 10 and 16, 0.02 for sources 11 and 17, 0.01 for sources 12 and 18. The aggregate peak rate of the total traffic thus was 2015 Mbps. The purpose of the experiment was to examine how successfully the compared schemes can cope with such stressful conditions when arrival rate to the switch output buffer can exceed 13 times the server capacity, while preserving the design goals. The output buffer threshold value used in AS scheme experiments was 200 cells. A MCR value used was PCR/100 (1% link bandwidth) - in practice, it is desirable to allow some minimum capacity for processing aggregate ABR traffic when there is contention. As all ABR traffic sources had the same PCR = 155 Mbps, in AS scheme experiments each of the active ABR traffic sources received periodically the same amount of the feedback equal to u(k)/(number of currently active ABR traffic sources). In the case of different PCRs, the formula above could be easily adjusted. In AS scheme as well as in ERICA scheme experiments, inactive ABR traffic sources were allocated MCR only, for two reasons mainly: in order to drain out their queues rapidly and because of the transmission delay the sources which may seem as inactive, could be in fact, active. In examining AS scheme the forgetting factor equal to 0.96 was used; initial estimates were $S_{a0} = S_{b0} = 1$ and $a_0 = b_0 = 0.1$.

Performance evaluation of the schemes showed that ERICA scheme achieved the average utilization (Fig. 16) on 1 km link 0.33% higher, on 10 km link 0.03% higher, on 100 km link 0.26% higher and on 1000 km link 1.39% higher owing to higher ABR utilization (Fig. 15). As any MCR > 0 contradicts the initial stipulation that VBR traffic can take the entire server capacity whenever it needs it, the MCR employed in this experiment brought about conflicting demands by VBR and ABR traffic classes, as VBR traffic class, albeit able to fill the entire server capacity (if all VBR traffic sources are simultaneously transmitting), was guaranteed only 88% of it. Obviously, although the MCR was guaranteed to all 12 ABR traffic sources, due to their bursty nature they did not use it all the time and not all of them at the same time, what allowed the VBR traffic to have enough bandwidth to flow smoothly and unabatedly. The number of VBR traffic cells received, for both schemes (Fig. 14) was practically identical. However, the utilization metric gives only a partial picture of efficiency. Ideally, an efficient scheme should also control queuing delays within acceptable limits. The delay varies according to load, but there is always a non-zero queuing delay. ERICA scheme (Fig. 2 and Fig. 10) had the mean queuing delay and mean queue length in the switch output buffer on 1 km link 18.7 times longer, on 10 km link 8.5 times longer, on 100 km link 1.7 times longer and on 1000 km link 4.7 times longer. ERICA scheme (Fig. 3) had the queuing delay variance in the switch output buffer on 1 km link 878 times bigger, on 10 km link 491 times bigger, on 100 km link 2.3 times bigger and on 1000 km link 7 times bigger. ERICA scheme (Fig. 8) had the maximum queue length in the switch output buffer on 1 km link 24.8 times longer, on 10 km link 15.8 times longer, on 100 km link 1% longer and on 1000 km link 1.2 times longer. The corresponding results only for the buffers of sources 7 (Figures 4, 5, 11, 12) and 12 (Figures 6, 7, 9, 13) are presented because the former is one of the two with the highest and the later one of the two with the lowest source utilization. Due to limited space the results for remaining buffers are not presented. By comparing Fig. 2 with Fig. 4 and 6, then Fig. 3 with Fig. 5 and 7, then Fig. 8 with Fig. 9 and 12, then Fig. 10 with Fig. 11 and 13, could be seen how AS scheme compared to ERICA scheme reduced markedly mean delay, delay variance and queue size in the ATM switch output buffer, aggravating at the same time corresponding parameters in the sources' buffers. However, this trade-off, while improving remarkably QoS for delay sensitive VBR traffic, did not harm ABR traffic because it is delay insensitive. With the sort and configuration of traffic generators employed throughout these experiments the ABR service class whose capacity and demand thus varied dynamically, was always in a transient state. For such a case there is currently no known model for quantifying fairness. Hence the issue of fairness could not be addressed in this study and for the issues that were addressed, the simple network model (Fig. 1) was appropriate. As the system was in a state of high variation and had no steady state, the aim was to keep the average utilization high, the average queue size small and prevent queuing delays from becoming unbounded. Under such stressful conditions both schemes were found to be robust, not allowing essential metrics to degrade to unacceptable levels. While ERICA scheme gave highest priority for maximizing the average utilization, AS scheme traded-off a slight reduction in average utilization for considerable reductions in queue size, mean queuing delay and particularly queuing delay variance in the ATM switch output buffer, on all four link lengths. It should be pointed out that the above cited fundamental principle in control theory is not practically applicable on 1 km link, because 10 μs control interval means that RM cells' share in the total number of generated cells (data and RM cells together) is 27.4% whereby data cells utilization of the server and output link falls to about 70 %. Therefore, in order to prevent such huge number of RM cells being generated, a sort of trade-off should be made by replacing the 10 μs interval with a longer one, e.g. 50 μs or 100 μs (as it is on 10 km link) with RM cells' share in the total number of generated cells 5.4% and 2.7% resp.. The total numbers of ABR and VBR cells received as well as the server/output link utilization would be lower, but the numbers of ABR and VBR data cells much higher and data cells utilization of the server and output link could reach and even exceed 90%.

5 Summary

Basic ERICA and proposed AS flow control schemes for ABR service in ATM networks are compared in the presence of two traffic classes - ABR and VBR, under heavy load conditions exceeding 0.95. The discussion relates to the traffic management at the segment of an ATM network between terminals generating traffic and the access switch. By ensuring many times shorter queues in the ATM switch output buffer, AS scheme provided for delay sensitive VBR traffic class sharply reduced mean queuing delay and queuing delay variance particularly on LAN links (up to 100 km), with only slightly decreased utilization. In this way the goal of this experiment i.e. the QoS improvement for VBR traffic class was achieved. The "curse" of long distances, besides the control loop segmentation which is more expensive solution as it demands intermediate switching elements, could be overcome by transmitting ABR traffic cells immediately as they are generated and queuing them in input buffer(s) of the ATM switch, where they should be waiting for the advice what their ACR is. As a truly integrated transport network for all services is wanted, an unpredictable load pattern is inevitable - therefore designing accurate predictive techniques should not be favored as a feasible solution. Future work should be focused on the implementation of AS scheme whereby its implementation complexity compared to ERICA's could be tested.

References

[1] The ATM Forum Technical Committee: Traffic Management Specification Version 4.0, April 1996.

[2] K. Kawahara, Y. Oie, M Murata, H. Miyahara: Performance Analysis of Reactive Congestion Control for ATM Networks, IEEE JSAC, vol. 13, May 1995.

[3] C. Ikeda, H Suzuki: Adaptive Congestion Control Schemes for ATM LANs, IEEE INFOCOM, June 1994.

[4] G. Pecelli, B. Kim: Dynamic Behavior of Feedback Congestion Control Schemes, IEEE INFOCOM, vol. 1, 1995.

[5] A. Kolarov, G. Ramamurthy: End-to-End Adaptive Rate Based Congestion Control Scheme for ABR Service in Wide Area ATM Networks, IEEE ICC, June 1995.

[6] J. Ren, J. Mark: Design and Analysis of a Credit Based Controller for Congestion Control in BISDN/ ATM Networks, IEEE INFOCOM, vol 1, 1995.

[7] H.T. Kung, R. Morris: Credit-Based Flow Control for ATM Networks, IEEE Network, March/April 1995.

[8] A. Arulambalam, X. Chen, N. Ansari: Allocating Fair Rates for Available Bit Rate Service in ATM Networks, IEEE Communication Magazine, November 1996.

[9] D. Gaiti, N. Boukhatem: Cooperative Congestion Control Schemes in ATM Networks, IEEE Communications Magazine, November 1996.

[10] Kalyanaraman, R. Jain, S.Fahmy, R Goyal, B.Vandalore: The ERICA Switch Algorithm for ABR Traffic Management in ATM Networks, IEEE/ACM Transactions on Networking, November 1997.

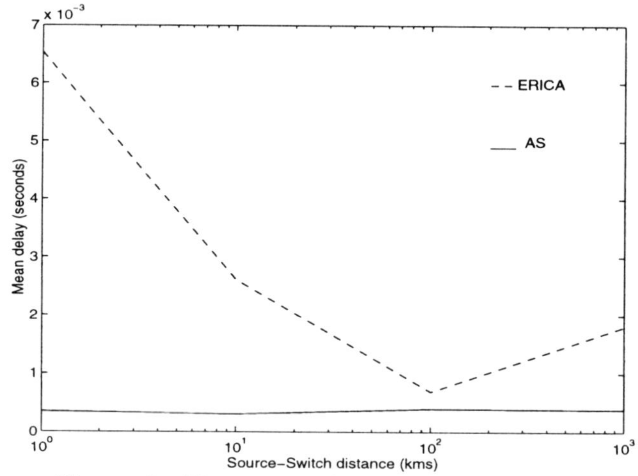

Figure 2: Mean queuing delay in the ATM switch output buffer

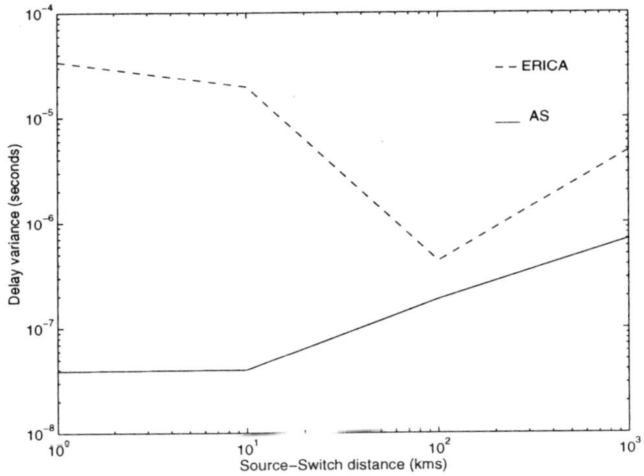

Figure 3: Queuing delay variance in the ATM switch output buffer

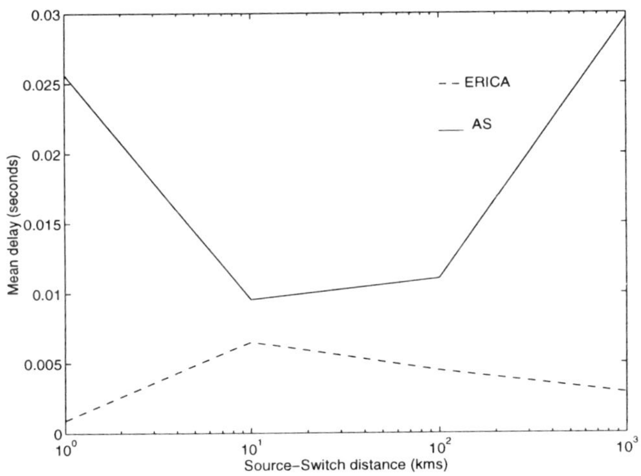

Figure 4: Mean queuing delay in the ABR traffic source 7 buffer

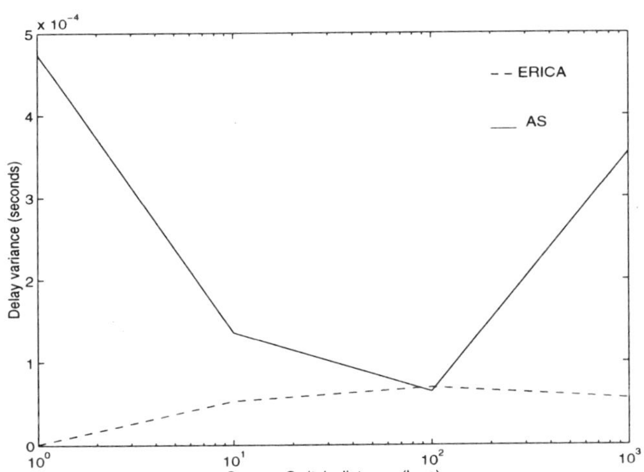

Figure 5: Queuing delay variance in the ABR traffic source 7 buffer

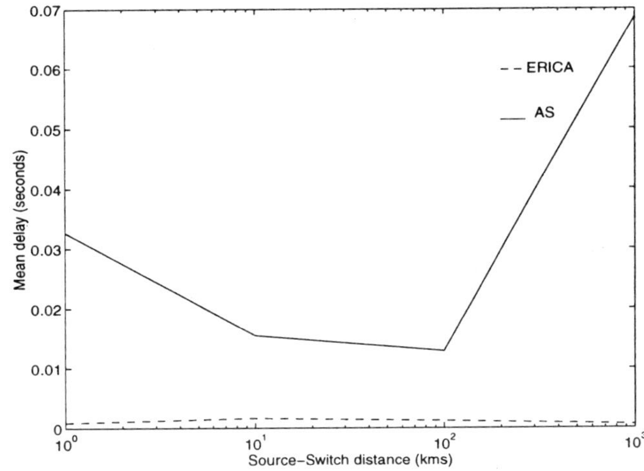

Figure 6: Mean queuing delay in the ABR traffic source 12 buffer

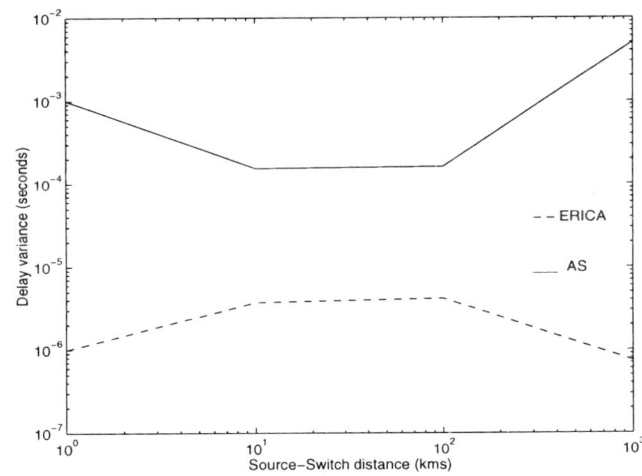

Figure 7: Queuing delay variance in the ABR traffic source 12 buffer

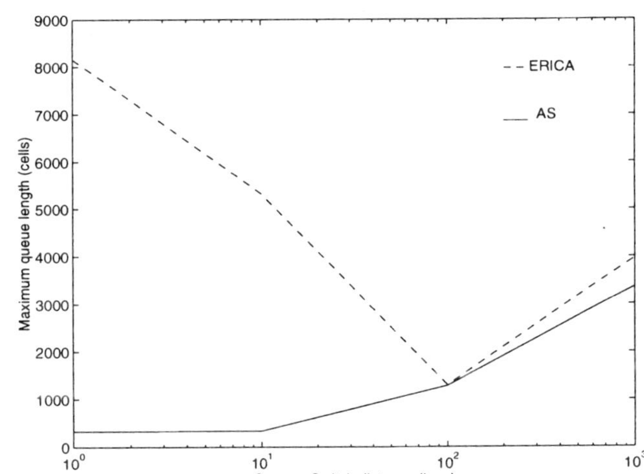

Figure 8: Maximum queue length in the ATM switch output buffer

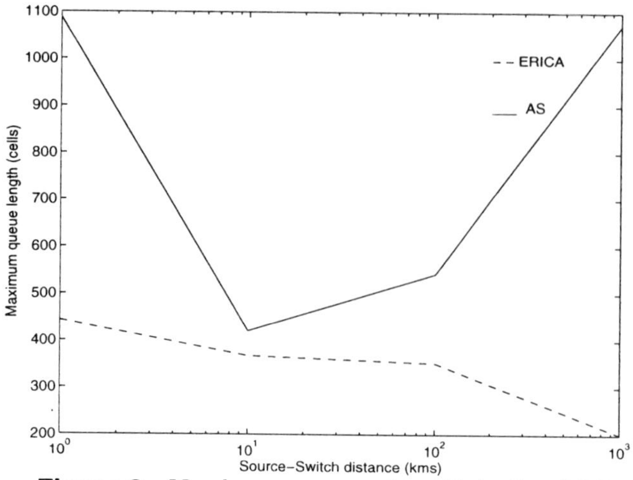

Figure 9: Maximum queue length in the ABR traffic source 12 buffer

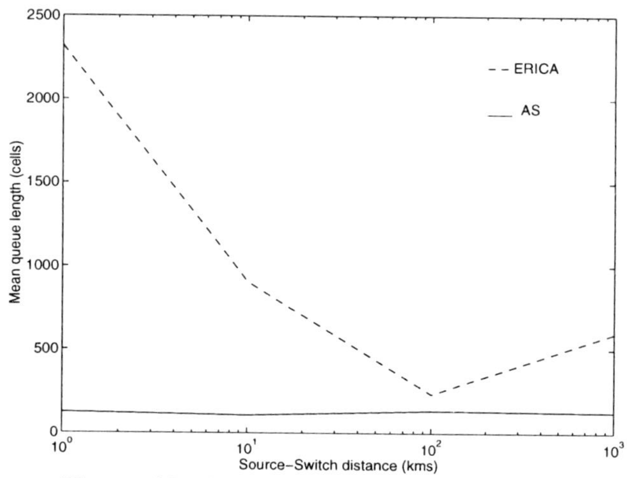

Figure 10: Mean queue length in the ATM switch output buffer

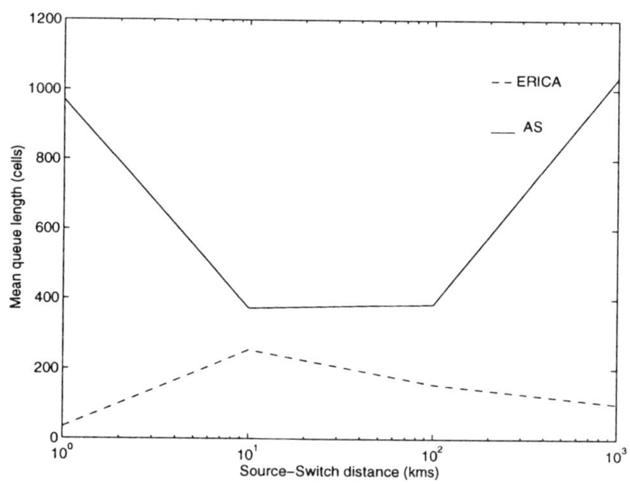

Figure 11: Mean queue length in the ABR traffic source 7 buffer

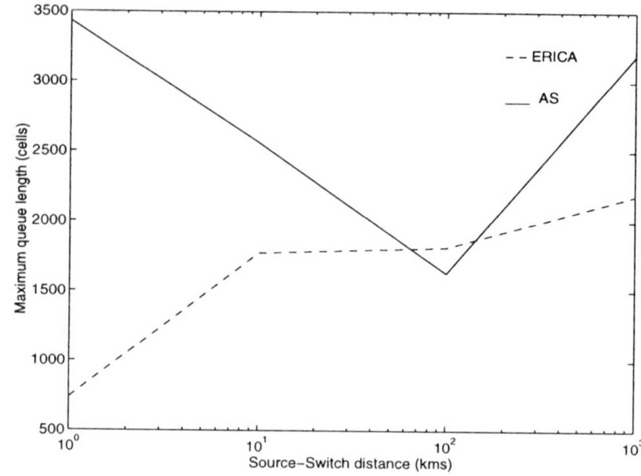

Figure 12: Maximum queue length in the ABR traffic source 7 buffer

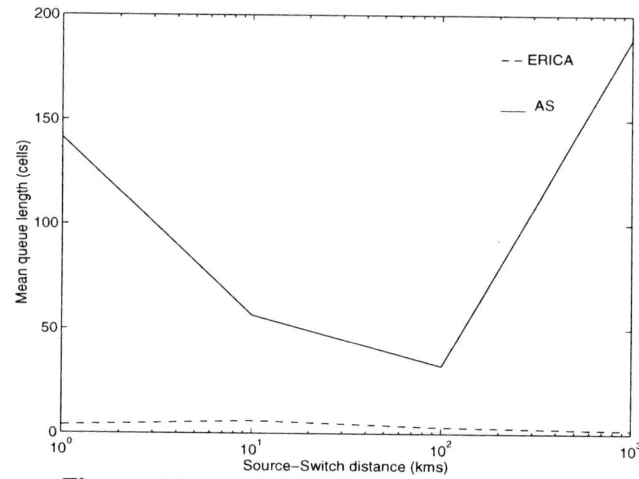

Figure 13: Mean queue length in the ABR traffic source 12 buffer

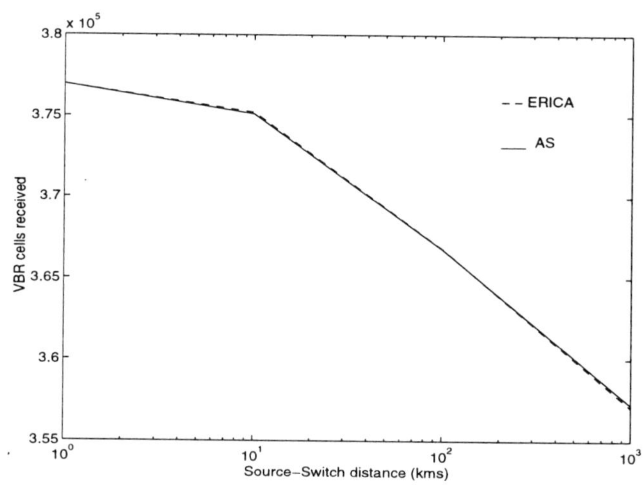

Figure 14: Number of VBR traffic cells received

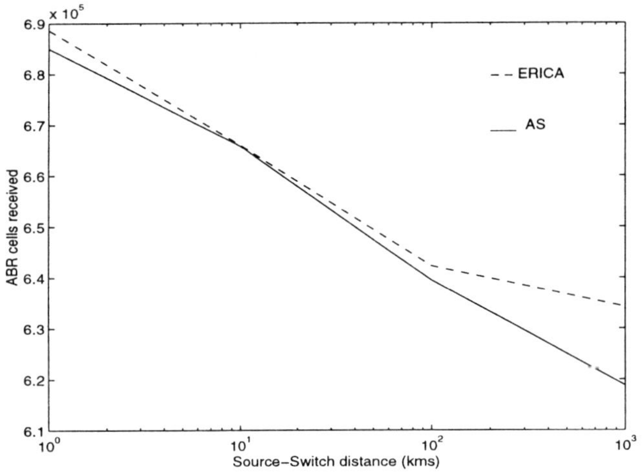

Figure 15: Number of ABR traffic cells received

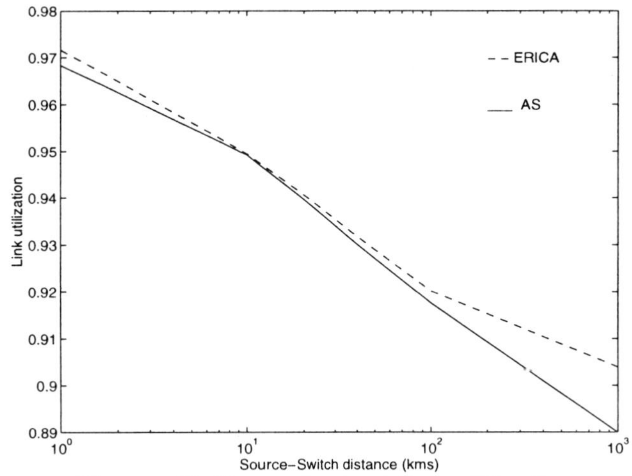

Figure 16: Server/output link utilization

Performance of TCP over ABR with Long-Range Dependent VBR Background Traffic over Terrestrial and Satellite ATM networks

Shivkumar Kalyanaraman*, Bobby Vandalore, Raj Jain, Rohit Goyal, Sonia Fahmy
The Ohio State University
Department of Computer and Information Science
Columbus, OH 43210-1277
E-mail: {shivkuma, vandalor, jain, goyal, fahmy}@cis.ohio-state.edu

Sastri Kota
Lockheed Martin Telecommunications,
1272 Borregas Avenue, Sunnyvale, CA 94088
Email: kota@lmsc.lockheed.com

Abstract

Compressed video is well known to be self-similar in nature. We model VBR carrying long-range dependent, multiplexed MPEG-2 video sources traffic. The actual traffic for the model is generated using fast-fourier transform of the fractional gaussian noise sequence. Our model of compressed video sources bears similarity to an MPEG-2 transport stream carrying video, i.e., it is long-range dependent and generates traffic in a piecewise constant bit rate manner. We study the effect of such VBR traffic on ABR carrying TCP traffic. The effect of such VBR traffic is that the ABR capacity is highly variant. We find that a switch algorithm like ERICA+ can tolerate this variance in ABR capacity while maintaining high throughput and low delay. We present simulation results for terrestrial and satellite configurations.

1. Introduction

Asynchronous transfer mode (ATM) is a connection-oriented, cell-switching, high-speed networking technology. It is widely used in the Internet backbone and campus backbones. ATM is the technology chosen for implementing the broadband integrated services digital network (B-ISDN). ATM supports different categories of services to meet different kind of traffic requirements. The available bit rate (ABR) service is used to transport data with minimum cell rate guarantees. ABR uses closed loop feedback to control the source rates. The source sends resource management (RM) cells periodically (every $Nrm - 1$ data cells) to collect network feedback information (Figure 1). The RM cell is turned around at the destination. The switches along the path indicate the rate which they can currently support in explicit rate field of the RM cell. When the source receives the (backward) RM cell, it adjusts its rate based on the feedback information.

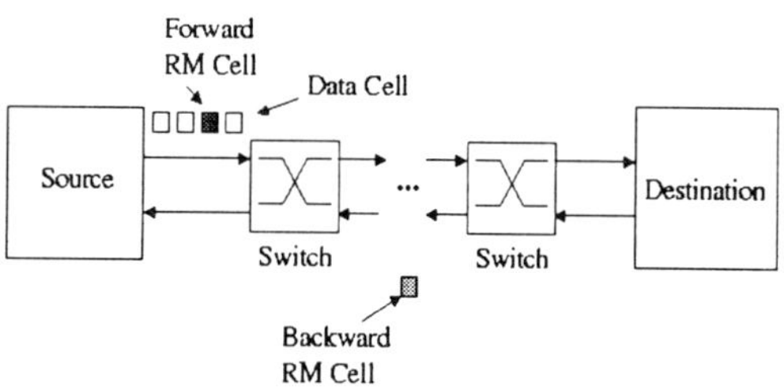

Figure 1. RM cell path

The ABR service has been extensively studied with different source traffic patterns like persistent sources, ON-OFF bursty sources, ping pong sources, TCP sources, long-range dependent (or self-similar) sources, and source-bottlenecked VCs. Many of these studies have also considered the performance in the presence of ON-OFF VBR background traffic [10].

In reality, VBR consists of multiplexed compressed audio and video application traffic, each shaped by leaky buckets at their respective sustained cell rate (SCR) and

*Shivkumar Kalyanaraman is now with Dept. of ECSE, Rensselaer Polytechnic Institute, Troy, NY 12180-3590

0-8186-8810-6/98 $10.00 © 1998 IEEE

peak cell rate (PCR) parameters. Compressed video has been shown to be long-range dependent by nature [5, 2]. Compressed audio and video streams belonging to a single program are expected to be carried over an ATM network using the MPEG-2 [1] transport stream facility as outlined in reference [7].

In this paper, we first present a model of multiplexed MPEG-2 transport streams carried over ATM using the VBR service. Each stream exhibits long-range dependence, i.e., correlation over large time scales. We then study the effect of this VBR background on ABR connections carrying TCP file transfer applications on WAN (wide area network) and satellite configurations.

2. Overview of MPEG-2 over ATM

In this section, we give a brief introduction to the MPEG-2 over ATM model and introduce some MPEG-2 terminology. For a detailed discussion, see reference [15].

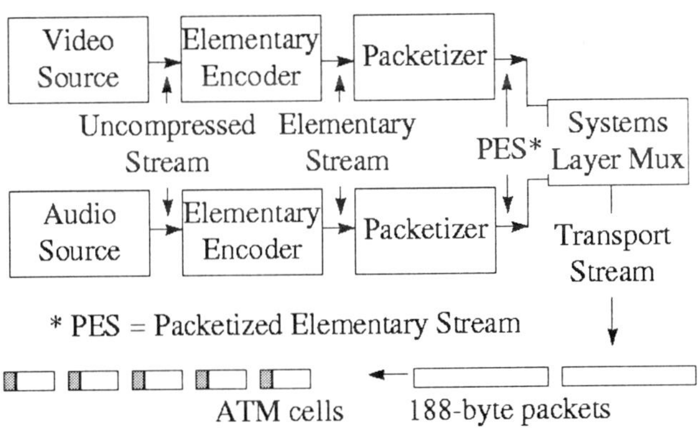

Figure 2. Overview of MPEG-2 Transport Streams

The MPEG-2 standard specifies two kinds of streams to carry coded video: the "Transport Stream" and the "Program Stream". The latter is used for compatibility with MPEG-1 (used for stored compressed video/audio), while the former is used to carry compressed video over networks which may not provide an end-to-end constant delay and jitter-free abstraction.

A Transport Stream can carry several programs multiplexed into one stream. Each program may consist of several "elementary streams," each containing MPEG-2 compressed video, audio, and other streams like close-captioned text, etc.

Figure 2 shows one such program stream formed by multiplexing a compressed video and a compressed audio elementary stream. Specifically, the figure shows the uncompressed video/audio stream going through the MPEG-2 elementary encoder to form the elementary stream. Typically, the uncompressed stream consists of frames generated at constant intervals (called "frame display times") of 33 ms (NTSC format) or 40 ms (PAL format). These frames (or "Group of Pictures" in MPEG-2 terminology) are called "Presentation Units." MPEG-2 compression produces three different types of frames: I, P and B frames, called "Access Units," as illustrated in Figure 3.

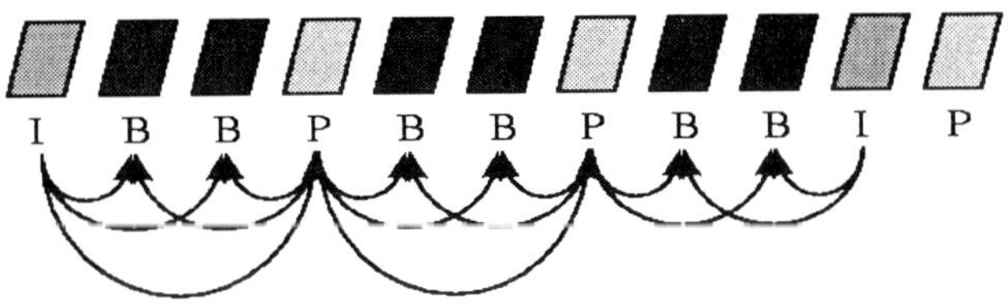

Figure 3. The I, P and B frames of MPEG-2

I (Intra-) frames are large. They contain the base picture, autonomously coded without need of a reference to another picture. They might take about 4-5 frame display times (approximately 160 ms) to be transmitted on the network depending upon the available rate [6].

P (Predictive-) frames are medium-sized. They are coded with respect to previous I or P frame. Transmission times for P frames is typically about 0.5-1 frame display times [6].

B (Bi-directionally predicted-) frames are very small. They are coded with respect to previous and later I or P frames and achieve maximum compression ratios (200:1). Transmission times for B frames is typically about 0.2 frame display times or even less [6].

As shown in Figure 2, the access units are packetized to form the "Packetized Elementary Stream (PES)". PES packets may be variable in length. The packetization process is implementation specific. PES packets may carry timestamps (called Presentation Timestamps (PTS) and Decoding Timestamps (DTS)) for long-term synchronization. The MPEG-2 standard specifies that PTS timestamps must appear at least once every 700 ms.

The next stage is the MPEG-2 Systems Layer which does the following four functions. First, it creates fixed size (188 byte) transport packets from PES packets. Second, the transport packets of different PESs belonging to one program are identified as such in the transport packet format. Third, it multiplexes several such programs to create a single Transport Stream. Fourth, it samples a system clock (running at 27 MHz) and encodes timestamps called "MPEG2 Program Clock References" (MPCRs, see [7]) in every multiplexed program. The time base for different programs may be different.

The MPCRs are used by the destination decoder to construct a Phase Locked Loop (PLL) and synchronize with the clock in the incoming stream. The MPEG-2 standard specifies that MPCRs must be generated at least once every 100 ms. Due to AAL5 (ATM adaptation layer) packetization considerations, vendors usually also fix a maximum rate of generation of MPCRs to 50 per second (i.e. no less than one MPCR per 20 ms).

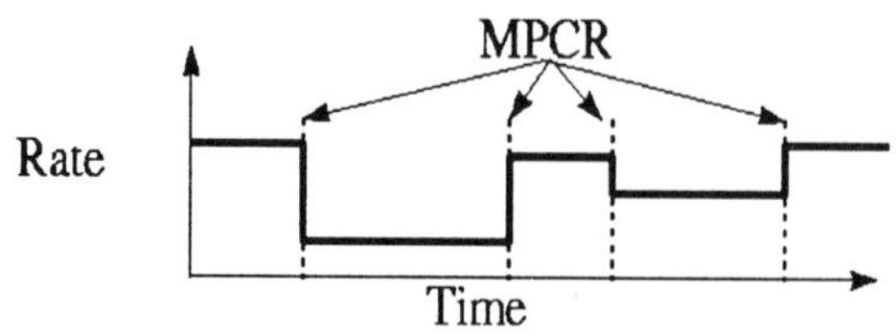

Figure 4. Piecewise constant nature of MPEG-2 Single Program Transport Streams

The key point is that the MPEG-2 rate is piecewise-CBR (the bandwidth requirement is constant in a piecewise manner). As shown in Figure 4, the program's rate (not the transport stream's rate) is constant between successive MPCRs. The maximum rate is bounded by a peak value (typically 15 Mbps for HDTV quality compressed video [15]). The choice of the rates between MPCRs is implementation specific, but in general depends upon the buffer occupancy, and the rate of generation of the elementary streams.

The transport stream packets are encapsulated in AAL5 PDU (protocol data unit) with two transport stream packets in a single AAL5 PDU (for efficiency). The encapsulation method does not look for MPCRs in a transport packet and might introduce some jitter in the process. Alternate methods and enhancements to the above method have been proposed [15, 9].

An ATM VBR connection can multiplex several transport streams, each containing several programs, which in turn can contain several elementary streams. We model the multiplexing of several transport streams over VBR. But in our model, we will have only one program per Transport Stream (called the "Single Program Transport Stream" or "SPTS").

MPEG-2 uses a constant end-to-end delay model. The decoder at the destination can use techniques which use a de-jittering buffer, or re-stamp the MPCRs to compensate for network jitter [15]. Phase locked loop at the destination locks onto the MPCR clock in the incoming stream. The piecewise-CBR requirement allows the recovered clock to be reliable. Engineering of ATM VBR VCs to provide best service for MPEG-2 transport streams and negotiation of rates (PCR, SCR) is currently an important open question.

3. VBR Video modeling

There have been several attempts to model compressed video, see references [2, 5, 3] and references therein. Beran et. al., [2] show that long-range dependence is an inherent characteristic of compressed VBR video. But, they do not consider MPEG-2 data. Garrett and Willinger [5] show that a combination of distributions is needed to model VBR video. Heyman and Lakshman [3] argue that simple markov chain models are sufficient for traffic engineering purposes even though the frame size distribution may exhibit long-range dependence. The video traffic on the network may be affected further by the multiplexing, renegotiation schemes, feedback schemes and the service category used. Examples of renegotiation, feedback schemes and best-effort video delivery are found in the literature, [8, 13, 4].

We believe that a general model of video traffic on the ATM network is yet to be discovered. In this paper, we are interested in the performance of ABR carrying TCP connections when affected by a long-range dependent, highly variable VBR background. We hence need a model for the video background. We have attempted to design the model to resemble the MPEG-2 Transport Stream.

There are three parameters in the model: the compressed video frame size, the inter-MPCR interval lengths, and the rates in these inter-MPCR intervals. In our model, the inter-MPCR intervals are uniformly distributed and the rates in the inter-MPCR intervals are long-range dependent. In real world, the rates are chosen depending upon the buffer occupancy at the encoder, which in turn depends upon the frame sizes of the latest set of frames generated. Further, the range of inter-MPCR intervals we generate follows implementation standards. We believe that this models the MPEG-2 Transport Stream, and still incorporates the long-range dependence property in the video streams. The effect of this VBR model on ABR is to introduce high variance in ABR capacity. As we shall see, the ERICA+ algorithm tolerates the variance in ABR capacity, and successfully bounds the maximum ABR queues, while maintaining high link utilizations.

4. Modeling MPEG-2 Transport Streams over VBR

We model a "video source" as consisting of a transport stream generator, also called encoder (E) and a network element. The encoder produces a Transport Stream as shown in Figure 2 and discussed in section 2. In our model, the Transport Stream consists of a single program stream. The network element encapsulates the transport packets into AAL5 PDUs and then fragments them into cells. The output of the network element goes to a leaky bucket which restricts the peak rate to 15 Mbps. This leaky bucket function can alternatively be done in the encoder, E (which does not send transport packets beyond a peak rate).

Several (N) such video sources are multiplexed to form the VBR traffic going into the network as shown in Figure 5. Each encoder generates MPCRs uniformly distributed between 20 ms and 100 ms. The reason for this choice (of

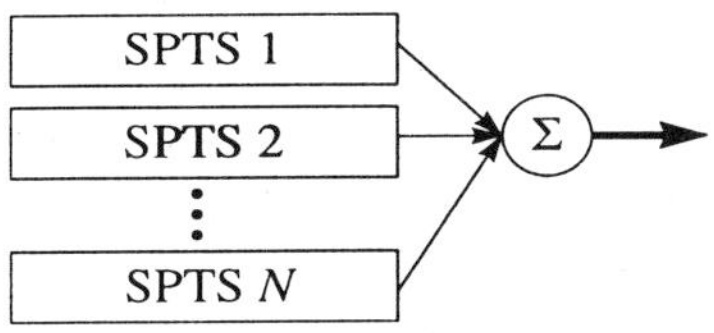

Figure 5. Multiplexing MPEG-2 Single Program Transport Streams (SPTSs) over VBR

maximum and minimum MPCRs) is explained in section 2. The rate of an encoder is piecewise-constant between successive pairs of MPCRs.

We generate the rates as follows: we choose the rate such that the sequence of rate values is long-range dependent. Specifically, we use a fast-fourier transform method [14] to generate the fractional gaussian noise (FGN) sequence (an independent sequence for each source). We ignore values above the maximum rate to 15 Mbps and below the minimum rate (0 Mbps). The reason for this choice is discussed in the following section. We choose different values of mean and standard deviation for the generation procedure. When we generate an inter-MPCR interval T_i and a corresponding rate R_i, the video source sends cells at a rate R_i uniformly spaced in the interval T_i. Due to the ignoring of some rate values, the actual mean of the generated stream may be slightly greater or lesser than the input means. We later measure the actual mean rate and use it to calculate the efficiency metric.

Though each video source sends piecewise-CBR cell streams, the aggregate VBR rate need not be piecewise-CBR. It has a mean (SCR) which is the sum of all the individual means. Similarly, it has a maximum rate (PCR) which is close to the sum of the peak rates (15 Mbps) of the individual video streams. These quantities depend upon the number of video sources. In our model, we use N equal to 9 to ensure that the PCR is about 80% of total capacity. VBR is given priority at any link, i.e, if there is a VBR cell, it is scheduled for output on the link before any waiting ABR cells are scheduled. Further, since each video stream is long-range dependent, the composite VBR stream is also long-range dependent. Therefore, the composite VBR stream and the ABR capacity has high variance.

4.1. Observations on the Long-Range Dependent Traffic Generation Technique

The long-range dependent generation technique described in [14] can result in negative values and values greater than the maximum possible rate value. This occurs especially when the variance of the distribution is high (of the order of the mean itself). Fortunately, there are a few approaches in avoiding negative values and bounding values within a maximum in such cases. We considered these approaches carefully before making a choice.

The first approach is to generate a long-range dependent sequence $x_1, x_2, ..., x_n$ and then use the sequence $e^{x_1}, e^{x_2}, ..., e^{x_n}$ in our simulation. The values e^{x_i} is rounded off to the nearest integer. This method always gives zero or positive numbers. The new distribution still exhibits long-range dependence, though it is no longer a fractional gaussian noise (FGN) (like the originally generated sequence) [14]. Another problem is that all significant negative values are truncated to zero leading to an impulse at zero in the new probability density function (pdf). Further, the mean of the new sequence is not the exponentiated value of the old mean. This makes it difficult to obtain a sequence having a desired mean.

A second technique is to avoid exponentiation, but simply truncate negative numbers to zero. This approach again has the problem of the pdf impulse at zero. Also the mean of the entire distribution has increased.

The third technique is a variation of the second, which truncates the negative numbers to zero, but subtracts a negative value from the subsequent positive value. This approach is aimed to keep the mean constant. But, it not only has the side-effect of inducing a pdf impulse at zero, but also changes the shape of the pdf, thus increasing the probability of small positive values.

The fourth and final technique is to simply ignore negative values and values greater than the maximum. This approach keeps the shape of the positive part of the pdf intact while not introducing a pdf impulse at zero. If the number of negative values is small, the mean and variance of the distribution would not have changed appreciably. Further, it can be shown that the new distribution is still long-range dependent.

We choose the fourth approach (of ignoring negative values and values greater than the maximum) in our simulations.

5 Overview of ERICA+

The ERICA+ switch scheme [11] operates at each output port of a switch. The switch periodically monitors the load on each link and determines a load factor, the available ABR capacity, and number of currently active sources or VCs. The measurement period is the "averaging interval". These measurements are used to calculate the feedback rate which is indicated in the backward RM cells. The measurements are done in the forward direction and feedback back is given in the backward direction. Only one feedback is calculated for every averaging interval. The algorithm tries to achieve 100% utilization with queuing delay equal to a target value using queue control. Dynamic queue control is done by varying the available ABR capacity dependent on queue size.

6 The "N Source + VBR" Configuration

The "N Source + VBR" configuration shown in Figure 6 has a single bottleneck link shared by the N ABR sources and a VBR VC carrying the multiplexed stream. Each ABR source is a large (infinite) file transfer application using TCP. All traffic is unidirectional. All links run at 149.76 Mbps (155.52 less the SONET overhead). The links traversed by the connections are symmetric i.e., each link on the path has the same length for all the VCs. In our simulations, N is 15 and the link lengths are 1000 km in WAN simulations. In satellite simulations, the feedback delay can be 550 ms (corresponds to a bottleneck after the satellite link) or 10 ms (corresponds to a bottleneck before the satellite link). This is illustrated in Figures 7 and 8.

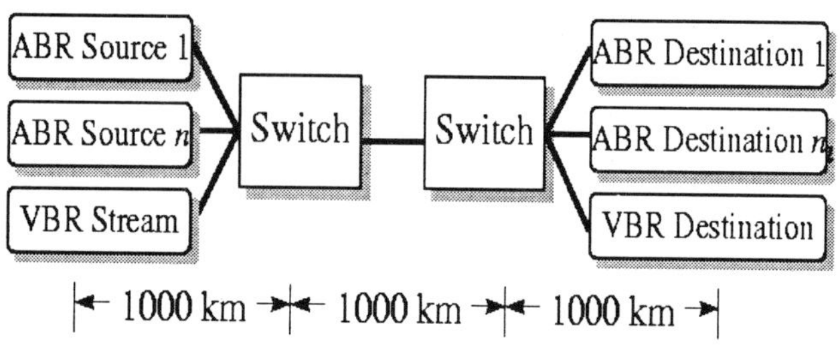

Figure 6. The "N Source + VBR" Configuration

The individual link lengths determine the round trip time (RTT) and the feedback delay. Feedback delay is the sum of the delay for feedback from the bottleneck switch to reach the source and the delay for the new load from the sources to reach the switch. It is at least twice the one-way propagation delay from the source to the bottleneck switch. The feedback delay determines how quickly the feedback is conveyed to the sources and how quickly the new load is sensed at the switch.

For the video sources, we choose means and standard deviations of video sources to have three sets of values, (7.5 Mbps, 7 Mbps), (10 Mbps, 5 Mbps) and (5 Mbps, 5 Mbps). This choice ensures that the variance in all cases is high, but the mean varies and hence the total VBR load varies. The number of video sources (N) is 9 which means that the maximum VBR load is 80% of 149.76 Mbps link capacity. As discussed later the effective mean and variance (after bounding the generated value to within 0 and 15 Mbps) may be slightly different and it affects the efficiency measure.

The Hurst parameter which determines the degree of long-range dependence for each video stream is chosen as 0.8 [2].

We also compare results with prior results using an ON-OFF VBR model [10]. In this model, the ON time and OFF time are defined in terms of a "duty cycle" and a "period". A pulse with a duty cycle of d and period of p has an ON time of $d \times p$ and OFF time of $(1\text{-}d) \times p$. When the duty cycle is 0.5, the ON time is equal to the OFF time. During the ON time, the VBR source operates at its maximum amplitude. The maximum amplitude of the VBR source is 124.41 Mbps (80% of link rate).

7. TCP and ERICA+ Parameters

We use a TCP maximum segment size (MSS) of 512 bytes. The window scaling option is used to obtain larger window sizes. For WAN simulations we used a window of 16×64 kB or 1024 kB which is greater than the product of the round trip time (RTT) and the bandwidth yielding a result of 454,875 bytes at 121.3 Mbps TCP payload rate (defined below) when the RTT is 30 ms. For satellite simulations, we used a window size of $256 \times 34000 = 8.704 \times 10^6$ bytes which is sufficient for an RTT of 550 ms at 121.3 Mbps TCP payload rate.

TCP data is encapsulated over ATM as follows. First, a set of headers and trailers are added to every TCP segment. We have 20 bytes of TCP header, 20 bytes of IP header, 8 bytes for the RFC1577 LLC/SNAP encapsulation, and 8 bytes of AAL5 information, a total of 56 bytes. Hence, every MSS of 512 bytes becomes 568 bytes of payload for transmission over ATM. This payload with padding requires 12 ATM cells of 48 data bytes each. The maximum throughput of TCP over raw ATM is (512 bytes/(12 cells $\times$ 53 bytes/cell)) = 80.5%. Further in ABR, we send FRM cells once every $Nrm - 1$ (31) cells. Hence, the maximum throughput is $31/32 \times 0.805 = 78\%$ of ABR capacity. For example, when the ABR capacity is 149.76 Mbps, the maximum TCP payload rate is 116.3 Mbps. Similarly, for a MSS of 9140 bytes, the maximum throughput is 87% of ABR capacity.

We use a metric called "efficiency" which is defined as the ratio of the TCP throughput achieved to the maximum throughput possible. As defined above the maximum throughput possible is $0.78 \times$(mean ABR capacity). The efficiency is calculated as follows. We first measure the aggregate mean VBR rate (since it is not the sum of the individual mean rates due to bounding the values to 0 and 15 Mbps). Subtract it from 149.76 Mbps to get the mean ABR capacity. Then multiply the ABR capacity by 0.78 (or 0.87) to get the maximum possible throughput. We then take the ratio of the measured TCP throughput and this calculated value to obtain the efficiency.

In our simulations, we have not used the "fast retransmit and recovery" algorithms. Since there is no loss, these algorithms are not exercised.

The ERICA+ parameters used in the simulations are as follows: the averaging intervals end either after the specified length or after a specified number of cells have been received, whichever happens first. In our simulations, these values default to 500 ABR input cells or 5 ms. The other parameters are used to define a function which scales the ABR capacity in order to achieve the desired goals. These include a target queuing delay (T0, set to 500 microseconds), two curve parameters (a = 1.15 and b = 1.05), and a factor which limits the amount of ABR capacity allocated to drain the queues (QDLF = 0.5).

8. Simulation Results

8.1. Effect of High Variance and Total VBR Load

In this section, we present simulation results where we vary the mean and the standard deviation of the individual video sources such that the total variance is always high, and the total maximum VBR load varies.

Table 1, and Table 2, show the maximum queue length, the total TCP throughput, and efficiency for three combinations of the mean and standard deviation. Table 1 is for TCP MSS = 512 bytes, while Table 2 is for TCP MSS = 9140 bytes.

Table 1. Effect of Variance and VBR Load (MSS = 512, 10 sec simulation)

	Video Sources		ABR Metrics		
#	Mean per-src rate Mbps	Std dev of rate	Max. switch Q len. in cells (× F/b del)	TCP thru-put Mbps	Eff. (% of Max thru put)
1.	5	5	6775 (1.8)	68.72	94.4%
2.	7.5	7	7078 (1.9)	59.62	94.1%
3.	10	5	5526 (1.5)	82.88	88.4%

By bounding the MPEG-2 SPTS source rate values between 0 and 15 Mbps, we ensure that the total VBR load is about 80% of the link capacity.

For row 1, measured VBR throughput was 56.44 Mbps (against 9 × 5 = 45 Mbps expected without bounding). For row 2, it was 68.51 Mbps (against 9 * 7.5 = 67.5 Mbps expected without bounding). For row 3, it was 82.28 Mbps (against 9 * 10 = 90 Mbps expected without bounding). Observe that when the input mean is higher, the expected aggregate value is lower and vice-versa.

The efficiency values (as defined in section 7) are calculated using these values of total VBR capacity. For example, in row 1 of Table 1, the ABR throughput is is 149.76 - 56.44 = 93.32 Mbps. For a MSS of 512, the maximum TCP throughput is 78% of ABR throughput = 72.78 Mbps (not shown in the table). Given that TCP throughput achieved is 68.72 Mbps (column 5), the efficiency is 68.72/72.78 = 94.4%. For Table 2, since the MSS is 9140 bytes, the maximum TCP throughput is 87% of ABR throughput as discussed in section 7, and this is the value used to compare the total TCP throughput against.

Table 2. Effect of Variance and VBR Load (MSS = 9140, 10 sec simulation)

	Video Sources		ABR Metrics		
#	Mean per-src rate Mbps	Std dev of rate	Max switch QLen in cells (× F/b del)	TCP thru-put Mbps	Eff. (% of Max thru put)
1.	5	5	5572 (1.5)	77.62	95.6%
2.	7.5	7	5512 (1.5)	67.14	95.0%
3.	10	5	5545 (1.5)	56.15	95.6%

Observe that the efficiency achieved in all cases is high (above 90%) in spite of the high variance in ABR capacity. Also observe that the total TCP throughput is higher (as well as the efficiency) for TCP MSS = 9140 bytes in all cases.

The maximum queue length is controlled to about three times the feedback delay (or one round trip time) worth of queue. The feedback delay for this configuration is 10 ms, which corresponds to (10 ms) × (367 cells/ms) = 3670 cells worth of queue when the network is on the average overloaded by a factor of 2 (as is the case with TCP). The round-trip time for this configuration is 30 ms.

The queue length is higher when the mean per-source rate is lower (i.e., when the average ABR rate is higher). This is explained as follows. Whenever there is variance in capacity, the switch algorithm may make errors in estimating the average capacity and may over-allocate rates temporarily. When the average ABR capacity is higher, each error in allocating rates will result in a larger backlog of cells to be cleared than for the corresponding case when the average ABR capacity is low. The combination of these backlogs may result in a larger maximum queue before the long-term queue reduction mechanism of the switch algorithm reduces the queues.

8.2. Comparison with ON-OFF VBR Results

In our earlier paper [10] and references therein, we had studied the behavior of TCP over ABR in the presence of ON-OFF VBR sources. We had studied ranges of ON-OFF periods from 1 ms through 100 ms. Further, we had looked at results where the ON period was not equal to the OFF period. The worst cases were seen in the latter simulations. However, with modifications to ERICA+ and a larger averaging interval we found that the maximum switch queue length was 5637 cells. This experiment has a duty cycle of 0.7 and a period of 20ms i.e., the ON time was 14 ms and the off time was 6 ms. Since we use the same switch algorithm parameters in this study, we can perform a comparison of the two studies.

We observe that, even in the presence of the long-range dependent VBR background traffic, the ABR switch queues do not increase substantially (beyond one round trip worth of queues) and the efficiency remains high (around 90%). This is because the ERICA+ switch algorithm has been refined and tuned to handle variance in the ABR capacity and ABR demand. These refinements allow the convergence of the ABR queues, without compromising on the efficiency.

8.3. Satellite simulations with Short Feedback Delay

In this section and the next, we repeat the experiments with some links being satellite links. In the first set of simulations, we replace the bottleneck link shared by 15 sources with a satellite link as shown in Figure 7. The links from the second switch to the destination nodes are 1 km each. The total round trip time is 550 ms, but the feedback delay remains 10 ms.

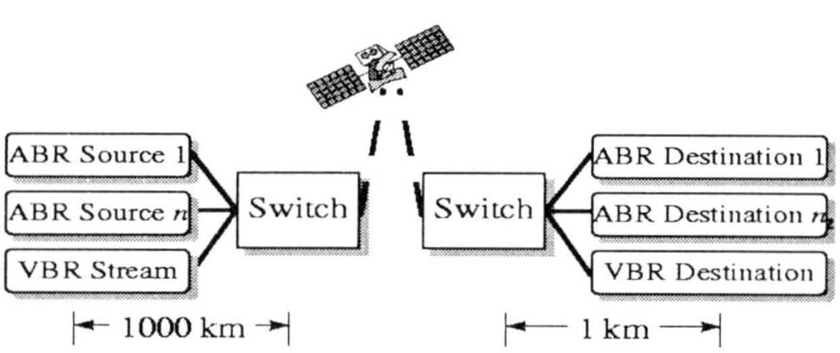

Figure 7. The "N Source + VBR" Configuration with a satellite link

Table 3 and Table 4 (similar to Tables 1 and 2) show the maximum switch queue length, the total TCP throughput, and efficiency for three combinations of the mean and standard deviation. Table 3 is for TCP MSS = 512 bytes, while Table 4 is for TCP MSS = 9140 bytes.

Note that the TCP startup time in this configuration is large because the round trip time (550 ms) is large and TCP requires multiple round trips to be able to use its full capacity. However, the effect on total TCP throughput is minimal since there is no loss and the feedback delays are small (10 ms) compared to round trip time, allowing ABR to control sources more effectively. Throughputs are high, and efficiency values are high.

Table 3. Max Queues for Satellite Networks with Short Feedback Delay (MSS=512, 170 sec)

	Video Sources		ABR Metrics		
#	Mean per-src rate Mbps	Std dev of rate	Max switch QLen in cells (× F/b del)	TCP thru-put Mbps	Eff. (% of Max thru put)
1.	5	5	5545 (1.5)	68.09	92.9%
2.	7.5	7	4416 (1.2)	59.16	82.5%
3.	10	5	4064 (1.1)	47.39	86.7%

Table 4. Max. Queues for Satellite Networks with Short Feedback Delay (MSS=9140, 170 sec)

	Video Sources		ABR Metrics		
#	Mean per-src rate Mbps	Std dev of rate	Max switch QLen in cells (× F/b del)	TCP thru-put Mbps	Eff. (% of Max thru put)
1.	5	5	5759 (1.6)	72.18	88.3%
2.	7.5	7	11366 (3.1)	67.23	84.1%
3.	10	5	13105 (3.6)	57.69	94.6%

The tables shows that maximum queues are small (in the order of three times the feedback delay), irrespective of the mean and variance. In such satellite configurations, we observe that the feedback delay is the dominant factor (over round trip time) in determining the maximum queue length. As discussed earlier, one feedback delay of 10 ms corresponds to 3670 cells of queue for TCP.

8.4. Satellite simulations with Long Feedback Delay

In our second set of satellite simulations, we examine the effect of longer feedback delays. Consider a switch A at the end of a satellite link or a switch downstream of A. It will have a feedback delay of about 550 ms. We use a new configuration as shown in Figure 8 by replacing the links in the feedback path to sources with satellite link. All other links are of length 1 km each. As a result, the round trip time and the feedback delay are both approximately equal to 550 ms.

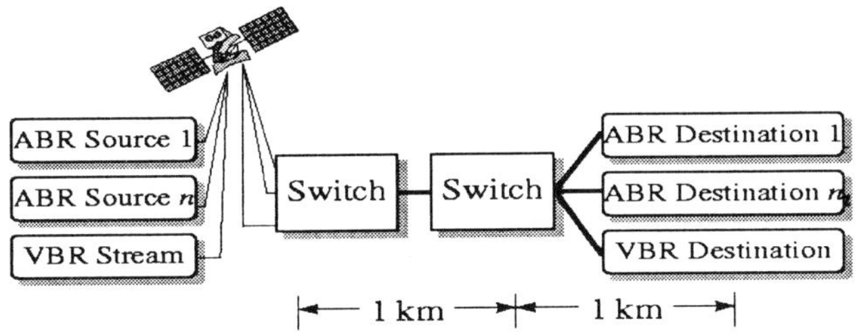

Figure 8. The "N Source + VBR" Configuration with satellite links and long feedback delays

Tables 5 and 6 (similar to Tables 1 and 2) show the maximum switch queue length, the total TCP throughput, and efficiency for three combinations of the mean and standard deviation. Table 5 is for TCP MSS = 512 bytes, while Table 6 is for TCP MSS = 9140 bytes.

Table 5. Max Queues for Satellite Networks with Long Feedback Delay (MSS=512, 170 sec)

	Video Sources		ABR Metrics		
#	Mean per-src rate Mbps	Std dev of rate	Max switch QLen in cells (× F/b del)	TCP thru-put Mbps	Eff. (% of Max thru put)
1.	5	5	299680 (1.5)	58.25	79.60%
2.	7.5	7	186931 (0.9)	49.50	80.53%
3.	10	5	156232 (0.8)	44.16	80.93%

Observe that the queue lengths are quite large, while the total TCP throughput and efficiency are smaller (by 6-13%) compared to the values in Tables 1 and 2 (1000 km feedback delay cases) respectively. The total queue is still a small multiple of the feedback delay or RTT (a feedback delay of 550 ms corresponds to 201850 cells). This indicates that satellite switches need to provide at least that much buffering to avoid loss on these high delay paths. A point to consider is that, these large queues should not be seen in downstream work-group or WAN switches, because they will not provide so much buffering. Satellite switches can isolate downstream switches from such large queues by implementing the VSVD option as described in our previous contribution [12].

9. Conclusions

Compressed video sources exhibit long-range dependence in the traffic patterns they generate. In this paper, we

Table 6. Max Queues for Satellite Networks with Long Feedback Delay (MSS=9140, 170 sec)

	Video Sources		ABR Metrics		
#	Mean per-src rate Mbps	Std dev of rate	Max switch QLen in cells (× F/b del)	TCP thru-put Mbps	Eff. (% of Max thru put)
1.	5	5	215786 (1.1)	65.96	80.81%
2.	7.5	7	233423 (1.2)	58.76	85.71%
3.	10	5	144362 (0.7)	49.67	81.61%

briefly survey VBR video modeling techniques, the MPEG-2 over ATM approach, and propose a model for MPEG-2 video over VBR which incorporates the long-range dependence property in compressed video. Long-range dependent traffic can be generated by combining the fractional gaussian noise sequences generated using fast fourier transforms. This traffic is used to model multiplexed MPEG-2 video sources. The generated long-range dependent traffic is transported over VBR service. The effect of this long-range dependent (background) traffic over VBR is to introduce high variance in the ABR capacity. However, a responsive switch scheme like ERICA+ is sufficient to handle this variance in ABR capacity. This results in controlled ABR queues and high utilization. The maximum ABR queue length is a function of the feedback delay and round trip time. This implies that switches terminating satellite links should provide buffers proportional to the length of the satellite link in order to deliver high performance. Further, if they implement the VSVD option, they can isolate downstream work-group switches from the effects of the long delay satellite path.

Acknowledgments

This research was sponsored in part by NSF Grant/Contract #NCR-9628438.

References

[1] I. 13818-2. Generic coding of moving pictures and assoicated audio information, 1994.

[2] J. Beran, R. Sherman, M. Taqqu, and W. Willinger. Long-range dependence in variable-bit-rate video traffic. *IEEE Transactions on Communications*, 43(2/3/4), Feb/March/April 1995.

[3] D.P.Heyman and T. Lakshman. What are the implications of long-range dependence for VBR-video traffic engineering ? *IEEE Transactions on Networking*, 4(3), June 1996.

[4] H. Eriksson. Mbone: the multicast backbone. *Communications of the ACM*, 37(8):54–60, August 1994.

[5] M. W. Garrett and W. Willinger. Analysis, modeling, and generation of self-similar VBR video traffic. In *Proc. of ACM SIGCOMM*, pages 269–280, Sept 1994.

[6] M. S. Goldman. private communication.

[7] M. S. Goldman. Variable bit rate MPEG-2 over ATM: Definitions and recommendations, October 1996.

[8] M. Grossglauser, S. Keshav, , and D. Tse. RCBR: a simple and efficient service for multiple time-scale traffic. In *Proc. of ACM SIGCOMM*, August 1995.

[9] S. Hrastar, H. Uzunalioglu, and W. Yen. Synchronization and de-jitter of MPEG-2 transport streams encapsulated in AAL5/ATM.

[10] S. Kalyanaraman, R. Jain, S. Fahmy, R. Goyal, J. Jiang, and S. Kim. Performance of TCP over ABR on ATM backbone and with various VBR traffic patterns. In *Proc. of IEEE ICC*, June 1997.

[11] S. Kalyanaraman, R. Jain, R. Goyal, S. Fahmy, and B. Vandalore. The ERICA switch algorithm for ABR traffic management in ATM networks. *Submitted to* IEEE/ACM Transactions on Networking, November 1997.

[12] S. Kalyanaraman, R. Jain, J. Jiang, R. Goyal, S. Fahmy, and P. Samudra. Design considerations for the virtual source/virtual destination (VS/VD) feature in the ABR service of ATM networks. *Computer Networks and ISDN Systems (to appear)*, 1998.

[13] T. Lakshman, P. Mishra, , and K. Ramakrishnan. Transporting compressed video over ATM networks with explicit rate feedback control. In *Proc. of IEEE INFOCOM*, 1997.

[14] V. Paxson. Fast approximation of self-similar network traffic, April 1995.

[15] C. Tryfonas. MPEG-2 transport over ATM networks. Master's thesis, UC Santa Cruz, Sept 1996.

Paper Session 2
Track A: Routing

Session Chair: Alden Jackson
BBN Technologies

Distributed Quality-of-Service Routing in High-Speed Networks Based on Selective Probing *

Shigang Chen, Klara Nahrstedt
Department of Computer Science
University of Illinois at Urbana-Champaign
Urbana, IL 61801
{s-chen5, klara} @cs.uiuc.edu

Abstract

We propose an integrated QoS routing framework based on selective probing for high-speed packet-switching networks. The framework is fully distributed and depends only on the local state maintained at every individual node. By using controlled diffusion computations, the framework captures the common messaging and computational structure of distributed QoS routing, and allows an efficient implementation due to its simplicity. Different distributed routing algorithms (DRAs) can be quickly developed by specifying only a few well-defined constraint-dependent parameters within the framework. Our simulation shows that the overhead of the proposed algorithms is stable and modest.

1 Introduction

Distributed multimedia applications have quality-of-service (QoS) requirements specified in terms of constraints on various metrics such as bandwidth, delay, delay jitter, cost, etc. The task of QoS routing is to find a path from the source node to the destination node which has sufficient resources to support the required end-to-end QoS.

The recent work in QoS routing has been following two main directions: *source routing* and *distributed routing*. In the source routing, each node maintains an image of the *global network state*, based on which a routing path is centrally computed at the source. The global network state is typically updated periodically by a link-state algorithm. In the distributed routing, the path is computed by a distributed computation during which control messages are exchanged among the nodes and the state information kept at each node is collectively used in order to find a path.

The source routing scheme [4, 6, 8] has several problems. First, the global network state has to be updated frequently enough to cope with the dynamics of network parameters such as bandwidth and delay, which makes the communication overhead excessively high for large scale networks. Second, the link-state algorithm commonly used in the source routing can only provide *approximate* global state due to the overhead concern and non-negligible propagation delay of state messages. The inaccuracy in the global state may cause the QoS routing fail. Third, the link-state algorithm has the scalability problem [1]. It is impractical for any single node to have access to detailed state information about all nodes and all links in large networks. The hierarchical routing is used as a solution [5]. However, the state aggregation increases the level of inaccuracy [6]. Fourth, the computation overhead at the source is excessively high, especially when multiple constraints are involved, considering that the QoS routing is typically done on a per-connection basis.

In the distributed routing, the path-selection computation is distributed among the intermediate nodes between the source and the destination. Hence, the routing response time can be made shorter and the algorithm is more scalable. However, most existing distributed routing algorithms [9, 11] still require each node to maintain a global network state, based on which the routing decision is made on a hop-by-hop basis. The routing performance heavily depends on the accuracy of the global state. Therefore, these algorithms more or less share the same problem of the source routing.

Multimedia applications tend to have diverse QoS requirements on bandwidth, delay, delay jitter, cost, path length, etc. From a network designer's point of view, it would be beneficial to accommodate different QoS routing algorithms in a single integrated framework, which captures the common messaging and computational structure. The framework should be *simple*, which enables an efficient implementation, and *extensible*, so that new QoS metrics can be easily added without affecting the existing ones. It should also support both unicast and multicast. Besides, a distributed framework whose correctness depends only on local states is preferred. To the best of our knowledge, all existing algorithms are tailored towards specific problem classes with a single or multiple specific routing constraints, and

*This work was supported by the Airforce grant under contract number F30602-97-2-0121 and the National Science Foundation Career grant under contract number NSF CCR 96-23867.

0-8186-8810-6/98 $10.00 © 1998 IEEE

none of them provides a framework with the above features.

In this paper, we present an integrated QoS routing framework, from which a family of fully distributed algorithms for unicast routing are derived. The framework is presented in the form of a *generic algorithm* based on *selective probing*. Every node in the network maintains its own local state and no global state is required. The algorithm uses a distributed computation to collectively utilize the most up-to-date local state at each node to find a path. It requires a single pass of messages to find a routing path which is always loop-free. A family of *concrete unicast routing algorithms* is derived from the generic algorithm by specifying a few well-defined open parameters that are constraint-dependent. We show the flexibility of our framework by discussing various algorithms on bandwidth, delay, cost and their combinations. We also discuss several optimization techniques which improve the routing performance. In addition, we describe a heuristic solution to the NP-complete multi-constrained routing problem. Our framework supports multicast routing as well, which was presented in [3].

The most related work is done by Shin and Chou [10] and by Hou [7][1]. Their flooding-based distributed algorithms also rely on local states for routing, but only the delay metric is considered and a large number of routing messages are required. Our framework provides an integrated approach to route connections with many different QoS constraints and improves the routing performance by optimizations such as topology-based routing table and iterative routing.

The rest of the paper is organized as follows. The network and QoS models are given in Section 2. A distributed QoS routing framework is proposed in Section 3, from which a family of unicast routing algorithms are derived in Section 4. Simulation results are presented in in Section 5. Finally, Section 6 concludes the paper. An early version of this paper can be found in [2].

2 Network and QoS Models

A network is modeled as a set V of nodes that are interconnected by a set E of communication links. Each node i has a routing table that has an entry $R_i(t)$ for every possible destination t. The routing table is constructed based on the connectivity (topology) of the network. For example, $R_i(t)$ can be $\{j \mid d_{i,t} = d_{j,t} + 1 \lor d_{i,t} = d_{j,t},\ \forall (i,j) \in E\}$, where $\forall x, y \in V$, $d_{x,y}$ is the distance between node x and node y. $R_i(t)$ consists of a subset of adjacent nodes of i.

The topology of the network can change, which however is *relatively infrequent* comparing to those QoS parameters such as bandwidth, delay and delay jitter. We assume that the topology information is updated by the distance-vector or link-state algorithm, which can be the same one used for non-QoS data-packet routing. That is, QoS routing and non-QoS routing are allowed to share state information and even routing tables. Throughout this paper, we only consider the logical network defined by the combination of the routing tables at all nodes. Those paths that are made possible by the underlying network but not by the routing tables are excluded.

[1] Hou's algorithm works in the context of the virtual path layout in an ATM network.

Definition 1 Concave and additive QoS metrics: Let $m(i,j)$ be a QoS metric for link (i,j). For a path $P = (s, i, j, ..., l, t)$, metric m is *concave* if $m(P) = min\{m(s,i), m(i,j), ..., m(l,t)\}$. Metric m is *additive* if $m(P) = m(s,i) + m(i,j) + ... + m(l,t)$.

Bandwidth is concave; delay, delay jitter and cost are additive. A connection request is represented by a tuple (Qos, s, t, cid), where Qos, s, t and cid are the quality-of-service requirement, the source, the destination and a system-wide unique identifier, respectively. cid consists of the source IP address, the port number and a sequence number. When an unsuccessful connection request is retried, a different sequence number is assigned.

The quality-of-service requirement (Qos) consists of a set of constraints, $\bigcup_{i=1}^{n} \{m_i \circ M_i\}$, where m_i is a metric and M_i is a constant. The purpose of routing is to find a path P which satisfies, $\forall i \in [1..n]$, $m_i(P)\ \mathcal{R}\ M_i$, where $\mathcal{R}$ is $<, \leq, >$ or $\geq$. Wang and Crowcroft [11] proved that if Qos contains at least two additive metrics then the routing is a NP-complete problem.

3 Distributed QoS Routing Framework

Our distributed QoS routing framework defines a protocol for exchanging routing messages among nodes, and provides a common basis for distributed QoS routing regardless the specific metrics involved. We have two goals in mind when designing the framework: (1) It must be general enough to accommodate various QoS metrics, and (2) it must be simple enough to enable a relatively easy implementation with acceptable overhead in the context of high-speed networks.

We present the framework in the form of a *generic algorithm* which implements the following two-phase protocol.

3.1 Two-phase connection establishment protocol

The connection establishment protocol used in this paper consists of two phases: *probing phase and acknowledgement phase*. The probing phase does the QoS routing and the routing path it selects is called the *tentative path*. The acknowledgement phase does the resource reservation. Three types of control messages, *probe, ack and failure*, are used.

The probing phase is started when a connection request (Qos, s, t, cid) arrives. *Probes* are sent from the source s toward the destination t to select a tentative routing path. There are three problems: (1) detecting the *eligible* paths that have sufficient resources to support the required Qos, (2) selecting a tentative path from the eligible paths based on certain optimization criteria, and (3) minimizing the routing overhead introduced by probes. Our solution to the above problems is *selective probing*, in which probes are flooded selectively only along those paths which satisfy the Qos and the optimization requirements. Since a probe proceeds only when the nodes and the links on the way have sufficient resources, every probe arriving at t detects an eligible routing path, which is the one the probe has just traversed from s to t. Upon receipt of probes, the destination t selects a tentative path among the detected eligible paths based on the optimization information carried by the probes.

In the acknowledgement phase, an *ack* message is sent back along the tentative path from t to s, and reserves resources along the way. When s receives the ack, the connection is successfully established. However, since the available resources of every link or node are dynamically changing, an intermediate node on the tentative path may not be able to reserve the required amount of resources at the time when it receives the ack. In such a case, the ack is turned around as a *failure* message and sent back to t to release the reserved resources.

3.2 Data Structures

A simplified data structure for a control (probe, ack or failure) message is $[k, Qos, s, t, cid]$, where k is the sender of the message, which can be the source or an intermediate node. For example, $probe[k, Qos, s, t, cid]$ represents a probe sent by k for connection cid whose source, destination and QoS requirement are s, t and Qos, respectively. When details are not of interest, we simply use $probe[cid]$ to refer to a probe for connection cid. Messages belonging to different connection requests may be sent over the network simultaneously. They are distinguished by their cids and thus no message interference will occur among different requests.

As a probe is sent from the source to the destination, we want to record the path the probe traverses. There are two approaches: one is to record the path in the probe itself, and the other is to record the path at the intermediate nodes on a hop-by-hop basis. The first approach requires larger size probes, and thus consumes more communication bandwidth and more memory space to store the probes when they are waiting in the queues. The second approach, however, requires memory space at the intermediate nodes to store the path. We choose the second approach, which is appropriate for an ATM network where a probe with a constant, smaller size is more likely to be able to fit into a single cell. Table 1 shows the variables declared at a node i. The variables for a connection cid are created upon the receipt of the first probe[cid]. The obsolete variables are deleted by a timeout mechanism.

3.3 Generic DRA

The function *genericDRA*() defined in the following implements the proposed two-phase protocol. It has two important parameters, ***forward condition*** in Line 8 and Δt in Line 9, which are constraint-dependent and thus left open. In Section 4, various *concrete DRAs* will be derived by specifying these parameters differently. The *forward condition* is a boolean function with three arguments (i, j, Qos), where i is the node with the DRA running, j is an adjacent node of i, and Qos is the quality-of-service requirement. A probe received by i is forwarded to j only when the forward condition is satisfied, which implements the *selective probing*. Δt is called the *probe waiting-time*. Let us assume it to be zero for the time being, which means that the probe is sent immediately to j without an artificially introduced delay. When we discuss the *additive* DRAs in Section 4.2, assigning non-zero values to Δt becomes crucial.

$\pi_i(cid)$	The node from which i receives a probe of connection cid. It is called the *predecessor* of i.
$n_i(cid)$	The node from which i receives an ack of connection cid. It is called the *successor* of i.
$f_i(cid)$	A boolean variable whose initial value is false. Whenever an intermediate node i forwards a received probe[cid], $f_i(cid)$ is set to be true.
$R_i(t)$	The routing-table entry indexed by t. $R_i(t)$ stores a subset of the adjacent nodes of i, to which data packets for t may be forwarded.

Table 1. Variable definition

genericDRA() at node i

```
1.  while true do
2.    block until receiving a message;
3.    switch (the received message)
4.    case 1: probe[k, Qos, s, t, cid]
5.      if i ≠ t and f_i(cid) = false then
          /* i has not forwarded a probe[cid] before. */
6.        π_i(cid) := k; /* record the predecessor */
7.        for every node j ∈ R_i(t), j ≠ k do
8.          if forward condition (i, j, Qos) is true then
9.            send j a probe[i, Qos, s, t, cid] after a delay Δt;
10.           f_i(cid) := true;
11.         endif
12.       endfor
13.     else if i = t and f_t(cid) = false then
          /* start the acknowledgement phase */
14.       send k an ack[i, Qos, s, t, cid];
15.       f_t(cid) := true;
16.     else
17.       discard the probe;
18.     endif
19.   case 2: ack[k, Qos, s, t, cid]
20.     if node i has the required resources then
21.       reserve resources for connection cid;
22.       n_i(cid) := k; /* record the successor */
23.       if i ≠ s then
24.         send π_i(cid) an ack[i, Qos, s, t, cid];
```

```
25.       else
26.         connection cid is successfully established;
27.       endif
28.     else
29.       send k a failure[i, Qos, s, t, cid];
30.     endif
31.   case 3: failure[k, Qos, s, t, cid]
32.     release resources reserved at i for connection cid;
33.     if i ≠ t then
34.       send n_i(cid) a failure[i, Qos, s, t, cid];
35.     endif
36. endswitch
37.endwhile
```

Case 1 describes the probing phase and cases 2 and 3 describe the acknowledgement phase. When a new connection request arrives, a probe is sent to the source to initiate the probing phase. By lines 5-12, *an intermediate node i forwards only the first received probe that satisfies the forward condition.* Lines 13-15 do the path selection. If two or more probes arrive at t, i.e., two or more paths satisfy the QoS requirement, only the first received probe counts and its path is selected as the tentative path, which is recorded by the $\pi_i(cid)$ variables at the intermediate nodes. Optimizing the path selection is discussed in Section 4. The probing phase terminates and the acknowledgement phase starts at Line 14.

The algorithm successfully establishes a connection when the source receives an ack and reserves the required resources successfully. If the source does not receive an ack during a timeout period, the rejection of the connection is assumed. The timeout period is set based on the time complexity of the algorithm (Section 3.4). An alternative approach for rejection indication is to send back a negative acknowledgement (nack) for each probe dropped. When an intermediate node receives a nack for every probe sent, it sends a nack to its predecessor. When the source receives a nack for every probe sent, it signals the rejection of the connection.

Theorem 1 If the generic DRA establishes a connection, the path of the connection must be loop-free.

Due to space limitation, we leave out the proof of all theorems. Interested readers can find the proof in [2].

3.4 Complexity analysis

The algorithm takes a single message round-trip time to establish a connection. If we assume that in normal conditions it takes at most one unit of time for a message to traverse one link including the buffering and processing time at nodes, then the time-complexity is $O(2l)$ units of time, where l is the length of the tentative path.[2]

The algorithm sends at most one probe per link in the sub-net consisting of all paths from the source to the destination. The total number of probes sent is thus bounded by e, where e is the total number of links in the sub-net. There are at most one ack and one failure message for each link on the tentative path. The total number of ack and failure messages is thus bounded by $2l$, where l is the length of the tentative path. Hence, the message complexity (number of control messages) of the algorithm is $O(e + 2l)$ for a single connection request.[3] The average message overhead is substantially lower than the worst-case one when optimization techniques are applied, which is shown by the simulation results in Section 5.

4 Distributed Unicast Routing Algorithms

From the generic DRA, we derive various concrete DRAs for different QoS metrics such as bandwidth, delay, cost, delay jitter, path length, etc. Concrete DRAs are classified into three categories: *concave-metric DRAs*, *additive-metric DRAs* and *multiple-metric DRAs*.

4.1 Concave-metric DRAs

We use the *bandwidth* metric as an example. DRAs on other concave metrics such as buffer space or *CPU time* can be defined similarly. For all concave DRAs, $\Delta t = 0$. The forward condition is specified as follows.

4.1.1 Bandwidth DRA

Let $bandwidth(i, j)$ be the residual (unused) bandwidth of link (i, j). Let B be the bandwidth requirement of a connection. The forward condition is

$$\textit{forward condition}\ (i, j, Qos\{bandwidth \circ B\}) : \\ bandwidth(i, j) \geq B$$

The resulting routing algorithm is called DRA(*bandwidth*).

It is hard to analyze the performance of a routing algorithm in a dynamic network where the bandwidth of each link may change at any time. For simplicity, we assume for the following theorem that the local states at nodes do not change during the process of routing a connection. The same assumption is made also for Theorems 3-4

Theorem 2 Given a connection request $(Qos\{bandwidth \circ B\}, s, t, cid)$, DRA(*bandwidth*) finds a tentative path P from s to t such that $bandwidth(P) \geq B$, if such a path exists.

[2] According to Lines 13-15 of genericDRA(), only the first probe received by t counts for the time complexity. It defines the tentative path and terminates the probing phase. All probes received by t successively are simply discarded and do not add up to the time complexity.

[3] Only a single run of the algorithm is considered in the complexity. The overhead of failure-and-retry is not included.

4.1.2 Optimization

When there exist many paths that satisfy the QoS requirement, the ***shortest*** path in terms of delay or number of hops or the ***widest*** path in terms of residual bandwidth [11] is often preferred. However, DRA(*bandwidth*) finds a tentative path blindly through the competition among probes. Whichever probe reaching the destination first defines the path. This scheme does not guarantee that the shortest or widest path is always selected as the tentative path, although we argue that our algorithm is statistically in favor of the shortest path, because a probe sent along a shorter path will be more likely to reach the destination earlier than a probe sent along a longer path when the two paths have similar congestion conditions. In the following, we discuss some optimization techniques, which are also applicable to all DRAs proposed later.

We define the *age* of a probe as the number of hops it has traversed. When a node i receives and forwards a probe$[k, B, s, t, cid]$, it not only keeps k in $\pi_i(cid)$ as its predecessor but also records the age of the probe. If another probe with a less age is received from k', i changes the value of $\pi_i(cid)$ to k' so that when an ack is received by i later, the ack is forwarded to k' instead of k and thus follows a shorter path to the source. The above scheme can also be applied to bandwidth. We define the *bandwidth* of a probe as the minimum bandwidth of all links it has traversed so far. When i receives a probe from k' with a larger bandwidth than that of the previously received probe, i changes its predecessor to k' which leads to a path with larger residual bandwidth.

Instead of keeping a single predecessor, a node i can declare $\pi_i(cid)$ as a set which keeps a group of predecessors. For every received probe$[k, B, s, t, cid]$, i adds k to its predecessor set.[4] When i receives an ack, it chooses a predecessor from the set to forward the ack. If i receives a failure message from that predecessor, it chooses another predecessor from the set to forward the ack again. Only after i receives a failure message from every one in the set, it passes the failure message to $n_i(cid)$. Multiple predecessors improve the chance for the connection to be successfully established when the network state dynamically changes. Further improvement on the above approach can be done as follows. When i receives a probe, information besides the predecessor, such as the age and/or the bandwidth of the probe, is also recorded. Such information can help i make a better choice on which one in the predecessor set should be selected to forward the ack.

In DRA(*bandwidth*), the destination sends an ack immediately after it receives the first probe even though successive probes may suggest better paths. We can improve the algorithm as follows. When the destination receives a probe, it checks the age and the bandwidth of the probe. If the quality of the corresponding path is good, for example, the age is equal to the shortest distance from the source to the destination or the bandwidth is greater than some large value, an ack is replied immediately. Otherwise, the destination waits for a short period of time for more probes and then chooses the best one to reply.

[4] Still, only the first probe which satisfies the forward condition is forwarded.

4.2 Additive-metric DRAs

We define an abstract additive metric, *length*, which can be delay, delay jitter, cost or number of hops. Let p be a probe and P be the path which p has traversed so far. We define $length(p) = length(P) = \sum_{(i,j)\in P} length(i, j)$.

We extend the structure of a probe and add a new field to keep $length(p)$, so that the receiver of p knows the value of $length(p)$. Initially, $length(p) := 0$. Whenever p proceeds for another link (i, j), $length(p) := length(p) + length(i, j)$. The forward condition for *length* is specified as

$$\begin{gathered} \textit{forward condition } (i, j, Qos\{length \circ M\}) : \\ length(i, j) + length(p) < M \end{gathered}$$

where p is the received probe and M is a constant.

4.2.1 Discussion of Δt

Besides the forward condition, specifying an appropriate non-zero Δt (Line 9 of genericDRA() in Section 3.3) is also important for an additive-metric DRA. If we let Δt be zero as we did for a concave-metric DRA, the algorithm does not work well sometimes. See Figure 1 for an example. The length of each link is labeled beside the link. Figure 1 (a) shows that the path $P = s \to i \to k \to h \to t$ satisfies the connection request $(Qos\{length \circ 5\}, s, t, cid)$ because $length(P) = 4$ and the length requirement is 5. In Figure 1 (b), suppose probe 2 arrives at node k earlier than probe 1. Probe 2 traverses $s \to j \to k \to h$, and is dropped by node h because $length(h, t) + length(probe\ 2) > 5$ and thus the forward condition is violated, where $length(probe\ 2) = length(s, j) + length(j, k) + length(k, h) = 5$ as defined previously. Probe 1 traverses $s \to i \to k$ and is dropped by node k because k has already forwarded probe 2.[5] Hence, no probe can reach t and the algorithm fails to find a tentative path.

We want probe 1 to arrive at node k earlier than probe 2. More generally, it should take less time for a probe to traverse a shorter path than a longer path. A simple approach is to introduce extra delay for each probe to traverse a link; the longer the length of the link, the longer the delay. That can be done by assigning an appropriate value for Δt (see Line 9 of genericDRA() in Section 3.3). How to specify Δt as well as the implementation issues will be discussed shortly when we study the delay DRA and the cost DRA. A performance advantage of doing so is that the shortest path will always be selected as the tentative path because the probe traversing the shortest path arrives at the

[5] By the construction of the algorithm, node k forwards at most one probe. After k forwards probe 2, it discards all successively received probes including probe 1.

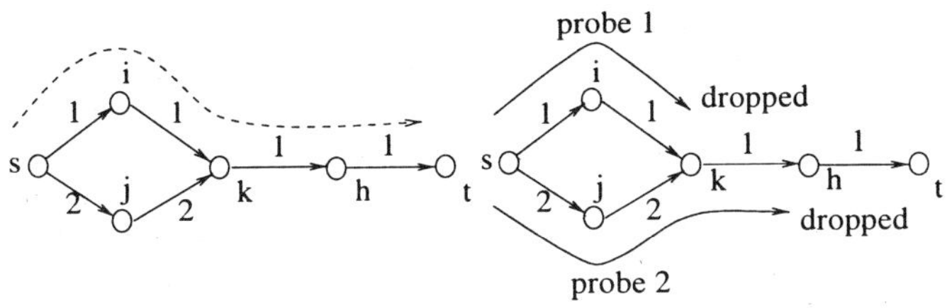

(a) (b)

Figure 1. (a) There exists an eligible path for the request ($Qos\{length \circ 5\}, s, t, cid$). (b) An additive-metric DRA fails in finding the path if $\Delta t = 0$.

destination first. The message (or computation) overhead for finding the shortest path is $O(e)$,[6] which is remarkably lower than $O(ve)$ of the distributed Bellman-Ford algorithm, where v is the number of nodes and e the number of links. However, the cost we pay is the time complexity, which is increased by the extra delay of the probes. Fortunately, as we will see shortly, the increase on the time complexity is controllable and can be adjusted to a modest range. In the following, we will use *delay* and *cost* as examples to show how to choose Δt.

4.2.2 Delay DRA

A quality-of-service requirement $Qos\{delay \circ D\}$ requires the end-to-end delay to be bounded by D. The end-to-end delay of a path is the summation of the *node-delay* at every node and the *link-delay* at every link on the path. *node-delay*(i,j) includes the protocol-processing time and the queueing delay of a normal data packet at node i for link (i,j). *link-delay*(i,j) is the propagation delay on link (i,j). The *delay* metric is defined as

$$delay(i,j) = node\text{-}delay(i,j) + link\text{-}delay(i,j)$$

Let p be a probe and suppose the path that p has traversed so far is $P = s \rightarrow k \rightarrow ... \rightarrow i \rightarrow j$.

$$delay(p) = delay(s,k) + ... + delay(i,j)$$

The forward condition for *delay* is

$$\text{forward condition } (i,j,Qos\{delay \circ D\}): \\ delay(i,j) + delay(p) < D$$

Let $\Delta t =$ *node-delay*(i,j), and the resulting DRA is called DRA(*delay*). Line 9 of genericDRA() becomes

$$\text{send } j \text{ a probe}[i, Qos\{delay \circ D\}, s, t, cid] \\ \text{after a delay of } node\text{-}delay(i,j) \qquad (1)$$

The probe has to be forwarded **after** a period of *node-delay*(i,j). This can be easily implemented by treating probes as *normal data packets* whose processing and queueing delay at node i is *node-delay*(i,j) by definition. However, this approach is applicable only to DRA(*delay*) but not to other additive-metric DRAs where a value other than *node-delay*(i,j) is assigned to Δt, as we shall see shortly in DRA(*cost*). A more general implementation is described as follows: Two queues, *data packet queue* and *control message queue*, are maintained at node i for link (i,j). The control message queue has a higher priority than the data packet queue. The statement (1) is non-blocking. It completes by inserting the probe with a timestamp Δt into the control message queue, in which probes are placed in the order of increasing timestamps. A timer is set appropriately for the first probe in the queue. When the timer is timed out, the probe is transmitted immediately.

Since probes travel at speeds according to the delays, a probe traveling along the minimum-delay path arrives first. The time complexity of the probing phase is bounded by $min\{D, delay(P^m_{s,t})\}$, where $P^m_{s,t}$ is the minimum-delay path from s to t. After time D, $delay(p) \geq D$ for every existing probe p of the connection and thus none of the probes can satisfy the forward condition any more. After $delay(P^m_{s,t})$, the probe traversing $P^m_{s,t}$ has already arrived at the destination, which terminates the probing phase by selecting $P^m_{s,t}$ as the tentative path.

Theorem 3 Given a connection request ($Qos\{delay \circ D\}, s, t, cid$), (1) DRA(*delay*) finds a tentative path P such that $delay(P) < D$, if such a path exists; (2) the tentative path must be the minimum-delay path from s to t.

4.2.3 Cost DRA

A quality-of-service requirement $Qos\{cost \circ C\}$ requires the end-to-end cost to be bounded by C. Let *cost*(i,j) be the cost of link (i,j) in dollars or by some other measurement, and *cost*(p) be the accumulated cost on the path that a probe p has traversed. The forward condition for *cost* is

$$\text{forward condition } (i,j,Qos\{cost \circ C\}): \\ cost(i,j) + cost(p) < C$$

Let $\Delta t = f(cost(i,j))$ where f is a monotonic non-decreasing function, and the resulting DRA is called DRA(*cost*). An example f is

$$f(cost(i,j)) = max\{\frac{cost(i,j)}{C} \times T - link\text{-}delay(i,j),\ 0\}$$

where T is a time constant. The time for a probe to traverse link (i,j) is

$$f(cost(i,j)) + link\text{-}delay(i,j) \\ = max\{\frac{cost(i,j)}{C} \times T,\ link\text{-}delay(i,j)\}$$

Ideally, we want to choose T such that $\frac{cost(i,j)}{C} \times T \geq$ *link-delay*(i,j), which makes the probing delay over (i,j)

[6] $O(e)$ is the message complexity of the probing phase. See Section 3.4.

directly proportional to $cost(i,j)$. However, there exists a tradeoff since a larger T makes the routing time longer. Let P be the tentative path. The time complexity of the probing phase can be measured by

$$\sum_{(i,j)\in P} max\{\frac{cost(i,j)}{C} \times T,\ link\text{-}delay(i,j)\}$$
$$= max\{\frac{\sum_{(i,j)\in P} cost(i,j)}{C} \times T,\ \sum_{(i,j)\in P} link\text{-}delay(i,j)\}$$
$$\leq max\{T,\ \sum_{(i,j)\in P} link\text{-}delay(i,j)\}$$

Generally, the value of T can be selected based on the estimated end-to-end delay from s to t.

4.3 Multiple-metric DRAs

We use two examples. The first one has one concave metric and one additive metric, and the second one has two additive metrics.

4.3.1 Bandwidth and delay DRA

We consider $Qos\{bandwidth \circ B, delay \circ D\}$ where the bandwidth requirement is B and the end-to-end delay requirement is D. The forward condition is

$$forward\ condition\ (i,j,Qos\{bandwidth \circ B, delay \circ D\}):$$
$$bandwidth(i,j) \geq B\ \wedge\ delay(i,j) + delay(p) < D$$

Let $\Delta t = node\text{-}delay(i,j)$ and the resulting DRA is called DRA(*bandwidth*, *delay*).

Theorem 4 Given a connection request $(Qos\{bandwidth \circ B, delay \circ D\}, s, t, cid)$, (1) DRA(*bandwidth*, *delay*) finds a tentative path P such that $bandwidth(P) \geq B$ and $delay(P) < D$, if such a path exists; (2) the tentative path has the minimum delay among all eligible paths from s to t.

4.3.2 Delay and cost DRA

It is a NP-complete problem to find a path that satisfies $Qos\{delay \circ D, cost \circ C\}$, which requires the end-to-end delay and the end-to-end cost to be bounded by D and C, respectively. DRA(*delay*, *cost*) provides a heuristic solution for this problem. The forward condition is

$$forward\ condition\ (i,j,Qos\{delay \circ D, cost \circ C\}):$$
$$delay(i,j) + delay(p) < D\ \wedge\ cost(i,j) + cost(p) < C$$

Determining Δt is tricky. A general form is

$$\Delta t = max\{\alpha \times delay(i,j) + \beta \times cost(i,j) - link\text{-}delay(i,j),\ 0\}$$

When the delay bound is hard to achieve but the cost bound is easy to achieve, we let $\alpha = 1$ and $\beta = 0$. Δt becomes the same as in DRA(*delay*). Hence, when probing for a tentative path, the algorithm is in favor of paths with short delays. When the cost bound is hard to achieve but the delay bound is easy to achieve, let $\alpha = 0$ and $\beta = T/C$, where T is a constant. Δt becomes the same as in DRA(*cost*). When both delay and cost bounds are difficult to achieve, which means D (C) is close to the minimum delay (cost) between the source and the destination, we let $\alpha = 1$ and $\beta = D/C$. [7] When the relative difficulties of achieving the two bounds are unknown, a general way of increasing the probability of finding a tentative path is to allow multiple executions of DRA(*delay*, *cost*) with different Δt's. When a connection request $(Qos\{delay \circ D, cost \circ C\}, s, t, cid)$ arrives, two pseudo requests are created:

$$(Qos\{delay \circ D, cost \circ C\}, s, t, cid')$$
$$(Qos\{delay \circ D, cost \circ C\}, s, t, cid'')$$

Hence, three instances of DRA(*delay*, *cost*) are executed and each uses a different Δt. The three Δt's are

$$\Delta t = node\text{-}delay(i,j)$$
$$\Delta t = max\{\frac{cost(i,j)}{C} \times T - link\text{-}delay(i,j),\ 0\}$$
$$\Delta t = node\text{-}delay(i,j) + \frac{D}{C} \times cost(i,j)$$

4.4 Iterative DRAs

We use DRA($*$) as a general term referring to *any* of the above concrete DRAs. DRA($*$) finds a tentative path through the competition among probes. The first probe reaching the destination defines the path, which however may not be the optimal one. When there exist many paths that satisfy the QoS requirement, the shortest path in terms of *number of hops* is often desired due to a better statistical performance [8]. We propose *iterative* DRAs to find the shortest tentative path. As an example, let us design an iterative version of DRA(*bandwidth*) first.

We define the *age* of a probe p as the number of hops it has traveled.[8] Initially, $age(p) := 0$. Whenever p passes a link, $age(p) := age(p) + 1$. We introduce a new forward condition for DRA(*bandwidth*):

$$forward\ condition\ (i,j,Qos\{bandwidth \circ B\}):$$
$$bandwidth(i,j) \geq B\ \wedge\ age(p) + d_{j,t} + 1 \leq L$$

where $d_{j,t}$ is the distance from j to the destination t and L is a constant no less than $d_{s,t}$.

Should p be forwarded to j, the length of the shortest possible path for p to reach t would be $age(p) + d_{j,t} + 1$, including the portion that p has already traversed from s to i. Hence, the above forward condition allows a probe

[7] The reason for β to be D/C instead of 1 is to balance the impacts of the two metrics on Δt so as to avoid one metric dominating the value of Δt.

[8] In Section 4.1.2, the ages of probes are used as an optimization technique for the intermediate nodes to choose their predecessors. Here, the same ages are used in an *end-to-end* manner to constrain the length of the tentative path by limiting the maximum number of hops the probes can travel.

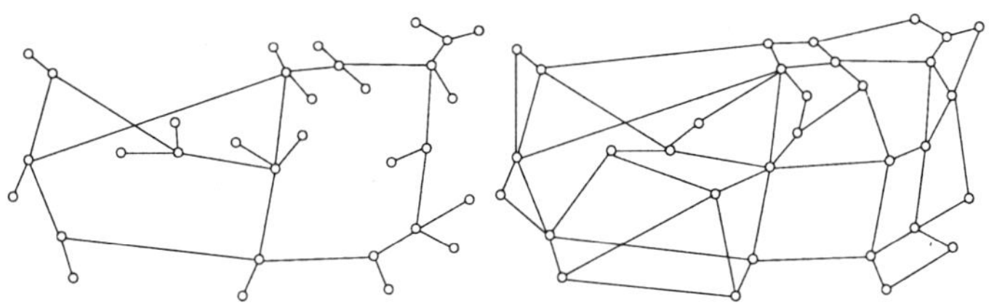

NET-1 NET-2

Figure 2. network topologies

to be forwarded only along those links which lead to paths whose lengths are bounded by L. When $L = d_{s,t}$, the algorithm forwards probes only along the shortest paths and the corresponding DRA is called

$$\text{DRA}(\textit{bandwidth}) \text{ WITH } L = d_{s,t}$$

A general form of our iterative DRA is

$$\text{DRA}(\textit{bandwidth}) \text{ ITERATIVE ON}$$
$$\{L = d_{s,t}, L = d_{s,t} + 1, ..., L = +\infty\}$$

It executes DRA(*bandwidth*) iteratively each time with an increasing value of L — $d_{s,t}, d_{s,t} + 1$, ..., and $+\infty$, in turn — until the connection is established.

Though many iterations are allowable, we only use two iterations in order to reduce the overhead. That is, we consider DRA(*bandwidth*) ITERATIVE ON $\{L = d_{s,t}, L = +\infty\}$ in this paper. DRA(*bandwidth*) WITH $L = d_{s,t}$ is first executed, which tries to find a shortest path P with $bandwidth(P) \geq B$. If it succeeds, *the next iteration is canceled.* If it fails, DRA(*bandwidth*) WITH $L = +\infty$ is executed to search all possible paths.

For an arbitrary DRA($*$), let Fcondition($*$) be its original forward condition. A new forward condition is defined as

$$\textit{forward condition } (i, j, Qos):$$
$$\text{Fcondition}(*) \wedge age(p) + d_{j,t} + 1 \leq L$$

The corresponding iterative DRA is denoted as

$$\text{DRA}(*) \text{ ITERATIVE ON } \{L = d_{s,t}, L = +\infty\}$$

Comparing to their non-iterative counterparts, the iterative DRAs not only find shorter routing paths but also reduce the average overhead significantly at the cost of longer routing time, which will be shown by the simulation results in the next section.

5 Simulation Results

5.1 Message overhead

The message overhead is one of the most important performance metrics for distributed routing algorithms. It has a direct impact on how applicable the algorithms are in the real world. The worst-case message overhead of our DRAs has been analyzed in Section 3.4. In this section, we study by simulation the *average* overhead, namely, the average number of probes sent per connection request.

Two network topologies, NET-1 and NET-2 (Figure 2), were used in the simulation. NET-1 is based on the major circuits in ANSNET and NET-2 increases the connectivity of NET-1 by additional links. Each link is full duplex with a bandwidth capacity of 155Mbps(OC3). The nodes are placed in a 3000×2400 Km^2 rectangle, roughly the size of USA, and the propagation speed through the links is two thirds of the light speed. The message overhead of DRA(*bandwidth*), DRA(*delay*) and their iterative versions will be presented. The results for other DRAs can be found in [2]. We use DRA($*$) ITERATIVE as an abbreviation of DRA($*$) ITERATIVE ON $\{L = d_{s,t}, L = +\infty\}$.

Figure 3 presents the results of four experiments: running DRA (*bandwidth*) and DRA(*bandwidth*) ITERATIVE on NET-1 and NET-2. The message overhead is plotted with respect to the average traffic load in the network. The source node, the destination node and the bandwidth requirement B of each connection request are randomly generated. B is uniformly distributed between 64Kbps $\sim$ 1.5Mbps. For each request, the background traffic load on every link is randomly generated from the range of [0.0, 155.0Mbps]. Each point in Figure 3 is taken by averaging the overhead of one thousand independent connection requests.

Both DRA(*bandwidth*) and DRA(*bandwidth*) ITERATIVE have higher overhead on NET-2 than on NET-1, because NET-2 is better connected and more probes are flooded during the routing. DRA(*bandwidth*) has a much higher average overhead than DRA(*bandwidth*) ITERATIVE though its worst-case overhead is lower (see Section 4.4). This can be explained by the following reasoning: When the network is not congested (average traffic load less than 145 Mbps in our simulation), DRA(*bandwidth*) ITERATIVE succeeds in its first iteration and thus probes are flooded only along the shortest paths. The overhead is certainly lower than DRA(*bandwidth*) which does a much broader flooding. When the traffic load grows heavier, the overhead of DRA(*bandwidth*) ITERATIVE may increase due to the second iteration.[9] However, the more the second iterations are required, the more the network is congested, which further implies that satisfying the forward condition becomes harder and harder due to the lack of bandwidth. The immediate result is more and more probes are discarded instead of being forwarded. Therefore, when the second iterations can not compensate the discarded probes, the average number of probes sent decreases, as observed in Figure 3. When the network is fully congested, hardly can any probes be sent out from the source nodes and the overhead reaches zero.

Figure 4 shows the results of running DRA(*delay*) and DRA(*delay*) ITERATIVE on NET-1 and NET-2. The de-

[9] The overhead increase is not observed for DRA(*bandwidth*) ITERATIVE on NET-1. This is because NET-1 is much sparser than NET-2 and thus the number of probes resulted from the second iterations are not many enough to offset the increasing number of discarded probes due to heavier background traffic.

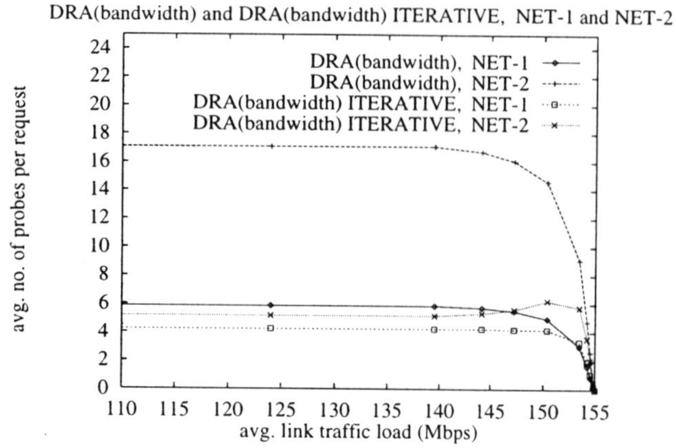

Figure 3. Average message overhead of DRA(bandwidth) and DRA(bandwidth) ITERATIVE

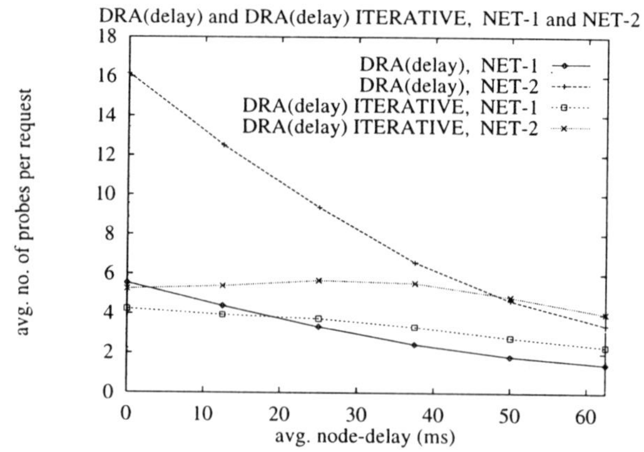

Figure 4. Average message overhead of DRA(delay) and DRA(delay) ITERATIVE

lay requirements of the experimental connection requests are uniformly distributed in the range of [0.0, 200.0ms]. The *node-delay* of each link is randomly generated from [0.0,125.0ms]; experiments show that larger *node-delay*'s make the forward condition hardly satisfied and thus of little interest to our simulation. Similar to Figure 3, the overhead of DRA(*delay*) ITERATIVE does not increase significantly with respect to the average *node-delay*. The reason is that although an increasing *node-delay* results in more second iterations, it also results in more discarded probes because the forward condition is harder to be saitisfied. On Net-2, DRA(*delay*) ITERATIVE has a much lower overhead than that of DRA(*delay*) when the average *node-delay* is relatively low. Experiments on other DRAs also reveal that the iterative DRAs have a better overall performance.

The average source-destination distance of all connection requests is 3.2 hops in our simulation. The average number of probes per request is always under 6.5 for any iterative DRA and any background traffic condition. Such a result indicates that the selective probing provides an efficient distributed routing approach, which has low overhead and does not rely on accurate global state.

5.2 Routing time

In this section, we use DRA(*delay*) and DRA(*delay*) ITERATIVE to study how long it takes to make the routing. For those connections that are successfully established, we measure the average time to find a tentative path, called the *average probing time*. For those connections that are rejected, we measure the average time to timeout and signal the rejection, called the *average rejection time*. DRA(*delay*) rejects a connection after a timeout period of $2D$ if no *ack* is received, where D is the delay requirement.[10] DRA(*delay*) ITERATIVE has two iterations: DRA(*delay*) WITH $L = d_{s,t}$ and DRA(*delay*) WITH $L = \infty$. Both of them have a timeout period of $2D$. Therefore, a connection will be rejected after $4D$.

Before presenting the simulation results, we make a simple analysis on the probing time of DRA(*delay*) first. Let Φ be the set of connection requests used in the simulation. Among the requests, the set of successful (accepted) ones is Φ_s and the set of rejected ones is Φ_r. Recall that probes in DRA(*delay*) travel at speeds according to the delays of their paths (Section 4.2.2). The probe traversing the minimum-delay path arrives at the destination first. Therefore, for a request $\{D, s, t, id\}$ in Φ, the probing time is $delay(P^m_{s,t})$, where $P^m_{s,t}$ is the minimum-delay path. The average probing time of successful requests is

$$\lambda = \frac{\sum_{\{D,s,t,id\}\in\Phi} delay(P^m_{s,t})}{|\Phi|}$$

Suppose s and t are uniformly selected from all nodes. If $\Phi_s = \Phi$, λ is expected to be equal to the *average end-to-end delay* between two nodes in the network, which is defined as

$$\eta = \frac{\sum_{s,t\in V, s\neq t} delay(P^m_{s,t})}{\sum_{s,t\in V, s\neq t} 1}$$

Now, let us consider the case $\Phi_s \subset \Phi$. A request $\{D, s, t, id\}$ with a large $delay(P^m_{s,t})$ is more likely to be rejected, because given the same D the constraint $delay(P^m_{s,t}) < D$ is harder to be satisfied. Therefore, Φ_s tends to have requests with smaller $delay(P^m_{s,t})$ and Φ_r tends to have requests with larger $delay(P^m_{s,t})$, and hence λ can be less than η, as we shall see in the simulation results.

The node-delay of a link is randomly generated from $[0.0, 60.0ms]$. Figure 5 shows the average probing times of DRA(*delay*) and DRA(*delay*) ITERATIVE with respect to the average delay requirement D. The probing time of DRA(*delay*) is bounded by η, 88.38ms in the figure. It converges to η as D increases. DRA(*delay*) ITERATIVE has

[10]Recall that the time complexity of the probing phase is bounded by D (Section 4.2.2). A timeout period of $2D$ leaves enough margin for the ack to travel back in time.

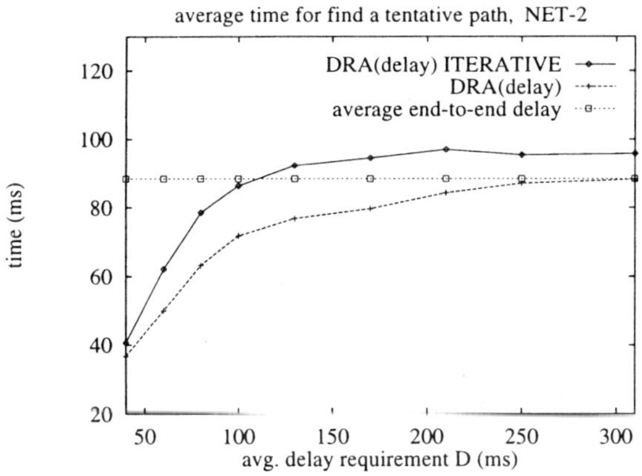

Figure 5. Average time to find a connection

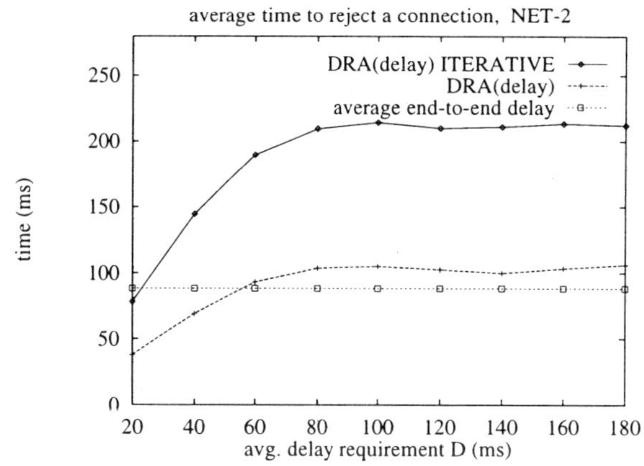

Figure 6. Average time to reject a connection

a larger probing time than DRA(*delay*) due to its two iterations. As D increases, the timeout between the two iterations increases and thus the probing time increases. On the other hand, larger D's allow more connections to be established by the first iterations, and less second iterations (less timeouts) are necessary. When the decrease in the number of timeouts compensates the increase in the length of timeout periods, the average probing time stops increasing. The probing time of DRA(*delay*) ITERATIVE goes slightly higher than η as shown in the figure.

Figure 6 shows the rejection times of DRA(*delay*) and DRA(*delay*) ITERATIVE. As D increases, the average rejection times increase due to longer timeouts. However, after D passes certain threshold (80ms in the figure), the average rejection times become stable and do not increase further. This is because connections with too large D will not be rejected and thus will not contribute to the rejection-time average. The rejection time of DRA(*delay*) ITERATIVE is about twice that of DRA(*delay*), which is comparable to the average end-to-end delay η between two nodes in the network. This can be illustrated by the following much simplied analysis. Consider a fictitious ideal simulation run where all connections with their delay requirements D_r less than η are rejected and all other connections are accepted. Suppose D_r's of the rejected connections are uniformly distributed in $[0..\eta]$. The average of D_r's will be $\overline{D_r} = \frac{1}{2}\eta$. Hence, it takes about $4\overline{D_r} = 2\eta$ on average for DRA(*delay*) ITERATIVE to timeout and signal the rejection, and it takes about $2\overline{D_r} = \eta$ on average for DRA(*delay*) to timeout.

In the actual simulation, not all D_r's fall in $[0..\eta]$. Some rejected connections have delay requirements larger than η, which makes $\overline{D_r}$ and thus the average rejection time larger than those in the above ideal case. In Figure 6, the rejection times of DRA(*delay*) ITERATIVE and DRA(*delay*) can go up to 2.4 and 1.2 times η, respectively.

6 Conclusion

In this paper, we described in detail a unique integrated and distributed QoS routing framework presented in the form of a generic DRA. From the framework, we derived three classes of unicast routing algorithms: concave-metric DRAs, additive-metric DRAs and multiple-metric DRAs. Each DRA has its iterative version. Simulations revealed that the iterative DRAs have a better overall performance than the non-iterative counterparts. The stable and modest overhead of the iterative DRAs makes them practical.

References

[1] J. Behrems and J. Garcia-Luna-Aceves. Distributed, scalable routing based on link-state vectors. *SIGCOMM*, pages 136–147, August 1994.

[2] S. Chen and K. Nahrstedt. Distributed qos routing. *Tech. Report UIUCDCS-R-97-2017, Department of Computer Science, University of Illinois at Urbana-Champaign*, July 1997.

[3] S. Chen and K. Nahrstedt. Distributed quality-of-service routing in high-speed networks based on selective probing. *Technical Report, University of Illinois at Urbana-Champaign, Department of Computer Science*, 1998.

[4] S. Chen and K. Nahrstedt. On finding multi-constrained paths. *IEEE International Conference on Communications*, June 1998.

[5] A. Forum. Private network network interface (pnni) v1.0 specifications. May 1996.

[6] R. Guerin and A. Orda. Qos-based routing in networks with inaccurate information: Theory and algorithms. *Infocom'97, Japan*, April 1997.

[7] C. Hou. Routing virtual circuits with timing requirements in virtual path based atm networks. *INFOCOM'96*, 1996.

[8] Q. Ma and P. Steenkiste. Quality-of-service routing with performance guarantees. *Proceedings of the 4th International IFIP Workshop on Quality of Service*, May 1997.

[9] H. F. Salama, D. S. Reeves, and Y. Viniotis. A distributed algorithm for delay-constrained unicast routing. *INFOCOM'97, Japan*, April 1997.

[10] K. G. Shin and C.-C. Chou. A distributed route-selection scheme for establishing real-time channel. *Sixth IFIP Int'l Conf. on High Performance Networking Conf. (HPN'95)*, pages 319–329, Sep. 1995.

[11] Z. Wang and J. Crowcroft. Qos routing for supporting resource reservation. *JSAC*, September 1996.

A Linear-Based Trunk Reservation Routing Algorithm for ATM Networks

Antonios F. Atlasis[1,2] Evangelos D. Baltatzis[1] Georgios I. Stassinopoulos[1] Iakovos Venieris[1]

1. National Technical University of Athens, Department of Electrical Engineering and Computer Science, Heroon Polytechniou 9, Zographou, GR-157 73 Athens, Greece. tel:+3 01 7722531, fax: +3 01 7722534 e-mail: atlasis@telecom.ece.ntua.gr, stassin@cs.ntua.gr, vbalta@telecom.ntua.gr, venieris@cs.ntua.gr.
2. Hellenic Air Force, Engineering Department

Abstract

In this paper an efficient heuristic routing algorithm is proposed that increase the network throughput irrespective of the network traffic load. Its effectiveness is based on an efficient cost metric, which achieves a successful trade-off between the use of the minimum-hop routes and the load balancing. Moreover, it employs the known Trunk Reservation concept according to a probability that increases linearly as the traffic load increases. This results in an effective compromise of the performance of the algorithm between light and heavy loads. Finally, its simplicity and its suitability for a real-time application render it as an efficient routing algorithm for ATM networks.

Keywords: *ATM, routing, Call Admission Control, Quality of Service, Virtual Path, Virtual Channel Connection, Trunk Reservation.*

1: Introduction

In ATM Networks, where various sources with diverse traffic characteristics and Quality of Service (QoS) constraints are statistically multiplexed at very high rates, a Call Admission Control (CAC) function is required in order to decide whether a new call request should be accepted or not. The route that the incoming call will use is selected by a routing algorithm, which is part of the CAC function [1]. The routing algorithm aims at the maximization of the network throughput (minimization of the call blocking rate) and the guarantee of the QoS requirements.

However, the statistical multiplexing of sources with different QoS constraints reduces the achieved statistical gain because the most stringent among them should be guaranteed for each source. Moreover, when sources with significantly different traffic characteristics are statistically multiplexed the resulted cell loss probabilities for individual traffic streams may differ more than an order of magnitude [7]. Hence, even in this case more stringent QoS should be provided than the ones they are actually required so as to ensure that all the Virtual Circuit Connections (VCCs) will be guaranteed the QoS that they negotiated during the call set-up phase.

The Virtual Path (VP) concept, which has been introduced to ATM networks, enables traffic classification, resulting in homogeneous traffic along the same VPs and thus, simplifying the routing problem. Each VP is usually assigned a specific traffic class, thus all the contained VCCs transfer the same type of traffic and have the same QoS requirements. In addition to this, the VP notion reduces significantly the complexity, the processing and the time required to establish new VCCs [2].

Many routing algorithms have been proposed so far suitable for ATM networks. The effectiveness of most of them depends on the loading conditions of the networks, while some other have increased hardware requirements or require considerable execution time which render them unsuitable for real-time applications. In this paper, a simple heuristic routing algorithm suitable for real-time applications is presented which, achieves an increased network throughput in comparison with the most known routing algorithms while guaranteeing the appropriate QoS support. Moreover, it is enhanced with the trunk reservation concept, which is applied according to a probability that is increased linearly as the network load increases; this policy aims at a better overall performance of the algorithm irrespective of the traffic load.

This paper is organized as follows: In section 2, some general aspects of the ATM routing problem and related work are discussed. In section 3, a new routing algorithm suitable for ATM networks is proposed, while, in section 4, a comparative performance study of this algorithm with some of the most known ones is presented. In section 5,

0-8186-8810-6/98 $10.00 © 1998 IEEE

the implementation and the deployment concept is discussed and finally, in section 6 we draw our conclusions and some directions for future work.

2: General concepts of the ATM routing problem and related work

In the dynamic environment of the ATM networks, where the traffic load and the network topology change significantly over the time, the use of a routing algorithm able to adapt to traffic changes is mandatory. As it is reported in [3], the goal of this algorithm should not be the optimization of the delay or the route distance of a single connection, but instead, the global optimization of the network performance. Specifically, since the CAC algorithm is responsible for deciding whether the requested QoS requirements can be guaranteed or not, the main target of the routing algorithm should be the minimization of the call blocking rate (which implies maximization of the network throughput). For this purpose, it should try to maintain the quality of the offered services at the routes to acceptable levels as much as possible while employing efficiently the network resources, because otherwise new call requests will be rejected by the CAC. Thus, the routing algorithm should co-operate with CAC in order to be QoS-oriented.

Moreover, the average call set-up time should be minimized and consequently, the average execution time, which is required by the routing algorithm to select a route, should be minimized too. This is an important feature that a routing algorithm should have, since it preserves the advantages that the high-speed trunks offer, without affecting the delay-sensitive calls. The complexity and the computation overhead should be minimized too, in order to avoid potential implementation and deployment bottlenecks.

The most classical routing algorithm found in the literature is the Shortest-Path. This algorithm chooses the route with the least cost. Least cost can be expressed in terms of hops (Minimum Hop algorithm), congestion (Least Loaded algorithm), delay, etc. Whenever the shortest-path route is not available, alternate routes are tried in order of preference. The most known algorithms used to find the shortest-path route are Bellman-Ford's, Dijkstra's, Floyd-Warshall's [5] and Fords-Fulkerson's [6]. The shortest-path route can either be computed dynamically, on demand, or it can be obtained by a routing table maintained at the source nodes. In the second case, a set of possible routes for every possible destination is computed using one of these algorithms, or one of the algorithms described in [8, 9]. However, the tables must be updated according to changes at the network topology and the traffic conditions. This can be done either periodically (for example according to a pre-specified time interval) or whenever a change occurs (after a link failure, when a new link is added to the network, etc.).

Furthermore, as it has been discussed in [4], routing based on delay metrics only cannot avoid network congestion and thus it is unsuitable for the ATM networks. On the other hand, as it has been shown in many papers in the literature, the Shortest Path algorithm based on minimum-hop count (Minimum Hop algorithm, also known as Alternate-Path) is very effective, especially when the traffic load increases, because it does not consume unnecessary resources. On the other hand, the Least Loaded algorithm (which tends to use the least congested route and thus to balance the traffic load) appears to be less efficient, especially as the traffic increases and the waste of network resources becomes crucial. Routing based on congestion only can result in oscillations, while the fact that it does not take into consideration the length of the route, in terms of number of hops, can lead to significant waste of network resources. So, at high loads load balancing should be reduced so as to exploit them better. However, at light loads alternate routes should also be used in order to avoid premature congestion. As it is evident from the above discussion, these two objectives (minimum-hop and load balancing) are in conflict and thus, an effective compromise between them is required. Furthermore, as it is proved in [3], the problems of establishing the routes so as to minimize the reserved bandwidth for a number of calls, as well as to maximize the number of the accepted calls without overloading the network, are NP complete and hence a heuristic approach is required.

A simple variation of the Minimum Hop is the Trunk Reservation algorithm, which employs a methodology adopted from the circuit-switched networks. The purpose of this methodology, which has also been used to some interesting approaches (i.e. in [4]), is to enhance the performance of a routing algorithm in heavy loading conditions. It is usually implemented using a threshold ρ_{trunk} of the link utilization. When the expected route utilization ρ^{+}_{route} (which is defined as the maximum expected utilization of the links that comprise this route) is bigger than the ρ_{trunk}, the call is established at this route only if this is a minimum-hop one. Otherwise, (that is if it is an alternate one) another route is tried. Its effectiveness is based on the fact that at heavy loads, where the saving of network resources is very critical, the high utilized links are used only for minimum-hop routes resulting in even better usage of the network resources. Thus, premature congestion is avoided and the network throughput is increased.

Summarizing, both the minimum-hop and the trunk

reservation concept aims at the avoidance of the premature congestion of the links (VPs) that belong to minimum-hop routes. They both prevent the waste of network resources and consequently lead to maximization of the network throughput, especially at heavy loads. However, they result in a deterioration of the performance of a routing algorithm at light loads. In both cases it's behavior in terms of handling future calls is considerably affected. Thus, an effective compromise is required when a routing algorithm decides upon using them or not. Aiming at this target, the following routing algorithm is proposed.

3: The proposed routing algorithm

3.1: Designing an efficient cost metric for the routing selection

As it was explained in the previous section, a routing algorithm should generally favour the minimum-hop routes under any type of loading conditions in order to avoid waste of network resources. However, when the traffic load is light, although the algorithm should favourably select the minimum-hop routes, it should also try to balance the load effectively since there are plenty of network resources. As the network load increases, it is usually undesirable to establish a VCC using an alternate (other than the minimum-hop) route, since it would utilize more network resources and hence, in the long term it can lead to earlier blocking of calls. Thus, alternate routes should be used much more selectively decreasing load balancing. So, available network resources are exploited much better and premature congestion is avoided. The better usage of network resources results in the acceptance of more calls at heavy loads and thus, the network throughput is increased.

As it is concluded from the above comments, when a new call request occurs, the routing algorithm should take into consideration the required resources and the congestion level of each route. When they are increased, the cost of this route should be increased too. The resources that are needed for the establishment of a call are increased as the number of the hops of the candidate route is increased. Moreover, its cost should also be increased as the available bandwidth decrease and generally, as the congestion level increase. These factors that influence the suitability of a route should be combined in a single relation efficiently in order to express the cost of the route. The cost function should achieve an effective trade-off between the minimum-hop and the least loaded concepts, meeting the requirements discussed above, whereas complicated procedures should be avoided. In order to achieve these objectives for each link we weight the required additional bandwidth that it should be reserved for the establishment of the call at this link in conjunction with the expected link's utilization. Thus, the cost of link i is defined as:

$$c_i = \rho_i^+ (W_i^+ - W_i)$$

where W_i is the already allocated (used) equivalent bandwidth at link i, ρ_i^+ and W_i^+ the expected link utilization and the expected equivalent bandwidth respectively in case that the new call request will be accepted. Then, adding the costs of each link that belong to the candidate route, we implicitly take into consideration the resources that are required in terms of the number of the hops of this route. Hence, the cost c^j of the route j is defined as:

$$c^j = \sum_{i \in j} [\rho_i^+ (W_i^+ - W_i)] \quad (1)$$

The difference $W_i^+ - W_i$ expresses the additional equivalent bandwidth that is required to establish the new call. This is not necessary equal with the equivalent bandwidth W_r that corresponds to the new call in case that the last one was considered independently of the already established calls. In fact, due to statistical multiplexing it generally holds:

$$W_i^+ \leq W_i + W_r \quad [10]$$

Observing equation (1), it can be noticed that the cost c^j of the route j increases as:

- The required additional bandwidth for establishing the new call increases.
- The congestion level of the links (expressed by their utilization factor) that comprise a specific route increases.
- The number of the hops of the particular route increases (since the number of the addenda that comprise the sum increases).

The above statements seem quite natural taking into account the above discussion. Thus, the proposed cost function combines the number of the hops (implicitly), the required equivalent bandwidth and the congestion level of the routes.

The values of ρ_i^+ and W_i^+ should be computed on a call set-up basis and they should be based on the traffic characteristics of the sources and not on real-time traffic measurements. The use of real-time measurements is not considered a good policy for preventing cell losses in the near future [4]. The high variations of the traffic at the VPs caused by the statistical multiplexing of Variable Bit Rate (VBR) sources can lead to fluctuations in the traffic measurements and consequently to inaccuracies as well as to oscillations as far as the selection of a route is concerned.

3.2: Linear employment of the Trunk Reservation concept

As it was explained in the previous section, the trunk reservation concept improves considerably the performance of a routing algorithm at heavy loads, preventing the use of the VPs by alternate routes when the traffic load increases. However, it affects negatively its performance at moderate and at light loads. As the value of the threshold ρ_{trunk} decrease, the performance of any routing algorithm that uses this concept is improved at heavy load and decrease at light load, and the contrary. That is because the smaller ρ_{trunk} blocks alternate routes earlier, resulting in an increased call blocking rate at light load (since when the minimum-hop routes are blocked, alternate routes cannot be used). However, when the alternate routes are blocked, there are more available network resources, which lead to an increased call acceptance rate at heavy load. The big difference between the performance of an algorithm that employs this concept at these two extreme conditions is due to the fact that, after the threshold ρ_{trunk} the behaviour of the routing algorithm diversifies sharply. Aiming at a better overall performance and at a balance of the behaviour between these two extremes, it is proposed that there should not be a crisp threshold that activates the trunk reservation concept, but instead, it should be activated smoothly. Specifically, it is proposed that after the threshold ρ_{trunk} the trunk reservation should be employed with a linear distributed probability that increases as the expected utilization of the route ρ^{+}_{route} increases. Specifically, this probability should be equal to zero below a value β of the ρ^{+}_{route}, while after that it should be increased linearly up to a point α (α>β) where the probability should take its maximum value (equal to 1). So, when $\rho^{+}_{route} \geq \alpha$ the trunk reservation concept should always be applied. The line which is determined by the points (β , 0) and (α , 1) is defined by the equation:

$$P = \frac{1}{\alpha - \beta}(\rho_{route} - \beta)$$

According to this probability the trunk reservation concept is applied by the proposed routing algorithm.

3.3: The Linear Trunk Weighted Shortest Path (LTWSP) algorithm

In order to minimize the processing required at the intermediate nodes, satisfying one of the main targets of the ATM networks, a call-level execution of the routing algorithm at the source nodes is proposed (source-routing).

In summary, the following on-line algorithm is defined:

When a new call request occurs:

1. For each candidate route estimate W_i^{+} and ρ_i^{+} of each link according to the CAC algorithm that is used.
2. Compute the cost c^j of each route j using equation (1).
3. Select the route with the minimum cost.
4. Apply the trunk reservation concept to the selected route with probability:

$$P_r = \begin{cases} 0, \text{ when } \rho_{route} < \beta \\ \frac{1}{\alpha - \beta}(\rho_{route} - \beta), \text{ when } \beta \leq \rho_{route} \leq \alpha \\ 1, \text{ when } \rho_{route} > \alpha \end{cases}$$

4.1. IF trunk reservation concept is applied.

IF the route is accepted by the CAC AND the route is a minimum-hop one establish the call.

ELSE select the route with the next minimum cost and run again step 4.

4.2. IF the trunk reservation concept is not applied.

IF the route is accepted by the CAC, establish the call

ELSE select the route with the next minimum cost and run again step 4.

5. IF all the routes have been rejected, the incoming call is blocked.

The computation and the selection of a route can be made either on-line by using one of the algorithms which were mentioned in section 2, or by using pre-computed routes included in a routing table that is maintained at each source node, as described in the same section. Nevertheless, a fully end-to-end adaptive source-routing algorithm is provided which does not suffer from looping and it is suitable for connection-oriented high-speed networks.

4: Simulation study

The confidence intervals of the measurements are 95% constructed with the method of independent replications. For the comparative study, the Least Loaded (LL), the Minimum Hop Only (MHO), the Minimum Hop

(MH), the Trunk Reservation (TR) and the Multi-Path (MUL) algorithm were used. A brief review of them can be found in [4]. In addition to these, the proposed algorithm was also compared with a shortest-path algorithm that uses the cost metric of equation (1) without employing the Trunk Reservation concept (Weighted Shortest-Path algorithm – WSP). Moreover, it was compared with a shortest-path algorithm that uses the same metric but it also applies the Trunk Reservation concept using a crisp threshold ρ_{trunk} just like RES and MUL algorithm do (Trunk Weighted Shortest-Path algorithm – TWSP) and not linearly as the proposed algorithm. The purpose of these last comparisons is to make clear the advantages of both the proposed cost metric and the linear employment of the Trunk Reservation concept.

As a network model the one of figure 1 was used, which enabled us to run the simulator at a cell basis, just like in [4]. The enlarging of the network size or the increase in the link speed was almost impossible since excessive computation time was required. On the other hand, although the network model that was used seems very simple for the representation of a real physical ATM network, it can be corresponded to a VP-sub-network that has been assigned to a particular traffic class. This results in homogeneous traffic and in an employment of the benefits described in the introduction. In that case the speed of the links corresponds to the bandwidth allocated to each VP, while each node corresponds to a VP terminating point. Consequently, both the network size and the speed of the links can be justified. Furthermore, bursty sources were assumed with exponentially burst inter-arrival time and constant burst size. The duration of an established call and the inter-arrival time of new call requests were also assumed to be exponentially distributed (Poisson arrival process). The network and traffic parameters are summarized in table 1. The propagation delay from a host to its neighbouring VP node, the cell processing time at switches and at hosts were assumed negligible, since they actually do not affect the overall comparative performance of the algorithms. Finally, output queuing was assumed, while the cells were served in accordance with the FCFS discipline.

The additional expected equivalent bandwidth required by an incoming call, for reasons of simplicity of our study, was estimated by the equation:

$$W_i^+ - W_i = P\frac{T_{ON}}{T_{ON} + T_{OFF}}$$

where P is the peak rate of the source, T_{ON} and T_{OFF} the average active and idle time respectively. The same expression normalized by the capacity of link i C_i is added to the current link utilization to estimate the expected link utilization, that is,

$$\rho_i^+ = \rho_i + \frac{P}{C_i}\frac{T_{ON}}{T_{ON} + T_{OFF}}$$

For CAC purposes, the simple algorithm used in [4] was employed. Specifically, a threshold of route utilization is specified such that, an incoming call is accepted as long as the ρ_{route}^+ remains lower than this threshold. Following [4] we assume that the threshold is 70%. Doing so, reliable statistics for the number of dropped cells can be obtained. The CAC algorithm, although very simple for a real ATM network, it does not affect the comparative performance study of the routing algorithms.

The utilization threshold ρ_{trunk} (which is used by the algorithms TR, MUL and TWSP) is set to 0.65, just like in [4]. The same value was used for the constant β of the LTWSP, while the constant α was tested for several values in the interval (0.65, 0.7]. The value 0.7 defines the maximum value of α because (as it was mentioned above) it is the CAC threshold. The best overall performance of the LTWSP algorithm was observed when α=0.66.

The compared routing algorithms were examined under various unbalanced traffic loads, which fully cover all the possible ranges of network load. At light load conditions two cases were examined with call arrival rates λ_I and λ_{II} (table 2). At moderate load conditions, the call arrival rates were assumed to be λ_{III}=1.5λ and λ_{IV}= 2.25λ_I, while at heavy load conditions call arrival rates become λ_V=4.5λ_I and λ_{VI}=6λ_I. Moreover, the algorithms were examined under time varying traffic loads. In this case it was assumed that the call arrival rate at each source node changes every 10 sec and that its value is uniformly distributed in the interval [0, λ_{VI}].

The algorithms were tested using the same stream of random numbers for the call requests so as to allow for a fair comparison and eliminate possible discrepancies due to differences in arrival patterns. The statistics that they were gathered regarded the number of the blocked calls and the network throughput in terms of the number of the cells that they were transmitted successfully (reached their destination node). We do not present the numerical results in percentage terms so as to observe more easily and accurately the differences between the performance of the examined routing algorithms. This does not introduce any inaccuracies because, as it was explained above, the same stream of random numbers was used.

Table 3 shows the performance of the eight tested routing algorithms in terms of the average number of the total blocked calls under the tested loading conditions. Based on these numerical results, the following observations can be made:

- The WSP shows a better performance than the MH

algorithm and the LL algorithm (the ones that does not use the trunk reservation concept) in five out of the seven examined loading scenarios. This means that the metric cost expressed by equation (1) is more efficient than the minimum-hop and the least loaded metric costs.

- Similarly, the TWSP exhibits a better performance than the TR and the MUL, the other two algorithms that uses the trunk reservation concept in exactly the same way as the TWSP does, in five out of the seven examined loading scenarios.
- Generally, the algorithms that uses the trunk reservation concept (TR, TWSP, MUL) exhibit better performance than the ones that do not use it (WSP, MH, LL), especially at moderate and at high loads. This observation demonstrates the effectiveness of the trunk reservation concept.
- The LTWSP achieves a better compromise than the algorithms mentioned above between light and heavy loads. Specifically, it exhibits the least blocked calls in five out of the seven examined loading scenarios and less blocked calls than the already known algorithms (MUL, MHO, TR, MH, LL) in six out of the seven cases. The only case that one of the already known algorithms blocks less calls than the LTWSP is the MH algorithm under light loading conditions (when the arrival rate is λ_1).

A general conclusion obtained by the above observations is that, although in some cases the differences between the performance of the routing algorithms which perform better in a single loading scenario are very slight, the performance of the LTWSP algorithm is always the best (or the second best) irrespective of the loading conditions. On the contrary, the performance of the other algorithms depends on the loading conditions considerably; thus, in some cases exhibit a very good one, while in some others exhibit one of the worst or even the worst. The efficiency of the LTWSP in comparison with the one of the other algorithms can be clearly observed at time varying loads, which indicates the case of the traffic at a real network.

We also measured the cells that arrive to their respective destination node, which can be considered as a metric of the throughput. The numerical results are presented in table 4. As it can be observed, the LTWSP exhibits the higher throughput in five out of the seven examined scenarios, while in all cases it achieves a higher throughput than the known routing algorithms. Consequently, it does not only minimize the number of the blocked calls, but besides this it maximizes the number of the cells that are transmitted successfully. This means that the cells generated by the additional accepted calls are not dropped due to congestion, which implies an efficient use of the network resources. Moreover, even in the first case (λ_1) that MH blocks 14,319.3-14,028.6=290.7 less calls than the LTWSP, which means that it generates 290.7x62.5=18,168.75 more cells, 16,455,935-16,412,613=43,322 less cells arrive to their destination. Consequently, even in this case the performance of the LTWSP is better than the one of the MH.

So, the LTWSP does not only minimize the number of blocked calls, but also it maximizes the number of cells transmitted successfully (achieving a higher throughput) under various loading scenarios. Thus, it does not only routes more calls than the other algorithms, but also the additional transmitted cells are not dropped due to congestion; on the contrary, they arrive successfully to their destination. This implies that LTWSP exploits much better the network resources irrespective of the traffic conditions.

5: Implementation and deployment considerations

In terms of implementation, the proposed algorithm is based on a metric information of the already allocated equivalent bandwidth and the link utilization for each link that belongs to a possible route.

In that sense the proposed algorithm should be combined with a network topology and link-state distribution mechanism responsible for delivering the required information to the source nodes where the routing algorithm is executed. The P-NNI routing protocol of the ATM-Forum includes topology information distribution mechanisms across switching elements of an ATM network. In addition to this, hierarchy mechanisms are included, which are used for scalability reasons, mainly by providing an aggregated view of clusters of switching elements (called peer-groups). A network that supports the P-NNI protocol provides the following services to its nodes:

Each node maintains a detailed topology database about all the other nodes of the same peer-group. Moreover, each node maintains a global view of the rest of the network (out of the peer group), but only aggregated topology information in terms of sub-networks. This view depends on the hierarchical clustering of the switching systems in peer-groups, by the network administrator.

Each node receives regularly detailed information about the link utilization of all the links of the peer group and aggregated information about other peer groups (hierarchical model).

However, the efficiency of the routing algorithm is heavily dependent on some CAC information of the nodes included in a candidate route. The importance of this information is twofold. First it is used on the estimation of ρ_i^+ and W_i^+, namely the estimated new (expected) link utilization and equivalent bandwidth respectively, in case that the new call will be accepted. Secondly, it can be used as an input to an algorithm that checks the validity of a candidate route in terms of the CAC. This functionality is particularly important since it is performed before the call set-up process is initiated. Taking into account that the CAC is performed individually by each node that belongs to a selected route during connection set-up, it is particularly important for the routing process to know a priori whether a selected route would be accepted by the individual CAC of the inter-mediate nodes. This mechanism would significantly reduce the possibility that a call would be rejected during the connection establishment procedure.

Normally, the routing algorithm requires that every switching system advertises detailed CAC information in order to produce likely to be accepted routes. However, there are two problems in this approach:

CAC parameters are not subjected to standardization between the different switching systems, so it is not possible for a routing algorithm to cope with potential specialties.

Detailed CAC information cannot be distributed to all nodes (that are responsible for running the routing algorithm) without significant network overloading.

The solution adopted by the P-NNI routing and signaling protocol is the definition of the Generic Connection Admission Control which defines a set of parameters that represents in a common and generic way the CAC status of the individual switching systems. In this way, a switching system may support the P-NNI protocol without revealing its detailed CAC parameters. Furthermore, groups of switching systems, organized in an hierarchical fashion, may provide an aggregated view of their CAC status, thus reducing the traffic load produced by advertising those parameters to all the nodes of the network. Consequently, the distribution of the CAC information of the switching elements (or clusters of them) is included within the information set of the P-NNI information distribution mechanisms, and can be used by the proposed routing algorithm in the same way as it is defined in the P-NNI's Generic CAC mechanism.

6: Conclusions and future work

In this paper, a dynamic adaptive routing algorithm was proposed suitable for homogeneous traffic in ATM networks. This heuristic algorithm, as it was shown through a simulation study, minimizes the number of the blocked calls while it also maximizes the number of the successfully transmitted cells under various loading scenarios. The cost metric that is employed although it is very simple, it achieves an efficient compromise between minimum-hop and load balancing. Its performance is enhanced from the fact that it employs the efficient trunk reservation concept according to a probability that is increased linearly as the expected load of the network increases. This results in an effective compromise of its performance between light and heavy loads as well as in an efficacious use of the network resources.

In a forthcoming paper the performance of the proposed algorithm will be examined in combination with a more efficient CAC algorithm under pre-specified values of the QoS parameters (both for cell loss and cell delay). Thus, a QoS-based integrated CAC-routing scheme will be presented suitable for ATM networks. The use of a better CAC algorithm will enable the call-level execution of the simulation and consequently, the use of a more complicated network model. Finally, a more accurate approximation of the equivalent bandwidth than the one used in this study will may lead to a more correct selection of a route and thus, to a better performance of the algorithm.

References

[1] ITU-T, Draft Recommendation I.371: "Traffic Control and Congestion Control in B-ISDN", Geneva, May 1996.

[2] ATM Forum, "Traffic Management Specification, version 4.0", April 1996.

[3] N.F. Huang, C.S. Wu, Y.J. Wu, "Some Routing Problems on Broadband ISDN" Computer Networks and ISDN systems 27, 1994, pp. 101-116.

[4] S. Bahk, M. El Zarki, "Congestion Control Based Dynamic Routing in ATM Networks", Computer Communications, vol.17, no.12, December 1994.

[5] D. Bertsekas, R. Gallager, "Data Networks", Prentice-Hall, 1987.

[6] L. Ford, D. Fulkerson, "Flows in Networks", Princeton: Princeton University Press, 1962.

[7] J. Bae, T. Suda, R. Simha, "Analysis of a Finite Buffer Queue With Heterogeneous Markov Modulated Arrival Process: A study of the Effects of Traffic Burstiness on Individual Packet Loss", IEEE INFOCOM'92, pp.219-230.

[8] D.Shier, "On Algorithms for Finding the k Shortest Paths in a Network", Netwoks, vol.9, 1979.

[9] D.Topkis, "A k Shortest Path Algorithm for Adaptive Routing in Communications Networks", IEEE Trans. On Communications, vol.36, no.7, July 1988.

[10] R.Guerin, H.Ahmadi, M.Naghshineh, "Equivalent capacity and its applications in high-speed networks", IEEE J-SAC, vol.9, no 7, pp.968-981, Sept. 1991.

Link Rate	Link Propagation Delay	Buffer Size at Host	Buffer Size at Switch
10.6 Mbps	10 msec	Infinite	32 cells
Peak rate	**Mean rate**	**Burst Duration**	**Average Call duration**
10.6 Mbps	106 Kbps	400 μsec	0.25 sec

Table 1: Traffic and network parameters

From Nodes	To nodes 1		2		3		4		5	
	λ_I	λ_{II}	λ_I	λ_{II}	λ_I	λ_{II}	λ_I	λ_{II}	λ_I	λ_{II}
1	X	X	80	100	160	200	80	100	80	100
2	80	100	X	X	160	200	80	100	80	100
3	80	100	80	100	X	X	160	200	160	200
4	80	100	80	100	80	100	X	X	80	100
5	80	100	80	100	80	100	80	100	X	X

Table 2: Offered call arrival rates (in calls/second) for unbalanced light loading condition.

	Unbalanced light load		Unbalanced moderate load		Unbalanced heavy load		Varying load
Arrival rate λ	λ_I	λ_{II}	λ_{III}	λ_{IV}	λ_V	λ_{VI}	
WSP	13,621.2 ± 293.367	64,278 ± 321.052	127,992 ± 379.404	331,908 ± 581.531	952,242 ± 591.982	1.36989e+06 ± 687.982	545,375.6 ± 14,609.6
TWSP	14,833.5 ± 273.972	55,202.2 ± 300.539	106,492 ± 264.891	286,186 ± 568.028	902,540 ± 580.094	1.3241e+06 ± 806.274	506,102.1 ± 13,464.7
LTWSP	14,319.3 ± 267.666	54,902.6 ± 282.935	106,349 ± 284.478	286,210 ± 697.475	902,348 ± 567.251	1.32382e+06 ±922.456	505,757.0556 ±13,871.6
MUL	15,183.8 ± 285.411	56,582.6 ± 228.13	107,765 ± 336.856	286,884 ± 450.08	902,574 ± 692.865	1.32404e+06 ± 742.59	507,176.5093 ±14,527.8
MHO	24,841.7 ± 288.367	65,203.6 ± 275.011	113,742 ± 191.715	287,223 ± 481.458	902,366 ± 769.845	1.32424e+06 ± 916.311	509,946 ±13,113
TR	14,877.6 ± 250.817	56,454.1 ± 270.701	107,690 ± 258.283	286,892 ± 509.639	902,443 ± 612.341	1.32425e+06 ± 757.497	507,003.0678 ±14,889.6
MH	14,028.6 ± 324.682	65,352.6 ± 242.426	129,430 ± 364.343	287,223 ± 481.458	952,251 ± 769.873	1.3701e+06 ± 701.293	545,844.9062 ±14,403.6
LL	19,044.7 ± 302.945	72,791.2 ± 310.504	135,114 ± 405.699	335,045 ± 582.632	902,574 ± 692.865	1.37026e+06 ± 689.175	546,463.1416 ±15,319.4

Table 3: Performance of the routing algorithms in terms of the average number of the total blocked calls under various unbalanced loading conditions.

Arrival rate λ	Unbalanced light load		Unbalanced moderate load		Unbalanced heavy load		Varying load
	λ_I	λ_{II}	λ_{III}	λ_{IV}	λ_V	λ_{VI}	
WSP	16,447,047	17,494,148	17,871,478	18,475,916	20,058,640	20,893,665.15	18,304,104
TWSP	16,436,363	18,179,502	19,322,510	21,272,258	22,999,341	23,602,723.31	20,728,499
LTWSP	16,455,935	18,183,712	19,316,804	21,262,603	23,013,681	23,615,925.45	20,737,569
MUL	16,379,400	18,082,362	19,244,898	21,233,806	22,999,574	23,604,825.72	20,637,639
MHO	15,892,766	17,665,950	18,972,454	21,236,135	23,012,789	23,592,380.68	20,534,776
TR	16,421,713	18,101,662	19,251,471	21,232,505	23,010,407	23,595,012.64	20,641,691
MH	16,412,613	17,426,069	17,787,730	21,092,533	20,054,695	20,881,098.00	18,277,294
LL	16,025,948	16,941,423	17,433,412	18,292,252	22,951,842	20,872,644.78	18,224,778

Table 4: Performance of the routing algorithms in terms of the number of the successfully transmitted cells under various unbalanced loading conditions.

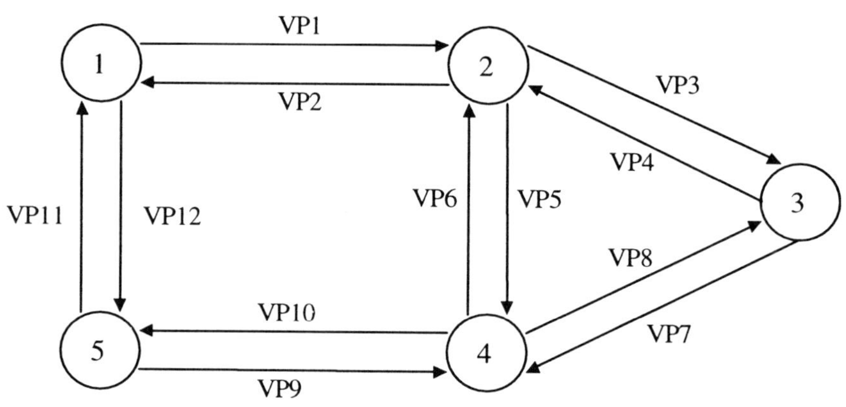

Figure 1: The Five-node network used in the simulation.

RISP: Address Resolution Protocol in Network Layer

N. Oguchi* Y.-M. Chen** J. Ogawa* T. Tsuruoka* T. Taniguchi** S. Nojima*

*Fujitsu Laboratories Ltd.
1-1, Kamikodanaka 4-Chome, Nakahara-ku, Kawasaki, 211-88, Japan
oguchi@flab.fujitsu.co.jp

**Fujitsu Laboratories of America, Inc.
595 Lawrence Expressway, Sunnyvale, California 94086, USA
ychen@fla.fujitsu.com

Abstract

Conventionally, the network layer (such as IP) to link layer (such as Ethernet and ATM) address translation is done in the link layer. This approach requires link technology-specific solutions such as ARP for Ethernet, and ATMARP or NHRP for ATM. By moving the address resolution function from link layer to network layer, this paper proposes a unified address resolution scheme applicable to current and future network technologies. For NBMA (Non-Broadcast Multi-Access) networks, this scheme achieves better implementation efficiency because the conventional scheme would require extra table lookups when the link layer has to consult with network-layer routing function to forward a request that cannot be resolved locally.

1. Introduction

Non-Broadcast Multiple Access (NBMA) networks such as ATM and Frame Relay have been used to transport IP data traffic by public carriers and Internet Service Providers (ISPs). This is mainly through the use of PVCs (Permanent Virtual Circuits). Recently, ATM has emerged as a LAN medium, through the SVC (Switch Virtual Circuit) service with IP running on top of it.

NBMA and broadcast networks such as the Ethernet have different transmission mechanisms. Consider conventional forwarding mechanism for IP packets. A host sends data packets in the following steps:

1. retrieving the routing table to decide the *logical interface* it should send packets to,
2. acquiring the destination data link layer address from the IP address with an address resolution mechanism, and
3. sending the packets using the frame transmission method peculiar to the underlying medium.

From the protocol stack point of view, the logical interface abstracts link layer seen by the network layer (i.e., the logical interface is the boundary between the two layers [1]). By treating address resolution as a link-layer issue, different address resolution mechanisms are prepared for Ethernet and ATM. In the case of Ethernet, ARP [2] resolves the MAC address from an IP address. In the case of ATM, ATMARP [3] or NHRP [4] resolves the ATM address from an IP address.

We think the difference between the network technologies is their frame transmission method, not necessarily the address inquiry function. For the frame transmission, Ethernet uses CSMA/CD without explicit signaling, while ATM signals a transmission path, encapsulates data frames, and then divides them into cells. Emerging network technologies such as xDSL, Cable Modem, FTTH, SONET, WDM, ... *et al* each will have its own frame transmission method. It is desirable to have a common address resolution protocol rather than inventing one for each technology.

In this paper, we show that it is possible to treat address resolution as a network-layer issue so that a common method applies to many link-layer technologies. We also provide evidence that this new approach simplifies implementation without sacrificing performance. Unlike the conventional "network" type (i.e., broadcast) logical interface for data link layer, our approach makes an abstraction of the link layer using the point-

0-8186-8810-6/98 $10.00 © 1998 IEEE

to-point logical interface. More precisely, we change the conventional IP-to-MAC and IP-to-ATM address mappings to the mapping of IP address to point-to-point logical interface. Then we map each such interface to a physical communication path to a destination host. In this way, we become able to treat any link layer in the same fashion. The performance advantage of this approach lies in the separation between address resolution and frame transmission. Address resolution can be implemented by a very efficient and robust network-layer protocol, while frame transmission can be optimized for specific link-layer technologies.

The remainder of this paper is organized as follows. In Section 2, we discuss the problem with the conventional approach to address resolution. That is, the conventional approach results in the inconvenience of requiring new address resolution protocols for new communication media. From the discussion, we extract design objectives for a new protocol. In Section 3, we present a protocol that meets the objectives. The protocol has been implemented and its performance evaluated. In Section 4, related work is cited and compared with our approach. Finally, summary of this paper as well as future work are provided in Section 5.

2. Problem statement

In this section, we provide rationale for a network-layer address resolution protocol.

2.1. Realization of address resolution

Many LAN services are based on packet broadcasting. Partitioning a network into subnetworks allows us to control broadcast traffic within its originating subnetwork. For NBMA networks, which do not have a native broadcast domain, a concept called Logical IP Subnetwork (LIS) was proposed in [3]. A LIS is a group of hosts functioning as a logical subnetwork, in the sense that they can send packets directly to each other. In this "classical" approach, hosts that belong to different LISs have to communicate via routers, although they can be connected directly via the link-layer switching devices such as ATM switches.

To set up a direct path between hosts, their NBMA addresses are required because these addresses are the entities communicated between link-layer devices to configure individual local switching decisions to form the end-to-end path. One can view an IP address as a *logical* address, that facilitates the management of a large number of network devices, while the corresponding data link layer address as the *physical* address used by physical devices to set up connection paths.

For NBMA networks to support the conventional LAN services and manageability, the concept of LIS is indeed indispensable. However, there are also benefits for not limiting the IP-to-NBMA address translation within a LIS. For example, direct end-to-end switched paths (a.k.a. *shortcut paths*) that cut across LIS boundaries can be used. While the LIS concept mandates dividing the NBMA network into LISs and using the routers located at LIS boundaries to provide data paths between each pair of stations, direct paths (that bypass router intervention in data forwarding) provide the benefit of high-speed and large-capacity data. A direct-path communication is also convenient for QoS guarantees because there is no concentration of traffic on routers.

Taking this view, a challenge remains for us is for a host to resolve the NBMA address for a destination outside the LIS boundary. However, when two devices are located in different LISs, there is no direct communication path for them to exchange data link layer addresses. The only way is to involve network-layer routing to communicate the address information. Therefore, address resolution (conventionally treated as a link-layer issue) requires the service of network-layer routing for sending address inquiry packets.

2.2. Abstraction of frame transmission interface

NBMA and legacy broadcast networks differ in IP data transmission mechanism. Consider a host A sending IP data packets destined for an IP address B. In a legacy broadcast network, the data link layer address of B is retrieved from an *address translation table* maintained at host A. The retrieval is done using IP address B as an index to the table. Afterwards, the data link layer address is put in the header of each packet before transmitting it on the communication medium. Now, change the setting to an NBMA network. The data link layer address (e.g., ATM address) of B is also acquired from an address translation table. However, here host A first *signals* [5, 6, 7] to make a direct path to B using its data-link address. After that the data packets are sent along this path. Note that although the mechanism for transmitting IP packets over a data-link medium is different between a broadcast network and an NBMA network, the need for an address translation table remains the same.

It is expected that as each new communication medium emerges, it will be necessary to equip it with the support of IP communication. It would be desirable to avoid individually developing address resolution mechanism, in addition to the media-dependent frame transmission mechanism, for each new medium. Note that address resolution mechanism can be considered as being composed of the management of the address translation table and an address inquiring function. We have shown that the management of the translation table is media-independent. The remaining task for us is to design an address inquiry mechanism that is media-independent, too.

A reasonable approach would be to make an abstraction of the frame transmission mechanism, so that address inquiry can access its service the same way for different communication media. The abstraction would require separating address resolution and frame transmission mechanisms into two protocol layers where the address resolution mechanism resides in the upper layer.

2.3. Implementation considerations

From the perspective of efficiency in protocol implementation, the conventional broadcast type logical interface fails to accommodate new communication media. The interface is used to abstract a physical medium for accessing multiple hosts on the same subnetwork. Since multiple destination hosts share an interface, to send an IP packet to a specific host, address translation table is used the following way. First, routing table entry for the IP destination is retrieved, which determines the logical interface for the packet. Second, the packet is passed to the interface and subsequently enters the link layer. In the link layer, the data-link layer address for the packet is acquired from the address translation table, using the host IP address as the index to the table. If there is no entry in the table for the packet, link-layer address resolution protocol is invoked.

The continued use of this interface for NBMA networks imposes challenges. Whenever there is no entry in the address translation table, approaches such as ATMARP and NHRP require that the source host sends an inquiry to address resolution servers in the NBMA network. The host can communicate directly with such a server because there is at least one server in each LIS and the host is configured with the data-link layer address of the server. Since the inquiry is sent from the link layer, the address resolution function looks as if it resided only in the data-link layer. However, to use direct paths exceeding the LIS boundary, this approach dictates an NBMA address resolution protocol such as NHRP that requires implementation extending over both network and data-link layers. This results in poor portability.

Consider the case where an address inquiry packet has to be sent beyond a LIS. To reach a server that can answer the inquiry, the inquirer has to check its routing table to decide which first-hop router to forward the inquiry packet. In other words, the inquiry forwarding decision cannot be made until routing table has been retrieved. Consider the example in Figure 1. Before the source host can send inquiry about the NBMA address of the destination host, its link-layer address resolution module has to consult with network-layer routing table to check whether Path 1 or 2 should be the one to send the inquiry packet. Therefore, using this conventional approach, the operation of address inquiry requires processing extended over two layers. Even worse, the link-layer inquiry mechanism requires service from its upper layer, which breaks the principle of protocol layering. This motivates our design of an inquiry protocol that allows implementation in a single layer.

2.4. Protocol design goal

In summary:

1. To achieve efficient IP communication over various data-link technologies including NBMA networks, inter-LIS address resolution is required.
2. Abstraction of frame transmission mechanisms is necessary so that address inquiry mechanism does not depend on the type of a data-link layer.
3. It is preferable to compose the address inquiry function in a single layer for better portability.

This paper outlines a solution to achieve these objectives.

3. The RISP system

We propose using a network-layer address resolution protocol, such as the Responder Initiated Shortcut Path (RISP) protocol to be described in this section, as the solution to the problem defined in the previous section. The RISP protocol enables direct paths that do not route packets through the routers connecting source and destination LISs. It also facilitates address resolution for an ATM network that is configured into multiple LISs.

3.1. Outline of system operation

Figure 2 illustrates the concept of RISP. It shows an ATM network composed of three LISs, and the state where the source host (Requester) in LIS-a tries to

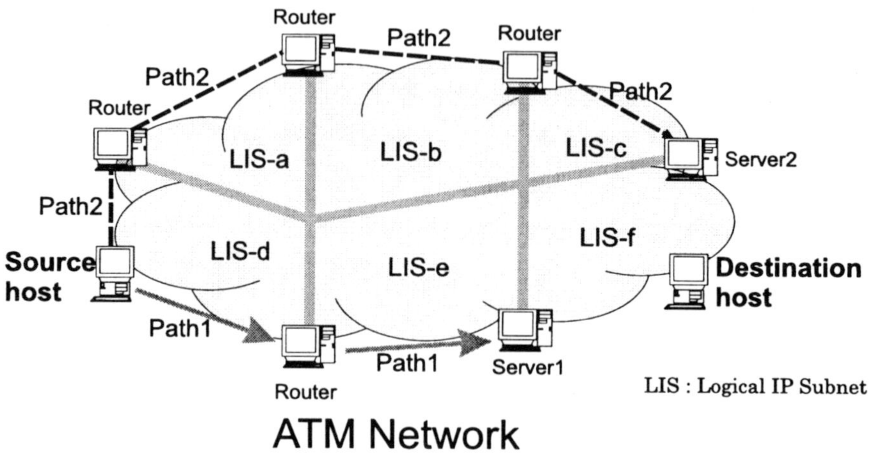

Figure 1. Network-layer routing providing service to address resolution

communicate with the destination host (Responder) in LIS-c. There are routers properly arranged to relay packets between each neighboring pair of LISs. Also, there has not yet been a direct path between the two hosts.

When there is need for the source host to send IP packets to the destination host through a direct path, the source host composes an inquiry packet, called the *Callback Request* packet,[1] and becomes a *requester*. The source host sends the packet to the destination host putting its own ATM address in the packet. This inquiry packet is relayed by the routers between LIS-a and c, and transmitted to the destination host (Step 1 in Figure 2). End-to-end address resolution and direct path setup are done in one shot by (*i*) performing an ATM signaling at the destination host (Step 2 in the figure), and (*ii*) sending the Callback Reply packet along this new path (Step 3 in the figure). At this moment, the destination host becomes the *responder* for the inquiry. After the requester receives the reply, it can start sending IP packets along this direct path (Step 4 in the figure). For manageability, only the requester is allowed to use the shortcut VC for data packets; the responder is not allowed unless itself first becomes a requester to send Callback Request.

While the usual way of responder signaling is preferred for optimized performance, an option is provided in RISP to allow requester signaling, which may be required by certain applications. One can set the option in the Callback Request message to indicate that the requester wants to signal the VC itself. In this case, Callback Reply will be sent back hop-by-hop from the responder. Upon receiving the reply, the requester can signal for the VC.

The discussion so far assumes that both the source and destination hosts are attached to the ATM network. In practice, RISP can be applied to situations where either or both hosts are not attached to the ATM network but connected to it via LANs. Then, ingress and egress routers would take the roles of source and destination hosts, respectively.

3.2. Internal operation at a host

To verify that the protocol indeed works in practice, we implemented it on UNIX OS, and constructed an end-to-end system composed of ATM switches, PC routers and RISP hosts (a *RISP host* refers to a host computer where RISP is implemented). Figure 3 shows the functional diagram of the software implemented in a RISP host. Not only functional blocks but also message flows are illustrated in the figure. The functional blocks can be roughly divided into three groups: 1) residing type (daemon) processes, 2) additional operations defined in the kernel, and 3) a management command program. Subsequently we will describe the three groups individually.

Daemon processes: The issuing and handling of the RISP protocol messages is implemented as a residing type process `rispd` in the user space to ease the job of prototyping (This implementation strategy was first adopted in [8]). The process is also responsible for the mapping of IP addresses to their

[1] RISP protocol uses similar packet formats as NHRP, so that authentication mechanism developed for NHRP might also be applicable to RISP. Moreover, it seems possible to introduce firewall in a RISP system by placing the firewall function in one of the intermediate routers. These items are for further study.

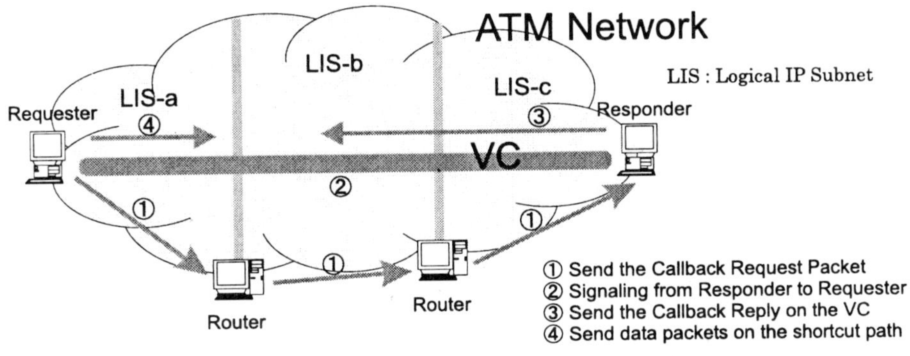

Figure 2. Basic steps of thc RISP operation

corresponding VCs. In addition to `rispd`, process `ilmid` acquires ATM address information from the ATM switch where the host is attached, and process `ATMsigd` creates and tears down SVCs based on the request from `rispd`.

Kernel: Two sockets are created to facilitate the communication between `rispd` and kernel. Upon receiving an IP or RISP packet from any socket at the "IP-forward" module, the kernel retrieves the proper entry from routing table, using destination IP address as index. If the entry has a link to VC table, meaning that a direct path exists for the IP address, the packet will be forwarded to the VC retrieved from the VC table. Otherwise, the packet is forwarded to the interface as indicated by the interface table (IF table). In addition, if the packet is IP, `rispd` is notified to determine whether a Callback Request should be issued for this IP address. Now, consider the receiving of packets. Upon receiving a LLC/SNAP-encapsulated frame from ATM driver at the "IP/RISP packet dispatcher" module, it passes the packet up to `rispd` through the SVC socket if the packet is a RISP protocol packet, or otherwise (i.e., an IP packet) to an appropriate application through the BSD socket.

Management command program: It is a user interface for accessing `rispd`.

We also made modifications to the structure of the routing table (in the network layer). In the routing table, there are three kinds of entries. Two are conventional – the network routes and host routes. A network route represents the path to a certain subnetwork. A host route identifies the path to a specific host. The third kind, called *direct host routes*, is an addition by RISP. A direct host route represents a path directly attached to a destination host in another LIS, not going through transit routers. Each routing table entry (network route, host route, or direct host route) is attached with an information piece called *output interface*. The output interface identifies the logical interface tied to the entry. Recall that logical interface is the interface between network layer and data-link layer. In Unix, there are two kinds of logical interfaces. One is the broadcast-type interface, which assumes many hosts connected to the interface. Ethernet interface is an example. The other is the point-to-point interface, which assumes that exactly one host is connected to the interface. A good example is the interface for a dial-up connection. In a RISP host, one point-to-point interface is allocated for each VC terminated at the host. Therefore, when a direct path (VC) is created and corresponds to a direct host route, the host allocates a new point-to-point interface for this path.

The possible processing flows for a host to send an IP packet are illustrated in Figure 4.

1. In its normal state, each RISP host maintains a VC to a router in each LIS where the host belongs. We call this router the *designated router* for the host in the LIS. The host allocates a point-to-point logical interface for the VC, and a routing table entry for the router. This enables the host to reach the network through the router. The router should also register the host to its routing table in order to forward packets destined for the host.

2. For sending IP packets, a RISP host first looks up the routing table. If it finds a "direct host route" entry for the destination IP address, it passes the packet to the logical interface represented by the routing entry.[2] In Figure 4, Flow (1) shows the

[2] In this implementation, the direct path is preferred over the

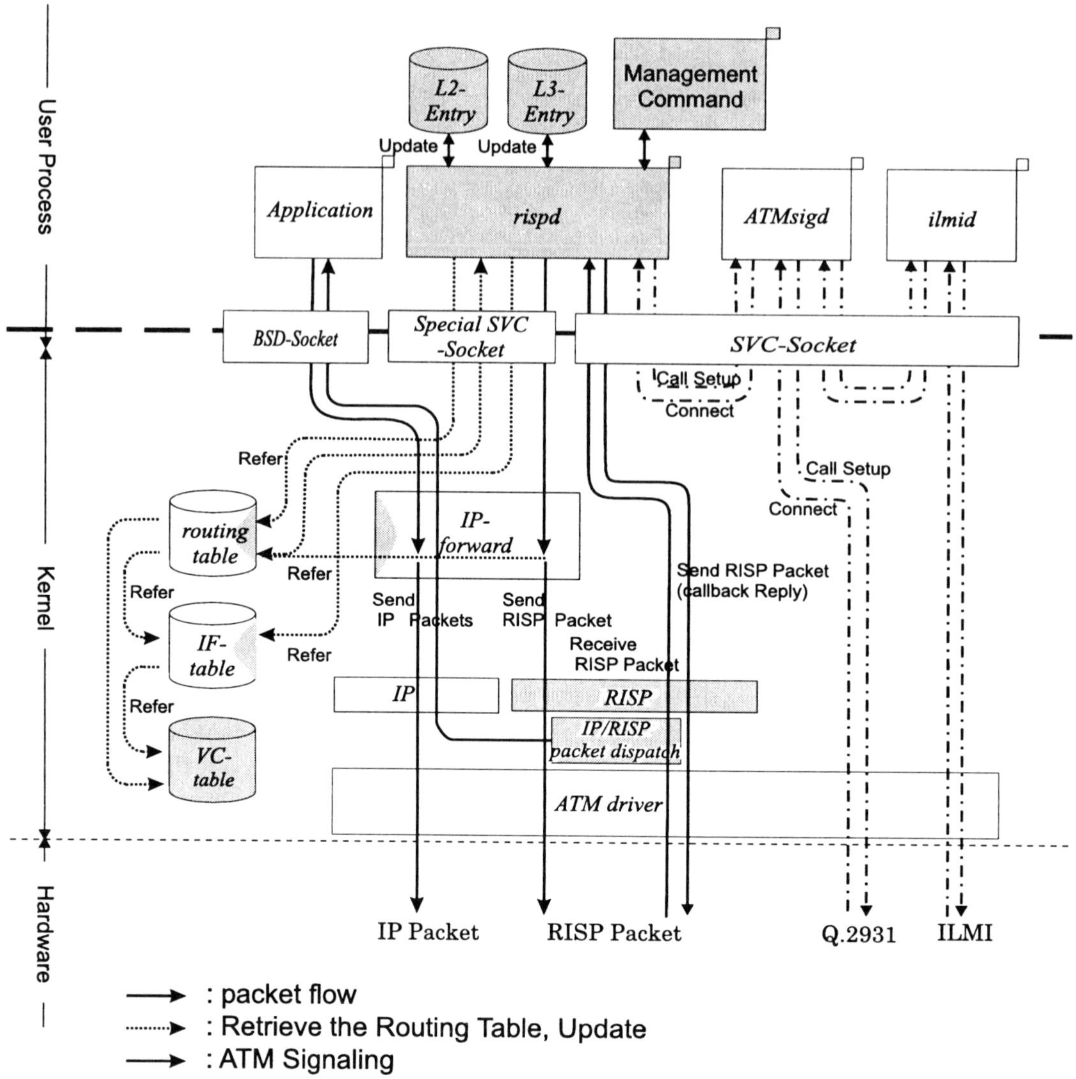

Figure 3. Software function blocks of a RISP host

case when a direct host route is found and the IP packet is sent to the corresponding logical interface #3.

3. If a direct host route entry cannot be found, network routes and host routes are searched. If one such entry matches the destination IP address, the data packet is transmitted to the logical interface indicated by the entry, and `rispd` is notified to possibly issue a Callback Request for the IP address. If a Callback Request is issued (i.e., the host becomes requester for the request), the IP address is put in the packet header, which will be used by routers to forward the packet. The most important piece of information in the packet is the own ATM address of this sending host (i.e., requester host), which will be used by the responder host to signal a VC. Naturally it is also possible to include other information items in the packet but it is beyond the scope of the paper. In Figure 4, Flow (2) shows that a Callback Request is first created and then sent to the logical interface #1 indicated by a host or network route entry in the routing table.

hop-by-hop routed path which traverses routers. This policy is not necessary and can be altered according to user preference. It is possible for a user to select case by case between the direct path and the routed path, through the use of a policy control module.

4. The routers between the source and destination

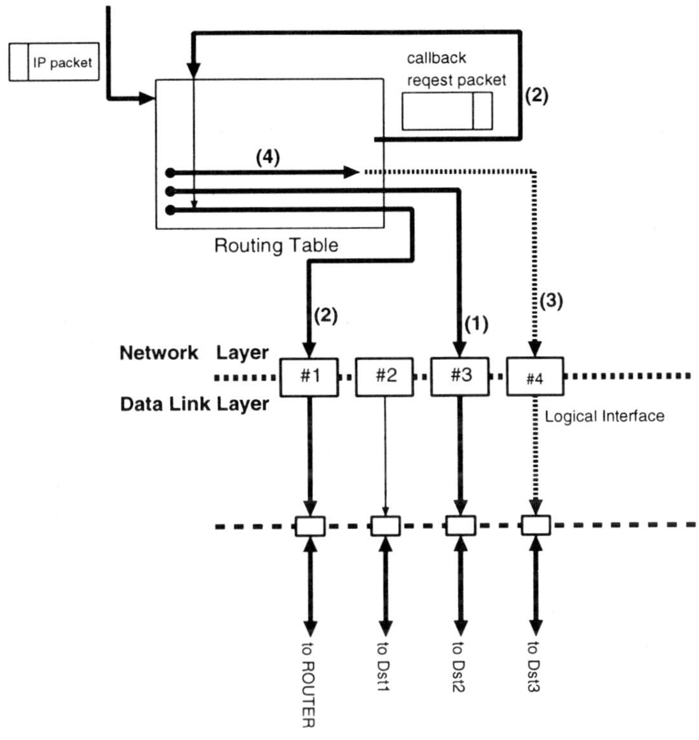

Figure 4. Packet transmission in a RISP host

LISs forward this Callback Request packet by normal IP routing. Each router uses the destination IP address written in the packet to identify the next-hop interface.

5. Upon receiving the Callback Request packet, the responder host signals a VC using the requester ATM address carried in the packet. It also composes a Callback Reply packet, and sends it back to the requester.

6. Upon accepting the VC and receiving the Callback Reply packet, the requester allocates a point-to-point logical interface to this direct path. Note that a point-to-point logical interface needs to be specified with an address pair (*own IP, destination IP*). Also note that the host has a point-to-point interface to its designated router. Let this interface be identified by pair (ip1,ip2). Then the "own IP" of the new point-to-point interface is set to ip1, and the "destination IP" is set to the IP address of the responder. After this address pair is specified, the interface is mapped to the underlying VC, and all future data packets to this interface will be transmitted on the VC to the destination host. In Figure 4, logical interface #4 is created for a new VC and Flow (3) indicates the mapping from a direct host route entry in the routing table to this new interface.

7. The host registers the direct host route entry in its routing table so that the logical interface created in the previous step can be used to transmit subsequent IP packets destined for the destination host. In the routing table, the IP address of the destination host is specified in the routing table entry information. Note that this IP address may be different from the responder IP address (which happens when the responder is the egress router for the destination host). The entry also needs to record an output interface, which is just the logical interface created for the VC.

8. Subsequent IP packets addressed to the destination host become able to use the direct VC since its corresponding logical interface is now referred by the routing table. This is illustrated as Flow (4) in Figure 4.

3.3. Network-layer address resolution

RISP accomplishes the protocol design objectives we outlined in Section 2.4, as follows.

- **End-to-end address resolution in an NBMA network:** RISP provides the functionality of end-to-end address resolution exceeding a LIS boundary. It does so by (*i*) sending the Callback Request packet to the destination host according to IP routing when a direct path to the destination host does not exist, (*ii*) making a direct path from the destination host to the source host, and (*iii*) composing and sending a callback reply packet to the source host as shown in procedures 3, 4, and 5, respectively in Section 3.2.

- **Abstraction of data link layer:** The RISP system realizes the abstraction of data link layer through the following three measures. First, it allocates a point-to-point logical interface to each direct path. Second, it abolishes the conventional way of address translation, which uses the address conversion table in data link layer. And finally, it performs the conversion from an IP address to a point-to-point interface through retrieving an entry in the network-layer routing table. Owing to this abstraction, it is expected that RISP can be applied to many link-layer technologies with different characteristics, including the emerging network technologies that we mentioned in the Introduction section.

- **Implementation only in network layer:** RISP combines the address table management and address inquiry as a single layer function in the network layer. It does so via the following two methods. First, it integrates the address mapping table, conventionally placed in the data link layer, with the routing table in the network layer. Second, it sends address inquiry packet to the next hop router using IP routing. In this way, it is fair to say that the protocol has good portability because it eliminates the complex interactions between function modules located in different protocol layers. The portability is a direct result of composing address resolution mechanism in a single layer.

3.4. Performance

Performance of RISP has been studied [9] and compared with the performance of NHRP. Note that the main difference between RISP and NHRP is that RISP (as a network-layer address resolution protocol) is universally applicable to emerging lower-layer technologies, whereas NHRP is a specific solution for MPOA. Hence the main advantage of RISP is the reduced engineering and development costs as well as time to market. However, our experiments also indicated that RISP has comparable performance.

In our testbed experiment, we tested the performance of data transfer under three configuration for an ATM network: (i) Classical IP (i.e., RFC1577), (ii) NHRP, (iii) RISP. (Implementations of (i) and (ii) were described in Ref. [8] and [10], respectively.) We measured the video frame rate when the load of an intermediate router was gradually increased by cross traffic. Under RISP and NHRP, the video remained at the same desired frame rate because the two protocols both provide direct paths to applications. However under Classical IP, video quality degraded as the load increased.

Another metric for comparison is the latency for setting up the direct paths. We configured the number of routers in the routed path from the ingress router to egress router. The setup latency in both RISP and NHRP were almost same, and the increase in latency due to extra intermediate router hops was not found to be significant, compared with the latency for ATM VC signaling alone.

Analysis showed that RISP is simpler in terms of communication and computation complexities. Details on the analysis, as well as aforementioned experiments, can be found in Appendix A.

3.5. RISP over a broadcast network

RISP can be applied to a switched Ethernet that is divided into logical subnetworks known as *Virtual LANs* or VLANs. When there is no direct host route to a destination host, a source host sends a Callback Request packet to the next hop router, with the MAC address of the source host written in the packet. Each router between the source and destination VLANs relays the packet towards the destination host, using IP routing. The destination host then sends back a Callback Reply packet to the source host using the source MAC address written in request packet. (Switched Ethernet network is able to send packets directly to their destinations only if the destination MAC addresses are written in the packets.) In the Callback Reply packet, the destination host writes its own MAC. When the source host receives the packet, it makes a point-to-point interface and keeps the destination MAC address as the interface information of this new interface. It then adds the direct host route entry to the routing table for this new interface and then it becomes able to send data packets to the destination along the direct, switched path.

4. Related work

A callback-based shortcut setup protocol called *Constrained NHRP* [11] or CNHRP has been proposed in ATM Forum. The main difference between CNHRP and RISP is the abstraction of VC at the end station. CNHRP abstracts a shortcut VC as one of the many possible paths composing a network type (i.e., broadcast LAN) interface. On the other hand, RISP treats each VC as an individual point-to-point interface.

The difference translates into better data forwarding efficiency in RISP, as follows. The procedure for a CNHRP-speaking host to send an IP packet consists of the following three steps. First, the host looks up its routing table to decide the "next hop" logical interface for the packet. Second, since the interface is of the network type, the host has to look up an IP-to-ATM address translation table (constructed from running the ATMARP or NHRP protocol) to acquire the ATM address for the "next hop" interface. Finally, the host decides which VC for this ATM address should be used to send the packet. In contrast, RISP allows a single routing table lookup to retrieve the VC suitable for the IP packet.

5. Conclusion

This work was derived from the observation that connectionless and connection-oriented networks currently require different address resolution mechanisms and different frame transmission mechanisms. In addition, there is difference between intra-LIS and inter-LIS address resolution mechanisms currently used for NBMA networks. With a goal to treat the differences with a unified method, we designed a network-layer address resolution protocol, RISP, as a proof of concept. We validated this concept by implementing the protocol and evaluating its performance.

In the future, the concept can be applied to emerging network technologies including xDSL, Cable Modem, FTTH, SONET, WDM, and others, whenever there is a need to run IP communication over these networks. Moreover, since it is possible to apply the concept of shortcut path to connection-less networks, it seems worth further investigation on applying the proposed address resolution method to a broadcast network that is divided into VLANs. Finally, extending the protocol to other types of communication paradigms such as broadcast, multicast, and QoS-guaranteed [12] communications are interesting subjects for further study.

Appendix

A. Performance of RISP

First, we tested the performance of data transfer under three configuration for the ATM network: (i) Classical IP (i.e., RFC1577), (ii) NHRP, (iii) RISP. In our testbed two Fast-Ethernet networks were connected to an ATM network. The ATM network consisted of ATM switches with 155Mbps links and was divided into two subnets (LISs). Fast-Ethernet networks also contain Ether Switches. We allocated two PC routers (266Mhz Pentium) between Fast-Ethernet networks and ATM network as the ingress and egress routers. In the ATM network a PC router (200Mhz Pentium) connected the two LISs, which was called the *intermediate router*. An AVI file (a 4min. 28sec. music video) stored in an Windows NT server on one of the Fast-Ethernet subnets was accessed from a Windows 95 client on the other Fast-Ethernet subnet. The intermediate router also had two Ethernet interfaces connecting itself to a traffic generator and sink. We measured the average video frame rate when the load (consisting of 512-Byte Ethernet frames) from the traffic generator was gradually increased from 4,000f/s to 15,000f/s. Under both RISP and NHRP, the video remained at the desired quality of 29.2 video frames per second. However under Classical IP, the average video frame rate degraded as the load increased.

This experiment illustrated that that both RISP and NHRP provide direct paths to applications so application performance such as delay and throughput is the same in both systems.

Another performance measurement for comparison is the latency for setting up the direct paths. To evaluate path setup latency, we used the same testbed above. We configured the number of routers in the routed path from the ingress router to egress router (the number ranged from 0 to 5, where "0" means that there is no intermediate router and so ingress and egress routers were directly connected.) Here, the setup latency is defined as the time elapsed from the time instant that the kernel at the ingress router notifies the daemon (`rispd` or `nhrpd`) that a short-cut path is needed, till the time that the daemon notifies the kernel that the shortcut path is ready for use. When measuring the latency for NHRP, we turned off the address resolution cache at NHSs so that the NHRP Resolution Request message always reached the NHS in the subnetwork of the egress router.

The setup latency in both RISP and NHRP were almost same, and the increase in latency due to extra intermediate router hops was not found to be significant, compared with the latency for ATM VC signaling alone. In Ref. [9] we showed that even if we turn the NHRP cache on, the setup latency for RISP stayed comparable with that for NHRP.

Therefore, as far as performance is concerned, the experiments demonstrated that RISP and NHRP are comparable. As mentioned in the paper, RISP is a simpler protocol, where the simplicity mainly lies in the fact that RISP requires neither special network devices to perform address resolution functions, nor overloading routers (already performance bottlenecks) with caching and address resolution functions.

To more closely examine the simplicity (or complexity) issue, we will compare RISP and NHRP in terms of 1) amount of control messages, 2) protocol overhead, and 3) protocol state machine.

1. RISP and NHRP issue the same amount of request and reply messages. Under NHRP, a request (and corresponding reply) message can possibly traverse fewer router hops, assuming server caching is effective. However, this trades message complexity for cache complexity. In our performance evaluation, we did not observe significant reduction in shortcut setup time because the dominant component of the setup time is the latency for VC signaling, which is the same in RISP and NHRP.

2. An intermediate router forwards a RISP message by a simple lookup of routing table. However, under NHRP, the router (a.k.a. Next Hop Server) has to search its address resolution cache and update some states if necessary.

3. Consider the state transition table for the process of establishing a shortcut VC. The table contains states necessary for massage transactions defined in the protocol, as well as states specific to the implementation style. The number of states is 28 in the case of a NHRP client, while the number is 11 for RISP. Since the implementation styles for the two protocols are not identical, which may give somewhat incoherent state counts, the numbers should be treated as a rough estimation. Still, the number of states is significant smaller in RISP.

References

[1] W.R. Stevens, *TCP/IP Illustrated Volume 1*, Addison-Wesley, Reading, Massachusetts, 1994.

[2] D. Plummer. "An Ethernet Address Resolution Protocol - or - Converting Network Addresses to 48.bit Ethernet Address for Transmission on Ethernet Hardware," *Request for Comments 826*, November 1982.

[3] M. Laubach. "Classical IP and ARP over ATM," *Request for Comments 1577*, January 1994.

[4] J.V. Luciani, D. Katz, D. Piscotello, and B. Cole. "NBMA Next Hops Resolution Protocol (NHRP)," *Request for Comments 2332*, April 1998.

[5] ATM Forum, *ATM User Network Interface (UNI) Specification Version 3.1*, Prentice Hall, En glewood Cliffs, NJ, June 1995.

[6] ITU-T Recommendation Q.2931. *Broadband Integrated Services Digital Network (B-ISDN) - Digital subscriber signalling system no. 2 (DSS2) - User-network interface (UNI) - Layer 3 specification for basic call/connection control*, ITU, October 1995.

[7] M. Perez, F. Liaw, A. Mankin, E. Hoffman, D. Grossman, and A. Malis. "ATM Signaling Support for IP over ATM," *Request For Comments 1755*, February 1995

[8] W. Almesberger, et al. "ATM on Linux," http://lrcwww.epfl.ch/linux-atm.

[9] Y.-M. Chen, J. Ogawa, N. Oguchi, et al. "Shortcut Routing for Networks with Heterogeneous Routing Mechanisms," *Proc. IEEE NetWorld+Interop'98 Engeneers Conference*, Las Vegas, May, 1998.

[10] T. Tsuruoka, N. Oguchi, Y. Nomura, and S. Nojima. "Implementation and Evaluation of NHRP," (in Japanese) *Technical Report of IEICE*, Kumamoto University, Kumamoto, Japan, Nov. 1997.

[11] W. Stoye "Constrained NHRP," *ATM FORUM Technical Committee MPOA Subworking Group*, August 7, 1996.

[12] T. Hamada, Y.-M. Chen, et al. "QRISP: a Protocol for Shortcut-based QoS Provisioning." *Proc. IEEE Globecom'98*, Sidney, Australia, November 1998.

Source-Initiated Adaptive Routing Algorithm (SARA) for Autonomous Wireless Local Area Networks[1]

Ranga Ramanujan, Sid Takkella, Jordan Bonney, and Ken Thurber

Architecture Technology Corporation
Minneapolis, Minnesota

Abstract

Conventional routing protocols used in wireline and wireless networks are not designed to operate in an autonomous (or ad hoc) wireless local area network (AWLAN) environment with asymmetric (i.e., unidirectional) links. This paper presents the design of a routing protocol called, Source-Initiated Adaptive Routing Algorithm(SARA), for AWLAN environments that may contain asymmetric links. To allow efficient operation in a symmetric network while ensuring correct operation in asymmetric networks, SARA supports two different modes of protocol operation: one optimized for symmetric networks and the other providing additional capabilities needed for operation in asymmetric networks at a higher cost. The ability of SARA to adapt its mode of operation and optimize its execution for each network environment is one of its major advantages and distinguishes it from existing routing protocols for wireless networks. Furthermore, within each of its operating modes, SARA supports best-effort as well as policy-based routing.

1. Introduction

An autonomous wireless local area network (AWLAN) is a collection of up to about 100 wireless computers (e.g., wearables) that can be rapidly deployed as a temporary local area network without the aid of any established infrastructure or centralized administration and without any user-initiated configuration actions. Examples of situations where such networks are needed include disaster recovery operations and the front lines in a battlefield, situations where the normal infrastructure may have been destroyed or may be unavailable. In such networks, some nodes wishing to communicate may be outside the communication range of one another. However, such "out-of-range nodes" may be able to communicate through intermediate nodes that act as routers relaying messages between the out-of-range nodes. Thus, the wireless nodes in an AWLAN must employ some sort of a routing protocol to discover multi-hop paths through the wireless network. Conventional routing algorithms for wireline and wireless networks do not adequately address all the requirements of routing in a general AWLAN environment, especially one containing asymmetric (i.e., unidirectional) network links. In his paper, we present a new routing protocol for AWLANs called the Source-Initiated Adaptive Routing Algorithm (SARA) to address this problem.

Section 2 presents the major requirements imposed by AWLANs for routing. Section 3 describes the limitations of existing routing schemes in addressing these requirements and motivates the need for SARA. Section 4 describes the design of SARA and Section 5 presents our conclusions.

2. Requirements for Routing in AWLANs

In an AWLAN, an existing route between two nodes may fail when any of the nodes on the path between these end nodes fails or moves out of the wireless transmission range of the next or previous hop along the route or cannot communicate with the next or previous hop for some other reason such as interference or terrain masking. When route failures happen, the routing protocol must be able to dynamically adapt (or repair) the routes by finding an alternate route if one exists. In other words, the routing protocol in an AWLAN must be self healing.

In an AWLAN environment, it is not uncommon to encounter asymmetric or unidirectional wireless links. For instance, a node A may be able to receive transmissions from a node B but the reverse may not be true. Such asymmetry in the wireless communication may be induced by several factors such as varying propagation characteristics of the transmission signals or differences in the transmission power of the nodes (e.g., node B in the above example may use high-power transmissions that reach A but the latter relies on low-power transmissions that cannot reach B). It is therefore necessary for a routing protocol

[1] This material is based upon work supported by DARPA under contract number DAAH01-96-R048. Any opinions, findings, and conclusions or recommendations expressed in this paper are those of the authors and do not necessarily reflect the views of DARPA.

in an AWLAN to operate correctly and generate valid routes in a wireless network with asymmetric (unidirectional) links.

The mobile computing devices in an AWLAN are generally resource constrained in terms of processing power and battery life and must be built to stringent size, weight, and power specifications. Therefore, the routing protocol in such networks must permit a lightweight implementation within such nodes that conserves usage of memory, processing, and power at the nodes.

Traditionally, routing algorithms are designed to generate routes that minimize the number of hops taken by messages to reach a destination. However, AWLAN applications may desire routes that optimize metrics such as the amount of power consumed in transporting a packet, the throughput of the route, or the signal stability of the links in the route. Different applications running at a node may use different route metrics. Hence, the routing algorithm in an AWLAN must facilitate the generation of routes optimized to application specific metrics.

In summary, any routing protocol for a general AWLAN environment must possess the following capabilities:

1. It must be autoconfiguring, i.e., require no manual administrative actions for its operation.
2. It must be self-healing
3. It must operate correctly in networks with asymmetric (unidirectional) links.
4. It must support application directed policy routing.
5. It must permit lightweight implementation within the resource constraints of a mobile node.
6. It must produce loop-free routes

3. Limitations of Existing Routing Solutions

Routing protocols used in the conventional wireline environment fall into two categories: those based on the link state protocols and those based on distance vector protocols. Examples of link state routing protocols include the replacement for the original ARPANET routing protocol [1], IS-IS (adopted by the ISO) [2], and OSPF (used in parts of the Internet) [3]. Examples of distance vector routing protocols include the original routing protocol for the ARPANET [4], and RIP (used in parts of the Internet [5], in Novell's IPX [6], and in Xerox's XNS [7]). These wireline oriented protocols are not suitable for AWLANs for the reasons outlined below.

In *link state routing,* each router monitors the cost of the link to each of its neighboring routers and periodically broadcasts an update of this information to all the routers in the network. Given this information on the cost of each link in the network, each router generates a picture of the topology of the entire network. A router then uses this locally generated topology to compute the lowest cost path to each possible destination. Link state algorithms have the capability to accommodate a variety of cost metrics for evaluating and selecting routes. However, in a multi-access broadcast network, such as wireless networks, the size of the link database that has to be maintained by a router grows exponentially with the number of routers in the network. To address this problem, protocols such as OSPF elect one router in each domain as the *designated router*; all other nodes in the broadcast domain are treated as virtual hosts connected to the designated router. While this addresses the scalability problem in traditional broadcast networks, it creates new problems for AWLANs. In such networks, the mobile node selected as the designated router must act as a hub for all the virtual hosts connected to it and has to route all the traffic originating at any of these hosts. This has several consequences. First, due to resource constraints, mobile nodes in an AWLAN may not be equipped to serve in that role. Second, the mobility of the nodes in an AWLAN may result in the need for frequent elections of designated routers generating additional traffic and the potential for periods of routing instability. Third, the use of the designated router approach precludes the generation of optimal routes. Another reason why link state algorithms are unsuited for tactical AWLANs is that they may generate invalid routes in wireless networks with unidirectional links.

In *distance vector* routing, each router periodically broadcasts its view of the distance to all the hosts to each of its neighboring routers. Each router computes the shortest path to each host based on the information advertised by its neighbors. The basic distance vector algorithm has been successfully used in some wireless networks [8,9,10]. To apply the conventional routing approach in a mobile wireless environment, each wireless mobile node (mobile host or wireless router) periodically broadcasts a routing update packet to any neighboring wireless node within its transmission range. The basic distance vector algorithm is not suitable for AWLAN environments because of three reasons: 1) In a dynamic wireless network, these algorithms are slow to converge and are prone to temporary routing loops; 2) They may calculate invalid routes in a network with unidirectional links; and 3) They do not support application specified policy routing. An extension to the basic distance vector routing algorithm, called Destination Sequenced Distance Vector (DSDV) algorithm [10], alleviates the slow convergence problem and eliminates temporary loops in mobile wireless networks. However, DSDV still does not support application directed policy routing. Also, it cannot guarantee correct routes in networks with unidirectional links.

The Mobile and Ad Hoc Networking (MANET) working group of the IETF is currently investigating a number of routing algorithms for ad hoc wireless networks. The candidate protocols include the Ad Hoc On-Demand Distance Vector (AODV) protocol [11], the Temporally Ordered Routing Algorithm (TORA) [12], the Zone Routing Protocol (ZRP) [13], and the Dynamic Source Routing (DSR) protocol [14]. AODV, TORA, and ZRP are all designed for networks with bi-directional links; they may produce invalid routes in networks with unidirectional links. Furthermore, they do not support application directed policy routing.

The DSR protocol uses source routing where every data packet to be routed carries in its header the complete ordered list of nodes that the packet must traverse to reach its destination from the source node. In contrast to other MANET protocols, DSR is designed to operate correctly in networks with unidirectional links. The protocol as defined currently does not allow application directed policy routing. However, it can be extended to support this capability. The major drawback of DSR for AWLAN environments is the residual overhead of the protocol associated with routing data packets. As the length of the route increases, the size of the data packet also becomes larger. When compared to hop-by-hop routing, the source routing approach used by DSR incurs larger steady state routing overhead in terms of the CPU cycles used and the power consumed by a node to forward a packet. Also, the source route information carried within the data packets consumes additional network bandwidth when compared to packets routed using hop-by-hop schemes.

Another routing protocol that has been designed for mobile wireless computing environments is the Wireless Routing Protocol (WRP) [15]. However, WRP does not support policy routing or operation in networks with unidirectional links.

4. Source-Initiated Adaptive Routing Algorithm (SARA)

SARA performs on-demand discovery of routes in the network. The route discovery process is initiated by the source node when the application at the source node initiates a communication session with a destination for which the source has no routes. This avoids periodic router advertisements and update messages, reducing the overhead of SARA in terms of network bandwidth and power consumption especially during periods when there is no movement of nodes within the network.

As noted earlier, a routing protocol for an AWLAN environment must be designed to operate correctly in a network with asymmetric links. Although a protocol designed for asymmetric networks would be sufficient for a symmetric network, its use in such a network would incur much higher routing overhead than a protocol that is optimized for symmetric networks. To allow efficient operation in a symmetric network while also ensuring correct operation in asymmetric networks, SARA supports two different modes of protocol operation, where one mode is optimized for symmetric networks and the other mode provides the additional capabilities needed for operation in asymmetric networks at a higher cost. SARA automatically determines the nature of a network environment (i.e., whether it is a symmetric or asymmetric network environment) and selects the appropriate mode of operation for the network. This ability to adapt its mode of operation and optimize its execution for each network environment is one of the major advantages of SARA and distinguishes it from existing routing protocols for wireless networks.

Within each mode, SARA facilitates another degree of dynamic tailoring of the protocol execution overhead by providing two sub-modes. These two sub-modes called *best-effort routing* and *policy routing* are implementations of SARA tailored for best-effort and policy routing respectively. The former incurs much less overhead than the latter. The choice of the sub-mode of operation for SARA is made by the application on a per session basis, the default sub-mode being best-effort. This allows applications to select the sub-mode that best meets their needs while at the same time optimizing the per packet overhead associated with routing data packets.

Thus, the two modes and two sub-modes of operation for SARA give rise to four operational regimes for SARA, i.e., 1) best effort routing for symmetric networks; 2) best effort routing for asymmetric networks; 3) policy routing for symmetric networks; and 4) policy routing for asymmetric networks.

Conceptually, one may view the SARA implementation as consisting of a routing agent that implements four sets of processing routines corresponding to the four operational regimes. Which set of routines is used to process an incoming routing control message or a data packet to be forwarded is determined by the routing agent by the value of *mode/sub-mode* field contained within each packet. The value of this field is set by the originator of the packet. The sub-mode, as indicated earlier, is determined by the sending application's routing needs. The value assigned to the mode is determined by the value of the Boolean variable, called *Asymmetric_Channel*, that is maintained by a routing agent. If the variable is set (i.e., has value of 1), the mode field of the transmitted packets is set to "asymmetric". If not, the mode field is set to "symmetric". Section 4.1 describes how SARA automatically determines the symmetry of the network and assigns the proper value to the Boolean variable Asymmetric_Channel. Section 4.2 introduces the routing control messages that are used by SARA to discover and maintain routes. These messages are common across the four operating regimes of the protocol. Sections 4.3 through 4.6 describe the four operating regimes of SARA.

4.1 Automatic Selection of Operational Mode

Each node in the network, transmits a *Link_Status* message to all nodes within its transmission range every *Link_Status_Interval* seconds. A node also maintains a list of all the nodes from which it has received a Link_Status message within the last 3*Link_Status_Interval seconds. This list is called the *neighbor list* for the node. The Link_Status message transmitted by a node A contains the identity of A as well as the identities of all nodes in the neighbor list maintained by A.

Another list maintained by a node is the *reachable neighbor list.* This is a subset of the neighbor list maintained by the node. A node I can belong to the reachable neighborhood list maintained by A if and only if the following two conditions are met by I:

1. I must be contained in the neighbor list maintained by A.
2. Within the last 3*Link_Status_Interval seconds, A must have received a Link_Status message from I indicating that A belongs to neighborhood list of I.

Before transmitting its periodic Link_Status message, a node examines the *neighbor list* and *reachable neighbor list* to ensure that the members of these lists meet the membership criteria. Any member not meeting the criteria is deleted from the list(s). Subsequently, the node checks whether all the members of the *neighbor list* are also contained in the *reachable neighbor list.* If not, it implies that the wireless network contains one or more uni-directional links. In this case, the node performs the following steps:

1. If the Aymmetric_Channel flag is not set, then the node sets the flag and initializes the timestamp associated with the flag to the value of the node's clock. It then performs an AWLAN-wide broadcast of the *Change_Mode* message that targets all the nodes in the AWLAN.
2. If the Aymmetric_Channel flag is set, then the node checks the timestamp associated with the flag to determine when it was set. If the flag was set more than 3*Link_Status_Interval seconds ago, the node updates the timestamp to the current local time and performs an AWLAN-wide broadcast of the Change_Mode message.

Before transmitting its periodic Link_Status message, a node checks the Aymmetric_Channel flag . If it is set and if the timestamp associated with the flag is older than 7*Link_Status_Interval seconds, the node resets the flag.

When a node receives a Change_Mode message, it sets its Aymmetric_Channel flag (even if it is already set) and initializes the timestamp associated with the flag to the value of the local clock.

4.2 SARA's Routing Control Messages

SARA uses two types of routing control messages: *route request* and *route update.* The functions of these messages and their processing by the routing agents varies with each operational regime of the protocol as described in Sections 4.3 through 4.6.

Each node maintains a state variable called the *update sequence number* that is incremented each time the node transmits a route update message. A node that does not have a route to a destination, D, that it needs to communicate with, broadcasts a route request. The fields in the route request message are defined below:

Mode/Sub-mode: This field is initialized by the sender of the route request and its function was described earlier.

Destination: This field contains the address of the target of the route request message, i.e., D.

Update Sequence Number: If the routing table at the node originating the route request has an existing (and potentially outdated) entry for the requested destination, the USN of the routing table entry is copied into this field by the originating node. If, on the other hand, the originating node has no entry for the destination this field of the route request message is set to null by the originating node.

Route Log: The route log field contains an ordered sequence of route records, one for each node traversed by the route request message including one for the originating node. As a route request message passes through a node, it appends to its log a route record containing the address of the node and the current value of its USN variable.

Piggyback Option: This optional field may be used by the sender of a route request to piggyback information destined for the destination D on to the route request message.

If a node receiving a route request message is the destination of the request, D, it responds with a route update message. The fields in the route update message are defined below.

Mode/Sub-mode: This field is initialized by the sender of the route update by copying the value of the corresponding field from the route request that triggered the generation of this route update.

Destination: This field contains the value of the destination field of the route request that triggered the generation of this route update

Update Sequence Number: This field contains the value of the USN variable of the destination node that generated this message.

Route Log: The route log field contains an ordered sequence of route records, one for each node traversed by the route update message including one for the node generating the route update. As a route update message passes through a node, it appends to its log a route record containing the address of the node and the current value of its USN variable.

The following paragraphs describe how the routing control messages described above are used to implement the four operational regimes for SARA.

4.2 Best-Effort Routing in Symmetric Wireless Networks (SARA/SB)

We abbreviate this operational regime of SARA as SARA/SB (where the two letter abbreviation SB stands for Symmetric, Best-Effort). The routines implementing the SARA/SB algorithm within a routing agent rely on each node to maintain a routing table. At any instance in time, the routing table at a wireless node contains an entry for each destination that may be reached through one or more hops from this node. Routing table entries maintain the next hop of the routes to such destinations. In addition to the destination and the next hop fields, each route entry contains three special fields, i.e., *update sequence number (USN)* field, the *timestamp* field, and the *route_pending* flag. The utility of these fields will become clear as we describe the operation of SARA/SB in the following paragraphs.

We first describe how the algorithm discovers a route between two nodes that did not have a previously established route. Subsequently, we describe how SARA/SB handles failures of existing routes.

Route Discovery. To find a route to a destination D, a node generates a route request message and broadcasts it to all nodes within its transmission range. The source node creates an entry for D in its routing table and sets the route_pending flag of the entry. The current value of the local clock is entered into the timestamp field of the entry.

If a node receiving a route request message is the destination D of the request, it broadcasts a route update message to all nodes that are within its transmission range and increments its USN variable. Otherwise, it performs the following steps:

1. For each route record contained in the route log of the route request message, the node determines whether it has a route entry for the address, say A, in the route record. If not, it creates a new route entry for the destination A. The next hop field for this entry is the neighbor from which the node received the route request, as indicated by the last entry in the route log of the route request message. The timestamp field of the route entry is set to the value of the local clock and the route_pending flag for the entry is cleared, if it was set.
2. If the routing table at the node has an existing entry for the address A in the route record, then the fields in the entry are updated as described above if the USN value in the route record for A is greater than the USN of the current route entry for that destination in the routing table.
3. If the routing table at the node has no entry for the destination, the node creates a new entry in the table and sets the request pending flag for the entry. The local time at the node is entered into the timestamp field of the route entry. The next hop field of the newly created entry is initialized to a null value.
4. If the routing table at the node has an existing entry for the destination and if the request pending flag for the entry is set, the node discards the route request message. If, however, the request pending flag for the entry is not set, the node compares the USN value carried by the route request to the value associated with the route entry. If the USN in the route request message is greater than or equal to the USN of the route entry, then the node appends a route record to the route log field of the message and broadcasts the route request message to all nodes within its transmission range. It then sets the request pending flag of the route entry at the node. If the USN in the route request message is less than that in the route table entry for the destination, the node broadcasts a route update message. The USN

in the route table entry is copied into the USN field of the route update.

When a route update message arrives at a node, it processes each route record in the route log just at it would for a route request. Let D be the value of the destination field in the route update. If the request pending flag of the route entry for D was set prior to the processing of the route log, the node appends its route record to the route log and broadcasts the route update to all nodes within its transmission range. Otherwise, the node discards the received route update message after processing the route log of the message.

Periodically, a node examines the timestamp field of the entries in its routing table. It deletes any entry with timestamp less than (current time – ROUTE_LIFETIME), where ROUTE_LIFETIME is a preset parameter of the routing protocol.

After generating a route request for a destination D, a node waits for a time period specified by the preset parameter ROUTE_REQUEST_TIMEOUT. If the route entry for D is not updated within this time (by an arriving route update or route request), the node retries the route request. The maximum number of retries that may be attempted by a node is given by the parameter MAX_RETRIES. If a route to D is not established within MAX_RETRIES attempts, the routing algorithm signals an error to the application indicating that D is not reachable.

Route Adaptation. An existing route may no longer work, for instance, if any of the nodes along the route should fail (or be powered off) or if the sender, the receiver, or one of the nodes along the route should move out of the transmission range of its next or previous hop. When a problem with an existing route is detected, SARA/SB's route adaptation scheme finds an alternate route, if one exists.

The route adaptation scheme relies on the periodic Link_Status messages transmitted by each node as described earlier. Each node in the wireless network maintains a neighbor table. Whenever a node receives a Link_Status message it determines whether the originator, O, of the message is contained in its neighbor table. If not, the node adds a new entry in the table. The node_ID and check-in time fields of this new entry hold the address of O and the local time when the Link_Status message was received by this node. If an entry for O already existed when the Link_Status message from O was received, then the node simply updates the check-in time field of the entry with the local time at which the route update message was received.

Periodically, a node examines its neighbor table. Any node in the table whose check-in time is less than (current time – 2* Link_Status_Interval) is marked as unreachable and its entry is deleted from the neighbor table. When a node detects an unreachable node, U, it invalidates all entries in its routing table that have U as the next hop, i.e., the route_pending flag for all these entries is set. Then, for each of the invalidated entries, it generates a route request message, copying the node address and USN fields of the routing table entry into the destination and USN fields respectively of the route request message.

4.4 Best-Effort Routing in Asymmetric Wireless Networks (SARA/AB)

The routines implementing SARA/AB within the routing agent maintain a routing table whose structure is identical to that for SARA/SB. We first describe how the algorithm discovers a route between two nodes that did not have a previously established route. Subsequently, we describe how SARA/AB handles failures of existing routes. In the following discussion, the mode/sub-mode field of all route request and route update messages generated by the execution of the algorithm carry a value reflecting the operating regime of the algorithm, i.e., AB.

Route Discovery. A node S that does not have a route to a destination D that it needs to communicate with, broadcasts a route request message. The structure of this message is identical to that describe earlier for SARA/SB.

The source node creates an entry for D in its routing table and sets the route_pending flag of the entry. The current value of the local clock is entered into the timestamp field of the entry.

When a node receives a route request message, it appends its route record to the route log of the route request. If the node receiving the route request message is the destination, D, of the request, it performs the following actions:

1. It assembles a route request message for S and piggybacks a route update message to it. The route log of the route request received from S is copied into the piggyback option field of the route update. The node D then broadcasts this route request for S to all the nodes within its transmission range. It then increments the USN variable at the node.
2. If the route request received from S contains a piggybacked route update, then the node D extracts the route update message from the received route request. The route log of this extracted route update contains the entire source route from D to S. Let D, n_1, n_2, n_3, ..., n_n, S represent the sequence of

nodes in this source route from D to S. For each node p following D in the source route (i.e. $p \in \{ n_1, n_2, n_3, \ldots\ldots, n_n, S\}$), the node D creates a new entry for p if one does not already exist and sets its next hop field to n_1. The USN field of the new entry is set to the value contained in the route record for p and the current value of the local clock is entered into the timestamp field of the entry. If p already has an entry in the routing table, then D updates the fields of the entry as described above if and only if the value USN of the route entry is less than the USN contained in the route record for p. The route_pending flag of the entry is cleared if it was set before. Subsequently, the node D transmits the route update message to the node n_1.

If a node receiving a route request message is not the destination of the request, it determines whether its routing table has an entry for the destination D of the request. If not, it creates an entry for D and sets the request_pending flag for the entry. It then adds its route record to the route log of the received message and transmits the route request to all nodes within its transmission range. If the node has an existing entry for D in its routing table and if the route_pending flag for the entry is set, the node discards the received route request message. If, however, the request_pending flag is not set the node does the following.

Let S be the originator of the route request received by this node. The node compares the USN of the route entry for D in its table to the USN of the received route request. If the USN of the route entry is greater than that of the received route request, the node generates a route request directed at S and piggybacks a route update message to the route request. The route log of the route request received from S is copied into the piggybacked route update. The node then broadcasts this route request for S to all the nodes within its transmission range. It then increments the USN variable at the node.

If the USN of the route entry is not greater than that in the received route request, the node sets the route_pending flag for the route entry for D and assigns the current value of the local clock to the timestamp field of the entry. It then broadcasts the route request message to all nodes within its transmission range.

When a node I receives a route update message, it examines the route log of the message. This contains a source route from some source node to a destination where I is either the destination of the source route or is as an intermediate hop on this source route. In the former case, I discards the received message. In the latter case, I processes the message as follows. Let the source route in the route log of the received route update message be denoted by $S, x_1, x_2, \ldots, I, i_1, i_2, \ldots, D$. For each node p following I in this source route, the node I creates a new entry for p if one does not already exist and sets its next hop field to i_1. The USN field of the new entry is set to the value contained in the route record for p and the current value of the local clock is entered into the timestamp field of the entry. If p already has an entry in the routing table and if the value of the USN of the route entry is less than the USN contained in the route record for p , then I updates the fields of the route entry and clears its route_pending flag. Then, irrespective of whether the routing table at I was updated or not, I transmits the route update message to the node i_1.

Route Adaptation. The route adaptation scheme relies on the use of end-to-end acknowledgements at higher layers to detect failures of existing routes. In this case, existing transport or application level replies from a destination may be used by the sender to deduce the status of the node's route to that destination.

On detecting a route failure, the source attempts to establish a new route to the destination by generating a route request for that destination.

4.5 Policy-Based Routing in Symmetric Wireless Networks (SARA/SP)

In the policy-driven mode of operation, SARA employs source routing of data packets. That is, each data packet carries with it the source route or the sequence of nodes that it must traverse to reach the destination from the source. The routing agent implementing SARA/PB maintains a *source route cache* in which it caches the source routes that it has learned. A source route within a route cache contains an ordered sequence of route records, one for each node on the source route. Each route record contains the identity of the node in the source route and an attribute list for the node describing the characteristics of the node. Examples of node characteristics contained in the attribute list include the average power consumed by the node for each packet that is transmitted or received, the maximum throughput of the node, and the length of time that the node has been stationary. If the route cache at a source node contains multiple source routes to a destination, the routing agent may use the information contained in the attribute lists of the nodes in the source routes to evaluate the route metrics (i.e., a measure of the goodness of the routes) of the alternate routes and select the route yielding the best metric. For example, the routing agent may select a route to minimize the total power consumption over the path traversed by the packets of an application session. The choice of the routing metric to be optimized in selecting a route may be specified by the application. Also, route evaluation may be performed on a per packet basis, per session basis, or per destination basis depending upon the needs of the application domain.

We first describe how the algorithm discovers a route between two nodes that did not have a previously established route. Subsequently, we describe how SARA/SP handles failures of existing routes. In the following discussion, the mode field of all route request and route update messages generated by the execution of the algorithm carry a value reflecting the operating mode of the algorithm, i.e., SP.

Route Discovery. When a node sends a packet to another node, the routing agent at the sending node first checks its *source route cache* for existing source routes to the destination. If multiple routes exist, it evaluates the application specified route metrics for the routes and selects the route yielding the best metric. It then sends the packet with this source route in its header. If no route is found, the sender may attempt to discover a route using a *route discovery* protocol. While waiting for the route discovery to complete, the node may continue normal processing and may continue to send and receive packets from other nodes. The node may buffer the original packet in order to transmit it once a route is found or it may discard the packet and rely on a higher-layer protocol to retransmit the packet.

During route discovery, the sender broadcasts a *route request* message that contains the four fields described earlier: i.e., mode, destination, USN, and route log. The source copies the value of the USN variable at the node into the USN field of the route request message. After transmitting the route request message the source increments the USN variable at the node.

A node receiving a route request message processes the request according to the following steps:

1. If this node's route record is already contained in the route log of the request, then discard the route request packet and do not process it further.
2. Else, if the destination, D, of the request matches this node's own address, then append the node's route record to the route log of the received message and create a route update message. As noted earlier, the route update message contains two fields, i.e., the USN and the route log. To create the route update message, the node copies the USN and the route log fields from the received route request message into the corresponding fields of the route update message. The destination also reverses the ordered list of route records in the received route request to create a source route from the destination to the source, S. It then adds this newly created route to its source route cache. Subsequently, the node transmits the newly created route update message to the neighbor that is on the newly created source route to S.
3. Else, append this node's own route record to the route log of the route request message, and re-broadcast this request.

When a node receives a route update message, it processes it as follows. Let S, I_1, I_2, ..., I_i, ..., I_n, D be the source route from the source S to the destination D that is contained in the route log of the received route update message. The node checks the route log of the message to determine which address in the route log matches its own address. If the matching address is S then the node adds the source route in the route log to its route cache. If the matching address is some I_k, where $1 \leq k \leq n$, then the node relays the route update message to the node that precedes I_k in the ordered list of nodes in the route log of the message.

The SARA/SP scheme described above allows for the discovery of multiple routes between a source and a destination, if such routes exist. All routes to a destination D that are known by a source S can then be evaluated by the routing agent at S in accordance with an application specified routing metric to select the route yielding the best metric.

If there are multiple paths from the sender S to the destination D, the latter node will receive multiple copies of the route request message originated by S, one for each of the existing routes between S and D. In this case, D returns to S a route update for each copy of the route request message received from S.

Route Adaptation. When a node is using any source route, it monitors the continued correct operation of that route. For instance, if the sender, the destination, or any of the other nodes named as hops along a route move out of the wireless transmission range of the next or previous hop along the route, the route can no longer be used to reach the destination. A route will also not work if any of the nodes along the route should fail or be powered off. When a problem with an existing route is detected, *route adaptation* is used to find an alternate route to the destination.

SARA/SP relies on higher layers of the communication protocol stack to detect the failure of a source route. For instance, existing transport or application level replies from the original destination may be used by the sender to deduce the status of this node's route to the destination. Once a higher layer entity at a sending node, S, deduces the failure of a route to a destination, D, it notifies the routing agent at S. The latter then purges all the source routes to D from its route cache and initiates route discovery for D using the scheme described above.

4.6 Policy-Based Routing in Asymmetric Wireless Networks (SARA/AP)

The AP regime of operation of SARA is very similar to that of the SP regime described above. The route discovery and route adaptation techniques used by SARA/AP differ from that used by SARA/SP only in the way that route update messages are generated by the target of a route request. In order for the destination D of a route request to return a route update packet to the initiator S of the route discovery, D must have a route to S. The node D cannot simply reverse the route from the S to D as in the case of the SP mode of operation because the route between this pair of nodes may not work in both directions. Therefore, if D does not already have a route to the sender in its *route cache*, it creates a route request to S and piggybacks the route update on to this route request.

5. Conclusions

This paper presented the design of a routing protocol for autonomous wireless local area networks(AWLANs), called Source-Initiated Adaptive Routing Algorithm (SARA), that is unique in its ability to operate over networks with asymmetric (unidirectional) links while supporting best-effort as well as policy routing. SARA supports two different modes of protocol operation, where one mode is optimized for symmetric networks and the other mode provides the additional capabilities needed for operation in asymmetric networks at a higher cost. SARA automatically determines the nature of a network environment (i.e., whether it is a symmetric or asymmetric network environment) and selects the appropriate mode of operation for the network. This ability to adapt its mode of operation and optimize its execution for each network environment is one of the major advantages of SARA. Furthermore, within each mode, SARA facilitates another degree of dynamic tailoring of the protocol execution overhead by providing two sub-modes. These two sub-modes called *best-effort routing* and *policy routing* are implementations of SARA tailored for best-effort and policy routing respectively. The former incurs much less overhead than the latter. This allows applications to choose the sub-mode that best meets their needs while optimizing the per packet overhead associated with routing data packets.

Another major advantage of SARA is that it is a lightweight protocol whose processing and memory requirements are very frugal. Consequently, it permits a number of implementation options for the routing functions. For instance, one can realize the routing functions entirely within software that executes on the CPU of the mobile wireless node, sharing the processing resources of the node with other applications executing on the node. Alternatively, the router function can be implemented within a low-cost, low-power add-on card for a mobile node. We have designed such a "router in a card" implementation using low-power commodity DSP chips [17]. The advantages of such a hardware implementation over a software implementation include increased throughput of the router, lower end-to-end packet delivery latencies, and lower power consumption for the router function within the mobile node. A third possible realization of the nomadic router is as a standalone relay whose only function is to forward messages destined for mobile hosts within the network. Unlike mobile hosts, relays do not run any applications that send or receive messages. SARA allows for such relays to be realized with low cost hardware [17].

We implemented packet level simulations to compare the performance of SARA with two well-known routing algorithms for ad hoc networks, i.e., DSDV[10] and TORA[12]. The results of the simulation are presented in another paper [16]. Configurable parameters of the simulation models included the number of wireless nodes, the initial placement and movement characteristics of the nodes, and the application traffic pattern. The number of nodes in the simulations was varied from 5 to 80. Four different movement scenarios and two different application traffic patterns were simulated.

The quantitative metrics characterizing the performance of the protocols that were derived by the simulations were: 1) the data delivery efficiency (i.e., a measure of the percentage of packets that were successfully delivered by the network to their intended destinations); and 2) the resource consumption indicator (i.e., a measure of the average energy expended by the network to deliver each packet). While the relative performance of the protocols varied over the set of scenarios that were simulated, the results of the simulation clearly established the potential of SARA to outperform DSDV and TORA while at the same time delivering capabilities that are not matched by these hop-by-hop routing schemes, i.e., the ability to accommodate uni-directional links and the ability to support policy routing.

7. References

[1] J.M. McQuillan, I. Richer, and E.C. Rosen, "The New Routing Algorithm for the ARPANET," IEEE Trans. on Communications, May 1980.

[2] International Standards Organization, "Intermediate System to Intermediate System Intra-Domain Routing Exchange Protocol for Use in Conjunction with the Protocol for Providing the Connectionless-Mode Network Service (ISO 8473)," ISO DP 10589, Feb. 1990.

[3] J. Moy, "OSPF version 2," Internet Request for Comments RFC 1247, Jul. 1991.

[4] J.M. McQuillan and D.C. Walden, "The ARPA Network Design Decisions," Computer Networks, Aug. 1977.

[5] C. Hedric, "Routing Information Protocol," Internet Request for Comments RFC 1058, Jun. 1988.

[6] P. Turner, "NetWare Communications Processes," *NetWare Application Notes*, Novell Research, Sept. 1990.

[7] Xerox Corporation, "Internet Transport Protocols," Xerox System Integration Standard 028112, Dec. 1981.

[8] J. Jubin and J.D. Tarnow, "The DARPA Packet Radio Network Protocols," Proc. of IEEE, Jan. 1987.

[9] D.M. Frank, "Transmission of IP Datagrams over NET/ROM Networks," in ARRL Amateur Radio 7th Computer Networking Conference, Oct. 1988.

[10] C.E. Perkins and P. Bhagwat, "Highly Dynamic Destination-Sequenced Distance-Vector Routing (DSDV) for Mobile Computers," in Proc. of SIGCOMM'94, Aug. 1994.

[11] C. Perkins "Ad Hoc On Demand Distance Vector (AODV) Routing," Internet Draft (work in progress), Nov. 1997.

[12] V. Park, and S. Corson, "Temporally-Ordered Routing Algorithm (TORA) Version 1 Functional Specification," Internet Draft (work in progress), Nov. 1997.

[13] Z. Haas, and M. Pearlman, "The Zone Routing Protocol for Ad Hoc Networks," Internet Draft (work in progress), Nov. 1997.

[14] J. Broch, D. Johnson, D. Maltz, "The Dynamic Source Routing Protocol for Mobile Ad Hoc Networks," Internet Draft (work in progress), Mar. 1998

[15] S.Murthy and J.J. Garcia-Luna-Aceves, "An Efficient Routing Protocol for Wireless Networks," ACM Mobile Networks and Applications Journal, 1996.

[16] R.Ramanujan, S. Takkella, J. Bonney, and K. Thurber, "Simulation of Routing Protocols for Autonomous Wireless Local Area Networks," Proceedings of MILCOM'98, Oct. 1998.

[17] R.Ramanujan, S. Takkella, J. Bonney, and K. Thurber, "Nomadic Routers for Rapidly Deployable Wireless Networks," Technical Report ATC-RD-98-001, Architecture Technology Corporation, March 1998.

Track B: Integrated Services/Multimedia

Session Chair: Christina Class
Swiss Federal Institute of Technology

New Approach of Resource Management to Provide Integrated Services over ATM Networks

Tetsuya Yokotani   Ken Murakami   Tatsuki Ichihashi   Shuichi Tonami
Information Technology R&D Center, Mitsubishi Electric Corporation

High-Speed Network Dept., Information Technology R&D center,
Mitsubishi Electric Corp.
5-1-1, Ofuna, Kamakura, 247-8501, Japan
E-mail: yokotani@kousoku.isl.melco.co.jp

Abstract

The cooperative action between RSVP and some protocols performed on ATM networks, is one of problems that should be solved to provide Integrated Services over ATM networks discussed in IETF. In this paper, after describing some schemes that map RSVP into these protocols to reserve resources over ATM networks, we compare these schemes and point out some problems therein. Next, we propose a new approach referred to as "the Direct Look-up Approach" to improve these schemes. The new approach removes overhead by the mapping between RSVP and protocols performed on ATM networks, and control messages of RSVP on ATM networks are directly examined. Finally, we discuss some issues for the implementation of this new approach.

1. Introduction

Recently, the number of subscribers to the Internet has rapidly increased, and the various new applications across the network have been introduced besides applications using the conventional data communication. Therefore, the resource reservation in the Internet has become one of the most interesting study items to guarantee the requested QoS (Quality of Service) of these subscribers or applications. In IETF (the Internet Engineering Task Force), the new service specifications with resource reservation, such as the guaranteed service [1] and the controlled load service [2], besides the conventional best effort service, have been discussed in the Integrated Service (intserv) and the Integrated Services over Specific Link Layers (issll) working groups. For these new services, FlowSpec [3], which is the set of some parameters to reserve resources, and RSVP (Resource Reservation Protocol) [4], which is the protocol to negotiate resource allocation in the network, have been specified.

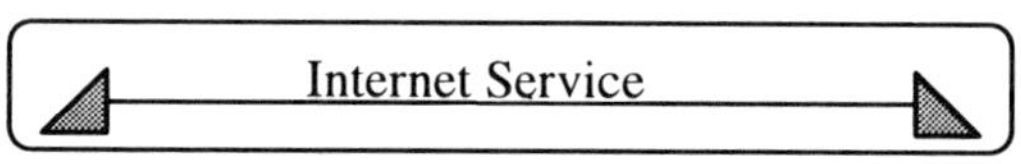

(a) Conventional service model

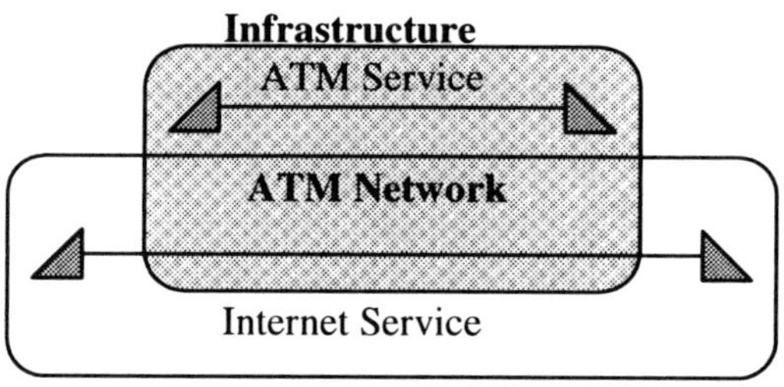

(b) New service model

Fig. 1 Service models

By the way, it has been expected that ATM networks are the most promising candidate of all of communication networks as an infrastructure. Figure 1 shows a service model based on ATM networks. Internet services with resource reservation are invoked on the ATM platform. However, the ATM network should also support services using the native ATM interface such as MPEG-2 over ATM. Both of these service types must own jointly an ATM network. However, there are still some problems that should be solved. An essential problem is protocol mapping for resource reservation from the Internet level to

0-8186-8810-6/98 $10.00 © 1998 IEEE

the ATM level. The Internet level intends to reserve resources by using protocols specified in this level such as RSVP, independent of protocols specified in the ATM level. On the other hand, resources for the native ATM service should be reserved in the ATM level. To solve this problem, it should be studied that RSVP is emulated effectively by some protocols performed on ATM networks to reserve resources in the ATM level. However, the solution of this problem is difficult due to a difference of architecture to reserve resources between the Internet and the ATM network. Although this point has been discussed in some literature, e.g., [5], it has not yet arrived at the goal. This paper proposes a new approach referred to as "the Direct Look-up Approach (DLA)" to solve this problem. DLA reduces the overhead by emulation of RSVP by some protocols on ATM networks. DLA provides the Internet services over ATM networks efficiently as well as the native ATM services.

The structure of this paper is as follows. Section 2 summarizes some approaches for resource reservation in ATM networks. Section 3 presents approaches with emulation of RSVP by some protocols in ATM networks and some issues in these approaches. Section 4 presents an outline of the proposed new approach, DLA. Section 5 presents some issues to implement DLA described in Section 4, and their solutions. Finally, Section 6 mentions applied network configurations of DLA, and operations of our proposal on these networks.

2. Resource Reservation in ATM Networks

Approaches of resource reservation in ATM networks are classified into the network oriented approach and the user oriented approach. In the network oriented approach represented by the ABR (Available Bit Rate) service specified in the ATM Forum [6], network resources are allocated depending on the condition of congestion in a network. In the user-oriented approach, users request needed resources to the network by using some protocols such as signalling procedures, e.g., [7]. When Internet services are provided on ATM networks, the best effort service may make use of the former approach. However, the guaranteed and the controlled-load services require the latter approach because the requested QoS does not depend on the traffic load in the network but depends on requirements from applications. We summarize schemes falling under the latter approach.

(1) Resource reservation by signalling procedures

Resources requested by a user are reserved when an ATM connection is established by signalling procedures, e.g., [7]. In short, when the connection is established, resources for this connection are determined statically. This scheme has some flexibility. We can change pre-reserved resources that are allocated in the connection-establishing phase by using the procedure specified in [8]. However, although some extensions of this procedure have been discussed, such as [9], PCR (Peak Cell Rate) in traffic descriptors can be changed only in this procedure. Moreover, it must be noted that signalling procedures can reserve resources for bi-directional communication path. Figure 2 shows a summary of the sequence chart of these procedures.

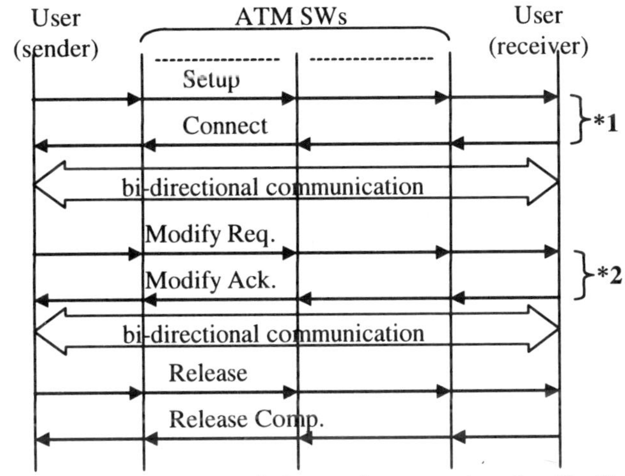

*1: Resource negotiation and reservation by Traffic descriptors and QoS parameters
*2: Modification of PCR in Traffic descriptors

Fig.2 An example of the sequence chart in signalling procedure

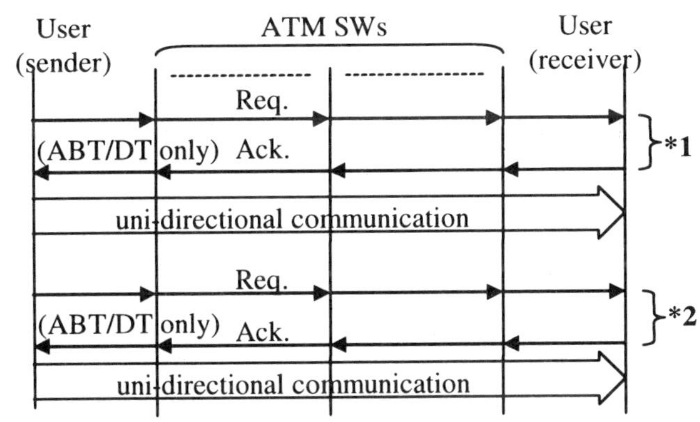

*1:Negotiation and Reservation of PCR in Traffic descriptors by RM cells
*2: Modification of PCR in Traffic descriptors by RM

Fig.3 An example of the sequence chart in ABT

(2) Resource reservation by ABT

Resources are not always reserved when the ATM connection is established. Resources can be reserved just before information is transferred. ABT (ATM Block Transfer) [10] can be applied to this reservation style.

ABT consists of two types, such as ABT/DT (ABT with Delay Transmission) and ABT/IT (ABT with Immediate Transmission). In ABT/DT, the sender transmits data after it has received the acknowledgment of resource reservation. However, in ABT/IT, this acknowledgment is not needed. Anyway, ABT can reserve resources for uni-directional communication path during two successive RM cells. Figure 3 shows a summary of sequence chart in ABT.

3. Approaches by Protocol Emulation and their Issues

When Internet services with resource reservation are provided over ATM networks, it is one of problems how to emulate RSVP on ATM networks. In this section, we discuss cooperative actions between RSVP and protocols on ATM networks to reserve resources described in the previous section and emulation of RSVP by using these protocols.

3.1 Classification of cooperative actions between RSVP and ATM protocols

Figure 4 shows a typical example of network configurations. In most cases, from the standpoint of overall cast, it is appropriate to establish connections to ATM networks users via Network Edge Devices (NEDs) such as routers with ATM interfaces. Therefore, although Internet services are provided between users, ATM services should be only provided between NEDs.

In this network configuration, cooperative actions between RSVP and protocols for resource reservation on ATM networks are classified into emulation of RSVP based on signalling procedures, and that based on ABT. Moreover, we can classify these operations from another viewpoint that NEDs terminate control messages of RSVP, or transfer them transparently in the ATM network. We present these cooperative actions based on the above-mentioned classifications after the next sub-sections, and compare these operations.

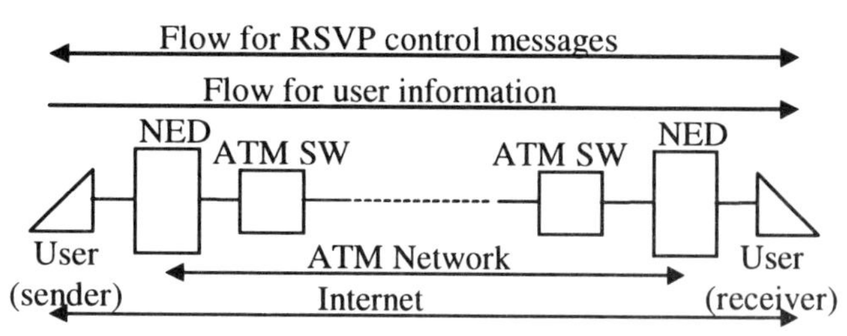

Fig. 4 A typical network configuration

3.2 Cooperative actions between RSVP and signalling procedures

Traffic descriptors which characterize a traffic source, and QoS parameters which specify requirements of QoS in End-to-End have been discussed in RSVP and protocols on ATM individually. However, these descriptors and parameters in RSVP can be mapped into those in the major ATM signaling procedure [7] by some techniques such as presented by [11]. Therefore, it seems that cooperative actions between RSVP and signaling procedures in ATM are simple. However, when we study cooperative actions between RSVP and signaling procedures, we understand that an essential problem is coordination between the soft state policy in RSVP and the hard state policy in ATM. In signaling procedures on ATM networks, resources are reserved basically by the hard state policy described in Section 2. If we try to reserve resources by using the soft state policy to harmonize RSVP, we can use the signaling procedure specified in [8] on ATM networks. Unfortunately, this procedure cannot cover capability to transfer traffic descriptors and QoS parameters that are specified in [3] and can be transferred by RSVP. This procedure can modify PCR only of traffic descriptors as presented in 2.1, and cannot modify other traffic descriptors, such as SCR (Sustainable Cell Rate) and MBS (Maximum Burst Size), and all of QoS parameters, such as CLR (Cell Loss Rate), maxCTD (maximum Cell Transfer Delay), and p-pCDV (peak-to-peak Cell Delay Variation). To apply this procedure for emulation of RSVP, this procedure should be enhanced so that it has the same capability to transfer and to negotiate parameters as the major procedure such as in [7]. When some information elements for traffic descriptors and QoS parameters in [7] are introduced in [8], this enhancement will be achieved easily.

Under the assumption that this enhancement is accepted, we discuss cooperative actions between RSVP and signaling procedures. There are two possible schemes as follows, based on termination of RSVP control messages at NEDs or non-termination of them.

(1) Non-termination of RSVP control messages : Scheme 1

Figure 5 shows a summary of a sequence chart of the case of non-termination of RSVP. In this case, NED1 becomes the connection owner, when the first packet from a sender arrives at NED1. Then, a bi-directional ATM connection is established by using the signaling procedure [7] and some techniques of IP over ATM [12]. At this time, a TCP session is also established. However, resources are not reserved at this phase. After that, the receiver invokes the Reserve message of RSVP control messages to reserve resources. When the message arrives at NED1 across the ATM network, the signaling procedure [8] is invoked. It should be noted that this procedure cannot be started from NED2 because this procedure must be invoked by the connection owner which is determined at the connection establish phase. After the resource to be reserved is negotiated by this procedure, the Reserve message is transferred to the sender. In the second and later rounds of resource negotiation, when requested resources are not changed, the signaling procedure is not invoked. In this case, the Reservation message is transferred from NED2 to NED1 directly. If NED2 does not receive the Reserve message from NED1, it invokes the signaling procedure, and releases resources.

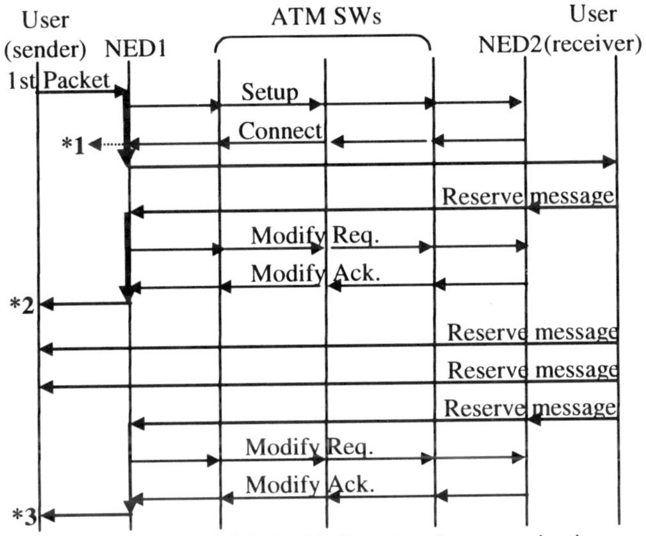

***1:** Connection establish for bi-directional communication

***2:** Resource reservation ***3:** Changing reserved resources

Fig. 5 The sequence chart in Scheme 1

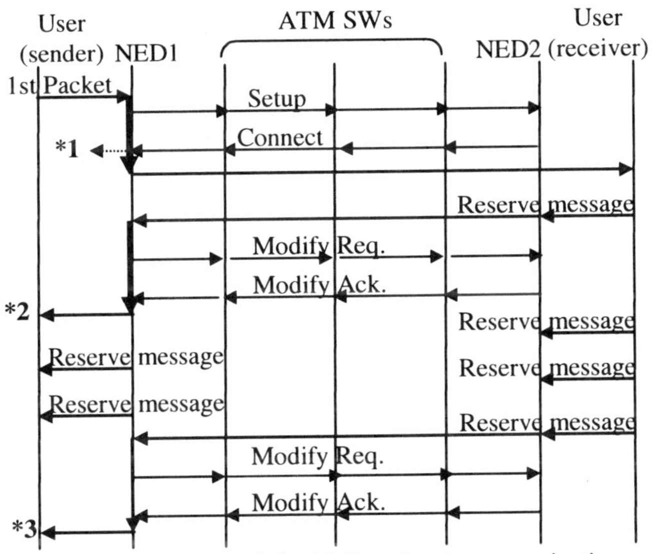

***1:** Connection establish for bi-directional communication

***2:** Resource reservation ***3:** Changing reserved resources

Fig. 6 The sequence chart in Scheme 2

(2) Termination of RSVP control messages : Scheme 2

Another approach terminates RSVP control messages at NEDs. Figure 6 shows a summary of a sequence chart in this case. Operations in this case are the same as those in the previous approach in the ATM connection establish phase and the first resource negotiation phase. After the second and later rounds of resource reservation, if requested resources are not changed from the previous round, NED2 does not transfer the Reserve message. Moreover, NED1 periodically issues Reserve messages to the sender as if these messages are transferred from NED1. In short, this approach basically provides no transfer of RSVP control messages except for the case that requested resources are changed. However, when some fields of RSVP control messages, such as the fields for refresh cycle, are changed, it may be needed that these messages are transferred across the ATM networks.

(3) Considerations of these approaches

In general, processing for a signaling procedure requires a heavy workload in each ATM switch. The delay for this processing is more than several milliseconds or over ten milliseconds, [13] and [14]. Therefore, these approaches need much overhead time due to processing delay of signalling procedures because resources are changed by using signalling procedures. Moreover, in these approaches, NEDs must translate the soft state to the hard state policies, or the hard state to soft state policies. Therefore, management between flows managed by RSVP and ATM connections, such as time keeping for interval RSVP messages and invoking signalling procedures by states of RSVP control messages, are much complicated.

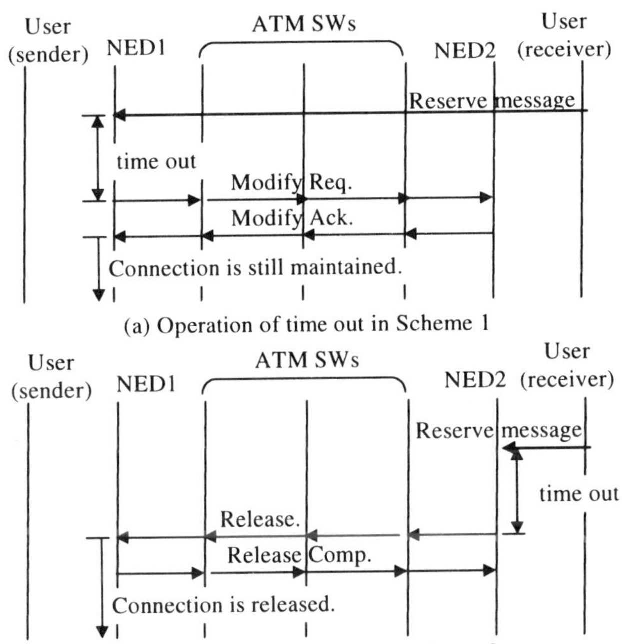

Fig. 7 Operations in the case of no receiving Reserve messages

In addition to common disadvantages of both approaches, the traffic load is increased in Scheme 1 because it always transfers RSVP control messages across the ATM network.

In Scheme 2, even if some of fields besides fields for resource reservation in these messages are changed, they should be transferred across ATM networks. Therefore, NEDs have to memorize all of fields in previous round messages. There is a more serious problem in this scheme as in Fig. 7. In the case of Scheme 1, when the receiver suspends issue of Reserve messages, NED1 can recognize this situation, and can release resources by using the signalling procedure [8] without connection release. However, when NED2 does not receive the Reserve message, NED2 cannot inform NED1 of this situation. It is the only way that NED2 invokes the procedure for connection release. When the receiver resumes the issue of Reserve messages, the procedure for connection establish spending much time must be invoked.

Therefore, we can conclude that these approaches, Scheme 1 and Scheme 2, are not so suitable for emulating RSVP and ATM networks.

3.3 Cooperative actions between RSVP and ABT

ABT has been applied to emulation of RSVP over ATM networks as another possible approach e.g., [15]. ABT provides resource reservation on uni-directional path same as RSVP. Moreover, since the protocol is very simple, processing delay of ABT may be smaller than that of signalling procedures. The case, that RSVP is emulated by ABT, can be also classified into two cases, non-termination, and termination of RSVP control message as well as the case described in 3.2. Emulation of RSVP by ABT seems to be one of good approaches. However, because ABT is performed by the RM cell that is one of types of OAM cells, the control field in this cell is very small. The current specification in ABT provides modification of PCR only. Unfortunately, it is difficult that control fields for other traffic descriptors and QoS parameters can be assigned in this cell. Therefore, there is a tight limitation on the approach using ABT. If two or more cells perform ABT, ABT loses most of its advantages, and will not be materialized on ATM networks.

4. Proposed Approach

We presented some approaches that emulate RSVP by using resource reservation protocols in ATM networks. However, we recognize that each approach has some problems. In this section, we propose a new approach referred to as DLA (the Direct Look-up Approach).

Figure 8 shows the configuration of an ATM switch using DLA. In this approach, the Resource manager is defined in each switch. When a communication path is established, two ATM connections, which transfer user data and RSVP control messages, are prepared. Because, in DLA, connection establishment and resource reservation are separated in each other, resources in the connection for user communication are not assigned at connection establish phase. The connection to transfer RSVP control messages, which are set via the Resource manager in each switch, is established. Some resources for the connection are assigned as a CBR or VBR connection in advance.

When the switch receives RSVP control messages, it transfers these messages to the Resource manager. The Resource manager recognizes Reserve messages of these messages by decoding the RSVP type field in the RSVP header. After that, the manager looks up Reserve messages, and assigns resources to the user connection that is controlled by this connection. In short, this approach does not require that the resource reservation protocol in the ATM level, such as signaling procedures and ABT, are invoked. It can look up the control messages of RSVP directly. In this approach, although the routing issue in the connection-establishing phase is resolved by the conventional signaling procedure, resource reservation by soft state policy is performed by investigating the RSVP control messages directly.

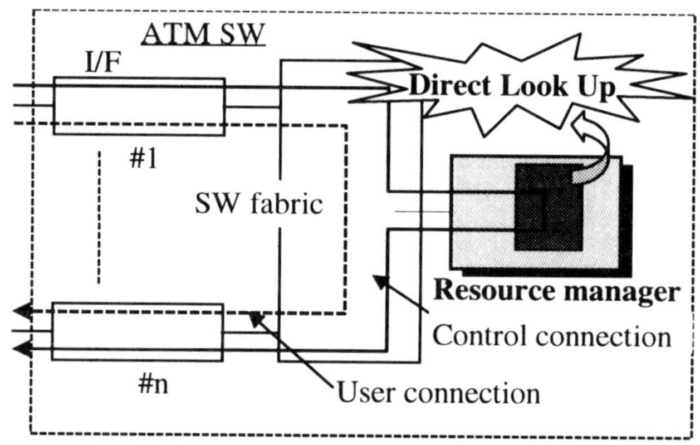

Fig. 8 Configuration of an ATM switch with the Resource manager

5. Issues in the Implementation and their Solutions

In this section, we point out some issues in the implementation of DLA, and study their solutions.

5.1 Data separation to each connection

RSVP is operated over IP or UDP as shown in Fig. 9. Control messages of RSVP must be distinguished from user data. Therefore, if RSVP is operated over IP, control messages of RSVP can be separated from user data by decoding protocol ID field in the IP header. If RSVP is operated over UDP, they can be separated from user data by decoding the port number for UDP. These mechanisms to distinguish these control messages from user data are implemented in NEDs according to our former study [16]. Figure 10 shows the configuration in an NED for these mechanisms. By these mechanisms, control messages of RSVP are transferred across the ATM network by a connection different from a connection to transfer user data. Therefore, control message of RSVP can be investigated by the Resource manager in each switch.

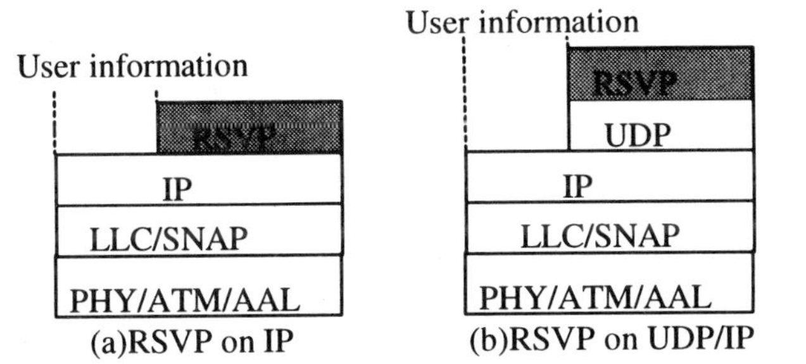

Fig. 9 Protocol stack of RSVP over ATM

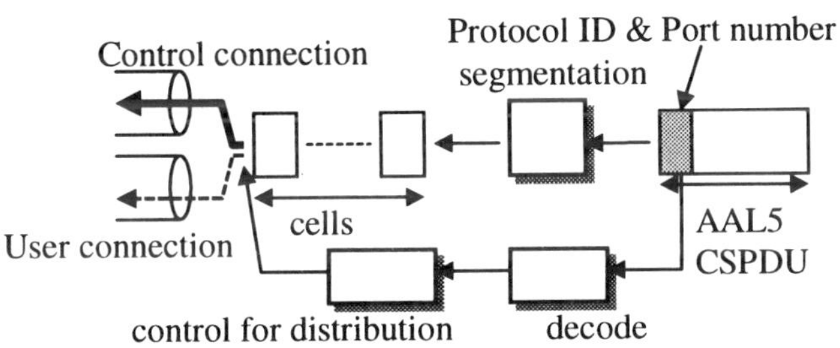

Fig. 10 Processing of RSVP control messages at an NED

5.2 Configuration and operations at the Resource manager

The next issue is the processing messages of RSVP in the Resource manager. Basically, in this approach, the whole of an RSVP control message should not be stored at the Resource manager to minimize transit delay in ATM networks. In the case of the hard state policy for resource reservation such as signalling procedures, the store of the whole of control messages may be tolerated, because the frequency of invoked operations for resource reservation is very small. However, in the case of soft state policy such as RSVP, operations for resource reservation are invoked frequently because this policy requires refreshment at every predetermined period. Therefore, the cut through method, which does not need the store of the whole of a message and has been applied to connectionless communication over ATM, e.g., [17] and [18], is suitable for the processing messages of RSVP in the Resource manager.

However, these messages are transferred across the network by several cells. The Resource manager recognizes Reserve messages of RSVP messages by decoding the RSVP type field at first. After this recognition, in the case of Reserve messages, because the resource manager understands the requirement of requested resources, it must decode the FlowSpec field. Therefore, some cells must be stored at least in the Resource manager. For example, the case, that RSVP is implemented over IPv4, is shown in Fig. 11.

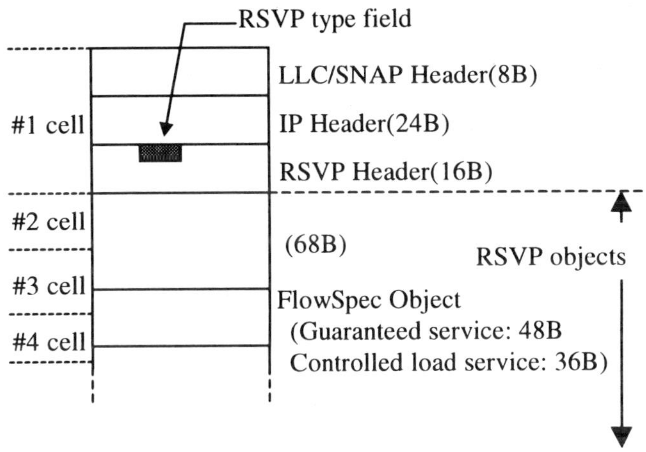

Fig. 11 Mapping the Reserve message into cells

On the other hand, the Resource manager must also work for other methods to reserve resources on the ATM network, such as ATM signaling procedures and ABT. Therefore, the Resource manager is configured as in Fig. 12. When signaling procedures and ABT are applied to reserve resources, information for resource reservation in these protocols is transferred to the CAC (Connection Admission Control) function directly. Then, the traffic descriptors and QoS parameters specified in the ATM network are recognized. Resources, which satisfy these parameters, are assigned in this function.

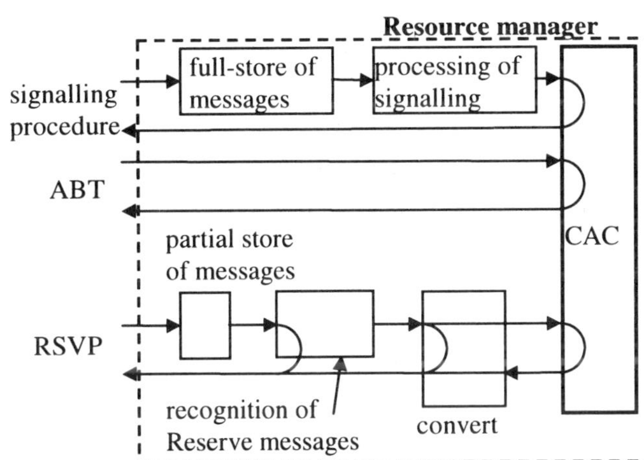

Fig. 12 Configuration of the Resource manager

In the case of RSVP, descriptors and parameters specified in FlowSpec are changed into the traffic descriptors and QoS parameters specified in the ATM network in Covert function by using [11]. In this function, they are compared with those values which were reported in the previous message. If modifications of these values are recognized, new values are transferred to the CAC function by using the local interface. Resources for this case are reserved in the same manner as resources for the ATM native service in the CAC function.

After resource reservation, if corruption of a message is detected by decoding the AAL5 trailer, reserved resources are released. Figure 13 summarizes the processing of the Reserve message at the Resource manager including processing corrupted message.

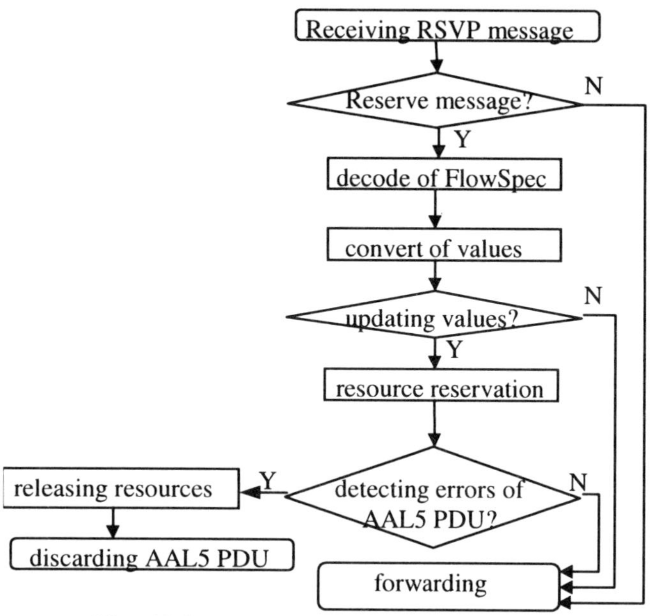

Fig. 13 Summary of the processing flow in the Resource manager

5.3 Reduction of the number of connections

Another issue is the number of ATM connections. DLA requires two ATM connections, connections for control messages of RSVP and user data, to transfer a flow. The number of available ATM connections on a physical link is less than thousands in general. To reduce the number of connections, we propose two schemes as follows.

(1) Scheme 1: Multiplexing by PT

Cells to transfer control messages of RSVP and to transfer user data are identified by values of PT (Payload Type) in each cell header. For example, a reserved value, 111, in the PT field may be assigned for control messages of RSVP. In this case, when each switch receives cells having this value in the PT field, it transfers these cells to the Resource manager. However, this scheme has some limitations. For example, this scheme cannot provide the congestion marking for this cell because of conflict of code points in the PT field.

(2) Scheme 2: Shared connection

Another scheme is the shared connection approach. In this scheme, a shared connection is established between an NED and a switch, and/or between switches, for multiple flows managed by RSVP. Figure 14 shows a connection configuration by this approach. This scheme requires clarification of the relationship between the user traffic transferred by the user connection and the management flow for this user flow transferred by the shared connection at the Resource manager. In order to clarify this relationship speedily, the Leading cell is introduced. This cell which contains VPI/VCI for the user connection managed by this cell, is inserted to a shared connection at consolidation points of multiple connections as in Fig. 15. The Leading cell is forwarded previously to control messages. The relationship, between the Leading cell and the control message indicated by this leading cell, can be recognized at the AAL level. CPI or CPCS-UU fields can be made available for this recognition. The VPI/VCI contained in the payload of this cell will be updated at each Resource manager according to updated VPI/VCI of user cells. In short, the Resource manager maps easily the control message into the user traffic managed by this message, by decoding the Leading cell only. We refer this scheme to as the enhanced scheme.

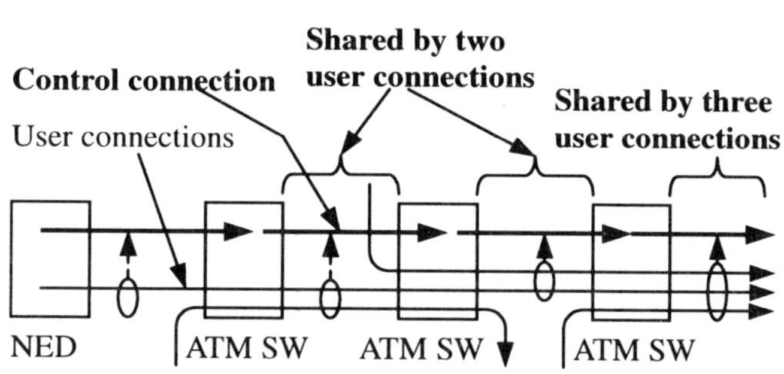

Fig. 14 Establishment of shared control connections

In the enhanced scheme, RSVP control messages should be transferred on the shared connection by message-by-message because multiplexing of traffic flows on an ATM connection by cell-by-cell cannot be provided by AAL5. Therefore, an RSVP control message should be re-assembled at each Resource manager, although the original scheme requires partial store of these messages instead of re-assembly of them. We study characteristics of transit delay for this scheme and the original scheme. These schemes can be modeled as in Fig. 16. If there are no bottlenecks at ATM switches, control messages are partially stored to decode RSVP header and FlowSpec object in Reserve messages. We understand, that the number of stored cells in this decode is 4 cells at least, by Fig, 11. On the other hand, in the case of the enhanced scheme, these messages should be stored in queues for re-assembling in every shared connection. After decode of messages, these messages are forwarded to queue to wait for transmission to the next shared connections.

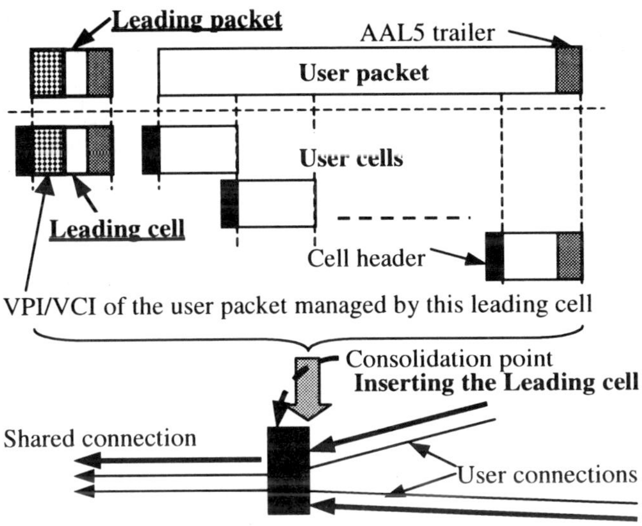

Fig. 15 The Leading cell and a user packet

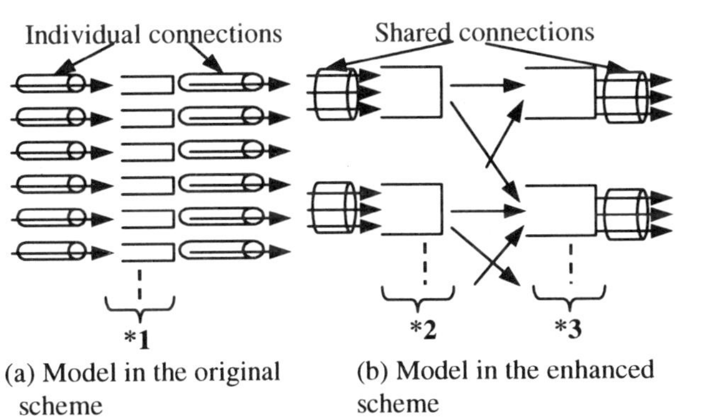

*1:Queues for partial store and forwarding of control messages
*2:Queues for full store of control messages
*3:Queues for forwarding of control messages

Fig. 16 Models in both schemes at the Resource manager

We assume that all of connections to transfer control messages are CBR, and have the same capability, C. Moreover, we suppose that the number of multiplexing connections to a shared connection is N, and the number of cells, which forms a control message including some RSVP objects, is 8 cells. Under these assumptions, characteristics of transit delay are shown in Figs. 17 and 18. In the case of the original scheme, the transit delay is partial store delay only, i.e., 4 cells. In the case of the enhanced scheme, transit delay consists of full store delay, and queueing delay which is derived from analysis of the M/D/1 queueing model, to transfer messages to the next shared connection. However, it is noted that the transfer rate for these messages is NC in these cases. These figures show that the total transit delay consisting of the stored delay and queueing delay in this scheme is smaller than that in the original scheme, for the most part, by gains of statistic multiplexing. Therefore, we can conclude that the enhanced scheme based on the shared connection approach is one of reasonable solutions for reduction of the number of control connections in DLA.

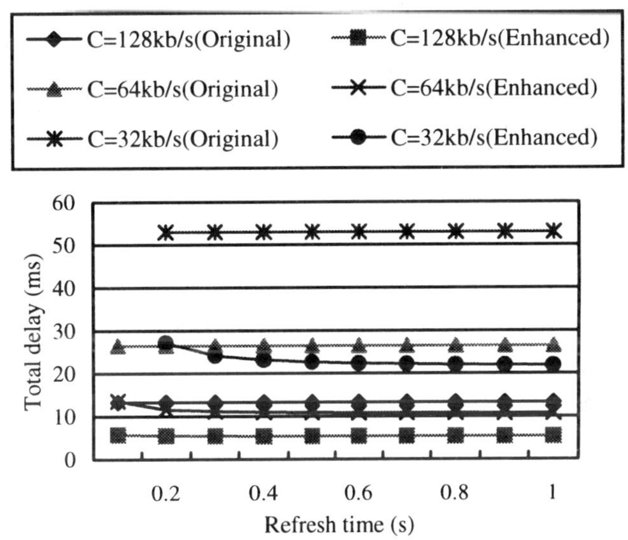

Fig. 17 Relationship between refresh time and total delay (N=10)

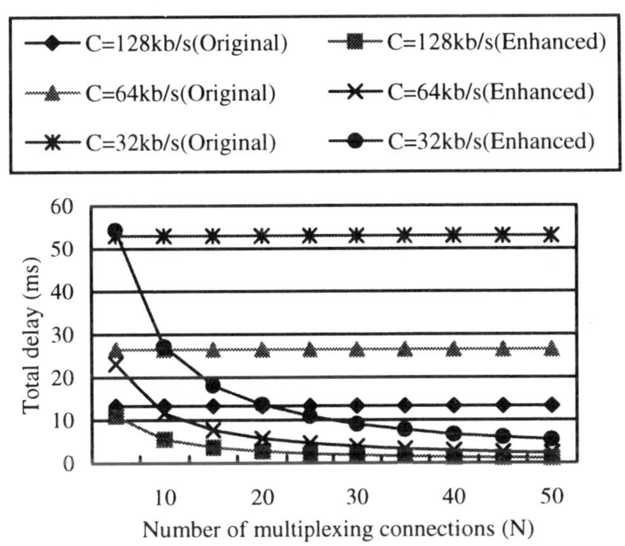

Fig. 18 Relationship between N (the number of multiplexing connections) and total delay (Refresh time = 200ms)

6. APPLICATIONS

DLA described in Sections 4 and 5 can be applied to IP over ATM as shown in Fig. 19. In this case, a router corresponds to an NED. Therefore, in this case, multicast on the ATM level is not needed, because it can be supported only on routers. However, if multicast on the ATM level is required because RSVP messages are transferred beyond a LIS (Logical IP Subnet) as in Fig. 20, the CAD (Consolidation And Distribution) manager is introduced to the switch as in Fig. 21. RSVP control messages from several interfaces are transferred to the CAD manager to consolidate them to one message before the Resource manager. After that, the consolidated message is transferred to the Resource manager. On the other hand, when one message is copied to several interfaces, the message that was processed at the Resource manager is transferred to the CAD manager.

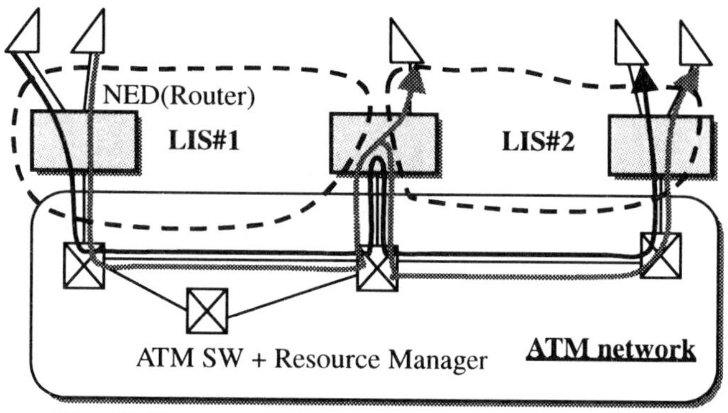

Fig. 19 Network configuration of IP over ATM by multiple LISs

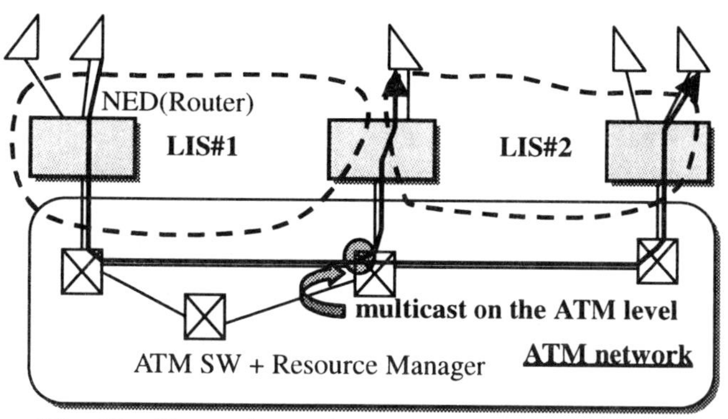

Fig. 20 Network configuration of IP over ATM with multicast on the ATM level

7. CONCLUSION

This paper has clarified mapping schemes between RSVP and some protocols on ATM networks such as signaling procedures and ABT, to provide integrated services over ATM networks. Then, it has pointed out some issues in these schemes and proposed the new approach referred to as DLA (the Direct Look-up Approach), which solves these issues. Moreover, it has presented some issues to implement DLA, and their solutions.

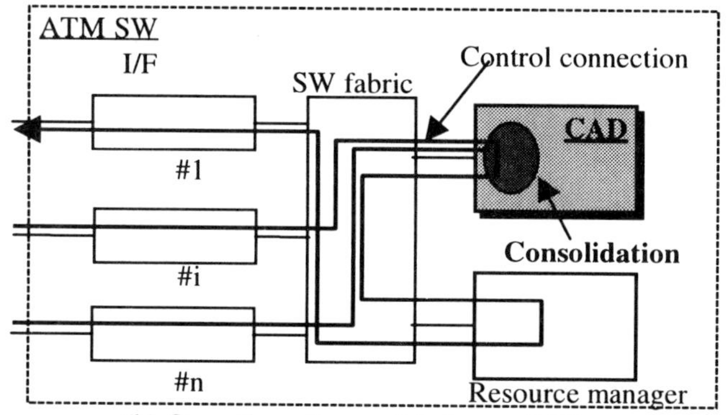

(a) Operation of distribution at CAD

(b) Operation of consolidation at CAD

Fig. 21 CAD and Resource manager

ACKNOWLEGEMENTS

Authors would like to thank Mr. M. Murotani of an Advisor of Corporate Research and Development in Mitsubishi Electric Corporation, and Mr. C. Matsuda of the Chief Researcher in their department in Mitsubishi Electric Corporation, for valuable discussions and comments.

REFERENCES

[1] S. Shenker, C. Partridge, R. Guerin, "Specification of Guaranteed Quality of Service", IETF RFC 2212, 1997

[2] J. Wroclawski, "Specification of the Controlled-Load Network Element Service", Internet draft, IETF RFC 2211, 1997

[3] S. Shenker, J. Wroclawski, "General Characterization Parameters for Integrated Service Network Elements", IETF RFC 2215, 1997

[4] R. Braden, L. Zhang, S. Berson, S. Herzog, S. Jamin, "Resource ReSerVation Protocol (RSVP) – Version 1 Functional Specification", IETF RFC 2205, 1997

[5] M. Suzuki, "Protocol and Implementation Specifications of RSVP - Ideal and Reality", IEICE Technical Report, IN97-61, 1997

[6] ATM Forum Specification, "Traffic Management Specification v4.0", 1996

[7] ATM Forum Specification, "ATM User-Network Interface (UNI) Signaling Specification v4.0", 1996

[8] ITU-T Draft Recommendation Q.2963, "B-ISDN, Digital Subscriber Signalling System No. 2 (DSS2), Connection Modification - Peak Cell Rate Modification by the Connection Owner", 1996

[9] K. Murakami, T. Yokotani, T. Ichihashi, S. Tonami, "Proposal of Signalling Procedure for Dynamic Bandwidth Control in Multicast Communication", IEICE Technical Report, SSE97-87, 1997

[10] ITU-T Recommendation I. 371, "Traffic Control and Congestion Control in B-ISDN", 1993

[11] M. Garrett, M. Borden, "Interoperation of Controlled-Load and Guaranteed Services with ATM", Internet draft, 1997
URL: ftp://ietf.org/internet-drafts/draft-ietf-issll-atm-mapping-02.txt

[12] D. Minoli, A. Alles, "LAN, ATM, and LAN Emulation Technologies", Artech House, 1996

[13] A. Battou, "Connection Establishment Latency: Measured Results", ATM Forum contribution, #96-1472, 1996

[14] J. Wu, Y. Hu, "The Estimation of Signaling Delay in ATM Networks", IEEE Communications Letters, Vol. 1, pp. 172-174, 1997

[15] K. Yamato, Y. Katsube, "A Study of RSVP Implementation over ATM Network", IEICE Technical Report, SSE95-200, 1996

[16] T. Yokotani, T. Ichihashi, C. Matsuda, M. Ishizaka. "Selectable Traffic Control Scheme for Burst Data Transmission using TCP/IP on ATM Networks", IEICE Transaction on Communication, E78-B, pp. 531-538, 1995

[17] K. Yamazaki, Y. Ikeda, "Connectionless Cell Switching Schemes for Broadband ISDN", ISS '90, Vol. VI, pp.5-10, 1990

[18] J. Murayama, H. Kitazume, N. Kukutsu, H. Hara, "Cell-Attached Frame Encapsulation Schemes for a Global Networking Service Platform", IEICE Transaction on Communication, E80-B, pp. 1429-1435, 1997

DQFS Service: A Tunable Scheme to Reduce Scheduling Overhead in Integrated Services Networks

Michael S. Boykin[†]
Taieb F. Znati[†,§]
[†]Department of Computer Science
[§]Telecommunications Program
University of Pittsburgh
Pittsburgh, PA 15260
{boykin1, znati}@cs.pitt.edu

Abstract

Discrete service disciplines have been shown capable of emulating the ideal Generalized Processor Sharing discipline within one maximum-sized packet's transmission time. As a result, the accuracy of such schemes increases with improvements in link speed due to the corresponding reduction in packet transmission delay. However, the merits of such accuracy diminish with improvements in link speed as its impact on call admission decisions decreases. Meanwhile, overhead, in terms of the number of scheduling decisions to be made per unit time, increases with the number of packets transmitted. In response, this paper will present the DQFS service discipline which enables GPS emulation servers to dynamically "tune" their service quanta based upon the QoS requirements of their currently supported applications rather than the network's maximum packet size. It will also demonstrate how the overhead of a GPS emulation server can be reduced in high speed networks without jeopardizing QoS guarantees or adversely impacting fairness.

Keywords: high-speed networks, scheduling, GPS emulation, service quantum

1. Introduction

Recent technological developments involving the standardization of the *Asynchronous Transfer Mode* (*ATM*) protocol have contributed a great deal towards paving the way for more efficient *Quality of Service* (*QoS*) support for heterogeneous multimedia applications. Within the *ATM* architecture, however, the task of scheduling has been left open as an implementation issue. To meet this requirement, the current trend has been to employ traditional scheduling disciplines such as *FIFO* or static multilevel priority schemes along with over-engineering of network resources. These schemes have been shown to provide low overhead approaches capable of furnishing guaranteed *QoS* support for multimedia applications.

Nevertheless, the functionality provided by such schemes comes at the expense of end-user applications through a reduction in the service flexibility afforded them. This lack of service flexibility is due to the network's static definition of its supported set of application classes and priority levels. Consequently, multimedia applications are forced to adapt their *QoS* requirements to levels supported by the underlying network architecture. This adaptation often leads applications to overstate their *QoS* requirements as they must choose among a set of priority levels which usually provide either insufficient or excessive resources in comparison to the application's actual resource need. Overstated application requirements, in turn, may results in a state of often underutilized network resources which is highly undesirable in expensive integrated services network (*ISN*) environments.

In [5, 6, 7], the *Generalized Processor Sharing* (*GPS*) service discipline was suggested as a framework to provide a wide range of heterogeneous application requirements in a fair manner. While clearly useful, the *GPS* discipline only represents an idealized service model which can not be implemented practically as it requires the server to service multiple connections simultaneously and in a fluid manner. Since its introduction, though, several scheduling schemes have sought to emulate the behavior of the *GPS* server through discrete, sequential service models. Two of the most well-known *GPS* emulation schemes are the *Weighted Fair Queueing* (*WFQ*) [3, 5] and *Worst Case Fair, Weighted Fair Queueing* (WF^2Q) [1, 2] service disciplines.

0-8186-8810-6/98 $10.00 © 1998 IEEE

The discrete service provided by *GPS* emulation schemes causes service unfairness to occur due to the discrepancies between the amount of service an ideal *GPS* server would have provided a given channel and that provided by the emulation server. Previous approaches from the literature sought to minimize the unfairness by having the server revisit its scheduling decision after providing each discrete unit of service. In this paper, however, we argue that statically attempting to minimize service unfairness in terms of the number of bits transmitted on behalf of a particular connection leads to frequent service interruptions and unacceptably high overhead in high speed *ISN*s. Moreover, we argue that such an approach is often unnecessary especially given the move to small, fixed-sized packets as specified by the *ATM* protocol standard. Instead of seeking to minimize service unfairness, the *Dynamic Quantum-based Fair-Share* (*DQFS*) service discipline attempts to efficiently define when scheduling decisions are to be made based upon the *QoS* requirements of the currently supported applications. This approach controls the resulting service unfairness yet facilitates a reduction in system overhead without jeopardizing *QoS* guarantees.

As scheduling decisions enable an emulation server to synchronize the level of service it provides to that provided by a *GPS* one, the points in time at which scheduling decisions occur may be referred to as a *service synchronization points*. To understand why packet-by-packet *service synchronization points* may lead to unacceptably high overhead or unnecessary service interruptions, note that due to the much lower ratio of maximum packet size to link transmission rate, many more packets are transmitted per unit time in an *ISN* environment as compared to legacy network environments. Therefore, schemes which dictate per packet *service synchronization points* have to make many more scheduling decisions. This leads to higher overhead in *ISN* environments than in those where the packet transmission delay is greater.

Further, an *ATM* network's small cell size coupled with its high link transmission rates reduces the need to ensure the difference between the number of bits transmitted on behalf of a given channel by an ideal *GPS* server and the number transmitted by a *GPS* emulation server is limited to a single cell. To illuminate this more, consider that human senses generally require time on the order of milliseconds to respond to a given stimulus. However, a maximum size 53 byte *ATM* cell only requires 424 nanoseconds (10^{-9}), less than one-half of one microsecond, to be transmitted onto a 1 Gbps link. Thus, over two thousand *ATM* cells could be transmitted prior to the human receiver becoming aware of the first transmission. Where the end-user is non-human, a certain amount of delay is still usually tolerable and increases in link speed do not necessarily change these tolerances. Therefore, maintaining fair discrete service levels which deviate from that provided by the *GPS* discipline by no more than a single cell may provide no noticeable service improvement for the user but will impose a great deal more overhead on the system.

The *DQFS* service discipline was developed to retain the beneficial characteristics of the *GPS* discipline while "tuning" its decision making methodology for use in a high-speed *ISN* environment. The goal of this discipline, like other *GPS* emulations, is to provide both fair and guaranteed service which is necessary for supporting a wide range of heterogeneous multimedia applications. Unlike other *GPS* emulations, the *DQFS* service discipline attempts to reduce the service overhead required to provide such support. This reduction is achieved based upon the use of dynamically-defined service quanta which enable the server to service multiple packets per scheduling decision. While the *DQFS* approach may potentially lead to an increase in the worst case end-to-end delay suffered by application traffic, we believe the larger delay is acceptable as long as the applications *QoS* requirements are met and a work conserving approach is maintained.

This paper will discuss the *DQFS* discipline's design parameters which allow a *DQFS* server to dynamically "tune" its service quanta based upon the most stringent application in its current workload. Further, it will demonstrate how such "tuning" enables the *DQFS* server to strike a balance between its desire to perform as few scheduling decisions as possible and the need to meet the *QoS* requirements of all supported applications with the system resources available. The following section discusses related work from the literature regarding *GPS* and its most well-known emulation servers. Next, in section 3, a discussion of the *Dynamic Quantum-based Fair-Share* service discipline's implementation and design issues is presented. This discussion will specifically describe the *DQFS* scheduling policy and methodology for reducing scheduling overhead while maintaining adequate application *QoS* support. Preliminary simulation results of the *DQFS* discipline's performance will be contrasted with another well-known scheme from the literature in section 4. Finally, section 5 will present a summary of the contributions made and some suggestions for future work.

2. Related Work

Recently several schemes which seek to provide a discrete, sequential service emulation of the fluid *GPS* discipline have appeared in the literature. In this section, the discussion begins with an overview of the *GPS* scheme itself and highlights the important aspects of its scheduling policy. Next, an overview of two of the more well-known emulation schemes are presented.

2.1. Generalized Processor Sharing

In [5], Parekh and Gallagher described a work conserving network multiplexing scheme referred to as *Generalized Processor Sharing*. In *GPS*, a logical service queue is associated with each connection. Intuitively, the *GPS* server operates by simultaneously servicing the packet at the head of each connection's service queue. Differentiated service is provided by assigning different service weights to each connection. Thus, the actual service rate received by each connection is computed as a function of the service weights of the backlogged connections and the server's rate R. A backlogged connection, in *GPS*, is any channel having traffic ready to transmit at the server.

Formally, a *GPS* server is characterized by N positive real numbers $\phi_1, \phi_2, \ldots$ and ϕ_n, where ϕ_i denotes connection i's service weight. The server is assumed to execute at a fixed rate R and is work conserving in nature. Next, let the function $S_i(\tau, t)$ represent the number of connection i bits transmitted during the interval of time denoted by $[\tau, t]$. A *GPS* server is then defined as a server for which Equation 1 holds for all connections, i, backlogged throughout the interval $[\tau, t]$.

$$\frac{S_i(\tau,t)}{S_j(\tau,t)} \geq \frac{\phi_i}{\phi_j} \tag{1}$$

Summing over all connections j, Equation 1 may be rewritten as:

$$S_i(\tau,t)\sum_j \phi_j \geq (t-\tau)R\phi_i$$

From this, it can be shown that a *GPS* server offers each connection i a guaranteed service rate, g_i, which is defined as:

$$g_i = \frac{\phi_i}{\sum_j \phi_j} R \tag{2}$$

The value g_i represents is the minimal guaranteed rate the server ensures connection i will receive. It was stated earlier that the *GPS* server services all backlogged connections simultaneously. Idle connections, hence, do not receive service and have their share divided among the backlogged channels. Thus, $r_i(t)$, referred to as the backlogged channel i's *instantaneous fair-share service rate* at a time t, is given by:

$$r_i(t) = \frac{\phi_i}{\sum_{j \in \mathcal{B}(t)} \phi_j} R \tag{3}$$

where $\mathcal{B}(t)$ denotes the set of all backlogged connections at time t. Although the features of the *GPS* scheme are desirable, its service definition represents an idealized discipline which can not be implemented in practice. However, it does offer a useful model by which to measure the fairness provided by other schemes.

2.2. WFQ and PGPS

Parekh and Gallagher described a realizable approximation of the *GPS* scheme they refer to as *Packetized GPS* or *PGPS*. In the literature, this scheme is also referred to as *Weighted Fair Queueing* (*WFQ*), an identical scheme presented earlier in [3]. The goal of both these emulations is to select, at each scheduling decision, the packet which would depart the *GPS* server next. One potential problem faced by these schemes, however, is that the packet which will depart the *GPS* server next may not have arrived at the time of the scheduling decision. To compensate for this fact, the *WFQ* discipline selects the packet which would depart the *GPS* server next given no additional arrivals occur in the future. By modifying the service definition in this way, it is possible to have the *WFQ* server maintain the work conserving nature of the *GPS* server.

Selecting the packet which will complete service next in the emulated *GPS* system is facilitated in *WFQ* implementations via the use of a non-decreasing, piecewise linear virtual time function, $\mathcal{V}(t)$. The *WFQ* virtual clock is updated with the occurrence of each scheduling event. Each *WFQ* scheduling event is defined to occur at the point in "real" time when either a currently queued packet departs the server or a new packet arrives. With this, packets are then stamped with their virtual starting and finishing times upon their arrival at the server. At each scheduling decision, the packet with the smallest virtual finishing time is selected to be serviced next.

In [5] it is shown that the number of bits this approximation services from each connection is, at most, L_{max} less than that provided by the ideal *GPS* server; where L_{max} equals the maximum network packet size. Hence, a connection must wait for L_{max} bits, at most, to be transmitted prior to receiving its fair share of service. Thus, the *WFQ* scheme causes connections to suffer no more than $\frac{L_{max}}{R}$ additional delay in the worst case than suffered under the ideal *GPS* scheme.

$$\delta_i^n = \frac{\sigma_i}{g_i^n} + \frac{L_{max}}{R_k} \tag{4}$$

In demonstrating *WFQ*'s applicability for use in *ISN* environments, Parekh and Gallagher showed the upper bound of δ_i^n, the worst-case delay a "leaky-bucket"-constrained connection i suffers at a *WFQ* server node n, is defined as shown in Equation 4; where σ_i denotes the maximum burst size, g_i^n denotes the guaranteed connection i service rate at node n and R_n denotes the service rate of the *WFQ* server node n. The first term of the equation denotes the largest delay suffered by a channel i burst. The second denotes the maximum amount of time a channel may be backlogged but unable to compete for service at a particular server.

2.3. WF²Q

In their work [2], Bennett and Zhang showed that the *WFQ* discipline, notwithstanding, exhibits a major shortcoming that can lead to a high degree of unfairness. While the proof in [5] shows the *WFQ* server never falls behind the *GPS* server by more than one maximum-sized packet, it does allow for the *WFQ* server to get far ahead of the *WFQ* server. Bennett and Zhang showed that the *WFQ* server may be on the order of $\mathcal{O}(N)$ packets ahead of the *GPS* server; where N is the number of supported connections.

Worst Case Fair, Weighted Fair Queueing, or WF^2Q, is an enhancement to the *WFQ* scheme which achieves an optimal emulation of the *GPS* scheme [1, 2]. WF^2Q achieves this by slightly modifying the scheduling policy used by *WFQ*. Instead of selecting the packet with the earliest finishing time, as is done by *WFQ*, WF^2Q selects the packet with the earliest finish time whose starting time is less than or equal to the current virtual time. By doing this, WF^2Q prevents the server from getting more than a single, maximum-sized packet ahead or behind the emulated *GPS* server in terms of the serviced provided to any particular connection.

Through their emulation of the *GPS* discipline, *WFQ* and WF^2Q servers achieve high levels of fairness along with the benefits of a work conserving approach. In both schemes, however, there is a potentially high price to be paid for the emulation of the *GPS* server. The overhead these schemes suffer due to their per packet scheduling requirement can prove too "heavy" for many processors to handle. This especially hold true on high speed links. As a result, many nodes resort to *FIFO*-based or other static priority scheduling schemes in order to enable the switch to process packets at a sufficiently high rate.

3. The DQFS Service Discipline

The *DQFS* service discipline has been designed to provide a work-conserving scheduling strategy that facilitates fair, low overhead service for heterogeneous multimedia applications. The basic *DQFS* discipline provides an optimal emulation of the *GPS* discipline similar to the *WF²Q* discipline. However, instead of defining fairness with regard to how close the discipline's service matches that of the *GPS* discipline, the *DQFS* discipline defines fairness based upon the consistency of its service with respect to that provided by *GPS*. By consistency, it is implied that the *DQFS* server treats all connections fairly with respect to their individual service weights and gets ahead of the emulated *GPS* server by no greater amount than it falls behind. As pointed out by Bennett and Zhang in [2], the *WFQ* discipline does not meet this definition of consistency as it allows the server to get ahead of the *GPS* server by a larger margin than it falls behind.

Like other *GPS* emulation schemes, the *DQFS* service discipline facilitates the establishment of communication channels for use by multimedia applications. These channels have associated minimum service rates and worst case end-to-end delay guarantees. Based on an individual channel's traffic and *QoS* parameters, the *DQFS* discipline dynamically measures how well the server has served each connection at prescribed *service synchronization points*. Afterwards, the server selects the connection in greatest need to receive service next. In performing these tasks, the *DQFS* discipline's intention is to not only meet the *QoS* requirements of the supported applications, but also to reduce the number of *service synchronization points* required.

3.1. The Basic DQFS Server

To select the channel which will receive service next, the *DQFS* server maintains three variables on behalf of each channel. These variables enable the server to monitor three aspects of the channel's service– the length of time the channel has been eligible for service, the amount of service it should have received during that time and the amount it actually received. The first parameter, *busy start time* usually denoted by t_0, records the start time of a channel's most recent busy interval at a particular node. Upon the arrival of a packet which causes a channel to change from being idle to being active, the *DQFS* server updates this parameter appropriately to record the start time and ensure the channel does not accumulate credits during silent periods. This update is performed by having the server remember the time of the *busy start time* when a channel transitions from being backlogged to being idle. At the time of the channel's next transition into an active state, the server determines the sign of the channel's *neediness deviation rate* which is discussed in detail below. If the computed value is non-negative, the server assigns the channel's *busy start time parameter* equal to the current time. By doing this, the server prevents the channel from accumulating service credits during silent periods. However, if the channel's *neediness deviation rate* is negative, the server keeps the old *busy start time* value. This also prevents the server from getting additional service credits. In this case, though, the credits would have been acquired because the channel's previous backlog interval ended and the current one is beginning with the channel having received more service than the *GPS* server would have provided.

The second parameter, the *committed equipartition service rate*, $\overline{EQ_m^n}(t_0, t_1)$, quantifies the service rate node n should have allocated to channel m during the interval $[t_0, t_1]$. Another way of interpreting this parameter's purpose is to view it as an idealized guaranteed service curve for channel m at node n from the *busy start time*, t_0, until a time t_1. As such, this curve measures the service rate a *GPS* server would have provided a backlogged channel m.

The *committed equipartition service rate* for a channel m at node n from time t_0 to time t_1 may be used to compute the number of bits the network should have transmitted on m's behalf between t_0 and t_1. This value, referred to as m's *committed equipartition service level* and denoted simply as, $EQ_m^n(t_0, t_1)$, may be computed as shown in Equation 5 below. In the equation, the time t_0 is taken to be m's *busy start time* at node n.

$$EQ_m^n(t_0, t_1) = \overline{EQ_m^n}(t_0, t_1) * (t_1 - t_0), \qquad (5)$$

The final scheduling parameter, the *node allocation service rate*, $\overline{A_m^n}(t_0, t_1)$, quantifies the actual service rate a node n has allocated to channel m during the period of $[t_0, t_1]$. Because a node services only one channel at a time at its maximum rate, the slope of a particular channel's *node allocation service rate* curve alternates between 0, when it is not receiving service, and the server's peak rate, R, when it is being serviced.

At a given node n, a *DQFS* server computes channel m's *node allocation service rate*, $\overline{A_m^n}(t_0, t_1)$, according to Equation 6 shown below. In the equation, the value of channel m's *node allocation service level* at node n, $A_m^n(t_0, t_1)$, denotes the actual number of bits n has transmitted on m's behalf during the interval $[t_0, t_1]$.

$$\overline{A_m^n}(t_0, t_1) = \frac{A_m^n(t_0, t_1)}{t_1 - t_0} \qquad (6)$$

Having maintained these three parameters for each connection, the *DQFS* discipline's selection of the next channel to be serviced is based on the concept of *neediness*. The *DQFS* server determines a channel's *neediness* based upon how far ahead or behind the system is in servicing that channel. To quantify the value of a particular channel's *neediness*, a *DQFS* server uses the three scheduling parameters associated with that channel in order to compute a *neediness deviation rate* from the time of its *busy start time*, t_0, until the current time, t_1. For a given channel, m, at a node, n, with a starting time, t_0, the *neediness deviation rate*, N, is computed according to Equation 7 assuming all packets in the network are of identical size. If network packets have non-uniform lengths, this value can be scaled to account for the different service times required to transmit the packets.

$$N_m^n(t_0, t_1) = \frac{\int_{t_0}^{t_1} \overline{EQ_m^n}(t_0, x) - \overline{A_m^n}(t_0, x)\, dx}{(t_1 - t_0)} \qquad (7)$$

Positive values of $N_m^n(t_0, t_1)$ indicate that m is owed service and that node n is behind in servicing it. Negative values, on the other hand, indicate that m has received service in excess of its rate specification and that node n is ahead in servicing channel m. Consequently, the *neediest* channel is the channel possessing the largest *neediness deviation rate* value. The *DQFS* scheduler selects this channel for service.

A closer look at Equation 7 reveals the value computed reflects the server's rate of deviation with respect to the service provided to a given channel and not the number of service credits accumulated. Using the rate, rather than the number of accumulated service credits, prevents channels from monopolizing a node's scheduling service by obtaining a large number of service credits during periods of idleness. Therefore, a potential cause of system instability is avoided [4].

Furthermore, it should also be noted that computing a channel's *neediness* based upon its *neediness deviation rate*, instead of merely the accumulated service credits, also allows the discipline to take into account how long it took for those service credits to be acquired. Thus, given two channels with the same number of service credits, the channel which acquired those credits in the smaller interval of time is assigned a higher priority. This policy is based upon the idea that it is more desirable to service the channel having accumulated those credits over the smaller interval because its *node allocation service rate* is deviating from its *committed equipartition service rate* at a faster rate. Thus, we limit the magnitude of the maximum deviation of all the backlogged channels by servicing the channel whose *neediness deviation rate* is accelerating fastest.

Finally, the service discrepancy accumulated by a basic *DQFS* server can be shown intuitively not to increase beyond a single maximum-sized packet in relation to the service specified by an ideal *GPS* server given that ϕ_i is reflected by channel i's *committed equipartition service rate*. This can be understood by noting that in order for the basic *DQFS* server to be ahead of the *GPS* server by more than one packet the *DQFS* server must select a channel with a negative *neediness deviation rate* as the neediest channel. However, this implies that the *DQFS* server is ahead of the *GPS* server with respect to each backlogged channel. This is impossible, though, since both servers are work conserving and bound by a maximum rate of R. From this, it can also be proven that the *DQFS* server does not fall behind the *GPS* server by more than a single maximum-sized packet either.

In the following subsection, the ability of the *DQFS* server to provide fair service within a single maximum-sized packet will be used as a building block for the server's synchronization efforts. In attempting to determine the period of synchronization, the objective of the *DQFS* discipline is to introduce *service synchronization points* only as required by a node's service rate and the *QoS* demands of its supported applications. By interposing *service synchronization points* as such, the service discipline can "tune" the server's behavior appropriately. When the server must provide highly synchronous service due to stringent *QoS* demands, the discipline can insert the necessary number of *service synchronization points*. Similarly, fewer *service synchronization points* are inserted if the *QoS* demands of the supported applications are less stringent.

3.2. Synchronizing DQFS Servers

The basic *DQFS* service discipline focused on minimizing the maximum drift between the service it provides and that provided by the ideal *GPS* server. We would, however, like to streamline this effort and enable the *DQFS* server to "tune" its maximum drift dynamically based upon the requirements set forth by the supported applications. Thus, the *synchronized DQFS* server will facilitate a service discrepancy equal to some integer number of maximum-sized packets. As will be shown later, this approach trades a reduced number of scheduling decisions for potentially larger per channel queue lengths. The idea is to service a selected channel for a period of time which sufficiently offsets the overhead encumbered selecting it and still maintain the necessary service flexibility to ensure the current set of *QoS* guarantees are upheld. As a result, supported channels are serviced by the *DQFS* server for longer periods of time enabling the number of scheduling decisions made over a given interval of time to be reduced. During the extended service interval, however, other channels have the opportunity to build longer queue lengths. Nevertheless, because both the *GPS* and *DQFS* disciplines are work conserving, the total system queue lengths are identical[1]. Therefore, the *DQFS* server's task is to balance its desire to reduce the number of service synchronization points with its need to ensure *QoS* guarantees are met

In order to ensure each application's specified *QoS* is met while reducing the number of *service synchronization points*, the *DQFS* discipline models each channel's two service curves as distributed virtual clocks. The discipline's aim, then, is to provide for synchronization between the two clocks and ensure the maximum drift between the two clocks is bound. Bounding the maximum drift, limits the unfairness any particular channel will suffer as a result of the discrete packet service provided by the *DQFS* node. Further, bounding the maximum drift also bounds the added delay induced by the *DQFS* discipline over the ideal *GPS* one.

[1]The actual *GPS* system queue length can be one maximum sized packet less than that a discrete emulator server as the *GPS* server can service bits immediately upon their arrival while the emulator, generally, must wait for the entire packet to be received.

3.2.1 Basic Clock Synchronization Model

The two virtual clocks used by the *DQFS* discipline for each channel m are labeled $\mathcal{E}_m(t_0, t)$ and $\mathcal{A}_m(t_0, t)$, representing the value of channel m's *committed equipartition service rate* and its *node allocation service rate* curves, respectively. The clocks' values denote the number of times the clock has ticked during the interval $[t_0, t]$. These values may also be interpreted as the number of bits serviced during the interval. The ratio of the values of the two respective clocks can be used to capture how fair the discipline is to a given channel with respect to the perfect *GPS* discipline.

To better understand how these clocks are used, recall by definition that:

$$\frac{\partial \mathcal{A}_m(t_0, t)}{\partial t} = \overline{A_m}(t_0, t) \tag{8}$$

This implies that during the interval from t_0 to time t, channel m's *node allocation clock*, $\mathcal{A}_m$, ticked at an average rate of $\overline{A_m}(t_0, t)$ ticks per unit time. Next, recall from section 2.1 that a *GPS* server services each backlogged channel at its *instantaneous fair-share service rate*, $r_m(t)$. Over an interval $[t_0, t]$, then, a backlogged channel m's *effective fair-share service rate*, denoted as $\overline{g_m}(t_0, t)$, during that interval may be defined as:

$$\overline{g_m}(t_0, t) = \frac{1}{(t - t_0)} \int_{t_0}^{t} r_m(x)\, dx \tag{9}$$

Note further that:

$$\frac{\partial \mathcal{E}_m(t_0, t)}{\partial t} = \overline{g_m}(t_0, t) \tag{10}$$

Thus, over an interval $[t_0, t]$, a channel's *committed equipartition clock*, $\mathcal{E}_m$, ticks at an average rate equal to its *effective fair-share service rate* during that interval. Therefore, the value

$$\frac{\frac{\partial \mathcal{A}_m(t_0,t)}{\partial t}}{\frac{\partial \mathcal{E}_m(t_0,t)}{\partial t}} = \frac{\partial \mathcal{A}_m(t_0, t)}{\partial \mathcal{E}_m(t_0, t)}$$

denotes the relation between the two service clocks at time t. This value can be rewritten as:

$$\frac{\partial \mathcal{A}_m(t_0, t)}{\partial \mathcal{E}_m(t_0, t)} = \frac{\overline{A_m}(t_0, t)}{\overline{g_m}(t_0, t)} \tag{11}$$

in order to depict the same relationship at time t but according to the rate of service provided by the *DQFS* server and that which would have been provided by an ideal *GPS* server.

In a *GPS* service model, the ratio of the two virtual service clocks always equals one as the two curves are identical by definition.

$$\frac{\partial \mathcal{A}_m(t_0,t)}{\partial \mathcal{E}_m(t_0,t)} = \frac{\overline{A_m}(t_0,t)}{\overline{g_m}(t_0,t)} = 1$$

Correspondingly, the goal of previous disciplines which seek to emulate *GPS*, including the basic *DQFS* discipline, has been to maintain this ratio as close to one as possible. Practically, however, the discrete nature of the service does not allow any emulation to match this value in the worst case. From the above definitions, a network server n's maximum drifting time may be defined, in general, by ρ^n as shown below.

$$(1-\rho^n) \leq \frac{\partial \mathcal{A}_m(t_0,t)}{\partial \mathcal{E}_m(t_0,t)} \leq (1+\rho^n) \qquad (12)$$

As the *WFQ* discipline does not meet our definition of consistency, the value of ρ^n for that discipline grows as a function of the number of supported connections. More precisely, the rightmost term of Equation 12 increases because the distance the *WFQ* server may get ahead of the *GPS* server grows with the number of accepted connections. The value of ρ^n in the leftmost term, on the other hand, is a function of a single maximum-sized packet as the *WFQ* server lags behind the *GPS* server by this much at most. Because of their tight consistency, the *DQFS* and *WF²Q* schemes provide an optimal emulation in this regard as they maintains a worst case ratio of:

$$\left[1-\left(\frac{\frac{s}{(t-t_0)}}{g_m}\right)\right] \leq \left[\frac{\partial \mathcal{A}_m(t_0,t)}{\partial \mathcal{E}_m(t_0,t)}\right] \leq \left[1+\left(\frac{\frac{s}{(t-t_0)}}{g_m}\right)\right]$$

where s is the maximum-size of a discrete unit of service and g_m is channel m's minimum guaranteed service rate. In the basic *DQFS* and *WF²Q* schemes, ρ^n is statically defined as a function of the maximum network packet size in both the rightmost and leftmost terms. Previous analysis has focused on the fact that, given a fixed packet size, the duration of the server drift goes to zero as the server's rate, R, goes to infinity; where server drift is defined as $\frac{s}{R}$. Hence, a discipline's emulation of the *GPS* discipline becomes increasingly exact as the server's rate increases.

Our analysis, however, also observes that the magnitude of the server's drift, denoted by the fraction $\frac{s}{(t-t_0)}$, goes to zero as well as the interval $[t_0, t]$ goes to infinity. This implies given a sufficiently large interval, ρ^n goes to zero regardless of s or the server's rate. In other words, over an adequately-sized observation interval, the difference in the rates of service provided by a *GPS* server and a discrete *GPS* emulation server goes to zero indicating their clocks become synchronized. This holds for *DQFS* service, *WF²Q* as well as *WFQ*.

Observing that s represents the maximum number of any channel's bits which the server may transmit sooner or later than the emulated *GPS* server does, the goal of the *DQFS* discipline is to determine a logical value of s which ensures application guarantees are fulfilled while enlarging the maximum discrete unit of service. This is based on the fact that the size of s not only plays a role in determining the time required for synchronization to be achieved, it also plays a major factor in determining the overhead encumbered achieving it. In regard to "tuning" the maximum drifting time, then, the *DQFS* discipline computes a logical value for s which is a function of the supported application's *QoS* requirements, the server's maximum rate and the maximum network packet size. This logical definition enables the *synchronized DQFS* server to service a larger number of packets between its *service synchronization points*, in turn, enabling it to reduce overhead.

3.2.2 Tuning ρ in DQFS servers

A service discipline can use several methods to compute the value of ρ^n. Considering the previously prescribed *DQFS* policy, however, the value of ρ^n should be based upon the most stringent *QoS* guarantee currently extended. By "tuning" the *DQFS* service clock to the precision level required by the most stringent application, other, less stringent applications, will automatically be "tuned" to an acceptable level of precision as well. This approach offers an added benefit in that it can reduce overhead without having to limit the number of application classes the server can support. Static priority schemes, on the other hand, often reduce the complexity of its scheduling decisions by limiting the number of distinct application classes it supports.

Recall from subsection 2.2 that δ_m^n, the worst-case delay suffered at a node n by a channel m with a guaranteed service rate g_m, is generally defined as:

$$\delta_m^n \leq \frac{\sigma_m}{g_m} + q_m\frac{s}{R} \qquad (13)$$

where q_m equals one for a basic *DQFS* server and the other values are as defined in subsection 2.2. The value $(q_m \cdot \frac{s}{R})$ denotes the maximum time the basic *DQFS* server may drift behind the *GPS* server before beginning to service channel m at its guaranteed rate, g_m. While the goal of the synchronized *DQFS* service discipline is to define a logical packet of size $(q_m \cdot s)$, we must not forget that each physical packet which composes this logical packet can have a different deadline by which it must be transmitted. This is in contrast to the constraints which would be present if the packet were actually $(q_m \cdot s)$ bits in length. If this were the case, there would be only one deadline for all bits of the packet.

In its efforts to compute ρ^n, therefore, the synchronized *DQFS* server modifies Equation 13 to account for the fact that packets towards the tail of a channel's queue may have a later finishing time than packets near the head of the queue. Consequently, the worst case delay equation used by a *DQFS* server is defined as follows:

$$\delta_m^n \leq \frac{\sigma_m}{g_m} + \frac{[(N-1) \cdot ((q_m - 1) \cdot s)]}{R} + \frac{s}{R} \tag{14}$$

where N is the number of supported connections. The second term in this equation accounts for the fact that, while the first packet in a channel's queue may have a smaller finishing time than the packet at the head of channel m's queue, the proceeding $(q_m - 1)$ cells of size s may all have a finishing time greater than the packet at the head of m's queue. Equation 14 helps guide the *DQFS* server in its determination of the maximum time channel m can tolerate it drifting behind the *GPS* server without violating its delay constraint, δ_m^n. In other words, the *DQFS* server computes the maximum q_m such that no channel's *QoS* guarantee is violated.

To understand the *DQFS* server's approach, observe Equation 15 below which is obtained from Equation 12 by substituting the derivatives of the two clocks with their actual values as defined in Equations 8 and 10. The n in the superscript of the variable denotes they are maintained at node n. Equations 16 and 17 are obtained, next, by multiplying Equation 15 by the value $\overline{g_m^n}(t_0, t)$.

$$(1 - \rho^n) \leq \frac{\overline{A_m^n}(t_0, t)}{\overline{g_m^n}(t_0, t)} \leq (1 + \rho^n) \tag{15}$$

$$[\, \overline{g_m^n}(t_0, t) - (\rho^n * \overline{g_m^n}(t_0, t))\,] \leq \overline{A_m^n}(t_0, t) \tag{16}$$

$$\overline{A_m^n}(t_0, t) \leq [\, \overline{g_m^n}(t_0, t) + (\rho^n * \overline{g_m^n}(t_0, t))\,] \tag{17}$$

From Equations 16 and 17, it can be observed that, over an interval of size Δ_m, channel m's *node allocation clock* may deviate from its *committed equipartition clock* by as many as:

$$[\rho^n * \overline{g_m^n}(t_0, t_0 + \Delta_m) * \Delta_m)] \tag{18}$$

clock ticks. This value may alternatively be viewed as the number of bits the emulation server is ahead or behind the *GPS* server. Separately, the value $(\rho^n * \Delta_m)$ denotes the size of the drift interval and $\overline{g_m^n}(t_0, t_0 + \Delta_m)$ denotes the effective rate at which m should receive service at node n during that interval. Denoting the value from Equation 18 by $\wp_m^n$ and substituting this value into Equation 14 for $(q_m * s)$, the following equation is obtained:

$$\delta_m^n \leq \frac{\sigma_m}{g_m^n} + \frac{[(N-1) \cdot (\wp_m^n - s)] + s}{R}$$

Assigning δ_m^n the value of channel m's delay requirements and solving for $\wp_m^n$ as shown in Equation 19, the maximum number of bits channel m can tolerate being transmitted prior to receiving its fair-share is computed. Alternatively this computed value when divided by R gives the longest tolerable drift interval that m may tolerate at node n without potentially having its delay constraint violated.

$$\wp_m^n \leq \left[\left(\delta_m^n - \frac{\sigma_m}{g_m^n} + \frac{(N-2)(S)}{R} \right) * \frac{R}{(N-1)} \right] \tag{19}$$

Finally, to compute, ρ^n, the quantum between two of *DQFS* server n's *service synchronization points*, Equation 20 shown below is used;

$$\rho^n = \{\min \ \wp_i^n \mid i \in \mathcal{S}^n(t)\} \tag{20}$$

where $\mathcal{S}^n(t)$ denotes the set of supported channels at node n at time t. Given ρ^n, a *DQFS* server in a packet network may continue servicing a selected channel's packets until either no more packets are queued or servicing the next packet will cause the server to exceed the maximum drift interval, ρ^n. In a cellular environment such as that defined by *ATM*, the *DQFS* server is allowed to service up to $\lfloor \frac{\rho^n}{s} \rfloor$ cells between *service synchronization points*. In doing so, the *DQFS* server is assured no channel's *QoS* guarantee will be violated. After the server completes service to the selected channel, the next *service synchronization point* takes place and a new channel selection is made. The value of ρ^n is updated each time a new connection is accepted or an old one is terminated. When this occurs, Equation 20 is used again with the new set of channels so that the new minimum synchronization interval can be selected and the system can remain "tuned".

4. Simulation and Analysis

To demonstrate the improved capabilities the *DQFS* discipline's approach provides, we implemented several *ISN* scheduling disciplines using the *CSIM* discrete-event simulation package. A representative example of the results of the simulation trials conducted is presented below. Due to space concerns, only the results of three *DQFS* server and the *WF*^{2}*Q* simulation trials are presented.

In the first simulation trial which lasted for 10 minutes of simulated time, a single server was configured to transmit 10,000 cells per second. The server provided support to ten connections, each with a guaranteed service rate of 1000 cells per second. All connections were assumed to tolerate a queueing delay of 20 milliseconds. In addition, each connection was allowed a maximum burst size of 10 cells. A connection's packets, therefore, were only permitted to occupy the maximum burst size number of buffers

Scheme	Num Synch. Points	Avg. Cells per Quantum	Num Late
DQFS	450,011	11.999	0
WF^2Q	5,400,111	1	0

Table 1. Trial One Results

Scheme	Num Synch. Points	Avg. Cells per Quantum	Num Late
DQFS	2,465,269	1.609	0
WF^2Q	4,018,156	1	0

Table 2. Trial Two Results

at any given time. Lastly, each connection was assumed to have an infinite capacity, dedicated, point-to-point link to the server enabling it to deposit packets at the server at the instant they are formed by the application.

Parekh and Gallagher computed the worst case delay any of these 10 channels may suffer to be 10.1 milliseconds according to equation 4. This worst case situation can be simulated to occur by having each of the channels continuously occupy their maximum number of buffers. By simulating this, the *DQFS* discipline's ability to ensure *QoS* support while reducing the number of service synchronization points can be observed.

In table 1, a chart is shown depicting the number of scheduling decisions made by each discipline, the average number of packets serviced between service synchronization points and the number of packets which missed the service deadline Based on the values in the chart, one can observe that the *DQFS* server required substantially fewer *service synchronization points* than the WF^2Q server. The value of $\lfloor \frac{\rho^n}{s} \rfloor$ for the *DQFS* server trial was 12. As depicted, the *DQFS* server serviced multiple cells between *service synchronization points* on average compared to the one cell serviced by the WF^2Q server. Notice too that the *DQFS* server's efforts to increase its quantum did not interfere with its ability to meet each channel's 20 millisecond delay constraint. With each trial, however, we noticed the average delay observed by packets serviced by the *DQFS* server increased over that observed by packets serviced by a WF^2Q server. Additionally, the size of the increase was directly related to increases in the average quantum size. Nevertheless, we feel this difference is acceptable since the application's *QoS* requirements were satisfied.

The results of the second trial are shown in table 2. The server's rate was again configured to be 10,000 cells per second. Instead of having all of the channels be continuously backlogged, only four of the channels in the trial transmitted the maximum number of packets. Two of these channels had a guaranteed rate of 1000 cells per second, while the other two had a guaranteed rate of 2000 cells per second. Two additional channels in the trial were also guaranteed a rate of 1000 cells per second but generated packets based on a geometric distribution. The probability of generating a packet during each cell time was assigned to be 0.1 while the probability of being idle was 0.9. The remaining two channels of the trial were also guaranteed 1000 cells per second but generated traffic according to an interrupted poisson process (*IPP*) where the length of the active state was drawn from a exponential distribution with a mean of 0.01 seconds and the length of the idle state was exponentially distributed with a mean of 0.09 seconds. In the active state, the *IPP* channels attempted to deposit a cell every $\frac{1}{10{,}000^{th}}$ of a second depending upon the number of packets they currently had queued at the server. Finally, the maximum burst size was defined to be 10 cells for the channels that were guaranteed 1000 cells per second. It was defined to be 20 cells for the channels which were guaranteed 2000 cells per second.

Scheme	Num Synch. Points	Avg. Cells per Quantum	Num Late
DQFS	2,973,638	1.332	0
WF^2Q	3,971,733	1	0

Table 3. Trial Three Results

Similar to the first trial, the *DQFS* server required fewer *service synchronization points* than the WF^2Q scheme and serviced more cells between each of them on average. Likewise, no cells were transmitted after their deadline. Though not shown in the chart, a fraction of the packets in this trial were dropped because the stochastic channels periodically exceeded their maximum burst size under both schemes. In this trial, the size of the service synchronization interval was equal to 15 due to the reduced number of channels considered in the trial. The average number of cells serviced per synchronization interval, although less than in the first trial, is still beneficial as a 60 percent increase in the number of cells transmitted per scheduling decision translates into 3750 fewer scheduling decisions per second on a 10,000 cell per second link. This percentage savings is especially useful since the computation of ρ^n need only be done when channels are accepted or terminated at a node.

In the third simulation trial, the server's rate was again configured to be 10,000 cells per second and each channel's guaranteed service rate was 1000 cells per second. In this trial, only three of the channels in the trial transmitted the maximum number of packets. Three other channels generated packets based on a geometric distribution, while the remaining four channels generated traffic according to an interrupted poisson process (*IPP*). The characteristics of these stochastic channels were identical to that described for the second trial.

As expected, the values in table 3 show no packets

missed their deadline under either of the schemes. Again, a fraction of the packets in this trial were dropped due to the stochastic channels periodically exceeding their maximum burst size. In this trial, we observed, once more, that the *DQFS* server performed fewer scheduling decisions than the WF^2Q server. Here the average number of packets serviced between service synchronization points was less than it was in the other trials as a result of the increased likelihood of channels having a backlog which was fewer than $\lfloor \frac{\rho^n}{s} \rfloor$ cells in length. However, the savings is still beneficial as less processing capacity is required for scheduling.

5. Conclusion

In summary, this paper has outlined the the scheduling policies and methodologies prescribed for use by a *DQFS* server. The *DQFS* service discipline was shown to be generalized and capable of providing support for real-time applications while reducing the overhead required for such support. Particular attention was paid to the *DQFS* synchronization model and the computation used to determine the interval between *service synchronization points*. Further, the *DQFS* discipline's *service synchronization points* were shown to enable a *DQFS* server to "tune" its scheduling quanta based upon its service rate and its supported channel's *QoS* demands. Finally, the paper contrasted results showing the *DQFS* discipline's performance and that of other well-known service disciplines.

In the future, the impact of the *DQFS* server's multi-packet service quantum will be assessed in relation to best-effort traffic. Because best-effort traffic is usually over-subscribed in *ISN*s, it is expected that best-effort connections should benefit greatly from the *DQFS* server's dynamic, yet fair, service quanta. Further, the implications of providing statistical and predictive service guarantees will be explored within the *DQFS* service model for applications which may tolerate *QoS* violations for some of its traffic. By providing service guarantees which are less stringent, it is thought that the *DQFS* server can obtain even higher efficiency both in terms of higher resource utilization and reduced overhead.

We are also considering making an implementation enhancement to facilitate improved service to best-effort applications while increasing the size of the actual service quanta. To do this, we are considering maintaining a FIFO queue consisting of the traffic from all best-effort channels supported by a *DQFS* node. Thus, each channel's traffic will be accessible from two service queues– one for the channel and another for all the best-effort traffic. Then, any time the selected channel does not possess a sufficient backlog to consume the quantum, we can attempt to consume the remaining quantum time by servicing traffic from the best-effort FIFO queue. As best-effort traffic is often over-subscribed and backlogged, this approach should prove useful for reducing the delay suffered by these applications. Furthermore, if this approach helps lengthen actual service quanta, it will also help reduce actual system overhead by limiting the actual number of scheduling decisions performed.

Lastly, we have been exploring the possibility of adapting an even more dynamic scheduling algorithm for future use. In the new version, we compute the scheduling quantum at the time of the scheduling decision based upon the current backlog at the server. The quantum is then adjusted appropriately with subsequent packet arrivals. With this approach, we expect to enlarge the average number of cells serviced service per quantum even further as the occurrence of the worst case traffic arrival pattern is often rare or infeasible.

References

[1] J.C.R. Bennett and H. Zhang. WF^2Q: Worst-case Fair Weighted Fair Queuing. In *Proceedings of INFOCOM '96*, March 1996.

[2] J.C.R. Bennett and H. Zhang. Why WFQ Is Not Good Enough for Integrated Services Networks? In *Proceedings of NOSSDAV '96*, April 1996.

[3] A. Demers, S. Keshav, and S. Shenker. Analysis and Simulation of a Fair Queueing Algorithm. In *ACM SIGCOMM '89*, pages 3–12, 1989.

[4] Cathy McCann, Raj Vaswani, and John Zahorjan. A Dynamic Processor Allocation Policy for Multiprogrammed Shared Memory Multiprocessors. *ACM Transactions on Computer Systems*, pages 146–178, 1993.

[5] A. Parekh. *A Generalized Processor Sharing Approach ti Flow Control in Integrated Services Networks*. PhD thesis, Laboratory for Information and Decision Systems, Massachusetts Institute of Technology, February 1992.

[6] A. K. Parekh and R. G. Gallager. A Generalized Processor Sharing Approach to Flow Control in Integrated Services Networks: The Single Node Case. *IEEE/ACM Transactions on Networking*, 1(3):344–357, June 1993.

[7] A. K. Parekh and R. G. Gallager. A Generalized Processor Sharing Approach to Flow Control in Integrated Services Networks: The Multiple Node Case. *IEEE/ACM Transactions on Networking*, 2(2):137–150, April 1994.

A Methodology to Assess Synchronization Algorithms for Distributed Applications

Christina Class, Burkhard Stiller
Computer Engineering and Networks Laboratory (TIK)
Swiss Federal Institute of Technology, ETH Zürich
Gloriastr. 35, 8092 Zürich, Switzerland
{class|stiller}@tik.ee.ethz.ch

Abstract

The need for algorithms providing synchronization between audio and video data was driven by the advent of multimedia applications in distributed environments. Numerous algorithms have been proposed, but there is a lack in methodologies to assess these algorithms, to compare them, and to determine algorithms best suited for a given networking and end-system environment and application.

In this paper a methodology to assess synchronization algorithms for distributed multimedia applications is presented. The methodology is based on four Quality of Service (QoS) parameters for synchronization comprising asynchrony, synchronization error probability, synchronization delays, and buffer requirements. An analytical analysis of these parameters is performed. A key feature of this methodology is that it parameterizes the network, the end-system, and the application. Thus, it allows for the assessment of any synchronization algorithm independent from network and end-system. Influences of the infrastructure on synchronization can be determined by the proposed methodology.
Keywords: *Quality of Service, Synchronization, Analysis, Distributed Multimedia Applications*

1 Introduction

The increasing development in computer engineering and technology leads to increased computing performance. Numerous *multimedia applications* became feasible like Video-on-Demand, Video-conferencing, Virtual Museums, and Teleeducation on top of a broad range of different communication networks. These applications are characterized by the integrated processing of different media types, such as audio and video. Some of these media are time dependent, *i.e.* change their values as a function of time. For this reason, recording, storing, and presentation of data must take into account the data's time component. The task of multimedia *synchronization* is to retain data's temporal relationships relative to each other or to a clock. In case of distributed multimedia applications this task is aggravated.

Multimedia applications need to provide a quality acceptable to the user. The quality must be provided by end-systems, the network as well as the application itself. The concept of Quality of Service (QoS) allows for the specification of the quality provided by a system or required by the user.

Different networks with varying characteristics support distributed multimedia applications. Within the literature many approaches and a huge range of synchronization algorithms exist. Firstly, there is a need to relate characteristics of the network and end-systems with characteristics of synchronization. This determines, if there exists a synchronization method that can, within a given environment, provide the required quality to the user. In response to this need, synchronization quality is defined comprising the QoS parameters asynchrony, buffer requirements, synchronization error probabilities, and synchronization delay. Secondly, there is also a need to classify and assess existing and future synchronization algorithms. Therefore, a methodology based on synchronization quality is defined to assess synchronization algorithms.

In this paper the methodology is presented as well as results of the analysis of two sample synchronization algorithms. These analytical results are required to apply the methodology. The application of the methodology to assessments of algorithms is not shown in this paper.

Following a brief discussion of related work in Section 2, Section 3 is devoted to specify characteristics of synchronization quality. Section 4 introduces the methodology based on synchronization quality parameters. While Section 5 determines an excerpt of results, Section 6 concludes the work and sketches future work.

0-8186-8810-6/98 $10.00

2 Related Work

Synchronization consists of two consecutive steps to be fulfilled. In a first step, synchronization has to be specified, *i.e.*, it has to be defined how data have to be played synchronously. Many approaches have been proposed, *e.g.*, the object composition Petri Net (OCPN) [10], the real-time synchronization model (RTSM) [22] and the inter-operable Petri Nets (IPN) [2]. [15] defines a temporal reference framework that allows for the classification of specification schemes.

The second step of synchronization is to retain the specified time relationships. Many different approaches are proposed in the literature for content-based, *e.g.* [13], event-based, *e.g.* [14], and temporal synchronization, *e.g.* [22], [23]. The two synchronization algorithms [17] and [20] analyzed in this paper are temporal synchronization approaches.

[3] describes a layered reference model for synchronization. [18] compares three basic synchronization methods (multiplexing, out-of-band, and time-stamping) according to a specified set of criteria. [6] defines different general types of synchronization services. [19] describes an approach to build a test environment for synchronization algorithms that measures skew, drift, jitter and losses. These approaches provide useful insight into synchronization but yet do not supply a general classification method for synchronization algorithms.

Quality of Service has been introduced as a powerful concept to define, monitor, and supervise the quality of communications. In particular, QoS is defined in Open Distributed Processing as "a set of quality requirements on the collective behavior of one or more objects" [9]. Slightly different definitions for QoS exist, *e.g.*, within [12]. The use of QoS parameters to determine general synchronization issues on an algorithmic level has been mentioned in [24], synchronization definitions in terms of skew and jitter are included in [21]. Several authors have included synchronization quality criteria in the discussion of their own work, *e.g.*,buffer utilization and delay [11], delay, losses and skew [17], buffer requirements [7], jitters [22], buffer size and delay [20], asynchrony and losses [16]. However, a detailed specification and utilization of generic synchronization quality parameters have not been reported yet.

Therefore, in this paper four generic QoS parameters for synchronization are defined and a general methodology is introduced that allows for the comparison of synchronization algorithms by analytical analyses.

3 Synchronization Quality

In this section basic terms are introduced and synchronization quality is defined.

3.1 Analytical Environment and Terminology

One *presentation unit (PU)* refers to the atomic information of a media stream. Examples of presentation units are video frames or audio samples. PUs are independent, *i.e.* no PU carries information relevant to others. In compression schemes like MPEG, compression is achieved by creating dependencies between PUs. To overcome these dependencies, the bit error probability has to be increased such as to cover also the probability that PUs cannot be presented due to a bit error in other PUs or due to loss of other PUs. Independent PUs can, thus, be modeled by an adequate bit error probability.

Multimedia applications are characterized by the integrated processing of different media types being *time dependent* or *time independent*. The *valid time interval* is defined as the interval in which a time dependent PU is valid.

The *media schedule* specifies the correct play-out time, called the *media time*, for each PU. The first PU of an application is assigned the media time 0. In applications handling stored data the media schedule must be specified explicitly, while in applications handling live data it is implicitly given by the capturing time.

In this paper, we assume that PUs are sent accordingly to their media schedule. Capturing live data and sending them instantaneously to the receiver is equivalent to data being sent accordingly to the media schedule. In case of stored data, the media schedule has to be read and interpreted on the sender's side and the data must be sent to the receiver accordingly to the media schedule. To do so, a local synchronization mechanism has to be applied in the sender, controlling the synchronized sending of the data.

Each PU i has different times assigned:

- The *sending time* denotes the time, the PU is sent ($t_{s,i}$).
- The *receiving time* specifies the time point the PU was received ($t_{r,i}$).
- The *presentation time* is the time the PU has to be presented ($t_{p,i}$). It is the target time of the synchronization and specifies the presentation time as achieved by the synchronization method.[1]

In case of different data streams that have to be distinguished, the indicator of the stream stands as additional index, *e.g.*, $t_{p,(l,i)}$ or $t_{p,(k,i)}$ for streams l and k.

The time in different end-systems is local and in general varies from a global reference time. Time differences and mappings can be clearly specified by the time model as introduced in [5]. This model allows for the analysis of

[1] If some constant time t_x is needed, *e.g.*, in a device to prepare data for presentation by decompressing data, the presentation has to be triggered at $t_{p,i} - t_x$. This can be substituted by a new presentation time. If t_x varies, the variation results in additional asynchrony.

algorithms based on the ideal assumption of perfect global clocks and for the consideration of local times and clock drifts in a second step.

Finally, one *synchronization group* encompasses all streams of an application that have to be synchronized. These streams do not have to be sent necessarily from the same sender. This definition is similar to the one provided in [17].

3.2 Quality of Synchronization (QoSy)

The concept of QoS is extended by parameters indicating the *Quality of Synchronization (QoSy)* [4]. These parameters encompass asynchrony, synchronization error probability, synchronization delays, and synchronization buffer requirements. They can be applied to describe the service quality offered by a given synchronization algorithm.

Asynchrony

The *presentation times interval* is defined as the time interval that elapses between the triggering of the play-out of two consecutive PUs in the receiver.[2] The *optimal presentation times interval* is defined as the time interval between the triggering of the play-out of two consecutive PUs according to the media schedule. *Asynchrony* is defined as the maximum difference of the length of presentation interval and optimal presentation interval as accepted by the synchronization algorithm.

The *maximum asynchrony for intra-stream synchronization* (or jitter) Δ_{ia} in a stream is defined by the maximum deviation of the presentation times interval of two subsequent PUs $(t_{p,i+1} - t_{p,i})$ from the optimal interval $(t_{s,i+1} - t_{s,i}$, as the sending of PUs follows the media schedule). Figure 1 depicts the minimum and maximum valid presentation times interval as well as the optimal presentation times interval. Out-of-order delivery of PUs is defined as a synchronization error and not accepted.

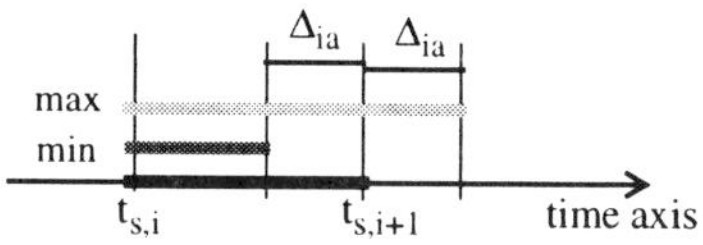

Figure 1. Intra-stream Asynchrony

The *maximum asynchrony for inter-stream synchronization* (or skew) Δ_{ie} for two streams k and l, which may originate from two different senders, is defined as the maximum deviation of the presentation interval of two PUs $(t_{k,p,i} - t_{l,p,j})$ from the optimal presentation interval $(t_{k,s,i} - t_{l,s,j})$.

[2] Note that a time interval can be of length zero to cover inter-stream asynchrony.

Synchronization Delays

The *delay* of data that is transmitted live, *e.g.*, during a video conference, as well as the delay before the first data is presented to the user, may be critical for the quality perceived by the user. Synchronization may increase these delays by buffering data to smooth the jitter.

Buffer Requirements

Whenever the network delay can vary, synchronization needs to buffer PUs arriving too early to ensure an in-time play-out of PUs. *Buffer requirements* can, thus, serve as an indication of the cost of synchronization algorithms within the given environment.

Synchronization Error Probability

In general, three different synchronization errors can be defined [4]:

1. There exist one or more consecutive valid time intervals of PUs in which the corresponding PU is not displayed. Reasons are late arriving PUs, losses of PUs, or unreliable end-systems.

2. One or more PUs are displayed outside their valid time intervals. This is referred to as *loss of synchronization*.

3. The mapping between the different time systems [5] is incorrect or the time systems are not mapped at all. In this case a *loss of time* occurs.

The synchronization error probability serves as an indicator for the quality of the synchronization scheme.

The following example illustrates the relevance for four synchronization parameters to synchronization quality:

Considering two scenarios it can be assumed a given synchronization mechanism based on global clocks and a known delay distribution for the communication as well as an error-free, loss-free data transmission over the network. In scenario A the receiver displays all data exactly at $t_{s,i}+\Delta_{\max}$, ($\Delta_{\max}$ known maximum delay). In scenario B the receiver displays data at $t_{s,i}+\Delta_{\min}$ ($\Delta_{\min}$ known minimum delay). In both cases the achievable asynchrony is 0, as all displayed PUs are displayed in time. Scenarios A and B describe extreme situations, but Table 3.2 indicates that one single synchronization quality parameter alone cannot serve as a valid indicator to describe the overall quality.

Table 1. Synchronization Quality Values

	Asynchrony	Delay	Buffer	Errors
A	0	maximum	maximum	0
B	0	minimum	minimum	maximum

4 The Methodology

In this section the synchronization model and the assessment scheme which underly the proposed methodology are presented.

4.1 A Model of Synchronization

In distributed multimedia applications five different components can be distinguished for the purpose of analyzing synchronization algorithms (cf. Fig. 2): (1) user, (2) application, (3) synchronization algorithm, (4) end-system, and (5) communication system or network.

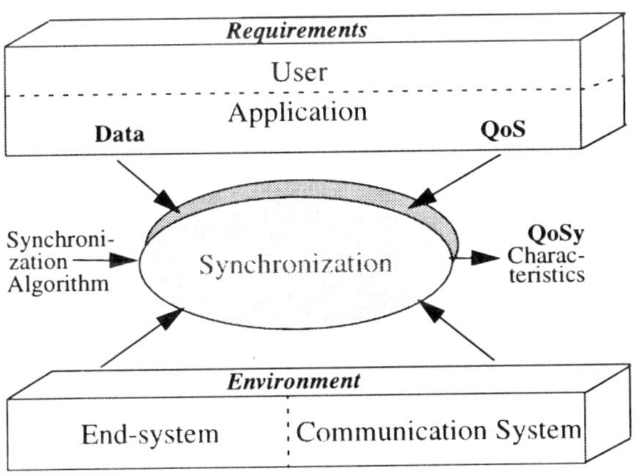

Figure 2. Model of Synchronization Analysis

Applications offer data, where at least a part of them is time dependent and, thus, require mechanisms to ensure a synchronized play-out. Data inherently own characteristics being relevant to synchronization, *e.g.*, the play-out period.

On one hand, the user of an application imposes requirements with respect to the entire application as well as to the synchronization itself. On the other hand, there exist a variety of characteristics of the underlying end-system and the communication system influencing the synchronization.

The network and the end-system offer a service with given characteristics concerning the synchronization investigation. In general, this service may not allow the application to play out data synchronously, particularly, if there exist delay variances in transmission. For this reason, synchronization methods have to be applied to fill the gap between application requirements and users and the "service" characteristics of the end-system and the network. To describe the quality offered by these synchronization mechanisms a method is required allowing for the evaluation of their quality, independently of the specific characteristics of network, end-system, and application.

4.2 Analytical Assessment

Applying the model above and the Quality of Synchronization parameters as defined in Section 3, synchronization algorithms can be analyzed.

Analyzing an algorithm is a demanding task which is not supported by rules or tools. However, clearly separated parameters allow for the direct calculation of the asynchrony. In a first step algorithms have to be analyzed, assuming perfectly synchronized clocks as the simplest case defined by the algorithm. Afterwards, all factors are taken into account step by step that aggravate synchronization by determining changes to the parameters introduced by these factors. The analysis was supported by the clear definition of different time systems [5].

The analysis remains independent of characteristics of the underlying network and end-system which are parameterized. Data characteristics in terms of parameters are included into the analysis, too.

The results of this analysis are expressions of parameters describing the environment (see Section 5.1 and Section 5.2). In this context environment refers to the environment of the synchronization algorithm, *i.e.* communication system, end-system, data, and application. In addition they determine, when evaluated, the synchronization quality characteristics of the analyzed algorithm within this specified environment. Furthermore a list of parameters describing characteristics of the environment and influencing the synchronization quality can be derived (see Section 5.3). These results allow for a deeper, analytical understanding of the synchronization service provided by the studied algorithm and they allow for an analytical assessment of the algorithm by evaluating parameter expressions.

For the analyses carried out, two synchronization methods belonging to two different classes of synchronization have been chosen. The *Concord* algorithm [20] belongs to the class of rigid synchronization algorithms, whereas the *Adaptive Synchronization Protocol (ASP)* [17] defines an adaptive synchronization algorithm. Since QoSy parameters as defined in Section 3.2 are referred to as guaranteed parameters, the analyses have to take into account the worst case.

The analyses have been performed for unicast communications and periodic live data or data that are sent according to a media schedule, respectively. Specially focussed on asynchrony synchronization errors, partly buffer requirements, and delays depend to a high degree on the communication system's characteristics. The transmission delay is analyzed, whereas the start-up delay is not considered, since this occurs only once during the beginning of a presentation and does not have an impact on the quality.[3] Since these analyses determine the synchronization quality in the receiver, resulting expressions also resolve the synchronization quality of one receiver in a multicast group. This holds as long at it is evaluated with end-system characteristics of this receiver and characteristics being valid for the transmission from the multicast sender(s) to this specific receiver.

The second type of synchronization errors (loss of synchronization) may occur due to synchronization information being modified by an unperceived bit error, errors in the synchronization function, or additional delays in the end-system. If the synchronization method is implemented correctly, these errors only occur due to problems in the end-system and are, therefore, not included in the analysis. For the same reason, an incorrect time mapping resulting in the third type of synchronization errors is not included in the analysis of synchronization quality. Thus, the parameter *synchronization error probability* is restricted for analysis purposes to the case in which a PU is not presented.

5 Determined Results

Central resulting expressions of the performed analyses are presented here while the detailed results can be found in [5].

5.1 Analyzing the Concord Algorithm

The *Concord algorithm* [20] is an easy-to-understand and easy-to-implement algorithm as it achieves synchronization by guaranteeing for a constant delay of packets for each data stream. As data is sent periodically, synchronization is simplified. Unknown network delays only play a role with respect to the first data packet.

The algorithm computes the delay each packet has to suffer and operates a synchronization buffer that is implemented as a shift register. A *total end-to-end delay* (Δ) is calculated, which is constant for every packet. This delay takes into account a specified maximum acceptable delay and a specified maximum packet loss rate. Three policies can be chosen to set the Δ of packets: to minimize the packet loss rate, to minimize Δ, or to minimize some sort of hybrid costs.

[3] This may be different, if schemes for stored data are analyzed allowing for the in advance transmission of data to minimize synchronization errors.

[20] assumes that packets are sent periodically with the period T_r which is specified in the media schedule. For analysis purposes, it is assumed that one packet refers to one PU. When a PU arrives, it is placed in the synchronization buffer to delay its play-out until the PU suffered the specified total end-to-end delay. If the delay of the first packet is not known, the total end-to-end delay cannot be calculated exactly and, depending on the error of the network delay, several packets need to be dropped. In case of different rates in the sender and the receiver, which result from clocks tuning at different speeds, PUs may need to be dropped or the play-out of PUs may need to be delayed.

Following parameters are required for the analysis:

λ	error in estimating the network delay of first packet
ϵ	bound on the clock asynchrony
Δ_{min}	minimum network delay
Δ_{opt}	total end-to-end delay specified by the algorithm
T_r	play-out period of the receiver (local time system)
τ_r	play-out period of the receiver (global time system)
τ_s	sending period of the sender (global time system)

In case of the basic Concord algorithm (cf. Table 2), synchronization can be retained by the algorithm and the total end-to-end delay is specified by Δ_{opt} which is optimal. The synchronization error is specified by the packet loss rate that was handed in by the user to determine Δ_{opt}. Buffer requirements per stream are defined by a buffer for $\left\lceil \frac{\Delta_{opt}-\Delta_{min}}{T_r} \right\rceil$ presentation units (for the basic algorithm).

Table 2. Characteristics of Concord for One Stream

asynchrony	0
delay	Δ_{opt} (depends on the delay distribution of the network)
synchronization error	specified packet loss rate
buffer requirements	$\left\lceil \frac{\Delta_{opt}-\Delta_{min}}{T_r} \right\rceil$ packets

In case the network delay of the first packet is not known, the total end-to-end delay is increased by the uncertainty in assuming the delay of the first packet. If this uncertainty is less than the play-out rate, other parameters are not influenced. In case the uncertainty is higher than the play-out rate, a buffer overflow may occur and in total $\left\lfloor \frac{\lambda}{T_r} \right\rfloor$ additional packets need to be thrown away, resulting in a momentary asynchrony. After these packets have been discarded, an asynchrony of 0 can be guaranteed by the algorithm.

Drifting clocks lead to an additional asynchrony of the clock drift's bound. They increase buffer requirements by the number of PUs that may be displayed during the time of the clock drift.

Different sending and play-out rates ($\tau_r \neq \tau_s$) require that every $\frac{\tau_r}{|\tau_r - \tau_s|}$-th packet has to be discarded or duplicated which adds to the asynchrony. In case of a faster receiver, the delay is slightly increased, but buffer requirements are not influenced.

In an environment that has, *e.g.*, unknown network delay and different production and service rates, values for QoSy parameters have to be combined to assess the algorithm for this specific environment.

The asynchrony of a synchronization group results in the maximum of all stream asynchronies plus ϵ in case of bounded clocks. The delay is specified to be the maximum delay of streams belonging to this synchronization group. The buffer requirement for the whole group is simply the sum of buffer requirements of all streams. Hereby it must be taken into account that buffer requirements per stream must be calculated with respect to the delay of the synchronization group. The buffer requirement for one isolated stream may be smaller, if its maximum network delay is smaller than the total end-to-end delay for the group.

5.2 Analyzing ASP

The *Adaptive Synchronization Protocol (ASP)* [17] is an adaptive synchronization algorithm with centralized control. It monitors the underlying network and adapts to changing network conditions. The control mechanism of this protocol is based on the buffer level. One synchronization group consists of one controller for the whole group and one agent per stream. An agent is a software entity controlling an individual stream. The packet sequence must not be changed by the underlying network.

ASP distinguished between one master stream and slave streams. A master stream defines a stream, where slave streams are synchronized to.

ASP is based on stream rates, *i.e.*, data is periodic. The controller sends a start message to source agents, and sink agents start the play-out of data after an initial delay of Δ. Δ is the maximum delay of all data transmissions plus the delay that is needed to fill the buffers to a minimum level.

ASP consists of four different protocols. The goal of the algorithm is to minimize the end-to-end delay or to minimize the data loss, respectively, depending on the synchronization policy chosen and the actual network state. To achieve this goal, a buffer area is defined in each play-out buffer. The buffer fill must be kept within this buffer area. Buffer regions below or above this area are critical. In the master stream a second buffer area is defined, a target buffer area. This area is within the buffer area of the master. The stream agent of the master tries to keep the buffer fill within this target area and adapts the play-out rate while the sending rate remains unchanged, whenever the buffer fill is outside the target area. The adaption is performed by sending an *Adapt* message to slave agents. The message contains the end time for the adaption phase as well as the media time that has to be valid at the end time. Master and slaves adapt their play-out rate, thus, that the specified media time is valid at the end of the adaption phase. In case a slave buffer fill enters a critical buffer region, the slave triggers an adaption phase and becomes a tentative master.

There are two different kinds of adaption phases. The goal of a *slowing down adaption* phase is to slow down the play-out rate for a given time interval to increase the buffer fill. If the buffer fill has to be decreased, the *speeding up adaption* increases the play-out rate during the adaption phase.

Following parameters are required in the analysis:

Δ_{min}	minimum network delay in the master stream[a]
Δ_{max}	maximum network delay in the master stream[a]
c	width of the target buffer area (1 in case of a tentative master)
j_M	accepted jitter of the master stream
j_S	accepted jitter of the slave stream
L_M	length of the adaption phase as defined by the master
l	time to rest in the slave stream for carrying out an adaption phase
$T_{r,M}$	play-out period of the master stream (in the local time system)
$T_{r,S}$	play-out period of the slave stream (in the local time system)
ϵ	bound for the clock asynchrony

[a] During a time interval.

If no adaption has to be performed, the intra-stream asynchrony achieved by ASP equals 0 or ϵ in case of bounded clocks. This is a similar result as for the rigid Concord algorithm. But the delay of the stream is smaller than the delay for the Concord algorithm. It is determined by $\Delta_{min} + \frac{1}{2} \cdot c \cdot j_M$ or $\Delta_{max} - \frac{1}{2} \cdot c \cdot j_M$, and it is smaller than the maximum total end-to-end delay, that can guarantee for a given data loss probability as, *e.g.* the delay in the Concord algorithm. Δ_{min} and Δ_{max} are not fixed, but can vary over time to adapt to the current network delay. The delay in all streams is determined by the delay of the master stream. The delay during an adaption phase and its changes depend highly on the current situation in which the adaption phase takes place.

The asynchrony can be calculated for different adaption phases. The value of the asynchrony depends on the length of the adaption phase in the master and also on the length of the adaption phase in the slave which may be shorter due to propagation delays of the *Adapt* message in the network. This can lead to a significantly higher asynchrony. The asynchrony also depends on the width of the target buffer or the buffer region in a tentative master. Tables 3 and 4 depict asynchrony and delay parameter values for master and slave streams.

Table 3. Characteristics of ASP for Master Stream

	Minimum Delay Policy	Minimum Loss Policy
	no adaption in progress	
asynchrony	0	
delay	$\Delta_{min} + \frac{1}{2} \cdot c \cdot j_M$	$\Delta_{max} - \frac{1}{2} \cdot c \cdot j_M$
	slowing down adaption	
asynchrony	$\frac{\frac{1}{2} \cdot c \cdot j_M}{L_M}$	
delay	increasing	
	speeding up adaption	
asynchrony	$T_{r,M} - \frac{T_{r,M} \cdot L_M}{\left\lceil \frac{\frac{1}{2} \cdot c \cdot j_M}{T_{r,M}} \right\rceil + L_M}$	
delay	decreasing	

The buffer fill smoothing function also influences the adaption phase, as this function determines, when an adaption phase is entered and how aggressive the stream agent reacts to delay differences in the network. The synchronization error probability depends on the buffer width in the stream, the above mentioned smoothing function, and the number of adaption phases, the delay of the network and the bit rate. If the adaption phase is not delayed until all slave agents received the *Adapt* message, the synchronization error probability is increased.

Concerning buffer requirements, $\left\lceil \frac{j_M}{T_{r,M}} \right\rceil$ and $\left\lceil \frac{j_S}{T_{r,S}} \right\rceil$ denote the buffer size in PUs for the buffer region in the master and the slave. Real buffer requirements are higher, as there exists also a critical buffer region below and above the buffer region which ASP takes into account.

The inter-stream asynchrony provided by ASP equals 0 or ϵ, in case of bounded clocks, if there is no adaption phase in progress. The inter-stream asynchrony in adaption phases is limited to $\frac{1}{2} \cdot c \cdot j_M$ which describes the value by which the media time has to be corrected during the adaption phase. This asynchrony may occur in case that one slave agent receives the *Adapt* message after or at the end of the adaption phase. If the adaption phase is delayed until all streams receive the *Adapt* message, the inter-stream asynchrony remains 0. In case of master switching, when a master and a tentative master may send contradicting *Adapt* messages, this inter-stream asynchrony is determined by the sum of the value by which both streams want to change the media time. The delay of the synchronization group is specified

Table 4. Characteristics of ASP for One Slave Stream

	Minimum Delay Policy	Minimum Loss Policy
	no adaption in progress	
asynchrony	0	
delay	$\Delta_{min} + \frac{1}{2} \cdot c \cdot j_M$	$\Delta_{max} - \frac{1}{2} \cdot c \cdot j_M$
	slowing down adaption	
asynchrony	$\frac{\frac{1}{2} \cdot c \cdot j_M}{\left\lceil \frac{l}{T_{r,S}} \right\rceil}$	
delay	increasing	
	speeding up adaption	
asynchrony	$T_{r,S} - \frac{T_{r,S} \cdot \left\lceil \frac{l}{T_{r,S}} \right\rceil}{\left\lceil \frac{\frac{1}{2} \cdot c \cdot j_M}{T_{r,S}} \right\rceil + \left\lceil \frac{l}{T_{r,S}} \right\rceil}$	
delay	decreasing	

by the delay of the master stream. As for the Concord algorithm, buffer requirements for single streams are added to obtain buffer requirements for the whole synchronization group.

5.3 Qualitative Results

The analyses presented so far result in formal results on an abstract level. As network, application, and end-system characteristics are numerically parameterized, they are to be included into the calculation of synchronization quality, *i.e.,* the synchronization quality expressions have to be evaluated by assigning values to these parameters.

The analyses carried out revealed relevant environment characteristics for the transformation from general results to specific numerical results. Figure 3 shows relevant influencing factors for the Concord algorithm, whereas Figure 4 displays these factors for the Adaptive Synchronization Protocol.

5.4 Assessment

The results of the analysis of the *Concord* algorithm concur with the values for buffer size and delay as discussed in [20], validating our results. As asynchrony has been partly discussed in [20], parts of our results concerning asynchrony as well as the discussion on synchronization errors provided in [5] and mentioned above determine new results. These results corroborated our assumptions on the quality and performance of the algorithm. The identified list of influencing parameters as depicted in Figure 3 determines for the first time parameters that should be tuned to

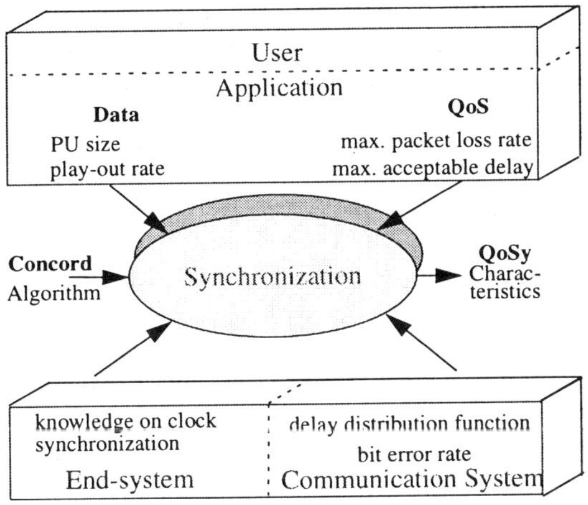

Figure 3. The Analysis Model Applied to Concord

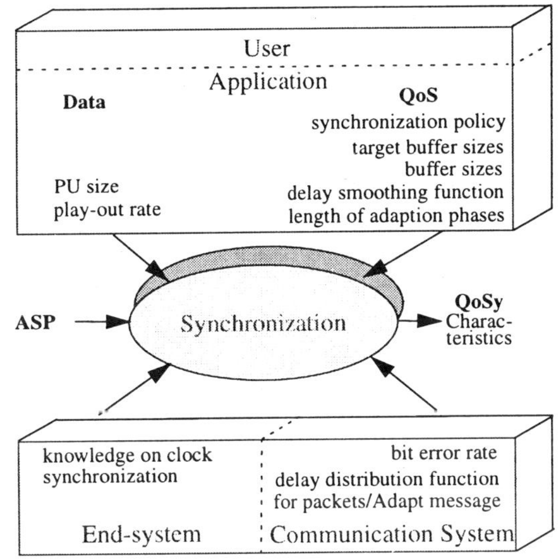

Figure 4. The Analysis Model Applied to ASP

improve synchronization quality in a given implementation providing insufficient quality.

Characteristics of the Concord algorithm have been directly derived from the description of the algorithm. In case of ASP this was not straight-forward, as there are many interdependent and changing parameters, influencing the behavior of the algorithm

Based on the simulation in the CINEMA environment [1], more detailed discussions on buffer requirements and stability issues of ASP are included in [8] and [17]. In contrast, the provided analytical results above, especially concern asynchrony. The list of influencing factors as depicted in Figure 4 together with the analysis results allows for the tuning of ASP to provide high quality synchronization. Asynchrony is necessarily introduced by entering an adaption phase. The obtained results illuminate the concrete effect of adaptation phases and illustrate that it is possible to remain largely within the asynchrony limits defined in [21] even during adaption phases. This was shown by simulation in [8] and [17].

6 Conclusions and Future Work

In this paper a methodology to assess synchronization algorithms is presented. The methodology is based on the concept of analyzing synchronization algorithms analytically. The analysis is performed by determining values for synchronization quality parameters, comprising asynchrony, synchronization delays, buffer requirements, and synchronization error probabilities. Characteristics of end-systems, the communication system, the application as well as the data are parameterized to allow for the analysis of the isolated synchronization algorithm and, thus, of the synchronization quality provided by this algorithm. Two exemplified analyses of a rigid synchronization algorithm (Concord) and an adaptive one (ASP) have been carried out for unicast applications including live data.

The fact that data may be retrieved in advance and can be stored in the receiver has not yet been taken into account determining future work. QoSy criteria will also be studied in multi-party applications, especially, in video-conferencing including a critical delay.

As numerous synchronization algorithms have been proposed in the literature, two problem fields can be identified: Firstly, a synchronization algorithm must be selected for a given problem field that can fill the gap between (1) application requirements concerning synchronization and presentation quality and (2) characteristics and guarantees provided by end-systems and the network. This task also includes the determination of the existence of such a synchronization algorithm. Secondly, existing synchronization algorithms need to be comparable with respect to different criteria which also include characteristics of applications, end-systems, and communication systems.

The presented methodology is a first step to answer both problem fields. To identify a synchronization algorithm that fills the gap between a given environment and application, parameter values describing the environment and the application can be included into expressions resulting from analyses of these algorithms. Thus, the synchronization quality parameters of these algorithms for a specific case can be evaluated. If these quality values fulfill specified criteria, *i.e.* the application/user requirements for synchronization, this algorithm solves the investigated problem. Based on parameter values for the analyzed algorithms the best suited algorithm for the given problem can be chosen.

In addition, a classification of synchronization algorithms can be undertaken based on the analysis of different sample parameter values. This will result in classes of synchronization algorithms focusing on different criteria as perfect synchronization, low delay, or low error rate. For instance, ASP focuses on (1) low delay and low buffer requirements or (2) low loss rate for the price of a less optimal synchronization during adaption phases.

The presented synchronization quality parameters QoSy provide means to better understand synchronization algorithms and to perform an analytical analysis. By this, future applications will profit since a perfectly suitable synchronization algorithm can be selected.

Acknowledgments The authors are grateful to Bernhard Plattner for the possibility to conduct the described research and Thomas Walter for commenting in detail on earlier versions of this work.

References

[1] CINEMA Project. http://www.informa-tik.uni-stuttgart.de/ipvr/vs/projekte/cine-ma.engl.html.

[2] Y. Y. Al-Salqan and C. K. Chang. Temporal Relations and Synchronization Agents. *IEEE Multimedia*, 3(2):30–39, Summer 1996.

[3] G. Blakowski and R. Steinmetz. A Media Synchronization Survey: Reference Model, Specification, and Case Studies. *IEEE Journal on Selected Areas in Communications*, 14(1):5–35, January 1996.

[4] C. Class. Synchronization Issues in Distributed Applications: Definitions, Problems, and Quality of Synchronization. Technical Report 31, Computer Engineering and Networks Laboratory, ETH Zürich, Switzerland, December 1997.

[5] C. Class. Analysis of the Concord Algorithm and the Adaptive Synchronization Protocol Using QoSy. Technical Report 37, Computer Engineering and Networks Laboratory, ETH Zürich, Switzerland, February 1998.

[6] L. F. Rust da Costa Carmo, P. de Saqui-Sannes, and J.-P. Courtiat. Basic Synchronization Concepts in Multimedia Systems. In P. V. Rangan, editor, *Network and Operating System Support for Digital Audio and Video, 3rd International Workshop*, pages 94–105, La Jolla, California, USA, November 1992.

[7] W. Geyer, C. Bernhardt, and E. Biersack. A Synchronization Scheme for Stored Multimedia Streams. In B. Butscher, E. Moeller, and H. Pusch, editors, *Interactive Distributed Multimedia Systems and Services, European Workshop IDMS'96*, pages 277–296, Berlin, Germany, March 1996. Springer.

[8] T. Helbig. *Kommunikation und Synchronisation multimedialer Datenströme in verteilten Systemen.* PhD thesis, Universität Stuttgart, Germany, June 1996.

[9] International Telecommunications Union Telecommunications Standardization Sector, Recommendation X.902. *Information Technology - Open Distributed Processing - Reference Model*, November 1995.

[10] T. D. C. Little and A. Ghafoor. Synchronization and Storage Models for Multimedia Objects. *IEEE Journal on Selected Areas in Communication*, 8(3):413 – 427, April 1990.

[11] T. D. C. Little and A. Ghafoor. Multimedia Synchronization Protocols for Broadband Integrated Services. *IEEE Journal on Selected Areas in Communications*, 9(9):1368–1381, December 1991.

[12] K. Nahrstedt and R. Steinmetz. Resource Management in Networked Multimedia Systems. *IEEE Computer*, 29(5):52–63, May 1995.

[13] D.-Y. Oh, S. S. Kumar, and P. V. Rangan. Content-based inter-media synchronization. In *Multimedia Computing and Networking 1995*, volume 2417, pages 202 – 214, San Jose, California, SPIE, February 1995.

[14] M. Papathomas, G. S. Blair, G. Coulson, and P. Robin. Addressing the real-time synchronization requirements of multimedia in an object-oriented framework. In *Multimedia Computing and Networking 1995*, volume 2417, pages 190 – 201, San Jose, California, SPIE, February 1995.

[15] M. J. Pérez-Luque and T. D. C. Little. A Temporal Reference Framework for Multimedia Synchronization. *IEEE Journal on Selected Areas in Communications*, 14(1):36–51, January 1996.

[16] S. Ramanathan and P. V. Rangan. Adaptive Feedback Techniques for Synchronized Multimedia Retrieval over Integrated Networks. *IEEE/ACM Transactions on Networking*, 1(2):246–259, April 1993.

[17] K. Rothermel and T. Helbig. An adaptive protocol for synchronizing media streams. *Multimedia Systems*, 5(5):324–336, September 1997.

[18] V. Saparamadu, A. Senevirante, and M. Fry. A review of inter media synchronization schemes. In *Proceedings of the First Int. Conf. on Multi-Media Modeling*, pages 229–239, Singapore, November 1995.

[19] B. K. Schmidt, J. D. Northcutt, and M. S. Lam. A Method and Apparatus for Measuring Media Synchronization. In *5th Int. Workshop on Network and Operating System Support for Digital Audio and Video*, pages 190–201, Durham, New Hampshire, USA, April 18-21, 1995.

[20] N. Shivakumar, C. J. Sreenan, B. Narendran, and P. Agrawal. The Concord Algorithm for Synchronization of Networked Multimedia Streams. In *Proceedings of the International Conference on Multimedia Computing and Systems*, pages 31–40. IEEE Computer Society Press, May 15 18, 1995.

[21] R. Steinmetz. Human perception of jitter and media synchronization. *IEEE Journal on Selected Areas in Communications*, 14(1):61–72, January 1996.

[22] C.-C. Yuan and J.-H. Huang. A Multimedia Synchronization Model and Its Implementation on Transport Protocols. *IEEE Journal on Selected Areas in Communications*, 14(1):212–225, January 1996.

[23] P. N. Zarros, M. J. Lee, and T. N. Saadawi. Interparticipant Synchronization in Real-Time Multimedia Conferencing Using Feedback. *IEEE/ACM Transactions on Networking*, 4(2):173–180, April 1996.

[24] M. Zitterbart, B. Stiller, and A. Tantawy. A Model for Flexible High-Performance Communication Subsystems. *IEEE Journal on Selected Areas in Communications*, 11(4):507–518, May 1993.

Multicasting Multimedia Streams with Active Networks*

Albert Banchs
Telefonica I+D
Emilio Vargas, 6
E – 28043 Madrid, Spain
banchs@tid.es

Wolfgang Effelsberg
University of Mannheim
Praktische Informatik IV
D – 68131 Mannheim, Germany
effelsberg@pi4.informatik.uni-mannheim.de

Christian Tschudin
University of Zurich
Computer Science Department
Winterthurerstrasse 190
CH – 8057 Zürich, Switzerland
tschudin@ifi.unizh.ch

Volker Turau
FH Wiesbaden
Fachbereich Informatik
Kurt-Schumacher-Ring 18
D – 65197 Wiesbaden, Germany
turau@informatik.fh-wiesbaden.de

Abstract

Active networks allow code to be loaded dynamically into network nodes at run-time. This code can perform tasks specific to a stream of packets or even a single packet. In this paper we compare two active network architectures: the Active Node Transfer System (ANTS) and the Messenger System (M0). We have implemented a robust audio multicast protocol and a layered video multicast protocol with both active network systems. We discuss the differences of the two systems, evaluate architectural strengths and weaknesses, compare the runtime performance, and report practical experience and lessons learned.

Keywords: *Active networks, ANTS, M0, robust audio, scalable video, layered video.*

1 Introduction

Active networks allow protocol processing code to be loaded into network nodes at run-time. Based on an identifier in each packet header, a specific piece of code is invoked as the packet travels through the node. The main advantage of active networks is the flexibility compared to traditional networks: It is very easy to implement a new protocol, to remove errors in network software, or even to provide specific processing just for the duration of one session.

The next generation of computer networks will have to handle a large variety of application traffic: audio, video, workflows, and many more. Many of them inherently require multicast. In order to support large numbers of receivers worldwide the multicast function will have to be provided in all network nodes. Such a node is already much more complex than a traditional router: it must handle packet duplication, group address management, dynamic joining and leaving of group members, and perhaps also QoS-based multicast routing. The amount of processing required for each incoming packet is increased considerably, and so is network management overhead. New architectures and protocols are being designed and implemented at a much faster rate than ever. Thus an active network architecture allowing the fast deployment of new services in internal network nodes (stream-specific processing, network management) seems very desirable.

Packets in current networks are passive entities carrying data. From a router's point of view the payload has no semantics, it is just a sequence of bits. An interpretation of the data is only performed by the applications at the end nodes. The lack of knowledge prevents a network from performing content–related actions, such as dropping B-frames, but not I-frames of an MPEG video in the case of network congestion. One central idea of active networks is to transform packets into objects that include the operations to be performed on them. In doing so, packets are converted from passive chunks of data to objects with specific semantics. We claim that network performance can be improved in many ways if the semantics of the data is made available to the network's internal nodes.

But active networks also have inherent drawbacks. Since a node loads and executes foreign code at runtime there is a serious security exposure (the Trojan Horse problem). Also, since the run-time code must be portable, it will typically be less efficient than code written and compiled specifically for the hardware of a node. And the resource management problem within the nodes becomes much harder: It is possible that the code loaded for one application stream competes with the code for another simultaneous application stream

*This research was done when the authors were at the *International Computer Science Institute*, 1947 Center Street, Berkeley, CA 94704, USA, http://www.icsi.berkeley.edu

0-8186-8810-6/98 $10.00 © 1998 IEEE

for buffer space, CPU cycles, etc. We will discuss these issues in detail when we present the ANTS and M0 active network architectures.

The main goal of our work is to gain practical experience with two major active network systems, the ANTS system developed at MIT [21] and the M0 system developed in Switzerland [18]. We have installed both systems on a network of Sun workstations, and we have implemented two experimental *multicast protocols* on each system. Both protocols inherently require processing within the internal nodes of a network and are thus good examples for our purpose. The first protocol is a robust audio protocol, adding a link-specific degree of redundancy to an audio packet stream, depending on the observed transmission quality. The second protocol transmits a layered, rate-adaptive multicast video stream. Here the idea is to optimize link load in the multicast tree. Receivers announce their requirements to their upstream node. Each active node requests the maximum of the requested rates to its upstream node and only forwards as much of the video bit rate as a subtree needs.

The remainder of this paper is structured as follows. In Section 2 we present the ANTS and M0 architectures in detail. Section 3 introduces the two protocol examples and their implementation. In Section 4 we discuss architectural insights, compare the performance of the two protocols on both systems, and report the lessons we learned. Section 5 presents related work, and Section 6 concludes the paper.

2 ANTS and M0: Two Architectures for Active Networks

ANTS (Active Node Transfer System) is a toolkit for prototyping active network applications. It was developed by the TNS group at MIT [21]. The description of the architecture and the code used in our project are based on the release of September 1997. ANTS is a distributed system running in user space on top of UDP. It is programmed in Java.

M0 (M-zero) was designed and implemented by C. Tschudin [18]. Its purpose is to provide a testbed for mobile code, with applications in networking and distributed systems. The M0 prototype also runs in user space. It is programmed in the M0 language, which has a flavor similar to Postscript.

In principle active network architectures can be classified into those where each packet carries its own code, to be executed as it passes an active node, and those where code is cached in a node and only loaded on demand. M0 falls into the first class, ANTS into the second.

2.1 The ANTS Architecture

The main purpose of ANTS is to enable an easy development and deployment of network protocols. The nodes in ANTS are called active nodes. Instead of passive packets ANTS has *capsules* which trigger specific processing when passing an active node. The piece of code to be executed is identified by a reference to the forwarding routine in the header field.

In ANTS code is loaded on demand by a sequence of capsules called a "code group", a collection of related capsule types whose forwarding routines are transferred as a unit by the code distribution system. A "protocol" is a collection of related code groups that are treated as a single unit of protection by the active nodes. All protocol code is written in Java using the ANTS API.

2.1.1 Node Structure

An active node in ANTS has two caches, a code cache storing Java byte code, and a "node cache" storing data. In addition it has a classical routing table that indicates the next hop to be taken to reach a destination node. When a capsule arrives at a node the channel thread picks it up and processes it until completion. Capsules have the right to spawn their own threads. The evaluate method of the class of which the capsule object is an instance is executed. Usually it performs some processing on the capsule's content and forwards it to another node or delivers it to an application. New capsules of the same protocol can also be generated and injected into the network. The structure of an active node is shown in Figure 1.

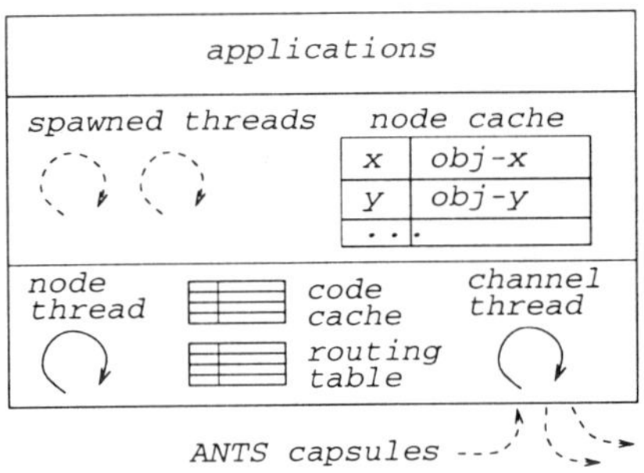

Figure 1. The structure of an ANTS node.

An instance of the Node class represents the local runtime for an active node. This class offers services that can be used during the processing of a capsule: access to the routing table, a cache for soft-states and registration of ANTS protocols.

2.1.2 Packet Structure

The structure of a capsule is very simple: It carries an identifier for its protocol and particular capsule type within that protocol, source and destination address, the remaining resource credits, the address of the previous active node, and application-specific data. Hence there is little overhead.

The ANTS Java API provides the abstract class Capsule for this representation. User-defined capsule types must be subclasses of this class and implement the "evaluate" method as well as serialization and deserialization methods.

That is, the bit stream representation of the capsule's data structure must be defined by the programmer.

2.1.3 Dynamic Code Management

The code representation in ANTS is the Java byte code format. If the code required by a capsule is found in the code cache, it is executed. If not, the active node generates a request capsule, sends it to the upstream neighbor and waits for the code group to be downloaded into the code cache. Once the code is there, it wakes up sleeping capsule threads, and they that execute the code. The rationale behind this concept is that at least the originator of a capsule should have the code required for its processing. Thus new code is injected into the network by the application that created the capsule. The loading is performed with a specialized network classloader. Code is removed from the cache according to the LRU principle.

2.1.4 Resource Management

Controlling the resources of an active node is the basis for guaranteeing quality of service. In ANTS each capsule carries a Time-To-Live (TTL) field initialized at creation time. The value is decreased every time a node puts data into the cache, generates a new capsule, or upon transfer to another node. Capsules with a negative TTL value are discarded. A capsule cannot access its own TTL field; this is an example where security is based on an implicit feature of the programming language. If a capsule spawns a child capsule the remaining TTL is distributed over the two. There is no constraint on the size of the data put into the cache by a capsule. Furthermore, there is no restriction on the processing time for each capsule.

2.1.5 Security

Security is a very critical issue in active networks since foreign and unknown code is executed in the nodes. One of the foundations for the security in ANTS lies in the Java system itself. Using a high-level programming language with well defined access rules has many advantages: Capsules can only be manipulated through the public interface provided, the services of an active node are also clearly defined and cannot be changed by a capsule, essential methods can be declared final such that subclasses cannot re-implement them, the Java virtual machine performs byte code verification to check whether the code comes from a compiler conforming to the language specification, the concept of the security manager of Java can be used to tailor the access of the capsules to the services of a node.

But active networks introduce other security risks which cannot be handled in a such a straight-forward manner. An example is protocol spoofing. To prevent this the ANTS system implements a clever security check: each capsule carries an identifier of its protocol that is based on a cryptographic fingerprint of the protocol code. Thus the probability of a capsule invoking the wrong piece of code is negligible. Some aspects such as name conflicts still have to be solved in the ANTS system.

2.2 The M0 Architecture

What is a capsule in the ANTS architectures is called a messenger in the M0 system: it is a program exchanged between M0 nodes. Messenger exchange was proposed as a replacement of the classical message exchange paradigm used in networks today; it favors an entirely instruction-based way of communication [17]. The M0 execution environment is an implementation of this approach.

2.2.1 Node Structure

There are four major elements inside an M0 node: concurrent messenger threads, a shared memory area, a simple synchronization mechanism (thread queues), and channels towards neighboring M0 nodes (see Figure 2).

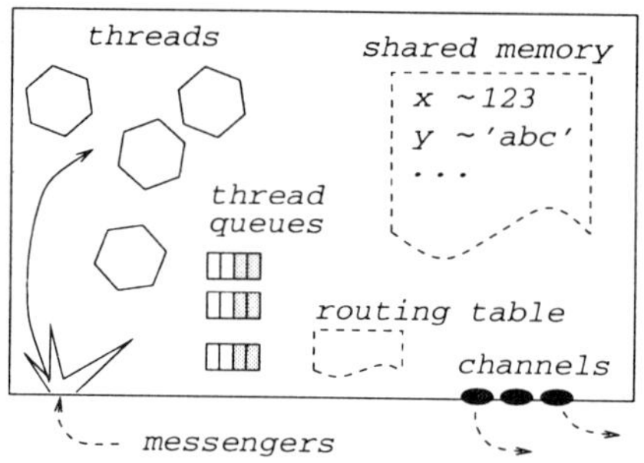

Figure 2. The structure of an M0 node.

On arrival, each messenger is executed by an independent and anonymous thread of control. These threads have their own private memory space and are fully protected from each other - they have no identifier under which they could be addressed. Messenger threads can coordinate their activities through the shared memory area where they can deposit arbitrary data structures under self-chosen names so that other threads can access them. Thread queues are a way to serialize the execution of threads in order to avoid race conditions. Channels enable messenger threads to send new messenger packets to neighboring nodes. The current M0 implementation maps messenger transmission to UDP, ANON [19], Ethernet or serial line communications. For the multicast applications described in this paper we have added support for an ANTS-like network with routing tables at the messenger level.

2.2.2 Packet Structure

M0 packets have a very simple format: a header, a code field and an optional data payload. The code field contains the program that the M0 platform has to execute. Messenger code is written in the compact M0 language. It is a high-level language that inherits from PostScript the main concepts of operand, dictionary and execution stack as well as the main data manipulation and flow control operators, but lacks everything related to rendering fonts and images. The M0 language also departs from PostScript with respect to the messenger–specific operators and a few new data types as well as the syntax. The M0 interpreter itself is written in C.

2.2.3 Dynamic Code Management

M0 deliberately has no explicit code caching or code loading functionality: it is argued that it is impossible to devise a dynamic code management scheme that suits all needs (prefetching or on–demand, best–effort or reliable, policy how long code should remain in the cache etc.). The basic execution model simply assumes that code is shipped with every messenger. This works quite well for small protocols where the compact code is only a few hundred bytes long. For more important code sizes the programmers have to implement their own caching method by storing the code in the shared memory area of a node under a self–chosen name (usually some random key): subsequent messengers carry this reference inside a minimal instruction sequence that looks up the stored code and executes it.

2.2.4 Resource Management

Each M0 node manages its internal resources independently of other nodes. M0 relies on an economy-based model of resource allocation [16]: all resources have price tags which depend on the node's actual load for a given resource, but also on the demand and offer from the running threads. Messenger threads are charged for their activities. When they run out of money they are silently removed from the system. On arrival, each messenger thread obtains an account with some start money. The amount is sufficient to do some exploration inside the node and eventually send out another messenger.

Accounts are also used for controlling the number of entries inside the shared memory area. Each entry must be "sponsored" by an account. Periodically, the system charges the sponsoring accounts depending on the amount of shared data space they sponsor. If for an entry there is insufficient money left on its sponsoring accounts, the entry is removed. This sponsoring model implements a user controllable 'memory decay' mechanism because messengers can add and/or refill sponsoring accounts.

2.2.5 Security

M0 puts emphasis on building security with messengers instead of providing rich services at the system level [20, 11]. There is no authentication between M0 nodes, nor has a messenger some identity attached to it that would allow authentication. Safety-related questions on resource consumption have to be handled by controlling the flow of money. Messengers can effectively protect themselves against other messengers by having full control on which information they pass on to others in which way. M0 provides basic cryptographic operators that can be invoked by a messenger. Currently these are DES and the MD5 hash function.

Table 1. Summary of main features of ANTS and M0.

	ANTS	M0
Runtime Environment	Java Virtual Machine	M0 interpreter
Requirements	JDK 1.0 or higher	UNIX, ANSI-C
Programming Language	Java	M0
Link Layer	UDP	UDP, ANON, ethernet, serial line
Code Distribution	system-supported, separated from normal capsules, code is cached	each messenger carries its code, cache can be implemented by messenger
Lifetime of capsule/msgr	user-defined TTL	potentially unlimited
Procreation limits	decrementing TTL for creating new capsule	none. new start money on arrival
Cache usage	decrementing TTL for entering data	load-dependent prices
Cache removal policy	user-specified TTL, LRU replacement policy	sponsoring of entries determines lifetime
CPU cycles	no control	limited by available money
Host protection	based on Java security mechanisms	based on M0 interpreter
Preventing code spoofing	via fingerprint, hashed over the code	no system support

2.3 Summary of Features of ANTS and M0

We summarize the most important features of ANTS and M0 in Table 1.

3 Two Protocol Examples

In this section we introduce two protocols for multimedia streams that we will use to demonstrate the usefulness of active networks. We have implemented both of them with ANTS and M0. The first protocol, Robust Multicast Audio, is an example of how the performance and efficiency of an existing protocol can be improved by adding application-specific compute power to internal nodes. The second, Layered Multicast Video, is an example of how active networks technology enables the quick development and deployment of a new protocol that optimizes network-internal bandwidth usage in multicast trees. Both applications involve continuous media, and both use the same multicast algorithm that we introduce in the following section.

3.1 An Active Multicast Protocol

Our multicast tree management is based on the algorithm provided with [21]. It uses two types of active packets (from now on we will use the term active packet as a common way to refer to capsules or messengers): *subscribe* active packets and *multicast* active packets. The subscribe active packets are sent periodically by the receivers towards the sender of the group they wish to join. Unlike [21] we accumulate subscribe packets in intermediate nodes to avoid a subscribe implosion problem at the sender. These active packets install forwarding pointers in the nodes they traverse. These pointers are removed if they are not refreshed on time. The multicast active packets carry the real multicast data. They are routed along the distribution tree built by the subscribe active packets. The multicast implementation is thus based on the softstate concept. The paths of these active packets are shown in Figure 3.

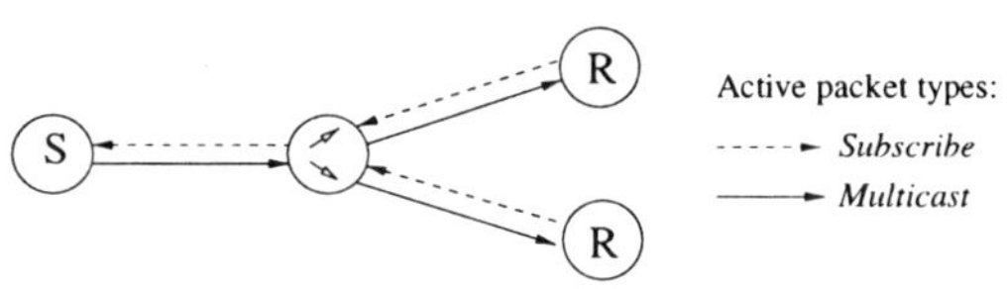

Figure 3. Multicast packet forwarding in an active node

3.2 Robust Multicast Audio

The first protocol we have implemented is Robust Multicast Audio (RMA). It is a protocol for improved–quality multicast audio transmission over best-effort networks, based on an encoder/decoder developed by M. Isenburg and H. Chordura at ICSI [5]. The encoding is based on wavelets, and the system is called WAR (Wavelet Audio Radio). We used ANTS and M0 to actively multicast a Berkeley radio station's music program.

In our protocol, the link between the audio server and each audio client is subdivided into several point-to-point links internal to the active network. On each internal link, the audio stream only carries the amount of redundancy optimal for the loss currently observed on that link. On an incoming link the active node reconstructs the original data, on the outgoing links it adds the appropriate amount of redundancy. Figure 4 illustrates the link-dependent redundancy in the RMA protocol.

The implementation of the RMA protocol uses three types of active packets: the *audio* active packets that carry the audio data, the *redundancy request* active packets that inform the active nodes about the losses on the internal point-to-point links, and the *subscribe* active packets that

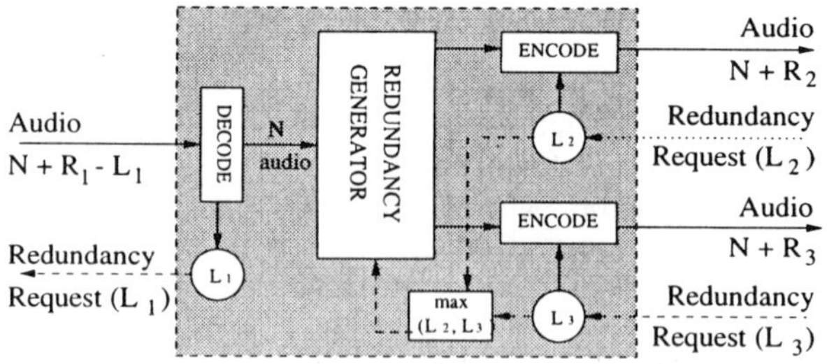

Figure 4. Link-dependent redundancy in the RMA protocol.

are used for multicast group subscription. The audio active packets are grouped in sequences, each consisting of $N + R_i$ active packets, where N is the number of original audio packets and R_i the number of redundancy packets added for internal link i. An active node waits until all the active packets belonging to a particular sequence have arrived. If L losses occurred it reconstructs as many of the N original packets as possible. Before sending the packets on each of the outgoing links the node adds the appropriate amount of redundancy for that particular link. Each active node is instructed to monitor the losses in the incoming data stream and transmits this monitored value to the upstream node, using a redundancy request active packet. This packet will adjust the amount of redundancy added on that link in the future (see Figure 4).

In order to avoid modifying the original WAR application programs we integrated them into the active network through gateways. The *client side gateways* are applications attached to an active node that provide a server interface for their communication with the receivers' WAR client software. The *server side gateway* is the root of the multicast tree: it plays the role of a WAR client in its interface with the WAR server. The main task of the gateways is to turn traditional packets into active packets and vice versa.

3.2.1 Discussion

Compared to the classical end-to-end solution one of the advantages of the RMA protocol is that it provides better performance since the losses on each internal link are recovered independently and thus do not add up. Another advantage is that redundancy is only added on those internal links where it is actually required, leading to a more efficient global use of the network resources than end-to-end redundancy.

A major advantage of multicasting a *radio* program is that delay is not a critical factor: a signal that arrives with a few seconds delay can still be said to be real-time since there is not immediate feedback from the receiver to the sender. In the original WAR system the redundancy is added at the end node; in our protocol it is added at the intermediate active nodes.

It would be very easy to replace the FEC scheme by an

ARQ retransmission scheme and experiment with a variety of algorithms, measuring delays, throughputs etc. [7]. Since the nodes are active we can even switch algorithms at runtime, a major advantage over passive networks. For example we could use ARQ when the link delay is very short, and FEC otherwise.

3.3 Layered Multicast Video

In a typical multicast session some users might have high-speed end systems and high-speed access to the network while others might have low–end PCs and ISDN or modem connections. Considerable bandwidth is wasted on links to low-speed receivers if the transmission rate of an upstream multicast node does not match the limited downstream capacity. Therefore it is desirable to set up a multicast tree with the optimal data rates for all receivers. This is illustrated in Figure 5.

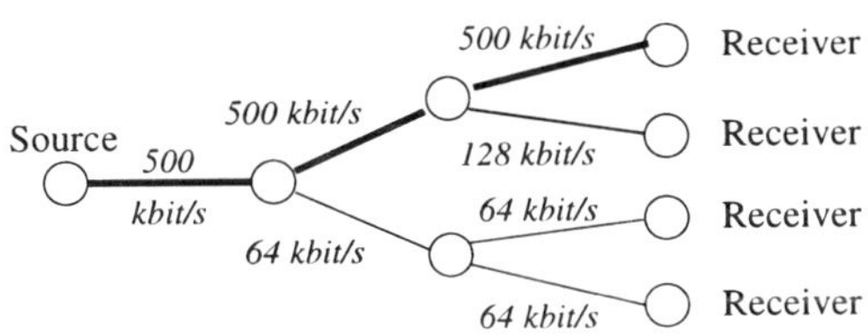

Figure 5. Distribution tree for layered multicast.

The second protocol we have implemented on top of the two active network systems is a layered, rate-adaptive multicast video protocol. The video is encoded in multiple layers such that layer 0 provides a minimum quality stream and each layer $i + 1$ adds more quality to layer i. Each active node participating in the multicast session understands the requirements of its subtrees and forwards only the corresponding video layers downstream. The nodes inform their upstream neighbors with active signaling packets about the layers they wish to receive (this is the maximum required by their subtrees and the local application). The active nodes filter out layer packets at runtime according to these requests.

We have used the Scalable Video Codec developed by W. Tan and A. Zakhor [13] in order to test this adaptive multicast protocol. The codec is based on subband coding, a non-standard but very efficient video coding technology [14]. Each packet in the encoded stream carries a layer identifier; the data in each packet belongs to one layer only. Thus the filtering in our active nodes is very simple: we can throw away entire packets if their data is not needed downstream. As a consequence our active filter code is very efficient.

The integration of this tool with the active network has been done in the same way as for the robust multicast audio protocol, i.e., using gateways for the interface between the tool and the active network. We use the same multicast tree mechanism: subscribe active packets to inform upstream neighbors about the layers needed, and video multicast active packets to carry the video data downstream.

In the video application the flexibility of active networks would also allow us to add enhancements to the protocol. For example, in a lossy network environment we could add redundancy to protect the data, giving a higher priority to the most important pieces of data by adding more redundancy to the lower layer packets. This would be similar to ICSI's Priority Encoding Transmission (PET) approach [1] but adapted for layered video and implemented hop-by-hop rather than end-to-end.

In [2] we illustrate the code the programmer has to write for each of the two active network systems: As an example we present the routine that filters the video multicast active packets at runtime.

4 Experimental Results and Lessons Learned

The implementation of the two multicast protocols with the two active network systems was a very interesting experience. It provided us with concrete insights into the practical consequences of architectural decisions and enabled us to evaluate the performance.

4.1 Architectural Comparison

ANTS and M0 are similar in their basic approach to active networking. However, they differ in several major architectural aspects such as programming language, application programmer interface and execution model which we will discuss in the following.

4.1.1 Language

The programming language used in ANTS is Java. Although capsules are processed in the same address space, an application programmer does not need to worry about uncontrolled manipulation of capsules: capsules in a node are objects that can only be manipulated by the public methods defined in the class. Developing an ANTS application is relatively easy because a user only has to write subclasses for given classes. Since development tools for Java are abundant, local testing and debugging is well supported. The Java skill base is increasing very quickly which allows protocol developers to concentrate on the protocol logic rather than new language concepts.

M0 on the other hand predates Java. PostScript had proven to be a successful portability technology. It is therefore quite logical to extend the approach of communicating with a printer or a screen to communication protocols in general. M0, like Java, is based on an interpreter which also supports multithreading. Compared to Java the code written in M0 is harder to understand, and the PostScript skill base is much smaller. M0 also has the disadvantage of not being object-oriented; in recent years object orientation has proven to be a powerful software engineering paradigm. On the other hand the programmer has more flexibility in M0;

for example dynamic code creation for compression or encryption purposes is easier.

4.1.2 Application Programmer Interface

A considerable advantage of ANTS is that applications can be written in Java and then execute in the same environment with the active network functionality: The application becomes an ANTS node. The M0 platform looks more like a router. The fact that the application code and the code for the active network nodes can be written in the same programming language avoids an 'impedance mismatch' at the programming level; it also avoids time-consuming and error-prone data representation transformations. For the video multicast application, the M0 implementation used three different languages: M0 for the multicast protocol, C to implement the gateway between the existing video software and Tcl/Tk to add a graphical user interface.

4.1.3 Execution Model

Both systems follow the same model in that upon arrival of an active packet the corresponding code is executed. M0 creates an independent thread for each incoming active packet to perform this processing, thereby providing different address spaces. In ANTS there is (by default) a single thread called ChannelThread which is used by all capsules. This has a disadvantage: if the processing of a capsule takes a long time (or even worse, an infinite loop occurs) the node is blocked, and incoming capsules may be lost due to buffer overflow. It is up to the capsule programmer to spawn his/her own threads should the expected processing time be long. For our video application the processing load was very low, so no new thread was created. In the audio application a thread was not created for every capsule, but only for calculating the redundancy. This flexibility proved to be very useful in the ANTS applications.

4.2 Packet Structure

ANTS and M0 rely on user-defined serialization, and in both cases it is easy to get things wrong. M0 provides a procedure for turning simple data types into an M0 code string that is able to recreate the encoded value. Serializing a sequence of simple values typically consists of concatenating the code strings. The ANTS API provides methods to serialize and deserialize simple types. Users must provide corresponding methods for their capsule classes. This can be difficult for complex classes. Using the Java 1.1 serialization package would ease this work and make applications more robust.

It is an open question whether fragmentation of large active packets should be under the control of the programmer. In our experiments we did not have the problem of limits in the size of an active packet: all ANTS capsules and M0 messengers fitted into a single UDP packet, which was the transport mechanism we used.

4.3 Dynamic Code Management

A major difference between ANTS and M0 is their respective approach to code distribution and caching. ANTS provides a code-on-demand mechanism and implements a code follows the path of the capsule policy. This has the advantage that the programmer does not have to program the code distribution for each new protocol. M0 has no system support for this. Messengers can carry their own code caching mechanism if desired.

M0's flexibility proved useful for the two multicast applications that we implemented. The *upstream* subscribe messengers that create the multicast tree are also responsible for code distribution; they install the code for the client-specific delivery of multicast messengers. The *downstream* multicast messengers consist of a very small lookup routine (12 bytes) for invoking this preinstalled code. In our opinion it is an open question whether code distribution by the sender or code distribution by the receiver is better for a receiver-oriented multicast scheme.

This is an example of how the code distribution mechanism provided by ANTS and M0 influenced our protocol implementations. Because M0 does not come with a standard code distribution protocol, it was possible to program the application such that the frequent multicast messengers become as small as possible. Because ANTS provides a convenient default code distribution mechanism, no attempts were made to implement code installation for downstream flows by upstream capsules. The difference in the code distribution philosophy is also visible at another level: because ANTS imposes that code executable by a capsule belongs to the same protocol it is not possible to have leaves push their proprietary delivery method into an already existing multicast tree. All possible 'methods' have to be known at protocol registration time.

4.4 Resource Management

In both architectures resource management is a subject for further study. In ANTS almost all critical resources are not covered yet. CPU time, for example, can not be bound, thread spawning is not monitored, bandwidth is not taken into account, nor is the amount of memory grabbed by a capsule. The handling of resource credits is simple; operations like storing data in the node cache always cost one unit, regardless of the current memory and cache utilization. In M0 the resources CPU time, bandwidth, thread creation and memory usage (local to a thread as well as shared memory) are all monitored, resource usage costs a price depending on the actual load for that resource.

ANTS' fixed-price model has the advantages of predictable cost and lower overhead whereas M0's variable-price model has the advantages of signaling the load and enabling money-based priorities. In both models it remains unclear how the initial amounts of money are assigned to the applications creating the active packets.

Table 2. Measurements for video/audio active packets

Throughput [pkts/s]	ANTS	M0
Video (1324 bytes/pkt)	133	195
Audio (1090 bytes/pkt)	100	155

4.5 Security

ANTS and M0 do not thoroughly handle security issues. We highlight some possible concerns.

Separate execution space for each active packet: Both systems provide separate execution spaces for each active packet. The only security exposure is the cache or shared memory in a node. Packets would have to guess the keys generated by other packets in order to intrude.

Access control: ANTS provides its own security manager based on the Java security model to restrict allowable operations. It is not necessary to restrict operations explicitly in M0 because the language only provides allowable operations (no file I/O, etc.).

Secure code shipping: This concern is not addressed in ANTS; in its current version it ships the code over the network in plain format. In M0 it is up to the programmer to encrypt the code.

Code integrity: ANTS uses fingerprints computed over the byte code to prevent code spoofing. In M0 there is no such protection.

Code authentication: Each ANTS capsule has a source address that cannot be changed from within the ANTS system. In M0 there is deliberately no source address field in messengers.

4.6 Runtime Efficiency

We evaluated the performance of our protocols in terms of throughput and overhead. Because ANTS and M0 are active network nodes running at the application level, their performance cannot be compared with the performance of an active or passive network running at the network layer. The purpose of our performance tests was to gain insight into the impact of the processing required by our protocols. We compared the relative performance of the two active network systems, and our measurements gave us hints how an active node reacts to changing processing requirements.

We ran most of our experiments on a single 10 Mbps Ethernet segment using Sun SPARC5 workstations under Solaris 2.5. In those cases where the Ethernet became the bottleneck we used a 155 Mbps ATM network. The Java version was JDK 1.1 without a JIT compiler. The first experimental setup consisted of a workstation generating packets, an intermediate workstation routing these packets, and a third workstation receiving them and making the measurements. We wanted to measure the maximum throughput the intermediate active node could route. In this scenario we tested both of our multicast protocols: we measured the maximum throughput that an active node could route with less than 0.1% losses. The results are shown in Table 2. The generation of packets at the source was done with bursts of packets with intervals of 20 ms between them. In the audio protocol we enforced the active node to always add 50% XOR redundancy in order to evaluate the impact of the redundancy computation (the throughput given in Table 2 includes these redundancy packets).

Table 3. Measurements for packet forwarding

Throughput (pkts/s)	Payload 1324 bytes	Payload 1090 bytes
C (ATM)	1000	1100
C (ethernet)	400	500
Java (ethernet)	200	200
ANTS (ethernet)	166	166
M0 (ethernet)	360	360

In order to better understand the decrease in throughput due to active network technology we also implemented small application programs that forwarded UDP packets with the same payload through the network. We did that in C and in Java. We also wrote versions of a protocol for ANTS and M0 that only forwarded packets without any further processing. The measurement results are shown in Table 3. We see that M0 provides a better throughput than ANTS. This is mainly due to the programming language used to implement the interpreter: C in the case of M0, Java in the case of ANTS. However, M0 pays a higher price for performing computations on the active packets in the node. This can be observed from the fact that its throughput decreases considerably in the full video and audio protocols (Table 2). It should be noted that the M0 node ran with resource management enabled while the ANTS node had virtually none.

Active networking introduces two types of overhead: code shipping and additional header fields. For our protocols the size of the code to be shipped was 800 bytes in M0 and between 1600 and 4000 bytes in ANTS. However, since the code is shipped infrequently (in ANTS it is loaded at the beginning of the session, in M0 it is sent with every subscribe capsule), this is not much of a burden to the network.

The overhead carried with each active multicast packet was 68 bytes in ANTS (all of them in the header) and 32 bytes in M0 (20 bytes in the header and 12 bytes of code). Considering that the data payload is 1090 bytes in the audio and 1324 bytes in the video this overhead is minimal.

4.7 Code Size and Reusability

The size of the code we had to write was relatively small. Table 4 gives an overview for the ANTS and M0 implementations. In designing our two applications we found that they have a lot in common, therefore code could be shared. Since both protocols are multicast protocols, the multicasting algorithm could be separated and the corresponding code reused.

The use of Java in ANTS made reuse of the multicast code very easy: A general multicast capsule class was implemented and refined for both applications. This would even allow us to experiment with different multicast protocols by just plugging in the new classes. It would also be possible to reuse a multicast class developed by a third party in our applications, as long as this class adhered to a fixed interface. We expect to see special APIs for protocol development in active networks in the future. These will make it even easier to develop and exchange new applications.

Table 4. Code sizes (in lines of code)

	Audio Multicast	Video Multicast
Capsule code (total) in Java	500	260
Gateway code (client and server) in Java	280	150
User interface in Java	450	280
Messenger code (total) in M0	170	170
Gateway code (client and server) in C	460	600
User interface in Tcl/Tk	n.a.	70

5 Related Work

The term active network is relatively young, but quite a few groups are already working on the topic. Good overviews of active network projects can be found in [15] and [9].

There are many similarities between active networks and mobile agent systems. A good overview of mobile agent projects can be found in [10]. The main difference is that active networks use the concepts for network layer processing whereas mobile agent systems run as application programs. Both have dynamic code deployment, caching, resource control and many other components in common.

In the area of multimedia communications the idea of media scaling and media filtering has found some attention in recent years although the algorithms and protocols proposed for it have never made their way into network products. For example a media scaling mechanism for MPEG video could be the dynamic adjustment of the quantization parameter at the encoding site as a function of the QoS parameters of a link. An example for media scaling can be found in [6], and filtering mechanisms are described in [23].

The RSVP protocol is designed to carry resource reservation packets in the Internet. The protocol itself does not specify what resources it deals with. The designers explicitly mention the inclusion of packet filters into the data path of an IP stream at each network node; all packets passing through a particular filter share a particular resource [24, 4]. In principle RSVP could be used to pipe an incoming packet stream through a video layer filter very similar to ours. However, the difference to our system would be that with RSVP, the code for the filters has to be installed in all routers beforehand. RSVP can only turn it on or off for a particular IP packet stream; there is no way to dynamically load filter code. Thus the overall design is much less flexible than ours. In a recent paper R. Wittmann and M. Zitterbart propose an active network extension to RSVP [22].

In his dissertation S. McCanne of UC Berkeley explicitly addresses the composition and transmission of video stream for multicast networks [8]. He also uses a layered video encoding scheme [13, 14], but assigns these layers to individual IP multicast groups: the more groups a user joins, the better his video quality will be. An advantage of this approach is that the internal network nodes can be normal multicast IP routers, forwarding the packets according to their group addresses. An inconvenience is that the session directory sdr will contain several entries for the same transmission, one for each layer of video, and the receivers have to deal with that. A more severe limitation is that too little semantics are known to the internal nodes. For example, with the subband coding of [13], if the packets for layer n are lost on a link, all packets of higher layers can be discarded downstream as useless, but the multi–group scheme is unable to handle such an optimization.

Some researchers oppose to the use of active network technology in the main data path; they claim that dynamically loadable code can never be efficient enough. In [3] B. Braden describes a signaling protocol based on active network technology; for signaling the code efficiency is not as critical as for the data path. Using active packets for network diagnostics, monitoring and auto-configuration is proposed in [12].

6 Conclusions

We have successfully implemented a robust audio multicast protocol and a layered video multicast protocol with the two active network systems ANTS and M0. It was surprisingly easy to get the code to work; all four implementations were done within four weeks by a team of three people.

Runtime efficiency was much better than expected: performance was sufficient to carry multimedia data streams. From our measurements we conclude that active network technology can be used not only for signaling protocols or network management but also in the data path of novel and experimental application protocols as long as the operations to be performed on each active packet remain simple. Multicast protocols are good candidates for active network technology. Compared to point-to-point protocols they inherently require more processing in internal nodes.

The comparison between ANTS and M0 revealed a

tradeoff between performance and other aspects such as security and resource management. The M0 architecture pays more attention than ANTS to the latter aspects but also receives a higher penalty for processing at the nodes. Another issue is the programming language: ANTS obtains portability and security facilities from Java but also pays a higher price in performance due to Java.

With the Java language in the ANTS system, the network is programmed in the same way as the application; this will allow to implement future network applications in an integrated manner, with part of the code running in internal nodes and other parts in the end systems. We consider this to be a powerful new programming paradigm for networked applications. The code deployment mechanism in M0 is more flexible than the "code follows the path of the capsule" mechanism of ANTS. For the implementation of receiver-specific filters in the multicast tree this proved to be an advantage.

We do not expect active network technology to completely replace existing high-performance implementations of protocols such as classical IP or multicast IP. But we can imagine hybrid router architectures offering standard handling of packet streams as well as secure "sandboxes" for user provided code to process application-specific protocols.

Acknowledgments

Martin Isenburg and Hartmut Chodura gave us their WAR code for robust audio encoding/decoding which we gratefully acknowledge. We would also like to thank Avideh Zakhor and Wai Tian Tan of UC Berkeley for letting us use their layering video encoder/decoder. Without their spontaneous help the experiments described in Section 3 would not have been possible.

References

[1] A. Albanese and M. Luby. PET - priority encoding transmission. In *High-Speed Networking for Multimedia Applications*. Kluwer Academic Publishers, Mar. 1996.

[2] A. Banchs, W. Effelsberg, C. Tschudin, and V. Turau. Multicasting multimedia streams with active networks. Technical report, International Computer Science Institute, Berkeley, Nov. 1997. TR 97-050, ftp://www.icsi.berkeley.edu/pub/techreports/1997/tr-97-050.ps.gz.

[3] B. Braden. Active signaling protocol. ftp://ftp.isi.edu/rsvp/active_signaling/ASP_overview.ps, June 1997.

[4] B. Braden, L. Zhang, D. Estrin, S. Herzog, and S. Jamin. Resource reservation protocol (RSVP), version 1 functional specification. Internet Draft, IETF, Aug. 1996.

[5] H. Chodura and M. Isenburg. WAR: Wavelet audio radio. http://www.icsi.berkeley.edu/~isenburg/papers/war.ps.gz, Aug. 1997.

[6] T. Käppner and L. Wolf. Media scaling in distributed multimedia object services. In R. Steinmetz, editor, *Multimedia Advanced Teleservices and High-Speed Communication Architectures*, pages 34–43. Springer, 1995.

[7] B. Lamparter, O. Böhrer, W. Effelsberg, and V. Turau. Adaptable forward error correction for multimedia data streams. Technical report, Dept. of Computer Science, University of Mannheim, Dec. 1993. TR 93-009, ftp://pi4.informatik.uni-mannheim.de/pub/techreports/1993/TR-93-009.ps.gz.

[8] S. R. McCanne. *Scalable Compression and Transmission of Internet Multicast Video*. PhD thesis, Computer Science Division, UC Berkeley, 1996. No. UCB/CSD-96-928, http://http.cs.berkeley.edu/~mccanne/phd-work/.

[9] S. Munir. Active networks - a survey. http://www.cis.ohio-state.edu/~jain/cis788-97/active_nets, Aug. 1997.

[10] K. Rothermel and R. Popescu-Zeletin, editors. *Mobile Agents. Proc. 1st International Workshop on Mobile Agents, Berlin*, LNCS 1219. Springer, Apr. 1997.

[11] T. Sander and C. Tschudin. Towards mobile cryptograph. In *IEEE Symposium on Security and Privacy*, May 1998.

[12] B. Schwartz, W. Zhou, A. Jackson, T. Strayer, D. Rockwell, and C. Partridge. Smart packets for active networks. http://www.net-tech.bbn.com/smtpkts/ smtpkts.ps.gz, Feb. 1998.

[13] W. Tan, E. Chang, and A. Zakhor. Realtime software implementation of scalable video codec. In *IEEE Int. Conf. on Image Processing, Lausanne, Switzerland*, volume 1, pages 985–988, Sept. 1996. http://www-video.eecs.berkeley.edu/~dtan/icip96.ps.gz.

[14] D. Taubman and A. Zakhor. Multirate 3-d subband coding of video. *IEEE Trans. Image Processing*, 3(5):572–588, 1994.

[15] D. Tennenhouse, J. Smith, D. Sincoskie, D. Wetherall, and G. Minden. A survey of active networks research. *IEEE Communications Magazine*, 35:80–86, Jan. 1997.

[16] C. Tschudin. Open resource allocation for mobile code. In *[10]*, pages 186–197.

[17] C. Tschudin. *On the Structuring of Computer Communications*. PhD thesis, University of Geneva, Switzerland, Sept. 1993. No. 2632, ftp://cui.unige.ch/pub/tschudin.

[18] C. Tschudin. The messenger environment M0 – a condensed description. In J. Vitek and C. Tschudin, editors, *Mobile Object Systems - Towards the Programmable Internet*, LNCS 1222, pages 149–156. Springer, Apr. 1997.

[19] C. Tschudin. ANON: A minimal overlay network for active networks experiments. Technical report, CS Department, University of Zurich, Aug. 1998.

[20] C. Tschudin, G. Di Marzo, M. M., and J. Harms. Welche Sicherheit für mobilen Code? In *Fachtagung Sicherheit in Informationssystemen (SIS'96), Vienna*, pages 291–307. vdf-Verlag, Mar. 1996.

[21] D. Wetherall, J. Guttag, and D. Tennenhouse. ANTS: A toolkit for building and dynamically deploying network protocols. In *IEEE OpenArch 98, San Francisco*, Apr. 1998. http://www.tns.lcs.mit.edu/publications/openarch98.html.

[22] R. Wittmann and M. Zitterbart. AMnet: Active multicast network. In A. Danthien and C. Diot, editors, *"From Multimedia Services to Network Services", 4th COST237 Workshop, Lisboa*, LNCS 1356, pages 154–164. Springer, Dec. 1997.

[23] N. Yeadon, A. Mauthe, D. Hutchison, and F. Garcia. QoS filters: Addressing the heterogeneity gap. In B. Butscher, M. E., and H. Pusch, editors, *Interactive Distributed Multimedia Systems, Berlin*, LCNS 1045, pages 227–244. Springer, 1996.

[24] L. Zhang, S. Deering, D. Estrin, S. Shenker, and D. Zappala. RSVP: A New ReSerVation Protocol. *IEEE Network*, Sept. 1993.

Paper Session 3
Track A: Network Architectures

Session Chair: Bikram Bakshi
Intel Corporation

Service Architecture for Utilizing TINA-based Public Network Services from the Internet Environment

Yuzo Koga, Kazunori Shiomi, Yutaka Matsushita
Matsushita Lab., Faculty of Science and Technology, Keio Univ.
3-14-1, Hiyoshi, Kouhoku-ku, Yokohama, 223-8522, Japan
yuzo@mos.ics.keio.ac.jp, shiomi@mos.ics.keio.ac.jp, on@mos.ics.keio.ac.jp

Abstract

In this paper, we assume that there will be two networks, the next-generation public network and the Internet, as the future information network infrastructure, and we propose the interworking architecture that allows users to utilize services on the next-generation public network from the Internet environment. Proposed architecture is constructed on the open distributed processing environment, based on TINA. We also constructed a platform, PLUS-TINA, especially for making use of services on the TINA-based public network from any Internet environment.

1. Introduction

Recently, it is said that we are faced with a historical turning point of the network infrastructure. As the realization of FTTH (Fiber to the Home) is getting realistically, the expectation to the next-generation public network is becoming larger. On this new public network, services, which uses multi media such as voice, video and data, will be deployed by several service provider. In such circumstances, because service providers will be requested to cope with users' needs quickly, it is indispensable to develop open environment that will be able to provide new services flexibly, easily and efficiently. Therefore, TINA (Telecommunications Information Networking Architecture) is paid attention to all over the world in place of legacy public network's architecture. TINA is studied/standardized in the TINA-C (TINA Consortium), that is organized with about 40 world companies, such as telecommunications operators, telecommunications manufacturers, computer manufacturers and software companies[2]. It is sure that next-generation public network, that is controlled/managed with the architecture like TINA, will become one of the future mainstay information network infrastructures.

On the other hand, there are the Internet as a representative new network infrastructure. The Internet, which was originally constructed for military purpose in DARPA, was getting larger from research/government facility's small network, and had included industries, and then has been abruptly developed due to the introduction of browsers, such as Mosaic and Netscape. In the present, several commercial services are being deployed on this network. Consequently, the Internet is now becoming the network which bear burden of the next-generation information network infrastructure.

To summarize the above discussion, there are two networks that can be the future multimedia information network infrastructure which are the next-generation public network and the Internet. However these two networks have originally developed independently, and now there exist services only on each networks. This means that it is impossible to utilize services on the Internet environment from the public network environment, and especially to utilize services on the public network from the Internet environment.

If these two networks continue to develop without having service interoperability between them, there will be two independent networks existing for users in the future. Accordingly, such circumstances might lead to the situation where a subscriber of the public network can not utilize the services usually available for her/him on the public network, when s/he moves to a place where s/he can only use the Internet environment. This will have a bad influence on the future multimedia network society. Consequently, we propose the interworking architecture for seamless service utilization between the next generation public network managed/controlled by a TINA-based architecture and the Internet.

2. TINA

With the development of new technologies, intelligent broadband-network has realized which can handle several media integrately, and now we have a chance where computers and networks are connected together. For realizing

0-8186-8810-6/98 $10.00 © 1998 IEEE

the new services, for example multimedia conference or video on demand, on such new networks, it is needed to have an architecture, which is more flexible than legacy's one with the access/management point of view, to introduce new services quickly and easily. With these concept described above, TINA-C was established in 1992. TINA is the next-generation networking architecture which integrates the telecommunications technologies, such as TMN (Telecommunications Management Network)[4], and the distributed computing technologies, such as ODP (Open Distributed Processing)[5][6] and CORBA (Common Object Request Broker Architecture)[7].

2.1. Classification of the Architecture

The architecture of the next-generation telecommunications network is very complicated, because it handle comprehensive matter and concept. Therefore TINA divides/classifies the architecture into four categories[3]:

Service Architecture: handles design, specification, implementation and management of the telecommunications services.

Network Architecture: handles design, specification, implementation and management of the transport networks.

Management Architecture: handles design, specification, implementation and management of the software system that manages services and resources.

Computing Architecture: handles design and construction of the environment for distributed software.

In these four architectures, The service architecture relates mostly to the interworking architecture that provides seamless service utilization between the next-generation public network, which is controlled/managed with TINA, and the Internet.

2.2. Service Architecture

The TINA architecture consists of a set of concepts, principles, rules and guidelines for constructing, deploying, and operating TINA services[10][11]. Here the term "service" means a meaningful set of capabilities provided by an existing or intended system to all business roles (refer to section 2.2.1) that utilize it. TINA services include at least the following types of services:

Telecommunication Service: This is a service based on the transport of bits of information between terminals attached to a telecommunication network. This service is responsible for the establishment of connections and processing of information related to the connections.

Management Service: This is a service responsible for management of TINA resources. It includes fault, configuration, accounting, performance and security functionalities, as well as service life cycle management service instance management and user life cycle management.

Information Service: This is a service that are able to handle information resources such as movie, sound or document. It includes the storage and the visualization such as billing, caching and all such services specific to the information resource are also considered as information services.

2.2.1 TINA Business Model

TINA defines the business model that divides the whole of telecommunication system into some business roles, according to the ODP enterprise view point[5]. Each business role has their own service view point, and one business role deploys their services utilizing services that is provided by other/same business roles. Fig. 1 depicts the scope of service architecture with respect to the set of business roles and their relations as defined in [8].

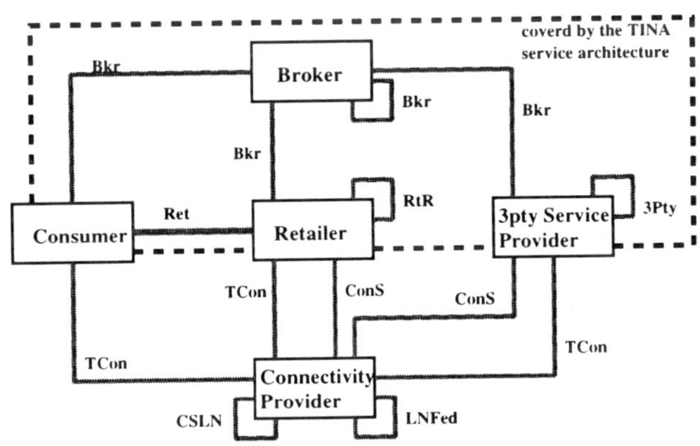

Figure 1. scope of the service architecture with respect to the business model

Each business roles can be explained as follows:

Consumer: is the business role that utilize services provided within the TINA system. Consumer make use of services provided by Broker or Retailer business role.

Broker: is the business role that provides the information of other services or service providers within TINA system.

Retailer: is the business role that allows consumer to make access to the services.

3rd Party Service Provider: is the business role that provides services to retailer or other 3rd party service provider.

Connectivity Provider: is the business role that actually manages the transport network or kTN (kernel Transport Network).

Moreover, TINA is now specifying the reference point, such as Ret, Bkr, 3pty and so on in Fig. 1, for application-systems/service-component of these business roles to be able to interact with other business roles on TINA DPE (Distributed Processing Environment). However, it is not described in this paper in detail.

2.2.2 TINA Session Concept

Basically, the interaction between SC's (Service Components) in the TINA service architecture can be divided into "access part" and "usage part". The interactions that authenticate users and allow users find/request the services are belong to access part. The interactions that control the service behavior, or deliver the stream contents are belong to usage part. The usage part can be divided more two parts, that is, "service part" and "communication part". These parts are the temporary relationship among a group of objects that are assigned to collectively fulfill a task for a period time, and are called "session" in TINA.

3. Proposed Architecture

In this section, we describe the proposed architecture which realize a seamless service offer from the Internet to the next-generation public network. As the next-generation public network and the Internet have different characteristics, we introduce an IWU (InterWorking Unit) that makes it possible to make access to each other (refer to fig2).

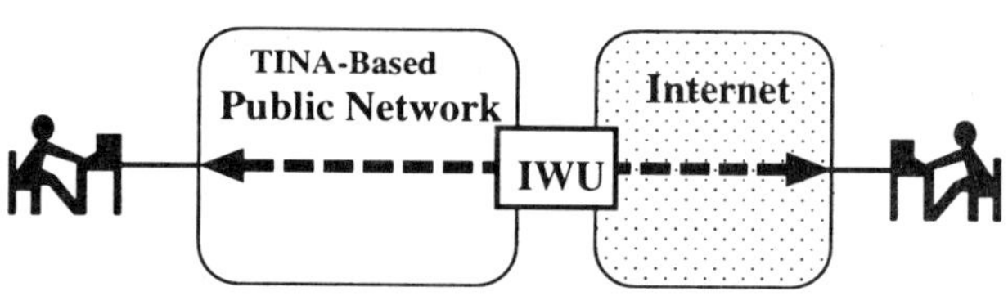

Figure 2. IWU between the TINA-based public network and the Internet

Figure 3 shows an overview of our proposed architecture. This proposed architecture is based on TINA concepts, and we arrange many SCs extended/redefined TINAs' on the distributed processing environment (TINA-DPE) in the public network environment. On the other hand, we developed and introduced PLUS-TINA (Platform for Utilizing Services on the TINA-Based Environment) as a platform for utilizing services on the public network environment from the Internet environment. Because PLUS-TINA is constructed with Java language, an user on the Internet environment can utilize services on the public network environment only by downloading it to her/his terminal.

In the Next, we describe SCs in each business role.

3.1. SCs in the Consumer Domain

UAP (User Application): is divided into the part for an authentication of users and the part which is related to service session which each service possess in access session of TINA.

TSM (Terminal Session Manager): coordinates the resource of the terminal, network and user. It interacts with SCs in the Retailer domain on access/service session. It also request an MMCM to reserve terminal resources which is essentially independent of telecommunication services.

MMCM (MultiMedia Control Manager): managed various devices, which is treated/controled as an object (DO: Device Object), in and end-user's terminal. In communication session, an MMCM interacts with a CSM in the retailer domain to establish end-to-end stream connections for actually utilizing multimedia services.

3.2. SCs in the Retailer Domain

UA (User Agent): is the SC which represents an user in the retailer domain, and exists corresponding to each of users. It is independent of services utilized by users, and manages user profile and session profile. In our proposed architecture, it also have the role of a USM (User Session Manager) defined in TINA. In the access session, it provides functions for authenticating an user and checking her/his profile which, for instance, includes user's subscription information. In the usage session, it provides functions for creating session profile and making request to corresponding SSM.

UCxt (Usage Context): manages the pool of knowledge for the association of an end user and her/his end systems. It keeps track of an end system which the user is using currently.

TE-A (Terminal Equipment Agent) represents user terminals in a provider domain, and it is created when the terminal connects to a network. It holds NAP's

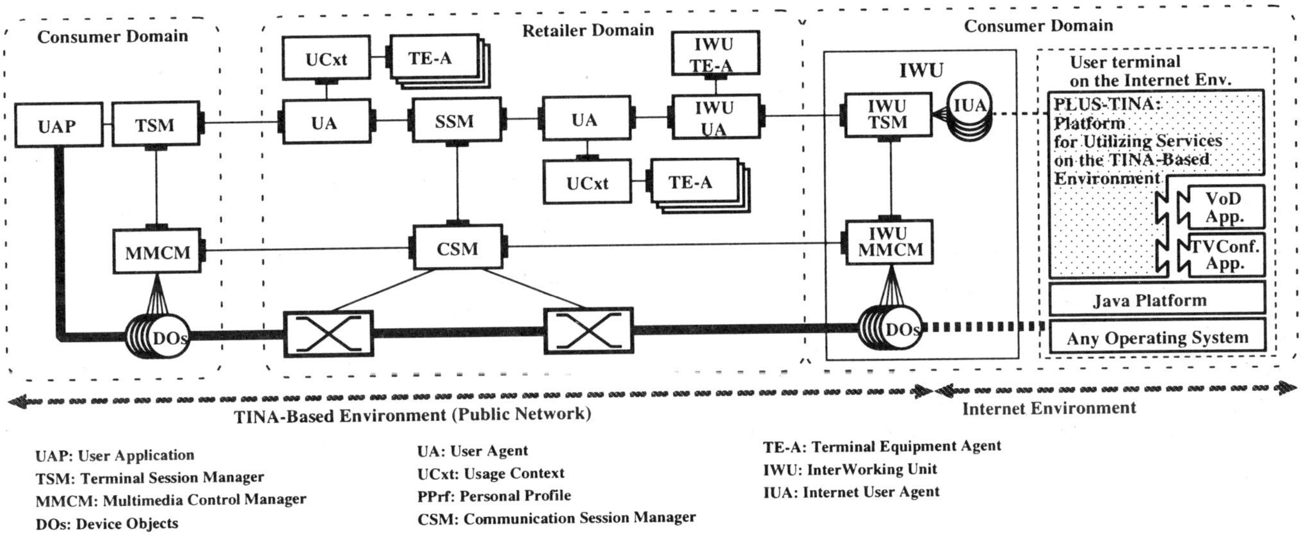

Figure 3. Overview of proposed architecture

(Network Access Point) and TAP's (Terminal Access Point) of the end systems.

SSM (Service Session Manager): manages/controls specific services. It is provided by 3rd party provider role in the TINA business model, and exists corresponding to each service. It performs important operations in a service session, holding service specific datas and managing a life cycle of the service session.

CSM (Communication Session Manager): performs an establishment, modification and release of connections that are requested by an SSM. At that time, it converts logical address treated in higher level to physical address.

IWU-UA: represents IWU in a retailer domain. We can consider the Internet as one of consumer domains from the public network (retailer domain) point of view. IWU-UA is responsible for sending control messages from other SCs in a retailer domain to appropriate IWU.

IWU-TE-A: represents a node of IWU, and manages NAP and TAP of corresponding IWU.

3.3. SCs in IWU

IWU controls the differences of protocols and data transfer technologies between the public network and the Internet. It consists of objects as follows:

IWU-TSM: is the entrance of the IWU from the public network environment. It manages/controls the whole IWU. It also transfers control messages from the public network to an appropriate IUA.

IWU-MMCM: manages devices in the IWU. Devices include DOs that convert streams on the public network to packets on the Internet, vice versa.

IUA (Internet User Agent): represents an user who exists on the Internet environment. It is created corresponding to each user, who exists on the managed Internet domain. It is the entrance of the IWU from the Internet environment.

These SCs interact/cooporate each other and provide various multimedia services for users.

4. Service Scenario for Utilization of the Services on the TINA-based Public Network from the Internet Environment

In this section, we describe the procedure to utilize services on the TINA-based public network, from the Internet environment.

4.1. Access Session from the Internet Environment

The public network can be used only by public network's subscriber, because it is provided by carriers with a commercial purpose. Consequently, the situations, where an user wants to utilize services on the public network from the Internet environment, is come out only when s/he (subscriber of the public network) moves to the place where s/he can only use the Internet environment. In this case, s/he must be authenticated by the public network operator. This authentication is performed in the TINA access session (see section 2.2.2). Followings are the procedure to authenticate users on the proposed architecture (see also Figure. 4).

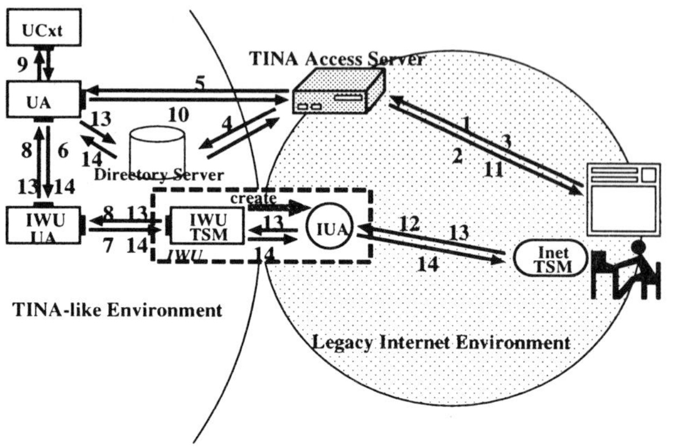

Figure 4. Procedure of the Access Session from the Internet Environment

1. An user (subscriber of the public network) who have moved to the Internet environment makes access to a TINA Access Server via browser (e.g., Netscape).
2. A Java applet for user authentication is downloaded to the browser.
3. The user sends her/his personal identification number (personal ID) and password for her/his authentication via the Java applet. The personal ID is allocated to each public network's subscriber to achieve user's personal mobility.
4. The TINA Access Server gets the password information of corresponding user, by making access to the directory server on the provider domain. Subsequently, it authenticates the user by comparing these passwords.
5. If the user is successfully authenticated, the TINA Access Server sends the login-request to her/his UA on the provider domain, with following information:

   personal ID

   hostname of the terminal which s/he is using on the Internet environment.
6. The UA makes request to the IWU-UA to register the user. In this case, the UA might make request to the Broker business role to get the location information of the appropriate IWU, because a lot of IWU's might exist distributively in the next-generation public network. The IWU-UA exists corresponding to each of the IWU's.
7. The IWU-UA makes request to the IWU-TSM to register the user. Subsequently, the IWU-TSM creates an IUA for the corresponding user in the IWU. The created IUA waits for the connecting request from the Internet terminal which the user uses with a certain port number (listen state).
8. The IWU-TSM makes response for the user-registration request, with following information:

   hostname of the IWU node

   port number with which IUA in the IWU is waiting as a "listen state"
9. The UA makes request to the UCxt to register the location of the user. In this case, the UCxt registers the IWU node as the terminal that the user is using at that time. With this way, the TINA-based environment can act as if the user exists at the corresponding IWU, when making a call which includes the user who actually exists on the Internet environment.
10. The UA makes response for the login-request.
11. If the registration of the user is successfully ended, the TINA Access Server displays the page, which informs about it to the user, on the browser. At the same time, following information is also displayed on the browser.

    hostname of the IWU node

    port number with which IUA in the IWU is waiting as a "listen state"

    These information is used the PLUS-TINA, which is the platform constructed with Java language for utilizing services on the public network, be connected to the IWU. The PLUS-TINA can be downloaded from this page.
12. The user downloads the PLUS-TINA, and connects it to the IUA in the IWU using the hostname and port number
13. The user makes request to the IUA to get the list of services s/he subscribed in the public network via the PLUS-TINA. This request is forwarded to IWU-TSM, IWU-UA and her/his UA.
14. The user gets the response for the service-list request.

With the procedure described above, the access session is completed. As a result of it, an user on the Internet environment can utilize services on the TINA-based public network, from the Internet environment.

4.2. Service Session for Utilizing Services on the Public Network

In this section, we show the procedure of the service session which allows user on the Internet environment to utilize services on the public network.

4.2.1 The Case in Which the User on the TINA-based Public Network Calls to the User on the Internet

Figure 5 depicts the interaction of the service session between service components when the user-a (caller) on the public network calls to the user-b (callee) on the Internet, for instance, to utilize the public network's multimedia conference service between them.

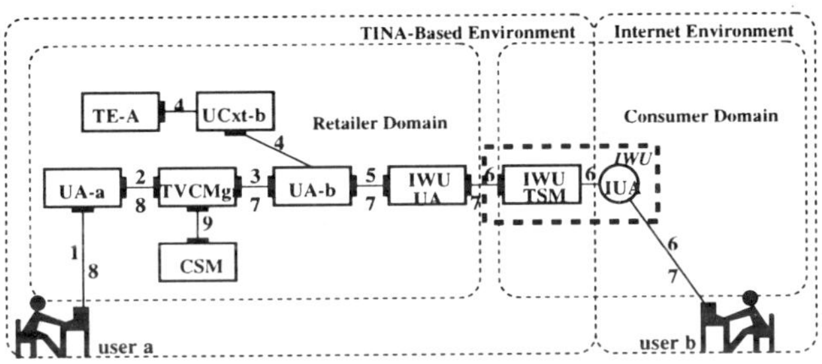

Figure 5. Interaction when the User on the TINA-based Public Network Calls to the User on the Internet

Followings are the procedures of the service session of this case:

1. An end-user on the TINA-based public network (user-a) requests of her/his UA (UA-a) to utilize the multimedia conference service with an user-b, via UAP and TSM within her/his terminal. In this case, if the user-a does not know where the user-b is, s/he can make this request only to specify user-b's personal ID.

2. The UA-a inquires into the service which the user-a wants to utilize, and requests of the corresponding SSM to make up the service session. In this case, we named the corresponding SSM TVCMgr.

3. The TVCMgr inquires into the participant of this call, and requests of the participant's UA (in this case, the UA-b) to join the call.

4. The UA-b make access to the UCxt-b to get the user-b's resource configuration information. With this action, it can know which terminal the user-b is actually using with the information of its TAP and NAP.

5. In this case, the UA-b can know that user-b is now on the Internet environment. It can also know the IWU in which user-b is registerd. Subsequently, It requests of the IWU-UA which is responsible for forwarding requests to the corresponding IWU.

6. The IWU-UA forwards the request to the IWU-TSM within the corresponding IWU. The IWU-TSM inquires into the participant's personal ID, and selects the user-b's IUA (actually the IUA connected to the terminal on the user-b's terminal). Then, the IWU-TSM makes invitation request to user-b on the Internet (actually, to the PLUS-TINA) to join the call, via selected IUA.

7. After receiving the request, user-b judges the call-invitation to accept or reject, and makes response to the IUA. If user-b accepts the call, but does not have an application to utilize the corresponding service, s/he can dynamically download the application modules (in this case, the application for utilizing the multimedia conference service) into the PLUS-TINA. Subsequently, the IUA forwards user-b's response to the TVCMgr via the IWU-TSM, IWU-UA and UA-b.

8. The TVCMgr sends the response to user-a via the UA-a. If the call is rejected by user-b, the service session is ended with this action.

9. If the call is accepted by user-b, the TVCMgr requests of the CSM to establish the stream connection for utilizing the multimedia conference service between user-a and user-b.

4.2.2 The Case in Which the User on the Internet Calls to the User on the TINA-based Public Network

Figure 6 depicts the interaction of the service session between service components when the user-b (caller) on the Internet call to the user-a (callee) on the TINA-based public network environment, for instance, to utilize the public network's multimedia conference service between them.

Followings are the procedure of the service session of this case:

1. An end-user on the Internet (user-b) requests of the IUA connected to the PLUS-TINA, to utilize the multimedia conference service with and user-a. In this case, if user-b does not have the application of this service, s/he has to download its modules. The IUA forwards the request to her/his UA (UA-b) on the TINA-based public network environment, via the IWU-TSM and IWU-UA.

2. The UA-b inquires into the service which the user-b wants to utilize, and requests to corresponding SSM to

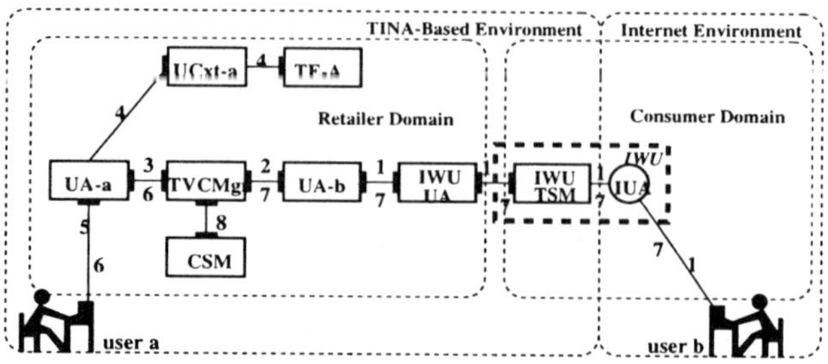

Figure 6. Interaction when the user on the Internet calls to the user on the TINA-based public network

make up the service session. In this case, we named the corresponding SSM TVCMgr.

3. The TVCMgr inquires into the participant of this call, and requests of the participant's UA (in this case, the UA-a) to join the call.

4. The UA-a make access to the UCxt-a to get the user-b's resource configuration information. With this action, it can know which terminal the user-a is actually using with the information of its TAP and NAP.

5. In this case, the UA-a can know that user-a is now on the TINA-based public network environment. It can also know the information of TAP and NAP of the terminal which user-a is using. Subsequently, the UA-a makes invitation request to user-a to join the multimedia conference service.

6. After receiving the request, user-a judges the call-invitation to accept or reject, and makes response to the UA-a. Then, the UA-a forwards the response to the TVCMgr.

7. TVCMgr forwards the response to the PLUS-TINA on the user-b's terminal, via the UA-b, IWU-UA, IWU-TSM and IUA. If user-a reject the call-invitation, the service session is ended with this action.

8. If the call is accepted by user-a, the TVCMgr requests of the CSM to establish the stream connection for utilizing the multimedia conference service between user-b and user-a.

4.3. Communication Session between the TINA-based Public Network and the Internet

In this section, we show the procedure of the communication session which makes it possible to communicate between an user on the TINA-based public network and an user on the Internet. In this paper, because we pay attention especially to the access session and service session, the communication session on proposed architecture is much simplified. It is processed by only one service component, called CSM, which has entire functionality for the communication session on the TINA-based environment.

On our proposed TINA-based public network, an ATM connection for utilizing services is ended at the IWU, since we assumed that the Internet (IP) environment does not support the ATM. Consequently, the service application on the Internet terminal is connected with the IWU using TCP/IP socket. If, in the future, ATM will be supported on the Internet (IP) environment using IP over ATM technologies, an end-to-end ATM connection between the terminal on the TINA-based public network environment and the terminal on the Internet environment can be established.

For establishing the TCP/IP connection between them, our proposed architecture does not use the TINA NRA (Network Resource Architecture), since we also assume that Internet environment and a terminal on it have no service component for TINA, especially for TINA NRA. However, if, in the future, TINA is also supported on the Internet environment, the end-to-end ATM connection between them, described above, can be established using TINA NRA concept.

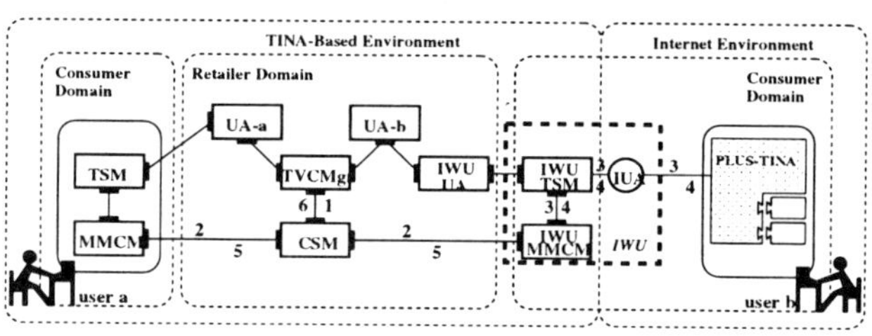

Figure 7. Procedure of the communication session between TINA-based public network and the Internet

1. The TVCMgr requests of the CSM to establish the stream connection for utilizing the service.

2. The CSM makes request to the MMCM within the terminal on the TINA-based public network and to the the IWU-MMCM within the IWU, to establish the ATM stream connection between them. Requests are sent corresponding to each of the medium, such as Audio and Video, with some information, such as media ID, QoS. Each MMCM creates channel for each media, managing the device in the terminal/node, and establish the connection between them.

3. The IWU-MMCM requests of the PLUS-TINA in the terminal on the Internet environment, via IWU-TSM and IUA, to establish the TCP/IP socket connection between the IWU and the service application on the Internet's terminal. In this case, requests are sent corresponding to each of the medium with some information, such as media ID, QoS level, hostname of the IWU node and the port number which is prepared in the IWU for the service by IWU-MMCM. Subsequently, the PLUS-TINA make up the TCP/IP socket connection corresponding to each of the medium between the IWU and the service application, using these information.

4. After establishing the TCP/IP socket connection between them, the PLUS-TINA makes response to the IWU-MMCM, via the IUA and IWU-TSM.

5. After establishing a media's connection, each MMCM makes response of the corresponding media to the CSM.

6. Finally, the CSM makes response to the TVCMgr to inform that all the media's connection is established and that communication is ready.

With these procedure of the communication session, users can utilize the the TINA-based public network's service between the public network environment and the Internet environment.

5. Evaluation and Implementation

5.1. Realization of the PLUS-TINA

In this section, we make mention of PLUS-TINA, the platform for utilizing public network's services from the Internet environment, when migrating to a place where s/he can only use the Internet environment. Considering such a situation, the kind of terminals/operating-systems s/he would use is indefinite factor. However, it is obviously desirable to be able to utilize the public network's services with any terminal/operating-system. Therefore, we constructed the PLUS-TINA by using Java language, which does not depend on the kind of terminal/operating-system.

When the user makes use of the PLUS-TINA, s/he has to download the module to the terminal which s/he is using, after being authenticated in the access session (refer to section 4.1). In this case, we can consider the following three approaches:

Approach 1: To download the PLUS-TINA as a Java application. In this way, IWU and the Java application are connected with a socket via TCP/IP.

Approach 2: To download the PLUS-TINA as a pure Java applet to a browser like Netscape. In this way, the web server and the applet are connected with socket via TCP/IP, and the user can make access to the public network services via the browser and the web server.

Approach 3: To download the PLUS-TINA as a Java applet constructed with CORBA stub. In this way, the applet itself can use the CORBA distributed processing environment as a CORBA client.

With any of these three approaches, the user has to download the service specific application (e.g., VoD application) onto the PLUS-TINA, and then make use of the public network's service. Naturally such service specific applications are developed and spread by their service provider. With approach 2 or 3 using Netscape Communicator, the plug-in functions/API's are available for specific applications. Moreover, there are some products from Netscape Communications Corporation, such as LiveConnect[15], which makes it easier to construct flexible browser-based service specific applications, so the user will be able to utilize various public network services via Netscape.

Table. 1 shows the comparison of these three approaches.

Considering the easy to use and widely spread browsers such as Netscape, approaches 2 and 3 seem more appropriate than approach 1. Moreover, it is possible to apply approaches 2 and 3, since with invocation -type service, such as Video On Demand, the user only has to send out a request for service. However, considering the exchangeability of the control message to allow users receive the call participation request, approaches 2 and 3 can not cope with it flexibly. The purpose of this paper is to realize the public network's terminal virtually on the Internet terminal. Although it can be possible to indicate users of the request they have received with the socket-connection between the web server and the applet on the browser, by using one a method of Java language which makes it possible to dynamically change the page of the browser, it is not realistic to leave the browser, such as Netscape, up and running from the performance point of view.

Because of these reasons, we have concluded to apply the approach 1 to construct the platform, PLUS-TINA, to seamlessly utilize public network's services from the Internet environment.

5.2. Implementation of the Proposed Architecture

We have implemented the proposed architecture on the work-stations (Sun SparcStation 20). To construct the environments, we have applied the IONA Orbix2.2MT[16] and IONA OrbixWeb3.0 as a TINA-DPE, and implement each SC with C++ (SPARCCompiler C++ 4.0.1) and Java (JDK

Table 1. the comparison of approches to utilize public network's services

items for the comparison	Approach 1	Approach 2	Approach 3
Performance of the terminal	Because Java is the interpreter language, the performance of platform (PLUS-TINA) and service application are worse than that of C/C++ language.	Adding the exponential load height of Java language, browser also has high load performance. Consequently, whole performance is much worse than approach 1.	
Generality/Scalability	Scalable within the range of Java language's capability.	A certain degree of the Generality and the Scalability is expected, using plug-in functions.	
Exchangeability of the control message	Coping with the pull-type and push-type of the message forwarding, users can become both of the caller and callee.	Because the applet and web server is connected with socket, it can indicate users to have received the call indication, using one of the Java's method that can dynamically change the page of the browser.	Because Java applet has only CORBA stub, the applet itself has only the function of the CORBA client, that is, other CORBA objects can not invocate the operation of this applet. With this reason, users can only be a caller.

1.1.4). As for the implementation of multimedia conference service and video on demand service on the proposed architecture, we have applied the Parallax XVideo2.0 as a video tool, ForeSystem ASX-200 as ATM switch for stream connection on the public network.

TINA kTN (kernel Transport Network) on the TINA-based environment of implemented system is realized using TCP/IP-based Orbix as TINA-DPE connecting each terminals with Ethernet (MAX 10 Mbps), and stream connection on the public network environment is realized connecting each terminals with optical fiber via ATM switch as depicted in Figure. 8

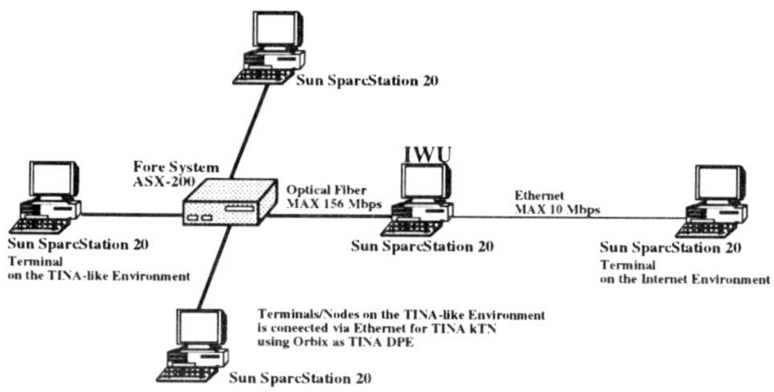

Figure 8. implemented environment

IIOP (Internet Inter-Operable Protocol) is used for the communication between components constructed with C++/Java on TINA-DPE. As for the components of our proposed architecture on the TINA-based environment, we have implemented redefined/extended components, referring the MINDS[17][18][19].

5.3. Picture of the Implementation

Figure. 9 shows the example of the services. It depicts the situation where user is utilizing the multimedia conference service, which is the service on the TINA-based public network, from the Internet environment. As depicted in the figure, user had done the access session via Netscape, and after successfully authenticated by the public network, then s/he had downloads the PLUS-TINA via Netscape. Subsequently, s/he made access to the multimedia conference service on the TINA-based public network environment.

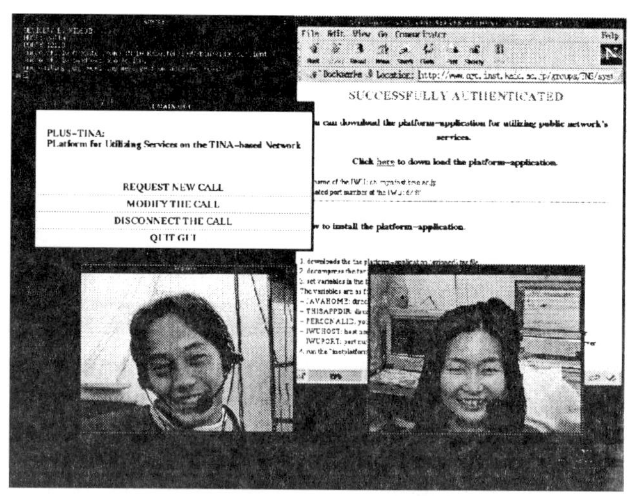

Figure 9. Service implementation

6. Conclusion

In this paper, we considered the two networks, that is, the next-generation public network and the Internet, as the next-generation information network infrastructure, and proposed the interworking architecture for utilizing services deployed on each of the networks from both of the networks seamlessly. We adopted TINA as next-generation public network's architecture, and propose the new architecture based on it. Especially, to utilize services on the TINA-based public network environment from the Internet environment, we also proposed and implemented the platform named PLUS-TINA. The PLUS-TINA is constructed with Java language so as to insure its portability.

In this study, we concentrated especially on the service architecture, and we apply the original way to establish the connections between the IWU and the terminal on the Internet environment. But, there are some works to apply the TINA NRA (Network Resource Architecture)[20] to the connection-less network such as the Internet, and it should be remarkable. However, to apply TINA NRA to the connection-less networks like the Internet, the end-user's terminal has to prepare the TINA-DPE and related service component within it. It is very doubtful that the terminal which users temporary use has such an environment. Therefore, the proposed approach described in this paper is one of the very useful solution to apply to the the connection management of the Internet environment, and for seamlessly utilize the services deployed on each of the networks.

References

[1] Barr, W.J., Boyd, T. and Inoue, Y.: TINA Initiative, IEEE Communications Magazine, pp. 70–81 (1993)

[2] TINA-C: The TINA Consortium, http://www.tinac.com/ (1997)

[3] TINA-C: Overall Concepts and Principles of TINA Version: 1.0, TINA-C Deliverable (1995)

[4] ITU-T Recommendation M.3010 : Principles for a Telecommunications Management Network (1993)

[5] ITU-T X.901-X.904: ISO/IEC 10746-1 ODP Reference Model Part 1-4 (1993-1995)

[6] Tetsuo NAKAKAWAJI, Akira TANAKA, Shoichiro ASANO: Overview of Standardization of Open Distributed Processing, Journal of IEICE, Vol. 77, No. 3, pp. 277–287 (1994)

[7] Object Management Group: The Common Object Request Broker: Architecture and Specification, CORBA Version 2.0 (1995)

[8] TINA-C: TINA Business Model and Reference Points Version: 4.0, TINA-C Public (1997)

[9] TINA-C: The Ret Reference Point Version: 0.3, TINA-C Internal (1997)

[10] TINA-C: Service Architecture Version: 4.0, TINA-C Deliverable (1996)

[11] TINA-C: Service Architecture Version: 5.0, TINA-C Deliverable (1997)

[12] P. Newman, W. Edwards, R. Hinden, E. Hoffman, F. Ching Liaw, T. Lyon and G. Minshall: Ipislon Flow Management Protocol Specification for IPv4 Version 1.0, RFC 1953 (1996)

[13] P. Newman, W. Edwards, R. Hinden, E. Hoffman, F. Ching Liaw, T. Lyon and G. Minshall: Transmission of Flow Labelled IPv4 on ATM Data Links Ipsilon Version 1.0, RFC 1954 (1996)

[14] ITU-T: Support of Broadband Connectionless Data Service on B-ISDN, ITU-T Recommendation I.364 (1993)

[15] Netscape Communicatsions Corporation: Live Connect, http://www.netscape.com/ (1997)

[16] IONA Technologies Ltd.: Iona Technologies - Products - Internet - Orbix, http://www.iona.com/products/orbix/ (1996)

[17] Hong, C.S., Honda, S., and Matsushita, Y.: Networking Architecture for Multimedia Services on a Distributed Processing Environment, Journal of IPSJ, Vol. 37, No. 3, pp. 439–450 (1996)

[18] Hong, C.S., Kashiwa, D., Koga, Y., Matsushita, Y.: A Novel Service Networking Architecture Using TINA Model and Its Realization to VoD Manager, Proceedings of SIG DPS, IPSJ, Vol. DPS-76, No. 29, pp. 169–174 (1996)

[19] Koga, Y., Hong, C.S., Matsushita, Y.: An Interworking Architecture between TINA-Like Model and Internet for Mobility Services, IEICE TRANSACTION COMMUNICATION, Vol. E80-B, No. 10, pp. 1393–1400 (1997)

[20] TINA-C: Network Resource Architecture Version: 3.0, TINA-C Deliverable (1997)

[21] Kim, H.C., Steegmans, F., Narayanan, N., Rajahalme, J., Wellesplein, F.: Managing TINA Streams that use Internet Transport, Proceeding of TINA'97 Conference (1997)

HIGII PERFORMANCE INTEGRATED NETWORK COMMUNICATIONS ARCHITECTURE - (INCA)

Klaus Schug[1], Anura Jayasumana[2] and Prasanth Gopalakrishnan[2]
[1]MiTech Incorporated, 8484 Georgia Ave Suite 950, Silver Spring, MD 20910-5604
kschug@mitechincorp.com
[2]Colorado State University, Department of Electrical Engineering, Fort Collins, CO 80523-1373
jayasuma@longs.lance.colostate.edu, prasanth@lamar.colostate.edu

ABSTRACT

Current communication subsystem mechanisms within workstation and PC class computers are limiting network communications throughput to a small percentage of the present network data rates. Even though CPU and computer network speeds have increased by more than an order of magnitude, the execution rate of computer functions and applications requiring network communications have increased only marginally. An integrated network communications architecture (INCA) is presented that is interoperable with all existing programs, computers and networks, and scales with network and CPU speeds. The INCA architecture minimizes internal system limitations and provides application level, as opposed to network interface level, internal machine data throughput rates near that of high speed network transmission rates. Test results of a software implementation of the INCA architecture on actual systems and networks are presented that show a 260% to 760% improvement in the application level throughput of network communicated data of workstation and PC class computers.

1. Introduction

In recent years, networks with media rates of 100 Megabits per second (Mbps) or more have become widely available: FastEthernet, Fiber Distributed Data Interface (FDDI), Asynchronous Transfer Mode (ATM) and Myrinet. Emerging network technologies are beginning to deliver bandwidths approaching 1 Gigabit per second (Gbps). Central processing units (CPUs) are now available in personal computer (PC) and workstation (WS) class computers that operate at 300 to 500 Megahertz (MHz) and execute more than 100 Million instructions per second (MIPS). Present internal network communication architectures are unable to provide anywhere near the application data throughput that networks can deliver and CPUs can process. The network data throughput limit of computers is the hardware limit imposed by the memory system bandwidth. Although present WS class computers have sustained data coping memory bandwidths in the 100 - 400 Mbps range [1], the present network communication architectures provide no more than several Mbps of network data to application programs. Networks can deliver data one to two orders of magnitude faster than computers can absorb, despite CPUs capable of operating at network speeds. The network and processing technology advances of recent years have shifted the network communications bottleneck to the internal computer architecture. Somewhere between the network interface and the CPU, the internal hardware and software architecture of computers is severely restricting data throughput and thereby negating network and CPU technology advances for network communication.

This paper presents the design and performance evaluation of a more efficient internal computer network communications architecture that can provide applications and distributed systems with a higher network data throughput and hence make use of high bandwidth, low latency networks and CPU technology advancements.

One difficult, but extremely useful requirement, interoperability, is added to the problem of defining a high performance, internal computer network communications architecture. Interoperability is defined as the ability to work with existing networks, communication protocols, computer systems (including operating systems and network interfaces), and application programs without requiring modification to any of these components.

As a result of the interoperability requirement, the described architecture presented is applicable to all computers connected to a network, whether the network connection is via a high speed link or via a slow speed dial up modem link. The higher the speed of the connection, the more noticeable becomes the performance improvement of the presented architecture. The remainder of section 1 includes a brief description of the major elements of computer internal network communications.

0-8186-8810-6/98 $10.00 © 1998 IEEE

Section 2 presents the INCA design with a description of the five major elements of the high performance INCA. Section 3 details the experiment setup and performance evaluation results. Section 4 provides a summary and conclusion.

1.1. Network communication

High performance network communication can be defined as high bandwidth (high data rate), low overhead and low latency information exchange between physically separated, networked computers. High bandwidth or high data rate is almost exclusively a function of the network technology employed to connect the machines of the network. Given that the selected network technology fixes the maximum data rate, network communications performance becomes a matter of minimizing communications overhead and latency. For purposes of this paper, the time spent in the actual network hardware, in network interface units (NIUs) and in the network (e.g., transmission time in a local area network), is defined as network communications latency. The time spent by the processor sending or receiving a message is defined as network communications overhead. For purposes of this paper, latency is defined as the time required to perform the data link and physical layer functions at both the sender and receiver, and the time required to travel through the network connection media. Overhead is therefore defined as the time to perform the Network, Transport, Session, Presentation and Application layer communication functions at both sender and receiver.

1.2. Overhead versus latency

To illustrate the cost of overhead vs. latency, consider the transmission of messages that are 1000 bytes long. The communications cost of one message in milliseconds (ms), considering only communications latency, is taken as the propagation delay time required for transmission (TX) of one 1000 byte (B) message, plus one NIU time at the sender, plus one NIU time at the receiver and plus any network switch delay. Message throughput in terms of messages per second (messages/s) is calculated as one second (s) divided by the communications cost of one message. Data throughput is calculated as the number of messages/s times 1000 bytes per message, times 8 bits per byte, yielding Mbps. Network latency reduces data throughput and efficiency by 65% (Ethernet) to 32% (Myrinet), for an average cost of 49% in communications throughput or efficiency. However, the performance reduction because of communications latency costs can potentially be reduced, perhaps to 0, by performing processor computations of network application code during this delay time.

In contrast, communication overhead is made up of processor cycles that cannot be used for computation or "to perform real work." To illustrate the relative effects of communications overhead versus communications latency, Table 1 depicts communication costs as a ratio of overhead versus latency. Communications overhead accounts for the differences in throughput and overall communications efficiency in Table 1. Communications overhead with communications (network) latency reduces data throughput and efficiency by 90% for Ethernet and to 99.6% for Myrinet. This places the cost of communications overhead plus latency at an average of 97.6% of the network transmission bandwidth or data transmission rate.

Table 1 clearly depicts communications overhead as the cause of poor network communications throughput. Communications overhead is responsible for 3.6 to 182 times the amount of communication performance degradation as is attributable to communications latency, even when latency includes Media Access Control (MAC) delays. The higher the data rate of the network, the greater the degradation due to communications overhead. This fact, combined with the physical limitations of improving communications latency and the ability to overlap latency with other computations, strongly suggests that communications overhead is the area to concentrate on for achieving efficient, fast network communications.

1.3. Internal communications architecture

Communications overhead begins at the NIU, inside the computer, and ends at the internal computer interface

Table 1. Communications Overhead versus Communications Latency Cost

	Network Technology			
	Ethernet	FDDI	ATM	Myrinet
Network TX Rate (Mbps)	10	100	155	640
Latency Data Throughput (Mbps)*	3.536	41.88	81.952	436.104
Latency + Overhead Data Throughput - Application Data Throughput (Mbps)	0.985	1.353	1.379	2.391
Overhead/Latency Cost Ratio	3.59	30.95	59.43	182.39

* Throughputs calculated and observed for typical network configurations and traffic patterns

to the application program. The hardware and software architecture through which data travels between the network and application can be defined as the internal computer network communications architecture.

The architecture can be divided into the following major software and hardware components: the NIU, the NIU interface to the internal computer system, communications protocols, the operating system (OS), the memory subsystem, the application program interface (API) and the CPU. From the previous discussion on communications latency and communications overhead, the NIU itself is considered to contribute only to communications latency and is therefore not included as a part of the INCA architecture. Since it is not a source of communications overhead and not a source of network data throughput limitation, nor likely to be either in the future, the CPU component is also not a part of the INCA architecture.

The overhead associated with internal network communications has been analyzed in a number of papers [2, 3]. Although it is difficult to compare the results because the measurements are made for different architectures, protocols, programming interfaces, and benchmarks, the conclusion is that there is no single dominating source of overhead. Implementing an efficient internal network communications architecture involves looking at the overhead impacting components of the internal communications architecture and their interaction. The research presented is therefore centered on defining and evaluating the performance of an internal computer network communications architecture that provides a more efficient software and hardware entity interaction in carrying out network communications overhead functions. Specifically, the NIU interface, protocol processing, the OS, memory management, cache operation and the API will be highlighted in the INCA architecture.

2. INCA

INCA is an all in one software architecture that combines the internal network communications functions into three major components: a computer network interface (CNI), Integrated Protocol Processing (IPP) and an API. All INCA components are available in the form of one software library for any existing application program to use with complete interoperability. INCA is a copy-once architecture because network data is copied only once before the application consumes the data. An overview of INCA is provided in Figure 1a.

The INCA is quite different from the current system architecture depicted in Figure 1b. The CNI handler contains a NIU driver to control the NIU and to set up the direct memory access (DMA) network data transfer from (for receiving) or to (for transmitting) the NIU and main memory - random access memory (RAM). In the receiving case, the CNI handler intercepts the NIU "message arrived" interrupt signal and sets up a DMA transfer to OS virtual memory space. The memory locations of the message buffers in the OS virtual memory (VM) address space are mapped into the application VM address space. No additional copy from OS to application address space is therefore required. As data becomes available in the message buffers, the CNI handler starts the IPP which currently includes the Internet protocol (IP), the user datagram protocol (UDP), the transport control protocol (TCP) and optionally, a presentation protocol - external data representation (XDR). The protocols reside in the application address space and read/write the data from the application address space VM locations to perform their processing.

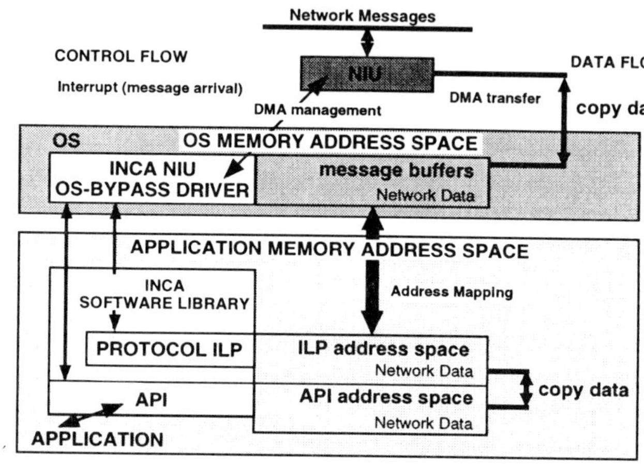

Figure 1a. INCA Network Communications

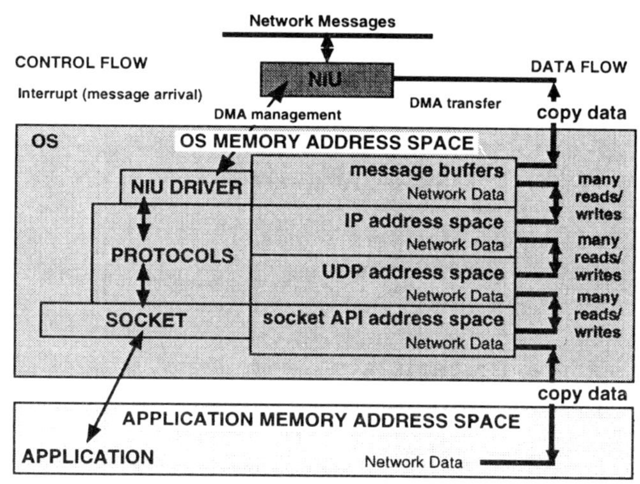

Figure 1b. Current System Network Communications

Unlike other efforts to move protocol processing into user space, such as X-kernel [4] and Mach [5], INCA makes the move to user space while retaining interoperability with existing operating systems, applications and other heavily invested in system components as well as providing a number of other performance improvements. Once the data processing is complete, the packets are demultiplexed to the corresponding protocol ports set up by the application through the use of the API calls.

2.1. CNI

The CNI functionality is accomplished via three main pieces of software, an NIU device driver, a semi OS-Bypass message handler [6, 7], and access via the INCA API. The NIU device driver is a software set of C programming language functions that support direct access to the network card. The driver also supports very low level communication primitives in which network packet reception and transmission can be tested and measured. The NIU driver has been implemented as a loadable module in the OS. The driver has features to support semi OS-Bypass and direct DMA transfer to the user space.

When the NIU signals via a hardware interrupt that a message has arrived, the INCA NIU driver sets up the DMA transfer from the NIU to the OS address space message buffer. In addition, the driver maps the OS message buffer addresses to the application making use of the INCA network communication library routines, which include the driver. The DMA network data transfer is accomplished with the message data buffers pointing to the application address space. Finally, the driver sets up an endpoint mechanism for data reception and transfer. The endpoint mechanism provides the user application with direct access to the NIU and for data reception and transfer. These endpoints are again created in the driver OS memory space and mapped on to the user address application memory space. Adding virtual memory buffer management functions to the CNI semi OS-Bypass handler would require changes in some or all of the internal network communications subsystem components such as the Commercial-off-the-shelf (COTS) OSs and NIUs.

To distinguish existing OS system calls from those that access the INCA OS replacement functions, the CNI driver and semi OS-Bypass functions are accessed via INCA library calls with different names from the OS system calls. One of these calls is used in place of endpoint tags to provide multiplexing of the incoming channels to different applications or different instantiations of the same application. This implements an OS-Bypass channel for network data routing. For existing applications that do not wish to modify their system calls, INCA allows the traditional system interfaces to applications (i.e., sockets).

2.2. Integrated protocol processing

IPP is an extension of integrated layer processing (ILP) to: 1) include protocols above the transport (e.g., UDP, TCP, TP0-5) layer, including the session, presentation (e.g., XDR) and optionally, the application layer and 2) integrate the ILP loop into the CNI message handler. The IPP INCA component performs protocol processing without invoking the OS resident protocols.

Earlier ILP research implementations [8, 9, 10] did not integrate ILP with a semi OS-Bypass message handler, did not add session and higher layers to the ILP loop, nor was ILP always performed in user application address space. Protocol execution inside the existing OSs and under the control of the OS is not used by INCA's IPP component. Modification of the OS to improve protocol processing efficiency would require changes that would violate interoperability. The purpose of any ILP based technique such as IPP, is to improve throughput performance by integrating protocol processing to eliminate one load and one store, a read and write, of every machine word (e.g., four to eight) bytes of network message data. To this performance goal, this research effort added the requirement for interoperability, requiring the IPP loops to use existing protocols and requiring INCA software libraries to accommodate the integration of all existing protocols into the IPP CNI message handler.

The interoperability requirement prevents integrating applications with the INCA IPP portion of the CNI message handler. Interoperability with existing protocols and integration introduces some amount of serial processing into an ILP loop in order to satisfy protocol processing ordering constraints. INCA executes protocols in three stages. The initial stages of a series of layers are executed serially, then the integrated data manipulations take place in one shared stage and then the final stages are executed serially. Message processing tasks are executed in the appropriate stages to satisfy the ordering constraints. Header processing is assigned to the initial stage. Data manipulation is assigned to the integrated stage. Header processing for sending and external behavior (e.g., error handling) are assigned to the final stage. Executing the tasks in the appropriate stages ensures that the external constraints protocols impose on each other cannot conflict with their internal constraints. The ILP loop has been implemented to start up directly after reception of data into the user message buffer. It does the integrated checksumming on data in the initial stage, protocol data manipulations and byte order conversions in the middle integrated stage, and flow control and error handling in the final stage.

The concept of delayed checksumming has been included in the loop. In the case of IP fragments, the checksumming is done only after reassembly.

Checksumming processing has been sped up in the INCA ILP loop through the use of a checksum routine optimized for reduced instruction set (RISC) CPUs. Once the data processing is complete, the packets are demultiplexed to the corresponding protocol ports set up by the application.

The INCA IPP protocol library consists of C computer language functions that implement the ILP loop and other pieces of the protocol control setting such as fragmentation, and in the case of TCP, maintaining the window, setting up time-out and retransmission, etc.

2.3. Memory management

INCA performs memory management three ways, by eliminating most network data copying, allowing the OS to perform virtual memory management, and performing its own message buffer management. The goal of memory management is to reduce data copying. INCA's CNI semi OS-Bypass message handler with embedded ILP loop protocol processing provides an integrated data path to achieve minimal data copying. The CNI, protocol processing, network message buffer management and API are integrated into one user level library routine. Network data is accessible for protocol processing without the current system data copies from the OS message buffer space to the protocol memory space and without the numerous reads and writes within the protocol processing entities. In the ILP loop, all protocols are executed before the data is written to another memory location. At the completion of the ILP loop, the data is written to the "incabuffers" structure in the application address space. The application accesses the data in the "incabuffers" and since the data is already in the program's address space, no copying of the data is required.

The CNI must be able to translate the virtual addresses to physical addresses, and for interoperability, the translations must be coordinated with the OS's VM subsystem. INCA has the OS perform VM management through the use of the UNIX mmap() or equivalent OS function. To enable the OS to perform VM management and address translation, the INCA driver must allocate message buffers in the OS address space initially as well as in the application address space to allow the OS to make the required mappings and perform its virtual memory management functions. Any other approach besides OS assisted VM management, e.g., NIU VM management or translation look-aside buffer (TLB) handler incorporation into the NIU, would seriously violate interoperability.

Message buffer management is performed by the CNI semi OS-Bypass handler. The CNI has complete control over the size, location, and alignment of physical buffers. In connections to networks such as FDDI or ATM that use message sizes of 4096 kilobytes (KB) and 53 bytes, respectively, then INCA's buffer manager can select an integer multiple of the network message size for the size of the message buffers. Each message is aligned to the beginning of message buffers with a single message per buffer for messages smaller than a chosen buffer size. For messages larger than the chosen buffer size, multiple buffers are used beginning with the first and intermediate buffers filled from start to end. The application specifies message buffers using offsets into the buffer region, which the network interface can easily bound-check and translate.

2.4. Cache operation

While caches are very effective in reducing memory accesses for many computations, the characteristics of strictly layered message processing are such that caching is not as effective, mainly because of poor data and instruction locality [1]. The cost of a cache miss tends to increase as processor speeds increase. The trend in CPU design to execute multiple instructions in a single cycle effectively increases the cost even more.

INCA increases cache effectiveness by increasing the cache hit ratio for network communications data processing through a number of methods inherent in the use of a single data copy, semi OS-Bypass handler CNI with integrated ILP. INCA's architecture and processing patterns reduce the cache performance degradation of four of the five main factors influencing cache performance: context switches, DMA transfers, TLB misses, self interference and not fitting into the cache. Each word is loaded and stored only once in the ILP loop, even though it is manipulated a number of times. Integration of protocols eliminates the load and store instructions themselves. This saves the time to transfer data between memory and the cache and saves the time to load the data from the cache and store data to the cache or a write buffer. Since there are fewer load and store instructions and they occur in an inner loop containing more instructions, the delay after a cache load is more likely to be overlapped with additional computations from the loop, and on machines with write-through caches and write buffers, stores are less likely to fill a write buffer. Finally, integration eliminates some buffer allocations and deallocations since data which would have been buffered between data manipulations is now streamed directly from one to the next. The result is that INCA provides a substantial improvement on cache operation by lowering the memory cycles per CPU instruction (mCPI).

2.5. API

The application program interface provides the connection between the network communications subsystem and the application programs. Since INCA bypasses some of the current system network communications subsystem functions, a new API is required to use the INCA library routines for high performance networking. Once again, the interoperability requirement dominates the design tradeoffs and implementation options.

The INCA API allows the application to: open a network by opening a NIU device driver, specify parameters to the NIU device driver, specify the protocols and their options, and set the characteristics of the data transfer through the OS-Bypass channel. The INCA API consists of alternative system calls for the current OS system calls such as socket(), connect() and listen(). The INCA API looks very much like the current UNIX OS API set of "open()", "read()", "write()" and "close()" named function calls. But these functions are not system calls, but rather are INCA specific functions that will implement ILP and semi OS-Bypass as a user level communication primitive that is transparent to the user.

INCA can incorporate all the application, presentation and session (replacement for socket and streams calls) functions into the IPP loop of the semi OS-Bypass message handler. In current systems, the application programs many times contain the application layer protocol (e.g., hypertext transport protocol - HTTP) and the presentation layer functions (e.g., XDR). Only the socket or streams system calls are the API. Placing all protocol functions into INCA's IPP loop would have the benefits of not requiring application program upgrades because of changes in the application, presentation and session layers, and the data throughput would be increased in these applications. In the future, incorporation of the higher layer protocols can be accomplished dynamically at run time through application selection of the protocol stack configuration. INCA's API can be located anywhere between the application and any protocol of the protocol stack.

3. Experiment setup and results

The INCA testbed consisted of a SUN Microsystems UltraSPARC1 WS with a 143 MHz UltraSPARC1 CPU, 64 megabytes (MB) of RAM, 512 KB of level 2 cache, the Solaris 2.5.1 OS (also known as SUN OS 5.5.1), with a SUN SBus FastEthernet Adapter 2.0 NIU. The UltraSPARC1 was connected via a private (no other machines or hubs) 100 Mbps FastEthernet to a Gateway 2000 PC. The two machines were connected with a dedicated 100 Mbps twisted pair category – 5 cable. The Gateway PC was configured with a 167 MHz Pentium Pro CPU, 32 MB of RAM, 256 KB of level 2 cache, the LINUX 2.0.29 OS, and with a 3Com FastEtherlink (parallel tasking peripheral component interconnect (PCI) bus 10/100Base-T) FastEthernet NIU. This test configuration uses actual machines, OSs, NIUs and networks found in many computing environments. The results should therefore have wide applicability.

3.1. Experiment setup

A number of experiments were performed using different size messages transmitted between the SUN WS and the Gateway PC. The only application running on the PC was the test application, the World Wide Web (WWW) Hypertext Markup Language (HTML) browser Chimera from the French national research institute INRIA. The SUN UltraSPARC1 was running the normal set of OS background processes and the INCA message generation application.

For measuring current PC and LINUX system performance, software probes were inserted in three locations: 1) in the LINUX FastEthernet card driver, 2) at the start of protocol processing and 3) at the point where the application began reading the data. The probes wrote the system time to memory when they were executed during the course of network message handling.

For INCA measurements, the INCA library was executed, including the FastEthernet driver, CNI handler and the IPP loop with standard, full implementations of IP, UDP, TCP and optionally XDR functions, all external and separate from the implementations in the OS. Probes were also placed in the same three locations: in the INCA FastEthernet card driver, at the start of the ILP loop and at the point where the application began reading the data. By subtracting the times of the probes, throughput measurements were made.

An INCA message generation program transmitted messages over the FastEthernet at various message sizes ranging from 10 bytes to 65,512 bytes. Messages larger than this were not considered in order to avoid violating interoperability with existing protocol implementations. Messages in the range of 10 to 200 bytes are given more emphasis since 89% of UDP and 99% of TCP network messages are below 200 bytes [11]. Each test at each message size was repeated six times and the lowest times, best throughput, for both INCA and the current system configurations were used for analysis of the results.

3.2. Measurement tools and software

The INCA experiments were conducted using the freely available "ttcp" software used to measure the network throughput between two nodes over a network. Many modification were done to the "ttcp" software to make it work with Solaris and LINUX. A separate test program was written similar to the "ttcp" software to run with the INCA library. The timing measurements were made using the function CLOCK_GETTIME library function in the portable operating system interface (POSIX) 4 library. This timing function is able to provide nanosecond time stamping. Microsecond resolution timers were available for timing measurements on the PC platform. The measurements were taken using a client-server test bench. In this model, a transmitter and a receiver were defined and data was transmitted by the client using the specified protocol and received by the server routine.

3.3. Results

The performance of the INCA network communications architecture running on current systems, the SUN UltraSPARC1/Solaris 2.5.1 and Gateway 2000/LINUX 2.0, is compared to the network communications architecture of the same systems without INCA.

3.3.1. INCA versus SUN UltraSPARC1/Solaris. Table 2 and Figure 2 depict the results of the INCA implementation on the SUN WS. The percent (%) gain with INCA is expressed as the percentage of the current system throughput that INCA achieves. Since 99% of TCP and 89% of UDP messages are below 200 bytes in size [11], the region of interest is up to and below the 200 byte message size. INCA increases SUN WS UDP Throughput by 760% at message sizes between 10 to 40 Bytes. Both Table 2 and Figure 2 show that INCA clearly provides significant performance improvements while maintaining interoperability.

Table 2. INCA Implementation Increases Solaris Network Data Throughput by up to 570%

INCA THROUGHPUT PERFORMANCE ON SUN ULTRASPARC1					
	SOLARIS 2.5.1		INCA		
Msg. Size (Bytes)	Proc. Time (nsec)	Thruput (Bytes /Sec)	Proc. Time (nsec)	Thruput (Bytes /Sec)	Gain (%)
TCP					
50	168384	296940	48781	1024989	345
100	170285	587251	49452	2022163	344
200	174873	1143687	49900	4008016	350
1000	182480	5480053	59298	16863975	308
1400	189418	7391061	61199	22876191	310
UDP					
50	81675	612182	14321	3491376	570
100	86079	1161724	16000	6250000	538
200	89059	2245702	19803	10099480	450
1000	99911	10008908	49564	20175934	202
1400	104163	13440473	65228	21463175	160

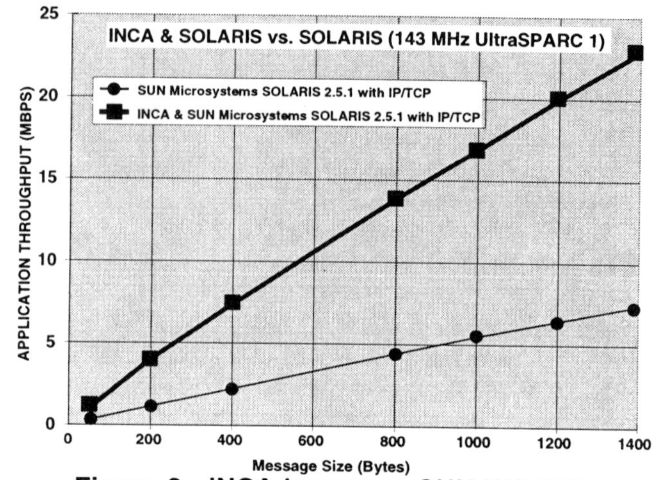

Figure 2. INCA Increases SUN WS TCP Throughput

3.3.2. INCA versus PC/LINUX 2.0. The overall network data application throughput performance improvement of the Gateway 2000 PC with LINUX running INCA versus the same system without INCA is listed in Table 3 and depicted in Figure 3. The percent (%) gain with INCA is expressed as the percentage of the current system throughput that INCA achieves.

INCA outperforms the present PC system anywhere from 255% to 587% depending upon the message size. The largest gain is in protocol processing, where INCA performs protocol processing 12,600% faster than LINUX without INCA.

It is apparent from the results in Table and Figure 3 that INCA performs protocol processing in a much more efficient manner than the current PC/LINUX system. An improvement by INCA of 12,600% for small message sizes and 1500% for large message sizes is quite substantial. Furthermore, the implementation of IP and UDP was retrofitted into INCA. A "from scratch" implementation of IP and UDP would optimize the protocol processing loop more, providing even greater throughput improvement with INCA.

Checksumming processing has been sped up in the INCA ILP loop through the use of a checksum routine optimized for a RISC CPU and through integration. In addition, the protocol data and control processing is separated.

Since the Pentium Pro is not a RISC processor, the protocol performance improvement comes mostly from the elimination of data copies (including many reads and writes within a protocol processing process), the ILP loop and the cache performance improvements from an integrated protocol processing loop.

As the number of protocols or protocol functions increase, INCA's performance over the base system increases even more. With additional protocol processing,

Table 3. INCA versus LINUX IP/UDP Performance Results

INCA VERSUS LINUX 2.0, 167 MHz Pentium Pro PC (IP and UDP Protocols)									
Message	CNI Main Memory Transfer			Protocol Processing			Application Throughput		
Size	(μs)		INCA	(μs)		INCA	Mbps		INCA
(Bytes)	LINUX	INCA	% Gain	LINUX	INCA	% Gain	LINUX	INCA	% Gain
10	1829	1344	73	1889	15	**12593**	0.02	0.06	274
100	1893	1506	80	1991	18	11061	0.21	0.52	**255**
200	2013	1517	75	2055	42	4893	0.39	1.03	261
500	2193	1551	71	2008	45	4462	0.95	2.51	263
1000	2569	1595	**62**	2029	79	2568	1.74	4.78	275
1500	3043	2069	68	3927	110	3570	1.72	5.51	320
2000	3043	2069	68	4357	160	2723	2.16	7.18	332
4000	3280	2306	70	7463	305	2447	2.98	12.26	411
10000	4228	3254	77	18347	663	2767	3.54	20.42	576
65000	13234	12260	**93**	95056	6186	**1537**	4.80	28.19	**587**

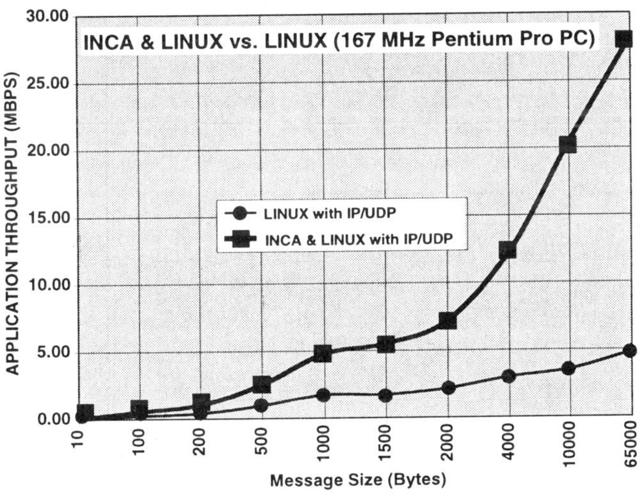

Figure 3a. INCA versus LINUX IP/UDP Application Throughput

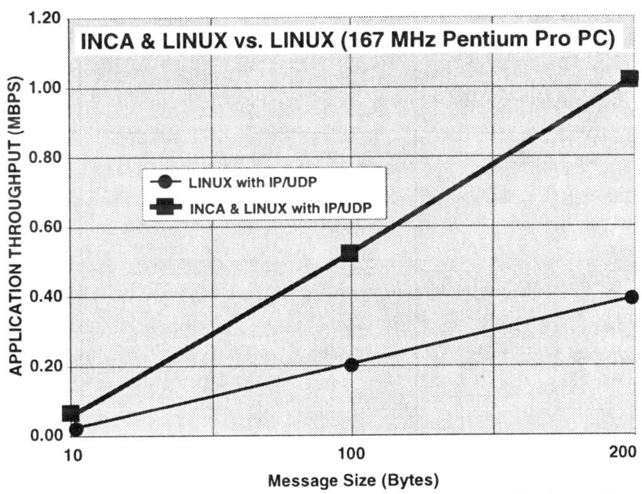

Figure 3b. INCA versus LINUX IP/UDP 10-200 Byte Application Throughput

such as XDR presentation formatting, INCA's and LINUX's throughput decreases. However, INCA's throughput decrease is half that of LINUX's. The improvement of INCA over LINUX increased from a maximum of 587% to a maximum of 613%.

The larger the message size, the more INCA improves throughput over the present LINUX system. The larger the messages, the more data to copy over the memory bus, the greater the performance improvement with INCA's reduced data copying. The more protocols that are used, for example the addition of XDR presentation protocol processing, the greater the performance improvement of INCA from the use of ILP.

Unlike many other performance techniques, INCA improves performance for small (≤ 200 byte) messages as well as for large messages.

4. Architectural considerations

The INCA architecture can be implemented within individual application programs, within the OS, or both. The software library comprising the architecture can be recompiled into applications/ linked to applications, or recompiled into the OS.

The amount of memory required for an application will increase by approximately the amount of the INCA library plus some additional RAM memory for intermediate data processing results. In light of the rate of increase in RAM densities (and hence capacities) and costs of a few dollars per Megabyte, the few additional Megabytes of memory required appear not to be a limiting issue. Even in a case of many large applications executing on one machine in a multi-tasking environment, virtual memory management and possible additional RAM can meet the need for more memory.

Data security may be somewhat reduced without an additional protection mechanism. As with any architecture that performs network data processing in user memory space, the effectiveness of existing OS protection mechanisms is reduced. Unauthorized access to user network data can become more likely.

The use of ILP affects protocol modularity in the sense of ease of swapping protocols in and out of the architecture. Unless designed for ILP, the incorporation of protocol modifications or new protocols will require manual coding, regardless of the implementation method. The process of integrating protocol changes could be automated at some point in the future.

INCA is bi-directional. One can transmit as well as receive using the INCA software library, thereby potentially doubling the performance benefit. For computers relying on a network connection in order to provide user services, such as a network computer, the INCA architecture would provide an even greater performance benefit. For such computers every application requires network data communication and processing. The INCA architecture becomes the processing path for an even greater percentage of user time, increasing the performance benefits of INCA.

5. Conclusions

Internal computer data processing overheads are limiting the throughput of network communicated data to a few megabits per second, despite the availability of near Gigabit networks and processors operating at near network speeds. Increased network communications throughput can be achieved through many design features, but the main options are optimizing the processing functions in the protocol architecture and reducing the number of data copies. Today's computer systems utilize the OS to perform both of these functions. Modifying the OS would result in major non interoperability costs and will not be supported by the commercial industry. Replacing the OS is also not an acceptable option. Good performance alone is not enough. Without the ability to interoperate with the existing application programs and machine/OS combinations by running application programs without modification, INCA research would suffer the consequences of almost all OS innovation research, a lack of applicability and a relegation to obscurity. Interoperability, including portability of the implementation, is required for acceptance and utilization of network communications performance improvements.

INCA improves network data throughput significantly without sacrificing interoperability. The combination of INCA architecture features and implementation methods: reduction in data copying between and within internal network data handling and protocol processing entities, message buffer management, checksumming and other protocol processing optimizations for RISC processors and level 1 "cache friendliness", make for substantial performance improvement.

Implementation on COTS WS and PC systems shows that INCA can function with all existing applications, OSs, communication protocols, machines, NIUs and networks while providing anywhere from 260% to near 760% greater data throughput than existing systems without INCA. The performance improvement is independent of the network link speed. Whether the network connection is via Gigabit or dial up modem speeds, or whether the machine requires the network in order to function (network computer), INCA provides the same percentage of improvement in data processing time.

INCA improves small message throughput as well as large message throughput by a significant percentage. The communication bandwidth of a system is often measured by sending a virtually infinite data stream from one node to another. While this may be representative of a few applications, the demand for high bandwidths when sending many small messages (e.g., a few hundred bytes) is increasing.

With such an improvement in network communications data throughput at the application program level, existing systems can utilize high speed networks and the exponentially increasing CPU power to provide a whole new realm of applications that require fast, high bandwidth network communications, either with many large messages or with many small messages.

As a stand-alone software only library, INCA can be ported to almost any existing and next generation machine, whether a home user's computer linked to a network via modem or whether a powerful server on a Gigabit link network. INCA performance scales with network, CPU and memory speed, memory bus bandwidth and NIU improvements, making the INCA results relevant for some time to come.

6. References

[1] P. Druschel, M. B. Abbott, M. A. Pagels, and L. L. Peterson, "Network Subsystem Design: A Case For An Integrated Data Path", IEEE Network (Special Issue on End-System Support for High Speed Networks), Vol. 7, No. 4, pp. 8-17, Jul. 1993.

[2] D. Mosberger, L. L. Peterson, and S. O'Malley, "Protocol Latency: MIPS And Reality", Technical Report TR 95-02, Department of Computer Science, The University of Arizona, Tucson, AZ, 1995.

[3] V. Roca, T. Braun and C. Diot, "Efficient Communication Architectures For Open Systems", Institut National De Recherche En Informatique Et En Automatique (INRIA), Sophia Antipolis, France, Jul. 1996.

[4] N. C. Hutchinson and L. L. Peterson, "The X-Kernel: An Architecture For Implementing Network Protocols", IEEE Trans. Soft. Eng., Vol. 17, Jan. 1991.

[5] M. Accetta, R. Baron, D. Golub, R. Rashid, A. Tevanian, and M. Young, "Mach: A New Kernel Foundation For UNIX Development", in Proceedings of the Summer 1986 USENIX Technical Conference and Exhibition, Jun. 1986.

[6] A. Mainwaring and D. Culler, "Active Message Applications Programming Interface And Communication Subsystem Organization", Draft Technical Report, Computer Science Division, University of California at Berkeley, 1996.

[7] T. von Eicken, A. Basu, V. Buch, and W. Vogels, "U-Net: A User-Level Network Interface For Parallel And Distributed Computing", Proc. of the 15th ACM Symposium on Operating Systems Principles, Copper Mountain, CO, Dec. 3-6, 1995.

[8] D. D. Clark and D. L. Tennenhouse, "Architectural Considerations For A New Generation Of Protocols," in ACM Communication Architectures, Protocols, and Applications (SIGCOMM '90), Philadelphia, PA, USA, Sep. 1990.

[9] M. B. Abbott and L. L. Peterson, "Increasing Network Throughput By Integrating Protocol Layers", EEE/ACM Transactions on Networking, Vol. 1, No. 5, pp. 600-610, Oct. 1993.

[10] T. Braun and C. Diot, "Performance Evaluation And Cache Analysis Of An ILP Protocol Implementation", IEEE/ACM Transaction on Networking, Jun. 1996.

[11] J. Kay and J. Pasquale, "The Importance Of Non-Data Touching Processing Overheads In TCP/IP", Proceedings of the ACM Communications Architectures and Protocols Conference (SIGCOMM), pp. 259-269, San Francisco, CA, Sep. 1993.

ATM Multipeer Communication Using a Two-Layer Architecture

Stefan Dresler
Institute for Telematics, University of Karlsruhe, Zirkel 2, D-76128 Karlsruhe, Germany
Phone: +49/721/608-6397, Fax: +49/721/388097
Email: dresler@telematik.informatik.uni-karlsruhe.de

Abstract

Applications deploying distributed database updates, distributed simulations, shared whiteboards, and forthcoming distributed interactive multi-user games have communication needs not satisfied by most available protocols or communication subsystems. These applications are different from classical applications in that they have potentially many senders and receivers. Although there has been a lot of research on unicast and recently on multicast protocols, only little work has been done in the area of multipeer communication, i.e., communication realizing an M:N communication service. Even fewer results are available for such a service on connection-oriented technologies like ATM (Asynchronous Transfer Mode). This paper describes the current situation, proposes a novel two-layer architecture especially suitable for ADSL and cable networks, which bridge the gap between LANs and the WAN, gives a first analysis, and presents open issues.

1. Introduction

Certain applications that maintain a complex communication scheme with several senders and several receivers, a so-called *multipeer* scheme, profit from a communication subsystem that guarantees certain properties of message delivery like an ordering relation on the messages. Examples of applications that may take advantage of such a system include distributed databases, distributed simulations, shared whiteboards, and forthcoming distributed interactive multi-user games.

Currently, these applications are facing the following situation:

- If the Internet Protocol (IP) is used and no further requirements regarding reliable, ordered or atomic delivery are imposed, the application can use the IP multicast architecture (which in the notation of this paper actually is a multi*peer* architecture) in LANs [1]. In WANs, the peers can connect to the MBone (Multicast Backbone) [2] to be able to deploy its multipeer service.
- If IP is used, but there are requirements with respect to reliable, ordered or atomic delivery, one of the available communication subsystems can be used (e.g., Horus [3], its predecessor Isis [4], Totem [5] and Transis [6]).
- If the sites are connected via e.g. ATM and the message and control overhead of using IP-over-ATM [7, 8, 9] – possibly enhanced by multicast extensions [10] – or MPOA (Multi-Protocol over ATM) [11] in this situation is considered too large, a native solution over ATM is required. A similar argument holds for other NBMA (non-broadcast – multiple access) technologies like Frame Relay, X.25, ISDN (Integrated Services Digital Network), ADSL (Asymmetric Digital Subscriber Line), etc.

Recently, some protocols have been proposed for some aspects of ATM multipeer communication, like SEAM [12], SMART [13], SPAM [14] and CRAM [15].

It turns out, however, that no protocol is readily available that implements an ordering service on top of ATM that at the same time takes into account the specific characteristics of ATM networks like connection-orientation, in-order delivery, bursty losses as dominating transmission error, and lack of a multipeer data distribution service, and which implements adequate traffic control functions and is tuned towards forthcoming access networks like ADSL and cable networks. This paper discusses aspects of realizing such a multipeer service on top on ATM.

The paper is organized as follows: First, the characteristics of multipeer communication are presented in detail. Following this, the endsystem view is contrasted with the needs of the multipeer group as a whole. Concentrating on ATM, the fourth chapter describes the specific situation of NBMA networks with respect to data distribution and robustness. Chapter five presents a novel two-layer architecture for multipeer communication especially suited for emerging applications used at home or in offices. Chapter six gives hints on open issues. The main thoughts and results of the paper are summarized at the end.

0-8186-8810-6/98 $10.00 © 1998 IEEE

2. Characteristics of multipeer communication

Multipeer communication is different from other communication relations (unicast (1:1), multicast (1:N), concast (M:1)) in several aspects, some of which are discussed below. These aspects are often not disjoint, but closely related. An approach using a token to pass the right to send, e.g., can use appropriate methods for ordering of messages, bandwidth allocation of senders, and failure detection.

2.1. Definition of an association and roles

Endsystems participating as peers in a multipeer communication can take the role of a *sender*, the role of a *receiver*, or both. In the following it is assumed that an endsystem can always take any of these roles. Depending on the concrete realization of the service and the parameters of the association, it is possible for an endsystem to change its role. Furthermore, it may be allowed to join late (referred to as dynamic join) or to leave a group, resp.

In multipeer communication, it is not always obvious what denotes an *M:N association.* (The expression "M:N connection" is often avoided because it does not hold for connectionless networks. We abstract from this here.) Is the association still up if a sender fails? Is it still up if a receiver fails? The answers to these questions strongly depend on the semantics of the communication relation as given by the application. A set of M terminals (senders) sending updates to a database distributed over N hosts (receivers), e.g., does not run into a dangerous situation if a terminal fails; integrity of the database might be endangered, however, if a receiver (a database host) fails.

2.2. Distributing data in multipeer communication

Distributing data from M senders to N receivers can be accomplished by several methods, e.g.:

- M*N 1:1 connections: This simple solution obviously suffers from a lot of state to be held in participating systems and the need for sending endsystems to duplicate data themselves. Since 1:1 connections (or associations, in connectionless networks) are supported by any communication system (directly or as a special case of broadcast communication), this solution can always be chosen, if resources allow.
- M 1:N connections: This approach uses less state space, but requires the physical interconnection (e.g., an Ethernet) or intermediate systems (e.g. routers) to be able to duplicate and forward multicast packets.
- One M:N connection: This seems to be the most elegant solution. It is realized in LANs based on Ethernet (layer 2 view), e.g., and over IP (layer 3 view) in global networks using the IP multicast mechanisms, as demonstrated by the MBone [2].
- Buffering system: Using an intermediate system collecting messages from M senders and forwarding these messages to N receivers is feasible, too. The connections from the senders to the buffering system can be of unicast type, while the connections from the buffering system are unicast or multicast.
- Hybrid approaches combine some of the solutions above. An architecture deploying buffering systems multicasting data to participants will be further discussed below.

The API (application programming interface), which offers the services of a communication subsystem realizing multipeer communication to the application, in general abstracts from the underlying topology.

2.3. Traffic management

In unicast communication, rate-based and credit-based solutions are well known, as in TCP (Transmission Control Protocol). For multicast communication, a number of solutions exists which offer specialized functionality for certain protocols. No commonly approved and widely used solution is available, however, exept a rate-based restriction imposed by MBone multicast routers. Concast communication is almost never mentioned explicitly, and there are no mechanisms in use to manage traffic. Accordingly, there are no traffic management functions available for multipeer communication, not counting implicit traffic management by routers dropping packets on queue overflow.

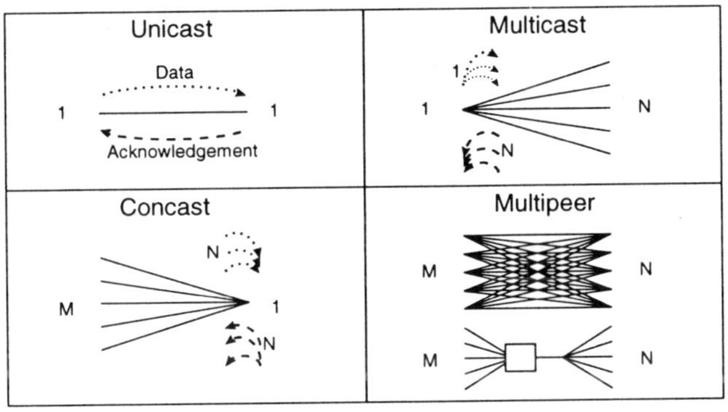

Figure 1. Traffic management in group communication.

Figure 1 shows the traffic management situation for different communication types. In unicast communication, a sender sends data (downstream) to a single receiver, which in turn sends acknowledgement information back to the sender (upstream). In multicast communication, a sender sends a message, which is in general duplicated on its way to the receivers. The N receivers generate N acknowledgements, which can also be used for flow and congestion control. A single send event downstream thus generates N responses sent upstream. In concast scenarios, M senders send data to a single receiver, which in turn sends acknowledgement information upstream. Here, M messages sent downstream result in M messages sent upstream, showing that concast is not just "the opposite" of multicast. Traffic management in multipeer communication realized by M*N unicast connections seems difficult, while using a concast to an intermediate, buffering system that distributes data via multicast allows to use mechanisms known from concast and multicast.

A way to realize flow control in concast and multipeer scenarios is to define a *network sliding window* [6] from which a send credit or a transmission delay can be derived.

2.4. Reliability and robustness

The probability for the loss of a packet on a connection (or association where connectionless networks are concerned) is not neglegible. In large multicast scenarios, it is not unlikely that any packet is not received by at least one host, requiring many retransmissions in prototols with ARQ (Automatic Repeat Request) and possibly resulting in the well-known implosion problem (a sender is swamped by lots of acknowledgements). The amount of status information to keep track of packets on an M:N association and the number of acknowledgements are even larger than for the multicast case, so that powerful mechanisms are necessary, especially involving FEC (Forward Error Correction). Furthermore, bursts (many packets close in time on the same link) are proliferated into the net whenever a single sender sends such a burst.

Further robustness issues concern the ability of the communication system to react to link failures causing network partitions.

2.5. Ordering

As soon as several senders are involved in a communication association, the question of ordering of messages arises. There are several semantics known, e.g.:

- FIFO (First In–First Out): in-order delivery of messages from each sender, no relation between messages of different senders. This is also commonly assumed for unicast communication.
- Causally ordered delivery: preservation of potential causal order among messages (compare definition of Leslie Lamport [16] or equivalent formulations [17]).
- Agreed delivery: unique order among every pair of messages in all of their destinations (also known as global or total order).
- Safe multicast: unique order of message delivery plus delay of delivery of messages until acknowledged by all group members.

Depending on the requirements of the application, a multicast communication subsystem can choose the appropriate mechanisms to ensure the required ordering of messages. As a rule of thumb, stricter requirements imply more expensive mechanisms, in terms of delay, bandwidth, number of messages, buffer state, and state space.

The Transis system [6], e.g., supports all of the four orderings for IP networks. [18] gives examples of the consequences of a security trading application and a fire detection system failing because necessary ordering criteria had not been met.

2.6. Support of heterogeneous scenarios

In scenarios with mobile participants (senders or receivers), especially those connected via a wireless link, transmission interrupts are not uncommon. If strict ordering or reliability requirements are needed, these interrupts are likely to also affect the multipeer service by delays or even communication breakdowns. This problem can be dealt with by a proxy taking part in the multipeer communication on behalf of the mobile user (more precisely the mobile terminal), thus blocking the interrupts from the communication group. A similar approach can be taken for users behind a slow link or with a slow terminal that is not able to cope with the management overhead.

2.7. Evaluation criteria

The aspects mentioned above already listed some criteria to evaluate the performance and resource use by multipeer protocols. Important (to varying degrees) criteria are:

- Average and minimum delay (latency) of messages for a given group
- Number of messages (user data plus ordering and error control overhead), also referred to as *message complexity*. Here the processing power of the hosts may be the limiting factor.
- Bandwidth consumption. There may be low limits on the link bandwidth to and from homes or offices that make participation in a group difficult or slow down the rest of the group.

- Number of connections needed to realize the service, contributing to the overhead
- Scalability with respect to
  - the number of participants (peers)
  - the number of groups
  - the size of the network
- Suitability for heterogeneous environments, as explained above
- Interoperability with existing hardware and network technology. Some systems proposed require changes to at least some of the network nodes, e.g. SEAM [12], SMART [13], SPAM [14] and CRAM [15].
- Type of ordering semantics, as listed above
- Flow and congestion control, if any. Criteria include fairness to other connections (which in turn requires a definition of fairness or friendliness, especially towards TCP in the Internet), operating safety (no negative impact on the stability of the network), and responsiveness (ability to react fast enough).
- Traffic concentration on links. Core nodes (pure transfer systems or buffers) and central links may become bottlenecks
- Assignment of unique identifiers for each sender, if not provided by the underlying communication system
- Possibilities of late join and of leave operations, depending on the semantics of the communication
- Latency for dynamic join
- Robustness against failures of links, plus impact on other multipeer participants. This is especially important in larger groups; depending on the ordering semantics, a failing host may affect the whole group.
- Two-layer or integrated approach for IP solutions over ATM
- Various security aspects, e.g. regarding users trying to gain an advantage over other peers by faking time stamps (if those are used) or serial numbers in messages

It is extremely difficult to assign relative importances to each of these criteria, because they strongly depend on the application and the network technology. The requirements of a low-bandwidth distributed application on a few hosts of a trusted local area network can be met more easily than those of time-critical applications on a large number of hosts connected by a public wide area network.

3. Endsystem view vs. network view

Endsystems have a view different from the situation for the whole group:

The endsystem is best served by a solution involving an error correction that is as simple as possible, using as little status information as possible, and being as robust as possible.

The network or the whole group, resp., however faces a diametrical situation: the communication relation is complex, possibly involving a lot of state information related to group membership (if the members of the group are known to all members, and especially if 1:1 connections are used in connection-oriented systems) and to packets sent and acknowledged. The issue of traffic control is important, but yet mainly unsolved, and actions have to be taken for providing an ordering of messages, e.g. by using a token controlling the right to send data.

These contrasting views were the main reasons for the development of the two-layer multipeer communication framework introduced below.

4. Multipeer communication over ATM

Most of the aspects of multipeer communication mentioned so far apply to IP networks as well as to connection-oriented networks like ATM. ATM networks, or most often any other NBMA network as well, have characteristics different from IP, however, that require special attention in multipeer scenarios. The main differences of IP and ATM networks are recalled in Table 1.

Table 1. Main differences of IP and ATM.

IP	ATM
connectionless	connection-oriented (out-of-band signaling)
variable length packets	variable length frames with fixed size cells
packet loss as dominating error	cell loss (due to congested queues) in general corrupts whole frame
out-of-order delivery possible	in-order delivery on each virtual circuit (VC)
multicast and broadcast in LAN (almost) for free	explicit multicast setup; broadcast only as special case of multicast

Multicast in IP over ATM networks can be achieved using the following mechanisms:

- IP over ATM [7, 8, 9] + MARS (Multicast Address Resolution Server) [10] concept: based on ATMARP and MARS (using a multicast server (MCS) or a mesh)
- LAN Emulation: using a Broadcast and Unknown Server (BUS) for multicast data distribution [19]
- MPOA: currently only supports unicast [11]

Problems of these approaches often involve the connection setups still being necessary for ATM, although IP is used on top of it, and a large number of connections for the mesh solution of MARS. Furthermore, error correction in these setups is not suited to multicast, and the solutions do not scale well with a large number of hosts or over wide area connections.

4.1. Connection management and distribution of data for a multipeer service over ATM

Focussing on ATM networks, the general mechanisms discussed above to distribute data in multipeer scenarios specialize as follows (compare Figure 2):

- M*N 1:1 connections: With ATM being connection-oriented, the number space available for connection identifiers is exhausted at a high rate with this approach. Furthermore, a lot of state in switches and endsystems is wasted, and endsystems duplicate packets themselves. Whenever a participating host fails, all other participants have a stale connection to this host. Similarly, whenever a new host joins, all other participants have to be contacted. Especially for larger groups, the initial establishment of all necessary connections takes time and non-negligible processing power on all hosts.
- M 1:N connections: This solution reduces the number of connections from $O(M^2)$ to $O(M)$. In the worst case – all ATM systems are connected by a single switch – the amount of state space is still not significantly reduced in this switch, however. The amount of work to be done for a sender in setting up a connection to all receivers is reduced if the *Leaf Initiated Join* (LIJ) mechanisms introduced in UNI 4.0 [20] are used. For unacknowledged multicast distribution, approaches that allow decentralized joins (joins the sender does not need to process or even initiate) [12] consume less state and less computing power than solutions that require the sender to add a receiver to the ATM connection.
- Common VC, AAL5: Using a common VC for multipeer communication over ATM is not covered by any standard and thus not readily available. With AAL5 as adaptation layer it has to be taken care that senders send in turn, not at the same time, – or at least that their packets do not overlap on intermediary links – because otherwise it is impossible to correctly reassemble the packets sent, unless each packet covers just a single ATM cell, which in general is not a valid assumption. This restriction is resolved in CRAM [15], which sends resource management (RM) cells (originally introduced by the ATM Available Bit-Rate (ABR) service) in front of user data frames to carry information about the sender of the frame. These RM cells are inserted at merge points. So-called source identifiers (SIDs) are assigned by the application or dynamically by the communication system.
- Common VC, AAL3/4: With an identifier field in AAL3/4 being available, the restriction mentioned for AAL5 does not apply here. The overhead/data ratio is worse, however. SPAM [14], a data forwarding model for multipeer connection support in ATM networks, uses a per-cell identifier, which in turn requires a new ATM adaptation layer, possibly making this approach a little inefficient because AAL functionality has to be provided in software.
- Buffering system: Using a buffering intermediate system is possible with ATM, too, and elaborated on below.
- VCs in VP: Another approach having been suggested is to route a Virtual Path (VP) and take different VCI values to distinguish between senders, as with AAL3/4, but with less overhead per cell [21, 22].

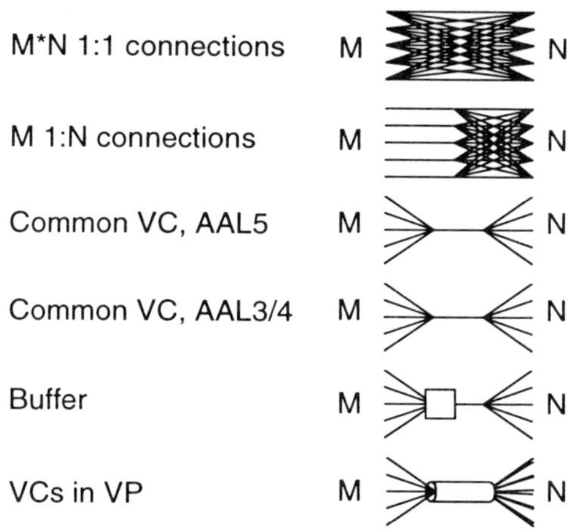

Figure 2. Possibilities to realize a multipeer data distribution service for ATM.

Access to the ATM Adaptation Layer (AAL) is realized through a native ATM interface [23] offering the services of the User Network Interface (UNI) [20, 24] or through an extended socket interface.

4.2. Reliability and robustness in ATM multipeer communication

Efficient error correction for multipeer ATM WAN scenarios is a nontrivial task. The dominating error in ATM networks is correlated cell loss due to buffer overflow in switches and endsystems. A remedy known from multicast solutions is to use FEC (Forward Error Correction), as it reduces (or even eliminates) the necessity to repeat packets (or cells) and avoids the implosion problem of multicast communication, at the cost of an initial overhead in the amount of data sent. This approach is taken e.g. in the Group Communication Server concept [25]. Some of the loss of cells can be avoided if the common source of buffer overflows – bursty traffic – is eliminated. This can partly be achieved by shaping traffic (introducing delays), or by dispersing traffic onto different sublinks, known as *network striping* or *multipath scheme* [26, 27, 28] (compare Figure 3). It has been shown that burstiness of traffic is reduced by the latter mechanism [29].

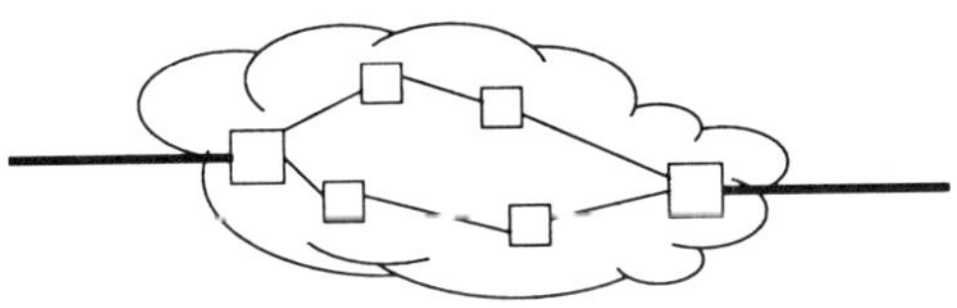

Figure 3. Network striping.

[30] describes a congestion control scheme for a multicast ABR service. Additional suggestions have been made in the ATM Forum.

5. Proposed server based approach using two layers

In smaller groups, usage of a buffering system, i.e., a server, as listed in the choices for distributing data in multipeer communication, seems to be a good solution. Reasons include:

- At any receiver, a single connection terminates, requiring less state space.
- Only a single reassembly buffer at the receiver side is necessary, instead of M buffers (for M senders).
- Taking the view of a peering endsystem, the approach is robust against loss of other connections (between a server and another endsystem).
- If a provider offers such a server as one of his or her machines, it does not necessarily have to be a single point of failure, because provider machines are often robust and have short down-times, especially if a provider can make money out of providing this service.
- A server does not necessarily have to be a point of delay, because receivers have to rearrange messages anyway for ordering services. Shortcutting frames (forwarding them as soon as the first cell has arrived) helps keeping the latency low [12].
- The server an endsystem connects to can provide a unique sender identification, if not already provided by the application.
- Traffic management functions can be located in the network, resulting in faster reaction to congestion than in scenarios involving functionality only in endsystems. Furthermore, the service is more robust against malicious over-use of resources, especially bandwidth, and against manipulation of sequence numbers or time stamps, if those are used to order messages.
- A server can act as a proxy for mobile terminals that may experience short interrupts in connectivity to the rest of the group, thus shielding the group from delays of messages or retransmissions.
- A server in front of a satellite link can merge message distribution requests of a group and schedule the messages for broadcasting.
- The approach does not require any changes to endsystems or intermediate systems, if regular switches are used combined with dedicated buffering systems.

An appropriate server can be found by endsystems by manually configuring an address, or by looking it up in some directory.

In wide area networks and for large groups, a set of servers can be used:

- These servers can perform retransmissions, without intervention of endsystems.
- The multipath concept can be deployed between servers, without bothering endsystems.
- The servers cooperate to provide an ordering service, if necessary.

The Totem system [5] is an example of a remotely related layered architecture for IP. It uses the notion of broadcast domains in the lower layer and of logical rings, and it is thus particularly useful for classical LANs. Furthermore, it provides a protocol connecting the rings.

The idea of placing ordering and error control intelligence on intermediate systems forms a realization of the *Active Networks* concept. If such functionality is not available, it is always possible to use regular workstations as servers.

Using an ADSL (Asymmetric Digital Subscriber Line) setup [31], the novel architecture sketched above is shown in more detail in Figure 4. Similarly, the architecture can be mapped onto other access technologies like cable networks and forthcoming networks using power lines to reach homes and offices. Figure 5 gives an example of a HFC (Hybrid Fiber Coax) setup [32].

Endsystems connect to servers via a simple unicast protocol, traversing the link provided by ADSL. The servers are located at the concentration points of the ADSL or HFC infrastructure. Server/server communication takes place via wide area ATM links. The servers are placed at the termination of the ADSL links at the telephone company or at central points within the telco network in case the logical ADSL connections are not terminated close to the physical ADSL end points but at some concentration point.

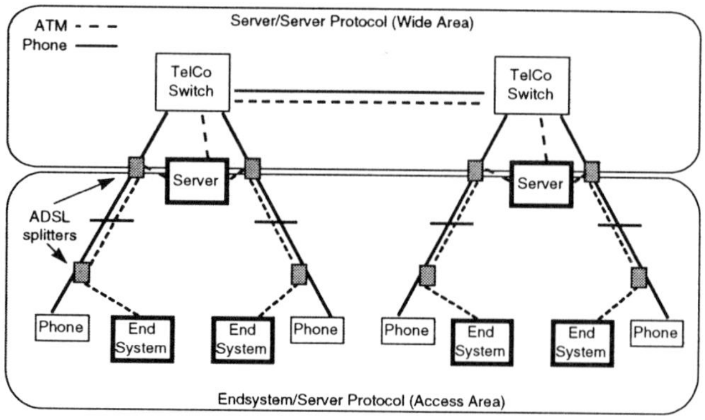

Figure 4. Two-layer architecture using ADSL as access network technology.

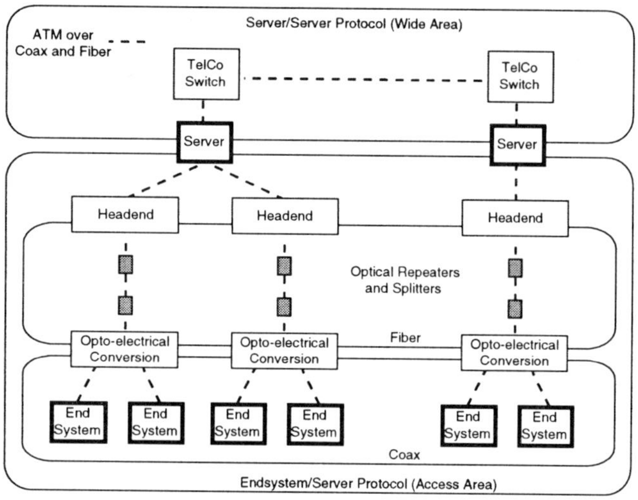

Figure 5. Hybrid fiber coax (HFC) as access network technology.

6. Research areas

Open issues related to the proposed architecture include:

- Which applications would profit most from such a service and such an architecture? More precisely: What exactly *are* the needs of the various applications like multi-user games, applications using distributed databases, CSCW (Computer Supported Cooperative Work) systems, distributed simulations, etc.? What should a service interface (and the API) look like?
- How can traffic control best (most efficiently) be realized for the server/server communication, i.e., how can several senders be coordinated among each other and with several receivers?
- How can an ordering service best (again most efficiently) be realized, for each of the various ordering semantics, and which semantic matches the architecture most closely?
- And leading further: What would an architecture look like realizing an ordered multipeer service using satellites for data distribution, possibly leaving control traffic to terrestrial links?

7. Conclusion

For multipeer communication scenarios, an efficient solution over ATM is desirable in order to take advantage of the special characteristics of this type of network and avoid the overhead of adaptation of e.g. IP to ATM.

The specific characteristics of ATM networks like connection-orientation, in-order delivery, bursty losses as dominating transmission error, and lack of a multipeer data distribution service ask for a dedicated solution to provide an ordering multipeer service. Not yet sufficiently addressed by most existing concepts are questions of error control, deployment in heterogeneous scenarios, efficient usage of non-classical data networks, traffic control for several senders, and security.

The approach proposed based on a two-layer architecture and a set of servers matches the needs of topologically distributed applications depending on a multipeer data distribution service by using a simple, robust protocol to endsystems typically located in homes or offices while being able to deploy powerful error control mechanisms in the wide area part of the communication.

8. References

[1] S. Deering, *Host Extensions for IP Multicasting*, STD 3, Request for Comments (RFC) 1112, Internet Engineering Task Force (IETF), August 1989.

[2] Vinay Kumar, *The MBone Information Web*, online at http://www.mbone.com/.

[3] R. van Renesse, K. P. Birman, and S. Maffeis, "Horus: A Flexible Group Communication System", *Communications of the ACM* 39(4), April 1996.

[4] K. P. Birman, R. Cooper, T. A. Joseph, K. P. Kane, and F. B. Schmuck, *ISIS – A Distributed Programming Environment*, June 1990.

[5] L. E. Moser, P. M. Melliar-Smith, D. A. Agarwal, R. K. Budhia, and C. A. Lingley-Papadopoulos, *Totem: A Fault-Tolerant Multicast Group Communication System*, Department of Electrical and Computer Engineering, University of California, Santa Barbara, *Communications of the ACM* 39(4), April 1996.

[6] D. Dolev and D. Malki, *The Design of the Transis System*, Computer Science Institute, Hebrew University, Jerusalem, Israel, 1995.

[7] J. Heinanen, *Multiprotocol Encapsulation over ATM Adaptation Layer 5*, Request for Comments (RFC) 1483, Internet Engineering Task Force (IETF), July 1993.

[8] M. Laubach, *Classical IP and ARP over ATM*, Request for Comments (RFC) 1577, Internet Engineering Task Force (IETF), December 1993.

[9] M. Perez, F. Liaw, D. Grossman, A. Mankin, E. Hoffman, and A. Malis, *ATM Signaling Support for IP over ATM*, Request for Comments (RFC) 1755, Internet Engineering Task Force (IETF), February 1995.

[10] G. Armitage, *Support for Multicast over UNI 3.0/3.1 based ATM networks*, Request for Comments (RFC) 2033, Internet Engineering Task Force (IETF), November 1996.

[11] ATM Forum, *Multi-Protocol over ATM – Version 1.0*, af-mpoa-0087.000, July 1997.

[12] M. Grossglauser and K. K. Ramakrishnan, "SEAM: Scalable and Efficient ATM Multicast", *Proceedings of IEEE Infocom '97*, April 7–11, 1997, Kobe, Japan.

[13] E. Gauthier, J. Y. Le Boudec, and P. Oechslin, "SMART: A Many-to-Many Multicast Protocol for ATM", *IEEE Journal on Selected Areas in Communications* 15(3), pp. 458–472, April 1997.

[14] S. Komandur and D. Mossé, "SPAM: A Data Forwarding Model for Multipoint-to-Multipoint Connection Support in ATM Networks", *Proceedings of the 6th International Conference on Computer Communications and Networks*, IEEE Computer Society, September 1997.

[15] S. Komandur, J. Crowcroft, and D. Mossé, *CRAM: Cell Relabeling at Merge-points for ATM Multicast*, IEEE International Conference on ATM (IPATM '98), June 22–24, 1998, Colmar, France.

[16] L. Lamport, "Time, Clocks, and the Ordering of Events in a Distributed System", *Communications of the ACM* 21(7), July 1978, pp. 558–565.

[17] B. Charron-Bost, F. Mattern, and G. Tel, *Synchronous, asynchronous, and causally ordered communication*, August 1995, 22 pages.

[18] R. Cooper, "Experience with Causally and Totally Ordered Communication Support – A cautionary tale", November 1, 1993, *Operating Systems Review* 28(1), pp. 28-31 (1994) .

[19] ATM Forum, *LAN Emulation over ATM – Version 1.0*, af-lane-0021.000, January 1995.

[20] ATM Forum, *ATM User-Network Interface (UNI) Specification Version 4.0*, af-sig-0061.000, July 1996.

[21] R. Venkateswaran, C. S. Raghavendra, X. Chen, and V. P. Kumar, *Support for Multiway Communications in ATM Networks*, The ATM Forum Technical Committee, Contribution 97-0316, April 28–May 2, 1997.

[22] R. Venkateswaran, C. S. Raghavendra, X. Chen, and V. P. Kumar, *Distributed Mechanisms for VCI Assignment in VP-based Multicast*, The ATM Forum Technical Committee, Contribution 97-0379, April 28–May 2, 1997.

[23] S. Dresler, M. Hofmann, C. Schmidt, and H. R. Wiltfang, "A Native ATM API suited for Multimedia Communication", *Proceedings of Fourth International Workshop on Interactive Distributed Multimedia Systems and Telecommunication Services (IDMS '97)*, September 10–12, 1997, Darmstadt, Germany.

[24] ATM Forum, *ATM User-Network Interface (UNI) Specification Version 3.1*, Prentice Hall, Englewood Cliffs, NJ, June 1995.

[25] G. Carle and S. Dresler, "High Performance Group Communication Services in ATM Networks", Chapter in *High-Speed Networks for Multimedia Applications*, W. Effelsberg, O. Spaniol, A. Danthine, D. Ferrari (Eds.), Kluwer Academic Publishers, Boston/Dordrecht/London, 1996, pp. 199–223.

[26] G. Carle, S. Dresler, and J. Schiller, "Multipath FEC Scheme for the ATM Adaptation Layer AAL5", IFIP TC6/WG6.2 Fourth International Conference on Broadband Communications '98 (BC'98), April 1-3, 1998, Stuttgart, Germany, Proceedings in: *Broadband Communications – The future of telecommunications*, Paul Kühn, Roya Ulrich (Eds.), Chapman & Hall, pp. 234-245.

[27] H. Adiseshu, G. Parulkar, and G. Varghese, *A Reliable and Scalable Striping Protocol*, Department of Computer Science, Washington University, St. Louis, USA, Sigcomm '96, pp. 131–141.

[28] C. B. S. Traw and J. M. Smith, *Striping Within the Network Subsystem*, IEEE Network, July/August 1995, pp. 22–29.

[29] Q. Ding and S. C. Liew, *A Performance Analysis of a Parallel Communications Scheme for ATM Networks*, The Chinese University of Hong Kong, H. K, IEEE Globecom '95, pp. 898–902.

[30] H.-Y. Tzeng and K.-Y. Siu, "On Max-Min Fair Congestion Control for Multicast ABR Service in ATM", *IEEE Journal on Selected Areas in Communications* 15(1), April 1997, pp. 545–556.

[31] ATM Forum, *Residential Broadband Architectural Framework*, af-rbb-0099.000, May 1998.

[32] C. Bisdikian, K. Maruyama, D. I. Seidman, and D. N. Serpanos, "Cable Access Beyond the Hype: On residential Broadband Data Services over HFC Networks", *IEEE Communications Magazine*, November 1996, pp. 128–135.

Physical and Logical Design of ATM Networks for Multimedia Traffic

Janelle J. Harms,
Department of Computing Science,
University of Alberta,
Edmonton, Alberta, Canada T6G 2H1
Email: harms@cs.ualberta.ca

Abstract

A logical Virtual Path-based network provides an effective way to facilitate the dynamic resource management in ATM networks. The physical topology of an ATM network should be designed to provide flexibility to the logical VP reconfiguration in order to adapt to changing traffic conditions Three different physical design algorithms are considered in this paper. Two parameters in the design control the spare capacity and the alternative path allocation providing the flexibility to the VPs. The algorithms are evaluated under both static and dynamic capacity allocation schemes using simulation.

1 Introduction

An ATM network is expected to accommodate multimedia traffic including traffic classes of: voice, video, data, and image which have different traffic characteristics, different qualities of service (QoS), and different bandwidth requirements. In addition, such a network should provide a mechanism for dynamic resource allocation in order to adapt to changing traffic conditions and possible network facility failures. The virtual path (VP) concept has been proposed to provide an effective mechanism for dynamic resource management control [14] [13]. A logical network topology can be designed to satisfy bandwidth requirements; while the QoS requirements for different classes of traffic are guaranteed. The logical network lends itself to re-design more readily than the physical network and can therefore adapt to changing traffic conditions more easily. Various strategies for logical network reconfiguration and dynamic capacity reallocation using the VP concept are reviewed in [2]. The physical topology of an ATM network should be designed to provide flexibility to the logical reconfiguration mechanism.

There are many physical topology design algorithms developed in the literature. In [3], an optimization problem is formulated and a low-cost topology design is found that determines the locations of the switch nodes and backbone links and also find routes for all source pairs. In [5], Gersht and Weihmayer provides a design to choose facility types, allocate capacity and route traffic to accommodate demand and performance requirements using a mixed integer linear programming formulation. Gerla *et al.* [4] and Lee and Yee [9] consider the logical topology design (network reconfiguration) for a given traffic scenario on an established ATM network. The logical reconfiguration problem is identified by Gerla *et al.* as a non-linear optimization problem where the physical routes and capacities of VP connections are determined to minimize the average packet delay. The problem formulated by Lee and Yee [9] is similar except they minimize the average packet number in the network. In all these optimization problems, tight capacity assignments and single path routing strategies are employed for better cost saving under a particular traffic scenario. Many algorithms have been developed to reconfigure VP overlays by changing VPs or reallocating capacity in order to adapt to changing traffic conditions or to provide the fault recovery in the case of link and node failures in ATM networks. Baba *et al.* [1] propose a dynamic VP bandwidth control method, where the bandwidth allocated to each VP is dynamically changed according to traffic fluctuation. Nakamura and Oda [12] develop an incremental assignment algorithm to provide multiple routes to each source pair and reserve the restoration capacity for survivable ATM networks. Murakami and Kim [11] develop an algorithm to find a VP configuration and bandwidth assignment that minimizes the expected amount of lost flow upon restoration from a network failure. However, few solutions for VP reconfiguration and dynamic capacity reallocations consider the affect of the underlying physical network.

In this paper, we address the problem of physical topology design for ATM networks with a view to facilitating the logical reconfiguration phase. To provide the flexibility for VP reconfiguration and dynamic re-

0-8186-8810-6/98 $10.00 © 1998 IEEE

allocation, the physical topology of an ATM network should be designed to be robust in the sense that multiple paths exist for each source pair and spare capacity is provided in each link. A design methodology for solving this problem for a single classes of service was developed by Hu and Harms in [7]. This will be extended in this paper to design new algorithms to support multimedia traffic. These new physical design algorithms are compared using logical design algorithms (capacity allocation schemes) through simulation.

The remainder of this paper is organized as follows. In Section 2, the single class physical topology design algorithm is described. In Section 3, algorithms to support multimedia traffic are described and, in Section 4, capacity allocation schemes are discussed. In Section 5, a simulation study is made comparing the flexibility of the physical design schemes for different capacity allocation schemes. Finally, Section 6 presents conclusions.

2 Physical design for a single class of service

In [7] a physical design strategy was described to find links, link capacities, and physical routes (which become virtual paths) for a backbone ATM network. This model assumes that a single class of service exists between each source pair. It can also be used for multiple classes of service multiplexed onto the same virtual path. The objective of the physical design methodology is to minimize cost and meet the traffic requirements. Besides low cost, another requirement is that the design be robust with respect to changing traffic conditions. Using the VP concept, we can construct a logical VP-based network. The routes found in the physical design become virtual paths (VPs). The physical network design can help the logical network to adapt in two ways:

- The physical network provides at least two disjoint routes for each switch node pair. This gives the routing algorithm more options for routing calls without needing to change the routes of the VPs. Providing alternative routes also helps in the case of network facility failures. In this section, the design algorithm finds one primary path and one alternative path between each source pair.
- Each transmission link should have some spare capacity. When the traffic demands change, spare capacity can be used to perform bandwidth reallocation.

We formulate an optimization problem for the physical ATM network design as follows. We assume that the network designer has found a set of switch locations for the backbone network. For a node pair (i,j), $i \neq j$, we use a_{ij} to represent the capacity cost per unit if a transmission link L_{ij} is established between the pair in the physical network. Intuitively this depends on the geographical distance of the link L_{ij}. The term b_{ij} is used to denote the initial set-up cost for the link L_{ij} and it is mainly related to the transmission trunk prices and installation charges which are also some functions of the physical distance of the link L_{ij}. In this paper, the capacity cost is equal to the distance between nodes and the set-up cost is proportional to the distance between nodes.

We denote by r_{ij} the traffic demand between the node pair (i,j), $i \neq j, i,j = 1,\cdots,n$. r_{ij} can represent the total multiplexing or accumulated bandwidth required for multiple classes of traffic between a node pair. Since the traffic in the network changes periodically, r_{ij} should be calculated as an average over a long time interval to make the physical network robust. Let N be the set of all the switch nodes and n the number of nodes. The physical topology design problem is to minimize the objective cost function:

$$\eta = \sum_i \sum_j \{a_{ij}c_{ij} + b_{ij}I(c_{ij} > 0)\}, \qquad (1)$$

subject to:

$$\begin{aligned} c_{ij} &= (1+\rho) \sum_{(k,h)\in P_{ij}^{(1)}} r_{kh} + \alpha \sum_{(k,h)\in P_{ij}^{(2)}} r_{kh} \\ &= (1+\rho)\sum_k \sum_h x_{ij}^{kh} r_{kh} + \alpha \sum_k \sum_h y_{ij}^{kh} r_{kh} \qquad (2) \end{aligned}$$

$\forall i,j \in N, i \neq j,$

$$x_{ij}^{kh}, y_{ij}^{kh} \in \{0,1\},\ \forall i,j \in N, i \neq j,\ \forall k,h \in N, k \neq h, \qquad (3)$$

$$x_{ij}^{kh} + y_{i'j'}^{kh} \leq 1,\ \text{for } i = i' \text{or } j = j', \forall k,h \in N, k \neq h, \qquad (4)$$

where c_{ij} is the total capacity assigned to the link L_{ij}. Note that the link capacities are continuous rather than discrete. Here $I(c_{ij} > 0)$ is the indicator function of the set $\{c_{ij} > 0\}$. $P_{ij}^{(1)}$ is the set of all the pairs using the link L_{ij} in the primary route, and $P_{ij}^{(2)}$ is the set of all the pairs using the link L_{ij} in the secondary (alternative) route. The constraint (3) means that x_{ij}^{kh} and y_{ij}^{kh} are 0-1 variables. $x_{ij}^{kh} = 1$ implies that the primary route for the node pair (k,h) traverses the link L_{ij}. $y_{ij}^{kh} = 1$ indicates that the secondary route for the node pair (k,h) traverses the link L_{ij}. In the above design problem, the topology of physical network and link capacity assignment are determined by the values of x_{ij}^{kh}, y_{ij}^{kh} and c_{ij}. The constraint (4) forces the primary and secondary routes for each pair to be node-disjoint. The primary and secondary routes are found based on shortest distance.

The two parameters ρ and α are included in the model (1) in order to control the amount of spare capacity assigned to the transmission links and the amount of bandwidth allocated to the alternative paths. The two parameters also affect the denseness of the topology because the capacity cost in the objective function is a function of the amount of link capacity. Roughly speaking, larger values of ρ and α result in more spare capacity allocated on the links and denser topology. A graph-based heuristic algorithm was used to provide a solution to this problem in [7] and the effect of the two parameters on the physical and logical design was studied and the model was validated for small network sizes.

3 Physical design for multimedia support

The model of Section 2 provides one primary route (a virtual path) and one alternative route (another virtual path) for each source pair. Therefore, if a voice connection is required between a particular source and destination, it will be placed on the same VP as a video connection. However, it has been shown that when similar traffic is multiplexed together, it is easier to characterize the traffic and provide quality of service guarantees. Therefore, different VPs should be given to different classes of service. Three broad classes of service: video, data and voice, are considered and three algorithms are developed to supporting these traffic classes.

The first algorithm, COMBINED, applies the model of Section 2 on the combined (sum of the) long term traffic requirement of all three classes of service. This provides one primary and secondary route between each source pair with enough bandwidth to meet the requirement of all the classes. The capacity is then divided appropriately onto three primary VPs and three alternative VPs. The second algorithm, SEPARATE, applies the model of Section 2 independently to each traffic class. The resulting physical networks are then combined into one network. Obviously the cost will no longer be optimal, however, the VPs between a source pair are no longer restricted to the same route.

The third algorithm, MERGED, applies the model of Section 2 to the most stringent class requirement (in this case, the video class) and then finds primary and secondary routes for the data and then voice on the physical network (which was designed for the video). The routes for each source pair are chosen based on minimising the cost (that is, capacity times distance similar to the objective of the physical design model of Section 2). The link capacities are updated as the routes are found. In this case, the routes are not restricted to the same path as in the COMBINED case but also, unlike in the SEPARATE case, the routes for the data traffic are chosen with knowledge of the video requirements and for the voice traffic with knowledge of both video and data.

4 Capacity allocation schemes

Once the physical network has been designed and provisioned, the network has the flexibility of routing on alternative paths and has spare capacity for reallocation of capacity. The basic algorithm is to check for capacity on the primary virtual path. If there is insufficient bandwidth, check if there is spare capacity on that path. If there is insufficient spare capacity, check if there is capacity on the alternative path. If this also fails, then the call is rejected.

One question of interest is how well the physical design facilitates the bandwidth allocation schemes. The physical design provisions the network to provide capacity of the long term traffic demand plus extra capacity (that is, $(1+\rho)r_{kh}$) on the primary route and a proportion of the long term traffic demand (that is, αr_{kh}) on the alternative route. The capacity allocation could be static or dynamic. In this paper, we consider three scenarios for allocating capacity to the primary VP. The alternative route is allocated a fixed capacity of αr_{kh}. For the primary route, static allocation (STAT) gives each primary VP the long term traffic requirement plus the extra capacity (that is, $(1+\rho)r_{kh}$). The capacity of a VP never changes and no spare capacity exists on the network. For the second algorithm (DYN1), the capacity of a VP is dynamic. In this algorithm, a base allocation is made to the primary VP (that is, r_{kh}) based on the long term traffic requirement and the spare capacity ρr_{kh} is pooled on each link. Another dynamic allocation algorithm, (DYN2), pools the spare capacity per class type. In this way, voice calls may not use spare bandwidth allocated for video calls but may share with other voice calls.

5 Performance evaluation

In this section, we study the effect of the physical design parameters (α and ρ), the physical design algorithms for multimedia traffic (COMBINED, SEPARATE and MERGED) and the capacity allocation schemes (STAT, DYN1 and DYN2) using a call-level simulation. To evaluate the design algorithms, we consider two performance measures: cost (as found by the physical design) and the fraction of blocked calls (as found by the simulation).

The physical network studied consists of 23 nodes and the long term traffic requirements were assigned as follows. Long term traffic requirements for the three classes are based on a mean bandwidth requirement multiplied by the number of expected calls between a source and destination. For video traffic, the mean bandwidth requirement was set at 2 Mbps and 2 or 3 calls were expected between each source and destination. For data, the mean requirement was 500 Kbps and the expected number of calls was 3 to 5. For voice, the mean requirement was 64kbps and the number of calls ranged from 2 to 10. To produce the traffic matrices for video, data and voice, a random choice was made of the combination of bandwidth and number of calls for each source pair. Thus, the physical network is designed for nonuniform traffic. The COMBINED algorithm uses the sum of the individual traffic matrices for input to the model of Section 2 and the SEPARATE algorithm applies the model to each of the three matrices independently. The MERGED algorithm applies the physical design algorithm to the video traffic matrix.

The simulation is at a call level. A call has attributes of a source, a destination, a bandwidth requirement and a duration. A call is accepted if there is enough available bandwidth given the particular capacity allocation scheme. Since the virtual paths are direct, this decision can be made immediately. It is assumed that spare capacity can be used immediately. If accepted, the bandwidth on the virtual path is reserved for the duration of the call. If there is not enough bandwidth, the call is rejected. The performance measures of interest are the cost of the physical design and the fraction of blocked calls. 95% confidence intervals were found for the simulation results but have been left off the graphs to improve readability.

The simulation was run using a different traffic pattern from that used in the physical design in order to study how well the network is able to adapt (through alternative paths and capacity reallocation). The video traffic requires bandwidth uniformly distributed between 1.5 and 2.5 Mbps, the data requires bandwidth uniformly distributed between 300 and 700 kbps and voice requires 64 kbps. This provides mean bandwidth requirements equal to the expected bandwidth of the long term traffic requirements. However, initially the simulation was run with a uniformly distributed number of calls of each type (regardless of its bandwidth requirement). Hence this does not match the physical design. Arrivals to the system and call durations were geometrically distributed.

In the first experiment, the cost was measured for the physical network for values of $\rho = 0.1, 0.2, 0.3, 0.4, 0.5$ and $\alpha = 0.6$ for the different multimedia algorithms. The results are plotted in Figure 1. Obviously as more extra bandwidth is allocated (increasing ρ) the cost increases for all the algorithms. SEPARATE has the highest cost since it designs the networks separately for each traffic type and the combination of networks does not pay attention to cost. The MERGED algorithm gives the lowest cost design. It improves on the COMBINED case by not constraining the different classes of service between a source pair to follow the same routes. An experiment (not shown here) provided similar results when α was varied.

In the second experiment (see Figure 2), the fraction of blocked calls was measured for the physical network for values of $\rho = 0.1, 0.2, 0.3, 0.4, 0.5$ when $\alpha = 0.6$ for the different multimedia algorithms and capacity allocation schemes. Obviously as more spare capacity is added, the blocking decreases. As expected, the static allocation has the highest blocking due to its inflexibility. The dynamic algorithm that pools all extra resources (DYN1), provides the lowest blocking since it is the most flexible. The blocking decreases more sharply with increased bandwidth for the dynamic algorithms because there is more flexibility in fitting in requests. The static allocation suffers from wasted capacity particularly for the large video calls. Once the extra capacity is large enough to fit more of these calls (at $\rho = 0.5$) the blocking drops significantly.

A similar experiment was run for varying the capacity on the alternative route (see Figure 3). The fraction blocked was measured for the physical network for values of $\alpha = 0.4, 0.5, 0.6, 0.7, 0.8$ and $\rho = 0.3$ for the different multimedia algorithms and capacity allocation schemes. Here the static allocation reacts more quickly to increased alternative path allocation. In particular, for the lowest α the extra capacity is not large enough to accommodate many video calls. The dynamic algorithms do not suffer as much from this since they share the spare capacity.

In the next experiment, blocking probability is measured for the different class types. In Figure 4, the STAT and DYN1 allocation schemes are compared for different values of ρ. It is clear that the video traffic is the main cause of the blocking. This is to be expected

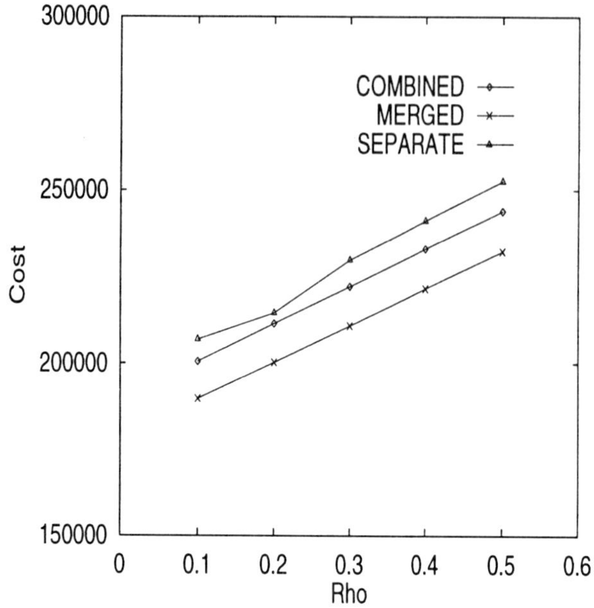

Figure 1: **Physical Design Cost for Varying Spare Capacity**

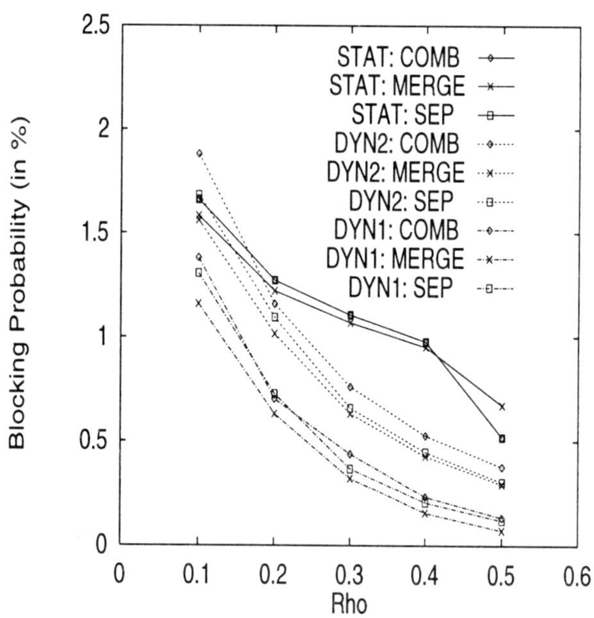

Figure 2: **Blocking for Varying Spare Capacity**

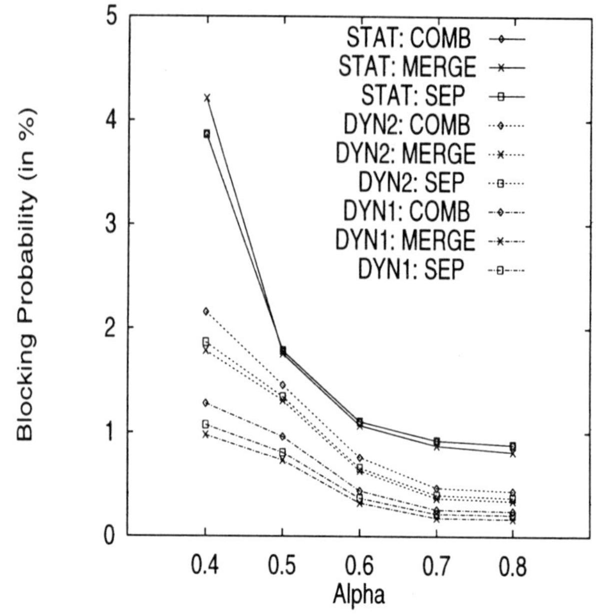

Figure 3: **Blocking for Varying Alternative Path Allocation**

since the networks were designed for only a few video calls but the simulation is being run with as many video calls as other types of traffic. For the static case, voice calls are also blocked. This is due to the inflexibility of the static allocation and the physical design where many sources expect only 2 voice calls. For the dynamic case, the voice call will use spare capacity possibly allocated for other traffic types. In another experiment, the proportion of calls for each type of traffic is more closely matched to the designed network. In this case 60% of the calls are voice, 25% are data and 16% are video. This matches the average requirements for the different traffic types in the physical design but not the specifics of particular sources. In Figure 5, it can be seen that the blocking is not as dominated by one call type for the dynamic case.

For the cases where the design for different traffic types is not combined (that is, MERGED and SEPARATE) there is flexibility to adjust ρ and α to a particular traffic type. In the next experiments, different traffic mixes are considered. In the first case, different values of ρ are considered. Mix 1 has: video $\rho = 0.25$ data $\rho = 0.45$ voice $\rho = 0.69$ and MIX2 has: video $\rho = 0.33$ data $\rho = 0.2$ voice $\rho = 0.14$. This is compared with the case where all values of $\rho = 0.3$. The offered load in each of these cases will be roughly the same. First the cost is shown in Figure 6. Note that the cost does not vary much for the different traffic mixes, however, offering more spare capacity to

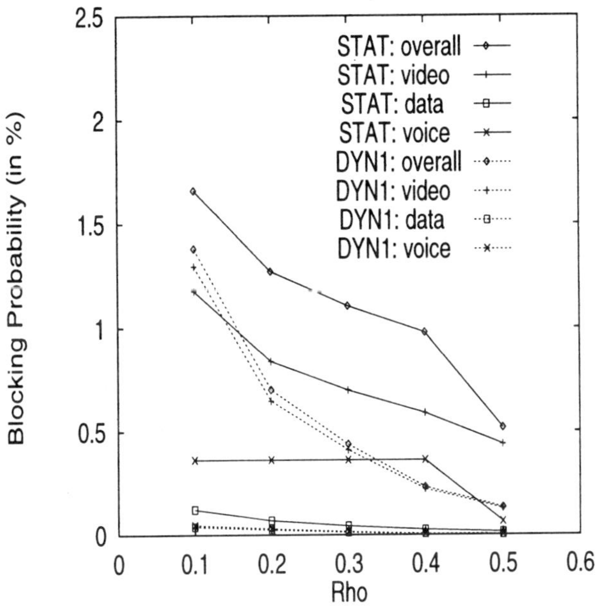

Figure 4: **Class Blocking: Static and Dynamic**

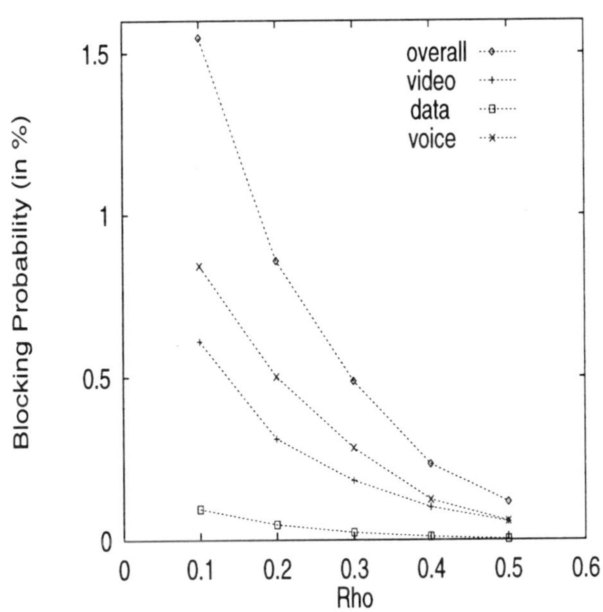

Figure 5: **Class Blocking: Dynamic (DYN1)**

the video does decrease the cost slightly. Again, the MERGED algorithm has the lowest cost. In Figure 7, the blocking for STAT and DYN are shown. The static reacts more to the different traffic mixes. In this case, for low video allocation, the higher data and voice allocations allow more calls to be accepted. For the dynamic case, there is less extreme performance differences when the mix is changed. In Figure 8, different values of α are considered. Mix 1 has: video $\alpha = 0.55$ data $\alpha = 0.85$ voice $\alpha = 0.21$ and MIX2 has: video $\alpha = 0.65$ data $\alpha = 0.38$ voice $\alpha = 0.77$. This is compared with the case where all values of $\alpha = 0.6$. Again, the offered load in each of these cases will be roughly the same. In this case, for Mix 1, the low α value for both video and voice causes many calls to be rejected for the static case. The dynamic case is able to adapt with the shared spare bandwidth. However, it also has higher blocking when the video is not allocated enough alternative path bandwidth.

6 Conclusions

In this paper, the problem of designing a physical topology for ATM networks in order to facilitate bandwidth allocation has been considered. Three physical design algorithms were developed for the support of different classes of traffic: a COMBINED method (where separate VPs for different classes follow the same route), a SEPARATE method (where the physical network is designed independently for each traffic class) and a MERGED method. The third algorithm merges the low bandwidth class requirements onto a network designed for the large bandwidth requirements and provides lower cost and slightly lower blocking than the other schemes.

In the physical design two parameters are used to control the extra capacity and capacity allocation on the alternative paths. A simulation was used to study the effect of static and dynamic capacity allocation on these physical designs. The simulation results showed that the physical network designed by this model helps the dynamic bandwidth allocation scheme to handle the traffic load changes. A small amount of extra capacity provides good flexibility when dynamic allocation is used. Having adequate capacity on the alternative paths becomes very important particularly in the static case where there is no ability to adapt.

In this paper, the dynamic allocation schemes are able to obtain spare capacity immediately. This may be unrealistic in a real system where delays in accepting a call may be unreasonable. Future work will be to consider more sophisticated capacity reallocation schemes that allocate resources before a call arrives.

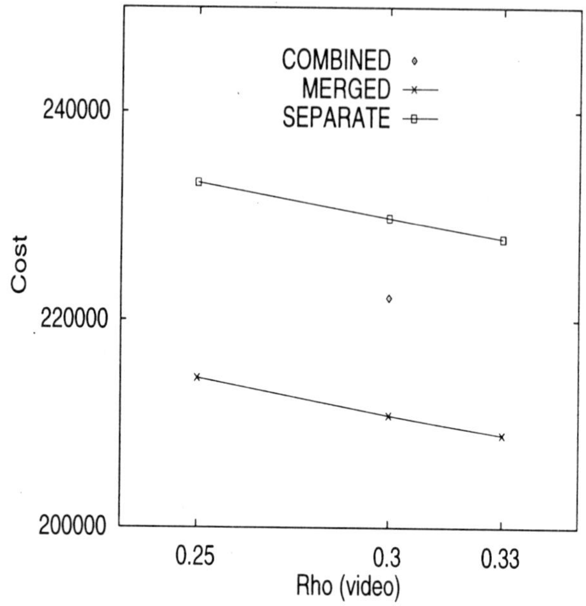

Figure 6: **Cost for Different Traffic Mixes**

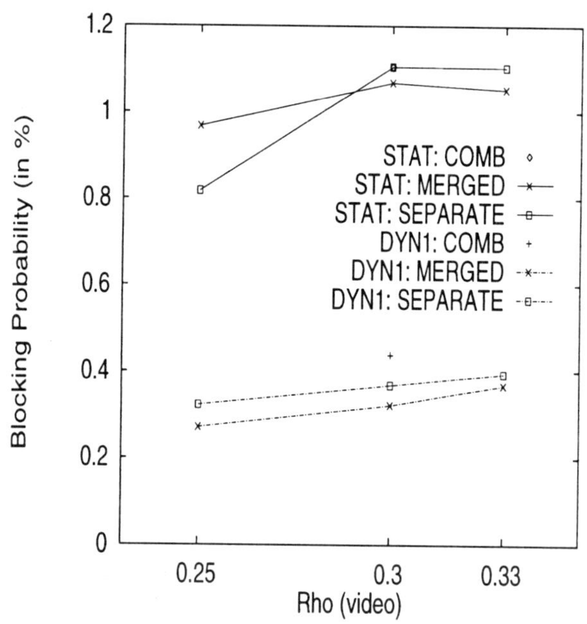

Figure 7: **Traffic Mix Blocking for Varying Spare Capacity**

7 Acknowledgement

Financial support for this research was provided by the Natural Science and Engineering Research Council of Canada.

References

[1] K. I. Baba, M. Murate, and H. Miyahara, "Performance analysis for the dynamic virtual path bandwidth control method in ATM networks," *International journal of Communication Systems,* vol. 7, no. 4, 1994, pp. 283-294.

[2] V. J. Friesen, J. J. Harms, and J. W. Wong, "Resource Management with Virtual Paths in ATM Networks," *IEEE Network,* Sept. 1996, pp. 10-20.

[3] B. Gavish, "Topological Design of Computer Communication Networks - The Overall Design Problem," *European Journal of Operational Research,* vol. 58, 1992, pp. 149-72.

[4] M. Gerla, J. A. S. Monteiro, and R. Pazos, "Topology Design and Bandwidth Allocation in ATM Networks," *IEEE J. Select. Areas Commun.,* vol. 7, no. 8, Oct. 1989, pp. 1253-62.

[5] A. Gersht and R. Weihmayer, "Joint Optimization of Data Network Design and Facility Selection," *IEEE J. Select. Areas Commun.,* vol. 8, no. 9, Dec. 1990, pp. 1667-81.

[6] R. Guerin, H. Ahmadi and M. Naghshineh, "Equivalent Capacity and Its Application to Bandwidth Allocation in High-Speed Networks," *IEEE J. Select. Areas Commun.,* vol. 9, 1991, pp. 968-81.

[7] C. Hu and J. Harms, "Topology Design for Reconfigurable ATM Networks", submitted to Discrete Applied Mathematics.

[8] A. Kershenbaum, *Telecommunications Network Design Algorithms.* McGraw-Hill, 1993.

[9] M. J. Lee and J. R. Yee, "A logical Topology and Discrete Capacity Assignment Algorithm for Reconfigurable Networks," *Operations Research,* vol.43, no.1, Jan.-Feb. 1995, pp. 102-16.

[10] D. Medhi, "Multi-Hour, Multi-Traffic Class Network Design for Virtual Path-Based Wide-Area Dynamically Reconfigurable ATM Networks," *IEEE/ACM Transactions on Networking,* vol. 3, no. 6, Dec. 1995, pp. 809-18.

[11] K. Murakami and H. S. Kim, "Virtual Path Routing for Survivable ATM Networks," *IEEE/ACM Transactions on Networking,* vol. 4, no. 1, Feb. 1996, pp. 22-39.

[12] H. Nakamura and T. Oda, "Optimization of Facility Planning and Circuit Routing for Survivable Transport Networks - An Approach Based on Genetic Algorithm and Incremental Assignment," *IEICE Trans. Commun.,* vol. E80-B, no. 2, Feb. 1997, pp. 240-251.

[13] S. Ohta and K. Sato, "Dynamic bandwidth control of virtual path in an asynchronous transfer mode network," *IEEE Trans. Commun.,* vol. 40, 1992, pp. 1239-47.

[14] K. I. Sato, S. Ohta and I. Tokizawa, "Broadband ATM Network Architecture Based on Virtual Paths," *IEEE Trans. Commun.,* vol. 38, 1990, pp. 1212-22.

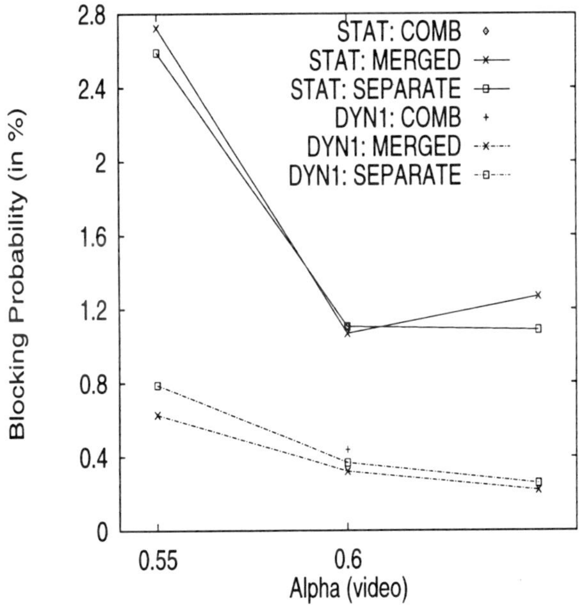

Figure 8: **Traffic Mix Blocking for Varying Alternative Path Allocation**

Track B: Modelling

Session Chair: Frank Huebner-Szabo de Bucs

AT&T Labs

Source Model for VBR Coded Video Traffic in ATM Networks

Gajendra Sisodia, Mark Hedley, Subrata De and Ling Guan

Abstract

In this paper, we present a new approach to modelling variable bit rate (VBR) coded video sources in asynchronous transfer mode (ATM) networks. Unlike the existing methods which model the number of cells generated by the coder for a sequence of video frames, the new approach improves modelling accuracy by considering the characteristics of different cells generated by the coder, and modelling the number of cells in each type of macroblocks of a frame separately. The model is tested by comparing the autocorrelation function and mean queue size in buffer in simulation of an ATM switch to mean queue size produced when traces generated by the model are used as the source. Comparison with the existing models are performed in the area of measuring the quality of their predictions for network performance and the grade of service experienced by a user.

Keywords: ATM, packet video, macroblocks, broadband traffic.

1 Introduction

The source modelling of variable bit rate (VBR) coded video is an active area of research. This is because video services are forecasted to be a substantial portion of the traffic on emerging broadband digital networks and there are considerable research activities aimed at designing VBR codecs and examining their feasibility in asynchronous transfer mode (ATM) networks [1]-[3]. Statistical source models of different types of video traffic are needed to design networks that achieve acceptable picture quality at minimum cost and to control and shape the output rate of the coder. One issue, for instance, is the problem of deciding whether a new video connection can be admitted into an ATM network and the consequent determination of the bandwidth that must be allocated to the connection to ensure adequate quality of service. Statistical source models are needed to resolve these admission control and bandwidth allocation issues.

Several different models based on the actual data measurement have been proposed for VBR video traffic (e.g. [4], [5], [6], [7], [8], [9]). The statistical performance for full motion and videoconferencing VBR video is studied by using those models.

In this paper, we implement some of those models and study the statistical performance. We are particularly interested in using model to predict mean queue size in ATM switch buffer. In real time video if mean queue size is high, each cell experience more delay in buffer before it is routed. This delay degrade the quality of real time video. We model H.263+ coded [10] VBR video traffic and discuss advantages and disadvantages of the models. Among these models DAR(1) [13] model has the advantage of being very general and can be used with any distribution for the number of cells per frame. This model can be used to model VBR videoconference and full motion type of video traffic. The disadvantage of this model is that it generate same number of cells for long sequences and its sample paths have flat spots, which is not a real case. We propose a new modelling approach to model VBR traffic which is a generalisation of a DAR(1) model. This new model is used to model the number of cells in each type of macroblocks of a frame separately and all macroblocks cells are added to get total number of cells in each frame. We find that this new model generate different number of cells per frame and do not have flat spots in its sample path. Some tests are performed to verify the new model, using video data derived from H.263+ coder. The simulation results for our new model are compared to those obtained using other models. It is found that this new model outperforms DAR(1) model in predicting network performance.

The video coding scheme used, and VBR statistics, are discussed in section 2. The previous source models which we use for our statistical analysis and simulation are discuss in section 3. In this section we also discussed the advantage, disadvantages and limitations of those models and how we fit our real data. In the section 4, we presented our new modelling approach of H.263+ coded data. In section 5, we discuss verification of models a using statistics of the real data, and data generated by using different models. The simulation study of mean queue size in ATM switch buffer is done in section 6 for real data, and each model data, using an ATM multiplexer switch.

0-8186-8810-6/98 $10.00 © 1998 IEEE

2 Source data

We acquired two long real video sequences for analysis with QCIF (176 × 144 pixels) resolution. They were:

A. A typical videoconference sequence showing head and shoulders of a speaker. This consists of 10,000 frames at 10 frames per second.

B. This is from a football game which has full camera movement. This consists of 10,000 frames at 15 frames per second.

These sequences were coded using a H.263+ coder (public domain software from the University of British Columbia, which in turn is based on the ITU TMN7 software [12]). There are a number of optional modes available, all of which were turned off. The quantisation parameter was set to 10, which provides a high degree of compression. The cells required per frame for the first five hundred frames of each sequence are shown in Fig. 3 and Fig. 6. Each frame is divided into a number of ATM packets (48 data bytes each), and the statistical properties of the number of cells per frame are shown in Table I. The frequency distributions of the sequences are shown in Fig. 1 and Fig. 2 respectively. As could be seen in both the sequences, the negative binomial distribution provides a good approximation to the distribution of the number of bits or cells per frame.

Table I
Summary statistics of coded data sequences

Parameter	Sequence 'A'	Sequence 'B'
Mean [cells]	4.04	28.38
Variance [cells]	1.41	272.13
Max [cells]	13	193
Min [cells]	2	10

3 Previous modelling work

Since the negative binomial is discrete analog of a gamma distribution, a discretized version of the latter can be used when it is more convenient to do so. The different source models can exploit this statistical behaviour of the sequences. We implemented three different models which exploit this property.

3.1 DAR(1) model

The source of the video using VBR encoding can be modelled as a multistate Markov chain. The Markov chain gives the number of cells in each frame and determined by three parameters; the mean and variance of the number of cells per frame and correlation between the number of cells in successive frames. These parameters can easily estimated from the mean and variance of the real data sequences. Although the DAR model [13] is effective as a source model when several sources are multiplexed, it is not effective as a source model for a single source in isolation because its sample paths have flat spots. This means that the model data

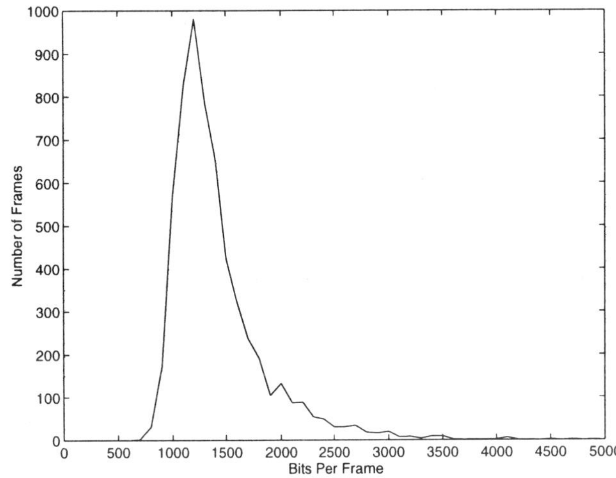

Fig. 1: The frequency distribution for the number of bits per frame for sequence 'A', with QP=10.

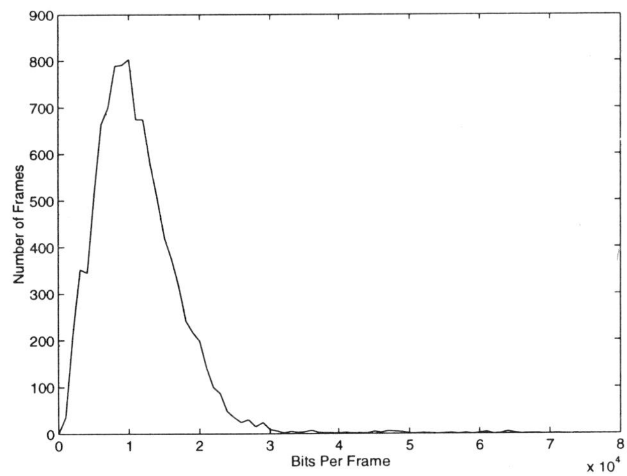

Fig. 2: The frequency distribution for the number of bits per frame for sequence 'B', with QP=10.

trace are constant for long interval, and do not look like the real data trace. This difference between model data and real data is mitigated when several sources are multiplexed. The DAR model was used successfully to compute effective bandwidth by Elwalid [14].

The DAR model is used to generate a sequence of cells per frame using a first order finite state Markov chain, determined using three parameters: mean, variance and correlation. The transition matrix P = (p_{ij}) of Markov chain is given by the

$$P = \rho I + (1 - \rho)Q \quad (1)$$

where ρ = autocorrelation factor (for first lag), I is the identity matrix and each row of Q consists of the negative binomial probabilities.

This model matches the autocorrelation function more closely and provides a more accurate estimation of cell loss probability than other Autoregressive models investigated [15].

3.2 GBAR Model

The GBAR(1) [16] process was introduced by McKenzie [17], which has inherent feature that the marginal distribution is gamma and the autocorrelation is geometric. The GBAR(1) model based on two well known results that the sum of independent Ga(α,λ) and Ga(β,λ) random variables is a Ga(α+β,λ) random variable and the product of independent Be(α,β-α) and Ga(β,λ) random variables is a Ga(α,λ) random variable. Thus if X_{n-1} is Ga(β,λ), A_n is Be(α,β-α), and B_n is Ga(β-α,λ), and these three are mutually independent, then

$$X_n = A_n X_{n-1} + B_n \quad (2)$$

defines a stationary stochastic process $\{X_n\}$ with a marginal Ge(α,λ) distribution. The process define by the (2) is called a GBAR(1) processes. This process is used as a source model by generating noninteger values from (2) and rounding to the nearest integer, which is a cells per frame. Table II shows the values obtained for the different parameters when the model is fitted to the real data.

Table II
GBAR model parameters

Parameter	Sequence 'A'
ρ	0.98
α	1.20
β	1.23
λ	0.305

3.3 SCENIC model

SCENIC model [8] is a generalised form of the DAR(1) model. This model is used to generate data for full motion type video sequences. In this model the scene is considered as a combination of frames. The scene boundary is defined to be where the bit rate changes sharply. The PDF of the scene length is taken to be:

$$p(x) = \frac{a}{x^n + b^2} \quad (3)$$

The mean and variance of this sequence can be calculated, and with this mean and variance, parameter r and p of the negative binomial distribution can be obtained. The parameter n and b were obtained by the application of a curve fitting technique to the histogram of the scene length. Table III shows the values obtained for the different parameters when the model is fitted to the real data.

Table III
SCENIC model parameters

Parameter	Sequence 'B'
ρ	0.91
r	3.29
p	0.104
b	52
n	2.8

4 New modelling approach

In previous modelling work, typically the number of cells generated by the video coder for each video frame is modelled. Among previous discussed models DAR(1) model has the advantage of being very general and can be used with any distribution for the number of cells per frame. This model can be used to model VBR videoconference and full motion type of video traffic. The disadvantage of this model is that it generates same number of cells for long sequences and its sample paths have flat spots (Fig. 4 and Fig. 7), which is not a real case. This (flat spots) affects the accuracy to predict the network performance by using this model. The accuracy of this model could be improved if the model do not have flat spots in its sample paths (cells per frame) and generate different number of cells per frame.

We suggested a new modelling approach to model the coded sequences at macroblock (MB) level which is a generalisation of DAR(1) model. As discussed before, we used H.263+ coder to code our two long video sequences of QCIF format. While coding each frame is divided into fix number of macroblocks (For example in QCIF format (in our case) each frame is divided into 99 macroblocks) and each MB in every frame is either intra coded (I-coded) or predictive coded (P-coded) or not coded (N-coded) at all. Therefore each frame has three types of coded macroblocks and the sum of these macroblocks is equal to the total number of Macroblocks in one frame (99 in our case).

When we coded our real video sequences, we separated the total number of coded bits for each type of coded MB in each frame. It was observed that the negative binomial distribution provided a good approximation to the distribution of the number of bits for each type of macroblocks (I-coded, P-coded and N-coded). We proposed a new model to model each type of MB which uses the negative binomial marginal distribution. This new model is named as DAR(M) model.

The DAR(M) model is used to generate the sequence of number of cell per frame associated with each type of MB, using finite state Markov chain. The Markov chain is determine by three parameters: the mean, variance and correlation factor. The transition matrix of this is given by

$$P = \rho I + (1 - \rho)Q \tag{4}$$

where P is the transition matrix. ρ is autocorrelation factor (for first lag), I is the identity matrix and each row of Q consists of the negative binomial probabilities is defined by

$$(f_0, f_1, f_2, \ldots\ldots\ldots\ldots\ldots\ldots f_k, f_K^c) \tag{5}$$

$$f_k = \binom{k+r-1}{k} p^r q^k \tag{6}$$

$$f_K^c = \sum_{k > K} f_k \tag{7}$$

where

$$p = \frac{mean}{variance} \quad \text{and} \quad r = mean \times \frac{p}{(1-p)}$$

Or mean (m) and variance (v) of the macroblocks distribution can be calculated as

$$m = \frac{r(1-p)}{p} \quad \text{and} \quad v = \frac{r(1-p)}{p^2}$$

k= 0,1,2,....... Here $0 < p < 1$, q= 1-p and $r > 0$. The parameter r need not be an integer. K represents the maximum number of cells that can be generated by the coder for one type of macroblocks in one frame.

This model generates separate number of bits for each type of MB (for both sequences). Let the total number of bits generated by the model for I-coded, P-coded and N-coded macroblocks are m_i, m_p and m_n respectively, then total number of bits per frame can be represented by

$$X_t = m_i + m_p + m_n \tag{8}$$

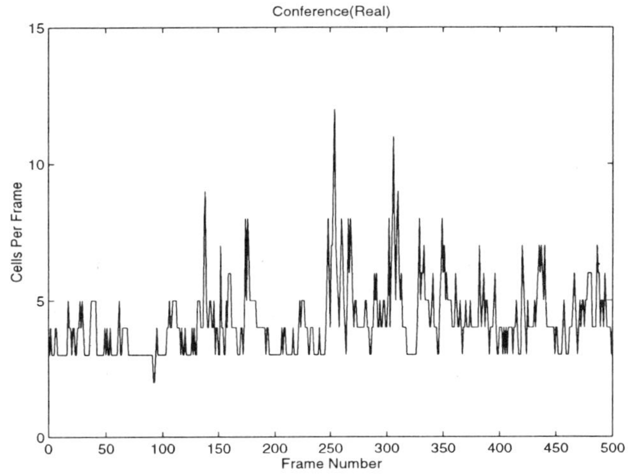

Fig. 3: Output traffic rate in terms of the number of cells per frame for sequence 'A', from frame 1 to 500.

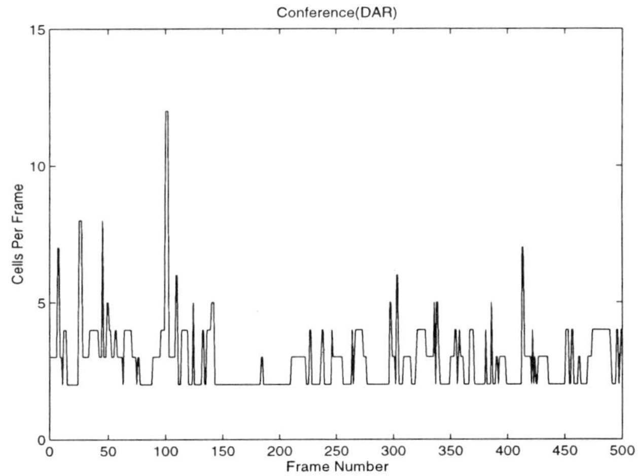

Fig. 4: Output traffic rate in terms of the number of cells per frame using DAR model for sequence 'A', from frame 1 to 500.

where X_t is the number of bits associated to each video frame.

The generated number of cells per frame for the first five hundred frames of each sequence are shown in Fig. 5 and Fig. 8. As it could be seen that this model generates different number of cells per frame and do not have flat spots in its sample path as compared to Fig. 4 and Fig. 7.

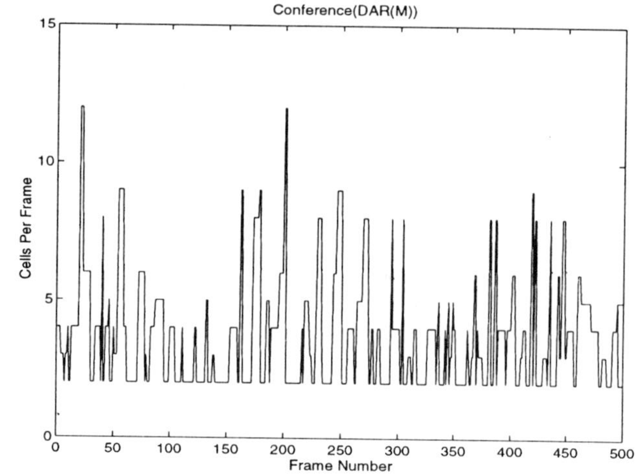

Fig. 5: Output traffic rate in terms of the number of cells per frame using DAR(M) model for sequence 'A', from frame 1 to 500.

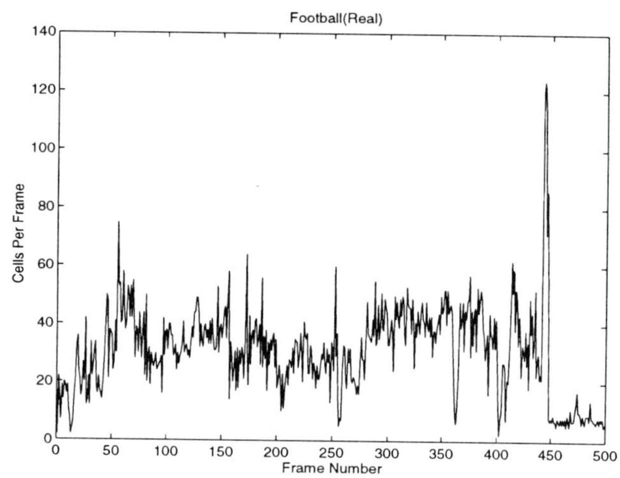

Fig. 6: Output traffic rate in terms of the number of cells per frame for sequence 'B', from frame 1 to 500.

5 Model verification

In this section, we will use two tests to verify the models. The first is to see if the autocorrelation function [19] matches well, the second to determine if the mean queue size predicted (section 6) by a model lies within the range of the real data.

The autocorrelation function of the generated sequences should be very close to the real data. Ideally, it should be the same as to the model data including the tail behaviour. As shown in the Fig. 9 and Fig. 10, this is not the case for the source models. The autocovarince is

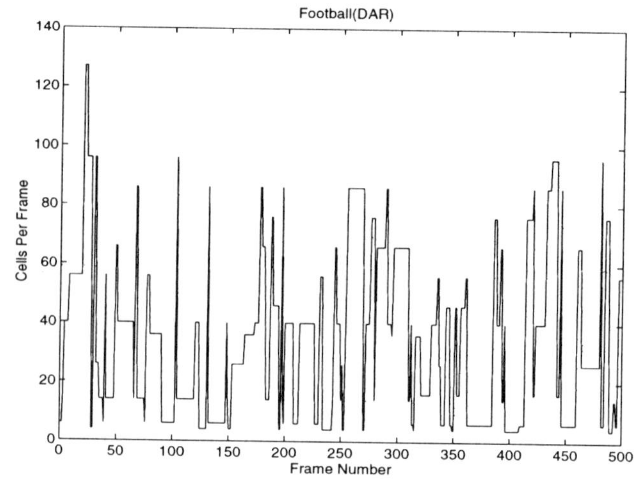

Fig. 7: Output traffic rate in terms of the number of cells per frame using DAR model for sequence 'B', from frame 1 to 500.

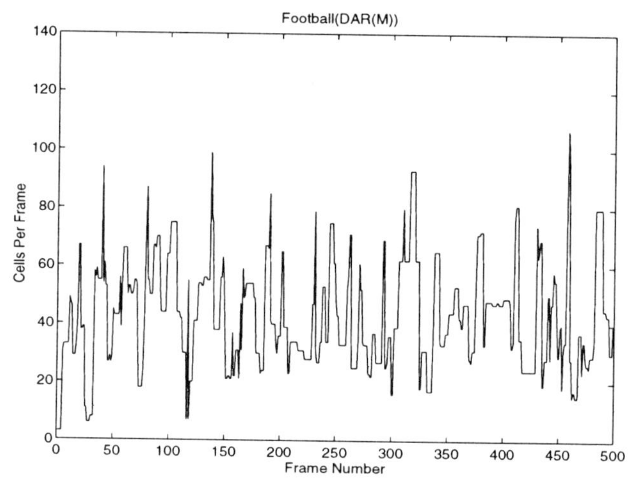

Fig. 8: Output traffic rate in terms of the number of cells per frame using DAR(M) model for sequence 'B', from frame 1 to 500.

computed for the real data sequences and, DAR(1), GBAR, SCENIC and DAR(M) model data sequences as a function of the lag measured in number of frames. Fig. 9 and Fig. 10 shows the autocovariance for sequence 'A' and 'B', and for the different models fitting to this sequence. For sequence 'A', the autocovariance for the DAR(1), GBAR and DAR(M) models decaying exponentially at large lags(video frame). Since GBAR model has only short range dependence [16], the autocovariance is not matching well for small lags(approximately 15 lags), but it matches well for large lags. It could be seen that autocovariance for the DAR(M) model is matching well for large leg as compared to other models. For the sequence 'B', the autocovariance for the DAR(1) and SCENIC is very close to the real data. It can be seen in the figure that DAR(M) model is matching well at the tail end of the real data. So the H.263+ coded real data sequences fits well to the sequences generated by the DAR(M) source models.

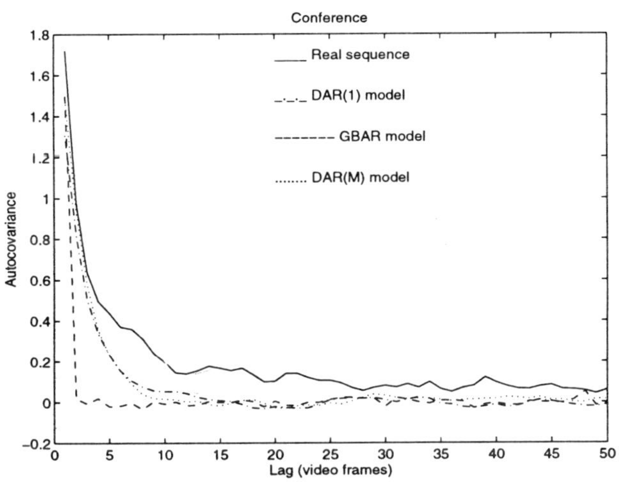

Fig. 9: Autocovariance function for sequence 'A' data and different models fitted to it.

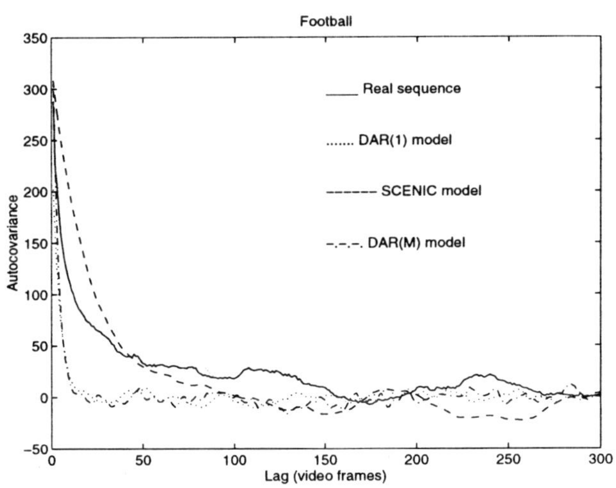

Fig. 10: Autocovariance function for sequence 'B' data and different models fitted to it.

6 Simulation

6.1 ATM multiplexer model

The usefulness of models for predicting mean queue size for different link utilisation was verified by simulation. The ATM multiplexer shown in the Fig. 11, was used for simulation. This model serves a number of independent video sources, and was used for the aggregate multiplexed video traffic analysis. In our case we used 16 number of input video sources, and individual VBR video source was modelled by using a same type of source model. All video sources used the same model data or real data, hence they were homogeneous sources. The cell arriving from these sources were assumed to be statistically multiplexed and were passed through the switch buffer and served by a common link. In our model all the video sources were transmitting data to a single destination.

The ATM switch buffer was used to store the cells temporarily, which were arriving from the source input. This buffer was a part of the ATM switch. The departure process of the buffer was deterministic with first in first out (FIFO) discipline. Since all used sources were video sources, no source had any priority over each other.

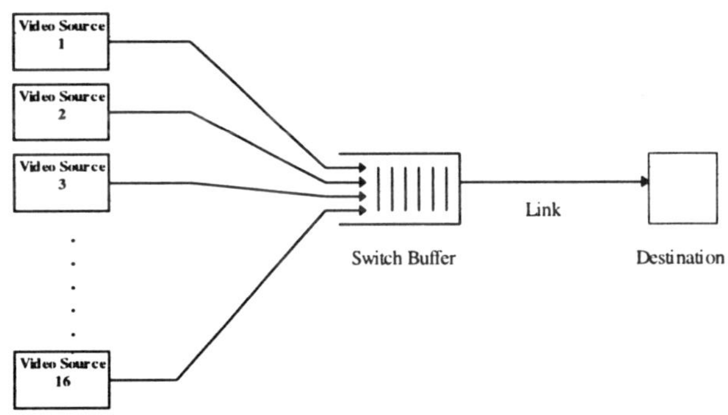

Fig. 11: The ATM multiplexer model.

6.2 Mean queue size predictions

We used mean queue size as another method to verify the DAR(M) model. As discussed before mean queue size is an important measurement for delay sensitive traffic like real time video. If mean queue size is large each cell experiences more delay in the buffer. We used the multiplexer model shown in Fig. 11 for simulation. The mean queue size is measured for different link utilisation factor for DAR(M) model and compared with real data and other models.

The mean queue size is computed for different link utilisation for sequence 'A' when buffer size was fixed to 10 cells. Fig. 12 shows the mean queue size vs buffer size for DAR(M) model and other models fitted to this sequence. It could be seen the DAR(M) model predicts mean queue size very close to real data and more accurately as compared to DAR(1) model. For this sequence DAR(1) model did not predict mean queue size well after 80% of link utilisation, whereas DAR(M) model predicts mean queue size well even for high link utilisation (for more that 80%).

Fig. 13 shows the mean queue size vs link utilisation for sequence 'B', and for DAR(M) model data. During the simulation buffer size was fixed to 500 cells. This figure shows that mean queue size predicted by DAR(M) model data is very close to real data. For this sequence DAR(1) model did not predict mean queue size well after 85% of link utilisation but DAR(M) model predicted mean queue size well even for 85% link utilisation and higher. This result confirms that data generated by the DAR(M) model is more close to a real data for both the sequences than the data generated by the DAR(1) model.

7 Conclusions

In this paper, we have proposed a new modelling approach for data generated by variable bit rate video coder and can be used to model videoconference and full motion video sequences. In this model, data was modelled at macroblock level instead of at frame level. This model generates data for each type of macroblock in every frame and all generated macroblock bits were added to get bits per frame. This new model has been shown to provide a more accurate approximations to the mean queue size and autocorrelation function than previous DAR(1) model on data from H.263+ video coder. We used this model and verified for multiplexed video traffic but this model could also be used as single source model and the performance of this model could be verified.

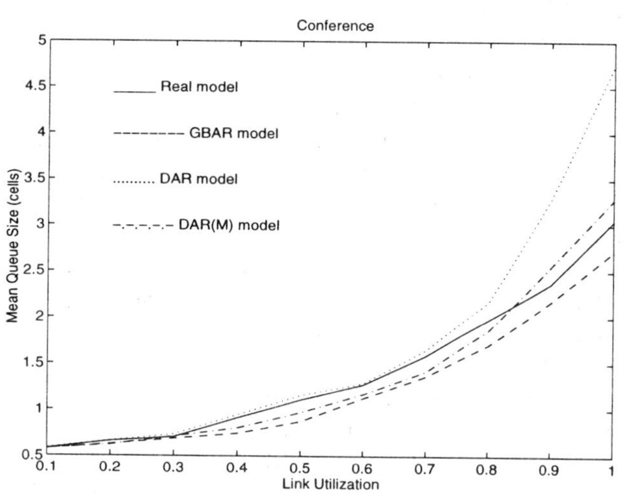

Fig. 12: Mean Queue Size vs. Link Utilisation for the sequence 'A', using real data and data generated by the various models.

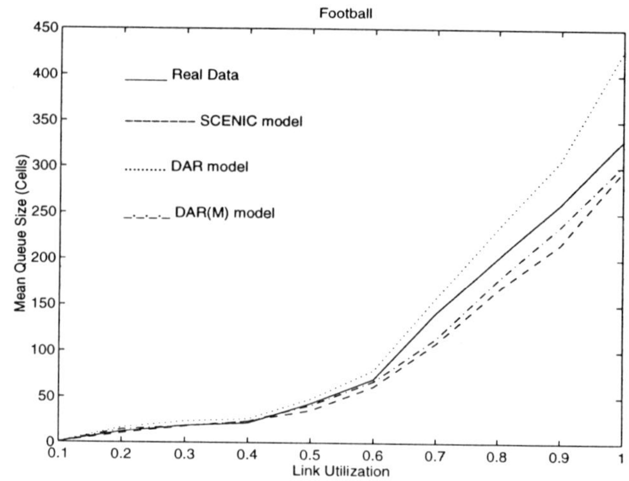

Fig. 13: Mean Queue Size vs. Link Utilisation for the sequence 'B', using real data and data generated by the various models.

References

[1] Verbiest, L. Pinnoo, and B. Voeten, "The impact of the ATM concept on video coding," *IEEE J. Selected Areas in Communications,* vol. 6, pp. 1623-1632, Dec. 1988.

[2] Zhang, W. Wu, K. Kim, R. Pickholtz, and J. Ramasastry, "Variable bit rate video transmission in the broadband ISDN environment," *Proc. of IEEE.* vol. 79, no. 2, pp. 214-222, feb. 1991.

[3] Special Issue on Packet Speech and Packet Video, vol. 7, no. 5, *IEEE J. Selected Areas in Communications.* June 1989.

[4] Maglaris, D. Anastassiou, P. Sen, G. Karlsson and J. D. Robbins, "Performance models of statistical multiplexing in packet video communications," *IEEE Tans. on Communications,* vol. 36, No. 7, July 1988.

[5] Marafih, Y. Q. Zhang and R. L. Pickholtz, "Modeling and queueing analysis of variable bit rate coded video sources in ATM networks," *IEEE Trans. Circuits and Syst. for Video Technol.,* vol. 4, No. 2, pp. 121-127, April. 1994.

[6] Cohen and D. P. Heyman, " A simulation study of video teleconferencing traffic in ATM networks," *IEEE INFOCOM,* vol. 3, 1993.

[7] Heyman, A. Tabatbai, T. V. Lakshman and H. Heeke, "Modeling teleconference traffic from VBR video coders," in *Proc. IEEE ICC'94,1994,* pp. 1744-1748.

[8] Frater, J. F. Arnold, P. Tan, " A new statistical model for traffic generated by VBR coders for television on the broadband ISDN," *IEEE Trans. Circuits and Syst. for Video Technol.,* vol. 4, pp. 521-526, Dec. 1994.

[9] Heyman and T. V. Lakshman, "Source models for VBR broadcast video traffic," *IEEE/ACM Trans. Networking,* vol. 5, pp. 40-48, Feb. 1996.

[10] ITU-T Recommendation. H263+, "Video coding for low bitrate communication, 1997.

[11] TMN encoder, University of British Columbia, Canada, http://www.ee.ubc.ca/Image, 1997.

[12] ITU-T , H.263+ Ad Hoc group, "Video Codec Test Near_Term, Version 7 (TMN7), 1997.

[13] Jacobs and P. A. W. Lewis, "Time series generated by mixtures," *J. Time Series Analysis,* vol. 4, No. 1, pp. 19-36, 1983.

[14] Elwalid, D. P. Heyman, T. V. Lakshman, D. Mitra, and A. Weiss, "Fundamental bounds and approximations for ATM multiplexing with applications to video teleconferencing," vol. 13, no. 6, *IEEE J. Selected Areas in Communications.* pp. 1004-1016, June 1989.

[15] Heyman, A. Tabatabai, and T. V. Lashman, "Statistical analysis and simulation study of video teleconference traffic in ATM networks," *IEEE Trans. Circuits and Syst. for Video Technol.,* vol. 2, pp. 49-59, Mar. 1992.

[16] Heyman, "The GBAR source model for VBR videoconferences," *IEEE/ACM Trans. Networking,* vol. 5, No. 4, pp. 554-560, August 1997.

[17] McKenzie, "Autoregressive moving-average processes with negative-binomial and geometric marginal distributions." *Adv. Appl. Prob.,* vol. 18, pp. 679-705, 1986.

[18] Bratley, B. L. Fox, and L. E. Schrage, *A Guide to Simulation.* Berlin: Springer-Verlag, 1987.

[19] Papoulis, "Probability, Random Variables, and Stochastic Process," *New York: McGraw Hill,* 1984.

Improving Network Simulation with Feedback

Kathleen M. Nichols
Bay Networks
Santa Clara, CA 95052-8185
knichols@baynetworks.com

Abstract

Since the publication of [1], it has become well known that real network traffic does not follow a poisson process and that feedback mechanisms in a network affect the traffic patterns. Yet much modeling and simulation work employs exponential interarrivals in open-loop traffic sources. Historically, these sources were chosen because they are amenable to analysis and easy to simulate, but they have serious shortcomings. Even when the source distribution is changed to reflect the burstiness of real traffic, we found that open-loop models fail to reproduce the detailed time structure and the crucial effects of feedback on traffic sources.

In this paper, evaluation of a Hybrid Fiber Coax (HFC) architecture is used to illustrate the inadequacy of traditional open-loop modeling. In addition, a promising intermediate technique of using "local feedback" is shown. Finally, using feedback models, the interaction of the HFC architecture with TCP dynamics was studied using web-browsing and file transfer applications. These studies led to a novel architectural improvement that would have been missed in an open-loop model.

1.0 Introduction

For many years network architectures have been studied in simulation by driving a model of the network with traffic sources where the message sizes and interarrival times are drawn from a random distribution, usually an exponential model. Since the publication of Leland et. al. [1], researchers have consistently found that real, measured data traffic does not follow a poisson distribution and some papers have additionally suggested probability distributions that capture the burstiness of real traffic [3,9,10] to replace the poisson arrivals. Despite the mounting evidence that poisson models are overly optimistic, significant amounts of network modeling and evaluation continue to be performed using such sources. Indeed, these models are widely used in industry and shipped with most commercial simulators. Our work adds to the body of evidence against poisson traffic sources and we have identified a further problem with commonly used simulation traffic models, their open-loop character. By *open-loop,* we mean the use of traffic sources which do not alter their behavior due to feedback from the network. These may be driven by a random or deterministic process or from a traffic trace or other measurement data. Traffic sources designed to respond to network feedback cannot be said to obey a particular apriori probability distribution since packet output will depend on information received in feedback. For example, in a TCP conversation the acknowledgements from a receiver are affected by network conditions experienced and in turn affect the sender's rate. When feedback is used, it is useful to think of *traffic* models rather than *source* models.

We make the case by focusing on the evaluation of Hybrid Fiber Coax (HFC) architectures. The performance evaluation criteria [2] submitted to the IEEE 802.14 Cable TV Media Access Control Working Group [8], one of the standards bodies working on broadband data delivery specifies open-loop traffic sources driven by exponential interarrivals. Another open-loop model, based on measured traffic and using a heavy-tailed interarrival distribution [3], was also used by the IEEE 802.14WG. We applied both these models and found them inadequate to evaluate crucial architectural features. To more appropriately evaluate HFC architectures, we began to use traffic models that respond to network feedback and found that

0-8186-8810-6/98 $10.00 © 1998 IEEE

open-loop and feedback traffic sources have very different network behavior characteristics. Our results show the failure of the open-loop models to accurately capture system dynamics. We identify two major problems with the use of traditional models: inaccurate conclusions about the system architecture and the lack of user-level performance metrics. To size system installations, we need a clear idea of how load variation affects the performance those users perceive. Although the shortcomings of open-loop traffic sources may be exacerbated due to the special characteristics of HFC architectures, clear general differences emerged.

Section 2 describes the HFC architecture we are simulating, section 3 covers the application of traditional open-loop source models to this architecture, and section 4 presents simulation results with feedback source models, comparing results for all simulations. In section 5 we show results obtained using closed-loop models of web-browsing and file transfer. We evaluate the performance effects of some TCP options and a novel architectural feature for HFC architectures. Section 6 summarizes.

2.0 The Simulated HFC Architecture

Hybrid Fiber-Coaxial cable TV networks are beginning to be utilized as a data delivery service to provide subscribers with Internet access. It is important to understand the behavior of these networks under expected data traffic loads in order to make appropriate architectural decisions and to provision installed systems. Background on the challenges of the HFC environment and of the on-going standards work in this area can be found elsewhere [4,5,8]; only salient architectural features are given here. The results presented in this paper are based on an HFC MAC protocol [6] having many features expected to be in the IEEE 802.14 standard.

A block diagram of an HFC network is shown in figure 1. Data is sent from the head-end to the stations *(downstream* channel) on a separate frequency from that on which the data is sent from the stations to the head-end *(upstream* channel). The propagation delay of the cable together with techniques to reduce channel noise impairment introduces delays in the round-trip path between head-end and stations of several milliseconds. In the upstream, a time-slotted channel is shared among the subscriber stations under the control of the head-end. Stations communicate with the head-end controller to request access to the upstream channel and the head-end controller's scheduling algorithm allocates these time slots using the requests from the stations and knowledge about the level of service of a particular subscriber. Stations can't communicate directly, so it's not possible to use a DQDB or CSMA MAC layer. The basic information unit sent in each upstream time slot is a 53 byte ATM cell augmented with 1 byte of management information, plus FEC and guardband bytes. The raw downstream channel bandwidth is 30 Mbps with a usable data payload of 23.9 Mbps. The downstream channel is shared by all the subscriber units for both user and management traffic. The raw upstream channel bandwidth is 2.56 Mbps with a usable data payload of 1.92 Mbps. The standards call for supporting 50-2000 stations on a single cable.

FIGURE 1. Block diagram of an HFC network

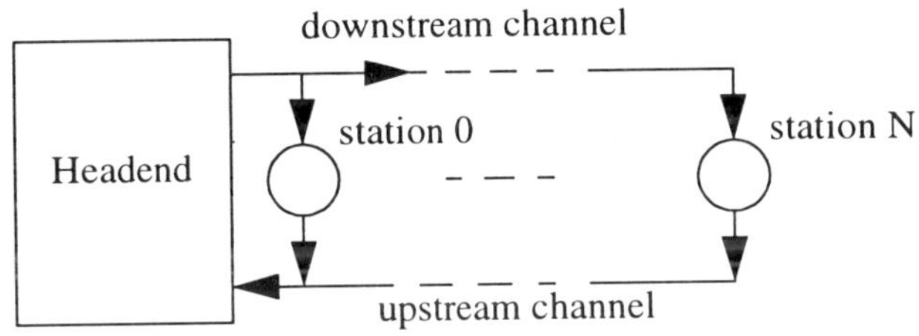

The headend controls the upstream channel by issuing *grants* that specify the station(s) and type of messages that can be sent in each upstream slot. Contention grants are issued to groups or to all stations to send requests for bandwidth. In response to successfully transmitted requests, direct grants are issued to individual stations to send data in a particular time slot on the upstream channel. Multiple grants (up to 15) can be packed into a single downstream cell. Random access algorithms are used to resolve contention when it occurs during bandwidth requests. Data is only sent in the directly granted slots. A block diagram of the request and grant flow is shown in figure 2. A scheduling algorithm is applied to the flow of resource requests using information about the type of service of each traffic flow and grants are then allocated to specific upstream cells. The head-end scheduler implements a sophisticated allocation model while the scheduler at the station schedules based on simple priority [13]. A scheduling period of 3.2 milliseconds was used throughout this paper. The cable modem sends its queue length in every upstream cell to be used by the head-end scheduler.

FIGURE 2. Simplified Diagram of Request and Grant Flow

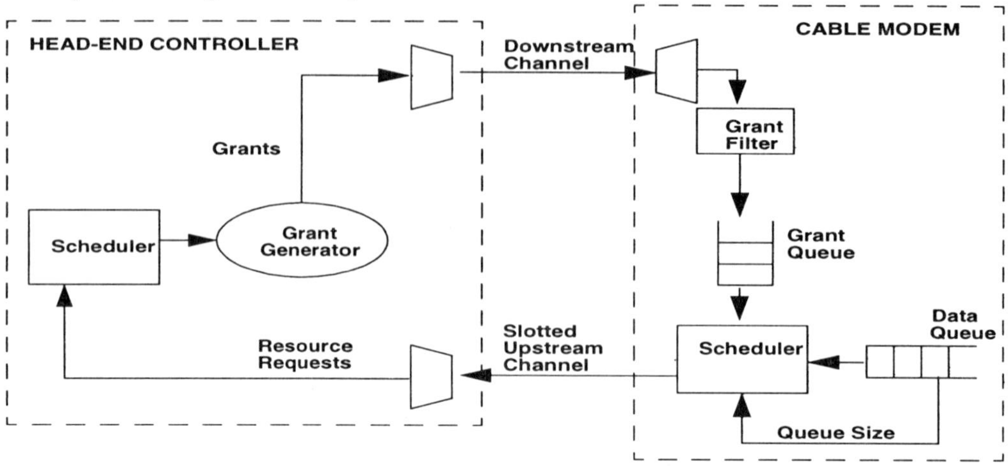

This makes it possible to *piggyback* data requests that arrive in the queue while it is being serviced without having to use a contention grant. This is desirable because requests made through contention are subject to collision, the resolution of which is costly in delays. Further, the physical effects of collisions on the channel may cause errors on other channels in the cable.

3.0 Traditional and Open-Loop Traffic Models applied to Cable Data Systems

Exponentially distributed packet arrivals (the popular poisson process) have been shown to represent traffic processes quite poorly and to give optimistic results (e.g., [9]), but it is often asserted that poisson modeling can be useful in evaluating a system during analysis and simulation. We begin by employing these traffic sources to model our HFC network. In the simulation, a headend module handles scheduling of the upstream channel and control of the contention resolution algorithm. Each subscriber station is modeled separately and includes both a model of the cable modem and an application model that sources traffic in the upstream direction. The upstream bus timing is modeled in detail, with time slots and propagation delays. The downstream bus was modeled only as messages passed from the head-end to the stations. The downstream messages include the major components of downstream delay, most notably FEC and interleaving delays, a total of 4.2 milliseconds in the simulations here. Variants of this basic simulation model were used by most of the participants in the 802.14 WG.

3.1 The simulator used in this paper.

Most of the 802.14 WG used Mil3's Opnet simulator. Initially, we followed this lead, but later found we needed something more "lightweight" and modifiable in order to carry out the kinds of investigations we needed. We gave up the friendly user interface and on-call support line for free source code, complete with bugs. This approach isn't for everyone, but we've been satisfied with the results. We selected Lawrence Berkeley Laboratories' *ns* simulator [14] as appearing the most germaine. Our reasons included its TCP simulation model and its use of C++, a language we were quite familiar with. Subsequently, we found we had to rewrite the TCP model and made major changes to the simulator's architecture, but that's the advantage of having source code. The major output from our simulator was trace files which we post-process in a number of ways to aid in analysis. We could create traces that looked very much like the output of a *tcpdump* on a real network, as well as other custom data. For the adventurous, further information on how to follow in our footsteps is included in section 6.0.

3.2 Exponentially distributed source models.

We implemented the "batch poisson" model suggested in [2] where the number of packet sizes selected is distributed randomly as follows: 60% of the packets are 64 bytes, 6% 128 bytes, 4% 256 bytes, 2% 512 bytes, 25% 1024 bytes, and 3% 1518. Packet interarrival times are exponentially distributed and the average can be varied.

About 12% of the channel will be dedicated to contention opportunities, leaving 1.7 Mbps available for data payload. Unallocated slots are designated as contention slots. [2] suggests performance modelers plot delay-throughput curves for 10, 50, and 200 stations, varying the arrival rate and using average packet delays; 200 stations are shown in figure 3. Since HFC networks are specified for up to 2000 connected stations, we ran a second set of simulations with the per station average bit-rate set to just under 1 Kbps and the number of stations varied from 100 to 1400. These results are labeled "fixed rate srcs". In figure 4 the median packet delays are shown. Median packet values are presented for consistency with other measures in this paper and are preferred for their stability. Note the differences at high throughput.

FIGURE 3. Average values for batch poisson

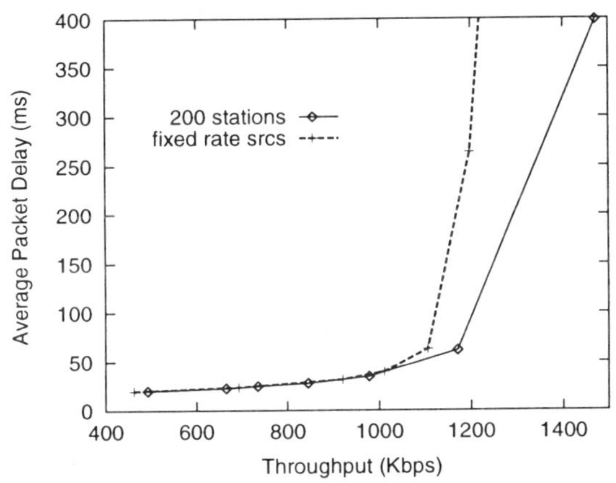

FIGURE 4. Median values for batch poisson

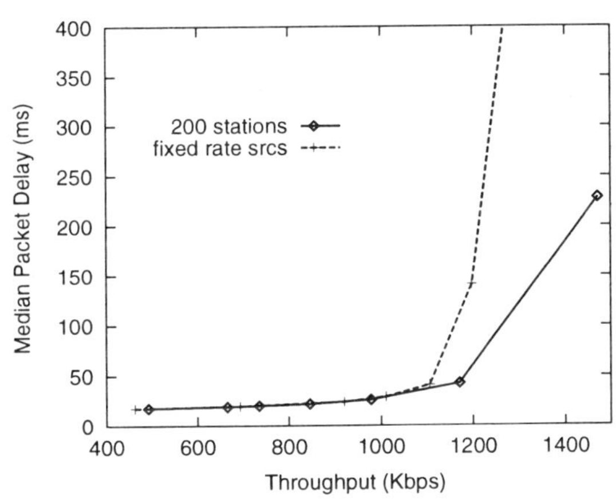

Architectural features dominate the delay at lighter loads, specifically the round trip time to get an allocation of upstream bandwidth from the headend, and as the load increases extra delays are introduced due to contention resolution. At the highest loads, the system becomes limited by the upstream bandwidth bottleneck and delays grow with station queue size. The two curves are initially coincident and diverge at higher throughput levels. We hypothesize that this is caused by the smaller likelihood of stations competing for the same contention grants when there are fewer stations and that more piggybacking occurs in the 200 station model. Since this model increases the load by decreasing the interarrival time, more packets arrive to a full queue and are thus piggybacked onto earlier requests. This hypothesis is verified by computing the ratio of all requests sent in contention slots to the number of total packets sent, a value that is 1.0 at light loads, 0.93 for the 1 Kbps sources at the highest throughputs, falling to 0.53 for the 200 source model. Nearly half of all packets are being piggybacked for the 200 source model!

The shape of these curves can be predicted by simple analysis. This is useful in model development as it helps validate the model's integrity, but the purpose of simulation is architectural insight. Spreading the traffic load across a larger number of clients results in different contention behavior, something that would have been missed if we'd relied only on the 200 station models. Could we be missing other behaviors? Measurement studies consistently show low *average* bandwidths per user and bursty application behavior. The next model was developed using measurements of such an application.

3.3 Deng's WWW traffic source model.

As in the larger internet, a large segment of the cable modem user population is expected to be spending on-line time accessing world wide web (WWW) pages. Web clients look quite different from poisson sources. Building on the WWW measurement and characterization work done by Cunha et. al. [10], Deng proposed a one-way client model of web browsing [3] and made an Opnet simulation model available to the 802.14 WG. It is an ON-OFF traffic source following these steps:

1. Start in the ON (browsing) state. The state changes to OFF at a delay (in seconds) taken from a Weibull distribution with parameters ($e^{4.5}$, 0.88). (Our model staggered the initial ON states to avoid synchronization.)

2.A URL request packet of size 250 bytes is produced after a delay picked from a Weibull distribution with parameters ($e^{1.5}$, 0.5).
3.Repeat step 2 until the state changes from ON to OFF.
4.Return to the ON state after a delay taken from a pareto distribution with parameters (60, 0.5).

Note that at least 60 seconds are spent in the OFF state, and at least 90 seconds are spent in the ON state. During the ON state, the minimum time between the fixed 250 byte (or 6 ATM cell) message is about 4.5 seconds, so the maximum source rate during the ON period is about 450 bps. This clearly produces a bursty model, though the burst sizes are not large. Though it models the user's actions, it is not possible to use this model to measure the delays a user would see as the number of clients increases. The emphasis is on reproducing the load the users put on the network in the upstream direction rather than on quantifying what the users see.

We next consider 1) how well does this model the dynamics of WWW browsing and 2) does this model produce additional information about the system being simulated that cannot be learned using the exponential sources? We experimented with this source model in our own simulator. In simulation the average source rate is about 34 bps. Although the number of stations varies from 100 to 2000, the average packet delay remains quite low, around 16 ms across all runs. This produces uninteresting results and the long OFF times require long simulation runs (3600 simulation seconds) for stable results ("Deng's srcs" in fig. 5).

FIGURE 5. Deng's WWW model

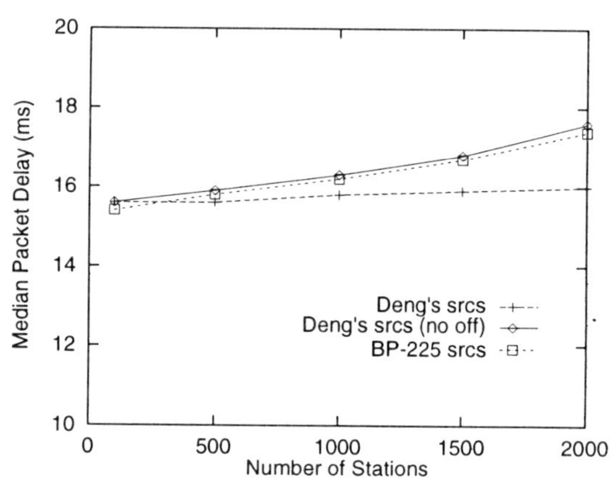

We are interested in the system dynamics under plausible, stressful loads and observe that only OFF times depend on the subject population. Thus we do away with the OFF times entirely and rerun the set of simulations. In this case, the average source load is about 225 bps and simulations can be shortened to 600 seconds. We compare it to batch poisson sources with an average data rate of 225bps (BP-225) to evaluate the utility of the bursty model. The delay curves for these experiments (figure 5) all have a very limited range (compare to figure 3). Little difference can be seen between the effects of each of these models on the architecture. None produced significant collisions on the upstream channel contention slots. The throughput curves are even less interesting so are omitted.

3.4 Summary

The open-loop web client model doesn't stress the modeled system. Further the upstream traffic due to the TCP protocol is not modeled, so it underestimates the upstream channel traffic. The batch poisson model can be made to drive the system into overload but we question whether the excessive piggybacking and its affect on contention dynamics well represents reality. We are concerned with how HFC architectures behave under the range of light through heavy loads and wish to determine where unacceptable overloads occur. We are convinced of the value of performing evaluations using realistic, bursty traffic, but it's unclear how to scale up Deng's measurement-based distribution since an increased source rate produces essentially the same behavior as in the batch poisson model. We need a bursty, realistic model that can be meaningfully scaled.

Also, although we can measure packet delays, upstream throughput, average queue sizes, etc., we cannot determine what these values mean to a typical user. It's difficult to say what a tripling or quadrupling of millisecond packet delays will mean to a user operating on timescales closer to seconds. System overloads are determined by the performance a user sees and we need to relate architectural features to that. To capture user level performance and create stressful but realistic source traffic, we moved to an approach based on a more faithful representation of the expected applications.

4.0 Adding Feedback to Traffic Models

4.1 Discussion of traffic models for HFC

What applications are most important for HFC networks? In the words of one anonymous reviewer, traffic mix "is dependent heavily on the country looked at or the persons using it." We chose to begin with web-browsing traffic for several reasons. Web-browsing is thought by many to be the major application of the target users (thus the use of Deng's model by 802.14). It is a network-stressful traffic pattern since it is bursty and has short transfers that seldom reap much advantage from piggybacking. Further, it is an interactive application so delay times matter. Interactive gaming has turned out to be a very important use of HFC networks and we encourage future studies with such a model. Long-lived FTPs are less interesting since they will capitilize on the request-grant architecture. The problem there is to prevent such applications from capturing most of the channel bandwidth (subject to economic factors). This is possible in HFC networks and we have published an approach [13].

Continuing with WWW modeling and our desire to more faithfully represent network traffic, we observe that the web browsing client-server conversation might be simulated, leading to a scalable model, more insights on system behavior and the ability to measure some quantities that pertain to application-level performance. Most of our work focused on web-browsing using http1.0. Our experiments and the published work of others indicates that this leads to more pessimistic assessments than using http1.1. In simulation, such pessimism can be useful to balance the necessary simplifications we make that cause results to be more optimistic than real-world measurements.

4.2 A more detailed client model for simulation

A typical process initiated when a user makes a request for a particular URL is:

1.User request for a URL results in opening of a TCP connection: a 40 byte SYN packet is sent.
2.The SYN is received by the remote server which returns a SYN acking the connection after some service time delay. Upon receipt of the SYN, the URL, typically 200-250 bytes, is sent to the remote server. (An ACK of this SYN may either be piggybacked with the URL or sent alone.)
3.After the service time delay, the remote server returns the requested page data including the in-lined URLs referenced on that page. As the data packets are received, ACK(s) and FIN are sent for this initial TCP connection. (When browsing in a "graphics off' mode, the page would be displayed and done at this time.) At the same time, SYNs are sent to open parallel connections for all the in-line URLs found on the page.
4.After the service time delay the remote server(s) return SYNs acking the connections and the in-lined URLs are sent from the requesting client.
5.After the service time delay, the remote server(s) returns the documents requested and FINs for the connections and the requesting client ACKs the data and the FINs. The number and spacing of ACKs depends on the size of the documents and, for larger documents, on the particular implementation of TCP. When the FINs have all been received by the client, it will be able to display the total page.
6.The user (or controlling process) delays some "think time" before making the next request, at which time, return to step 1.

For a web-browsing user, the performance measure of interest is how long it takes to "see something". The complete page can be displayed once all the data associated with all the URLs in the page have been received (step 5; step 3 for "graphics off"). Ignoring host and display time, this measure is a rough estimate of the delay a user sees in a real system.

4.3 Assumptions

We now have a model with figures of merit that have meaning at the user level. To implement it, we must model the downstream channel and add a model of transport layer behavior. We also need representative values for the web browsing parameters. In addition to the pioneering work of Cunha et at [10], work on measurement and modeling of WWW clients is continuing by other researchers. Mah at U.C. Berkeley has done measurements on some campus network segments and used these in trace-driven simulations [12]. We combine the measurements of Cunha and Mah to obtain representative values.

Some assumptions were made to expedite the simulation. In steps 2 and 4 all URLs were assumed to fit into six ATM cells (250 bytes). Further step 4 uses exactly three in-lined URLs, a pessimal value consistent with Mah [12]. In steps 3, 4 and 5 a fixed server delay time is used. Although this departs radically from behavior seen today, there are reasons it is justified for this study. First, companies planning data network services over cable are investing in large caching servers to provide response time acceptable for a commercial service and secondly, server and network delays are beyond the control of the architecture we are considering.

The document size distributions used in steps 3 and 5 were based on information from both Cunha and Mah. Mah found that the distribution of document sizes returned in response to the initial URL had different parameters than that of document sizes returned in response to in-line requests so we use a different document size distribution in step 3 than in step 5. However the largest outliers are clamped since we want our simulations to be test of the network's architecture not a completely faithful representation of web browsing. In step 5, the distribution is used to pick each of the three document sizes which are then converted to a number of maximum sized ethernet packets (1460 data bytes per packet).

Particular TCP implementations vary in the number of ACKs sent and whether ACKs are piggybacked on FINs and SYNs [151. We assume the client sends an acknowledgment every two packets and combines FINs and ACKs in a single packet.

A difficult problem is picking the average "think time"; that is, the average amount of time a user waits before selecting another page. Although [3] has some measurements of this value, it is unclear how well these apply. It could be extraced from the traces at [11] but these were taken using an unconventional browser, mosaic. A broader question is whether measured values for this timing are useful. Knowing how often users are active is useful in provisioning a system, but it can be misleading. Future developments in browsers might affect these times. Home web-surfers might be found to use the web differently from work and school web-surfers (picture the "couch potato" web surfer doing the equivalent of rapid channel surfing). There may be coincident use patterns so that designing to the average is dangerous underprovisioning. With our goal of exercising architectures in mind, think time was set to be random and uniformly distributed between one and 30 seconds, a fairly conservative (or pessimal) assumption. Altering the think time makes it possible to increase traffic levels while preserving the application behavior.

To speed evaluation, an intermediate approach was taken initially. The web-browsing interaction was used as the basis for a *local feedback (LF)* source model where backpressure from the modem queues provides feedback to the traffic sources. At each packet send, the LF source sends a message to the cable modem then *waits until the modem signals that its queue is empty* before it adds the server delay and goes on to the next step. Neither the upstream transmission delay of the last cell nor the downstream transmission delay is included in this model. Only part of the transport protocol behavior is modeled and simplifying assumptions were required. The number of ACKs was computed as the document size divided by 1460 bytes per packet and that result divided by 2 packets per ACK. Acknowledgments for a window's worth of packets for each TCP connection is sent after each empty queue signal plus server delay. This clearly ignores significant transport protocol interactions, possibly causing the page delay time to be underestimated.

4.4 Two-way world wide web client-server model

Full two-way (FT) client-server interaction necessitated rewriting the TCP model in the ns simulator distribution to set up and take down connections, to handle bidirectional traffic, and to handle variable packet sizes. WWW client models generate URL requests and hand the packets to the TCP connection management which generates the appropriate SYNs, FINs, and ACKs and returns the transferred document size to the client. Packets are segmented into cells and sent through the upstream channel to a server model attached to the headend. The server generates a protocol or data packet which is sent on a downstream channel to the appropriate station. The server delay (again 20 ms) is charged on the trip to the server from the headend and the server selects document sizes to return in the downstream.

Results of these experiments are in figures 6 and 7. The average rate for an LF client in a lightly loaded system is about 920 bps and the average rate for an FT client 980 bps, much higher than in Deng's model. For comparison, a batch poisson model with 925 bps sources (BP-925) is shown. The curves are very similar at light loads, but as the number of stations increases and delays and contention increase, both types of feedback stations cut back their rates as real clients would. Thus median packet delays differ significantly above 750 stations.

FIGURE 6. Local Feedback, Full Two-way, and Batch Poisson

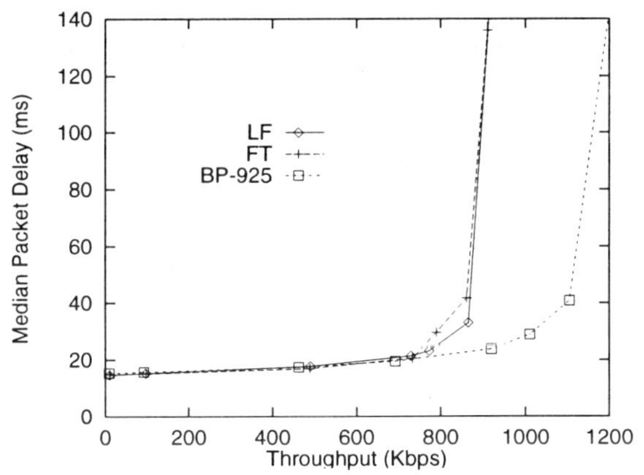

FIGURE 7. Throughput vs. station count

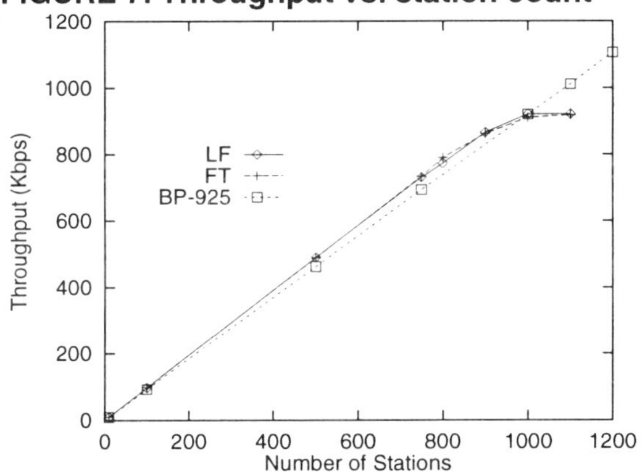

LF and FT models' throughput levels off around 1000 stations because feedback will not allow them to send packets into a saturated network. The open-loop BP model continues to put out the same average data rate per source and shows a sloping curve, approaching upstream bandwidth saturation while the feedback models quickly approach vertical. More differences between open-loop and feedback models will be shown later.

4.5 User-level metrics

A further advantage of the feedback model is that we can measure the user-level metric of page delay (see figure 8). There is a clear knee point after which additional clients result in extreme additional delays, but the exact location of this knee is particularly dependent on assumptions about the user think time distribution. The two models produce similar results for this metric, due in part to the fairly detailed LF model used and in part to not modeling the FT path beyond the headend.

FIGURE 8. Page Delay

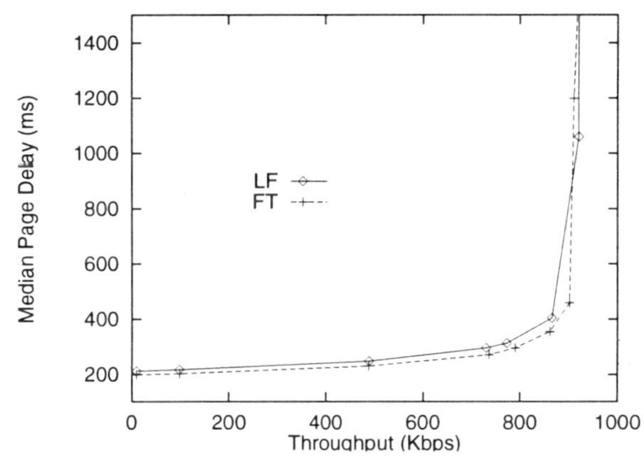

4.6 Comparing the models

We further explore similarities and differences across the models. Five models are used: Deng's sources with no OFF state (DENG), the local feedback web browser model (LF), the web browser with a full TCP model (FT) and two batch poisson models (BP-225 and BP-925). We start with throughput-delay curves (figure 9). We simulated DENG sources with up to 4500 stations (unrealisticly large) in order to evaluate effects of its heavy-tailed distribution. At

FIGURE 9. Throughput-Delay Comparison

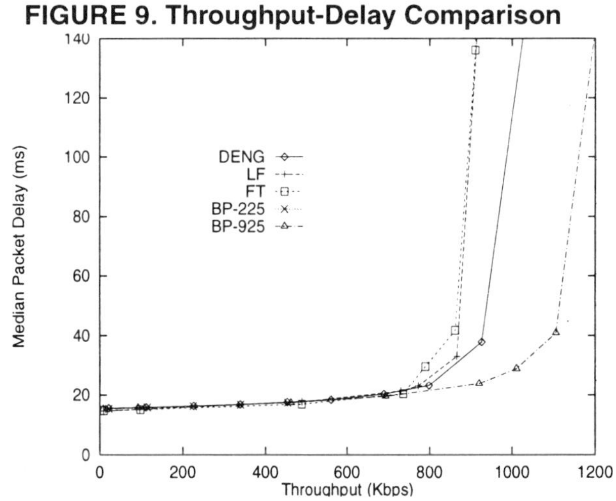

lower throughput all the curves are coincident, showing delay is primarily a function of throughput in that region. As throughput increases the traffic model becomes more important. The BPs are the most optimistic, below and to the right of the other curves. BP-225 is difficult to see as it has a maximum throughput of about 450 Kbps. DENG has a packet delay that lies above the BP curve closer to the feedback curves, but rises to the right of the feedback curves and with a slope that more resembles that of the BP curve.

Next we look at the upstream packet buffers. For each simulation, the maximum per-station buffer occupancy in cells was recorded. In figure 10, this metric is shown as a function of throughput and in figure 11 as a function of the total number of stations. Previously, we saw that piggybacking increases in open-loop models under heavy load. This is confirmed in figure 10 where maximum buffer size increases with throughput for all of the open loop models, but stays flat for the feedback models. These large buffer sizes cause a "false" piggybacking effect because this is not behavior exhibited in a real system. True piggybacking occurs in the feedback WWW models at all traffic intensities resulting both from opening all of the in-line connections at the same time and from getting windows of ACKs on parallel connections. We know the amount of piggybacking cannot be any greater than this due to the TCP/IP dynamics between the client and server. Real-life clients throttle back under load and/or data is dropped.

FIGURE 10. Maximum buffer (in ATM cells)

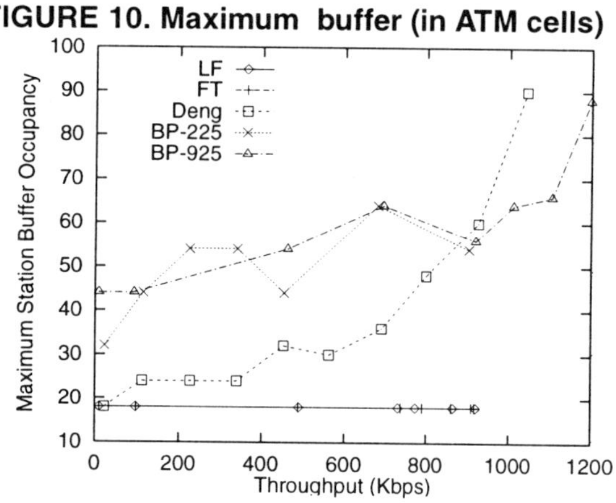

Contention behavior is critical in HFC architectures. The collision rate was recorded for each second of simulation time after the start-up period of 30 seconds (figure 12). At any value of total throughput, models with lower per-station rates should have more collisions since they require more simultaneously active stations to achieve the total. In the FT and LF models, upstream packets are either 64 byte protocol packets or 250 byte URLs, compared to the much wider BP packet size distribution (section 3.0). Because of the smaller packet sizes, we expect additional contention and channel utilization differences.

FIGURE 11. Maximum per-station buffer (cells)

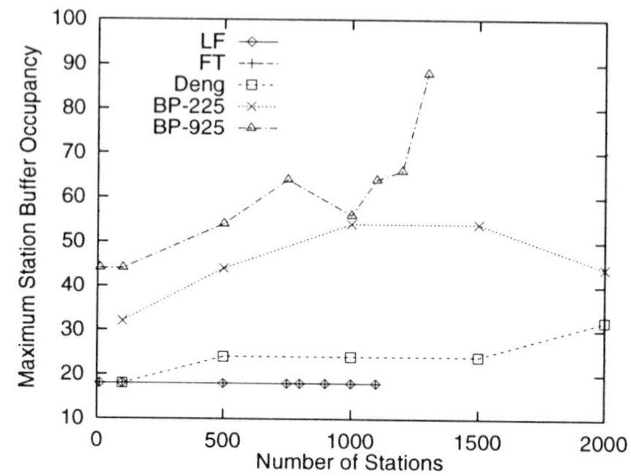

FIGURE 12. Collision rate comparison

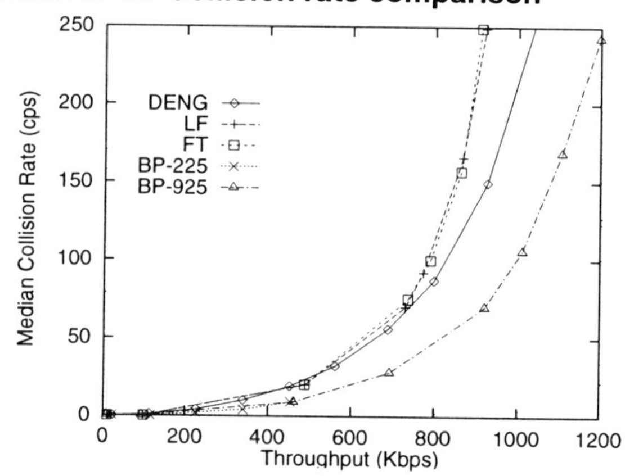

To compare collision rates using both the importance of station count and of throughput, the median collision rate was also normalized by the number of stations and plotted against the total average throughput (figure 13). This represents the normalized collision rate the upstream channel sees not the rate at which each station has a collision, since each collision represents two or more stations.

FIGURE 13. Normalized collision rates

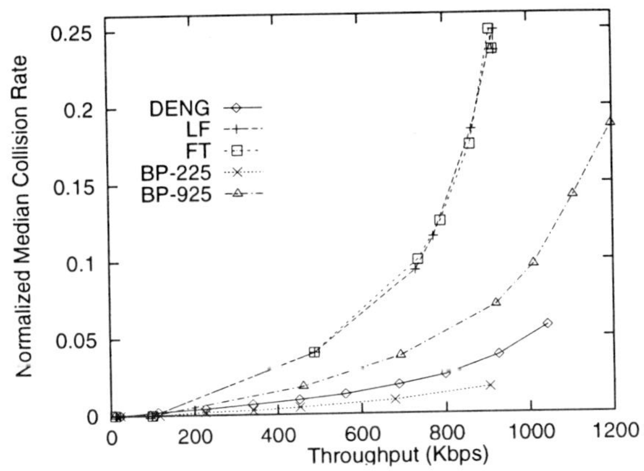

The two feedback models are strikingly similar in both graphs. DENG has a total median collision rate curve that is identical to the feedback models at lower throughputs, then diverges. Keep in mind that the DENG values came from many more stations than for the feedback models which becomes apparent in the normalized graph. The feedback models' curves fold back onto themselves at the top of the curve where the total system load caused clients to throttle back sufficiently to decrease the median contention rate per station. The open-loop models instead start to flatten out as the piggybacking rate goes up. Open-loop models produce little contention when the load and number of stations is close to that of feedback models. DENG has no significant collision rate at numbers of stations within the limit of 2000 stations.

4.7 Discussion

Open-loop sources create traffic (packets, cells) according to some pattern or probability distribution and the output is queued at the cable modem until it can be sent. If the traffic level is too high for the available bandwidth, it will cause large backlogs in an infinite queue system (most models) or be discarded in a finite queue system. Large backlogs are problematic because they will cause packet delays that primarily reflect queuing delays and because piggybacking completely removes these backlogged stations from the contention process and thus mitigates the critical loading on the contention resolution mechanism. There are few real applications that function this way since feedback is a major part of the network system dynamics. Real applications enter into a transport protocol level conversation with a remote peer thus will not continue to fill a cable modem's queue beyond the amount proscribed by the transport protocol. Applications based on TCP/IP will not have more than one window of data outstanding (a maximum of 16-64 Kbytes, depending on the implementation).

In most cases, an open-loop model using a heavy-tailed distribution (DENG) produces performance curves that lie between those of feedback and exponential models. The open-loop source model Deng developed by fitting data from network traces to heavy-tailed probability distributions faithfully captures some of the burstiness of the original application but fails to reproduce the behavior as sources adapt to network characteristics through interaction with the architecture and other network flows. Further, the sources cannot be meaningfully scaled to represent heavier usage per source. Deng's model ignores the TCP-based packet traffic, which accounts for most of the upstream traffic during web-browsing and does not permit measurement of user-oriented metrics.

The local feedback model closely tracks the upstream traffic produced by the full two-way TCP model. Though local feedback can be easily added to any model that is presently using open-loop models, they have three major drawbacks. First, the feedback structure needs to be customized to the application. For example, to create a file transfer model, the client model must be rewritten, including its TCP portions. Second, the return traffic path is not modeled so we cannot see its effects on system and application performance. Third, it is not possible to model server contention or resource-sharing problems beyond the upstream channel. A final caveat is that the fidelity of the LF curve fit to a full two-way feedback model will depend on the application modeled and how well it can be represented with an LF model. For example, an earlier version of the LF model had a less faithful TCP model, Though it produced curves that were similar in shape to those of the FT model and much more like FT than open-loop models, they were noticeably more optimistic than the FT curves.

Though metrics based on throughput can be useful, we are particularly concerned with how user perception of performance is affected as the number of users and their network use varies. We expect the number of stations that are active to change with time of day and HFC systems need to adapt accordingly and to avoid the worst performance ranges. Feedback models can be used to help understand how installed systems will function.

5.0 Results using the Feedback Model

A full, two-way TCP model makes it possible to add new application types and to observe the effects of parameter and architectural changes on them. Focusing on two applications, the web browsers of the last section and an FTP source, we show the effects of an increase in the initial TCP slow start window value on web-browsing sources and the effects of TCP window size changes on ftp throughput. In addition we describe and present the effects of a MAC layer architectural enhancement that uses knowledge about transport protocol behavior to improve performance by predicting when a station will be requesting a grant. This allows us to speed up response times and decrease contention.

5.1 Changing the initial window

The TCP used in the experiments sends at least one ACK for every two packets, uses a 2-packet initial slow-start window, and an 8 Kbyte (6 packet) maximum window. Figure 14 shows the results of increasing the slow-start initial window to 4 Kbytes on median page delays of web-browsing clients, a change that has been proposed for TCP [16]. The improvement in median page delays varies from 4% at the lightest loads to 16% at 1100 stations. The 4K slow start allows three packets to be sent in the first window of data, only one additional packet. The dramatic

FIGURE 14. Effects of slow start window changes on page delays in web browsing

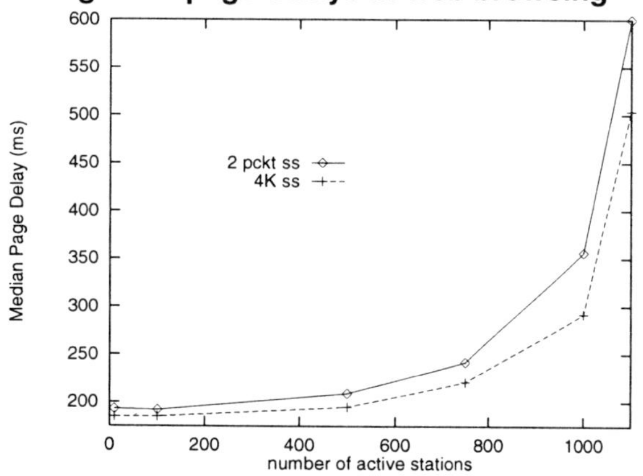

effect as the number of stations increases results from saving about one contention per URL fetched. In addition, the entire response fits in the 4 Kbytes more than 50% of the time.

5.2 Debugging prototypes

It is straightforward to use the full TCP model in an FTP application, a client and server where a file is transferred to the client from the server. A single client-server pair was used to help evaluate measurement results on initial products; simulation and measurement traces were correlated for insights on performance. Increasing the maximum TCP window fills more of the bandwidth-delay pipe and greatly improves throughput (table 1). Note the bandwidth-delay pipe is kept full with a 48 packet window. In addition, at this window size, all the upstream ACKs have their requests piggybacked on earlier ACKs, considerably reducing round-trip delay. The upstream direction saturates before the downstream since about 50 times as much data must be sent in that direction and the bandwidth asymmetry is only a factor of 10. Table 1 shows the upstream and downstream average data throughput for a range of window sizes given in number of packets.

TABLE 1. Channel throughput for different window sizes

	6	12	24	36	42	48
upstream (Kbps)	55	109	239	388	460	500
dwnstream (Mbps)	2.6	5.2	11.4	18.4	21.8	23.7

5.3 Architectural enhancements

The ability to evaluate architectures and to find opportunities for their enhancements is an important benefit of a realistic simulation. Testbed results were cross checked with simulator results to develop our intuition about traffic behavior for this architecture and to understand how to improve performance. One novel technique emerged as we noted that, in general, a data packet downstream results in an acknowledgment upstream. This observation was used to allow the headend to predict appropriate times to give grants to stations without waiting for them to contend. There are several ways to implement this feature, details are not given here. A conservative version of grant prediction was simulated for both web-browsing and for FTPs.

Figure 15 shows the result of repeating the experiments of figure 14 using predicted grants, including the 2 packet curve from figure 11 for ease of reference. Using predicted grants decreases page delays and supports more stations. In this case, the slow-start window increase results in a smaller range of improvements, 4% to 8%, since contention is already reduced. Thus these values reflect the more architecture-independent effects of increasing the window size. The median page delays are nearly the same at 1300 stations once upstream channel utilization becomes quite large, but this is the beginning of overload effects.

FIGURE 15. Effects of prediction grants on median page delays for web browsing

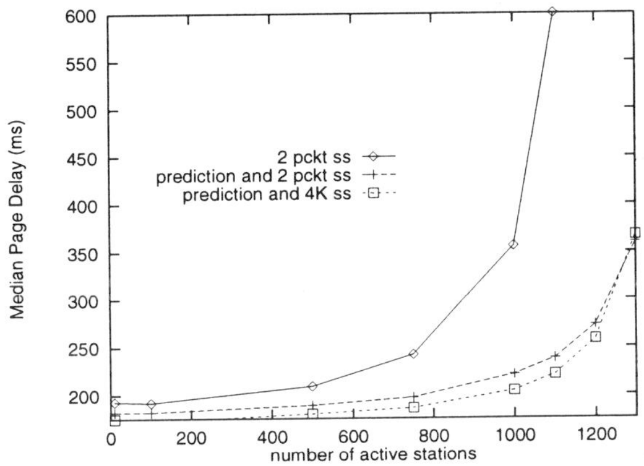

Predicted grants remove much of the contention from an HFC network. Not only does this reduce delays, it can improve fairness. The latter is best illustrated using FTPs. Average up- and downstream throughputs are listed in table 2 for 1, 5, and 10 active stations, both aggregate and per station values. Table 3 shows the same data when prediction grants are used.

TABLE 2. FTPs throughput without prediction

N	agg up	agg dwn	sta up	sta dwn
1	55 Kbps	2.6 Mbps	55 Kbps	2.6 Mbps
5	263	12.5	53	2.5
10	478	22.7	48	2.3

In this scenario, the channel is shared fairly, both with and without predicted grants (differences between the per station rates are less than 1%). Predicted grants result in about 10% more throughput because they lower the round trip delay. The small number of stations means there are few collisions, so the gain in performance comes almost solely from decreasing the time to request a grant and not from saving the time to resolve a collision. For 10 active stations, the downstream data payload reaches saturation, but the upstream channel is only about 25% utilized.

TABLE 3. FTP throughput with prediction

N	agg up	agg dwn	sta up	sta dwn
1	60 Kbps	2.9 Mbps	60 Kbps	2.9 Mbps
5	300	14.2	60	2.9
10	500	23.7	50	2.4

To congest the upstream channel, we did a "reverse" FTP (file transfer from station to HE). The MAC layer scheduling ensures all stations with packets to send get a minimum share of the channel but does not upper bound station traffic when there is channel bandwidth available. The reverse FTP uses all the upstream bandwidth it can get, reducing the contention slot allocation to its minimum value of 12% of the upstream channel. Table 4 lists results for a single reverse FTP: alone and with one and two "normal" FTPs. Table 5 adds prediction. Prediction has no effect on the reverse FTP because all of its packets are piggybacked, using no contention grants. The "normal" FTPs suffer without predicted grants because the reduced number of contention slots results in extra delay at each contention, thus extra round trip delay. Prediction removes this delay, increasing the downstream throughput from 1.8 Mbps to 3.0 Mbps per station, a fairer channel use.

TABLE 4. Throughput with a "reverse" FTP

	station to HE		HE to station	
FTPs	up	down	up	down
0	1.7 Mbps	34 Kbps	-	-
1	1.6	34	38 Kbps	1.8 Mbps
2	1.6	33	37	1.8

TABLE 5. Throughput with a "reverse" FTP and prediction

	station to HE		HE to station	
FTPs	up	down	up	down
0	1.7 Mbps	34 Kbps	-	-
1	1.6	34	64 Kbps	3.0 Mbps
2	1.5	32	59	2.8

It's important to balance the potential gain of sending a predicted grant against the cost of inaccurately predicting a grant and wasting the time slot on the upstream channel. The examples shown here had very few of these misallocated slots, but these applications lend themselves to the use of this feature. The predicted grant implementation was a conservative one. More sophisticated implementations might have traffic "learning" features included.

Bypassing contention is crucial in order to reliably deliver committed service tiers to different stations. This, in addition to its other performance properties, makes prediction an important technique to pursue. Intelligent use of predictive grants in concert with the delivery of different service tiers requires some further study. This feature cannot be meaningfully studied without a realistic closed-loop simulation. In addition to discovering this predicted grant mechanism, these experiments helped us to understand many aspects of the dynamic behavior of the architecture.

6.0 Summary and Pointers to Models

6.1 Summary

When constructing a simulation model, there is a danger of oversimplifying and arriving at inaccurate conclusions. Previous researchers have warned that poisson models do not well represent real traffic though some performance modelers still feel they give valuable system information. When applied to our architecture, we found the poisson models gave us performance numbers that are clearly wrong and dangerously optimistic. Further, we found that using open-loop models in general appears to give optimistic performance and doesn't allow us to measure the kind of quantities we need to evaluate user-level metrics. Our investigations convinced us that we must model MAC layer protocols with sufficient features of the application and transport protocol behavior to design architectures that will function well when deployed in the real world. Open-loop models can be useful in simulation model development, but should be approached with extreme caution for architectural appraisal.

A promising technique intermediate to a full two-way model is to use "local feedback". In our case local feedback is achieved by monitoring the status of the station queues that feed the upstream channel. For several important performance measures, this gives results quite close to the two-way model. It can be much easier to add this type of feedback to an existing model by modifying the source models than to make a full two-way model. For some simulators, this may also be preferable so that the simulation run-time does not become prohibitively long. Drawbacks are that local feedback must be customized for an architecture and a particular type of source, and that delays and congestion of the return traffic path is not modeled.

The original impetus for this work was twofold: to understand the effects of realistic traffic on our architecture and to make it possible to study more thoroughly the delivery of different tiers of service to different stations, work we initially reported on in [13]. In pursuing models for this purpose, we found several architectural interactions of interest and performance improvement techniques, including the predicted grants described in section 5.

This paper has presented summary statistics, but working with the model showed the dynamic behavior of the models are more divergent. It is difficult to capture and present these results. Future work might look at comparisons of open-loop and feedback models with more emphasis on dynamic behavior differences.

6.2 Pointers to useful simulation models

Although we started with a public domain simulator, it is not possible, or even desirable, for others to pick up the code used here. One problems is that the MAC model used here is proprietary to Com21. The ns version used here was changed in many ways from the original distribution: the TCP model was greatly enhanced, a more efficient event queue was added (the original had a linked list), web and file transfer clients and servers were created, and major architectural changes were made to the simulator to make it easier to add a MAC model. It is still possible for interested readers to perform simulations similar to those reported on here. Since this work was begun, the ns simulator has been superseded by the ns-2 simulator [17], which has a basic architecture more similar to the Com21 custom ns and includes some MAC models (but not, as of this writing, an HFC one). Further, we rewrote one of the TCP models of ns-2 to be an even closer model of reality. This model and web and FTP traffic models were used to study effects of changing the TCP initial window size. This was reported on to the Internet Engineering Task Force's (IETF) TCP Implementors Working Group and written up in an Internet Draft (which is expected to soon become an informational RFC). We've made these models available at the ns-2 "contributed code" web site [18]. We recommend use of ns-2 with our code modules for those who want a simulation environment close to that described in this paper.

7.0 Acknowledgements

The author was at Com21, Inc. when this work was done and would like to thank Mark Laubach of Com21 for encouragement to persist with traffic-oriented models. In addition, Van Jacobson of Lawrence Berkeley National Laboratory shared much advice, tools for viewing data, and informed many of this paper's insights.

8.0 References

[I] W.E. Leland, M.S. Taqqu, W. Willinger, and D.V. Wilson, "On the Self-Similar Nature of Ethernet Traffic," Proceedings of ACM SIGCOMM '93, pp. 183-193.

[21 J. Limb, et. al., "Performance Evaluation Process for MAC Protocols", IEEE 802.14 working group document 96/83R2

[3] S. Deng, "Empirical Model of WWW Document Arrivals at Access Link", IEEE ICC '96.

[41 D. Sala and J.0. Limb, "A Protocol for Efficient Transfer of Data over Fiber/Cable Systems", Proceedings of Infocom 1996, p 904.

[5] M. Laubach, "To Foster Residential Area BroadBand Internet Technology", Connexions, February 1996 Vol 10, no. 2, p 18-30.

[61 M. Laubach, *The UPSTREAMS Protocol for HFC Networks,* proposed to IEEE 802.14 Working Group, contribution number IEEE802.14-95/152RI, January, 1996.

[8] See http://walkingdog.com for further information about IEEE 802.14.

[9] V. Paxson and S. Floyd, "Wide Area Traffic: The Failure of Poisson Modeling", IEEE Transactions on Networking, June 1995, pp. 226-244,

[10] C.R. Cunha, A. Bestavros, M.E. Crovella, "Characteristics of WWW Client-based Traces", Boston University Computer Science Technical Report BU-CS-95-0 10, July 18, 1995.

[11] Traces at ftp://cs-ftp.bu.edu/techreports/95-010-web-client-traces.tar.gz

[12] B. Mah, "An Empirical Model of HTTP Network Traffic", *to appear in* Proceedings of INFOCOM '97, Kobe, Japan, April 7-11, 1997.

[13] K.M. Nichols and M. Laubach, "On Quality of Service in HFC Networks", IEEE ATM'96, San Francisco, CA, August, 1996

[14] Available at http: //www-nrg.ee.lbl.gov/ns

[15] V. Paxson, "Measurements and Analysis of End-to-End Internet Dynamics", Ph.D. dissertation, University of California, Berkeley.

[16] http://www-nrg.ee.lbl.gov/floyd/tcp_init_win.html

[17] Available at http://www-mash.cs.berkeley.edu/ns/

[18] Available at http://www-mash.cs.berkeley.edu/ns/ns-contributed.html

Performance Comparison of Reliable Multicast Protocols using the Network Simulator ns-2

Christoph Hänle
Vrije Universiteit Amsterdam
De Boelelaan 1081A,
1081 HV Amsterdam, Netherlands
chris@cs.vu.nl

Markus Hofmann
University of Karlsruhe*
Zirkel 2,
76128 Karlsruhe, Germany
hofmann@acm.org

Abstract

Reliable multicast protocols on top of the MBone are presently subject to intensive research. In the past, numerous protocols have been developed and their respective performance been analysed. Little progress has been made, though, to compare different approaches. In this paper, we use the network simulator ns-2 *to evaluate the performance of three protocols, namely* Scalable Reliable Multicast (SRM), Multicast File Transfer Protocol (MFTP) *and an enhanced version of the latter, called* Multicast File Transfer Protocol with Erasure Correction (MFTP/EC). *We also compare the results to each other and test the suitability for multicast file distribution.*

Keywords: Reliable Multicast, Network Simulator, Scalability

1 Introduction

Protocols for the reliable one-to-many data transfer can be constructed in various ways, and existing protocol architectures in fact use completely different techniques. As a consequence, they differ in bandwidth consumption and quality of service they offer to the application. Roughly speaking, reliable multicast protocols over the MBone all use IP's best effort multicast delivery service and provide mechanisms at least for error recovery, and possibly for flow control or congestion control as well.

The main difficulty is to cope with *scalability* and *heterogeneity*: The protocol should perform reasonably well even in large groups and for group members of greatly different Internet connectivity. These requirements are hard to encounter and the difficulties can not be completely hidden behind the interface to the application. For example, each receiving application might want to reliably receive packets in correct sequence and with minimum delay, and have the transmission rate be adapted to whatever rate it can handle. The sending application might require receivers to be kept in sync or might want to allow late joining. The ultimate protocol would achieve these service qualities using only little extra bandwidth for error recovery and would act fair to other network traffic. The criteria, however, are often competing aims and no single reliable multicast protocol architecture can meet them all simulataneously. Today, there is no *one-size-fits-all* protocol that can optimally serve the needs of all types of multicast applications. Instead, most multicast protocols are designed with stress on some criteria while neglecting others.

Application Level Framing (ALF) [3] has been proposed to help adapt transport-level services, such as reliability, to the needs of specific applications. ALF-based communication architectures are more flexible because they give the application more control over the end-to-end transmission. For example, ALF-based protocols normally do not try to put incoming packets back in order before handing them up to the application; they leave it to the application to deal with unsequenced packets in a clever way. Shifting the difficulty of coping with unordered packets to the applications is highly efficient, because the application can react in the most flexible way. This also means, however, that writing the application becomes more complicated [6]. In particular, the sending application has to partition data into units and to label each unit in an application context specific manner, such that out-of-order packets become meaningful enough for the receiving application to process them in a useful manner [7].

Another service quality that could be sacrified is quick loss recovery. For some types of applications such as multicast file distribution, there is no need for a receiver to

*Currently member of the Networking Software Research Department at Bell Laboratories, Holmdel, NJ, USA

0-8186-8810-6/98 $10.00 © 1998 IEEE

quickly be provided with a repair packet; it is acceptable to leave space for the missing packet, wait until the end of the regular transmission and then fill the gap.

Because different multicast protocols often offer different service qualities, there is generally no superiority of one protocol over the other. By looking at parameters such as the number of duplicate packets processed, however, the extra cost can be calculated that one protocol requires for offering a better service than another protocol.

An issue of great importance is congestion control for reliable multicast. The Reliable Multicast Research Group of the IRTF is currently defining a set of reference simulations to assess different congestion conrol schemes [9]. While congestion control is fundamental to any transport-level multicast protocol, none of the protocols examined in this paper does yet integrate appropriate mechanisms. We expect this will change in the future.

At least three different ways exist to measure protocol performance, namely *analytical evaluation*, *experiments* and *simulations*. In the past, extensive work has been done to measure analytical performance [21, 1, 10]. Likewise, numerous results from experiments over the MBone have been reported [12, 15, 26, 8]. In general, analytical results can demonstrate well the implications on a protocol's performance when modifying parameters such as the number of receivers or their respective loss rates, because these parameters generally are inputs to the formulae. Analytical evaluation, however, only works for greatly simplified models of the network and background traffic and results therefore always remain questionable.

The approach frequently adopted is to run experiments over the MBone, so that the measured outcome is realistic by definition. This technique, however, does not allow to vary network load in an arbitrary way. Therefore, measurements reflect the protocol behavior in more or less typical cases, but performance evaluation under exceptional circumstances is hardly possible. Little can therefore be said about the protocol's robustness in atypical circumstances. Further, while re-running the experiment with a different multicast protocol, identical background traffic and network behavior is required for a fair comparison of protocol performance, and this can not be enforced in the MBone.

The way we took was to use a simulator that models the MBone in great detail. This technique lets us gain power over all parts of the network and yields the greatest insight. For example, we can easily set up a topology and vary network load arbitrarily while monitoring link loss rates. We can further place the multicast sender and the receivers anywhere within the network and measure the protocol's performance. It is simple to exchange one multicast protocol for the other and re-run the simulator, thus guaranteeing identical background traffic when drawing the protocol comparison. It is essential that the simulator models the MBone appropriately, or else the results become unrealistic. Related work on multicast protocol simulations include [14] and [13], which focuse on the impact of subgrouping and overlay structures on multicast performance, and [17], which introduces MESH and compares it to different approaches (centralized, tree-based and unstructured organization of group members).

The main motivation behind using a network simulator is that many multicast protocols greatly depend on temporal and spatial packet loss correlation. Getting these parameters wrong quickly leads to wrong conclusions. By simulating packet flows and losses in a realistic way, we expected the loss characteristics to be comparable to the MBone, given a preconfigured network load. We will investigate later in this paper whether or not this assumption holds. Using the simulation approach, the MBone's characteristics are not only modeled for typical network loads, but the behavior can even be extrapolated to atypical high or low traffic patterns. Simulations can therefore anticipate protocol behaviour in exceptional cases.

Our simulation models of the MBone have been used to compare the performance of three reliable multicast protocols to each other. Sections 2 and 3 introduce these protocols and the simulation environment, respectively. In Section 4, we compare the loss characteristics of the simulated network with traces taken from the MBone and give evidence that our simulation models are quite realistic. Section 5 measures bandwidth requirements for each protocol and draws a comparison. Also presented are measurements of SRM's packet loss recovery times. Section 6 gives a conclusion.

2 Reliable Multicast Protocols

Recently, a large number of reliable multicast protocols have been proposed [19]. In this paper, we compare three of them to each other, namely *Scalable Reliable Multicast (SRM)* [5], *Multicast File Transport Protocol (MFTP)* [18] and *Multicast File Transport Protocol with Erasure Correction (MFTP/EC)* [10], based on the results obtained from running tests with the network simulator ns-2. These protocols have been chosen because their source code has been available for integration into ns-2. Unfortunately, we have not been able to compare these receiver-initiated, NACK-based protocols to multicast protocols with subgroup-based error recovery. The only hierarchical, subgroup-based protocol featuring local error recovery and publicly available source code is the *Local Group based Multicast Protocol (LGMP)* [11, 13]. However, the highly multi-threaded implementation architecture of LGMP causes some major difficulties for the integration into the network simulator ns-2. Therefore, we have not yet been able to evaluate LGMP using ns-2. Nevertheless, LGMP has been analyzed using a different simulation tool [14] and extensive measurements on the worldwide MBone have been performed [12]. More work needs to be done to put these results in relation with the results presented in this paper. Tree-based multicast protocols, such as RMTP [15] or TMTP [27], have not been included in our simulations because we did not have any access to their respective source code.

The protocols included in our simulations all use a receiver-initiated error recovery scheme, but they differ in the way feedback traffic is reduced: SRM uses a slotting and damping technique. MFTP packs multiple NACKs into a single PDU, using one bit per data packet. Finally, MFTP/EC also packs multiple NACKs into a PDU, but further reduces NACK traffic because each bit reflects the status of a *group* of packets.

2.1 SRM

SRM [5] provides reliable many-to-many multicast packet delivery. That is, each participant can act as a sender and a receiver simultaneously. SRM is based on the ALF principle, that is, the protocol does not put received packets back in order (neither packets from a specific source nor packets from different sources). Rather, the application has to deal with unsequenced packets. Though SRM gives no timing guarantees, its design aims at quick packet loss recovery.

Lost packets are detected when gaps in the sequence number space occur. For this to work, SRM participants need a separate counter for every source. Detection works well unless losses occur immediately before the end of a packet sequence. SRM solves this problem by having all participants periodically disseminate low-rate *session messages*, each one containing the sender's own highest sequence number sent so far and the respective highest sequence number heard from every other known participant. Session messages are also needed for round-trip time measurements and to estimate the current number of participants.

To perform loss recovery, participants set a timer for every detected packet loss. If the timer expires, they transmit a NACK (SRM calls it *repair request*) to the whole multicast group. If participants receive a repair request before timer expiration, they cancel the timer and send no repair request instead (NACK suppression). Participants that receive a repair request for which they hold the corresponding data packet are called *responders*. They enter a repair phase for the data packet requested. Similar to sending a repair request, they set up a timer and transmit the data packet (SRM calls retransmitted packets *repair packets*) only when the timer has expired and no such repair packet has been received in the meanwhile. This mechanism is to avoid repair packet implosion. Like repair requests, repair packets are sent using global (unrestricted) multicast.

Crucial to SRM is the configuration of the timers, that is, the decision of how long to delay a request packet or a repair packet before eventually sending it. Floyd *et al.* [5] discuss this issue in detail. In essence, suppose that participant A sets a request timer to recover from a lost packet originating from sender S and assume that $d_{S,A}$ is A's current estimated propagation delay for the distance between A and S. Then A sets its timer to some random value in the interval $3^i \cdot [C_1 \cdot d_{S,A}, (C_1 + C_2) \cdot d_{S,A}]$ where C_1 and C_2 are variables that SRM continually adapts using past statistics of duplicate request detections. i dictates the number of backoffs, starting with 0: if A sends the request, it increments i and reschedules a request packet, using the broader interval to select the expiration time. This is necessary in order to cope with multiple losses. Further, if A receives a request packet prior to timer expiration and is not in a so-called *deaf period*, it cancels the timer, increments i and reschedules a new timer. A deaf period lasts half as long as the timer interval and is to avoid further backoffs due to duplicate requests. For details, see [5, 25].

A responder B — upon receiving a repair request — sets a timer to some value randomly chosen from the interval $[D_1 \cdot d_{A,B}, (D_1 + D_2) \cdot d_{A,B}]$, where $d_{A,B}$ is B's estimated distance to the requestor A and D_1 and D_2 are numbers that SRM continually adapts. There is no concept of backoff for repair timers. After sending or receiving a repair packet, however, B enters a deaf period of time $3d_{S,B}$ (S being the original sender or the first requestor) to avoid sending multiple repair packets for duplicate requests.

SRM senders send at some fixed rate, that is, there are no flow control or congestion control mechanisms.

2.2 MFTP

MFTP [18] is a protocol for the reliable file distribution to a large number of receivers (that is, up to the order of a few thousands) using multicast transmission. The protocol partitions the file into packets and builds equally-sized blocks of packets. Each block consists of as many packets as bits fit into an IP-packet of maximum size. For example, if the network can handle packets of at most 1500 bytes, then blocks cover roughly 12000 packets.

The sender initially multicasts all packets in a first pass. Receivers write all data to a file and leave appropriate space whenever they detect a packet loss. Later, they fill the gaps when the appropriate repair packet arrives. For each block with at least one missing packet, receivers send back in unicast mode a NACK-bitmap, reflecting the status (received/missed) of each data packet within the block. Receivers randomly delay the NACK transmission by up to 2s to reduce the implosion problem. The sender collects all NACK-packets, determines the set of data packets being requested at least once and retransmits those in a second pass. Again, at the end of the second pass, receivers send back NACK bitmaps. The procedure continues possibly with a third or forth pass, etc., until all receivers have completely received the file. Receivers leave the multicast group as soon as they have completed reception, causing the multicast tree to prune back.

Because the sender does not stop sending packets until the end of a pass, the protocol is insensitive to high round-trip delays (unless a pass becomes very short). Also note that error recovery does not start before all regular data has been sent. This does not pose a problem when packets are stored on disk, because disk seeks can arbitrarily access any file position.

Congestion control is performed by setting a threshold and having receivers drop out if their loss rate exceeds the threshold. In a future version, the sender will then set up a second session on a different channel and will send the data at a lower rate.

2.3 MFTP/EC

MFTP/EC was derived from MFTP and uses erasure correction methods to perform loss recovery more efficiently. Sender and receivers partition the set of data packets into groups of k packets each and build blocks of approximately 12000 groups. (k is some small integer and is discussed at the end of this section.) After a complete file transmission, receivers send back NACK-bitmaps, where each bit indicates whether or not all packets of a group have been received successfully. The sender multicasts in a second pass one redundancy packet for each NACK'ed group. Therefore, recovery passes in MFTP/EC only last up to a fraction of $1/k$ of a full MFTP pass (although in general, more passes than in MFTP will be needed).

Redundancy packets are computed by XOR'ing together a *subset* of the original packets for the requested group, according to a bit-vector $\mathbf{g} \in \mathbb{F}_2^k$. For example, if $\mathbf{g}$ is $(0,0,1,0,1,0,0,1)^T$, then the 3rd, 5th and 8th original packet get XOR'ed to produce the redundancy packet.

Receivers, in turn, use the redundancy packets to repair lost packets. To do this, they keep track of which original and redundancy packets were received and gradually fill (for every group) a matrix $\mathbf{G} \in \mathbf{M}_{\mathbb{F}_2}(k \times k)$ by copying the vector $\mathbf{g}$ from the packet header into the next free column of the matrix.[1] A redundancy packet is rejected if either the matrix is already complete or if the new vector would be a linear combination of the vectors already stored the matrix. In both cases, the receiver discards the packet. A receiver has completed reception if the matrices for all groups are filled.

[1] Original packets are assigned a vector $\mathbf{g}$ too, namely the i-th original packet is assigned the i-th unit vector.

Let $\mathbf{s}_i \in \mathbb{F}_2^{12000}$, $i = 1, ..., k$ be the original data packets (for some group) in binary representation and let $\mathbf{c}_i \in \mathbb{F}_2^{12000}$, $i = 1, ..., k$ be the set of received (original and redundancy) packets. Then the following property holds:

$$(\mathbf{s}_1, ..., \mathbf{s}_k) \cdot \mathbf{G} = (\mathbf{c}_1, ..., \mathbf{c}_k)$$

As a final step, the receiver determines the original packets by solving the equation for the $\mathbf{s}_i$, which can be done because $\mathbf{G}$ is regular by construction. In effect, this again requires XOR'ing together a set of packets, this time redundancy packets though.

The number k of packets per group determines the efficiency of erasure correction. Higher values are generally feasible, because received redundancy packets become increasingly likely to repair a lost packet within the group it belongs to; they require, however, more processing power and disk activity, especially for the sender. See [10] for details. Lower values for k cause the gain of erasure correction to gradually vanish. At an extreme, if $k = 1$, then MFTP/EC effectively becomes MFTP. In our simulations k was always 16.

The sender's selection of $\mathbf{g}$ is also crucial to the protocol's efficiency and is performed before every new pass. $\mathbf{g}$ does not change within a pass. Badly chosen values for $\mathbf{g}$ will frequently result in linear dependencies. We found that codesets with a large Hamming distance are also feasible for the set of values that can be assigned to $\mathbf{g}$ in order to avoid dependencies. For details see [10]. We will measure how often linear dependencies occurred in Section 5.2.

3 Simulation environment

We have used the simulator ns-2 [25] from U.C. Berkeley/LBNL to simulate network and protocol behavior. In ns-2, the user defines arbitrary network topologies, composed of routers, links and shared media. Protocol instances can then be attached to nodes. A rich set of protocols is available. For example, there are several TCP flavors, UDP, SRM and RTP. Likewise, the user may choose between various types of applications. Among them are FTP, Telnet, and HTTP, which use TCP as the underlying transport protocol, and applications requiring a constant bit rate (CBR) traffic pattern, which use the UDP transport protocol. Multiple router policies can be configured, among them are drop-tail, early random detect and fair queuing. The routing model can be static or dynamic and there is support for multicast routing. The simulator is event driven and runs in a non-real-time fashion. Packet losses are simulated by buffer overflows in routers, which is also the dominant way packets get lost in the Internet. There is also support for error models other than losses through buffer overflows.

Tiers [4, 2] was used to create "realistic" network topologies in an automated way. Tiers generates a fully connected network made up of three different categories: One is the backbone or *WAN*, to which the *MANs* are attached. Routers that belong to MANs, in turn, are points of attachment for *LANs*. Each category consists of several nodes, connected by point-to-point links. There exist various configuration parameters for the size of the network and the connectivity. Based on the parameters, Tiers generates a random network topology. Tiers also assigns links a bandwidth based on its category and a signal propagation delay based on both the category and the distance between the two endpoints.

We have developed a graphical, interactive tool for setting up and supervising simulations based on the network editor Tkined [23]. Our tool helps the user to set up simulations quickly and intuitively and to monitor several parameters of the network or the protocol instances visually, such as packet losses, link utilization, queue sizes (per link) and number of received packets (per multicast protocol instance).

4 Network and Simulation Characteristics

In this section, we give evidence that the characteristics of our simulation models correspond fairly well to the characteristics of real networks. We compare the behavior of our simulated networks to the MBone traces from Handley [8] and Yajnik *et al.* [26]. Similar characteristics for modeled and real networks are essential when deriving conclusions from simulations. In particular, we examine packet loss rates and packet loss correlations (both spatial and temporal).

Let's start looking at the generation of random network topologies. Figure 1 depicts one of the topologies used in our simulations. All topologies were created by running Tiers with different configuration parameters.[2] The figure shows one WAN, consisting of 5 backbone nodes (depicted by a large square), which are connected by 6 backbone links in a redundant way. These WAN-links were assigned a bandwidth of 34368 kbps for each direction, thus representing an E3 carrier. The medium-sized nodes made up the 25 MAN networks, which consisted of 3 nodes each. Links between MAN nodes and those connecting a MAN to a WAN were given a bandwidth of 8448 kbps (E2 carrier). Finally, each of the 300 LANs consisted of 2 nodes, connected by a 10 Mbps link and attached to a MAN by an E1 carrier (2048 kbps).

All links were assigned a buffer for each direction, which was capable of queueing up to 50 packets for transmission. A queue size of 50 packets is also the ns-2 default value. Routing tables were computed prior to the start of the simulation using the distance vector multicast routing protocol (DVMRP) and did not change during the simulation. The routing policy was FIFO.

[2]The nodes were repositioned later by hand to achieve better readability, but the structure remained unchanged.

We defined background traffic for all topologies. In particular, TCP-Reno- and UDP-protocol instances were set up between two randomly elected nodes. To reflect the heuristic that servers are more often concentrated on single machines (think of an ftp server for example) whereas clients are usually spread all over the network, we have placed the servers (in one test scenario) on a randomly elected subset (60%) of all nodes. Server election was performed independently for TCP and UDP traffic.

4.1 Packet loss rates

We have monitored packet loss rates on a link basis. Simulation results show that hardly any packet was dropped when each node was assigned only few (say 1 to 5) TCP connections. Packet loss was below 1% on most bottleneck links while link usage was over 90%. This low loss rate certainly does not match well with the MBone. When more traffic was set up, loss rates increased. The labels on the links in Figure 1 show the average link loss rates for the scenario depicted in the right column of Table 1. Numbers are only shown for values $\geq$0.05%. If two numbers appear in the same label, then each one represents the loss rate for one direction. The average was taken over a period of ca. 450 simulated seconds. The figure shows link loss rates between 0% and 21.5%.

Moderate link loss rates (that is, $<$10%) occurred in most cases, even though 40000 TCP-Reno connections (running FTP instances) and 4000 UDP sources (running a CBR instances) were simulated on the 680 nodes, each protocol instance starting at a time chosen from the uniform distribution on the interval $[0, 300s]$ (for details, refer to Table 1). Obviously, it is not realistic to assume that the average number of TCP-connections originating from a host within only a few minutes is more than 60.

So why don't occur substantial packet losses unless there is an unrealistic high number of TCP connections active? First of all, it reveals the strength of TCP's congestion control scheme. Secondly, configuring 60 wide-area connections per host is unrealistic (except perhaps for servers), but assuming 60 outgoing connections per LAN or per intranetwork is much more pragmatic. It was mentioned above that we modeled LANs by two nodes only, which is probably not accurate in today's Internet. We also didn't model LAN traffic properly. If we view a single LAN-node as a representant of a whole LAN or even of an intranetwork and consider the outgoing connections to originate from some host within that LAN, then 60 TCP connections become much more realistic. Put it this way, the network grows considerably in size, because each LANs in Figure 1 then aggregates several nodes.

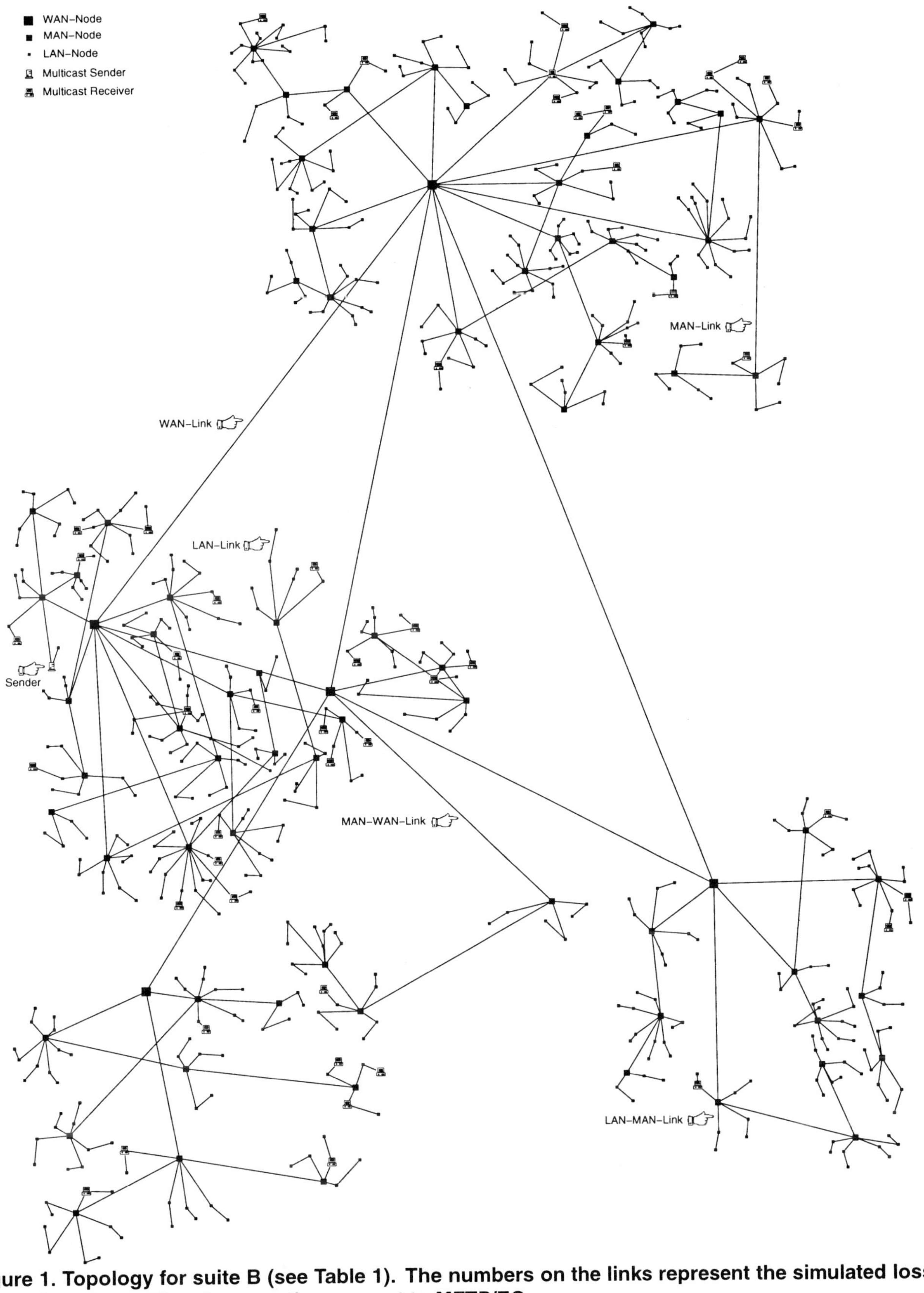

Figure 1. Topology for suite B (see Table 1). The numbers on the links represent the simulated loss rates when the multicast connection was set to MFTP/EC.

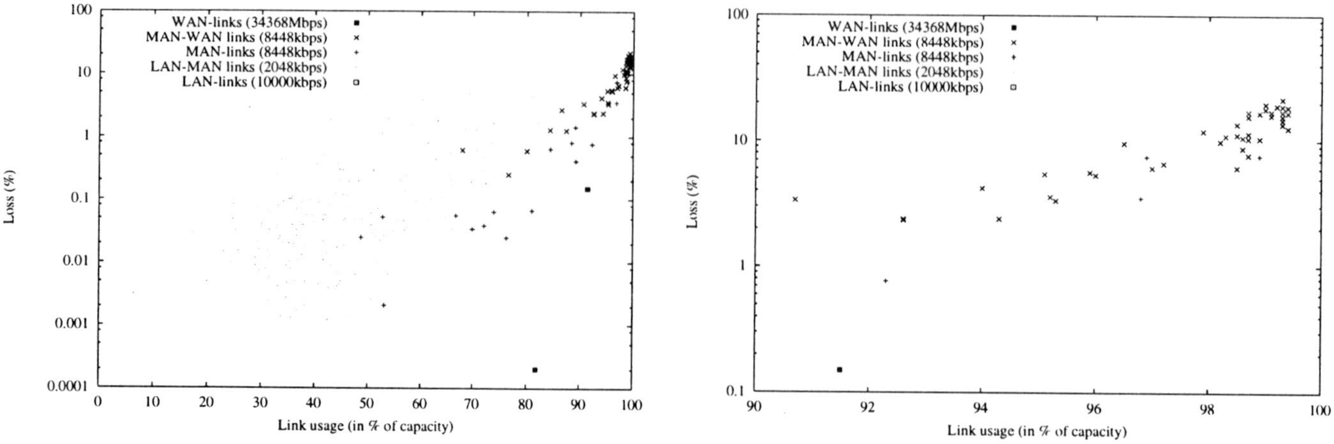

Figure 2. Link loss vs. usage for suite B. The right figure shows a part of the left figure in greater detail.

4.2 Spatial packet loss correlation

Let's look at the places where packets got lost in the MBone and where in our simulations.

Yajnik *et al.* [26] analyzed packet losses from MBone traces logged by audio multicast sessions over the MBone. The authors have used three different audio sources with up to 17 receivers that were spread all over the USA and Europe. Their measurements showed that only few packet losses occurred on the backbone links of the MBone. In general, the observed link loss rates ranged from 0.002% to 0.4% (with one notable exception of 6.6%)[3]. The rate at which packets got lost between the receivers and the backbone was much higher, ranging from 0.01% to 21.25%. Yajnik *et al.* further noted that very few packets were lost by only one receiver, that is, packets were unlikely to be dropped in the leaves of the network. In general, Yajnik *et al.* find that "spatially correlated loss in the network is low except for the loss next to the source".

Handley's MBone traces [8] are based on packet losses logged during multiple video sessions using the *vic video conferencing tool*. During the sessions, receivers were sending loss statistic reports to the monitoring workstation. Handley found that 50% of the receivers had a mean loss rate of 10% or lower, but that there were times when the loss rate was above 20% at 80% of the receivers and even that periods existed in which the loss rate was greater than 95% at 30% of the receivers. For most of the day, however, 25% of the receivers hardly lost any packets and the average loss rate was somewhere between 5% and 10%. 25% of the receivers experienced packet loss rates of more than 15% over hours. Handley also noticed that a small number of links are responsible for "larger scale correlation" of packet losses between receivers and that a large number of links existed with low loss rates, confirming that losses occur mainly spatially independently.

For a comparison to our simulations, refer to Figure 2, which shows the *link utilization/packet loss* relationship of the simulation in Figure 1. A different marker is used for each type of link. Links that did not drop any packets are not shown. We observe that no single packet was lost on LANs. Moderate packet losses occurred on links that connected a LAN to a MAN. Packet losses ranged from 0% to 6.7%, a typical value being around 0.1%. MAN-links lost packets from 0% to 7.5%. Packets were lost on MAN-WAN connections at loss rates up to 21.4%. Finally, only two WAN links lost packets with loss rates of 0.15% and 0.0002%, respectively.

Essentially, packets were dropped mostly on MAN-WAN links in our simulations, i.e. in branches that lead to or away from the backbone. Further, the large number of links closer to the leaves of the network lost packets at low rates. These properties meet well the MBone traces and therefore, we expect quite realistic spatial packet loss correlations. We will consequently see in Section 5.3 in accordance with Yajnik that losses show some component for high correlation between receivers, but mainly still occur independently.

The figure also reveals a moderate relationship between link utilization and loss rate: The higher the utilization, the more frequent do losses occur (although this appears to be only a rough trend). Interestingly, different types of links seem to have a different loss-utilization relationship. For example, a loss rate of 0.07% occurred on LAN-MAN links

[3]Yajnik's multicast tree only depicts a graph constructed of *virtual* links, where virtual links aggregate a series of physical links.

when they were used around 30-60% to their capacity on the average. The same loss rate occurred on MAN-links when the usage was approximately 50-80% and for a WAN-link to produce 0.07% packet losses, traffic had to exceed ca. 80-90% of the link's capacity. Among the WAN links which are not represented in the figure (because they did not drop any packet), one exceeded 73.1% and another one exceeded 63.6% of the link's capacity. Why the network behaves this way and whether or not the MBone has similar properties is a matter for further research.

4.3 Temporal packet loss correlation

We now examine in how far packet losses tended to occur in bursts. To measure the temporal correlation of packet losses at receivers, a multicast sender was set up in our simulations. It disseminated test packets to a set of receivers. The receivers logged the reception of each packet. The logfile was later examined in order to derive the number of burst errors of length n, $n = 0, 1, ...$[4]

Figure 3 shows the results of two scenarios that we have set up. For each burst of length n, the number of its occurrences is shown (as an aggregated value over all receivers). The straight lines in the graphs show how the curve would look like if losses were independently distributed in time. For example, if the average loss rate were q and N packets were sent, then burst errors of length $n = 5$ would be expected to occur $N \cdot (q^5 \cdot (1-q))$ times for the average receiver. Note that the scale in the graphs is logarithmic. All graphs clearly show that packet losses are more likely to occur in bursts rather than being independently distributed in time.

Handley and Yajnik also observed that packet losses in the MBone show a trend towards longer bursts than what would be expected from an independent loss distribution. Handley also reports that the "base losses" were superimposed by burst losses of length 7 to 10 packets, which occurred every 30s and which contributed to the average loss rate to 1.5%. Yajnik *et al.* make a similar statement. They both assume that this phenomenon is the result of a bug in some routers that occurs during the time of processing route updates. The bug was not modeled in our static routing model and was also not recognized. Moreover, Yajnik detected some rare, but very long burst losses, covering up to several hundred packets, which could also not be observed in our simulations.

As a conclusion, the simulation yields a burst loss distribution that is comparable with traces taken from the MBone as far as the base loss is concerned.

[4]Counting burst losses of length $n = 0$ means counting pairs of consecutively received packets (plus one if the very first packet was received).

5 Protocol Performance Measurements

In this chapter, the performance of SRM, MFTP and MFTP/EC is evaluated.

We discuss two different test suites, referred to as A and B, each one consisting of three simulations with an identical network topology, identical background (that is, unicast) traffic and one multicast connection with comparable settings. The simulations within a test suite only differed in the *type* of the multicast connection, which was one of SRM, MFTP or MFTP/EC. Setting up different multicast protocols in otherwise identical environments allows for a fair comparison. Refer to Table 1 for the configuration details.

The focus was on one-to-many burst data transfer. Therefore, there was only one SRM sender of fresh data, even though SRM provides a many-to-many service. Of course, when it came to retransmissions, all participants could eventually become a sender of repair packets.

5.1 Receiver loss rates

Figure 4 shows the loss rates that each receiver has experienced. The upper figure belongs to test suite A. Because little background traffic was configured, packet loss rates were moderate. In particular, the average receiver loss rate was 11%, 10.6% and 10.7% for SRM, MFTP and MFTP/EC, respectively. The lower figure belongs to suite B, where we see high packet loss rates, due to higher background traffic. Here, the respective average loss rates were 36.6%, 22.8% and 23.1%.

The reason why receiver loss rates are very similar between MFTP and MFTP/EC receivers and quite different from SRM receivers in both test suites is because of the different ways the protocols work and because the generated multicast traffic affects the network's characteristics and therefore the loss rates. For example, both MFTP- and MFTP/EC-senders multicast data packets and receivers send back NACK-packets in unicast mode at the end of each pass. The generated traffic pattern is therefore quite similar, although the same receiver generally needs different times to complete reception. SRM's traffic pattern, however, looks very different: Request packets (NACKs) are *multicast* to the entire group rather than sent in unicast mode, and repair packets may originate from any participant, not just from the original sender. Moreover, SRM's loss recovery starts right upon loss detection. In contrast, recovery in MFTP and MFTP/EC is not before the end of the regular transmission. Finally, SRM participants send session messages every 2s, which is unique to SRM.[5]

[5]The period defaults to 1s in the ns-2 SRM implementation [25]. However, this period was considered too short, because the relationship between bandwidth used for session messages would almost have exceeded

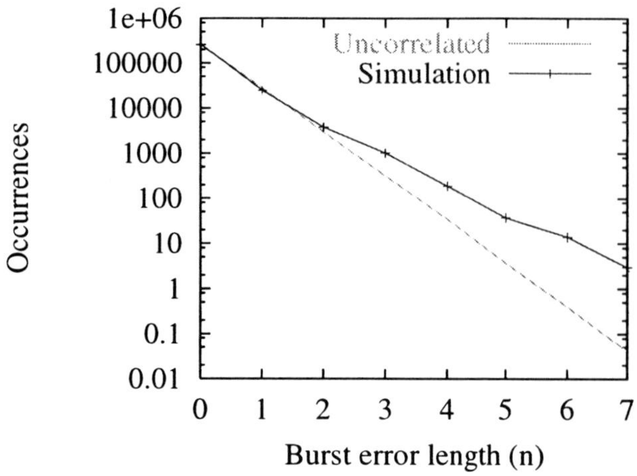

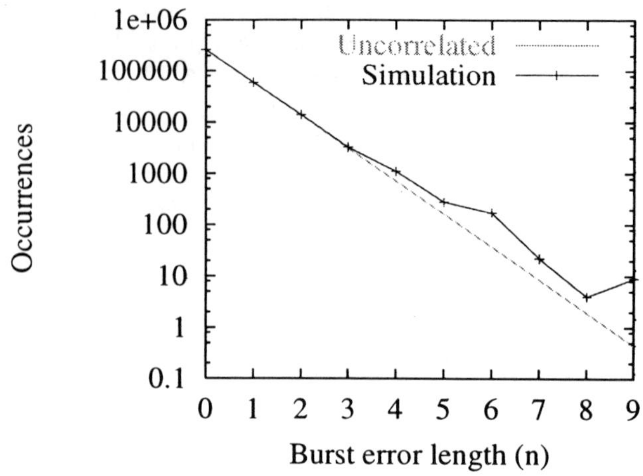

Figure 3. Distribution of burst errors for suites A (left) and B (right) with MFTP

In essence, we see slight differences in the receiver loss rates between MFTP and MFTP/EC and bigger differences between SRM and MFTP or MFTP/EC. The effect is visible in the upper figure. The reason why loss rates in the lower figure are generally much higher in SRM than in MFTP or MFTP/EC is because the current SRM implementation for ns-2 floods the network with repair packets substantially when loss rates are high, resulting in even higher loss rates due to additional traffic. We will further discuss this point below. However, SRM is a framework for reliable multicast that is still in progress. Recent proposals address the problems mentioned above by introducing a two-level hierarchy for session messages [24] and by using local error recovery, respectively [16]. Our simulation results clearly show the need for such enhanced mechanisms.

5.2 Bandwidth consumption

Let's take a look at bandwidth utilization. In all three protocols, data and repair packets are multicast to the whole group. It needs to be said that future revisions of SRM will probably include mechanisms to restrict retransmissions to a local scope. However, the current implementation addresses retransmissions to the whole group. Unlike SRM, MFTP's and MFTP/EC's repair phase starts at the end of the regular transmission, and receivers leave the multicast group as soon as they have completed the reception. Leaving the group causes the multicast tree to prune back, thus reducing unnecessary traffic. Therefore, to compare the cost of network utilization, we look at the *number of received packets* per receiver in each protocol. Using these statistics as an indicator for network utilization frees us from assessing and counting the cost for each individual packet flow within the network.

Receiver statistics also show evidence about which receivers suffer most from bad protocol performance, that is, which receivers must process a lot of *useless* packets. In SRM and MFTP, a useless packet is a double received packet. In MFTP/EC, a useless packet is one which transmission group is already complete or for which a linear dependence among the vectors $\mathbf{g}_i$ of the incoming and the already received packets arises (see Section 2.3). A packet is *useful* if it is not useless. For the following discussion, we neither consider repair requests in SRM nor NACK-packets in MFTP and MFTP/EC.

Figure 5 shows the result. Because the data transfer is reliable, all receivers have received the same number of useful packets, namely 4000 in both test suites. The six charts demonstrate that receivers with high loss rates showed a trend towards reception of only few useless packets. For example, receiver 30 in suite B experienced a high packet loss rate (see Figure 4 b) in all three protocols. Consequently, it received only few duplicate packets (see Figures 5 d,e,f), because a large number of missing packets meant that retransmissions often repaired a loss, and therefore did not count as useless packets.

For receivers with low loss rates, however, the number of useless packets is different in SRM as compared to MFTP or MFTP/EC. For example, receiver 20 in suite B experienced hardly any packet losses (see Figure 4 b). Figure 5 d demonstrates that this receiver had to process many double received packets with SRM while Figures 5 e,f show that it

the bandwidth used for data packets: A session message consists of $51 \cdot 4$ integers, that is, 816 byte (plus some header information) and gets multicast by each of the 51 participants to all group members. Therefore, in addition to 512 kbps data transmission rate, another 333 kbps would have been used for session messages. By doubling the interval, the session messages consumed only 166kbps of bandwidth. The shorter interval did not turn out to be a disadvantage to SRM in our tests.

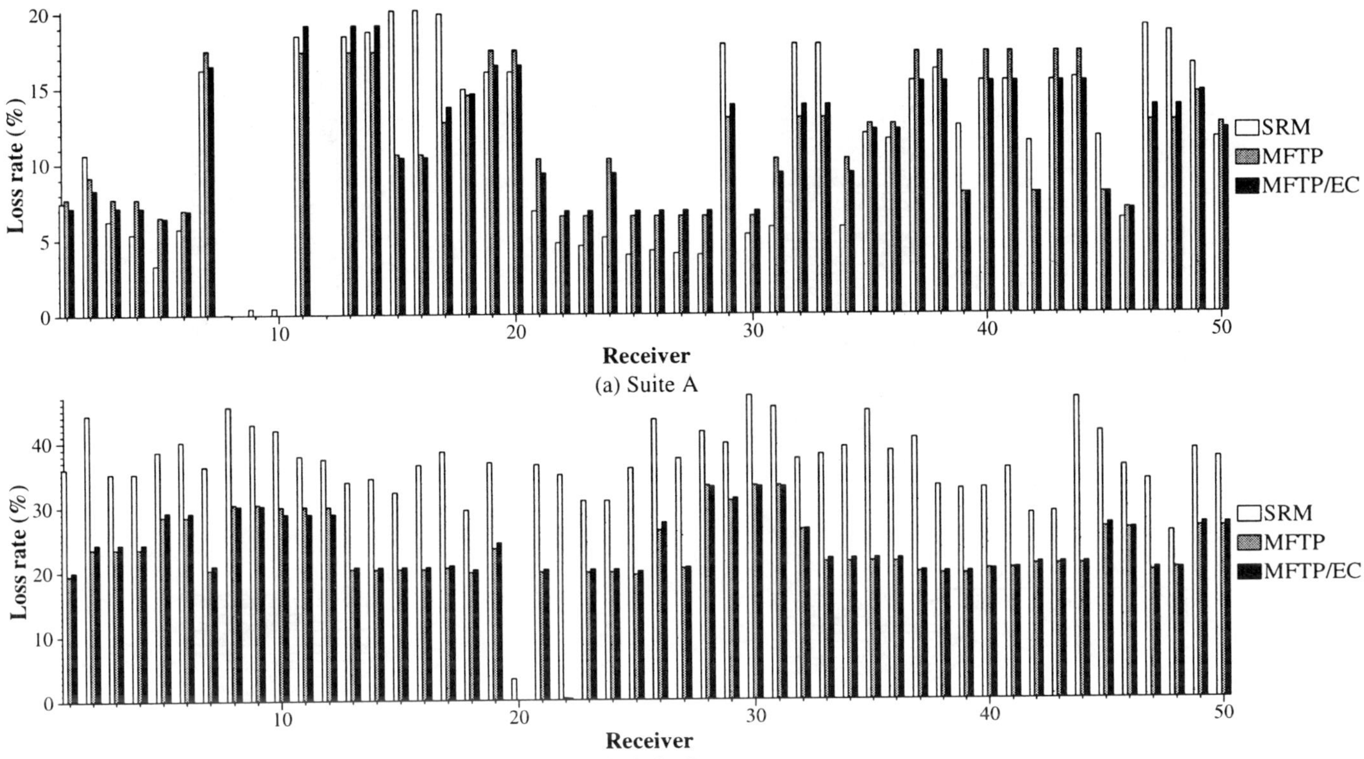

(a) Suite A

(b) Suite B

Figure 4. Receiver loss rates

	Suite A	Suite B
Topology	726 nodes (6 WAN, 60 MAN, 660 LAN) 727 links	680 nodes (5 WAN, 75 MAN, 600 LAN) 681 links
Background traffic	15000 TCP/FTP senders spread all over receivers spread all over 768 byte packet size 0...2048 kb file size 0...300 s start time	40000 TCP/FTP senders placed on 390 hosts receivers spread all over 1024 byte packet size 0...2048 kB file size 0...300 s start time
	2000 UDP/CBR senders spread all over receivers spread all over 1024 byte packet size 256 kbps transmission rate 1...100 s duration	4000 UDP/CBR senders placed on 390 hosts receivers spread all over 768 byte packet size 256 kbps transmission rate 1...100 s duration
Multicast traffic	One of SRM, MFTP, MFTP/EC 50 receivers 512 byte packet size 256 kbps transmission rate start time at 60 s 2000 kB file size Session messages frequency 2s (SRM) group size k=16 (MFTP/EC)	One of SRM, MFTP, MFTP/EC 50 receivers 512 byte packet size 256 kbps transmission rate start time at 60 s 2000 kB file size Session messages frequency 2s (SRM) group size k=16 (MFTP/EC)

Table 1. Test suite configuration details

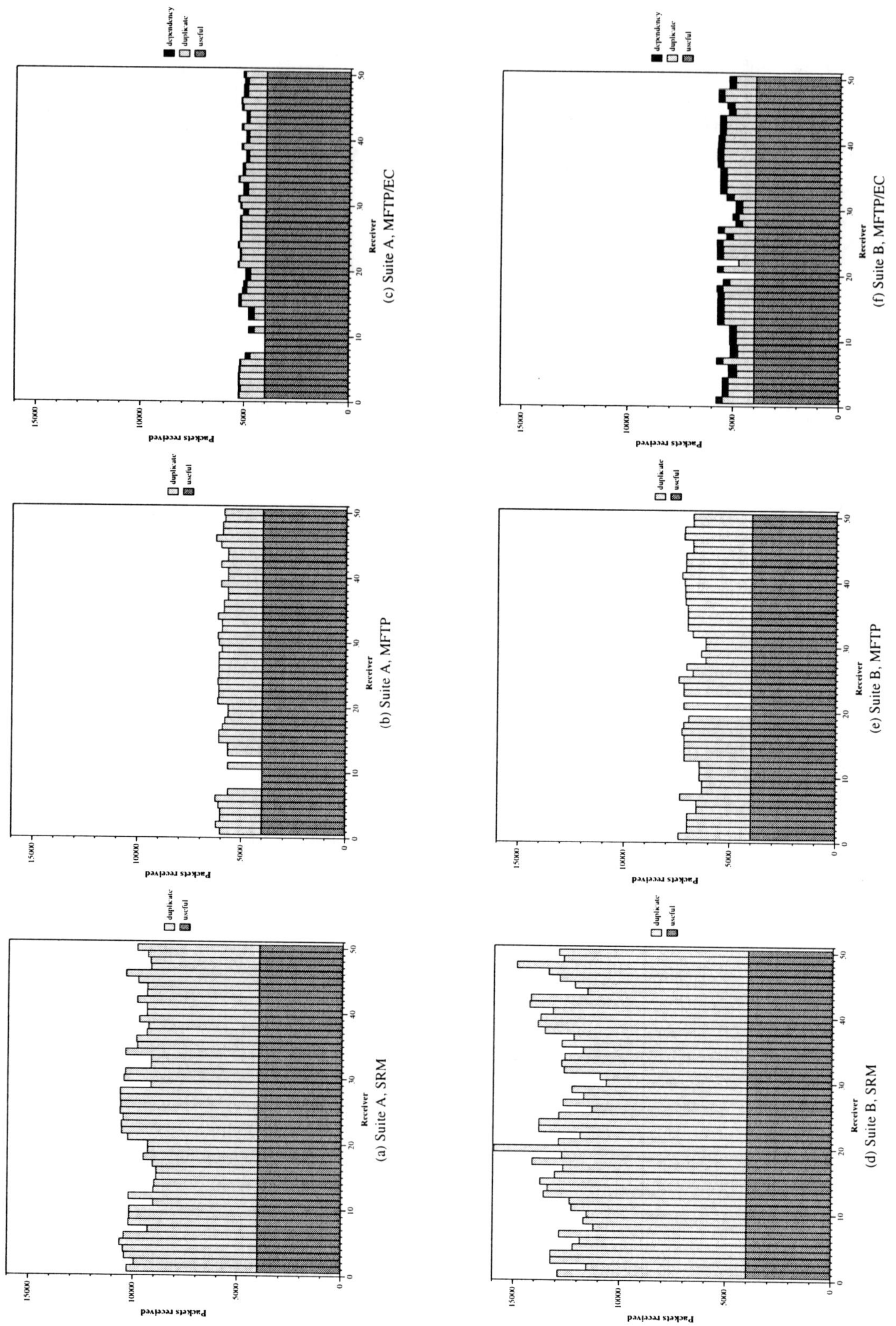

Figure 5. Receiver statistics for test suites A and B

received no duplicate packet at all with MFTP or MFTP/EC. The reason is that in MFTP or MFTP/EC, receivers with few losses finish reception quickly. Once they are done, they leave the multicast group and skip the repair phase. In contrast, because SRM's loss recovery takes place during the regular data transfer, receivers have no way to escape repair traffic. These results clearly show the need for enhanced error correction schemes when doing error recovery on the fly. These schemes might either provide some kind of local error recovery [14, 15, 27] or might use an FEC-based scheme as proposed in [20].

Looking at the general outcome, Figure 5 illustrates that MFTP/EC receivers needed the fewest number of repair packets for loss recovery. MFTP did a good job, too. We also see that the number of packets useless to an MFTP/EC receiver due to a linear dependence has only a minor impact on the protocol's efficiency. Our XOR-based erasure correction scheme is less efficient than the Reed-Solomon erasure correction scheme described in [22], because packets becoming useless this way could have been avoided. For practical reasons, though, our XOR-based approach is still a good alternative, because it requires much less computation power for the necessary coding and decoding of packets.[6] SRM receivers needed by far the most repair packets. Where does this come from?

SRM can easily run into a situation in which multiple repair packets are multicast in response to a single retransmission request. SRM tries to avoid this undesirable situation by setting and adapting various parameters, but by design, the problem still remains.[7] In contrast, the MFTP or MFTP/EC sender always multicasts just one repair packet (unless it got lost another time). Therefore, it is not surprising that SRM causes more network traffic. In return, SRM receivers recover from losses during the data transfer, not afterwards. This allows to use SRM for applications others than a simple file transfer.

5.3 Packet statistics in SRM

This section focuses on the issue of duplicate transmissions of request and repair packets in SRM.

Figure 6 presents two charts, corresponding to suite A and B. There is a thin column for each data packet, consisting of three bars of different colors. The grey bar indicates how many receivers lost the packet; the lengths of the black bar and the light grey bar on top represent the number of repair requests and repair packets being sent, respectively. The packets were sorted in decreasing order by the number of receivers that detected a loss.

[6] The XOR-based scheme works approximately 5 times faster than the Reed-Solomon based scheme from [22] if packets are cached in memory (that is, if they need not be re-read from disk). See [10] for details.

[7] Indeed, there is a trade-off in SRM between duplicate packet flow and loss recovery speed. We discuss SRM's recovery performance later on.

In each figure, we identify two categories of lost data packets, namely packets that almost all receivers have lost and those that rarely got lost. For example, in the upper figure, 132 packets were lost by 46 to 48 receivers while the remaining 2968 packets were lost by 1 to 22 receivers. (The remaining 900 data packets were received by all participants). Clearly, because the former set of packets show highly spatial correlation, they got lost on an uplink near the multicast sender. The latter set of packets show little spatial loss correlation and therefore got lost on a downlink near the receivers. The sharp contrast is due to the absence of substantial packet losses on backbone links, which was also found to be characteristic for the MBone [26]. We call the former set of packets *frequently lost packets* and the latter set *scarcely lost packets*.

In the upper figure, for each frequently lost packet, repair requests were sent between 2 and 12 times, the average being 6.3. Each scarcely lost packets was requested between 1 and 8 times, the average was 2.1. The number of repair packets sent was between 1 and 7 times for the frequently lost packets (average: 2.5) and between 1 and 10 times for the scarcely lost packets (average: 2.3).

The values for the lower figure are higher, as expected: Repair requests were sent for the frequently lost packets between 1 and 18 times, 6.6 on the average and between 1 and 11 times for the scarcely lost packets (2.6 on the average). Each frequently lost packet was repaired between 1 and 11 times (average: 4.3) and each scarcely lost packet between 1 and 10 times (average: 3.4).

For both suites, we conclude that the values for the average number of repair requests differs between frequently lost packets and scarcely lost packets while the values for the average number of repair packets is similar. The reason is that the number of receivers which miss a data packet and schedule a request is usually low. Therefore, SRM can set tight bounds for the request timer interval (by adapting parameters C_1 and C_2) while still preventing duplicate repair requests reasonably well. Occasionally, however, a packet gets lost by the majority of the receivers, and then the request timers settings are too tight, causing a lot of duplicate repair requests.

In contrast, repair packets are scheduled upon reception of a request, and the set of potential responders is usually almost all group members. This causes SRM to widen the timer interval for transmission of repair packets (parameters D_1 and D_2). If occasionally, however, only few receivers receive the request packet, then the repair timers will certainly take longer than necessary to expire, but this will not introduce a high duplicate packet flow.

If request or repair packets get lost, then receivers will require additional rounds for loss recovery. They will send a second, third, etc. request packet. If this happened in the simulations, the additional request and repair packets were

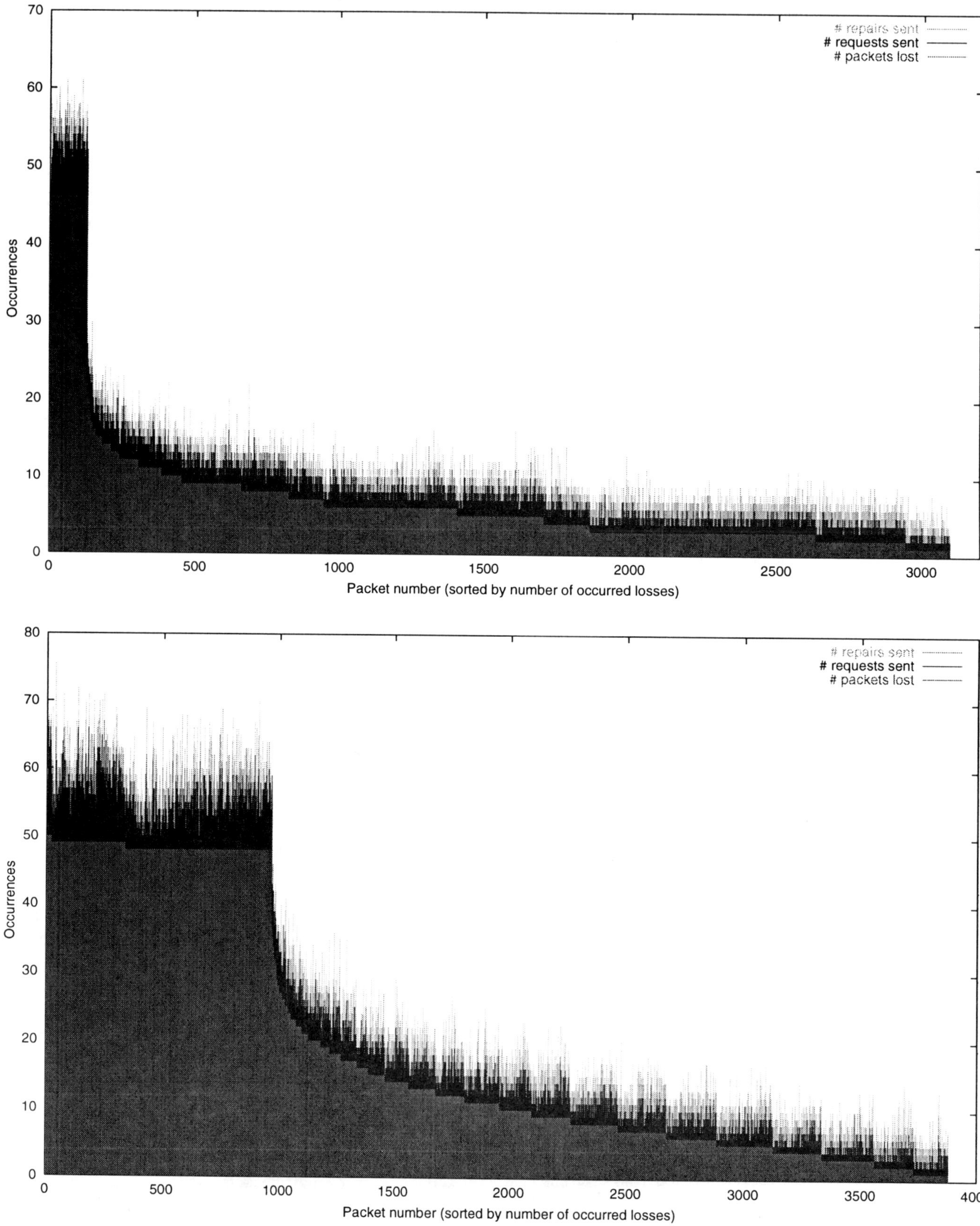

Figure 6. SRM's packet loss statistics for suites A (above) and B (below)

added to the ones from the first round to yield the figures.

As a conclusion, every lost packet triggered 2.27 request packets and 2.33 repair packets on average in suite A. Lost packets in suite B needed an average of 3.56 request packets and 3.62 repair packets for recovery.

5.4 Recovery speed in SRM

Until now, we have ignored the better service that SRM offers to the application: SRM hands up packets "roughly" in order, as opposed to MFTP and MFTP/EC, which can completely scramble the proper sequence. For this reason, SRM is suitable for a wider range of applications.[8]

One example could be a multicast file transfer where data is read from or written to streaming devices such as tapes, that is, where data cannot be randomly accessed. SRM can also be deployed in real-time applications in which it is feasible to buffer incoming data for several seconds. For example, radio over the MBone is a candidate application for SRM: By buffering incoming packets, receivers have in many cases enough time to recover from lost packets before the packet's contents is used to play the sound. Therefore, the receivers can improve reception quality with SRM at the expense of a delayed playback.

Let's see how close SRM gets to a perfectly sequenced delivery. Have a look at Figure 7. Each graph shows the packet reception times (that is, either the time at which the original packet or a repair packet was first received) for three receivers with different loss rates. The higher a peek in the figure is, the longer it took the receiver to receive a repair packet. We have chosen the receivers with the lowest positive, the highest and some middle packet loss rate. Note that all receivers started reception at time 60s, though we have separated the curves for better readability by shifting them 20s up or down.

The upper graph shows good recovery for the receiver with a loss rate of 3.3%. Recovery worked worse for the other receivers: Although most of the time, packet recovery was quick, there are some rare, but high peeks of approximately 20s. Moreover, there was one exceptional high peek of 67.7s for packet number 3841, meaning that recovery took more than a minute.

The lower figure again shows that packet recovery was quick for the receiver with a low loss rate of 3.4%. It could almost seamlessly hand up packets in order. The receiver with 25.9% recovered from most lost packets within 20s, and the receiver with the highest loss rate, 47.1% got the last missing packet at time 172.9s, long after the regular data transfer. If the application needed packets in order, it would have to wait a long time and to buffer a lot of packets.

[8] Another benefit is that SRM provides a many-to-many multicast service, as opposed to MFTP and MFTP/EC, but we did not use this feature for our simulations.

6 Conclusion

With the appearance of a large variety of multicast protocols, appropriate methods for evaluation and assessment become more and more essential. While real network experiments in a large scale are pretty complicated, simple mathematical analysis is not sufficient for evaluation of complex multicast behavior. Network simulation is a promising approach, especially for large-scale multicast communication. However, it is essential to carefully design realistic network models that reflect real network behavior.

We have described the design and the implementation of a large-scale network model for multicast communication using the network simulator ns-2. We have focused on the provision of realistic network simulations which model the network and protocol instances in great detail. Network topology, link capacities, propagation delays and background traffic were chosen in a way that yielded roughly similar loss properties with the MBone.

The simulation models have been used to evaluate three example multicast protocols, namely SRM, MFTP, and MFTP/EC. These protocols were chosen because their source code has been available for integration into ns-2. We have run simulations for two different test suites, one with light and the other one with intensive background traffic.

The simulation results clearly show that multicasting repair packets to the entire global group can cause significant bandwidth usage. MFTP tries to treat this problem by simply delaying error recovery until the end of each pass. Receivers leave the multicast communication as soon as they are done, thus reducing reception of unnecessary repair packets. Network load could be further decreased by using a parity based error recovery scheme such as in MFTP/EC. Bandwidth usage of SRM has been quite high. However, we expect improvements by integrating local error recovery and hierarchical session message distribution into SRM.

The simplicity and the benefits of MFTP and MFTP/EC come for the cost of flexibility. Both protocols are restricted to file transfer applications, where data can randomly be accessed. (StarBurst has recently developed a special type of "streaming mode" service for MFTP, though.) Writing received data to streaming devices such as tapes causes additional problems. SRM is much more flexible in that it supports many-to-many communication and streaming-mode applications. In particular, SRM recovers from losses as soon as they are detected. SRM can therefore be deployed for interactive applications, especially if minor deviations from a perfectly sequenced packet stream can be tolerated.

Our simulations yield short loss recovery times for SRM, most often below 2s when loss rates were around 10%, and within 10s when loss rates were around 30%. However, some rare, but long recovery times occurred, longer than 60s. Those recovery times were due to multiple losses of

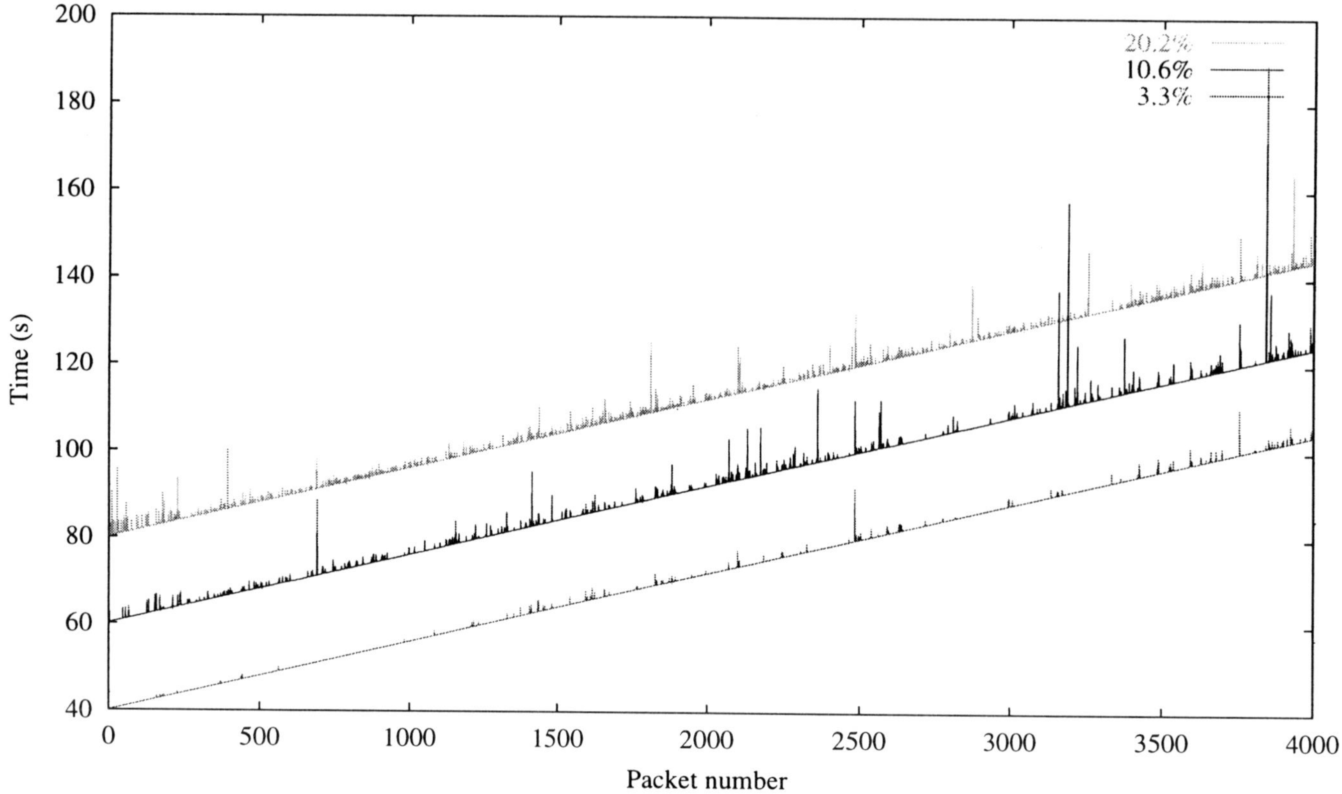

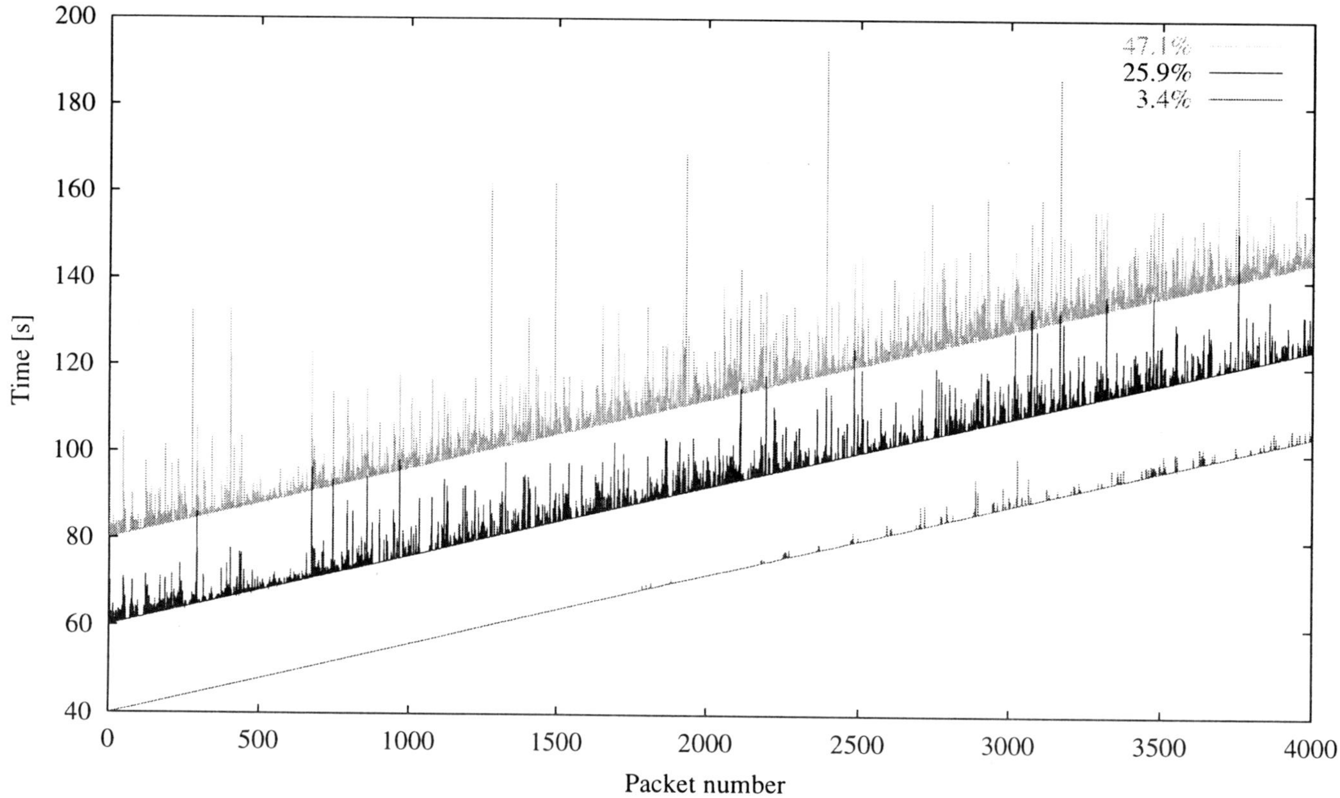

Figure 7. Packet recovery times for suites A (above) and B (below)

request or repair packets, causing receivers to backoff several times (for example, 3 or 4 backoffs were not unusual). If it is expensive for the application to conceal lost packets for a long time from the user, this might be a drawback.

We did not investigate scalability issues due to resource limitations: Some simulations had memory requirements of more than 1GB and ran for roughly one day on a 2x296Mhz Sparc Ultra. In larger sessions, we expect that NACK implosion becomes a problem for MFTP or MFTP/EC and session message traffic for SRM. In addition, more work needs to be done in order to compare these protocols to other approaches. In particular, it would be very interesting to simulate sub-group based and tree-based multicast protocols, none of which has yet been ported to ns-2. We hope that this will change in the future.

References

[1] M. H. Ammar. Improving the Throughput of Point-to-Multipoint ARQ Protocols Through Destination Set Splitting. Technical report, Georgia Institute of Technology, 1992. Also available as `http://mmlab.snu.ac.kr/~yslee/multicast/GIT-CC-92-13.ps.gz`.

[2] K. L. Calvert, M. B. Doar, and E. W. Zegura. Modeling Internet Topology. *IEEE Communications Magazine*, June 1997. Also available as `http://www.geocities.com/ResearchTriangle/3867/publications.html`.

[3] D. Clark and D. Tennenhouse. Architectural considerations for a New Generation of Protocols. In *Proceedings of ACM SIGCOMM*, pages 201–208, Sept 1990.

[4] M. B. Doar. A Better Model for Generating Test Networks. In *Proceedings of Globecom*, Nov 1996. Also available as `ftp://ftp.nexen.com/pub/papers`.

[5] S. Floyd, V. Jacobson, C.-G. Liu, S. McCanne, and L. Zhang. A Reliable Multicast Framework for Light-weight Sessions and Application Level Framing. In *ACM Sigcomm Conference*, pages 342–356, Aug 1995.

[6] M. Fuchs, C. Diot, T. Turletti, and M. Hofmann. A Framework for Reliable Multicast in the Internet. Technical Report RR-3363, INRIA, Sophia Antipolis, France, February 1998.

[7] M. Fuchs, C. Diot, T. Turletti, and M.Hofmann. A Naming Approach for ALF Design. In *Third International Workshop on High Performance Protocol Architectures (HIPPARCH)*, London, England, June 15-16, 1998.

[8] M. Handley. An Examination of MBone Performance. `http://north.east.isi.edu/~mjh/mbone.ps`, Jan 1997.

[9] M. Handley. Reference Simulations for Reliable Multicast Congestion Control Schemes. Draft Notes presented at IRTF RM Group Meeting, London, United Kingdom, July 6-7 1998.

[10] C. Hänle. A Comparison of Architecture and Performance between Reliable Multicast Protocols over the MBone. masters thesis, `http://www.cs.vu.nl/~chris/Thesis/Thesis.ps.gz`, Institut für Telematik, University of Karlsruhe, 1997.

[11] M. Hofmann. Homepage of the Local Group Concept (LGC). `http://www.telematik.informatik.uni-karlsruhe.de/~hofmann/LocalGroups.html`.

[12] M. Hofmann. *Worldwide MBone Experiments using LGMP*. Third IRTF RM Meeting, Orlando, FL, USA, February 22-24, 1998, Slides available at `http://www.east.isi.edu/rm/`.

[13] M. Hofmann. *Scalable Multicast Communication in Wide Area Networks*. Ph.D Thesis (in German), Institute of Telematics, University of Karlsruhe, Germany, Infix Publisher, Feb 1998.

[14] M. Hofmann and M.Rohrmüller. Impact of Virtual Group Structure on Multicast Performance. In A. Danthine and C. Diot, editors, *From Multimedia Services to Network Services*, number 1356 in Lecture Notes in Computer Science, pages 165–180. Springer Verlag, 1997. Proc. of Fourth International COST 237 Workshop, December 15-19, 1997, Lisboa, Portugal.

[15] J. C. Lin and S. Paul. RMTP: A Reliable Multicast Transport Protocol. In *Proceedings of IEEE INFOCOM*, pages 1414–1424, Mar 1996.

[16] C. Liu, D. Estrin, S. Shenker, and L. Zhang. Local error recovery in srm: Comparison of two approaches. Technical Report 97-648, USC Computer Science Department, January 1997.

[17] M. T. Lucas. *Efficient Data Distribution in Large-Scale Multicast Networks*. Ph.D Thesis, University of Virginia, May 1998.

[18] K. Miller, K. Robertson, A. Tweedly, and M. White. StarBurst Multicast File Transfer Protocol (MFTP) Specification. `draft-miller-mftp-spec-02.txt`, Jan 1997.

[19] MIST. Multicast Implementation Study. `http://www.tascnets.com/mist/`.

[20] J. Nonnenmacher, E. W. Biersack, and D. Towsley. Parity-based loss recovery for reliable multicast transmission. In *Proceedings of ACM SIGCOMM'97, Cannes, France*, 1997.

[21] S. Pingali, D. F. Towsley, and J. F. Kurose. A Comparison of Sender-Initiated and Receiver-Initiated Reliable Multicast Protocols. In *SIGMETRICS*, pages 221–230, 1994.

[22] L. Rizzo. Effective erasure codes for reliable computer communication protocols. *Computer Communication Review*, April 1997. Also available as `http://www.iet.unipi.it/~luigi/fec_ccr.ps.gz`.

[23] J. Schönwälder. Scotty, Tkined, Tnm. `http://wwwsnmp.cs.utwente.nl/~schoenw/scotty`.

[24] P. Sharma, D. Estrin, S. Floyd, and L. Zhang. Scalable Session Messages in SRM. Technical report, USC Computer Science Department, February 1998.

[25] UCB/LBNL/VINT. Network Simulator ns-2. `http://www-mash.cs.berkeley.edu/ns/`.

[26] M. Yajnik, J. Kurose, and D. Towsley. Packet Loss Correlation in the Mbone Multicast Network. In *Proceedings IEEE Global Internet Conference*, London, Nov 1996.

[27] R. Yavatkar, J. Griffioen, and M. Suda. A Reliable Dissemination Protocol for Interactive Collaborative Application. In *Proceedings of the ACM Multimedia '95 Conference*, November, 1995.

Adaptive Sampling Methods to Determine Network Traffic Statistics including the Hurst Parameter

Jack Drobisz and Kenneth J. Christensen
Department of Computer Science and Engineering
University of South Florida
Tampa, FL 33620
Email: {*drobisz, christen*}*@csee.usf.edu*

Abstract

Accurate traffic characterization by packet source is needed to predict network behavior and to properly allocate network resources to achieve a desired Quality of Service for all network users. As networks have become faster, the processing load required for complete packet sampling has also grown. In some cases, for example Gigabit Ethernet, the network can deliver packets faster than a network management subsystem can process them. In order to prevent inaccurate traffic statistics due to "clipping" of traffic peaks, Claffy et al. applied several static sampling strategies to network traffic characterization. As shown in this paper, static sampling may produce inaccurate traffic statistics. In this paper, adaptive sampling methods are developed and evaluated to address inaccuracies of static sampling. In addition, the estimation of the Hurst parameter, a measure of traffic self-similarity, is studied for static and adaptive sampling. It is shown that adaptive sampling results in a more accurate estimation of the mean, variance, and Hurst parameter for packet counts.

1. Introduction

With the advent of Gigabit Ethernet and other high-speed network technologies, direct measurement of packet-switched traffic by packet origin has become impossible unless a very fast processor is dedicated to traffic measurement. A slower, and thus less expensive, processor may be used if statistical sampling of network traffic is implemented. With sampling, not all packets are received and "measured" by a network management node, but only a selected fraction of all packets. Future high-speed networks are likely to carry many distinct types of traffic including bulk data transfer, real-time voice and video, and playback video. Recent work (see [2] and [8]) have shown that network traffic may exhibit properties of Long-Range Dependence (LRD) or self-similarity. Self-similar traffic exhibits bursts at multiple time scales and results in greater resource requirements than if simple Poisson models are used for network capacity planning. One measure of self-similarity is the Hurst parameter (see [8]). Being able to estimate the Hurst parameter as part of ongoing traffic measurement is important.

Statistical sampling of network traffic was first used by Claffy et al. (see [4]) in the early 1990's for traffic measurement on the NSFNET backbone. Claffy et al. studied classical event and time driven static sampling methods to reduce the number of packets that would need to be received and processed by a network management node. With sampling during periods of peak traffic the network management processor would not be over-utilized resulting in missed packets, or "clipped" peaks. However, during periods of low traffic, the network management processor may have idle capacity that could be used to more accurately characterize network traffic given a finer sampling granularity. This is the key observation to our research, that static sampling may result in under-utilization of a network management processor and inaccurate traffic measurements. In addition, Claffy et al. did not characterize network traffic by packet origin and did not estimate measures of self-similarity. In this paper an adaptive sampling method is developed that will be shown to more effectively utilize network management processing capabilities and result in better estimates of traffic measures than static sampling.

The remainder of this paper is organized as follows. Section 2 reviews static sampling methods and Section 3 reviews self-similarity. Section 4 describes the Network

0-8186-8810-6/98 $10.00 © 1998 IEEE

Management Subsystem (NMS) which implements traffic sampling. This NMS can be implemented as part of a switch, repeater, or other network component. Section 5 describes the new adaptive sampling methods and Section 6 describes the comparative evaluation of the sampling methods. Section 7 is a summary followed by references.

2. Review of Static Sampling Methods

In the early 1990's, the T1 NFS backbone traffic statistics collected using the NNStat collection mechanism (see [3]) were shown to occasionally result in a loss of statistical information during periods of high backbone utilization. Sampling every 50th packet resulted in a significant improvement in accuracy of statistics taken under high utilization periods [4]. In [4] Claffy et al. describe the application of event and timed-based sampling to network traffic measurement. The three algorithms studied were, systematic, stratified random, and simple random and are shown in Figure 1. In event based or "packet triggered" sampling, packets are counted to determine when the next packet is to be sampled, whereas in timer-based sampling a "timer trigger" is used. Time-based sampling was shown to be less accurate than event-based. Of the event-based sampling methods, all three algorithms could be used for characterizing network traffic.

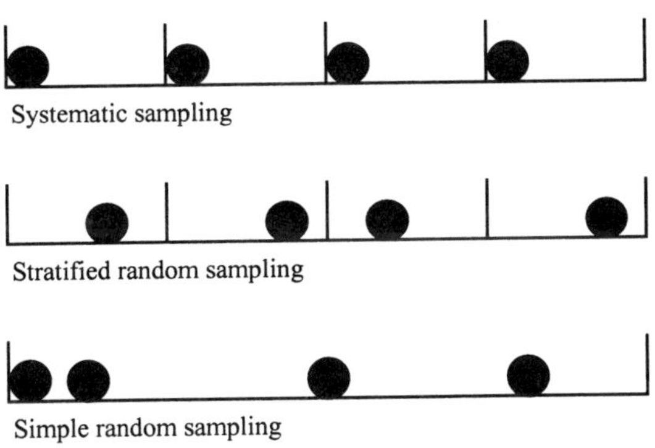

Figure 1 - Fixed granularity sampling (from [4])

3. Self Similarity of Network Traffic

The concept of self-similarity in the communications field was first introduced by Mandelbrot [9]. He proposed a fractal like model of random error perturbations that appeared to come in bursts not unlike those observed in the early hydrological data studied by Hurst [1]. In 1994, Leland, Taqqu, Willinger and Wilson demonstrated the presence of slowly decaying packet count bursts across all time scales in traffic on an operational corporate Ethernet LAN [8]. Time series with these characteristics are considered to exhibit LRD and are termed "self similar". Figure 2 shows event counts of Poisson and Pareto distributions for multiple time scales. For each series, the mean number of events per second is 1000. It can be seen that the Poisson time series becomes "smoother" as the aggregation level increases, however the Pareto series maintains its bursty appearance and is hence "self-similar" across multiple time scales.

In the past few years, several non-conventional models such as fractional Brownian motion, fractional Auto-Regressive Integrated Moving Average (ARIMA) and chaotic maps had been proposed to simulate self-similar network traffic. Recently, it was shown that a simpler model based on a Pareto distribution might be sufficient. Gordon et al. [7] stipulated that self-similar network traffic is a consequence of power law tails in packet inter-arrival times. Based on this insight, a model based on the Pareto distribution is,

$$Pareto(x) = \frac{\beta^{\alpha}}{(\beta + x)^{\alpha}} \qquad (1)$$

where, α and β are constants and x ranges from 0 to ∞. This distribution can be used to generate self-similar synthetic network traffic (i.e., packet inter-arrival times). In this work, the *inverse-transform method* was used to generate a continuous random variate having distribution function:

$$Pareto^{-1}(x) = -\beta + \frac{\beta}{U^{\frac{1}{\alpha}}}. \qquad (2)$$

The four measures considered in this study are the packet count mean, variance, peak-to-mean ratio (PMR), and Hurst parameter. The PMR is calculated by comparing the peak value with the average value from the population and it is often used as a measure of traffic burstiness, where high PMR means a high burstiness of traffic. This statistic is heavily dependent on the size of the intervals, and therefore may or may not represent the actual traffic [5]. A more accurate indicator of traffic burstiness is given by the Hurst parameter, which can be derived from the re-scaled adjusted range (R/S) statistic.

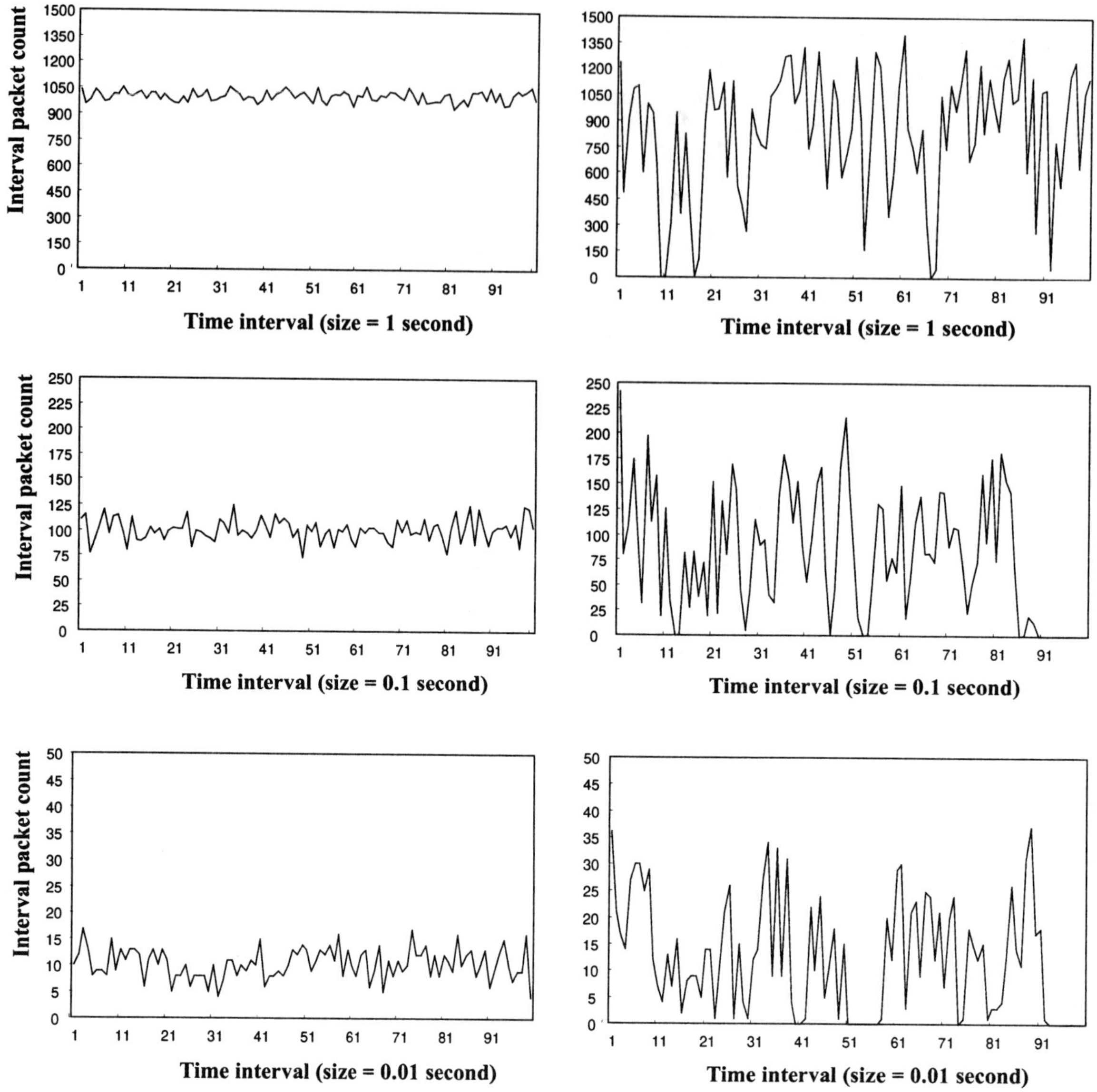

Figure 2 - Illustration of self-similarity (Poisson with $\lambda = 1000$ versus inverse-Pareto with $\alpha = 1.1$ and $\beta = 0.0002$)

The *R/S* statistic is one of several methods to estimate the Hurst parameter (see also [1] and [6]). Hurst discovered that many naturally occurring time series are well represented by the relation,

$$E[R(n)/S(n)] \approx cn^{H} \tag{3}$$

where as $n \to \infty$ c is an integer constant and H is a Hurst parameter ($0.50 < H < 1.0$). The estimation of H values can be based on a heuristic graphical approach involving linear regression as described in [8]. The data sets resulting in H values between 0.70 and 1.0 are considered to exhibit self-similarity.

4. A Network Management Subsystem

Traffic sampling can be implemented within network devices such as repeaters, switches, routers and so on. Such a device would contain a network management subsystem (NMS) with functionality similar to that shown in Figure 3. Existing standards such as SNMP and RMON already address collection of network management data at remote nodes. Collected network management data, including traffic statistics, are the periodically transmitted from the remote nodes to a central "network manager" host that formats and presents the data to a network administrator.

As shown in Figure 3, a hardware *counter* is used to count down all incoming packets and to open the processor register *gate* as dictated by the sampling strategy. During processing time in the *CPU*, the packet header is parsed and its source address is determined.

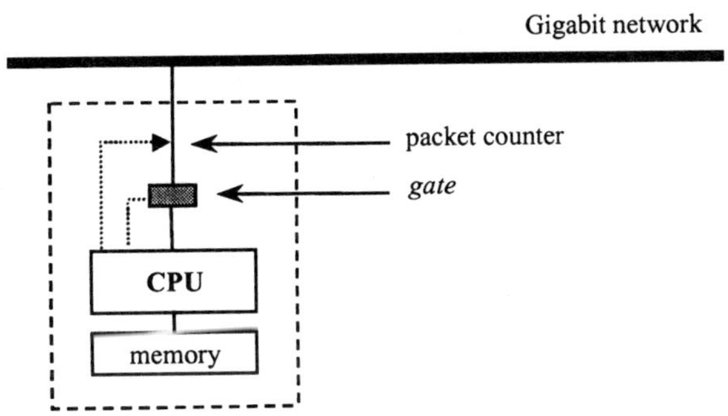

Figure 3 - Network management subsystem (NMS)

The packet source is used to group the packets and it could be represented by the IP or MAC address of a machine where the traffic originated. Once the packet is processed and its source is known, it is added to the corresponding time "bucket" in the internal *memory* to be used in future traffic characterization by source as requested by the NMS software. Figure 4 shows the timing diagram for packet sampling. The fixed processing time of each packet is a constant t_{proc}. The time until the next sample should be taken is t_{susp} and the delay until the packet actually arrives at the gate is t_{wait}. The total time *T* between two samples is:

$$T = t_{proc} + t_{susp} + t_{wait} \tag{4}$$

and the CPU utilization for traffic measurements is given by:

$$U_{CPU} = \frac{t_{proc}}{T} \tag{5}$$

After each packet is processed, the packet *counter* in the NMS is reset to a value determined by the sampling strategy. Packets may be of a variable length, but for the purpose of this study it was assumed that they take a fixed time to parse (e.g., based only on the first 64 bytes which contain the routing information used to group samples together). The *gate* is closed during the packet processing, or t_{proc}. This constant amount of time depends on the speed of the processor used as well as the number of instructions required to parse and process the packet. During t_{proc} the following steps are performed:

- Receive the packet into to the NMS
- Parse the packet header and determined its source address
- Locate (e.g., via a hashing algorithm) and increment the current source counter in memory
- Compute and set the value of the packet *counter*

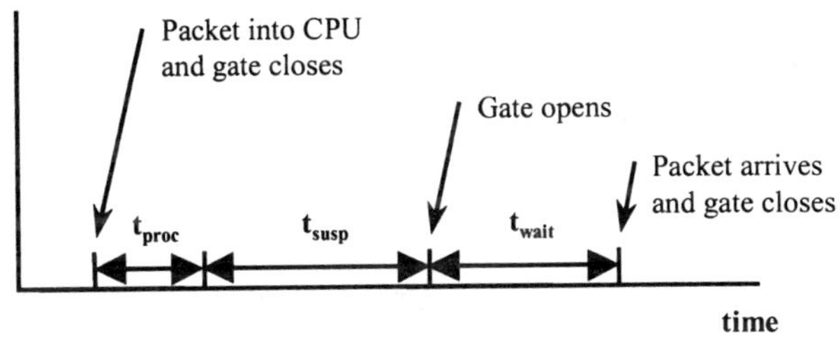

Figure 4 - Deterministic packet sampling timing

We estimate 50 to 200 lines of assembly code to perform the processing steps for a packet. In a Gigabit Ethernet, a 64-byte packet with 8 byte preamble and 12 byte interpacket gap is 672 nanoseconds in length, which equates to 1,488,095 packets per second maximum throughput. Thus, in a worst-case of 100% network throughput with all small packets, an NMS that samples and processes all packets would require approximate 75 to 300 million instructions per second (MIPS) processing power, or greater processing power than even high-end 1998 PC and workstation processors. Even at lower network throughputs and with larger packet sizes, the amount of processing power needed for sampling and processing all packets is non-trivial.

In this study we assume a 50 MIPS processor and an optimistic 50 instructions to receive and process a packet resulting in $t_{proc} = 1$ microsecond. Since the network management subsystem will perform tasks other than traffic measurement, the CPU was assumed to be available only half the time resulting in a target 50% CPU utilization for the sampling task and up to 25% of the traffic sampled. Allocating 50% of the CPU time for the task of static traffic measurement. Since wire utilization is likely to vary greatly over time, it seems logical that a better approach would be to let the NMS sampling algorithm fully utilize the CPU within a desired limit. This is the basis of the three new adaptive sampling methods described in the next section.

5. Development of Adaptive Sampling

In [4] the developed sampling methods were use to characterize a traffic stream independent of packet origins. This greatly reduces the processing required per packet (e.g., the packet source address does not have to be parsed and counted). It is desirable to be able to characterize traffic by packet origin to be able to determine if one or many sources are contributing to a specific traffic characteristic, and which applications and hosts are identified with those characteristics. Packet origin could be characterized by MAC address or IP address. Address pairs could also be monitored. The proposed adaptive sampling methods extend the work in [4] by adding source characterization and varying sampling granularity to control processor utilization. In this study Poisson and self-similar traffic streams are combined. Then, using sampling methods the characteristics of each stream are estimated. Figure 5 shows fixed granularity systematic sampling from [4].

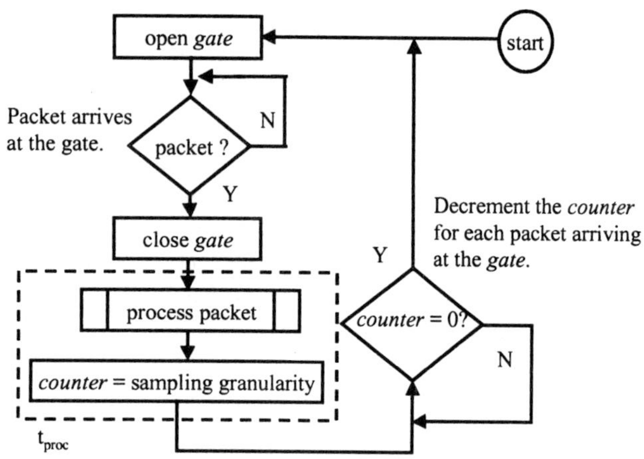

Figure 5 - Systematic sampling with processing delay.

Figure 6 shows the "CPU guard" adaptive sampling method where the sampling granularity as controlled by the counter is a function of CPU utilization. If CPU utilization is low (due to a low rate of packet arrivals), the counter set value is reduced for the next sample with a limit of complete sampling (i.e., all packets are sampled). Alternatively, if the CPU utilization is above a preset desired utilization, the counter set value is increased. The actual CPU utilization is calculated by dividing the desired processing time by the average time between two samples since the beginning of the trace. The second and third adaptive methods are partially based on the expectation that the network traffic exhibits temporal and source locality. In [6] it is observed that most traffic peaks are preceded by warning signs of increasingly higher congestion. This decrease in the inter-arrival time rate was used to replace the CPU utilization ratio with an Interarrival time ratio to "anticipate" the incoming "burst". Figure 7 shows the "IT guard" (IT = packet interarrival time) method. The last method combines the CPU and IT guard methods and is not shown in order to save space.

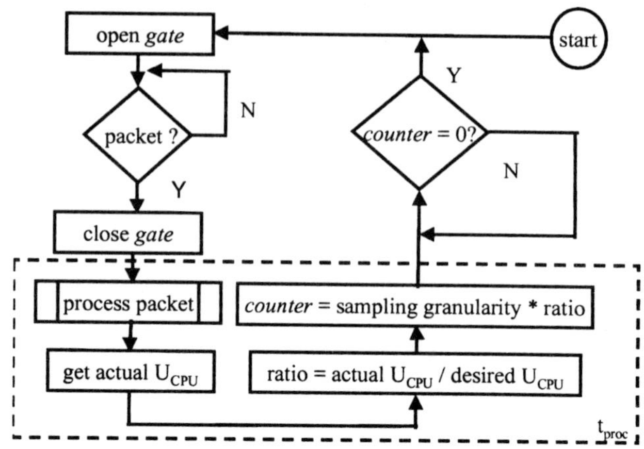

Figure 6 - Adaptive sampling with "CPU guard"

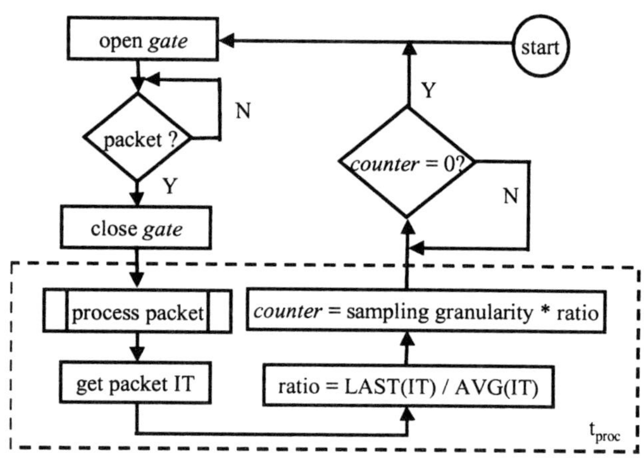

Figure 7 - Adaptive sampling with "IT guard"

In summary, the four methods of interest are:

- **Method #1** - Fixed granularity systematic sampling (Figure 5)
- **Method #2** - Adaptive sampling with "CPU guard" (Figure 6)
- **Method #3** - Adaptive sampling with "IT guard" (Figure 7)
- **Method #4** - Adaptive sampling with combined "CPU guard" and "IT guard" (not shown)

Name	Contribution	Description	1000 Packet Counts (1 millisecond each)			
			Mean	Variance	PMR	Hurst
ds01	50%	Exponential distribution of 97768 Its generated over 1 second interval with $\lambda = 97500$.	97.768	99.676	1.30922	0.59306
ds02	50%	Self-Similar distribution of 97279 Its generated over 1 second interval with $\alpha = 1.1$ and $\beta = 0.00000173$.	97.277	4743.40	2.67278	0.74572
ds0102	100%	195045 ITs merged from ds01 and ds02.	195.05	4861.54	1.87649	0.75542
ds03	10%	Exponential distribution of 19572 Its generated over 1 second interval with $\lambda = 19500$.	19.571	19.813	1.68617	0.58275
ds04	90%	Self-Similar distribution of 175431 Its generated over 1 second interval with $\alpha = 1.1$ and $\beta = 0.00000101$.	175.419	10583.5	2.26885	0.71506
ds0304	100%	194990 ITs merged from ds03 and ds04.	194.99	10626.8	2.1437	0.71444
ds05	90%	Exponential distribution of 176046 Its generated over 1 second interval with $\lambda = 175500$.	176.046	183.814	1.22127	0.59678
ds06	10%	Self-Similar distribution of 19220 Its generated over 1 second interval with $\alpha = 1.1$ and $\beta = 0.00000710$.	19.22	508.284	4.68262	0.81721
ds0506	100%	195266 ITs merged from ds05 and ds06.	195.266	665.837	1.38273	0.73654

Table 1 - Population measures for experimental traffic

6. Evaluation of Adaptive Sampling

Table 1 contains a summary of the traffic data used in this study. The three data sets, ds0102, ds0304 and ds0506 each consists of an exponential and self-similar components based on 50/50, 10/90, and 90/10 percent packet contributions. The data sets were generated using Poisson and inverse-Pareto distribution as described earlier in this paper.

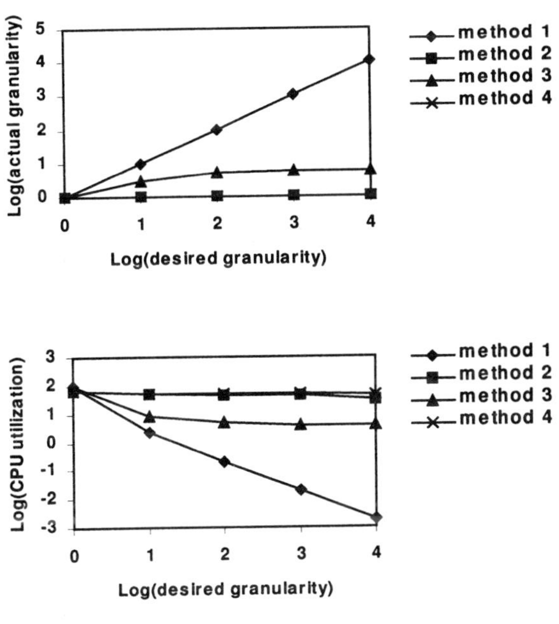

Figure 8 - Evaluation of CPU utilization

The four sampling method were implemented in ANSI C with the simulated traffic input from a file. First, the CPU utilization study was performed. The graph in Figure 8 shows the behavior of the adaptive methods with respect to sampling granularity and CPU utilization based on the aggregate data set ds0102. The static sampling method maintains the same sampling granularity and the CPU utilization decreases as the desired sampling granularity increases. In contrast, the other three methods attempt to sample as much as possible within the limit set on CPU utilization.

In the second set of experiments the accuracy of the computed mean, variance, PMR, and Hurst parameter for the three data sets were conducted. The following figures show plots of the four statistics for the exponential and self-similar components of data sets ds0102 and ds0304 over increasing sampling granularity. The last two graphs summarize the percent errors. Figures 9, 10, 11, and 12 show the accuracy of the four sampling methods in estimating the mean, variance, PMR, and Hurst parameter. Figures 9 and 10 shows the estimates for the exponential and self similar components of dataset ds0102 (50% exponential and 50% Pareto), Figures 11 and 12 for dataset ds0304 (10% exponential and 90% Pareto). In all cases, the population statistic is indicated on the Y-axis with Log(0) sampling granularity (i.e., all packets are sampled). As the sampling granularity increases, the accuracy of each method deviates from the population statistic, however in all cases except for PMR, the adaptive methods (method #'s 2, 3, and 4) are more accurate than the static method (method #1). For example, for the Hurst parameter method #'s 2, 3, and 4 are all approximately equal in accuracy and all better than method #1.

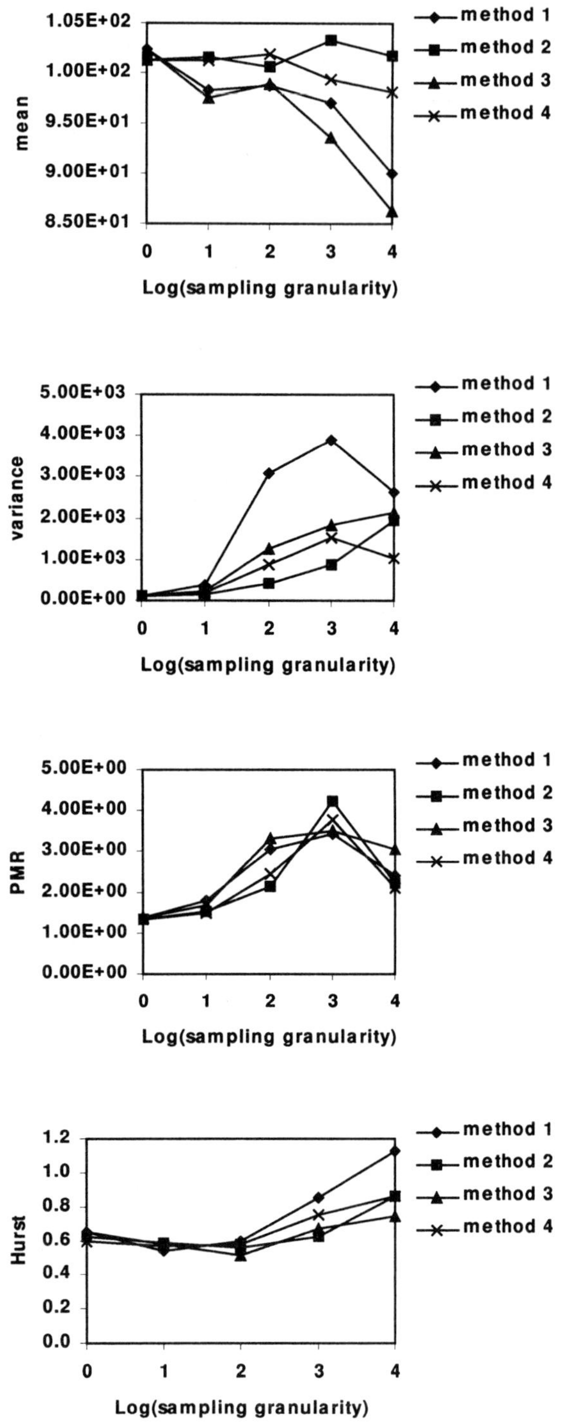

Figure 9 - Exponential component of ds0102

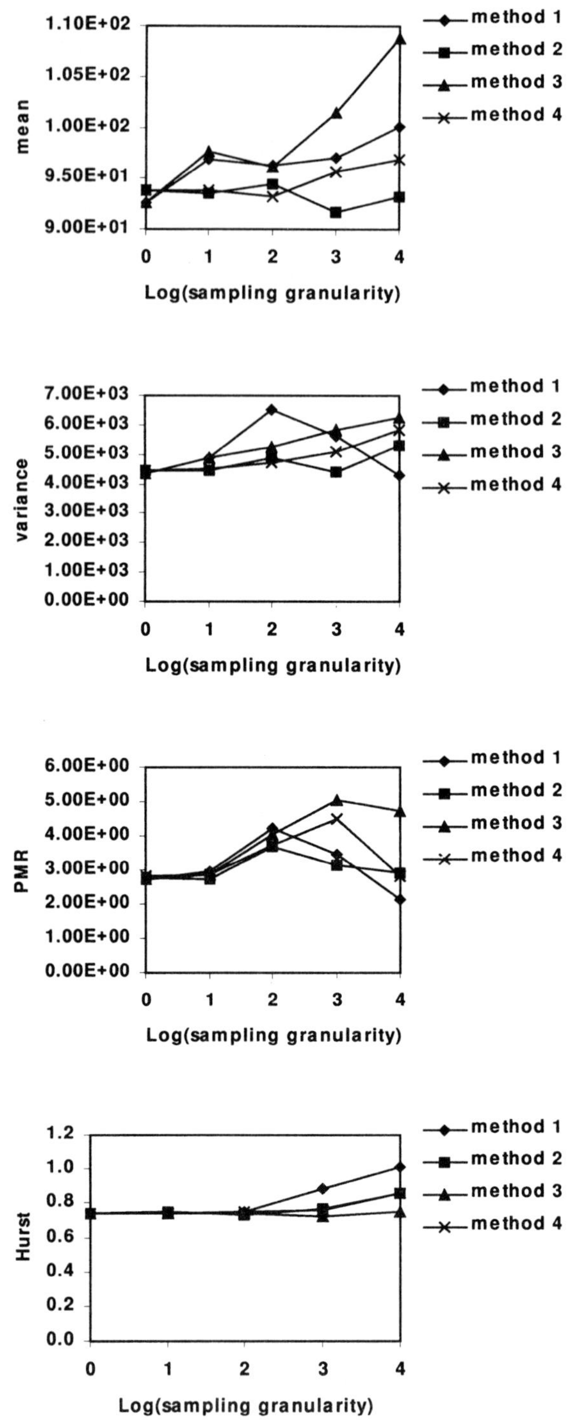

Figure 10 - Self-similar component of ds0102

From the graphs in Figures 9 through 12 we observe that adaptive sampling methods are better suited to estimating both Poisson and self-similar inter-arrival times under a high initial sampling granularity.

Resulting plots for methods using the CPU guard and IT guard are generally more consistent and more accurate than static sampling plots.

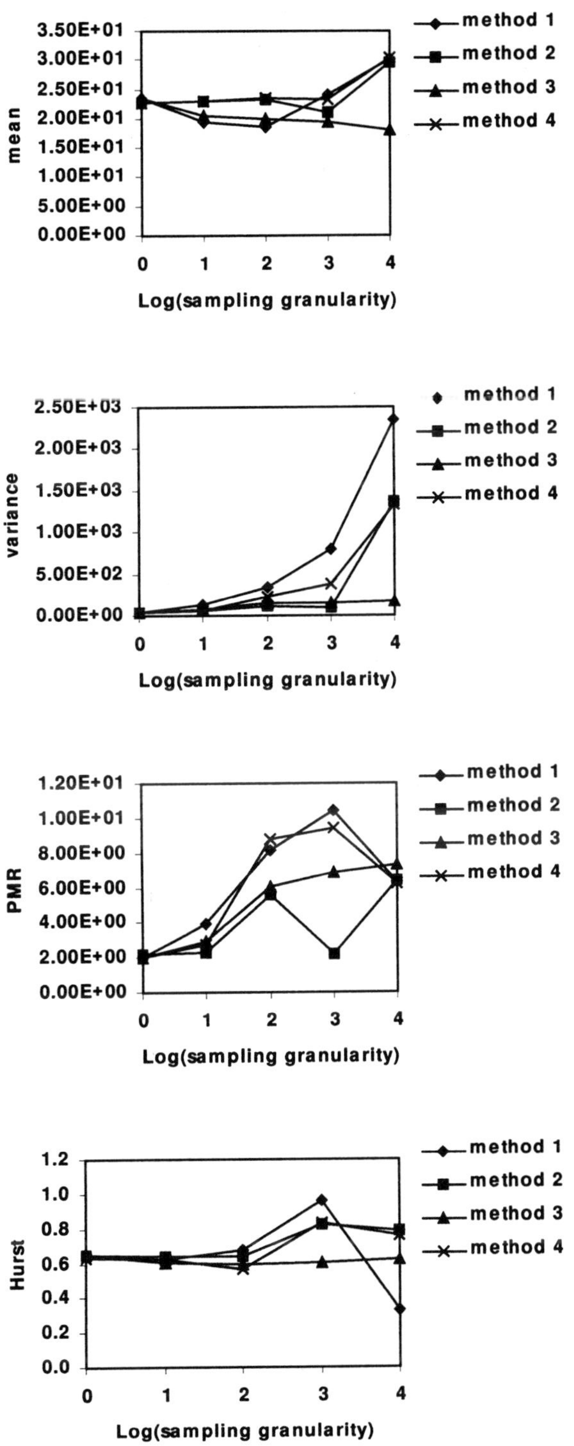

Figure 11 - Exponential component of ds0304

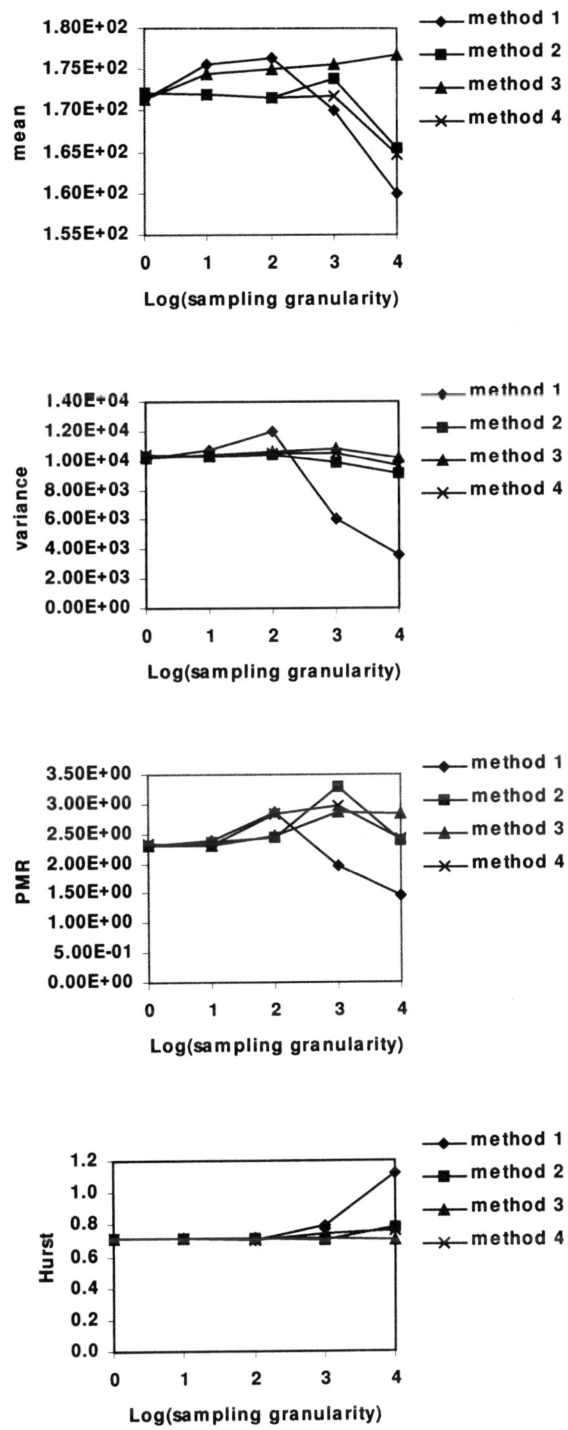

Figure 12 - Self-similar component of ds0304

Additional graphs for data set ds0506 (90% exponential and 10% Pareto) are not shown in this paper, but show the same results as the previous graphs.

Figures 13 and 14 quantify the percentage error in the estimates versus population statistics for the three datasets, ds0102, ds0304, and ds0506. The static method (method #1) results in the highest percent error in the Hurst parameter and also higher error in variance than the adaptive methods. This could be the result of "lost" congestion periods spread-out over a number of sampling intervals. Percentage error for the mean statistic are very low and about the same for all four methods. However, we notice that the adaptive method 3 which is based solely on the IT guard does not perform as well over the self-similar data set. The very high percentage error of the PMR statistic points out that it may not be a good indicator of traffic burstiness when sampling granularity is high. The Hurst parameter and the coefficient of variance (square root of variance divided by mean) can serve as good measures of traffic burstiness.

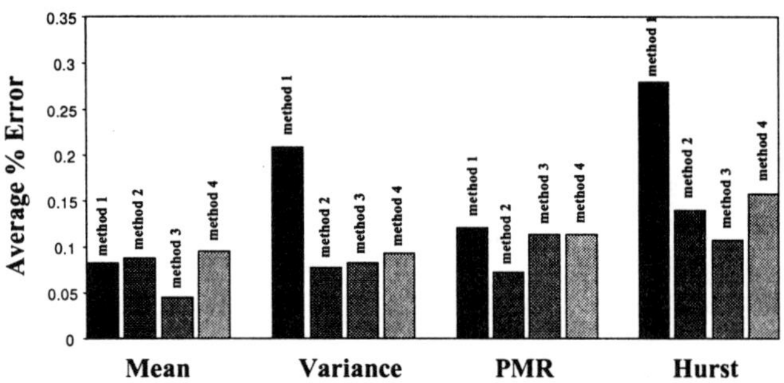

Figure 13 - Percentage error in exponential traffic. Variance and PMR data scaled down by 100 and 10.

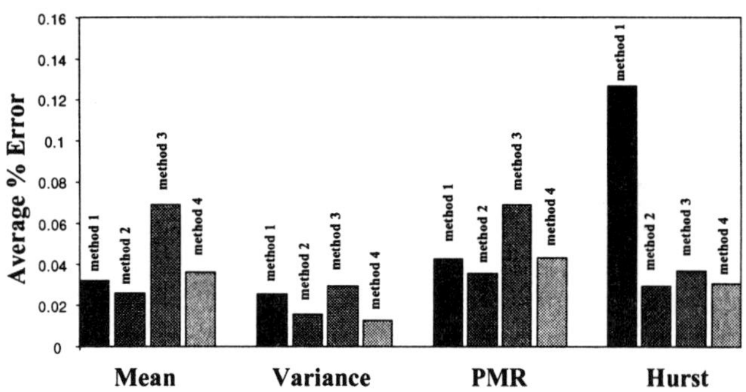

Figure 14 - Percentage error in self-similar traffic. Variance and PMR data scaled down by 100 and 10.

7. Summary

Estimating traffic characteristics is an important task of network management of LANs. Traffic characteristics of interest include mean, variance, peak-to-mean ratio, and Hurst parameter of packet counts. These traffic characteristics are used for capacity planning of network resources. Determining these traffic measures based on population measurements (i.e., processing of all packets) on a high-speed network, such as Gigabit Ethernet, is computationally expensive. Sampling methods can reduce the computational burden, as first demonstrated in [4] using fixed granularity sampling. The accuracy of the sample measures can be improved by extending fixed granularity sampling to adaptive sampling where the CPU utilization of the network management subsystem is set to a target, or desired, level. The adaptive sampling methods developed in this paper were shown to 1) be able to maintain a network management processor at a desired CPU utilization, and 2) generate more accurate traffic measures (especially for the Hurst parameter) than a static sampling method. Future work will address implementing the adaptive methods in existing network management systems.

References

[1] J. Beran, "Statistical Methods for Data with Long-Range Dependence", *Statistical Science*, Vol. 7, No. 4., pp. 404 - 416, 1992.

[2] J. Beran, R. Sherman, and T. Murad, "Long-Range Dependence in Variable -Bit-Rate Video Traffic", *IEEE Transactions on Communications*, Vol.43, pp. 1566 - 1579, 1995.

[3] R. Braden and A. Deschon, "NNStat: Internet Statistics Collection Package, Introduction and User's Guide," *Technical Report RR-88-206*, ISI, USC, 1988.

[4] K. Claffy, G. Polyzos, and H. Braum, "Application of Sampling Methodologies to Network Traffic Characterization", *Computer Communication Review*, Vol. 23, No. 4, pp. 194 - 203, 1993.

[5] A. Erramilli and J. Wang, "Monitoring Packet Traffic Levels", *Proceedings of IEEE GLOBECOM*, Vol. 1, pp. 274 - 280, 1994.

[6] H. Fowler and W. Leland, "Local Area Network Traffic Characteristics, with Implications for Broadband Network Congestion Management", *IEEE Journal on Selected Areas in Communications*, Vol. 9, No. 7, pp. 1139 - 1149, September 1991.

[7] J. Gordon, "Pareto Process as a Model of Self-Similar Packet Traffic," *Proceedings of IEEE GLOBECOM,* pp. 2232 - 2236, 1996.

[8] W. Leland, M. Taqqu, W. Willinger, and D. Wilson, "On the Self-Similar Nature of Ethernet Traffic (Extended Version)", *IEEE ACM Transactions on Networking*, Vol.2, No.1, pp. 1 - 15, February 1994.

[9] B. Mandelbrot, "Self-Similar Error Clusters in Communication Systems and the concept of Conditional Stationarity." *IEEE Transactions on Communication Technology,* Vol. COM-13, pp. 71 - 90, 1965.

Paper Session 4
Track A: Middleware

Session Chair: Alfred Weaver
University of Virginia

Replication in an Object-Oriented System

Marwan Sabbouh
OneSource Information Services, 150 CambridgePark drive, Cambridge, MA 02140
Professor Kanti Prasad, Ph.D.
University of Massachusetts Lowell, One University Avenue, Lowell, MA 01854
William Thompson III, Ph.D.
OneSource Information Services, 150 CambridgePark Drive, Cambridge, MA 02140

Abstract

After two decades of research, reliable computing remains a property of specialized systems and too costly to implement in many applications. In this paper, we present an object-oriented, and fault tolerant distributed system. This system is based on open standards and hides programming complexities. Our technique for delivering replication to programmers is based on typed objects, inheritance and protocol composition. Additionally, this technique uses reliable unordered communication for message delivery.

1. Introduction

Despite the deployment of object-oriented techniques to distributed systems, programming these systems remains difficult, as reliability and availability complexities are not hidden from the programmer. To solve these problems, many systems [1,2,3,4] introduced the concept of object grouping based on UDP multicast or IP-multicast [5]. Although object grouping is essential to achieving fault tolerance, these systems rely on applications programming interfaces (API) to give users the means to achieve replication. As a result, programming these systems remains difficult. Solutions based on CORBA services and DCOM facilitate service location and interaction, but they do not isolate the application programmers from the complexities of reliability and availability. Other systems such as Shadows [7] use inheritance to accomplish fault-tolerance. However, in this system, it is the programmer's responsibility to call the objects in order to attain reliability. The Friends [8] system uses reflection [9] and object-orientation architecture for fault-tolerance, however the system is dependent on the language used (Open C++). In this paper, we show that, object types, subtyping, and protocol composition can easily accomplish high availability based on software replication. Subtyping is concerned with the sharing of abstract behavior in the form of interfaces. The protocol composition property gives the system the ability to compose different protocol stacks for different objects.

In order to achieve this, we set out to add a "Replica" object type to the Inter-Language Unification (ILU) system [11]. The Replica object type offers methods that are used to implement our own replication technique. We also introduce a group communication protocol (GCP) for the ILU. The GCP provides for the unordered, reliable delivery of data and offers a send-to-n and a receive-from-n semantics. A user of this system is able to benefit from these additions simply by declaring the object to be a subtype of the Replica object. This is done using ILU's Interface Specification Language (ISL). The user does not call the methods on the Replica objects directly; rather the kernel calls these methods.

This research provides replication for an object-oriented system, where object types, subtyping, and protocol compositions are the essential properties. The object type and the subtyping properties hide the complexity of the system, and simplify its design, resulting in a more efficient system. The object type is encapsulated in every method invocation. This allows the kernel to intercept these invocations and invoke the replication technique for replica objects. The protocol composition property allows the use of open protocol standards for various object types. The two properties combined allow the system to become extensible. Furthermore, we make no assumptions concerning the language we use. This work innovates by making replication completely transparent to application programmers. The programmer provides a non-replicated implementation and needs only to specify his object to be a subtype of the Replica object. In short, there are no new APIs for the programmer, nor does the programmer call any replication object.

This research uses a reliable and unordered multicast protocol to implement the replication technique. Although, this technique is less general than a totally ordered reliable multicast, such as the one introduced by Isis [12], however it is well suited for grouping homogeneous objects, where clients are distinct from

0-8186-8810-6/98 $10.00 © 1998 IEEE

servers. This technique is implemented using standard protocols such as UDP, ONC RPC [13], HTTP, and IP-Multicast [5]. Currently, there is no standard for a group multicast protocol. The implementation of this technique is novel and takes advantage of the rich semantics of object-oriented programming. For instance, request messages are easily identified in our system, since the object type, and method ids are encapsulated in every request. We refer to the modified system as Fault Tolerant ILU or FT-ILU to distinguish it from the ILU. In the next section, we compare this work with previous work in this area. We will then briefly describe the ILU. We will then describe the replication protocol used in the FT-ILU. In conclusion we will summarize future work.

2. Background

This work builds on or uses results found in various disciplines. In particular, this work encompasses fields such as, object-oriented systems [6,7,14,15], group communication system [1,2,3,4], processor group membership [16,17,18,19], and replication techniques [21,22]. In the last decade, we saw an explosion of object-oriented systems and group communication systems. These systems include Arjuna [6], Shadows [7], COOL [14], and Network Objects [15].

The Arjuna system is object-oriented. The system provides user with classes that implement concurrency control, persistence and object recovery. Arjuna objects can be replicated. However, the Arjuna system is not language neutral. Additionally, object type is not at the heart of the system. Furthermore the programmer uses the objects provided by Arjuna to implement the properties required by atomic actions.

The Shadows evolved from the Arjuna system. The architecture in Shadows is based on three key concepts: objects servers, object migration, and location transparency. The authors of Shadows show that these properties provide adequate facilities to building more important properties such as persistence, durability, and concurrency.

The Chorus [20] Object Oriented Layer (COOL) is built on top of the Chorus micro-kernel to provide object-oriented support for applications. COOL is composed of three layers, the COOL-base layer, generic run-time layer, and the language specific layer.

The COOL-base layer presents two abstractions, clusters and clusters space. The COOL generic layer implements a generic object oriented computational model. This layer provides support for a generic RPC interface that is mapped onto the base layer. The language specific runtime layer deals with mapping a particular language model onto the generic runtime object model. COOL is language independent. However, COOL is tightly integrated with the Chorus system.

There are other systems, such as Isis, Horus, Totem, and Transis that distinguished themselves by providing solution for the processor membership problems by using a totally ordered, atomic broadcast protocols. These systems assume that operations are asynchronous, and that network partitioning occurs in the system. Some systems, such as Totem and Transis handle the merging of different partitions.

Isis was the first system to accomplish fault tolerance by replication. Isis was also first to support different ordering requirements on different operations. The system supported three different ordering requirements: Group broadcast, atomic broadcast, and minimal broadcast. The Isis also introduced the virtual synchrony execution model [23]. The virtual synchrony paradigm ensures the correctness of the primary-backup replication technique in the presence of unreliable failure detectors in an asynchronous system.

Horus evolved from the Isis toolkit. Horus is a flexible group communication system. The protocol layers in Horus can be varied to support application specific requirements. Horus builds on the protocol stack concepts introduced by the x-kernel [10]. However, it substitutes group communication for point-to-point communication.

Transis and Totem extends on the virtual synchrony property introduced by Isis. Horus, Totem and Transis attempt to reach agreement on group membership in asynchronous system where partitions occur due to process failure and network partitioning. Their solutions extend the virtual synchrony property.

Current research shows that the group membership problem cannot be solved in asynchronous systems with crash failure in the primary partition model [24]. However, Cristian showed the problem can be solved in a synchronous system, using atomic broadcast [19]. Later, Cristian extended his model to solve the problem in a timed asynchronous system [20].

In the FT-ILU system, to solve the above problem while ensuring progress and safety, we assume clocks that are loosely synchronized running on clients and servers. A protocol such as the network time protocol, NTP [25], could be used to synchronize clocks running on different machines. We also assume that partitions occur only due to failure and not to network partitions. In the event of network partitioning, processing can continue in one partition. Network partitioning is discussed in section 5. Both of these assumptions are reasonable, since our method is a replication technique, in which homogeneous objects are grouped, and where clients are distinct from servers. Additionally, it is assumed that the state of the object is held in the surrogate server or the client side.

3. Inter-language unification system

ILU is a multi-language object interface system [11]. ILU object interfaces can be specified in either the Object Management Group (OMG) Interface Definition Language (IDL) or ILU's Interface Specification Language (ISL). These interfaces are then subjected to a tool that generated language specific files. These files are then linked with the ILU kernel, language specific runtime and application specific code to generate the server and client modules. In this fashion, ILU hides implementation distinctions between different languages, different address spaces, and between different operating systems.

ILU is a layered system. The layers in ILU are the transport layer, the protocol layer, the security layer when applicable, and the application layer. The transport layer is a delivery layer and a filter layer. It deals with the sending and receiving of data. It can also act as a filter that changes the behavior of the transport layer. For instance the transport layer can consist of a TCP layer and a Record Marking layer [13] to implement a reliable, message oriented stack. The protocol layer handles the marshaling of method invocations. The application layer is where the programmer implements his objects.

ILU is object-oriented. Although different systems define object-oriented differently, ILU satisfies the Location, Access, and Migration transparency properties [26,27]. In addition to the above properties, FT-ILU satisfies the Replication and Failure transparency properties, as depicted in Table 1.

3.1. Object communications in ILU

In ILU, the object type system provides the sharing of abstract behavior in the form of interfaces. The ILU supports the object server model. The module that implements the method of an object is called a server. The module that calls another object's method is called a client [11]. A server may contain several objects each identified uniquely by a server identifier and an object handle. A server publishes the protocol, transport, and the endpoint by which a client communicates with a particular object. The protocol and transport information determines the protocol and the transport layer to use. A pair of endpoints determines a particular connection to the object. A client object needs only to know the server and the object handle, and then it is able to deduce the means by which to communicate with that object by looking up the object in a system wide registry.

Properties	FT-ILU implementation
Location	The object location is published in a registry
Access	Objects are accessed via methods
Migration	Object location is re-published upon relocation
Concurrency	Users must support concurrent access. Object state is held in the surrogate server
Replication	Hybrid schemes combine active and passive replication
Failure	FT-ILU implements a Group Communication Protocol that works on top of UDP, in addition to the Replica object type

Table 1 Transparency properties of FT-ILU

4. Group communication protocol

In order to implement software based replications; the ILU is extended with a Group Communication Protocol (GCP). This protocol ensures reliable delivery of packets. It also offers a send-to-n and a receive-from-n semantics, as well as a send-to-1 and a receive-from-1 semantics. This protocol is based on IP-multicasting and works on top of UDP. GCP ensures the delivery of data, providing a defined service to the marshaling layer. GCP is sender oriented. The sender ensures that all servers have received a copy of the request. This works since membership information is published in a system wide registry. GCP can be configured to support the reliable delivery of the request to a server in the group. This feature will be used extensively in FT-ILU. For instance, the FT-ILU kernel takes advantage of this feature when handling concurrent requests. Actually, our replication technique makes it possible to use this feature for all client method invocations. This is because a method invocation received by a primary server is propagated to other servers. GCP supports unordered delivery. Unordered delivery does not make guarantees on the order in which packets are delivered to the receiver. Unordered delivery is sufficient since it is the replication layer that provides for the ordered handling of method invocations by various clients. Section 5.1 details the replication properties, and Table 2 summarizes these properties. In the context of ILU, GCP maps into a transport layer. The marshaling layer deals with the marshaling of methods and their arguments. It also masks the differences between different machine architectures and different operating systems. The replication layer works on top of GCP. The replication layer implements the technique that will ensure the consistency of replicated objects. The figure 1 shows the layered architecture of FT-ILU.

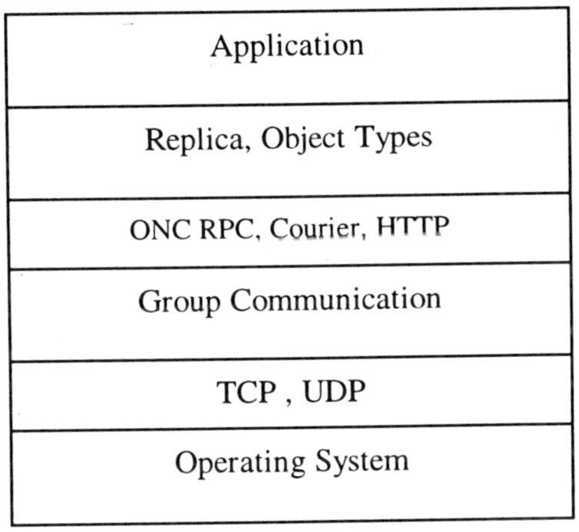

Figure 1 Layered architecture of FT-ILU

5. Fault tolerant ILU, FT-ILU

Fault tolerance in FT-ILU is accomplished by replicating a server on different machines. In the FT-ILU, fault tolerance is understood as no failed process causes application to take unsafe actions, and the application is able to make progress despite partial failure. This replication technique uses a hybrid scheme that combines both primary-backup and active replication. Primary-backup divides the server group into a primary replica, and secondary replicas. In active replication, all replicas belonging to a group have the same role [28].

This technique divides the server group into a primary server, and secondary servers. Furthermore, this system is synchronous. This assumption is valid since we group homogeneous objects running on a local area network and impose a limit on all communication delays and process speed. When a client invokes a method on a replica object, the request is sent to all servers. In turn, the servers put the request in a queue and wait for a notification event, which is sent by the primary to all servers in the group, including itself. Having received this event, the servers process the request and send the reply to the client, which is waiting for a reply to arrive from a server. The notification event uniquely identifies a method invocation. The operation of the system is shown in figure 2. In the server group, a server is identified uniquely by its IP address and a rank. The primary server has a rank equal to 1. A secondary server whose rank is two is the server that will assume the primary role in case of a primary server failure. We refer to a server whose rank is n as Server n.

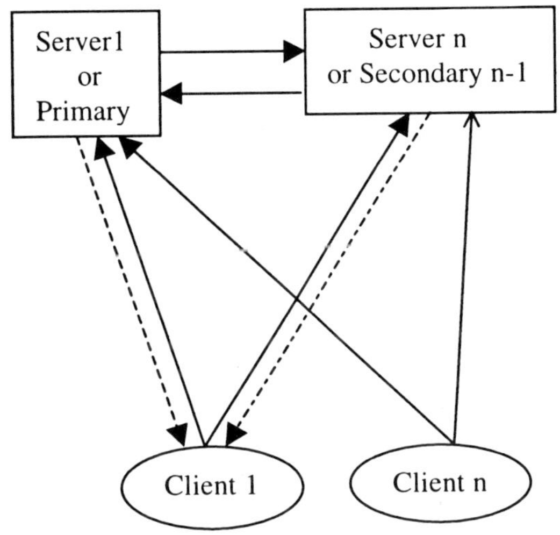

Figure 2 Method invocations in FT-ILU

5.1 Replication properties

The properties of this technique are summarized in the Table 2:

Atomicity	Given method invocation by client p1 on replica Server 1, every correct replica handles the method invocation, or none does.
Termination	All correct servers handling a request arrives at an answer
Synchronous	We impose a limit on all communication delays and process speed. Clocks are loosely synchronized using NTP
Membership	Allows the removal of an object from the group
Order	Given two method invocations by Client 1 and by Client 2, and if Server 1 and Server 2 both handle the invocations then they both handle them in the same order

Table 2 Properties of FT-ILU replication technique

The above properties ensure that if all of the servers are exposed to the same input, then the servers will process these invocations in the same order, thus maintaining a consistent internal state. In this case, method invocations will succeed despite partial failure in the system. This replication technique detects the Fail-Stop failure documented by Schneider [29]. We do not handle the Byzantine failure described by Lamport [30]. In addition to the Fail-Stop assumption, the synchronous assumption makes it possible to detect failure by implementing timeouts on notification packets. In the server group, we distinguish between two scenarios for failure detection.

In the first scenario, a primary server fails. Server 2 detects the primary sever failure. When a method invocation arrives at Server 2, and if it does not receive the notification event for that invocation, Server 2 sends a packet to Server 1 and waits for a reply. If that request times out, Server 2 will then send a special packet to all servers announcing that Server 1 is dead and that it is now the primary server. Consequently, all servers will decrement their rank by one. For example, Server 2 becomes Server1 and so on. Also, each secondary server responds to the new primary with the last request it processed successfully. The newly elected primary server uses this information to determine which event to notify next. This is necessary in order to handle the case where a primary server fails right after sending a notification that was not received by all the secondary servers. This technique gives the newly elected server a chance to re-send the notification event to the secondary servers that had not received it. To illustrate the point made above, consider a server group of three members S1, S2, and S3. Let us assume that S1 fails right after sending a notification event, EV1, to S2 and S3. Furthermore assume that S2 receives EV1 and S3 does not. S2 proceeds to answer the request that corresponds to the notification event, but S3 times out waiting for EV1. S3 then attempts to establish the liveliness of S2 by sending a special packet. S2 responds and S3 takes no further action. Now suppose that another request arrives to the group. Both S2 and S3 time out waiting for the notification event EV2. S2 determines that S1 is dead and proceeds to declare it dead. Consequently, S3 decrements it's rank by one. It also responds with the last event it processed successfully. In this case, it is EV0. S2 then sends the notification event EV1 before sending EV2. This causes S3 to process EV1 before EV2 and the remaining servers maintain a consistent state. At this point S2 becomes S1 and S3 becomes S2. Figure 3 shows the notification event format.

In the second scenario, a secondary server fails. Server 1 detects the failure when the failed server does not acknowledge any of its notification packets. Server 1 then informs other servers of the failed server removal from the group. Consequently, secondary servers whose ranks are higher than the failed server decrement their ranks by one.

This failure detection mechanism allows the removal of servers from the group. In this scheme, we really can't distinguish between a server that is too slow and a server that actually failed. In this situation, consider what happens as this scenario leads to partitioning in the system. The servers, including the primary server, time out waiting for a notification event. When that happens, the primary server changes its "IsPrimary" flag to false and removes itself from the group. In this fashion, when the primary server recovers, it will take no further action on outstanding requests. The secondary servers proceed with the protocol as explained above. The removal of a primary server will lead to a blockage in the system until the secondary server assumes the primary server's role.

Here, it is worth noting that a client may choose to wait for all servers to answer or just a server to answer. Furthermore, the client can't distinguish between a secondary and a primary server. This means that client processing can continue despite partial failure in the system.

The notification event format is shown in figure 3. The client port number and its IP address uniquely identify a process by an endpoint in the distributed system. The serial number (SN) of the request coupled with the above endpoint uniquely identifies a method invocation by the client process. The method and its arguments being invoked by the request are sent in the notification packet to handle the possibility that the primary server has received a request and one of the secondary servers has not received it yet. This handles the case of a client failure when sending a method invocation.

SN	Client port	Client IP	Object type, Method(arg)

Figure 3 Notification event format

5.2 Implementation details

This technique is based on the kernel being able to intercept method invocations. Since every method invocation encapsulates the object type and the method identifier, the kernel is then able to distinguish between different object types and different methods invoked on a particular object. Additionally, the kernel is able to deduce a unique event identifier from the method invocation to distinguish between different clients invoking the same method. When a server is implemented, the programmer calls ILU_C_InitializeServer. Note that this function is called in the non-replicated case as well. This function in turn calls several functions that prepare the server for handling method invocations. Figure 4 shows the progression of function calls for a non-replica method invocation. The application programmer calls the later function. It, in turn, calls a language specific runtime functions. These functions call some kernel functions that prepare the server for handling method invocations. Note that the server and the kernel implementation operate in a multithreaded environment. The _ILU_C_ReadConnectionRequests function blocks until a method invocation arrives at a server. At this point, _ILU_C_RunConnection is executed to read the method invocation. This method manages the transport and the protocol layer to input and marshal the incoming data. Once that is done, a call is setup to process the method and to return its result to the caller. This is the task of _ILU_ReceiveRequest. This is also where the kernel intercepts the incoming call. At this point, the kernel knows the object type and the method being executed. The kernel also knows the serial number of the call, as well as the caller in terms of its IP address and port number. So instead of proceeding directly to invoke the method, the kernel hashes the function call, then the primary sends a notification event to all the servers in the group indicating which event to process next. At the same time, the kernel starts a timer on the call. This timer will trigger if the method was not handled after time x has elapsed.

Figure 5 shows how the interception mechanism works in the FT-ILU. The rectangular boxes represent work done by a thread. Mutexes and conditions variables are used to synchronize the various threads. The _ILU_ReceiveRequest thread records the method invocation, by putting it in a hash table. The thread then increments a counter, that keep track of the number of notifications to be sent to servers, and starts a timer on the methods that triggers if the request was not serviced after time x has elapsed. Finally, the thread notifies a condition variable that causes the thread _ILU_NotifyServer to run. This thread, in turn, decrements the counter, po_req_rcvd, and sends the notification event to all servers in the group, including the primary server. Receiving a notification event causes the thread _ILU_HandleNotifyEx to run. This thread acknowledges the receipt of the notification event and records the time of the receipt of the notification packet in a counter used to determine the liveness of the primary server. The thread then stops the timer set by the _ILU_ReceiveRequest and notifies the _ILU_C_DoInvocation thread. This thread proceeds by invoking the method. It also signals the kernel that it is ready to process another method. This is the purpose of the po_sn_expected counter. Finally the reply is sent back to the client.

It is important to note that _ILU_C_DoInvocation is called eventually just as in the non- replica case. In this case, _ILU_C_DoInvocation is called only after the notification event arrives. The notification event causes Ilu_HandleNotifyEx to signal _ILU_C_DoInvocation to continue with its work.

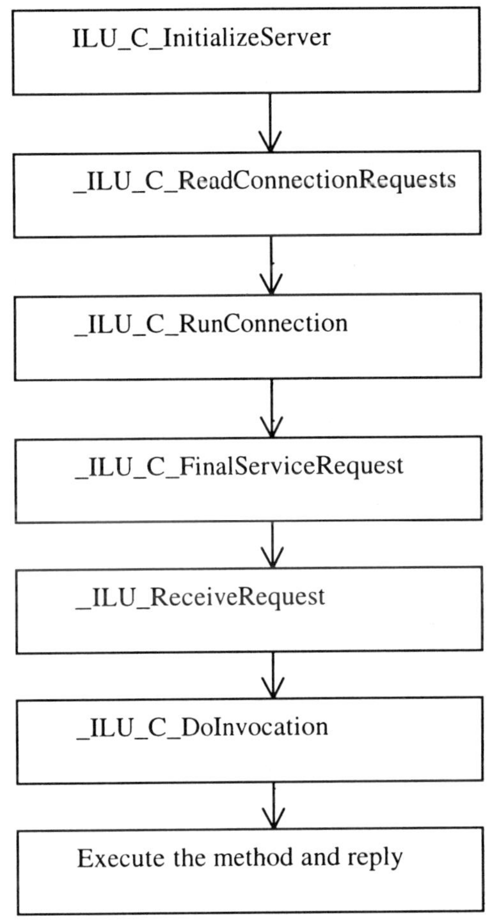

Figure 4 ILU_C_InitializeServer

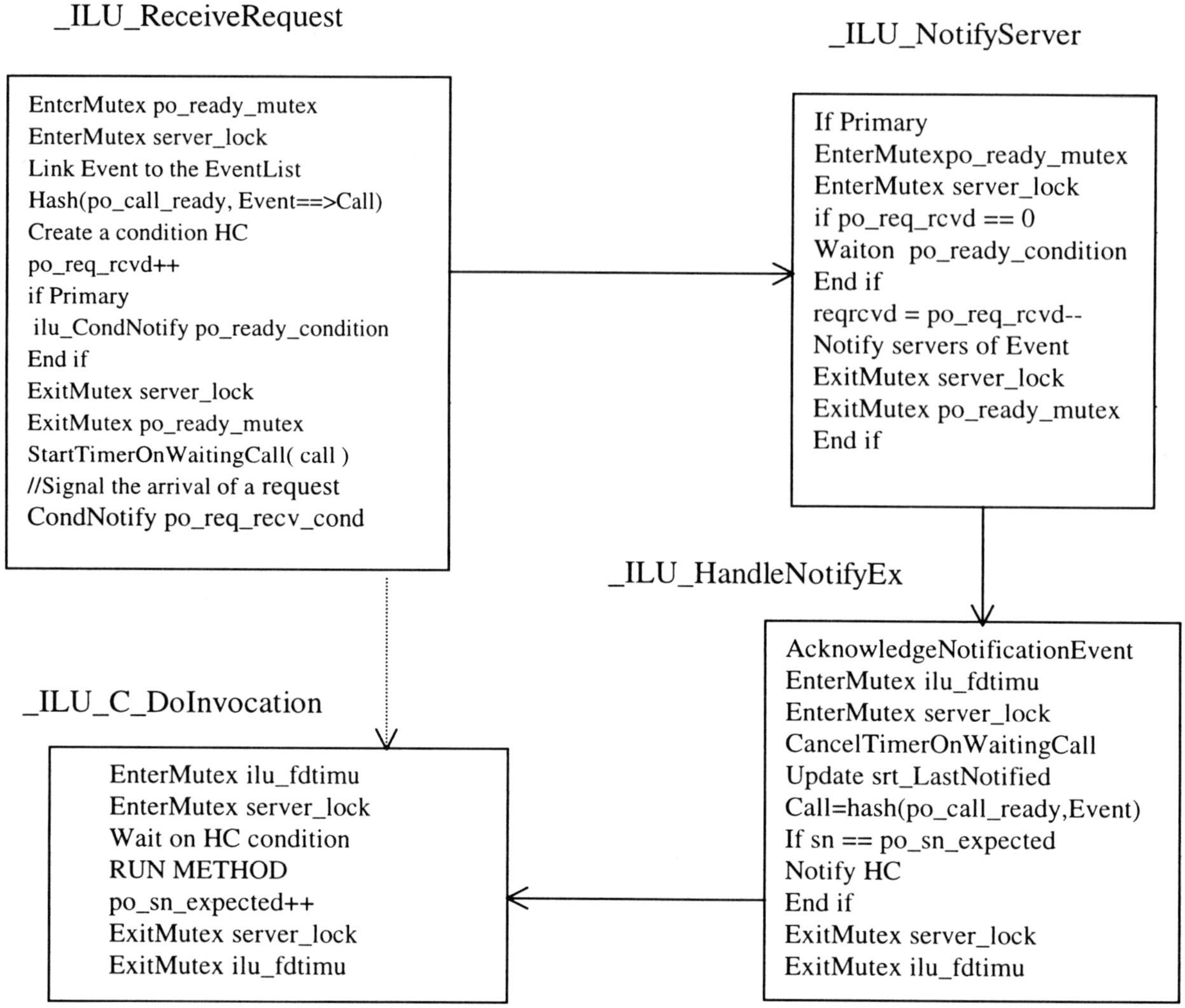

Figure 5 Interception mechanism

5.3 Experimental results

In this experiment, two servers were run in a group. The primary server was fully invoking the interception mechanism in order to notify itself and the secondary server of a receipt of an event. The arrival rate of method invocations was varied in order to study the behavior of the system under various load conditions. Additionally, this experiment is designed to determine the capacity of the system. The server and clients were connected using 802.3 Ethernet standard running at 10 Mbits per second. The server and client configurations are shown in Table 3.

Machine	Processor	Memory	Operating System
Primary Server	Pentium Pro 150 MHz	64 MB	NT 4.0
Secondary Server	Pentium Pro 150 MHz	260 MB	NT 4.0
Client	Pentium Pro 150 MHz Dual	146 MB	NT 4.0
Client	Pentium Pro 200 MHz Dual	196 MB	NT 4.0
Client	Pentium Pro 150 MHz	244 MB	NT 4.0

Table 3- Machine configurations

In the first experiment, the system was configured to run with piggybacking up to 25 notification packets and no Idempotent method invocations. Figure 6 shows the results. Each point, A (x, y) on the graph corresponds to a run of the system. During the run, the FT-ILU was subjected to one or more clients requesting operations. In a particular run, the x coordinate is an average of the number of operations per second. The x coordinate is computed by dividing the number of operations by the total time of the run. The y coordinate is computed by summing the elapsed time of each invocation and dividing it by the number of method invocation. The time of each invocation is the time elapsed when the _ILU_ReceiveRequest was first entered and the time _ILU_C_DoInvocation was run.

Figure 6 shows that the system capacity to be 58 operations per second. In the range between 23 and 43 operations per second, the elapsed time is almost a constant ranging between 47 and 59 milliseconds. At rates higher than 43 operations per second, the elapsed time increases linearly until it saturates at 58 operations per second.

In another experiment, the system was run with no piggybacking. In this scenario the capacity of the system was reduced to 52 operations per second and the minimum response time was 63 milliseconds. These findings show that piggybacking improves the system capacity and reduces the response time on the servers. For Idempotent method invocations, the capacity of the system was found to be 145 operations per second, and the minimum response time was 1 millisecond. The kernel recognizes an Idempotent method if it is tagged with the Idempotent keyword. When a client invokes an Idempotent method on an object group, any server in the group can then handle the request.

The above measurement shows that the interception mechanism and the replication technique increase the load of the server. In turn, this translates into a higher average response time and a reduced system capacity. This is not unexpected, as the replication technique invokes replication methods for incoming requests, adding to the system load. Note that the primary server is a client of the secondary servers. In the case with no piggybacking, the replication technique doubles the number of method invocation on a primary server, as each incoming request causes a notification to be sent to secondary servers. However, better results were obtained when the primary server piggybacked the notification events.

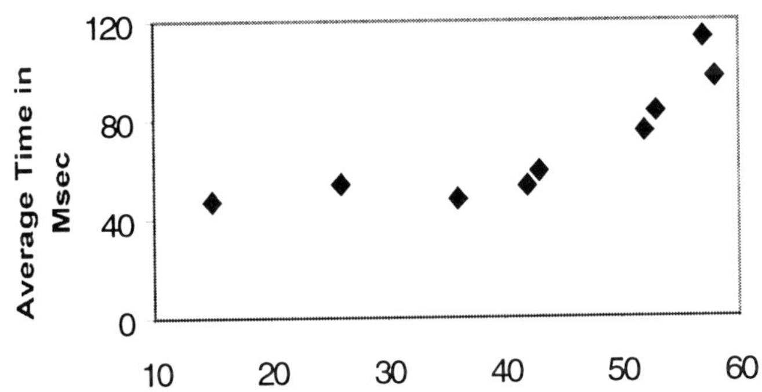

Figure 6 FT-ILU throughput

6. Conclusion and future work

A user who writes to this system takes advantage of the replication technique by declaring his object to be a subtype of the replica object. This is done using the ILU specification language (ISL). It can also be accomplished with a modified version of OMG IDL.

The replication technique, its failure detection algorithm, and the election algorithm when primary server fails have been implemented. To illustrate the ease of use of this system, the Test1 example that shipped with ILU 2.0alpha9, has run with the FT-ILU kernel. Primary server failure and secondary server failures have been detected successfully by the FT-ILU kernel. Upon a primary failure, secondary server 2 has assumed the role of the primary. Also, client processes have succeeded despite the failure of a secondary server. The system blocks for a primary server failure before it recovers.

The FT-ILU innovates in the use of the object types, protocol composition, and inheritance properties. The above properties were used to produce a fault-tolerant, cross-platform, language neutral, and object oriented distributed system. The use of these properties resulted in a system that is based on open standards, and one that hides programming complexity. In the FT-ILU, the programmer provides a non-replicated implementation of the object, and tags the object with the Replica tag. The FT-ILU is then capable of distinguishing this object from any other object, and invoking the replication technique. The object type is used to identify a particular method invocation. It is also used to trigger the interception mechanism and the replication technique. As a result, the object type simplifies the design and implementation of distributed systems. This is evident in the format of the notification event. The protocol composition properties allow the system to be based on open standards and make the system extensible. This property allows the use of the GCP with the replica object type. The use of inheritance is well documented in many systems.

These results can be applied to many other types of objects. For instance, its should be easy to see how the above properties can be used to simplify the task of programming concurrent objects, persistent objects, quality of service objects, and transactional objects. In the concurrent object case, the system is capable of obtaining the correct locks for the appropriate objects. In traditional system, the programmer would have to do that himself.

Although the approach used in the FT-ILU proved useful, few enhancements can be made to the system. Specifically, the use of other replication technique in the FT-ILU should be investigated. The latter work would be aimed at improving the response time and at supporting the merging of server groups. For example, the lazy replication technique [22] implemented in Argus supports three level of causality compared to the two supported by the FT-ILU. The system should also allow for the addition of a server to the group, not just the removal. Additionally, the implementation of the replication technique should have object granularity as opposed to server granularity. Recall that a server manages multiple objects. If replication were implemented at the object level, this would permit different objects in a server to participate in different groups. Furthermore, a server would then be a primary server for one object and a secondary server for another object. This would better balance the loads between multiple servers.

This research is exciting since its results are far reaching. The results of this work can be applied to various distributed object frameworks, such as DCOM and CORBA. In particular, the attribute based programming paradigm presented here for replica objects can be extended to support other object attributes, such as a secure attribute to support security, or a concurrent attribute to support a concurrency model. For example, A DCOM programmer would tag his object with the desired attribute and then the DCOM run time would invoke the corresponding meta-object at the right time. Also the protocol composition property proved very useful. The World Wide Web (WWW) is an example of a distributed system lacking the protocol composition property. The WWW can be improved by alleviating its dependency on the HTTP/TCP protocol stack. For instance, to bring replication to the WWW, the protocol can be changed to negotiate the protocol stack to use that best support replication. In this case, HTTP can be used on top of a group communication protocol. For static web page, the protocol defaults to using HTTP/TCP.

7. Acknowledgments

The authors wish to thank OneSource Information Services for allowing the use of company equipment for this research. We also wish to thank the referees for their valuable suggestions and comments on how to improve this paper.

8. References

[1] R. Van Renesse, K. P. Birman and S. Maffeis, "Horus: A Flexible Group Communication System", Communications of the ACM, vol. 39, no. 4, April 1996, pp. 76-83.

[2] D. Dolev and D. Malki, "The Transis Approach to High Availability Cluster Communication", Communication of ACM, vol. 39, no. 4, April 1996, April 1996, pp. 64-70.

[3] M.F. Kaashoek and A.S. Tanenbaum, "An Evaluation of the Amoeba Group Communication System", proceedings of the 16th International Conference on Distributed Computing Systems, May 27-30, 1996, pp 436-447.

[4] L. E.Moser, P. M.Melliar-Smith, D. A.Agarwal , R. K.Budhia, and C. A.Lingley-Papadopoulos, "Totem a fault-tolerant multicast group communication system", Communication of the. ACM, vol. *39*, no.4, April 1996, pp. 54 - 63.

[5] S.E. Deering, "Host extensions for IP multicating", RFC 1112, SRI Network Information Center.

[6] G.D. Parrington, et al., "The design and implementation of Arjuna", Usenix Computing Systems Journal, vol. 8, no. 3, 1995, pp. 255-308.

[7] S. J Caughey, G.D. Parrington, S.K. Shrivastava, "SHADOWS-A flexible support system for objects in distributed systems", Proceedings of the Third International Workshop On Object Orientation in Operating Systems, Pages 73-81, Ashville NC., 1993

[8] J.C. Fabre and T. Perennou, "A MetaObject Architecture for Fault-tolerant Distributed Systems: The Friends Approach", IEEE Transactions On Computers, vol. 47, no. 1, Jan 1998, pp. 78-95.

[9] G. Kiczales and J. Des Riviere, "The Art of the MetaObject protocol", MIT Press 1991

[10] L.L. Peterson and N. Hutchinson, "The x-Kernel: An architecture for implementing network protocols", IEEE Transactions on Software Engineering, vol. 17, no. 1, Jan. 1991, pp. 64-76.

[11] B. Jansen and M. Spreitzer, "Inter-Language Unification System", July 1996.

[12] K. Birman and T. Joseph, "Reliable communication in the presence of failures", ACM Transactions on Computer Systems, vol. 5, no. 1, February 1987, pp. 47-76.

[13] R. Srinivasan, "RPC: Remote Procedure Call Protocol", Specification Version 2, Internet RFC 1831, August 1995.

[14] R. Lea, P.Amaral and C. Jacquemont, "COOL-2: an object oriented support platform built above the CHORUS Micro-Kernel", Proceedings of the International Workshop On Object Orientation in Operating Systems IWOOS, Palo Alto, CA October 1991.

[15] A. Birrell, C. Nelson and S. Owicki and E. Wobber, "Network Objects", Digital Equipment Corporation technical report, Dec. 4 , 1995

[16] A. Riccardi and K. Birman, "Process membership in asynchronous environment", Cornell technical report, TR 93-1328

[17] G.Neiger, "A new look at membership services", in proceedings of the Fifteenth ACM Symposium on Principles of Distributed Computing, Philadelphia, PA, USA. 1996

[18] F. Cristian, "Reaching agreement on processor group membership in synchronous distributed systems", Distributed Computing, vol. 4, no. 4, April 1991, pp. 175-187.

[19] F. Cristian, F. Schmuck "Agreeing on processor group membership in timed asynchronous systems", University of California, San Diego technical report CSE95-428, 1995

[20] M. Guillemont, J. Lipkis, D. Orr and M. Rozier, "CHORUS: A second generation Micro-Kernel based on Unix; lessons in performance and compatibility, proceedings of the Usenix Winter 92 Conference, Dallas, Texas, January 1991

[21] R. Ladin, B. Liskov, S. Ghemawat, "Providing Availability using lazy replication", ACM Transactions on Computer Systems, Vol 10. No. 4. P.360-391, Nov 1992

[22] K. Birman, "Replication anad availability in Isis", Operating Systems Review, vol 19, no. 5, Dec. 1985, pp. 79-86.

[23] K. Birman, T. Joseph, "Exploiting virtual synchrony in distributed systems", proceedings of the 11th Annual Symposium Operating Systems Principles, pp. 123-138, Austin, TX (Nov. 1987)

[24] T. Chandra, V. Hadzilacos and S. Toueg, "On the impossibility of group membership", proceedings of the fifteenth ACM Symposium on Principles of Distributed Computing, Philadelphia, PA, USA. 1996

[25] D.L. Mills, "Network time protocol, specification and implementation", DARPA, Internet RFC 1059, July 1988

[26] G.S. Blair and R. Lea, "The impact of distribution on the object-oriented approach to software development", IEE/BCS Software Engineering Journal, vol. 7, no. 2, March 1992, pp. 130-138.

[27] ANSA reference manual, Cambridge, U.K., 1991.

[28] R. Guerraroui and A. Schipper, "Software-based replication for fault tolerance", Computer Vol. 30, No. 4, April 1997.

[29] F.B. Schneider, "Byzantine Generals in action. Implementing Fail-Stop processors", ACM Trans. On Computer Systems, Vol 2, No. 2, May 1984, pp. 145-154.

[30] L. Lamport, R.E. Shostak and M. Pease, "The Byzantine generals problem", ACM Transactions on Programming Languages and Systems, 4(3):382-401, July 1982.

[31] F.B. Schneider, " Implementing Fault-tolerant services using the state machine approach: A tutorial", ACM Computing Surveys, vol. 22, no. 4, Dec 1990.

[32] T. Chandra and S. Toueg, "Unreliable failure detectors for asynchronous systems", proceedings of the Tenth ACM Symposium on Principles of Distributed Computing, pp. 325-340, August 1991.

A Network Protocol for Cluster Computing

Alfred C. Weaver
Department of Computer Science
Thornton Hall
University of Virginia
Charlottesville, VA 22903

Abstract

The Xpress Transport Protocol (XTP) is designed to support the types of data exchanges typically found in cluster computing applications. It provides all the classic functionality of a transport protocol, plus new services such as transport multicast, multicast group management, transport layer priorities, traffic descriptions for quality-of service negotiation, rate and burst control, and selectable error and flow control mechanisms. XTP has wide interconnectivity because it operates over any network layer (IP, CLNP), any datalink layer (LLC, MAC), or directly on top of the AAL of ATM. In general, XTP avoids coupling policy with mechanism; XTP offers services but the user's application defines what communications paradigm is most appropriate for its particular environment. In spite of its richer functionality, XTP's reliable data transfer modes have performance characteristics similar to TCP and XTP's unacknowledged transfer mode has performance similar to UDP. Since XTP can run simultaneously with other transport protocols, and can run over whatever network layer (if any) is provided, it represents a low-risk way to exploit the increased functionality required for cluster computing without sacrificing connectedness or interoperability.

1: Network services

In the OSI Reference Model [11], each layer of the model is responsible for providing a specific set of services to the layers above and below it. For the transport layer, those responsibilities include:

- *client identification* -- multiplexing multiple users of the transport layer and keeping their data streams separate;
- *segmentation* -- dividing an arbitrarily long message into packets that are of a convenient size for the underlying network;
- *reliability* -- implementing a transport checksum that is used to verify the accuracy of data received, and rejecting data received with errors; and
- *ordering* -- assuring that the delivered data stream is sequential, with no lost data and no duplicate data.

In the Internet world, the Transmission Control Protocol (TCP) [3] provides these functions, and it is typically used for data exchange that requires full reliability (like file transfer). In addition, the User Datagram Protocol (UDP) [2] is available for less demanding applications; it handles a single message of up to 64 KB on a "best-effort" (unacknowledged) basis and is used for data that does not require guaranteed delivery. Both TCP and UDP require the services of the Internet Protocol (IP) [4] in the network layer below them to route messages to their destination. In the ISO world, the Transport Protocol class 4 (TP4) [12] and the Connectionless Network Protocol (CLNP) [13] provide similar services. TCP, UDP, and IP are very important and very valuable protocols in the networking world; even though they are neither national nor international standards, they are *defacto* standards in the Internet. Having been designed years ago, however, TCP/UDP/TP4 did not anticipate cluster computing applications that now require fast interconnection across LANs (and, sometimes, clusters connected across MANs and WANs). Thus, when these protocols are applied to some modern applications (e.g., interconnection of distributed applications, delivery of synchronized multimedia data streams, transmission of identical data to multiple destinations) they show some deficiencies. For example:

1. TCP supports only peer-to-peer connections (that is, one transmitter talking to one receiver) so a communication from, say, one transmitter to ten receivers requires ten connections and ten independent transmissions. There is no concept of *multicast*. In cluster computing, it is increasingly common for many

0-8186-8810-6/98 $10.00 © 1998 IEEE

applications on different hosts to share a common data stream (e.g., sensor data, multimedia).

2. Since TCP and TP4 do not support multicast, they have no concept of multicast group management, i.e., there is no ability to define a group of transmitters and receivers or for the application program to define the reliability requirements of the group members. Cluster multicast applications should have the option of knowing the identity and/or the status of the multicast receivers.

3. TCP provides little support for priority or latency control, both crucial for tightly-coupled or real-time systems. Cluster applications that source or sink real-time data profit from having the data on the network inherit the priority of the task that produced it.

4. TCP supports only fully reliable transmission (i.e., it repeats missing data until it finally arrives at the destination, no matter how long it takes) which is too strong for some applications. UDP supports only a "best-effort" service (i.e., the transmitter never knows if the receiver got the data) which is too weak for some applications. Data reliability is defined by the protocol, not by the application. Cluster applications should be able to define their own reliability paradigm on a connection-by-connection basis.

5. To send a single message reliably (as with transactions), TCP requires the exchange of six packets (two to set up and acknowledge the connection, two to send and acknowledge the data, and two to close the connection). This slows the exchange of data for short-lived connections since connection setup and tear-down are accomplished separately from data transfer. For cluster applications, transactions need to be fast and efficient.

6. When errors do occur, some TCP implementations recover using a *go-back-n* algorithm that retransmits all data beginning at the point of loss. That works well for LANs, where the round-trip time is short, but for those clusters interconnected via long-haul links or satellites this leads to inefficient use of the network when data previously sent and correctly received is nevertheless resent, only to be discarded at the destination as duplicate data. Instead of this scheme, clusters can use a selective retransmission algorithm that retransmits only the lost data. Recognizing this advantage, newer versions of TCP have implemented a similar scheme.

7. TCP, UDP, and TP4 all implement fixed policies defined by the protocol, not the application. For example, all connections are governed by flow control, which restricts the amount of data the transmitter can send. While this is usually correct, nevertheless there are some "streaming" applications within clusters that would benefit from unrestricted flow, but that option is simply not available. The point is that TCP and UDP embed policy with mechanism, and the two can not be untangled. For cluster computing, we think that the protocol should provide mechanisms, and the distributed applications should set policy.

2: A new approach

In search of a better match between application requirements and transport protocol functionalities, an international group of protocol designers, composed of representatives from industry, academia, military, and government, has defined the Xpress Transport Protocol [19, 21] which provides, all in one transport protocol, the traditional services found in previous transport protocols, plus important new functionality usable in cluster applications. XTP has been adopted as part of MIL-STD-2204, the U.S. military standard mission-critical, networked computers.

It is important to note that XTP is not intended as a replacement for TCP or UDP or TP4; rather it is simply another transport protocol with its own unique functionality which is available as an option for the system designer. Just as TCP and UDP operate side-by-side above IP, XTP operates simultaneously with other transport protocols, and utilizes the services of the network layer below it (if any). XTP operates over IP (which makes it usable in any Internet environment), over CLNP (which covers the ISO networks), directly over the LLC or MAC of any LAN (which covers Ethernet, token ring, FDDI, and ATM LAN emulation), and directly over the adaptation layer of an Asynchronous Transfer Mode (ATM) network. The possible interplay of transport protocols, network protocols, and networks is shown in Figure 1.

3: XTP functionality

If XTP has value to cluster computing, it is because it satisfies some need of the user's application. We examine these new functionalities and how they might be gainfully employed in a cluster application.

3.1: Multicast

Traditional transport protocols support only a unicast paradigm, that is, one transmitter talking to one receiver. As applications become more distributed, there is a need for network nodes to form groups that share certain types of data. For example, the cluster of

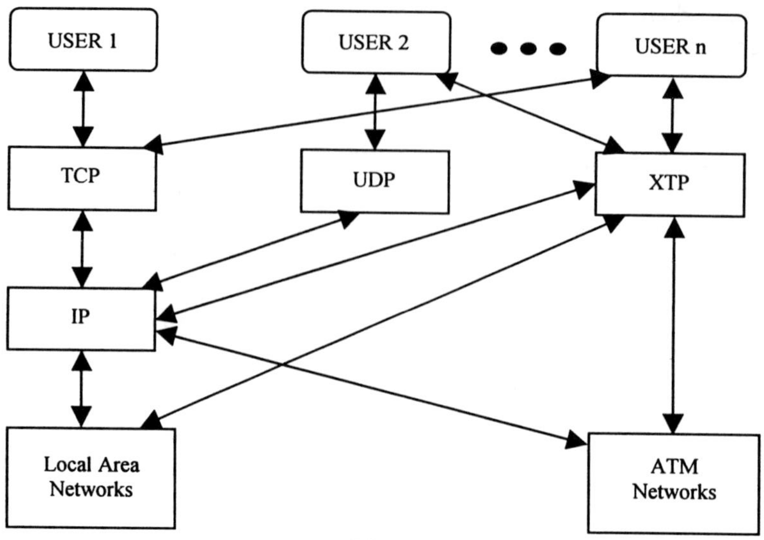

Figure 1.
Interplay of Protocols and Network

computers on a ship's bridge share data among the navigation system, the autopilot, the collision-avoidance system, and the weapons systems. Rather than broadcasting this information to all computers (which requires each node to inspect and interpret it in software, and then discard it if it is not needed), the modern approach is to form a multicast group consisting of one transmitter and arbitrarily many receivers. Then every transmission to the multicast group goes only to those applications that have registered themselves as receivers of the data. Security algorithms can be employed here to monitor and/or enforce group membership. Receivers can join, leave, and rejoin an on-going multicast group as permitted by the multicast group manager (see the next section on Multicast Group Management). The reliability of data delivery is independent of whether the transmission is unicast or multicast and is controlled by the user's selection of the error control mechanism (see the section on Selectable Error Control).

Figure 2(a) represents a traditional unicast, whereas Figure 2(b) shows the basic one-to-many approach of multicast. Figure 2(c) shows an N-to-M multicast. Groups that require more than a single transmitter can be synthesized by using N l-to-N multicast groups to form a N-to-N multicast capability as shown in Figure 2(d).

3.2: Multicast group management

An application may form, or may join, any number of multicast groups. Membership in the group is controlled by the multicast group manager, and it in turn is controlled by the transmitting application. Using MGM, the user can selectively allow or deny the admission of any node to the multicast group; therefore, the resulting dynamic group membership can be known at all times (if desired). The user controls the reaction of the protocol when group members fail or voluntarily leave the group. If the members of a multicast group are required to be fully reliable, then the failure of any group member destroys the integrity of the multicast group, resulting in a failure report to the transmitting application. The application determines the consequences of group membership failure; it may choose to delete the failed member from the group and continue, or abandon transmission entirely, or take some other action that the application deems appropriate. See [5] and [6].

Note how inappropriate it would be to have the protocol manage group membership via some predefined policy. Only the application can appreciate the side-effects of a change in group membership, so XTP reports group membership changes to the transmitting application and lets it decide what should be done. Since group membership is under program control, one could define a multicast group in which, say, three particular members must receive all data reliably and all other members may eavesdrop as they wish. Given that definition, XTP MGM would report failure of any of the three essential nodes, but would ignore the joining and leaving of other non-essential listeners. Also, we note that the reliability of group

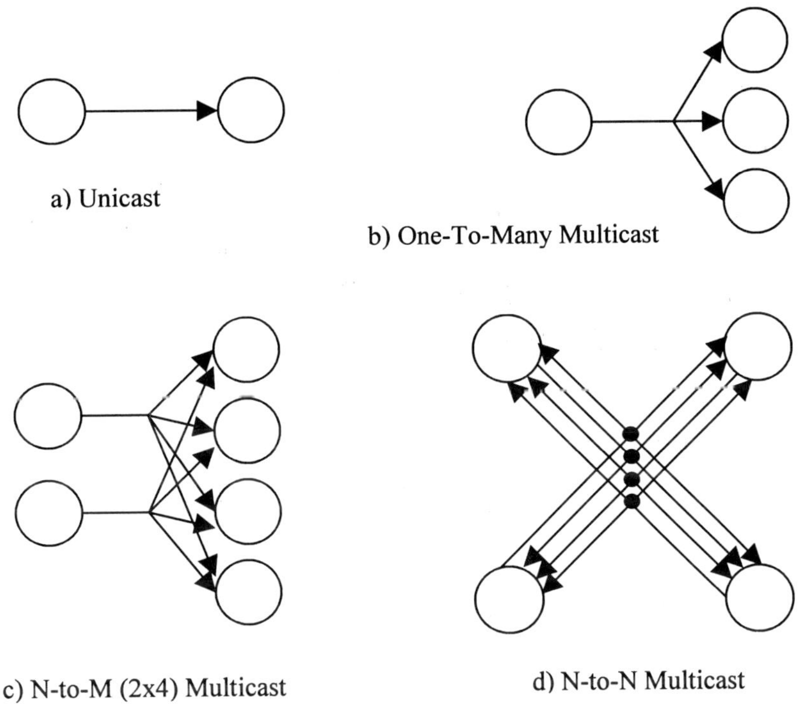

Figure 2.
XTP Multicast Paradigms

membership is orthogonal to the reliability of data transfer within a multicast group. As discussed in the section on selectable error control, XTP supports multiple paradigms for error control, but these are independent of the group membership issues.

3.3: Priority

A rich priority subsystem allows applications to define the importance of their data according to a system-wide scheme; XTP then operates on its most important data first. When XTP is coupled with a real-time operating system and a network that supports priorities, the system designer can then bound end-to-end delivery latencies for high-priority messages (see Figure 3). XTP puts a bit in the packet header that indicates whether or not each packet is participating in the overall priority scheme. If so, then an adjacent field indicates the relative priority of this packet compared to all other packets. XTP examines the priority bit and its associated numeric field and then processes that packet in accordance with its defined importance. One can say that, to a granularity of one packet's transmission time on the network, XTP is always operating on its most important packet. This is true not only in the end-systems, but also in all interior routers if they support the necessary mechanisms to detect and respond to XTP priority (see the section on Applications).

The XTP priority scheme is based on a static priority encoded in a 16-bit numeric field; the lower the numerical value, the higher the importance. By defining the priority system this way, putting a delivery timestamp in the priority field automatically implements an earliest-deadline-first delivery policy with no additional work on the part of the user. Users generate messages of varying importance; XTP sorts those messages internally and emits them in the order of most important message first.

3.4: Rate and burst control

In a cluster environment interconnected via a modern fiber optic network, the usual source of errors is not bit errors on the medium but rather buffer overruns in the receiver or congestion in the routers. Recognizing this fundamental paradigm shift, XTP adds a mechanism for error prevention in addition to the classic mechanisms for error detection (e.g., CRCs) and correction (e.g., retransmission). When using XTP, a receiver can dynamically throttle a transmitter by using rate and burst control. The rate control parameter limits the amount of data that can be transmitted per unit time, while the burst parameter limits the size of data that can be sent (i.e., rate and burst control together control inter-packet gaps). Figure 4 shows the effect of rate and burst control on the total amount of data transmitted over time.

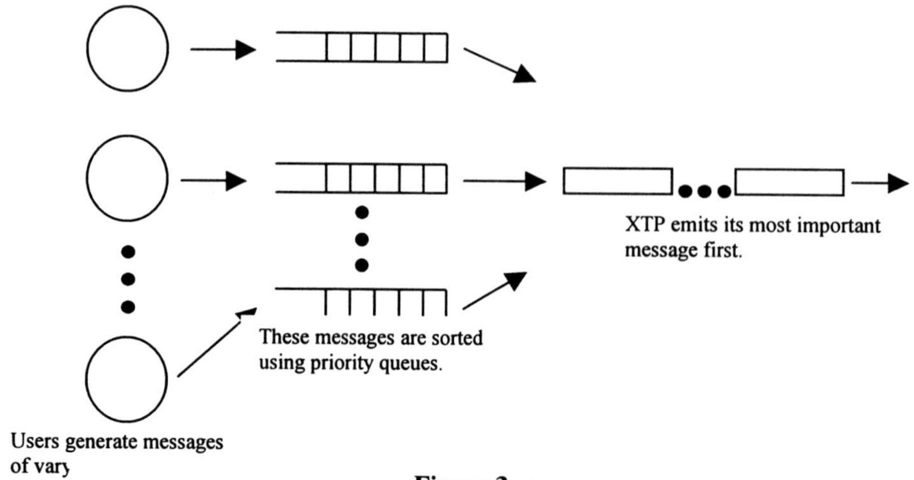

Figure 3.
XTP Priority Mechanism

When using TCP, a slow receiver's protection from a fast transmitter has to be synthesized by flow control; that is, the opening and closing of credit windows. This causes dynamic throughput fluctuation as transmission starts and stops in accordance with the demands of the flow control window. In contrast, rate control allows a steady stream of data to be emitted at a rate known to be acceptable to the receiver (and that rate can be dynamically adjusted to reflect changing conditions). Additionally, conventional flow control is only active end-to-end; that is, routers do not participate. Thus a receiver with spare capacity can open a large flow control window to invite rapid transmission, but this might only result in further congestion of some intermediate router. XTP's rate and burst control algorithms allow the routers to participate; a congested router could temporarily reduce the rate control parameter of its incoming connections until the period of congestion has passed.

3.5: Connection management

TCP and TP4 require the exchange of six data packets to transmit one data element reliably (two to set up and acknowledge the connection, two to send and acknowledge the data, and two to close the connection). XTP achieves the equivalent bi-directional reliability with only three packets because of XTP's powerful connection establishment mechanisms. In the XTP paradigm, host A sends its first packet which requests the connection with host B and sends its data, all in the same packet. Host B may then respond with packets flowing in the reverse direction. When the data transfer ends, the last packet from A to B is marked as such, which closes one side of the connection. Host B acknowledges having received the last data element from A and then closes the connection in the A-to-B direction. Traffic now flows in the reverse B-to-A direction until it ends, at which point the last packet is so marked. Host A acknowledges the receipt of the last packet from B and closes the connection in the B-to-A direction.

Thus, XTP needs only three packets to deliver one piece of data reliably: one to open the connections, send the data, and request the closure of the connection; one to acknowledge the data; and one to acknowledge connection closure. In the special case of a transaction, XTP requires only two packets. Host A sends its first packet to B that opens the connection and transfers the data (the transaction request); host B replies by sending its data (the transaction response) and closing the connection.

3.6: Selectable error control

XTP supports not one but three types of error control:

(a) a fully reliable mode like TCP and TP4, which would normally be used for applications such as file transfer;
(b) a UDP-like service, in which the receiver does not acknowledge transmission and thus the transmitter never knows whether the data was successfully delivered (i.e., a datagram); and
(c) a special mode called fast negative acknowledgment that can improve error repair in certain situations.

In a clustered environment with computers connected via a LAN, out-of-sequence data delivery is much more likely to mean that the missing data is truly lost, as opposed to delayed (as it might be by taking an alternate path in a WAN). Using the *fastnak* option, a receiver that identifies out-of-sequence delivery immediately (without waiting for any time-outs) sends

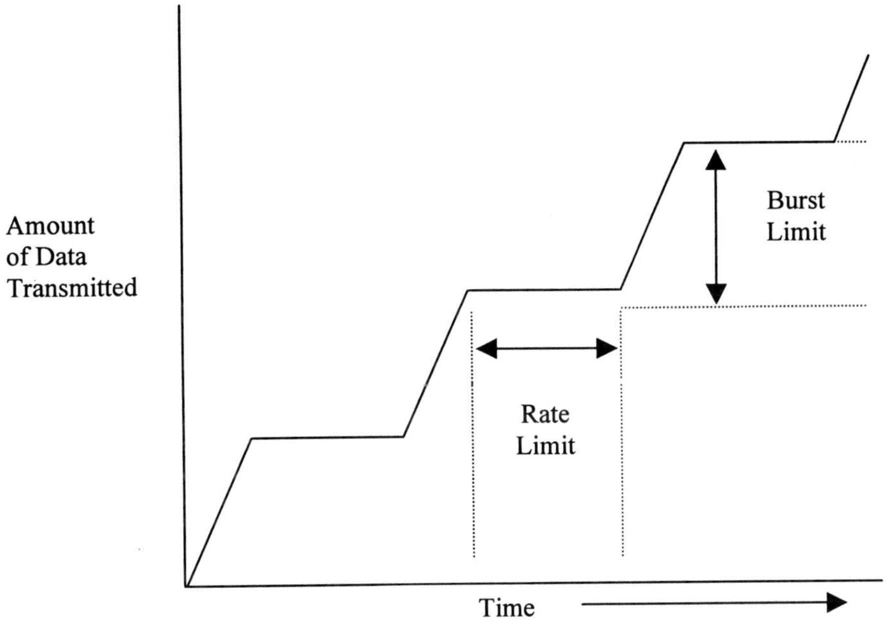

Figure 4.
Rate and Burst Control

a control packet that informs the transmitter about the missing data. The transmitter then immediately resends only the missing data.

Another independent option is *noerror* mode that suspends the normal retransmission scheme. Correctly received data is properly sequenced, but gaps, if any, are not retransmitted. This mode is useful for digitized voice. Not only does XTP provide a range of data reliability options, it does so in a single protocol. Each connection can support an independent choice of error control strategy, and the choice is entirely under the control of the application.

3.7: Selectable flow control

As with error control, three orthogonal options are provided. Traditional flow control based on credit windows is available for normal data. *Reservation mode* practices a conservative flow control policy whereby the receiver may only issue a credit for buffers dedicated to a particular connection; this assures that data will not be lost due to buffer starvation at the destination. The third mechanism is to disable flow control entirely by using the *noflow* option. Note that such a "free flow" or "streaming" mode of operation is not available in other protocols; this mode is useful for intra-cluster multimedia applications.

3.8: Selective retransmission

Older TCP implementations respond to errors by using a *go-back-n* algorithm in which the transmission window is reset and begins again with the first byte which was lost or received in error. While this works well for local area networks with short delivery latencies, it is less efficient with networks that have either high capacity (fiber optic networks) or long delivery latencies (satellite networks) or both. On these networks, *go-back-n* may retransmit data that has already been received correctly. XTP can use either *go-back-n* or *selective retransmission;* in the latter, the receiver acknowledges spans of correctly received data and the sender retransmits only the gaps. The user selects which scheme to use, if any (recall that retransmission does not occur when using *noerror* mode).

Historically, retransmission has been regarded as either inappropriate or ineffective for jitter control in multimedia systems, and this may well be true if TCP-style retransmission is used. However, we have shown in [7,8,9,10] that retransmission, layered on top of an efficient retransmission mechanism like that in XTP, can be very effective for controlling packet loss in delay-sensitive streams.

3.9: Selective acknowledgment

Acknowledging every packet assumes that the network often loses packets, assumes that the transmitter wants acknowledgments, and embeds policy with mechanism. XTP allows the user to decide if and when acknowledgments are desirable. Acknowledgments are provided whenever the transmitter requests them, thereby allowing the user to select an acknowledgment frequency ranging from always to sometimes to never. Philosophically, acknowledgment generation from the receiver is decoupled from data arrivals or window sizes. Whenever the transmitter wants to know the status of the connection, it asks; when the receiver responds, it tells everything it knows about its current status.

3.10: Maximum transmission unit (MTU) detection

A common problem with the independence of layers introduced by the OSI model is that the transport layer may segment a message into packets for the network layer, only to have the network layer fragment each of those packets into still smaller packets that are appropriate for a particular data link. XTP avoids this double effort by negotiating the proper MTU for the route in use. Both end-systems and routers can declare their MTU for a particular link, and the transmitter will select the minimum of all MTUs encountered on any given path.

3.11: Out-of-band data

It is sometimes useful to send information about the data stream without embedding it within the data stream itself. As an option, XTP can carry with each packet up to eight bytes of tagged data. Tagged data is passed from the transmitter to the receiver, and its presence is indicated to the receiver, but it is never interpreted by XTP. Tagged data can be used by the application for providing semantic information about the data. For cluster computing applications that handle real-time data, tagged data is an elegant way to associate a 64-bit timestamp with each packet transmitted.

3.12: Alignment

Although it is a simple notion, data alignment pays big dividends by avoiding excess data copies. The major fields of the XTP header are aligned on 4-byte boundaries; this minimizes the number of memory accesses needed to retrieve a field. The data segment begins and ends on 4-byte boundaries, and a length field identifies the last byte of the user data.

3.13: Traffic descriptors

We anticipate that packet-switched networks like the Internet will eventually support quality-of-service requests from transmitters; the ATM Forum is already grappling with the problem of how to implement QoS in ATM networks. Since XTP is designed to work in both environments, it defines a traffic descriptor field that can be used to communicate QoS parameters among routers and end-systems. While XTP itself does not perform explicit resource reservation, it can supply the necessary information to other resource reservation protocols. Because resource reservation work is still a research topic, we expect the form and content of the traffic descriptor field to evolve over time.

4: Performance

Protocol performance measurement is a tricky subject; it is difficult to achieve a true "apples-to-apples" measurement unless the same person or group designed and implemented both protocols in the same environment. Since XTP has more functionality than TCP/UDP/TP4, one might predict that it would run slower, but that has not been our experience. For a particular real-time application running under pSOS+ on a cluster of 133 MHz Pentium-based PCs connected by FDDI interfaces, we measured the following when comparing TCP vs. XTP vs. UDP.

As shown in Figure 5, throughput for all protocols is similar for small messages, for which throughput is governed by operating systems overhead more than message size. For larger messages, protocol and network overhead do influence throughput, and in this particular measurement XTP's reliable delivery mode performed slightly better than TCP.

Figure 6 shows a comparison of how fast the various protocols can transmit messages of varying size. The need to transmit many small messages very quickly is very common for real-time control applications (e.g., a cluster computing fly-by-wire control outputs on an airplane). For large messages, the performance of all protocols is similar because performance is dominated by getting the message transmitted on the network. For small messages, however, XTP shows a striking performance advantage (here a factor of two) over TCP and UDP.

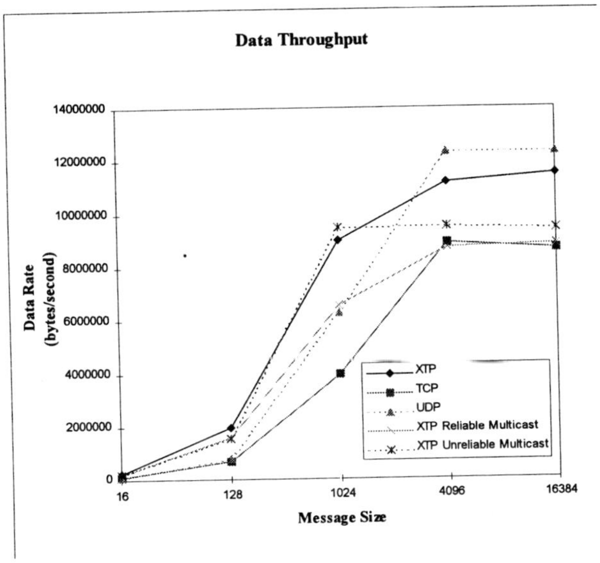

Figure 5.
Throughput of XTP, TCP, and UDP

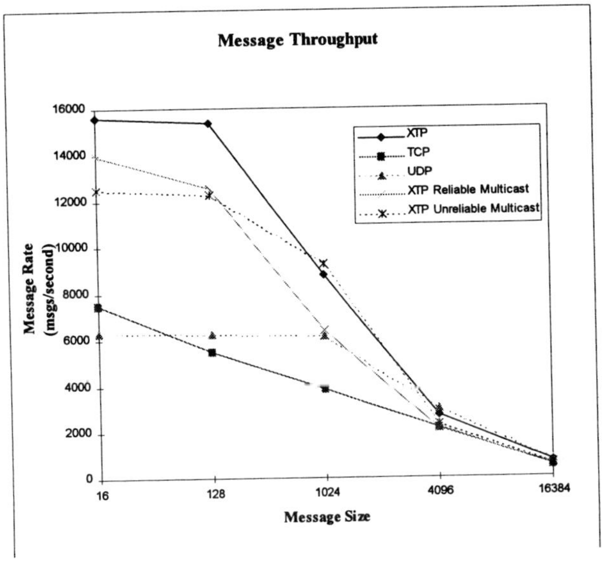

Figure 6.
Message Rate Comparison

Figure 7 confirms that XTP can deliver messages quickly. In this measurement, the user-memory-to-user-memory one-way latency varies from an average of 228 microseconds for 16-byte messages to 1.6 ms for 16k-byte messages. TCP and UDP timings are comparable.

In general, our experience has been that a skillful XTP implementation delivers to the application approximately 80-96% of the raw network bandwidth available at the level of the MAC device driver. Nevertheless, because it is difficult to separate the skill of the implementers from the inherent power of the protocol, XTP does not make the claim that it is faster than any particular protocol; the measured performance simply speaks for itself. XTP is a tool, just like TCP and UDP are tools, and all of them should be used wherever they are most appropriate. In my opinion, XTP's major contribution is not so much its performance but its functionality. The ability to utilize many different communications paradigms, all in the same protocol, and all under the user's control, is a major advantage for the system designer.

5: Applications

XTP has been utilized in a number of commercial and military applications. Its use is growing as application designers see its functional advantages (e.g., multicast, group management) in distributed systems. Here are some examples of how commercial companies and government agencies have used XTP's capabilities to achieve specific goals.

5.1: Multicast. A government contractor needed to interconnect a cluster of 22 CRAY supercomputers, all riding the belly of a C-130 aircraft, to form a flying signal intelligence center. Since this environment required sending identical data streams to multiple processors, they chose XTP so that they could utilize its multicast capabilities. Each multicast transmission consumes only a fraction of the network bandwidth that would otherwise have been required by N serial unicasts.

5.2: Gigabyte files. A commercial company needed to transfer gigabyte files routinely across a satellite-based network that connected clusters of computers located on different continents. They chose XTP to utilize its selective retransmission capability. When errors corrupt the satellite channel, XTP retransmits only the data that was lost; it does not restart the data stream from the point of loss.

5.3: High performance. A government agency needed a communications protocol that would support the real-time environment of weapons control. They chose XTP based on its low end-to-end latency characteristics. Being able to reliably send modest size messages with sub-millisecond latencies allowed them to write effective feedback control loops even in a packet-switched networking environment.

5.4: Image distribution. One company faced the problem of having to send very high resolution medical images over an FDDI-based network. They

User data message size (bytes)	Minimum latency (ms)	Average latency (ms)	Maximum latency (ms)
16	201	228	325
128	216	241	322
1024	313	336	452
4096	636	657	815
16384	1638	1656	1780

Figure 7.
XTP End-to-End Latency

needed to move multiple mammography images (40 MB each) to a work station cluster for simultaneous review by a staff of radiologists. They chose XTP for its combination of high throughput and multicast distribution.

5.5: Digital telephony. A government contractor wanted to operate a digital telephone/intercom system over an existing FDDI data network. The system had to support 120 simultaneous bi-directional conversations (64 Kbits/s each), and each conversation had to have the capability of being sent to any combination of destinations. They chose XTP because its multicast feature would allow any number of receivers to join a multicast group (under the supervision and control of the transmitter), thus making it simple to implement the cross-communications requirement.

5.6: Video file server. A company needed the capability to send and receive "video mail" (synchronized audio/video) throughout their corporate network, in addition to their traditional text-based electronic mail. They chose XTP because it handled the multimedia requirements with ease. Personal computers were able to mount a remote disk drive (the file server) and retrieve a compressed multimedia stream in real time.

5.7: Priority support. A government research lab required that its packet-switched network be able to support digital multimedia streams in addition to file transfer and electronic mail. They used XTP in combination with an XTP-aware IP router [1] to achieve this goal. This IP router identifies XTP packets and handles them in accordance with the XTP priority option.

5.8: Real-time systems. A government contractor needed to design a ship-board network, based on MIL-STD-2204, that would handle time-critical command and control messages, multimedia streams, background file transfer, and data distribution from one source to multiple destinations. They chose XTP because it provided latency control, message-level priorities, multimedia support, high overall performance, and multicast capabilities to handle the distribution of identical data streams.

5.9: Interoperability. Desiring to preserve the connectedness and interoperability associated with the classic protocols, one government contractor built a MIL-STD-2204 network incorporating TCP and UDP and XTP, all operating over IP. Another vendor provided TP4 and XTP, both over CLNP. Yet another vendor, working with real-time data on a single-segment LAN, put XTP directly on top of the MAC of FDDI.

6: XTP's Future in Cluster Computing

XTP offers significant new functionality (especially the transport layer multicast, multicast group management, and transport layer priorities) that has already been shown to be of significant benefit to cluster computing applications.

In an effort to speed the deployment of XTP, a public domain version has been developed at Sandia National Laboratories [20]; information is freely available from http://www.ca.sandia.gov/xtp/SandiaXTP. Commercial versions are available now from at least two sources [18, 14]. Commercial and military products developed from these XTP implementations are currently in everyday use.

7: References

[1] Christie, R.W. and Weaver, A.C., "Design of an XTP-Aware IP Router," Distributed Technology Exchange, NCCOSC RDT&E Division (NRaD), San Diego, CA, March 13-17, 1995.

[2] Postel, J., ed., "User Datagram Protocol," RFC 768, USC/Information Sciences Institute, August 1980.

[3] Postel, J., ed., "Transmission Control Protocol--DARPA Internet Program Protocol Specification," RFC 793, USC/Information Sciences Institute, September 1981.

[4] Postel, J., ed., "Internet Protocol-DARPA Internet Program Protocol Specification," RFC 791, USC/Information Sciences Institute, September 1981.

[5] Dempsey, B.J., Fenton, J.C., and Weaver, A.C., "The Multidriver: A Reliable Multicast Service for the Xpress Transfer Protocol," 15th Local Computer Networks Conference, Minneapolis, Minnesota, October 1-3,1990.

[6] Dempsey, B.J., "An Analysis of Multicast and Multicast Group Management," M.S. thesis, Department of Computer Science, University of Virginia, January 1991.

[7] Dempsey, B.J., Lucas, M.T., and Weaver, A.C., "An Empirical Study of Packet Voice Distribution over a Campus-Wide Network," 19th IEEE Local Computer Networks Conference, Minneapolis, Minnesota, October 1994.

[8] Dempsey, B.J., Lucas, M.T., and Weaver, A.C., ""Design and Implementation of a High Quality Video Distribution System using XTP Reliable Multicast," Second International Workshop on Advanced Communications and Applications for High-Speed Networks, Heidelberg, Germany, September 1994.

[9] Dempsey, B.J., *Retransmission-Based Error Control for Continuous Media Traffic in Packet-Switched Networks*, Ph.D. dissertation, Computer Networks Laboratory, Department of Computer Science, University of Virginia, May 1994.

[10] Dempsey, B.J., Liebeherr, J., and Weaver, A.C., "A New Error Control Scheme for Packetized Voice over High-Speed Local Area Networks," 18th IEEE Local Computer Networks Conference, Minneapolis, Minnesota, September 1993.

[11] International Organization for Standardization, "Information Processing Systems-Open Systems Interconnection-Basic Reference Model," International Standard 7498, October 1984.

[12] International Organization for Standardization, "Information Processing Systems—Open Systems Interconnection-Transport Protocol Specifications," International Standard 8073, July 1986.

[13] International Organization for Standardization, "Information Processing Systems—Open Systems Interconnection-Data Communications Protocol for Providing the Connectionless Mode Network Service, International Standard 8473, March 1986.

[14] Mentat, Inc., http://www.mentat.com/.

[15] Michel, J., Waterman, A., and Weaver, A., "Performance Evaluation of an Off-Host Communications Architecture," High Performance Communication Subsystems, Williamsburg, VA, September 1-3, 1993.

[16] Michel, J., Waterman, A., and Weaver, A.C., "Performance Evaluation of an Off-Host Communications System," 18th Local Computer Networks Conference, Minneapolis, MN, September 19-22, 1993.

[17] Survivable Adaptable Fiber Optic Network, U.S. Department of Defense Military Standard MIL-STD-2204, October 1992.

[18] "Xpress Transport Protocol", http://www.cs.virginia.edu/~acw/netx/.

[19] Strayer, W.T., Dempsey, B.J., and Weaver, A.C., *XTP: The Xpress Transfer Protocol,* Addison-Wesley, 1992.

[20] Strayer, W.T., Gray, S., and Cline, R.E., Jr., "An Object-Oriented Implementation of the Xpress Transfer Protocol," Proceedings of the Second International Workshop on Advanced Communications and Applications for High-Speed Networks (IWACA'94), Heidelberg, Germany, September 26-28, 1994.

[21] Strayer, W.T., ed., "Xpress Transport Protocol 4.0 Specification," http://www.ca.sandia.gov/xtp/.

CommBridge – An Enterprise Application Integration Architecture for Electronic Government

Jack Hornfeldt,
CIO and Director of
Information Technology Services,
Executive Office of Health and
Human Services,
Commonwealth of
Massachusetts
Jack.Hornfeldt@state.ma.us

Mark Heumann,
Application Development
Manager, Enterprise
Applications Bureau,
Information Technology
Division, Commonwealth of
Massachusetts
Mark.Heumann@state.ma.us

William P. Wilson, Jr.
Director,
Technology and Systems
Architecture,
Systems Engineering, Inc.
wwilson@sengi.com

Abstract

Driven largely by the re-engineering of Health and Human Services information systems for Welfare Reform and Y2K, the Commonwealth of Massachusetts is implementing an enterprise-wide infrastructure named CommBridge to meet application data and functional integration requirements mandated by law. The architecture uses a standards-based infrastructure (TCP/IP, LDAP, X.500, and X.509), and 80% of the inter-application transaction requirements can be met with a few easy-to-use API primitives. The project's pilot phase demonstrated the feasibility of the architecture, and a broader implementation was planned. Several interagency application interfaces for a new HS case management system are now in production. The architecture implements robust communication between applications using Message Oriented Middleware (MOM), a PKI security mechanism, a centralized directory for addressing and configuration information, incremental deployment, and centralized infrastructure management. Current development will incorporate enterprise-level information management capabilities based on the common interchange mechanism and access to enterprise data via the WWW.

Keywords

Enterprise Application Interoperability, Legacy Systems, Middleware, Message Oriented Middleware, MOM, Directory Services, LDAP, x.500, Encryption, PKI, X.509, TCP/IP, Government, Human Services, Financial Systems.

The Human Services Business Problem

Ever since the advent of "Open Systems", Information Technology Managers have been seeking to achieve transparent interoperability between disparate hardware and software platforms. The need to move information from one department, division, location, or enterprise to another is not new. What has elevated the call for interoperability is the contrast between the high speed and efficiency of processing and the slow-down caused by 'sneaker net', 'snail mail', and other human-speed delivery methods.

This paper presents business requirements for one enterprise, the Commonwealth of Massachusetts, and a configuration of technologies to achieve a network of system-to-system data interchanges that require no human intervention for successful operation, and can be applied to establish or modify a new interchange with minimal programmer activity.

File transfer and format translation are not new. Whether accomplished by tape mounts and conversion programs, or ftp over Internet connections, the movement of data has been taking place for decades. What differentiates **CommBridge** is that human intervention is not required for operation, that modification or addition of functions is facilitated so that standard application programmer skill-sets are sufficient to accomplish that goal, and that the cost to user agencies is limited to the installation of software and the one-time development of request or service application programs for each interface.

0-8186-8810-6/98 $10.00 © 1998 IEEE

In Massachusetts, the Executive Office of Health and Human Services (EOHHS) oversees fifteen agencies that deliver benefits and services to eligible residents of the state. Collectively, these agencies account for almost one-half of the Commonwealth's $16 Billion annual operating budget, and serve between 750,000 and 800,000 individuals at a particular time (12 to 13% of the population).

Due to federal requirements for various eligibility verifications, the Department of Transitional Assistance (DTA) must insure that client Social Security numbers are correct, that recipients of financial assistance or food stamps do not have income exceeding a minimal amount, and that clients are entitled to child support payments. The answers to these questions require matching of data with systems operated by other state agencies or, in the SSN verification instance, the federal Social Security Administration (SSA).

Similarly, the Department of Social Services (DSS), which must sometimes remove a child or children from a home in order to provide them with safety and a nurturing environment, must inform "welfare" since the removal of dependents would effect the benefits received by the adult(s). Children placed in foster care must receive Medicaid cards. In preparing the design of its new child welfare information system, DSS identified more than 20 interfaces with other agencies – all of which could be electronic.

The Division of Medical Assistance (DMA), in issuing Medicaid benefits, must also validate and verify each SSN. Its "partnership" with the Department of Mental Health provides a "safety net" for needy individuals – again, verification of identity and need are required.

Several agencies must submit identifying information to the Social Security Administration for verification of Social Security Numbers. The DTA and DMA also obtain additional data for eligibility determination. The daily file transmission from Boston to Baltimore is electronic, but the delivery of file extracts for assembly into a daily transport file has taken place through tape exchange. Return information from the SSA has been parsed and delivered to originating agencies by a tape exchange as well. The elimination of two human interventions each, at the agency and Data Center, is highly desirable.

The Executive Office of Health and Human Services has developed a "Client Index" – a warehouse-like database containing an unduplicated list of clients served by one or more of the HHS agencies. During initial development, semi-annual batch extracts from agency databases have been merged. In the second phase, CommBridge is used to update the "Index" on a regular basis without operator intervention. This makes timely data available for analysis, administrative oversight, and program planning.

The agencies involved in these data exchanges have systems running in MVS, UNIX (both HP/UX and AIX), and Windows NT. Some are operated at a Data Center managed by the State's Information Technology Division; others in agency offices. Some agencies are operating legacy systems, others have recently completed new implementations, and still others are in the midst of development. The impracticality of requiring all agencies to standardize on a particular platform is obvious. Achieving interoperability is the only feasible approach to such diversity. Seamless interoperability is, of course, the most desirable situation. EOHHS has found that CommBridge affords an optimal, almost ideal, solution. The cost to an individual agency is reasonable. The MQSeries™ software – in various platform "flavors" is low cost, and runs on a low-end server or as a second process on a large (e.g. database) server. The CommBridge implementation includes a repository of Application Program Interfaces and Request and Service specifications. Agency application programmers must write the program necessary to extract data necessary to respond to a request or to process received data. Once these tasks are accomplished, the queuing functions operate without intervention and system-to-system communication is established.

The Enterprise Technology Infrastructure

Not unlike other large enterprises, Massachusetts state government has built an impressive collection of computer systems developed to meet the immediate needs and mandates of each individual agency. Many of these single purpose systems, however, utilize antiquated, proprietary technology which, while meeting the immediate needs of the organization, allow little or no ability to take advantage of advances in enterprise computing. These "legacy" systems create significant barriers for quickly developing new applications, connecting to other agency and state systems, and responding to the changing needs of the public. Additionally, a wide range of hardware platforms (IBM 3090 mainframe, Windows NT servers, HP9000, RISC System 6000) were purchased to run these systems.

Disparate computer systems and the need for an enterprise strategic direction were some of the impetus behind the 1994 concept of the Massachusetts Access to Government Network or MAGNet. As part of the MAGNet vision, agency interworking services provide "peer-to-peer" connections between multiple cooperating applications across any combination of LAN LAN/WAN sub-networks. The network would support ordered delivery of messages, transparently managing platform-specific differences in data architectures. MAGNet also proposed using standardized message formats to promote data interchange.

This MAGNet vision spawned the Communication Bridge Project (CommBridge). CommBridge provides a mechanism for applications to communicate with other applications in a consistent, standardized manner. It enables real-time queries and updates, as well as data streaming. Backup and recovery, store and forward, security, auditing, and protocol conversion are also provided. Additionally, CommBridge utilizes other MAGNet standards including TCP/IP, X.500 directory services and PKI encryption standards.

CommBridge

In the winter of 1995, to address the Human Service business problem within the MAGNet interoperability vision discussed earlier in this paper, the IS management in the Commonwealth Department of Social Services funded a study to "... focus on interoperability requirements that represent elements of risk in initiating a large-scale project to link HHS agency information systems ... the central theme would be data exchange across heterogeneous systems ... the deliverables would focus on concrete demonstrable prototypes to stimulate interest, credibility, and agency participation to prepare for impending pushes for system integration."

The project was managed by the CIO of the Executive Office of Health and Human Services. The final report identified various HHS agencies that could benefit from such an infrastructure, analyzed and abstracted the types of transactions required across agency information systems, and addressed the infrastructure requirements and information flows which would take place. One of the key results was a Human Services Interoperability Architecture (HSIA) [Figure 1] that was later generalized into the enterprise-wide solution to be named CommBridge.

The study identified a number of requirements for the infrastructure technology base. It needed to support a variety of hardware and software platforms including several mainframe architectures, a variety of UNIX implementations, and Windows. It also needed to be able to integrate existing (legacy) applications as well as new ones. It needed to be minimally disruptive to a broad variety of application architectures. It had to be constructed using stable standards-based technologies. It had to address information security. It needed to be incrementally deployable, distributed in nature but centrally manageable. And it needed to be robust and fault tolerant.

Technologies that could be the basis for such an infrastructure were researched and critiqued. Researchers considered FTP and TCP/IP Sockets, Message Oriented Middleware (MOM), Object Request Brokers (ORB's), and Transaction Monitors (TM's). MOM was deemed to be the most appropriate technology given the current state of the art. There were several deployed implementations that met many of the desired criteria. IBM's MQSeries™ was chosen because of the breadth of platforms and the stability of the product.

A pilot project was completed under the management of the Commonwealth's Information Technology Division to test the network communication of data between two existing applications already exchanging information using magnetic tape. This pilot project demonstrates the feasibility of the CommBridge concept while further developing the architecture and constructing re-usable components for future expansion of the infrastructure.

The architecture of CommBridge embodies several key concepts. A department agrees to provide a "service" to those departments authorized to "request" it. For example, the Department of Revenue can offer wage information (in the same format) to all human service departments that have been authorized to receive this data. Each department's computer system is autonomous and no control is given up. Each department continues to manage its own systems, and applications are developed, driven by departmental business requirements. A set of "toolkits" are used to integrate CommBridge functionality into departmental applications without making any significant or time-consuming changes to the application programs.

Service and requester software components are reusable, resulting in great efficiencies once the core set of components are built and ready to be reused.

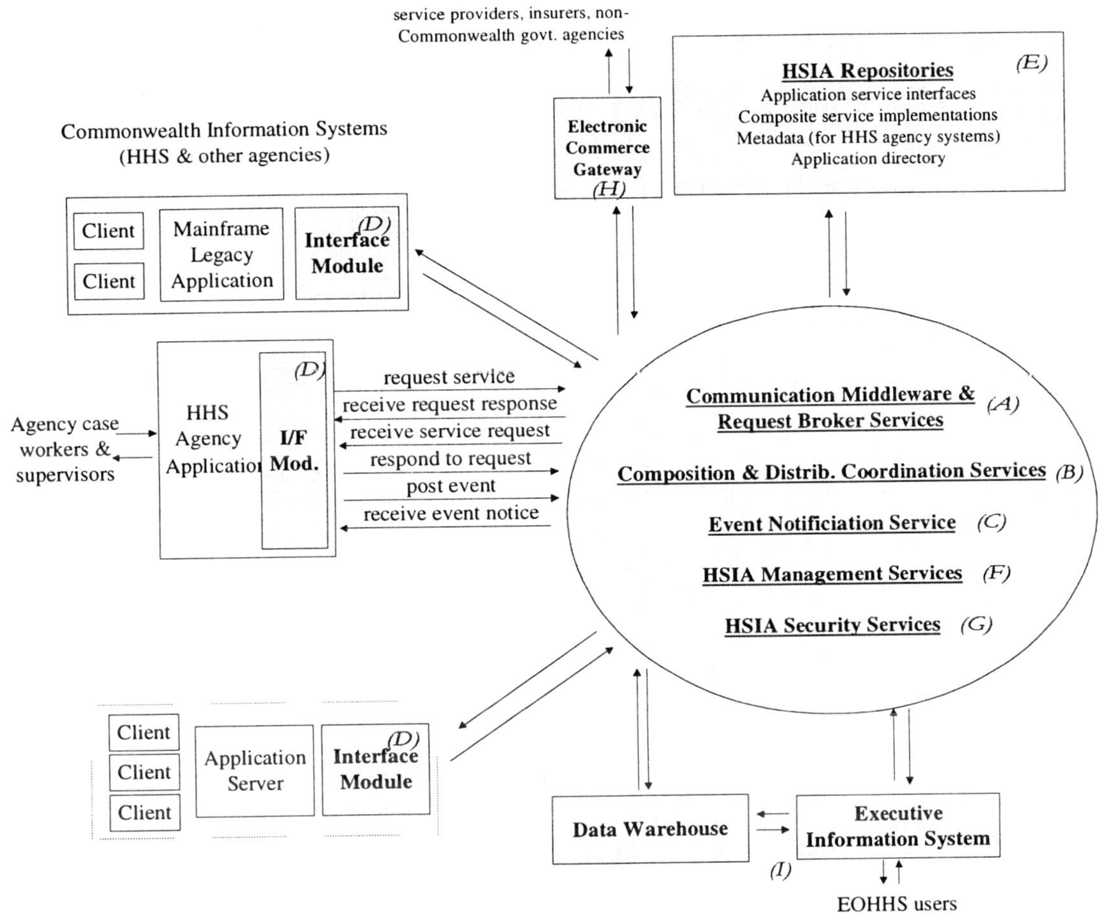

• **Figure 1: Human Services Interoperability Architecture (HSIA)**

The realization of CommBridge is based on re-usable API toolkits designed to handle the most commonly anticipated intersystem transaction models. These toolkits are constructed using a common API that integrates and hides the middleware and enterprise communications infrastructure from the toolkit designer and application developer. The overall structure is expressed in the CommBridge Layered Architecture shown in Figure 2.

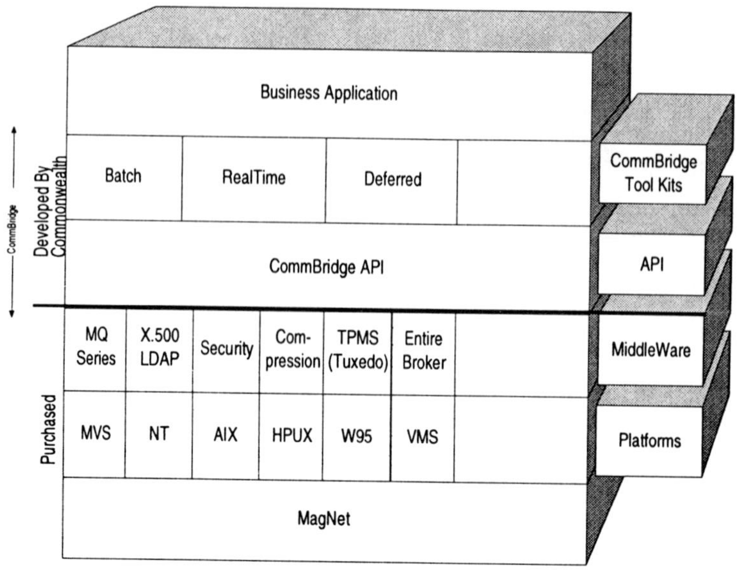

• **Figure 2: The CommBridge Layered Architecture**

The Transaction Paradigms

In order to isolate application programmers as much as possible from the complexities of the infrastructure, a set of toolkits were defined that represent standard approaches to be used to implement transactions between applications. The requirements for the common API used to construct these toolkits was abstracted from the initial set of 3 paradigms: Batch (file transfer), as shown in Figure 3; Real-time (synchronous), and Deferred (asynchronous) as shown in Figure 4.. A transaction toolkit consists of all of the components needed to implement the components of an interface.

All of the toolkit interfaces rely on common capabilities in the CommBridge API for security (Encryption and Authentication) which is based on standard PKI technology via the Entrust™ File security toolkit from NORTEL. Directory and configuration services are provided via LDAP access to the Commonwealth's X.500 directory. Message routing is specified outside of the application entirely using infrastructure configuration tools and managed out of the ITD data center on a 7x24 basis.

The transaction paradigms are structured around the idea that there are two participants in any transaction: a requester which initiates and receives primary benefit from the transaction, and a service which provides or consumes data and may perform business logic at the behest of the requester. Each requester has a requester component and a response handler component to receive replies. Each service has a service component to receive requests and a responder component to generate responses. A single service may handle multiple simultaneous requesters. Services are named and have published interface specifications that detail the data and process requirements necessary to access the service.

The Batch paradigm recognizes that many applications, especially legacy applications, operate around a periodic batch cycle. To effectively integrate with applications that operate in this way, a mechanism for sharing data via a file transfer mechanism is required. CommBridge provides a reliable file transfer capability using the assured delivery of Message Oriented Middleware. The Batch toolkit contains components to provide for interplatform record format conversions and signaling mechanisms to allow for automatic scheduling of business logic when a file is received. In cases where file exchange is already being used, no application code changes are required. CommBridge simply replaces manual file movement, with assured delivery over the wide area network. Signaling features interact with batch schedulers to eliminate the need for human intervention. In the CommBridge pilot, the time to complete a weekly magnetic tape-based data match between two agencies was reduced from several days to less than two hours.

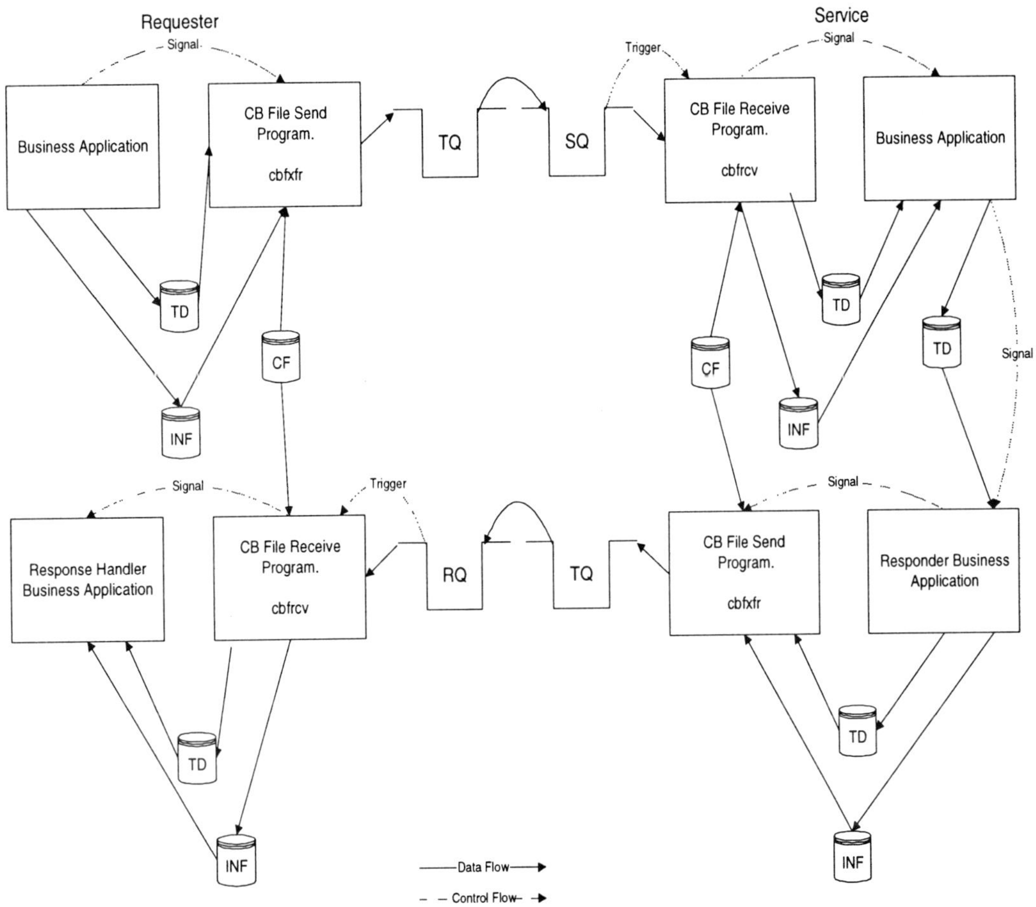

• Figure 3: CommBridge Batch Transaction Paradigm

Real-time and Deferred interface tools are intended to support on-line transactions where the exchange of information is initiated within the normal business flow rather than flagged or logged for later processing in a batch cycle. To this end, the toolkit API to initiate and process transactions is called directly from the business logic. Real-time transactions are intended to be used in two-tier interactive applications where the business logic on a client workstation needs to interact with another system in order to satisfy the data needs of a human operator. It is also useful with multi-step transactions that require verification to complete. In the real-time case, it is required that the business application wait or poll for a reply.

In the deferred case, the business application continues about its business and depends on CommBridge to deliver the transactions and activate an appropriate business application function when a response is received. The deferred transaction model uses static queues and persistent messaging to provide assured message delivery. Figure 4 shows the structure of a real-time transaction where the two business logic components at each end of the application are combined into a single execution unit. In the deferred case, the business logic for requester and service may be in separate execution units from the response handler and responder.

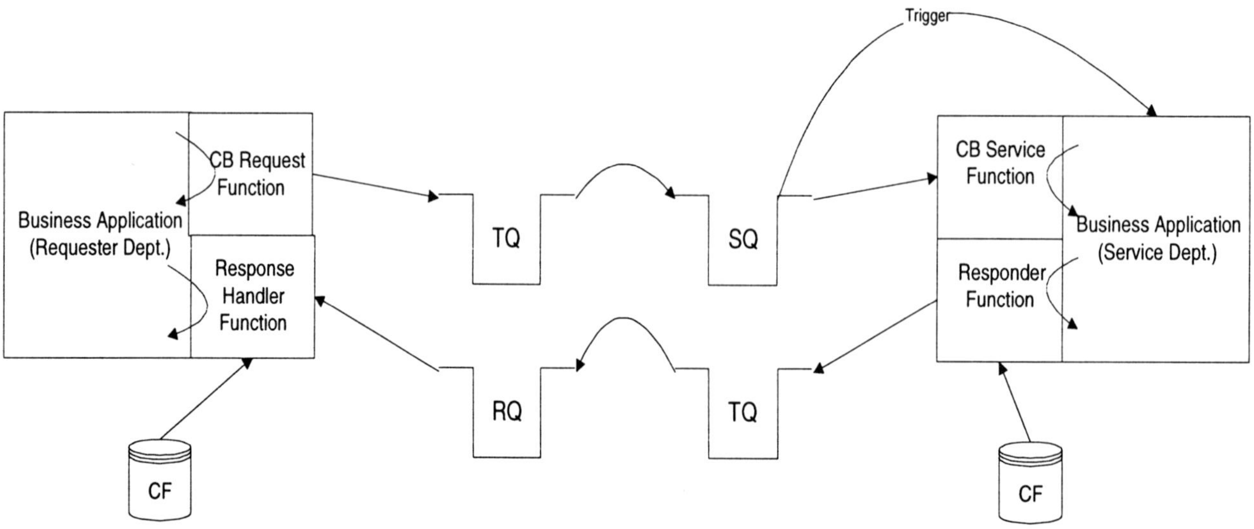

• Figure 4: CommBridge Real-time Transaction Paradigm

Reaching for the Web

By providing information access using CommBridge toolkits, a service application may provide the same capabilities to human requesters via the WWW. CommBridge can map the transaction data from these services to web pages through web-to-MOM servers that act in concert with web servers and Message Queue Managers. This has the substantial benefit of extending the utility of legacy applications, making them accessible from the web at the same time that they are made accessible to other applications. Existing MOM products provide a number of tools for integrating applications with the WWW, including web server-to-queue manager interface engines that allow Post Forms to be handled via asynchronous messages. Client and Server side messaging can also be performed through the use of JAVA and ActiveX interfacing tools.

Application Synergy

Once a comprehensive system of message-based application interfaces is in place, enterprise-level functions may be implemented that can "tap" data in transit for warehousing, initiate event-driven "publication" or notification services, allow for the integration of multiple transactions into simpler 'composite' transactions or sequenced 'workflows'. These functions may be implemented independently, allowing line-of-business applications to focus on solving key business problems without complicating the design to account for the more global potential infrastructure requirements.

Implementation Case Studies

The Department of Social Services (DSS) is the state agency responsible for child welfare in Massachusetts. In February 1998, the DSS implemented a new comprehensive child welfare client/server application named FamilyNet. One of the functions of FamilyNet is to capture information on consumers, including which services were provided to whom, when they were provided and when they were payable. State regulations require that all payees and all payments be recorded in the state accounting system, Massachusetts Management Accounting & Reporting System (MMARS) which resides on an IBM/3090. The business problem in this situation was how to send vendor and payment requests to MMARS, and how to update FamilyNet with payment information, keeping both applications in synch. CommBridge provided an easy solution to this business requirement. The State Comptroller's Office built a service, which they called MMARSLoad, which would allow departments wishing to interface with MMARS a predefined format for sending transactions. As part of the MMARSLoad service, a response would be generated for each request, giving the requester information on the status of each transaction (i.e. accepted or rejected, with reasons and dates, as well as payment dates and check numbers). FamilyNet was able to develop programs that, for example, would build a payment voucher transaction in the MMARS format every time a child received service from a vendor. These transactions would then be transmitted to MMARS on a daily basis at an appointed time (using the system scheduler). CommBridge on the MMARS end would receive and process the transactions as they arrived and would respond to FamilyNet on a system-scheduled basis. Acting as a response handler, FamilyNet would process the response file from MMARS as it arrived and update the FamilyNet database with the check number and payment date.

The Department of Transitional Assistance (DTA) is the state agency responsible for the welfare caseload in Massachusetts. The DTA is required to verify whether any of its clients are receiving earned income by performing a match against the Department of Revenue's (DOR) wage reporting database. This process, performed on a weekly basis, had required that the DTA download data about its clients to magnetic tape, hand carry the tape to the DOR (due to security requirements), have the tape loaded, perform a match against the DOR database, generate a response tape, hand carry the response back to the DTA, load the response tape, and update the DTA database. Needless to say, this process was not only tedious and error prone (tapes were sometimes misplaced or illegible) but also could take as long as a week.

Again CommBridge provided an ideal solution. The DOR established a CommBridge service named WageMatch and allowed the DTA to be a requester. DTA client data stored on an IBM/3090, rather than written to tape, invokes the CommBridge transfer executable, which encrypts the data and transmits it through the DOR firewall to an NT server where the CommBridge receiving process decrypts the data and creates a file. The DOR is then able to do the match against its database on the Unisys/2200, create a response file, and invoke the CommBridge transfer process that encrypts the data and transmits it back through the firewall to the DTA. The entire process, from creating the request to updating the DTA database with the response, takes only several hours.

Conclusion

CommBridge has achieved interoperability in a heterogeneous enterprise between applications operating on various platforms using a variety of commercially available standards-based technologies. The result of this capability is a great saving in time and greater efficiency in the delivery of government services. Future benefits are likely to be even more substantial as agencies take advantage of the common infrastructure to coordinate their services.

A New Scheme of Credit Based Payment for Electronic Commerce

Yi Mu and Vijay Varadharajan
School of Computing and IT, University of Western Sydney, Nepean,
PO Box 10, Kingswood, N.S.W. 2747, Australia
Email: {yimu,vijay}@cit.nepean.uws.edu.au

Abstract

This paper describes a new credit card system, which presents a promise for us to develop a new method of protecting secret information, such as credit card number, PIN and identification. Our credit cards are anonymous. That is, the identity of a card holder and credit card information are not revealed during a payment process. One important feature of our system lies in the fact that, unlike normal electronic credit based systems such as SET, iKP and NetCard, the involvement of the on-line financial institution that runs the payment system is reduced to a minimum.

1 Introduction

A fundamental requirement for the Internet to really become an open marketplace for goods and services in practice is the need for secure charging and payment mechanisms. Given the explosive growth in the use of the Internet, and in the services and applications being offered over the Internet, the mechanisms enabling secure commercial transactions form the foundation stone of this electronic information revolution. Needless to say security aspects become critical to the successful operation of any of these electronic payment schemes. Broadly speaking, there are two classes of electronic payment schemes. Schemes such as DigiCash [1, 2] and NetCash [3] consider cash-based electronic payments. Others such as iKP [4], NetBill [5], NetCheque [6], CyberCash [7], STT[8], SEPP [9], and SET [10] consider credit and debit based electronic payments. Our focus in this paper is on credit based electronic payment systems.

In general, an on-line credit card payment system involves at least the following parties: *Clients* (Service Users) requesting services from *Merchants* who provide the services, and *Banks* (or Financial Institutions) providing guarantee and transfer of cash and credits between *Clients* and *Merchants*. STT, SEPP, and SET refer to the Financial Institution as the *Acquirer* whereas *i*KP models this using a *Gateway* that acts as an intermediary to the existing financial network.

We use generic terms such as offer, order and slip in describing the payment schemes. The Merchant presents the information about the service in terms of an *Offer*. When the Client wishes to make a purchase, s/he sends an *Order* and a payment *Slip* to the Merchant. The *Offer* is intended for the merchant whereas the *Slip* is passed on to the Financial Institution. The Merchant requests the authorization from the Financial Institution, and upon receipt of the authorization, the Merchant confirms to the Client the conclusion of the payment transactions. This is then followed by the service delivery. Under these systems, the financial institution must be on-line, where it serves as a trusted authentication center for merchants and customers by verifying the authenticity of payment slips. The obvious reason for needing an on-line server is that merchants do not have the right to access the PINs and credit card numbers of clients. However, the cost of an on-line service has to be taken into account in the overall assessment.

In this paper, we propose three novel credit based systems that present a promise for merchants not to use an on-line banking service during the processing of a payment. In other words, in our systems merchants can ensure the authenticity of the credit cards without any help from the financial institution that provides the credit card service. Merchant can contact the online authentication server for a higher level of assurance, but the option is chosen only if merchants want to have a further confirmation from the financial institution before delivering the goods or providing service. The significance of our schemes have not been shared by the existing schemes mentioned above.

Our schemes are based on the methods of proof of knowledge on the equality of logarithms (for convenience, we refer to it as *equality proof of knowledge*[11] and *non-interactive equality proof*[12]). The idea behind our scheme is that when purchases an item from

0-8186-8810-6/98 $10.00 © 1998 IEEE

a merchant, a client can prove his PIN and credit card number embedded in his electronic credit card to the merchant without revealing the secrets. In particular, we will also show that using this technique we can make clients in our payment system anonymous. Our first scheme, using the interactive equality proof[11], is somewhat similar to Chuam's electronic wallet, but the scheme is used to a different payment system. However, the second and the third schemes are entirely new: The second scheme, using the non-interactive equality proof, reduces communication flows between client and merchant. The third scheme achieves anonymous credit cards.

The rest of this paper is organized as follows. In Section 2, we introduce the scheme of equality proof of knowledge. In Section 3, we construct our protocol without considering the anonymity of clients. In Section 4, we introduce non-interactive equality proof of knowledge and construct an improved payment protocol. In Section 5, we consider clients anonymity, based on the equality proof of several secrets, and propose a new protocol.

2 Equality Proof of Knowledge

The credit based payment scheme that will be introduced in this paper is based on the scheme of proving knowledge without revealing anything about the content that has been proven. This scheme of proof was initially proposed by Chaum and Pedersen [11] and Verheul and Tilborg [12].

We assume that the prover is P and the verifier is V. The common knowledge includes the the generators $g_i \in G$ $(1 \leq i \leq n)$. The P can prove that she knows a secret x from $h_i = g_i^x \bmod q$ without revealing the secret, where q is large prime. A confidence parameter l is used to specify the level of the confidence of the protocol. The protocol is given below.

Protocol 1

P		V
$r \in_R \mathcal{Z}_p$ $a_i = g_i^r \bmod q$ $(1 \leq i \leq n)$		
	$\xrightarrow{a_i}$	chooses c $(0 < c \leq l)$
	$\xleftarrow{c}$	
$z = cx + r \pmod{p}$		
	$\xrightarrow{z}$	$\forall i,\ g_i^z \stackrel{?}{=} h_i^c a_i$

In Protocol 1, the prover P chooses a number $r \in_R \mathcal{Z}_p$, computes a_i, in terms of $a_i = g_i^r \bmod q$, $(1 \leq i \leq n)$, and sends it to V. V then chooses a challenge $c \in l$ and sends it to P. Upon receipt of c, P computes $z = cx + r \pmod{q}$ as a response and then sends it to V, where q is a large prime number. V checks if the equality $g_i^z = h_i^c a_i$ holds for all i. If it does, the V will accept it. If not, then there is a probability less than $1/l$ that it will still be accepted by V. This protocol proves the knowledge of x to V without revealing x. The verification of completeness, soundness, and security of the protocol is given in [12].

For convenience, we introduce the definition of knowledge of equality proof.

Definition 1 *Given a challenge c and a corresponding response z,*

$$k[x, c, z] \equiv \{g_1, ..., g_n, h_1, ..., h_n, a_1, ..., a_n, z, c\}$$

is the knowledge of equality proof of the secret x from $\{g_i^x\}$.

With $k[x, c, z]$, the verifier can verify the authenticity of the secret without knowing the secret.

3 Construction of Our Protocol

Our protocol is based on the equality proof of knowledge given above and does not need an on-line authentication server such as a bank that runs the system. The authenticity of the credit cards is based on knowing the secret data embedded in the credit card. The secret data is constructed by concatenating the PIN number, credit number, and salt shared with the financial institution. The client can prove to the merchant that he knows the PIN number and the credit card number without revealing them to the merchant.

The notations that will be used in the description of the protocols are as follows:

- C: Client,
- M: Merchant,
- B: Bank,
- TA: Trusted Certification Authority,
- t_p: Timestamp generated by party P,
- d_p: Private Key of user P,
- e_p: Public Key of user P (associated with d_p),
- $\langle ... \rangle_{e_p}$: Public Key Encryption using e_p,
- $\langle ... \rangle_{d_p}$: Public Key based Signature using d_p.

3.1 Construction of Credit Card and Payment Tokens

An electronic credit card is obtained by a client at the stage of registration with the bank. This can be done either through a secure channel or via physical contact with the bank.

The information embedded in a credit card is as follows:

- client's ID (C),
- confidence level (l),
- $h_i = g_i^x \bmod q$, $i = 1, 2, ..., n$, where g_i are the common generators ($g_i \in G$) and x is the concatenation of PIN number, credit card number and salt,
- expiry date ($\mathcal{E}$), and
- the maximum amount ($\mathcal{A}$) that can be used.

The credit is denoted by symbol $\mathcal{C}$ expressed as follows:

$$\mathcal{C} = \langle C, l, h_1, ..., h_n, \mathcal{E}, \mathcal{A} \rangle_{d_b} \quad (1)$$

The credit card is digitally signed by the bank using its secret key d_b. We have assumed that the number of generators (n) is fixed by the bank. Therefore, it is unique in the system. The salt embedded in the credit card is unique for each client. The owner of the credit card knows the secret x. When using the credit card, the client must prove to the merchant that she knows x without revealing the secret to the merchant.

When a client wants to use the credit card for a purchase, she constructs a payment slip ($\mathcal{S}$). The payment slip contains the credit card information, the ID of merchant (M), order ($\mathcal{O}$), the amount \$ (including currency type) and a timestamp (t_c).

$$\mathcal{S} = \langle \mathcal{C}, M, \mathcal{O}, \$, t_c \rangle_{d_c} \quad (2)$$

is signed by the client. After client has paid for the goods, the merchant sends the client a receipt ($\mathcal{R}$) as a undeniable proof of the receipt of the payment. The receipt contains hashed credit card information, hashed amount that has been paid, hashed order, the challenge, and a timestamp. The receipt for client C is given by

$$\mathcal{R}_c = \langle H(\mathcal{C}), H(\$), H(\mathcal{O}), c, t_m \rangle_{d_m} \quad (3)$$

The receipt is signed by the merchant.

3.2 System Setup

Assume that there exists a trusted certificate authority (TA) such as a bank B that runs the payment system and issues certificates for all parties involved in the system. The TA could be an authorized department in the financial institution. Therefore, it is reasonable to assume that all parties involved in our system have a pair of legitimate public/secret keys (e_p, d_p) and the corresponding public key certificate ($Cert_p$) signed by the TA, where the subscript p denotes a party P. The certificate token for party P is constructed as follows:

$$Cert_p = \langle P, e_p, t, t', B \rangle_{d_b}, \quad (4)$$

where t and t' denote a timestamp and expiry time respectively.

Consider a client C who has registered with the financial institution that runs the system. In other words, C possesses his electronic credit card issued by the bank. The client and the bank share information on the credit card such as the credit card number, PIN, and salt (we refer to the concatenation of these data as x). However, there could be an option that the bank keeps only $g^x \bmod q$ and deletes x. Once a client can prove that she knows x by using an equality proof of knowledge, she will be allowed to use the credit card.

Consider a merchant M who has registered with the bank B and can provide the credit based payment service. This means that the merchant is ready to act as a verifier of the equality proof of knowledge. As mentioned before, the merchant should not know x, but she will be convinced by the client that the client who makes the payment is a legitimate party and the owner of the credit card.

The bank B is the authority that runs the system. The bank is on-line, but it might not be necessary to get involved in the actual payment process. It could get involved only if it is absolutely necessary. That is, when the merchant asks it to do so. An example of this situation would be the case when the amount of payment is large, thus the bank should check the available amount remaining on the client's account. This situation is the same as the existing non-electronic credit card systems.

Protocol 2

C		M
	$\xleftarrow{\langle Offer\rangle_{d_m},\ Cert_m}$	
$r \in \mathcal{Z}_p$ $a_i = g_i^r \bmod q$ $(1 \leq i \leq n)$ $w = \langle \mathcal{S},\ a_i,\ n_c\rangle_{d_c}$	$\xrightarrow{Cert_c,\ \langle w\rangle_{e_m}}$	$c =$ $\mathcal{D}\|t\|M\|L$ $(1 \leq L \leq l)$
	$\xleftarrow{\langle c, n_c\rangle_{d_m}}$	
$z = cx + r \ (\bmod p)$	$\xrightarrow{\langle z, n_c\rangle_{d_c}}$	$\forall i,\ g_i^z \stackrel{?}{=} h_i^c a_i$
	$\xleftarrow{goods,\ \langle C, n_c, k_s\rangle_{e_C},\ \mathcal{R}_c}$	

3.3 The Protocol

Protocol 2 describs the payment protocol. The merchant M broadcasts the offers through the Internet. The offers have been signed by the merchant using his private key. When the client decides to purchase an item described in an offer, she sends the merchant his payment slip containing the information on an order and the electronic credit card. Once a payment has been received, the merchant verifies the client's signatures in the slip and implements the equality proof of knowledge for the secret x. The goods and receipt will be sent to the client, provided every check is successful. The provision of goods/service is encrypted with a symmetric session key k_s, which has been protected using C's public key.

Note that the challenge c sent to the client is a bit concatenation of current date, time, the merchant's ID, and a random number R. This construction is important, since it removes the risk of occurrence of two identical challenges in different payments. Increasing the size of the data does not change the confidence level, since only R is randomly chosen.

The system functions in a similar fashion to a non-electronic credit card system such as Visa or MasterCard. The payment received by the merchant can be deposited to the bank later on; for instance at the end of each day. There could be an additional option that the merchant contacts the bank for the verification of the authenticity of the credit card before delivering the goods. This could happen when the payment is large. However, for a large number of small payments, the merchant might not need to contact the bank for reducing the cost of transactions.

In the deposit phase, the merchant sends the knowledge of equality proof $k[x, c, z]$ along with the payment slip to the bank. The deposit token is constructed as follows:

$$\{Cert_m, Cert_c, \langle\langle w, k[x, c, z], t_m\rangle_{d_m}\rangle_{e_b}\}$$

The bank returns a receipt with respect to the transaction. The receipt is constructed as follows:

$$\mathcal{R}_b = \langle C, M, w, H(\mathcal{S}), t_b\rangle_{d_b}$$

The bank keeps w and c as evidence of the transaction.

4 The Scheme Using Non-interactive Proofs

In the previous scheme, the merchant needs to send a challenge to the client. In this section, we show an improved scheme that does not require the involvement of the merchant in an equality proof using the non-interactive method of equality proof of knowledge [13].

4.1 Non-interactive Equality Proof

In the non-interactive method, the prover and verifier do not need to interact each other. In other words, the verifier does not need to send a challenge in the process of a proof. The challenge is actually computed by the prover itself.

One again assumes that the prover is P and the verifier is V. The common knowledge is the generators $g_i \in G$ $(1 \leq i \leq n)$. P will prove that she knows the secret x from $h_i = g_i^x \bmod q$ without revealing the secret.

Definition 2 *A pair (c, z) satisfying*

$$c = H(g_1\|...\|g_n\|a_1\|...\|a_n\|h_1\|...\|h_n) \tag{5}$$

and

$$z = cx + r \tag{6}$$

is the knowledge of an equality proof of x, denoted by $K[1{:}n, g_i, a_i, h_i]$.

H denotes a strong one-way hash function. $\{a_i\}$, c, and z are called commitment, challenge, and response respectively. $K[1{:}n, g_i, a_i, h_i]$ can only be given if the secret x is known, according to equations (5) and (6). With $K[1{:}n, g_i, a_i, h_i]$, one can verify the knowledge of equality proof, by checking $g_i^z = h_i^c a_i$ $(i = 1, ..., n)$.

The idea behind this is the fact that a $K[\ ]$ can be forged if the challenge c is known before the computation of the commitment a_i. Since c can only be computed after a group of $\{a_i\}$ has been computed or r has been chosen, the equality proof is equivalent to the one studied previously and cannot be forged.

4.2 The Payment Protocol

The algebraic setting is the same as in Protocol 2. We assume that the client wants to purchase an item from the merchant. To generate the knowledge of equality proof of x, the client executes an initializing run (RUN) that has the following steps:

RUN:

The client:

- chooses r at random in $\mathcal{Z}_p$ and defines $r \equiv \mathcal{D}||t||r$,
- computes $a_i = g_i^r \bmod q, \ 1 \le i \le n$, and
- computes $(c, z) = K[1{:}n, g_i, a_i, h_i]$.

In the initializing run, the client needs to make sure that the r has not been used before. One possible solution is to concatenate the current date and time to r. The payment protocol is illustrated as follows (Protocol 3):

Protocol 3

C		M
	$\xleftarrow{\langle Offer \rangle_{d_m},\ Cert_m}$	
executes RUN		
$w = \langle \mathcal{S}, K[.], n_c \rangle_{d_c}$	$\xrightarrow{Cert_c,\ \langle w \rangle_{e_m}}$	$\forall i,\ g_i^z \stackrel{?}{=} h_i^c a_i$
	$\xleftarrow{goods,\ \langle C, k_s, n_c \rangle_{e_c},\ \mathcal{R}_c}$	

In Protocol 3, once the client wants to purchase an item listed in the offer, she needs to execute the initializing run to obtain a current $K[.]$. In step two, the client sends the merchant the slip and the knowledge of equality proof on x. These information are signed by the client using his private key and then encrypted using the public key of the merchant. Upon receipt of this information, the merchant verifies all signatures therein and the authenticity of the knowledge of equality proof. If the checks are successful, the merchant sends the client the encrypted goods, encrypted delivery key k_s, and a receipt. Note that $K[.]$ must be signed along with the current payment slip $\mathcal{S}$ by the client. This will remove the risk of a dishonest merchant reusing it. Note that the confidence level defined previously is not applicable in the present system, and hence has been removed from the credit card token.

In the deposit phase, the merchant sends w to the bank. The deposit token is constructed as follows:

$$\{Cert_m, Cert_c, \langle \langle w, t_m \rangle_{d_m} \rangle_{e_b}\}$$

The bank checks the correctness of w and ensures that the set $\{a_i\}$ has not been used before. If the checks are successful, it provides a receipt with respect to the deposit made to the merchant. The receipt is constructed as follows:

$$\mathcal{R}_b = \langle C, M, w, H(\mathcal{S}), t_b \rangle_{d_b}$$

The bank needs to keep w as evidence of the transaction.

5 Anonymous Electronic Credit Card

In this section, we consider client anonymity. This is, clients' IDs are not revealed to the merchant when processing a purchase run. The anonymity of clients is based on the non-interactive equality proof studied in Section 4.

5.1 Anonymous Certificate

The client should obtain an anonymous public key certificate from the bank, the trusted certificate authority. The certificate contains an anonymous ID of the client ($\hat{C} = \{g_1^{C||s}, g_2^{C||s}, ..., g_n^{C||s}\}$), the public key, a timestamp, expiry time, and the ID of the issuer:

$$Cert'_c = \langle \hat{C}, e_c, t, t', B \rangle_{d_b} \qquad (7)$$

s is salt that is shared by the client and TA. The authenticity of the anonymous certificate is based on an equality proof of knowledge on C, namely the proof of the owner of the certificate without revealing the ID of the owner to the verifier.

The bank has the mapping between $\hat{C}$ and the real ID of the client. Therefore, the anonymity is only against merchants. This could be sufficient in a credit based payment system. However, if clients are allowed to have anonymous accounts with the bank, it is possible to make the credit card payments entirely anonymous. We will not consider this topic further in this paper.

5.2 Construction of Anonymous Credit Card

When an electronic credit card becomes anonymous, merchants are not able to know the ID of the card holder. The structure of a credit card is similar to the one studied in the previous section; the only difference is that it uses the anonymous ID of the client.

$$\hat{\mathcal{C}} = \langle \hat{C}, h_1, ..., h_n, \mathcal{E}, \mathcal{A} \rangle_{d_b} \qquad (8)$$

The authenticity of the credit card relies upon two equality proofs of knowledge of $C||s$ and x. The first proof ensures that the client is the owner of the credit card. The second proof shows that the client knows the secret data x. Now the payment slip and receipt tokens have $\hat{\mathcal{C}}$ instead of $\mathcal{C}$.

5.3 The Knowledge of Proof of Several Secret Numbers

In this subsection, we define and formalize the building blocks of our scheme. They are based on the non-interactive equality proofs of knowledge. The definition of the knowledge of proof of m secret numbers is as follows:

Definition 3 *A $m+1$ tuple $(c, z_1, ..., z_m)$ satisfying*

$$c = H(g_1||...||g_n||a_1||...||a_n||h_1^{(1)}||...||h_n^{(1)}||...||h_1^{(m)}||...||h_n^{(m)})$$

and

$$z_1 = cx_1 + r, \; ... \; z_m = cx_m + r.$$

is the knowledge of equality proof of $x_1, ..., x_m$, denoted by $K[1{:}n, g_i, a_i, h_i^{(1)}, ..., h_i^{(m)}]$.

Each response z_i corresponds to a secret number x_i, while the challenge c and the commitment r are unique. With the knowledge of the proof, one can verify the authenticity of $x_1, ..., x_m$, by checking $g_i^{z_j} \stackrel{?}{=} (h_i^{(j)})^c a_i$ $(i = 1, ..., n; j = 1, ..., m)$

5.4 Anonymous Protocol

The anonymous protocol is similar to the non-anonymous one, except that the client now needs to prove to the merchant both the ID and the secret x using the proof given in Definition 3.

RUN:

The client:

- chooses r at random in $\mathcal{Z}_p$ and defines $r \equiv \mathcal{D}||t||r$,
- computes $a_i = g_i^r \bmod q, \; (1 \leq i \leq n)$, and
- computes $(c, z_1, ..., z_m) = K[1{:}n, g_i, a_i, h_i^{(1)}, ..., h_i^{(m)}]$.

The protocol is given as follows:

Protocol 4

C		M
	$\xleftarrow{\langle Offer \rangle_{d_m},\; Cert_m}$	
executes RUN $(m = 2)$		
$w = \langle \mathcal{S}, K[.], n_c \rangle_{d_c}$	$\xrightarrow{Cert'_c,\; \langle w \rangle_{e_m}}$	$\forall i,\; g_i^{z_1} \stackrel{?}{=} (\hat{C})^c a_i$ $\forall i,\; g_i^{z_2} \stackrel{?}{=} h_i^c a'_i$
	$\xleftarrow{goods,\; \langle C, k, n_c \rangle_{e_c},\; \mathcal{R}_c}$	

The client's signature is verified using his public key e_c embedded in the anonymous public key certificate. In the deposit phase, the merchant sends w to the bank. The deposit token is constructed as follows:

$$\{Cert_m, Cert'_c, \langle\langle w, t_m \rangle_{d_m} \rangle_{e_b}\}$$

The bank needs to check all the information in w including the authenticity of the client and the validity of the credit card and then returns a receipt with respect to the deposit made to the merchant. The receipt is constructed as follows:

$$\mathcal{R}_b = \langle \hat{C}, M, w, H(\mathcal{S}), t_b \rangle_{d_b}$$

6 Conclusion

We have introduced three methods for the establishment of credit based electronic payment systems over Internet, using the techniques of equality proof of knowledge. In particular, we have presented a construction of payment that allows anonymity of clients. The major feature of the system lies in the purchase phase where the merchant involved can ensure the authenticity of the credit card information without any help from the financial institution that runs the system. This has given a greater flexibility to the payment system as it gives a further choice to the merchants whether to use the on-line bank or not.

References

[1] D. Chaum, A. Fait, and M. Naor, "Untraceable electronic cash," in *Advances in Cryptology – CRYPTO '88 Proceedings*, pp. 319–327, 1990.

[2] D. L. Chaum, "Achieving electronic privacy," *Scientific American*, pp. 96–101, August 1992.

[3] G. Medvinsky and B. C. Neuman, "Netcash: A design for practical electronic currency on the Internet," in *Proceedings of the ACM Conference on*

Computer and Communication Security, November 1993.

[4] G. Medvinsky and B. C. Neuman, "iKP - a family of secure electronic payment protocols," 1995. <http://www.zurich.ibm.com/Technology/Security/extern/ecommerce/>.

[5] M. Sirbu and J. D. Tygar, "Netbill: An Internet commerce system optimized or network delivered services," <http://www.ini.cmu.edu/ netbill>.

[6] B. C. Neuman and G. Medvinsky, "Requirements for network payment: The netcheque^{tm} perspective," in *Proceedings of the IEEE CompCon'95*, March 1995.

[7] CyberCash, "The cybercash^{tm} system - how it works," <http://www.cybercash.com/cybercash/cyber2.html>.

[8] STT, "Secure transaction technology," 1995. <http://www.visa.com/Visa-stt/ Stt-os.html>.

[9] SEPP, "Secure electronic payment protocol," 1995. <http://www.mastercard.com/Sepp/>.

[10] "Secure electronic transactions," in *VISA and MasterCard*, 1996.
<http://www.mastercard.com/SET/>.

[11] D. Chaum and T. P. Pedersen, "Wallet databases with observers," in *Advances in Cryptology – CRYPTO '92 Proceedings*, pp. 89–105, Springer-Verlag, 1992.

[12] E. R. Verheul and H. C. A. van Tilborg, "Binding Elgamal: A fraud-detectable alternative to key-escrow proposals," in *Advances in Cryptology – EUROCRYPTO '97 Proceedings*, pp. 119–133, Springer-Verlag, 1997.

[13] J. Camenisch, "Efficient and generalized group signatures," in *Advances in cryptology - EUROCRYPT'97, Lecture Notes in Computer Science 1233*, pp. 465–479, Springer-Verlag, Berlin, 1997.

Track B: Quality of Service

Session Chair: Rose Tsang
Sandia National Laboratories

EQuB—Ethernet Quality of Service Using Black Bursts

João Luís Sobrinho
Instituto de Telecomunicações
Torre Norte, IST, Av. Rovisco Pais
1096 Lisboa Codex, PORTUGAL
Email: joao.sobrinho@lx.it.pt

A. S. Krishnakumar
Bell Laboratories, Lucent Technologies
600 Mountain Ave.
Murray Hill NJ, USA
Email: askbl@lucent.com

Abstract

EQuB is an overlay mechanism to Ethernet's MAC protocol that provides QoS guarantees to real-time applications. In its basic form, EQuB relies on the sensing and collision detection abilities of standard network interface cards and, in addition, requires only that those cards be capable of sending jam signals—so called black bursts—of pre-specified durations. EQuB gives access priority to real-time traffic, provides round-robin service among real-time hosts and guarantees a small, bounded delay to real-time packets. We also discuss enhancements to the basic EQuB mechanism that improve its performance.

Simulation results are presented that assess the performance of 10 and 100BASE-T Ethernet LANs with a mixed population of data and real-time hosts. We conclude that, in spite of the priority attained by real-time traffic, data packet delays are not significantly affected as data load is traded for real-time load, and this is because EQuB dispatches packets to the channel much more efficiently than Ethernet's MAC protocol.

1. Introduction

Ethernet has become the most popular Local Area Network (LAN) technology since its inception in the late 70s. Ethernet was initially targeted for providing communication among a large number of slow hosts, with a 10 Mbps line speed deemed more than satisfactory. Over the years, the processing power of the hosts attached to Ethernets has increased by several orders of magnitude and new types of communication, emphasizing real-time voice and video, have been brought to the desktop. Ethernet technology likewise evolved with the specification of switched Ethernet and 100 Mbps Fast Ethernet, but not much has been achieved in providing Quality of Service (QoS) guarantees to the applications now driving Ethernet hosts.

The heart and soul of shared Ethernet is its medium access method, known as Carrier Sense Multiple Access with Collision Detection (CSMA/CD) [3]. With CSMA/CD, a host having a packet ready will only start its transmission if the channel is not already sensed occupied with a transmission from another host. Collisions are part of the operation of CSMA/CD. Ethernet uses a truncated Binary Exponential Backoff (BEB) algorithm to deal with the retransmission of packets that suffered collisions. It is known, both in theory and practice, that under moderate to high loads, BEB produces a so-called channel capture effect whereby one single host may send many packets in succession while the packets from other hosts are doomed to wait long times for access to the channel [1, 6]. This behavior is an artifact of Ethernet and accounts for its large packet delay variance. It also makes Ethernet unsuitable to support real-time applications, like voice and video, with their stringent end-to-end delay requirements.

The prevailing success of Ethernet is due, in part, to its simplicity and ubiquity. Any proposed enhancement to Ethernet's Medium Access Control (MAC) procedures has to provide backward compatibility so that hosts equipped with new Network Interface Cards (NICs) can co-exist with conventional Ethernet hosts, repeaters and switches. Several proposals have appeared aimed at providing some priority mechanism to real-time traffic [11, 12, 8], but most of them either require changing all the NICs or they do not make hard QoS guarantees to real-time traffic. Some exceptions are the Movable Slot TDM scheme [4], proposed by Maxemchuk, and the scheme proposed by Chlamtac [2] and further elaborated upon in [10]. The first is simple and ingenious in that it implements a distributed TDM scheme with no explicit slot assignment or clock synchronization. But it constrains data packets to be shorter than real-time packets and does not scale well with Ethernet speed. Chlamtac's scheme envisions chaining the packet transmissions from the real-time hosts as well as preemption of ongoing data packet transmissions. This scheme can heavily degrade data traffic performance and it is not flexible in supporting real-

0-8186-8810-6/98 $10.00 © 1998 IEEE

time hosts with varying source rates. Another, recent, proposal appears in [7] but it is only suitable to environments with a small number of real-time hosts.

In this paper, we propose EQuB, an overlay mechanism to Ethernet's medium access control protocol that provides QoS guarantees to real-time traffic. In its basic form, EQuB relies on the ability of the network interface cards to sense activity on the shared medium and, in addition, requires only that those cards be capable of sending jam signals—so called black bursts—of pre-specified duration. The algorithm is totally distributed and ensures that real-time packets never have to be randomly rescheduled. EQuB guarantees bounded access delays to real-time applications, priority access to real-time traffic, and round-robin service among the active real-time hosts.

In Section 2, we briefly review Ethernet's MAC protocol and we show its performance curves. The basic EQuB mechanism is described in Section 3 and enhancements to it are covered in Section 4. Results on EQuB are presented in Section 5 and conclusions are drawn in Section 6.

2. Ethernet

2.1. Topology

Ethernet technology is specified for both linear and star topologies. The latter have become very popular and can be operated at either 10 or 100 Mbps, as specified by the IEEE 803.3 standards 10BASE-T and 100BASE-T, respectively. The *path delay* between two hosts is the time it takes for a bit to travel from the sending to the receiving NIC. It takes into account both the cable propagation delay and the latencies introduced at the NICs and repeaters. We denote by τ the maximum value of the path delay found in a network. Proper operation of CSMA/CD requires that the maximum round-trip path delay, 2τ, be less than or equal to the *slot time*, t_{slot}, set at 512 bits. This, in turn, constrains the maximum *network diameter* of an Ethernet LAN to be 2.5 km and 250 m, for the 10 and 100 Mbps versions, respectively.

2.2. Medium access control

Consider a host with a packet ready for transmission at a given time. If the medium has been sensed idle during the previous interframe interval, of length t_{ifs}, $t_{\text{ifs}} = 96$ bits, the host immediately starts the transmission of its packet. Otherwise, the host waits until the medium becomes idle for the duration of an interframe interval and only then starts transmitting its packet. Due to the path delays separating the hosts a collision may occur. If a transmitting host detects a collision it aborts its own packet transmission and sends a jam signal, of length t_{jam}, $t_{\text{jam}} = 32$ bits, to reinforce that collision. This is the CSMA/CD part of Ethernet's medium access control protocol. After a collision, the host uses the truncated BEB scheme to schedule its next attempt to transmit the packet. A host waits a random number of slots, uniformly distributed between 0 and $2^{\min(c,10)} - 1$, before attempting again to acquire access to the channel according to the CSMA/CD rules, where c counts the number of collisions incurred by the current packet. That is, the interval of time allowed for scheduling a retransmission attempt is doubled at each new collision up to the 10-th collision and from then on remains fixed for 5 more collisions. The packet is discarded if it experienced 16 unsuccessful transmissions attempts.

We have simulated Ethernet's MAC protocol in a 10BASE-T LAN with N_{dh} data hosts, $N_{\text{dh}} = 10$. Each host runs a 100 m cable to a common repeater, resulting in a path delay of $\tau = 2.3\ \mu$s (23 bits). Table 1 summarizes the parameter values used, where the overhead bits per packet, h, contain the preamble (8 bytes), the destination address (6), the source address (6), the type/length field (2) and the frame check sequence (4), for a total of 26 bytes or 208 bits. Figure 1 shows the average and standard deviation of the data packet delays as a function of data load. We considered both *non-bursty* and *bursty* data traffic. In the non-bursty case, messages of 1 kbytes arrive at the hosts according to a Poisson process. Each message is transmitted in a single Ethernet frame. In the bursty case, the messages contain 9 kbytes and have to be fragmented into 6 frames each 1.5 kbytes long, the maximum allowed Ethernet frame length. We observe that the moments of packet delay worsen in the presence of bursty traffic and that the standard deviation can be several orders of magnitude greater than the average. This is a consequence of the almost-LIFO discipline produced by BEB: if a packet which has already suffered a number of collisions collides again with a recently arrived packet, the new packet will attempt retransmission within a window of two time slots whereas the older packet will attempt retransmission over a much larger window and, therefore, is unlikely to grab the medium before the new packet. The results of Figure 1 make it clear that real-time hosts with stringent delay requirements cannot be embedded in this environment unless the load is very small.

3. Basic EQuB mechanism

3.1. Black burst contention

Real-time hosts generate a continuous stream of information bits during long periods of times, designated *sessions*. During a session, real-time hosts expect to have undisputed access to the shared medium at more-or-less regular intervals of time and this is achieved with EQuB. At the beginning of a session a real-time host follows conventional

Parameter	Symbol	Nominal value
Slot time	t_{slot}	512 bits
Interframe spacing	t_{ifs}	96 bits
Jam signal	t_{jam}	32 bits
Overhead bits per pkt	h	208 bits
Channel bit rate	r_c	10 Mbps
Path delay	τ	2.3 μs
Data hosts	N_{dh}	10 hosts

Table 1. Nominal values for the parameters of the system.

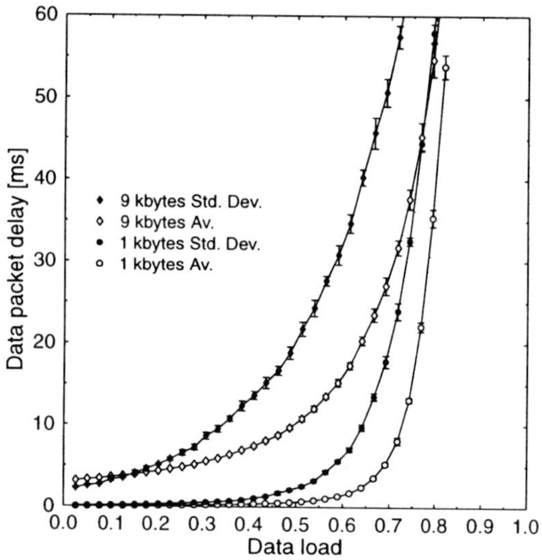

Figure 1. Average and standard deviation of data packet delays as a function of data load, for non-bursty and bursty traffic.

Ethernet rules, possibly using a more expedite retransmission algorithm, to transmit its first packet. Subsequent packets are transmitted according to the mechanisms herein described, until the session is dropped.

Each real-time packet is required to last for at least t_{pkt} when transmitted on the channel. Whenever a real-time host transmits a packet it further schedules its next attempt to access the channel to a time t_{acc} in the future. Suppose, then, that a real-time host has scheduled an access attempt for the present time. If the channel has been idle during the previous interframe interval, of length t_{ifs}, the host immediately starts the transmission of the packet. On the other hand, if the channel has not been idle for t_{ifs}, the host waits until that condition is satisfied and only then starts the transmission of its packet, in much the same way as in the Ethernet case. However, if the host subsequently detects a collision it withholds its packet transmission but continues to jam the channel up to a pre-specified maximum allowed interval of time. The jamming signal transmitted by a real-time host upon detecting a collision is called a *black burst*. The maximum duration of a black burst, b, that can be transmitted by a real-time host is a direct function of its *contention delay*, d_{cont}, measured from the time that the access attempt has been scheduled until the host perceives the medium to be idle for t_{ifs}:

$$\begin{aligned} b(d_{cont}) &= t_{jam} + n(d_{cont})t_{bslot}, \\ n(d_{cont}) &= 1 + \left\lfloor \frac{d_{cont}}{t_{unit}} \right\rfloor, \end{aligned}$$

where t_{bslot}, $t_{bslot} \geq 2\tau$, is the length of a *black slot*, $n(d_{cont})$ is the number of black slots in a black burst, the parameter t_{unit} is the unit of time used to convert contention delays into an integral number of black slots, and $\lfloor x \rfloor$ is the floor of x, i.e., the greatest integer not greater than x. We will show shortly that correct operation of EQuB requires $t_{unit} \leq t_{pkt}$. If, during the transmission of its black burst, a host no longer perceives a collision it aborts the transmission of the black burst and rather re-initiates the transmission of its packet which is now successful. On the other hand, if the host exhausts its black burst transmission without seeing that the other hosts have stopped transmitting it waits for the channel to become idle again and repeats the algorithm. The flowchart of the mechanism is given in Figure 2.

Note that the start of packet transmissions from different hosts are shifted in time by at least t_{pkt}. Since it is only when a host starts the transmission of a packet that it schedules the next transmission attempt to a time t_{acc} in the future, the contention delays of different hosts will likewise differ by at least t_{pkt}. Therefore, taking $t_{unit} = t_{pkt}$, the computed black bursts of different hosts differ by at least one black slot and, thus, every black burst contention period produces a unique winner. That winner is the host that has been waiting the longest for access to the channel. In the next section we show formally the correctness of these statements. The time diagram of Figure 3 illustrates the operation of EQuB. In this figure, real-time hosts 1 and 2 have their attempts to access the medium delayed by a data packet transmission. An interframe interval past the end of the data packet transmission, hosts 1 and 2 contend with black bursts. Host 2 has incurred a longer contention delay and hence is prepared to send a longer black burst than host 1. It starts the transmission of its packet as soon as it detects that host 1 is no longer jamming the channel. Host 1 loses the first black burst contention period and waits until it sees the channel become idle again. Its contention delay has increased and after a collision with a new data packet it successfully transmits its packet. Once more, the black burst

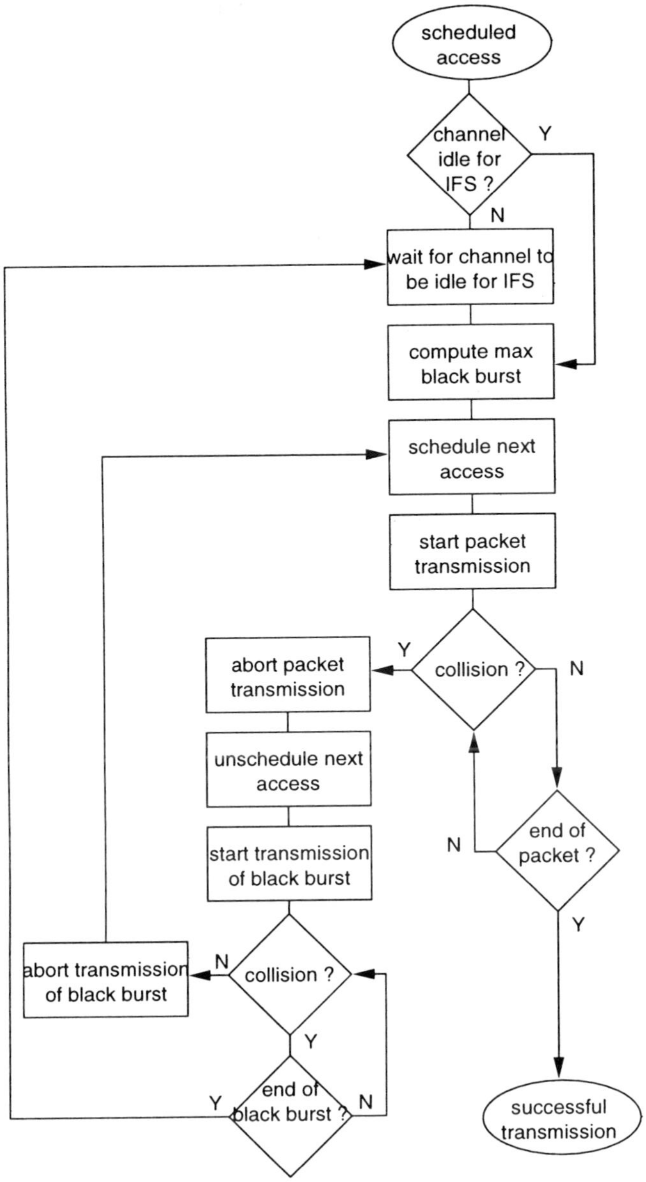

Figure 2. Flowchart for black burst contention.

with which host 1 asserts its priority access to the channel ends-up to be shorter than the maximum allowed.

The black burst contention mechanism gives priority to real-time traffic, enforces a round-robin discipline among the real-time hosts and results in bounded access delays to real-time packets. The latter property is because real-time packets never have to be randomly re-scheduled. In addition, this mechanism can be overlaid on a standard Ethernet implementation with only minor changes required at the real-time hosts: the BEB algorithm is turned off and, in substitution, we only require that the NICs at the real-time hosts be capable of sending black bursts the lengths of which are a function of the contention delay.

With straightforward modifications EQuB can also be operated at Ethernet switches, thus allowing its use in heterogeneous networks (switched/shared.) We will not elaborate this aspect further in this paper.

3.2. Correctness of the black burst contention mechanism

The path delay between hosts i and j is denoted by τ_{ij}. For all network topologies the following properties are satisfied, whatever i, j and k:

$$\tau_{ij} > 0, \qquad \tau_{ij} = \tau_{ji}, \qquad \tau_{ik} + \tau_{kj} > \tau_{ij}.$$

The inequalities are strict in this set of conditions, even for linear networks, since it takes at least a delay of one bit to copy information from a sending to a receiving NIC. Recall that $\tau \triangleq \max(\tau_{ij})$, and that $t_{\mathrm{bslot}} \geq 2\tau$. From the previous conditions together with the deferral rules of CSMA it can be shown that the transmission of host i started at time t_s^i is successful (no collision) if and only if no host j, $j \neq i$, initiates a transmission during the interval $(t_s^i - \tau_{ij}, t_s^i + \tau_{ij})$.

We now sketch the proof of correctness of the black burst contention mechanism, subdivided into three propositions.

Proposition 1 *Whenever a real-time host and a number of data hosts are involved in a collision, the real-time host will be able to successfully transmit its packet past the end of its black burst.*

Proof: Let real-time host i initiate a transmission at time t_s^i. We have to show that host i stops detecting a collision before its black burst timer expires. Suppose that data host j initiates a transmission during the interval $(t_s^i - \tau_{ij}, t_s^i + \tau_{ij})$. Host j detects a collision at a time not later than $(t_s^i + \tau_{ij})$ and, therefore, the end of the jam signal from host j reaches host i at time t_e^i, such that $t_e^i \leq t_s^i + t_{\mathrm{jam}} + 2\tau_{ij}$. Host i detects the collision at time t_c^i, $t_c^i > t_s^i$, and its black burst has a maximum duration b^i, with $b^i \geq t_{\mathrm{jam}} + t_{\mathrm{bslot}}$. Now,

$$t_e^i \leq t_s^i + t_{\mathrm{jam}} + 2\tau_{ij} < t_c^i + t_{\mathrm{jam}} + 2\tau_{ij} \leq t_c^i + b^i,$$

which concludes the proof. ∎

Proposition 2 *Whenever a real-time host is involved in a collision with other real-time hosts having a smaller number of black slots in their black bursts, the former host will successfully transmit its packet past the end of its black burst.*

Proof: Let real-time host i start transmitting at time t_s^i and be prepared to send n^i black slots in its black burst. Let

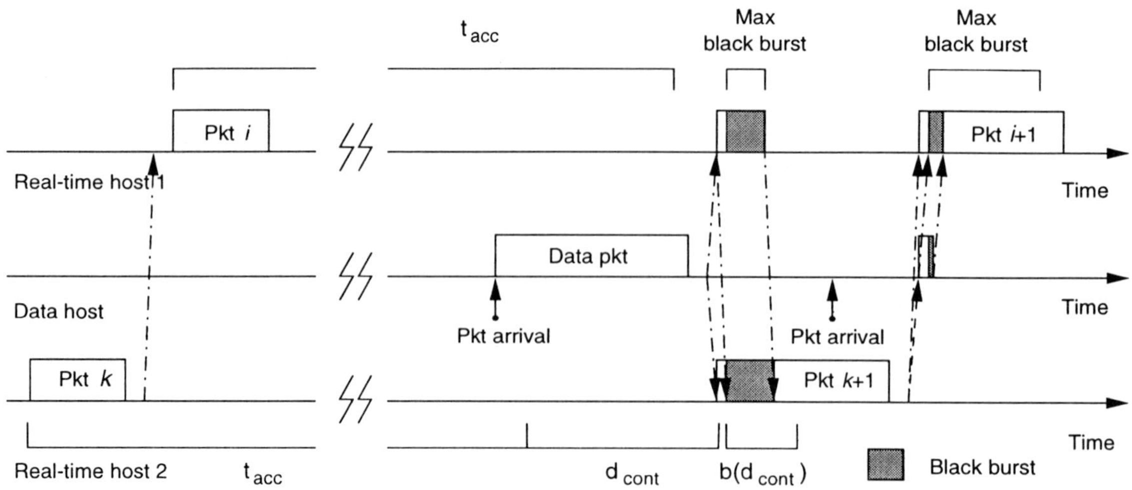

Figure 3. Time diagram illustrating black burst contention.

another real-time host, say host j, transmit in the interval $(t_s^i - \tau_{ij}, t_s^i + \tau_{ij})$. Host j is prepared to send only n^j black slots, $n^j < n^i$, implying that $b^i \geq b^j + t_{\text{bslot}}$, where b^i and b^j denote the maximum black burst lengths of hosts i and j, respectively. At a time not later than $(t_s^i + \tau_{ij})$ a collision is detected by host j. The end of the black burst of host j reaches host i at time t_e^i, with $t_e^i \leq t_s^i + b^j + 2\tau_{ij}$. Host i detects a collision at time t_c^i, $t_c^i > t_s^i$, and, therefore,

$$t_e^i \leq t_s^i + b^j + 2\tau_{ij} < t_c^i + b^j + 2\tau_{ij} \leq t_c^i + b^i,$$

which concludes the proof. ■

Proposition 3 *Of the real-time hosts involved in a collision the one that has been waiting the longest for access to the channel will successfully transmit a packet past the end of its black burst.*

Proof: Consider a set, $\mathcal{C}$, of real-time hosts involved in a collision. Let t_s^k denote the time at which host k, $k \in \mathcal{C}$, starts transmitting and t_o^k, $t_o^k \leq t_s^k - t_{\text{acc}}$, denote the last time that host k, $k \in \mathcal{C}$, successfully transmitted a packet. Choose host i, $i \in \mathcal{C}$, to be the oldest host with a pending request to access the channel, i.e., $t_o^i < t_o^k$, $k \in \mathcal{C}$, $k \neq i$, and let j be any of the other hosts involved in the collision. We have that $t_s^j \in (t_s^i - \tau_{ij}, t_s^i + \tau_{ij})$. In addition, for station j to have successfully transmitted a packet back at time t_o^j, we must have had $t_o^j \geq t_o^i + t_{\text{pkt}} + t_{\text{ifs}} + \tau_{ij}$. The contention delays of hosts i and j are $d_{\text{cont}}^i = t_s^i - (t_o^i + t_{\text{acc}})$ and $d_{\text{cont}}^j = t_s^j - (t_o^j + t_{\text{acc}})$, respectively, and their difference is

$$d_{\text{cont}}^i - d_{\text{cont}}^j = t_s^i - t_s^j + t_o^j - t_o^i \geq$$
$$t_s^i - t_s^j + \tau_{ij} + t_{\text{pkt}} + t_{\text{ifs}} > t_{\text{pkt}} + t_{\text{ifs}} \geq t_{\text{unit}}.$$

In conclusion, the black burst of host i will have at least one more black slot than that of host j, and, by Proposition 2, it will be able to successfully transmit its packet. ■

3.3. Interaction with higher layers

The *access delay* incurred at a real-time host is the time that elapses between the instant when a transmission attempt has been scheduled and the instant when the host gains uncontested access to the channel to transmit a packet. For $n \geq 2$, the n-th access delay associated with a session is denoted by d_n and is given by $d_n = (t_n - t_{n-1} - t_{\text{acc}})$, where t_n is the instant of time when the host started the (successful) transmission of its n-th packet. As we discuss further in Section 5.1, given the maximum length of the data packets, the number and rate of the real-time sessions, the black burst mechanism guarantees that the access delays are bounded, and usually by a very small value, d_M.

Typically, a real-time application generates blocks of information bits at regular intervals of time, of length much smaller than t_{acc}. The *transmission delay* is the time interval that elapses from the moment an information block is made available by the application until it is successfully transmitted at the MAC layer. The relation between access and transmission delays depends on how the application blocks of information are packetized for transmission at the MAC layer. It would be advantageous to have the MAC layer convey in a packet all the information blocks generated by the application up to the point when the host has acquired uncontested access to the channel. If this is possible, the transmission delay of the oldest block conveyed in a packet would consist of the scheduling interval, t_{acc}, plus the corresponding access delay: the transmission delay would never exceed $(t_{\text{acc}} + d_M)$. In general, however, it is not feasible to assemble a packet at the time that its transmission should start and, further, the MAC layer usually contains a single buffer which we must ensure to be filled with a packet by the time access to the channel is granted.

For a realistic alternative, consider a simplified communication architecture in which the real-time application puts its generated blocks of information into an application buffer. These blocks are grouped into frames by a transport layer which, in turn, delivers them to the MAC layer one by one. Whenever the MAC layer successfully transmits a packet, the transport layer will prepare itself to assemble the next frame containing all the blocks of information currently queued at the application buffer plus the blocks that will be generated during the next scheduling interval, of length t_{acc}. After this interval of time has elapsed the transport layer has a ready frame which it delivers to the MAC layer. With this procedure, the MAC layer will have a packet ready for transmission by the time an access attempt has been scheduled. Suppose that the access attempt for the n-th packet has been scheduled for time t_n^*, $t_n^* = (t_n - d_n)$. The contents of the $(n+1)$-th packet are the application blocks generated between t_n^* and $(t_n + t_{acc})$. The $(n+1)$-th frame further incurs an access delay equal to d_{n+1}. Therefore, the transmission delay of the oldest block conveyed in the $(n+1)$-th packet is not greater than $t_{n+1} - t_n^* = d_n + t_{acc} + d_{n+1}$. The transmission delay during a session never exceeds $(t_{acc} + 2d_M)$.

It is also clear that the basic EQuB mechanism supports hosts with different information generation rates and hosts with variable bit rate applications. The number of blocks of information conveyed in a packet may differ from host to host, and within a host from one access instant to another. The only constraint is for the length of each real-time packet to be at least the pre-specified value t_{pkt}.

4. Enhancements to EQuB

4.1. Chains

In this section, we discuss a scheme that reduces the number of real-time hosts that have to contend with black bursts by grouping real-time transmissions into *chains*. A chain is a sequence of real-time packets where each packet invites the next for transmission. In order to support chains, each real-time frame possesses two new fields: a send host ID (SID), which contains the identity of the host transmitting the packet and a next host ID (NID) which contains the identity of the host invited to transmit next. Both of these fields may assume the special value NIL. The SID field is set to NIL in the first and last packets of a session. After sending its first packet, a real-time host observes, during the ensuing cycle, the identity of each of the other active hosts. Therefore, by the time it transmits its second packet it is able to choose a unique identifier for itself, which it keeps for the duration of the session. Its last packet also has the ID field set to NIL. The NID field is NIL at every packet which is at the tail of a chain.

It is important to ensure that the data hosts perceive the medium to be continuously busy while the packets comprising a chain are being transmitted. A solution for this consists in having the inviting host append a black slot to the end of its packet transmission while the invited host prepends a black slot to the beginning of its packet transmission. The invited host starts transmission of its black slot immediately after reception of the packet from the inviting host, thus inducing a collision, and guaranteeing that there is always an overlap between the appending and prepending black slots whatever the location in the network. A refinement to this handshaking procedure is given in [2].

The dynamics of chain creation and segregation are achieved through a distributed algorithm running at each host. Two basic operations can be performed on chains: *splitting* and *concatenation*. Splitting occurs when a host ends a session and leaves the chain to which it belongs, possibly dividing it into two new chains. The last packet of the departing host has the SID field set to NIL as a way of notifying the next host in turn to assume the role of head host in the following cycles. Concatenation occurs when two distinct chains are merged into a longer one for the purposes of efficiency.

It is up to the tail host of a chain to decide whether or not to pull towards itself the next chain on the channel. Upon transmission of a packet, a tail host observes the channel for a cycle time. It will identify the potential host to be invited in the next cycle, this being the first non-departing host, i.e., SID not NIL, found on the channel. Then, it has to verify that at least one of the hosts following the first non-departing host has either its SID or NID field set to NIL. This condition prevents the formation of closed loops. While that condition is mandatory, others may also be desired. For example, concatenation should ensure that the number of hosts in a chain never exceeds a pre-specified maximum, so as to also provide timely access to data hosts. Moreover, concatenation should only be effected between chains that are already too close in time.

4.2. Virtual sensing

Chaining improves the efficiency of EQuB by restricting contention to the hosts that are at the head of a chain; they serve as contention proxies for the other hosts in their chains.

Another parameter that impacts the performance is the unit of time used to measure contention delays, t_{unit}. The correctness of the black burst scheme requires that t_{unit} be smaller than or equal to the transmission time of a real-time packet, t_{pkt}. Therefore, t_{unit} will depend on the coding rate of real-time applications, r_s, the scheduling interval, t_{acc}, and the medium bit rate, r_c. We would like to be able to choose t_{unit} independently of the other system parameters. This is achieved with *virtual sensing*. Virtual sensing requires that each real-time packet has an additional virtual sensing field which is either ON or OFF. Only the real-time hosts that are at the head of a chain have the virtual sensing field turned ON to indicate to the other real-time hosts, and only to those, that the channel is to be considered busy for a period of time of length t_{unit}, $t_{\text{unit}} > t_{\text{pkt}}$. Thus, the real-time hosts that are at the heads of chains, i.e., those that contend with black bursts based on the activity on the channel, will be separated in time by at least t_{unit} which ensures the correctness of the black burst contention mechanism.

Virtual sensing does not constrain the access of data hosts to the channel since only the real-time hosts interpret the virtual sensing field. In general, it does not constrain the access of real-time hosts either. If we choose t_{unit} to be shorter than the duration of a chain then the medium is occupied with real-time transmissions even during the virtual sensing interval. When a chain breaks in the midst of a virtual sensing interval, the head of the second sub-chain would have detected that the virtual sensing field was ON at the head of the first sub-chain, and will correspondingly delay itself until the heads of the two new chains are guaranteed to be separated by t_{unit}; it will then turn ON its own virtual sensing field.

5. Results

5.1. Modeling assumptions

We consider a BASE-T Ethernet LAN operating at transmission rate r_c (either 10 or 100 Mbps) and with numbers N_{dh} and N_{rth} of data and real-time hosts, respectively. The arrival of data packets to a data host is given by a Poisson process with parameter λ, and each has payload b_{pkt}, $b_{\text{pkt}} = 1$ kbyte. The real-time hosts generate information bits at a constant coding rate r_s. Therefore, the data and real-time loads are given by $\rho_{\text{d}} = N_{\text{dh}}\lambda b_{\text{pkt}}/r_c$ and $\rho_{\text{rt}} = N_{\text{rth}} r_s/r_c$, respectively. Each host is at the maximum allowed distance of 100 m from the repeater. Taking into account the channel propagation delay and latencies at NICs and repeaters, the path delay between any pair of hosts is assumed to be 2.3 μs. The standard parameter values of Ethernet are summarized in Table 1. EQuB introduces new parameters for the access of real-time hosts: (i) the black slot time, t_{bslot}; (ii) the scheduling interval, t_{acc}; (iii) the distribution of real-time hosts among the chains; (iv) and the minimum guaranteed time separation between the heads of distinct chains, t_{unit}. For 10BASE-T Ethernet we take $t_{\text{bslot}} = 96$ bits which would allow for a LAN of depth two, in which the path between two hosts may cross up to three repeaters, whereas for 100BASE-T we have $t_{\text{bslot}} = t_{\text{slot}} = 512$ bits. Overhead other than that from the MAC layer is neglected resulting in a minimum real-time packet length $t_{\text{pkt}} = (h/r_c + t_{\text{acc}} r_s/r_c)$. The length of a real-time packet grows linearly with the access delay incurred by the host so as to accommodate the information bits generated up to the actual time of access. We take t_{unit} to be an integral multiple, v, of t_{pkt}, i.e., $t_{\text{unit}} = v t_{\text{pkt}}$. Operation without virtual sensing is obtained with $v = 1$. For simplicity, each real-time chain consists of m real-time hosts and we do not model explicitly the processes of chain creation and segregation. Operation without chains is obtained with $m = 1$.

Depending on the real-time parameters, the access delays of real-time hosts may exhibit a discontinuous behavior. Up to a certain number of real-time hosts the access delays are bounded, and typically by a very small value. However, there may be values of N_{rth} for which the black bursts used to assert real-time priority access to the channel grow without bounds. EQuB is called *stable* if it operates in the former regime; otherwise, it is *unstable*. The reasons for this behavior are presented in [9] where a similar problem arises. For a short explanation, assume that the channel is packed with real-time transmissions and that a long data packet comes in between two of them. The first real-time host to be delayed has a contention delay which is essentially the length of the perturbing data packet. After the first real-time successful transmission, the second host to be delayed adds the black burst of the first to its contention delay. The third real-time host to be delayed wins uncontested access to the channel after a contention delay equal to that of the first plus the black bursts of the first and second hosts, and so forth. This suggests that in a very packed channel the contention delays, and hence the access delays, may begin to grow beyond recovery. Since EQuB confers non-preemptive priority to real-time hosts, its stability properties do not depend on the data load but only on the maximum length of a data packet (obtained with $b_{\text{pkt}} = 1.5$ kbytes).

5.2. Ethernet at 10 Mbps

First, consider an example where real-time hosts have low-rate sessions at 64 kbps. The scheduling interval is $t_{\text{acc}} = 25$ ms, there are $m = 4$ real-time hosts per chain and no virtual sensing ($v = 1$). In Figure 4, we plot the maximum access delay experienced by real-time hosts, d_M, as a function of the fraction of real-time load, $\rho_{\text{rt}}/(\rho_{\text{rt}}+\rho_{\text{d}})$, keeping the total load (data plus real-time) constant. We observe that the maximum access delays are very small—less than 3 ms—even at high network loads. This is not surprising since EQuB confers non-preemptive priority to real-time traffic which, in addition, is statistically very *regular*, i.e., non-bursty. However, the same reasoning would lead us to expect that the average data packet delay would increase with the fraction of real-time load. As shown in Figure 5, that is not so: the average data packet delay does not increase significantly, and may even decrease, as data load is

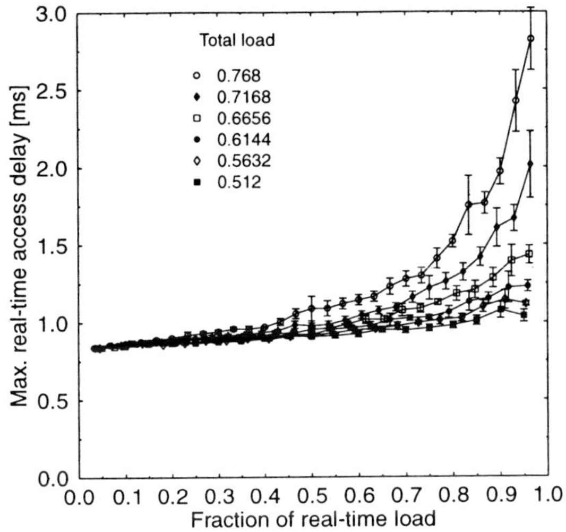

Figure 4. Maximum real-time access delay as a function of the fraction of real-time load, $r_c = 10$ Mbps, $r_s = 64$ kbps.

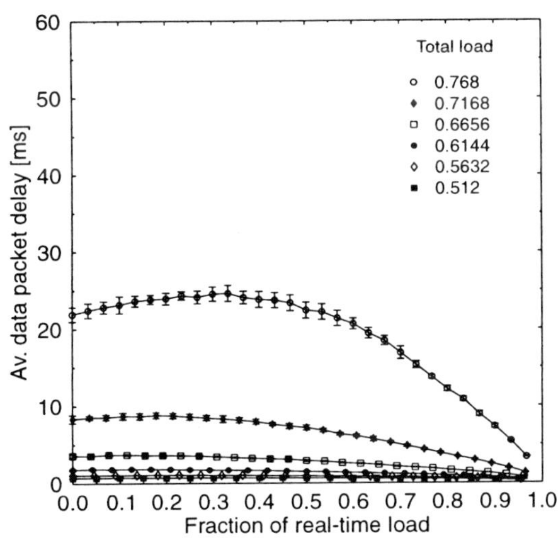

Figure 5. Average data packet delay as a function of the fraction of real-time load, $r_c = 10$ Mbps, $r_s = 64$ kbps.

traded for real-time load. This is because real-time traffic is served with EQuB which is more efficient than BEB. As we trade data for real-time load, a larger volume of traffic gets priority over data but that new traffic is dispatched to the channel very efficiently causing essentially no alteration to the average data packet delay. Figure 6 shows conventional throughput-delay curves for data traffic having as parameter the number of real-time hosts. We see, for example, that for

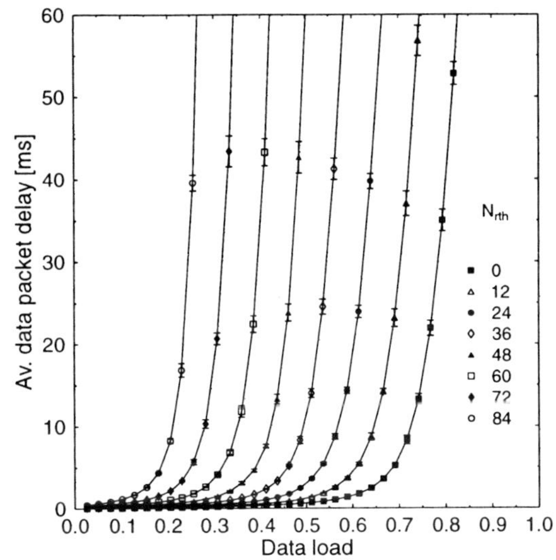

Figure 6. Average data packet delay as a function of data load, $r_c = 10$ Mbps, $r_s = 64$ kbps.

a target average data packet delay of 10 ms we can support data loads of 0.64 and 0.41 in the presence of 12 and 48 real-time hosts, respectively.

We now study the impact of the real-time parameters on the performance of the system. In Table 2, we show the maximum number of real-time hosts that can be supported, in the limiting case of very low data load, for two values of the scheduling interval, t_{acc}, and several combinations of the number of hosts per chain, m, and the virtual sensing parameter, v. The maximum number of supported real-time hosts increases with t_{acc}, m and v, but the rate of increase is higher in the order t_{acc}, m and v. For example, at $t_{\text{acc}} = 25$ ms, $m = 2$ and $v = 1$, 90 real-time hosts can be supported. Doubling either t_{acc}, m and v, while keeping the other parameters fixed, results in an increase in the number of supported real-time hosts to 126, 114 and 108, respectively. Doubling t_{acc} reduces by half the number of contending real-time hosts per second, almost doubles the virtual sensing interval, t_{unit}, implying shorter black bursts for the same contention delay, and reduces the relative overhead per real-time packet. Doubling m reduces by half the number of contending real-time hosts per second. Finally, doubling v only doubles the virtual sensing interval, t_{unit}, leading to smaller black bursts.

An extensive set of simulations has been ran that confirm that under low to moderate loads the basic EQuB mechanism (no chains and no virtual sensing) does not degrade data delay performance while it always ensures small access delays to real-time applications. The system parameters pertaining to real-time access only have a significant

$t_{acc} = 25$ ms

v \ m	1	2	3	4	5
5					130
4				128	130
3			123	127	129
2		108	117	124	128
1	64	90	103	114	121

$t_{acc} = 50$ ms

v \ m	1	2	3	4	5
5					140
4				140	140
3			138	140	143
2		134	138	140	143
1	106	126	134	140	143

Table 2. Maximum number of real-time hosts supported with m hosts per chain and a virtual sensing interval equal to v times the transmission time of a packet.

impact on data packet delay performance at high network loads. In the latter regime, and at fixed data and real-time loads, two conflicting factors affect data packet delay performance: the rate at which real-time chains contend for access to the channel and the length of the real-time chain transmissions. If real-time traffic is fragmented into many short chains then there is a high likelihood of collisions between real-time and data packets. Since a data host goes into backoff for every collision, large data packet delays may be incurred. On the other hand, if the rate at which chains contend for access to the channel is small but the chains are long then data packets may have to wait a long time for access to the channel. Moreover, when they finally do access it, they are likely to collide with the other data packets that have also been waiting for the channel to become idle. This trade-off is illustrated in Figure 7 where the average data packet delay is plotted as a function of the number of real-time hosts per chain for $t_{acc} = 25$ ms, no virtual sensing and two values of network load. The delays have a flat minimum at approximately 6 real-time hosts per chain, that is, when the total length of a real-time chain is about the length of a data packet. Having a small number of real-time hosts per chain also has the benefit of not being demanding to the procedures for concatenating real-time chains (an issue not addressed in this model).

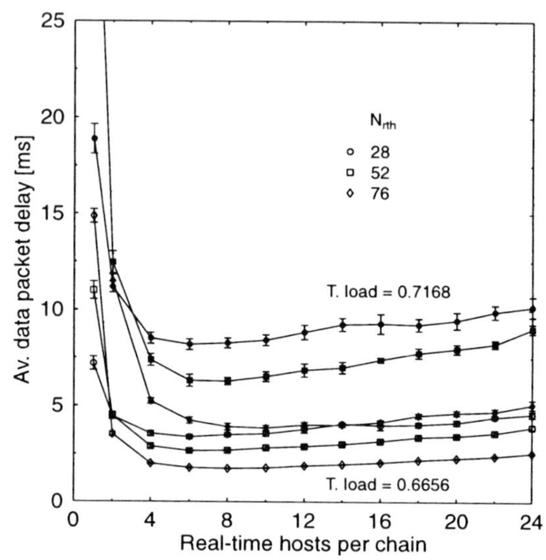

Figure 7. Average data packet delay as a function of the number of real-time hosts per chain, $r_c = 10$ Mbps, $r_s = 64$ kbps.

Figure 8 compares data packet delay performance for various combinations of t_{acc}, m and v, when the chains are short and the dominant factor affecting the performance is the number of contending real-time hosts per second. From the figure, we confirm that the sets of parameter values that yield less real-time chains per unit of time, namely $t_{acc} = 50$ ms, $m = 2$, $v = 1$, and $t_{acc} = 25$ ms, $m = 4$, $v = 1$, produce much better data delay performance. For $t_{acc} = 50$ ms, the relative overhead is smaller than that for $t_{acc} = 25$ ms thus resulting in an additional improvement in performance. Also, observe that the virtual sensing only improves the system when the real-time load is very high and black burst contention among the real-time hosts becomes frequent.

Finally, in Figure 9, we show data packet delay performance in the presence of medium-rate real-time sessions with coding rate $r_s = 256$ kbps, and $m = 1$, $v = 1$. Excellent performance is attained at high loads even without chaining or virtual sensing, since real-time packets are about four times larger than when $r_s = 64$ kbps.

5.3. Fast Ethernet

We now consider a Fast Ethernet LAN operating at $r_c = 100$ Mbps, and high-rate real-time sessions with $r_s = 1024$ kbps. We assume that real-time hosts can send a few Ethernet frames back-to-back, so that all information bits generated during an interval of time of length $t_{acc} = 25$ ms can be sent in succession once the host acquires access to the channel. This is similar to the *frame bursting* technique proposed for Gigabit Ethernets [5]. Figures 10 and 11 show data packet delay performance with the basic EQuB mechanism. From Figure 10, it is clear that

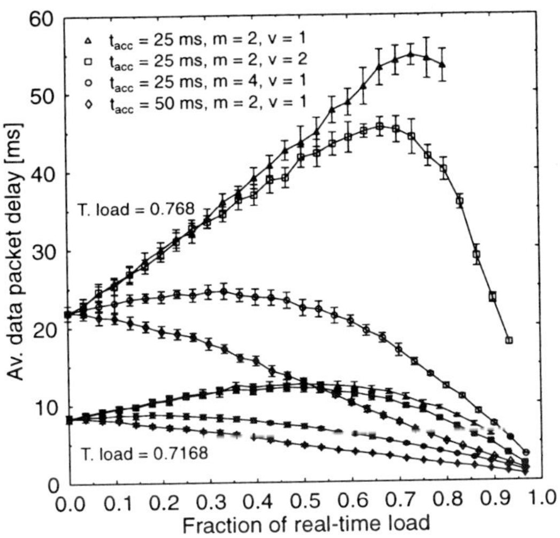

Figure 8. Average data packet delay as a function of the fraction of real-time load for various system parameters, $r_c = 10$ Mbps, $r_s = 64$ kbps.

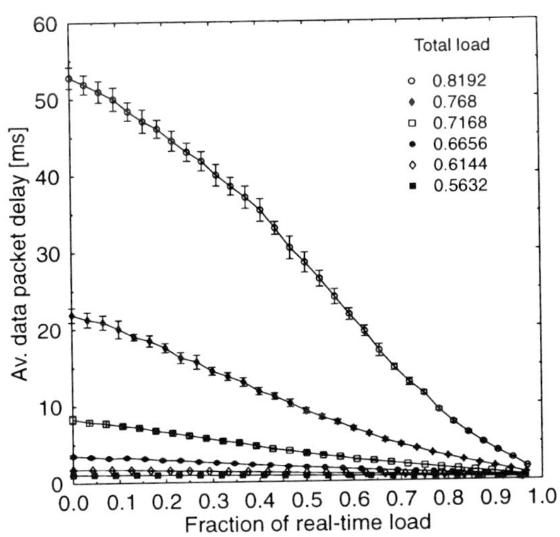

Figure 9. Average data packet delay as a function of the fraction of real-time load, $r_c = 10$ Mbps, $r_s = 256$ kbps.

the performance of the system improves as real-time load is traded for data load. This is both because, for the same load, the rate of real-time transmissions is less than that of data transmissions and because the access of the former transmissions is regulated by the efficient EQuB mechanism.

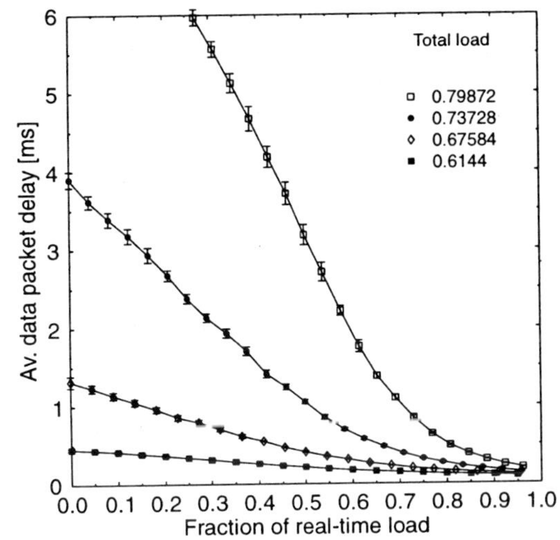

Figure 10. Average data packet delay as a function of the fraction of real-time load, $r_c = 100$ Mbps, $r_s = 1024$ kbps.

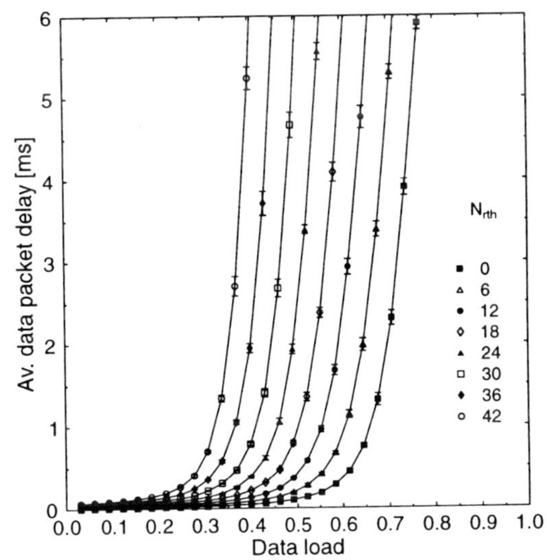

Figure 11. Average data packet delay as a function of data load, $r_c = 100$ Mbps, $r_s = 1024$ kbps.

6. Conclusions

EQuB is an overlay mechanism to the Ethernet standard that confers QoS guarantees to real-time applications. With EQuB real-time hosts contend for access to the channel using black bursts, the maximum durations of which are a linear function of the time that the host had to wait for the channel to become idle. EQuB gives non-preemptive priority to real-time traffic, guarantees bounded access delays to real-time transmissions and enforces a round-robin discipline among the real-time hosts. EQuB was designed to co-exist with standard Ethernet NICs and, since it relies solely on sensing and collision detection capabilities, it is both simple to implement and resilient to network failures.

Simulation results show that the basic EQuB mechanism by itself can support real-time traffic with reasonable efficiency on existing 10 and 100 Mbps Ethernet networks. The performance of the basic mechanism can be improved by grouping real-time packet transmissions from different hosts into chains. A distributed algorithm running at each host deals with the formation or concatenation of chains. Virtual sensing is another solution to improve the efficiency of the system.

The simulations studied the performance of EQuB on 10 and 100 Mbps Ethernet LANs, covering a large range of parameter values and real-time coding rates. In general, we conclude that although EQuB gives priority to real-time traffic, the average data packet delays may also improve, for a given total load, since EQuB dispatches packets to the channel much more efficiently than Ethernet's BEB. At high network loads, data packet delay performance depends mainly on the size of the real-time chains or, equivalently, on the rate at which real-time chains access the channel. As long as the typical length of a real-time chain is of the order of magnitude of the length of a data packet excellent performance is obtained for data traffic, while real-time traffic is always conveyed across the LAN with a very low and bounded delay.

References

[1] G. T. Almes and E. D. Lazowska. The behaviour of Ethernet-like computer communication networks. In *Proc. 7th Symp. on Operating Systems Principles*, pages 66–81, 1979.

[2] I. Chlamtac. An Ethernet compatible protocol for real-time voice/data integration. *Computer Networks and ISDN systems*, 10:81–96, 1985.

[3] The Institute of Electrical and Electronics Engineers, Inc., 345 East 47th Street, New York, NY 10017, USA. *ANSI/IEEE Std 802.3-Carrier sense multiple access with collision detection (CSMA/CD) access method and physical layer specifications*, 1996 Edition.

[4] N. F. Maxemchuk. A variation on CSMA/CD that yields movable TDM slots in integrated voice/data local. *The Bell System Technical J.*, 61(7):1527–1549, Sep. 1982.

[5] M. Molle, M. Kalkunte, and J. Kadambi. Frame bursting: a technique for scaling CSMA/CD to gigabit speeds. *IEEE Network*, pages 6–15, Jul./Aug. 1997.

[6] K. K. Ramakrishnan and H. Yang. The Ethernet capture effect: analysis and solution. In *Proc. 19th Conf. on Local Computer Networks*, pages 228–240, Minneapolis, MN USA, Oct. 1994.

[7] O. Sharon and M. Spratt. A CSMA/CD compatible MAC for real-time transmissions based on varying collision intervals. In *Proc. INFOCOM 98 Conf.*, pages 1265–1272, San Francisco, CA USA, Apr. 1998.

[8] S. M. Sharrock and D. H.-C. Du. Efficient CSMA/CD-based protocols for multiple priority classes. *IEEE Trans. on Computers*, 38(7):943–954, Jul. 1989.

[9] J. L. Sobrinho and A. S. Krishnakumar. Real-time traffic over the IEEE 802.11 medium access control layer. *Bell Labs Technical Journal*, 1(2):172–187, Autumn 1996.

[10] C. Szabo. An Ethernet compatible protocol to support real-time traffic and multimedia applications. *Computer Networks and ISDN Systems*, 29:335–342, 1997.

[11] F. A. Tobagi. Carrier sense multiple access with message-based priority functions. *IEEE Trans. on Commun.*, COM-30(1):185–200, Jan. 1982.

[12] W. Zhao and K. Ramamritham. Virtual time CSMA protocols for hard real-time communication. *IEEE Trans. on SW Eng.*, SE-13(8):938–952, Aug. 1987.

On optimal design of network topology

V.Kaminsky L.Kacnelson I.Gerlovin A.Zanis
Department of Mathematics and Computer Science,
Bar-Ilan University, Ramat-Gan 52900, Israel
kamin@macs.biu.ac.il

Abstract

This paper describes an implementation of the general flexible interactive method of optimal network topology design with simultaneous calculation of network equipment parameters which depend on the network topology. The initial information on the projected network contains the following data: single and corporate users location, the structure and the quantity of their information flows to the different corporate users (as senders-receivers) and QoS of all users. The structure and the quantity of information flows must be presented in the form of probability characteristics of these flows applied to each traffic type. The algorithm of the proposed method is based on use of two complex potential functions and a solving of flow problems. The proposed method is integrated into the complex software tool for network design. There are numerical experiments.

1. Introduction and problem formulation

1.1. Review

The optimal topology design and the topology extension of high-speed communication networks are presented in number of works with different problem formulations. One of them is considered in [1], [4], [5] and [8] (network components location are predefined). In this case, the problem is connected with traffic estimation, optimal choice of link capacities and most effective routing strategy. Another formulation considers the topology as surplus graphs, where switching nodes location is given and links have to be chosen according to different constraints [2] and [6].

Our problem formulation differs from the mentioned above in the following point: we do not know the location of switching elements and links, which connect them. User/network nodes are characterized by number of input/output ports, capacity and performance. However, in our formulation we use only nodes capacities, since we do not consider flow and congestion control constraints (such as call blocking probability, propagation delay, cell loss probability etc). Links/nodes capacities express upper bound to the total information flow in the network. Therefore, our approach can be used both as in the preliminary stage of methods from [1], [4], [5] and [8] as in independent method of topology optimization.

We use the continuous mathematics methods in order to solve the discrete mathematics problem. Potential users are given by their flow types, QoS and geographical locations. These users can be represented both by single users and by corporate ones (i.e., set of users that are connected into one LAN). We use budget and reliability constraints as optimization criterions and obtain (as results of the considered method) the number, the type and the location of user/network nodes and links as well as links and nodes capacities. Besides, we can group single hosts into corporate LAN. We assume, that links are inexpensive relative to other network components, but link cost increases significantly as far as its length grows. The proposed method provides solutions for additional sub-problems: a) one combines close hosts together, b) another shows future local networking with active information exchange between hosts and c) the third determines optimal equipment properties which are economically reasonable. In addition, basing on this method, it is possible to reduce congestion situations and increase performance of networks with unbalanced load. One practical usage of the proposed method is MANs design where LAN/MAN interconnection is based on ATM. The proposed method is based on results from [9].

1.2. Input information

Let $\mathbb{S} = \{a^{(i)} = (a_1^{(i)}; a_2^{(i)})\}_{i=1}^{I}$ be a system of corporate users located into the rectangle π on the plane in points $a^{(i)} \in \pi$ $(i = 1, 2, ..., I)$ with their "masses" $q^{(i)} = \sum_{j \in Q(i)} q_{ij}$, where q_{ij} is the information flows from the user i to the user j, $Q(i)$ means the set of all receivers or senders which associated with the user i by information flows according to all traffic types. We characterize random pro-

0-8186-8810-6/98 $10.00

cesses of an information transmission by means of the following characteristics: the sustainable bit rate $\bar{q}_\nu(i,j)$ and the burst size $\sigma_\nu(i,j)$ for the sender i, the receiver j by traffic type ν ($\nu = 1,2,3,4,5$) corresponding to voice, video, computer data, compressed voice and compressed video. We possess also an information on nodes in the form of the standard nodes menu $\dot{Q}$ ($\dot{Q} = (\dot{Q}_1; \dot{Q}_2; \dot{Q}_3; \dot{Q}_4; \dot{Q}_5)$, where $\dot{Q}_i$ is a capacity of an available switching device).

1.3. Problem formulation

Solving main problem three following results could be obtained: 1) the optimal choice of equipment for the projected network on account of the standard nodes menu, 2) the optimal arrangement of network and user nodes in the region of the projected network on account of dominating information flows and the "density" of information sources, 3) the optimal layout of the future information network. We take into account both the initial data about network flows and the final results of the solution per second.

2. Algorithm brief description

It is well known that the discrete mathematics problems are difficult solvable, in particular, when their dimension is sufficiency high. On the other hand, the continuous mathematics methods have big advantages in comparison with the discrete mathematics methods because we can use powerful concepts such as gradient, potential function and other. Therefore, in our problem we pass (in the solving procedure only) from the discrete formulation to the continuous one, but we preserve integral correlation between discrete and continuous concepts in the same areas $\omega \subset \pi$.

The main idea of our approach is based on following principles: 1) A transformation of point-wise information sources and drains on the plane to the "spread" form of these sources and drains, i.e., to their density function on the plane (in our consideration, those are potential functions, or simply potentials $P_i(x)$ $i = 4,5$ $x \in \pi$). 2) The similar transformation of one dimensional information flows on the plane into the "spread" form of these flows on the plane, but now in the vector form (the potential $P_i(x)$ $i = 1,2,3,$ $x \in \pi$). 3) We use so-called operator of kernel smoothing with-well known kernel function in order to obtain a transmission from the discrete given data to the transformed data (now in the continuous form i.e., in the form of a density). Integral correlation is preserved (for example, for any given circle $\sum_{i \in s} q^{(i)} = \int_s P_5(x)ds$). 4) We consider two "layers" of information flows: local flows and transit ones (see the potential function $P_4(x,y)$), correspondingly, for design of the planar network graph part and transit links of this network.

In the following we use two abbreviations: (CS) - a computer solution, if a corresponding parameter is obtained by a computer calculations and (DS) - a designer solution, if this solution is set by designer.

Our algorithm is interactive; it consists of initial stage **(i)** and three additional stages **(ii)-(iv)** which are realized in the certain recursive process.

(i). In the initial stage we define the approximate number of network nodes and user nodes, which are necessary to provide prescribed information flow. In this stage we obtain the initial number of nodes (which may be changed in following iterations) with their characteristics (selecting these nodes from the standard nodes menu) and so-called the radius of "attachment" ρ. Later on we use this radius for two purposes: in order to smooth certain given functions out and to create the virtual user nodes system for the next recursive process. The initial stage is to be realized in the form of (CS)+(DS).

In each following recursion we improve both the location of network and users nodes in the area π and the network topology (connections of information origins by means of links).

(ii). The first stage aim is to create a refined information for designer regarding information flows and information origins location. For this purpose, we construct five continuous functions defined at all points $x \in \pi$: $P_1(x)$ (the indicator of the horizontal flow projection), $P_2(x)$ (the indicator of the vertical flow projection), $P_3(x)$ (the flows potential), $P_4(x;y)$ (the indicator of so-called transit flows; this function is defined on pair of points sender-receiver, receiver-sender) and $P_5(x)$ (the origins potential). The calculation of $P_i(\cdot)$ for $i = 1,...,5$ is performed by (CS).

(iii). Designer (DS) performs the second stage. The main target of designer is to locate nodes (for the chosen number of nodes) by using the functions $P_i(\cdot)$ $i = 1,...,5$ which were obtained earlier on the first stage. After that, a designer must connect selected nodes by links and distribute all corporate users to different user nodes using also these functions P_i for $i = 1,...,5$. In addition, two supplementary procedures (also by (CS)) may be used by designer for the calculation: 1) virtual nodes load variation which is depended on those virtual nodes displacements and the chosen radius ρ, 2) virtual links load variation under conditions of fixed parameters of the virtual network. In the second stage endpoint, a designer obtains the certain network topology with current parameters which were fixed for this iteration.

(iv). The third stage solves the flow problem for obtained network with respect to corporate users $q^{(i)}$ $i = 1,...,I$ which work as random senders or random receivers. This stage is performed by (CS). In view of solution obtained on the third stage, a designer can introduce the network topology variation or nodes location, then he can begin the new recursion, i.e., pass to the first **(ii)** stage but with new parameters.

3. Preliminary stage of nodes number obtaining

We assume that a corporate user is realized in the form of a local network or a servers system, which are connected with one of user nodes. In addition, the users number in the local network or in the servers system is sufficiently large. Using the limit theorems of the probability theory, we obtain probabilistic characteristics of flows from each corporate user. Summing these characteristics over all information origins and taking into account statistical distributions of paths lengths in similar networks, we obtain the general flow Q per second in the projected network as the random vector of known characteristics. Hence, using the standard nodes menu (i.e., $\dot{Q} = (\dot{Q}_1; \dot{Q}_2; \dot{Q}_3; \dot{Q}_4; \dot{Q}_5)$), we can define the minimal nodes number allowing the future network functioning. This choice is realized by (DS) in the form $\tilde{N} = \frac{\kappa_1 \hat{Q}}{\dot{Q}_i}$, where $i \in \{1;2;3;4;5\}$, $\hat{Q}$ is the mathematical expectation of Q and κ_1 is the coefficient which is depended on the Q characteristics.

Restricting oneself, for example, $N = \tilde{N} + N^*$ nodes in the network (where N^* depends on the network topology and flows), a designer can change this number in accordance with given nodes menu in the following iterations.

4. Algorithm for the potentials $P_i(\cdot)$ $i = 1, 2, 3$.

The potential flow function helps to localize the best switching nodes installation place.

Let D_1 and D_2 be projections of the area π on the axes x and y, and $\pi = D_1 \bigotimes D_2$ is the rectangle containing all users. Fixing sufficiently small number δ, we partition D_1 and D_2 by means of a mesh so that $r = 1, ..., R$; $s = 1, ..., S$ and $\pi_{rs} = \{x = (x_1; x_2) \in \pi : r\delta \leq x_1 \leq (r+1)\delta; s\delta \leq x_2 \leq (s+1)\delta\}$; then it is clear, that $\pi = \bigcup_{r=1}^{R} \bigcup_{s=1}^{S} \pi_{rs}$. Introduce the following notations for the oriented pair i and j (sender-receiver): $\alpha(i,j) = (a^{(i)}; a^{(j)})$ is the shortest connection of users i and j, i.e., the segment on the plane with ends $a^{(i)}$ and $a^{(j)}$, $e^{(1)} = (1;0)$, $e^{(2)} = (0;1)$, $G(r,s) = \{(i,j) : \alpha(i;j) \cap \pi_{rs} \neq \emptyset\}$. Then the functions $P_i(x)$ for $i = 1, 2, 3$ can be calculated in the following form:

$$P_1(\xi_{rs}) = c_1 \sum_{(i,j)\in G(r,s)} \frac{|\langle \alpha(i,j); e^{(1)} \rangle|}{\|\alpha(i,j)\|} q_{ij}$$

$$and \qquad (1)$$

$$P_2(\xi_{rs}) = c_1 \sum_{(i,j)\in G(r,s)} \frac{|\langle \alpha(i,j); e^{(2)} \rangle|}{\|\alpha(i,j)\|} q_{ij}$$

where $\langle \cdot ; \cdot \rangle$ is a scalar product, $\|x\| = \|x\|_{\mathbb{R}^2} = \sqrt{x_1^2 + x_2^2}$ is a norm of the vector x;

$$P_3(\xi_{rs}) = c_1 \sqrt{P_1^2(\xi_{rs}) + P_2^2(\xi_{rs})} \qquad (2)$$

where $q_{ij} = \sum_{\nu=1}^{5} [\bar{q}_\nu(i,j) + \mu_\nu(i,j) \cdot \sigma_\nu(i,j)]$; $\mu_\nu(i,j)$ is the reliability weight coefficient for delivery of information flow of the type ν from i to j: $\nu = 1, ..., 5$; $i, j = 1, ..., I$; c_1 is a normalizing multiplier. Recall in this point that ν is a traffic type and I is the number of all users and we do not consider $i = j$. These weight coefficients are connected with QoS and data characteristics of the sender "i" and the greater coefficient $\mu_\nu(i,j)$ corresponds to the greater value of QoS by other coinciding conditions.

Remark 1. In view of approximation of the potential $P_i(x)$ for $i = 1, 2, 3$ by linear splines, the level lines of this potential are direct. Therefore, each of them is represented in the form of a piecewise linear line and, hence, its position is defined by finite sequence of points.

Consider all directions e_{rs} from the point-knot $x_{rs} \in \pi$ and select the direction e^*_{rs} such that the variation of $P_i(\cdot)$ for $i = 1, 2, 3$ is minimal (in essence, this direction coincides with the level line from the point x_{rs}).

Remark 2. In view of the same causes that are mentioned by us in Remark 1, there exists the class of piecewise linear splines on π (which is generated by segments-edges of the given mesh) such that the variation of P_i for $i = 1, 2, 3$ is minimal along these lines. We shall call similar lines the piecewise splines of the minimal gradient.

5. Algorithm for the potential functions $P_4(\cdot)$ and $P_5(\cdot)$

The transit flows indicator $P_4(x;y)$ is defined on $\pi^2 \subset \mathbb{R}^2 \bigotimes \mathbb{R}^2 = \mathbb{R}^4$ by means of the averaging with the kernel function $f(x)$ $(x \in \mathbb{R}^1)$ depending on the following factors: installation conditions of servers to the user nodes, cost of user and network nodes. Recall that the user i is located in the point $a^{(i)} \in \pi$.

Let $s = s(x;\rho) = \{\xi \in \pi : \|\xi - x\|_B \leq \rho\}$ be a "ball" centered in the point x of the radius ρ, where $\|x\|_B = \max\{|x_1|; |x_2|\}$ for $x = (x_1; x_2)$, and let $H_{(rs),(kl)}(\rho) =$

$\{(i;j) : a^{(i)} \in s(x_{rs};\rho); a^{(j)} \in s(y_{kl};\rho); s(x_{rs};\rho) \cap s(y_{kl};\rho) = \emptyset; q_{ij} > 0\}$ be a set of nonempty connections between $s(x_{rs};\rho)$ and $s(y_{kl};\rho)$. At first we define the function $P_4(x;y)$ (where $x, y \in \mathbb{R}^2$) only in the points-knots of the mesh $\{(x_{rs};y_{kl})\}_{(r=1;s=1),(k=1;l=1)}^{R;S} \in \pi^2 \subset \mathbb{R}^4$ by means of the following operator which symmetric with respect to the different knots $x_{rs} \neq y_{kl}$ (links resources are shared by both flow directions):

$$P_4(x_{rs};y_{kl}) = \frac{c_2}{16\rho^4} \sum_{(i;j)\in H_{(rs),(kl)}(\rho)} q_{ij} \cdot \cdot f(\|a^{(i)} - x_{rs}\|) f(\|a^{(j)} - y_{kl}\|) \quad (3)$$

where $f(\cdot)$ means the kernel function used by us for averaging in order to construct the continuous analogy of discretely distributed origins, $\|\cdot\|$ means the usual eucledian norm in the finite-dimensional space $\mathbb{R}^4$ and c_2 is a normalizing multiplier.

Now we pass to construction of $P_5(\cdot)$. Noting by $q = \{q^{(i)}\}_{i=1}^{I}$, we introduce the measure $\tilde{\mu}$ generated by means of the pair $(\mathbb{S}, q)$. This measure is Stilt'es's measure with the support $\mathbb{S}$. In order to construct the continuous function $P_5(\cdot)$ (the user potential) from the measure $\tilde{\mu}$ defined in the discrete form, we use the following smoothing operator $P_5(x) = \int\limits_{s(x;\rho)} \mu dt$, where the integral is the Stilt'es's integral (i.e. as a sum), $s = s(x;\rho) = \{t \in \pi : \|t - x\| \leq \rho\}$ and $\|t - x\| = \max\{|t_1 - x_1|; |t_2 - x_2|\}$. By using this operator in the points-knots $\{x_{rs}\}_{r=1;s=1}^{R;S}$ of the mesh mentioned in Sect. 4, we obtain the values of the function P_5

$$P_5(\xi_{rs}) = \frac{c_3}{4\rho^2} \sum_{i\in s(x_{rs};\rho)} q^{(i)} \quad (4)$$

in these points-knots, where c_3 is a normalizing multiplier. Further we extend the function P_5 from these nodal points up to the function P_5 defined on the whole rectangle π in the same way that was mentioned in Sect. 4 (i.e., by means of the linear-spline interpolation). In the case, when the number of corporate users is very big, the function P_5 shows the real density of information flows origins.

Remark 3. Similarly to the conclusions mentioned in Remarks 1 and 2, the level lines of $P_4(x)$ and $P_5(x)$ consist of direct lines segments, hence, their positions are defined by finite sequences of points. Besides, there exists the class of piecewise linear splines on π (which is generated by segments-edges of the given mesh) such that the variations of $P_4(x)$ and $P_5(x)$ are minimal along these lines.

The potential functions $P_3(\cdot)$ and $P_5(\cdot)$ must be normed so that the classical "Kirchhoff conditions" for the network hold (see Principle 4, Sect. 2), i.e.

$$|\sum_{k=1}^{\tilde{K}} \int_{\tilde{s}_k} P_5(x)dx - \int_{\pi} P_3(x)dx| \leq \varepsilon\tilde{Q}, \quad (5)$$

where $\tilde{Q} = \int\limits_{\pi} P_5(x)dx$ is all the user generated information. Constants c_1 and c_3 can be obtained approximately from conditions (5) and (6) for $\varepsilon = 0$ (this is flow balance).

6. Design steps and regulation criterions

Design process is recursive (every next iteration has been directed to an improvement of the general state of the considered network, i.e., to a lowering of the total (summarized) flow across all nodes - Criterion C^*). Designer also uses several options-procedures allowing to calculate the average of information flows across the "circle" $s = s(x;\rho)$ as a function of the point-center x and the radius ρ (see Sect. 5).

Let a number $\varepsilon > 0$ be the small prescribed number which defines the part of information flows located sufficiently inconveniently with respect to nodes. We call the circles family $\{s_k = s(x^{(k)};\rho_k)\}_{k=1}^{K}$ the covering Σ_ε if the following inequality holds

$$|\sum_{k=1}^{K} \int_{s_k} P_3(x)dx - \int_{D} P_3(x)dx| \leq \varepsilon Q, \quad (6)$$

where $Q = \int\limits_{D} P_3(x)dx = \sum\limits_{i=1}^{I} q^{(i)}$ is the general flow in the considered network. Generally speaking, partition of all nodes into two groups (users nodes and network nodes) is sufficiently conditional, since, in most cases, the nodes are realized as both user nodes and network nodes in the same time. Therefore we partition all nodes into two groups virtually. Designer actions are consisted of the following steps:

Step 1 (Virtual network nodes arrangement of the planar network layer). Using Remarks 1,2 and the function $P_3(\cdot)$ under condition of restriction on the switching nodes number, a designer defines the virtual network nodes location (DS). We select a network node location criterion in the following way.

a) The network node must be located in the points of the local maximum of the function $P_3(\cdot)$. It is motivated by an easy cause - the density of data processing is maximal in this point and in its certain neighborhood (of course, under condition that the function values in these points are sufficiently large).

b) If the local maximum points number n^* is large, i.e. $n^* \geq N$, then a designer defines the location of network nodes in order to reach the maximal value of the total flow in the covering $\Sigma_\varepsilon = \{\bar{s}_k = s(\bar{x}_k;\bar{\rho})\}_{k=1}^{\bar{K}}$ (DS). Here a designer uses integration procedures of the function $P_3(\cdot)$ on this covering which satisfies conditions (5) and (6) on the account of the potential functions P_1 and P_2 (CS). The users $\tilde{i} \notin \Sigma_\varepsilon$ can be connected with any selected nodes in the network using other criterions.

Step 2 (Virtual user nodes arrangement of the planar network layer). Using Remark 3 and the function $P_5(\cdot)$ under condition of a restriction on the switching nodes number, a designer defines the location of virtual user nodes (DS). In this case, he uses also options-procedures allowing to calculate the integral of the information generation "density" from origins on the circle $s(x;\rho)$.

The user node must be located in the area with the high information generation density $P_5(\cdot)$ because of all connections between this user node and servers of close users will be short. Then, in this case, it is possible to reach the easiest service.

Step 3 (Coordination of virtual network and user nodes to real nodes) This step is the most important in the design. On the first and second steps we obtained the location of virtual nodes only (network and user nodes separately), but this situation is not real. The virtual nodes location is the only desired one and now a designer must agree on the real nodes location. In this process a designer can reduce two neighboring nodes (network node and user node) to one node on account of (1),(2) and the standard nodes menu (DS). In the end of the process a designer must obtain the system of nodes so that the following requirements are satisfied: 1) The general nodes number n located by designer is such that $n \leq N$, where N is the nodes number accepted by designer on the design beginning. 2) All nodes can be represented by two groups (the first of them contains network nodes only, the second group consists of nodes functioning as user and network nodes at the same time). 3) Nodes power must correspond to the general information flow density in the circles around node location points (CS).

To reach the stated target, a designer uses the Lebesgue sets of functions $P_i(\cdot)$ for $i = 3, 5$, i.e., $L_3(h_3) = \{x \in \pi : P_3(x) \geq h_3\}$ and $L_5(h_5) = \{x \in \pi : P_5(x) \geq h_5\}$ correspondingly, where h_3 and h_5 are prescribed (sufficiently high) levels which may be defined from earlier calculated P_3 and P_5. It is useful to construct and to use the intersection $L_{35}(h_3;h_5) = L_3(h_3) \cap L_5(h_5)$ (CS). High data processing density of the information flow and high density of the information generation characterize this set.

The location of all nodes must be correlated with the functions $P_1(\cdot)$ and $P_2(\cdot)$ (CS), as well.

Step 4 (Links construction) At first we construct so-called "transit" links (i.e., sufficiently long links) by means of the function $P_4(\cdot)$ using points of its local maximums and its Lebesgue's set $L_4(h_4)$ for sufficiently big values h_4 (CS+DS). The local maximum point of the function $P_4(x, y)$ together with its certain neighborhood $s((x_0, y_0); r) = s(x_0, \rho) \bigoplus s(y_0; \rho)$ shows power transit links, definitely, under condition $s(x_0, \rho) \bigcap s(y_0; \rho) = \emptyset$ (i.e., when the distance between x_0 and y_0 is sufficiently long). A designer has a possibility to select one or several transit links in concord with nodes and links which are already in the presence. We have here $r = \sqrt{2}\rho$ in view of (2). Then we construct so-called "local" links (i.e., links connecting close nodes) taking into account two factors (DS+CS): functions $P_1(\cdot)$, $P_2(\cdot)$ and transit links obtained already. In addition, we use the certain procedure of distributed flows collection on the plane to one direction. Define the option-procedure of the join of continuously distributed flows to the united flow with discrete direction. Let θ^{k_1} and θ^{k_2} be two nodes connected with the link $[\theta^{k_1}, \theta^{k_2}]$, let two two-dimensional simplexes (two triangles) $\Delta(\theta^{k_1}, \theta^{k'}, \theta^{k_2})$ and $\Delta(\theta^{k_1}, \theta^{k''}, \theta^{k_2})$ be conjugate with the common edge $[\theta^{k_1}, \theta^{k_2}]$, let $\beta' = \frac{1}{3}(\theta^{k_1} + \theta^{k'} + \theta^{k_2})$ and $\beta'' = \frac{1}{3}(\theta^{k_1} + \theta^{k''} + \theta^{k_2})$ be centers of these simplexes.

Let $\Omega = \Omega(\theta^{k_1}, \theta^{k_2}) = \Delta(\theta^{k_1}, \theta^{k'}, \theta^{k_2}) \cup \Delta(\theta^{k_1}, \theta^{k''}, \theta^{k_2})$ be a domain that associated with the virtual link $[\theta^{k_1}, \theta^{k_2}]$; then the information flow in this link can be estimate as

$$F(\theta^{k_1}, \theta^{k_2}) = \int\limits_{\Omega(\theta^{k_1}, \theta^{k_2})} [\lambda_1 P_1(x) + \lambda_2 P_2(x)] dx, \qquad (7)$$

where $x = (x_1; x_2) \in \pi$, $a^{k_1} = (a_1^{k_1}; a_2^{k_1}) \in \pi$, $a^{k_2} = (a_1^{k_2}; a_2^{k_2}) \in \pi$, coefficients λ_1 and λ_2 depend on the ratio $\frac{a_1^{(k_2)} - a_1^{(k_1)}}{a_2^{(k_1)} - a_2^{(k_2)}}$. A designer aims to connect nodes such that: 1) the flow condensed on the area Ω has the sufficiently large value, 2) the links number is sufficiently small. In essence, the last ratio defines an angle coordinated with the direction of the considered link and integral (7) means the vector part of the whole flow that is "absorbed" by this link.

It is necessary to correct the functions $P_i(\cdot)$ for $i = 1, 2, 3$ after the construction of each real link by means of the mentioned procedure (CS).

Step 5 (Flow problem solving) In this last step of recursive process, we solve the linear problem (for the case of constant flows) with an object function according to the criterion C^*. Each iteration ends with this problem solution.

7. Numerical results

We consider the problem of network construction on geographical area π where corporate users are distributed uniformly. There are n_ν users so that each of them has traffic characteristics given by t_ν. Assuming that links cost is sufficiently low in comparison with network nodes cost, our goal is to minimize amount of network equipment (calculated as summary of switching capacities) simultaneously taking into account links length. We follow to the example considered in [3]. In our example $\nu = 2$, $n_1 = 120$, $n_2 = 40$, t_1 is an aggregated traffic from 15 standard 64

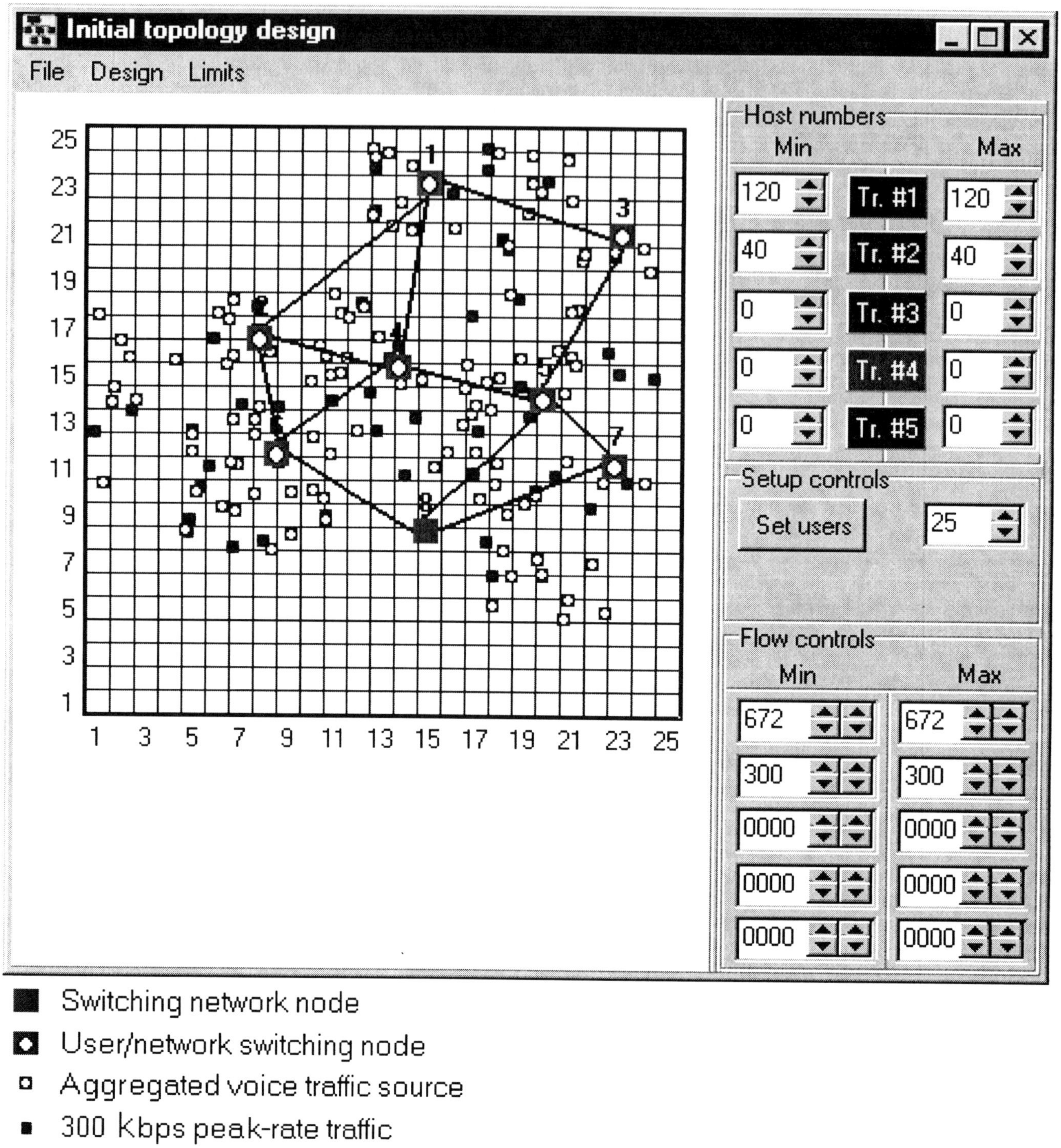

Figure 1. Result topology.

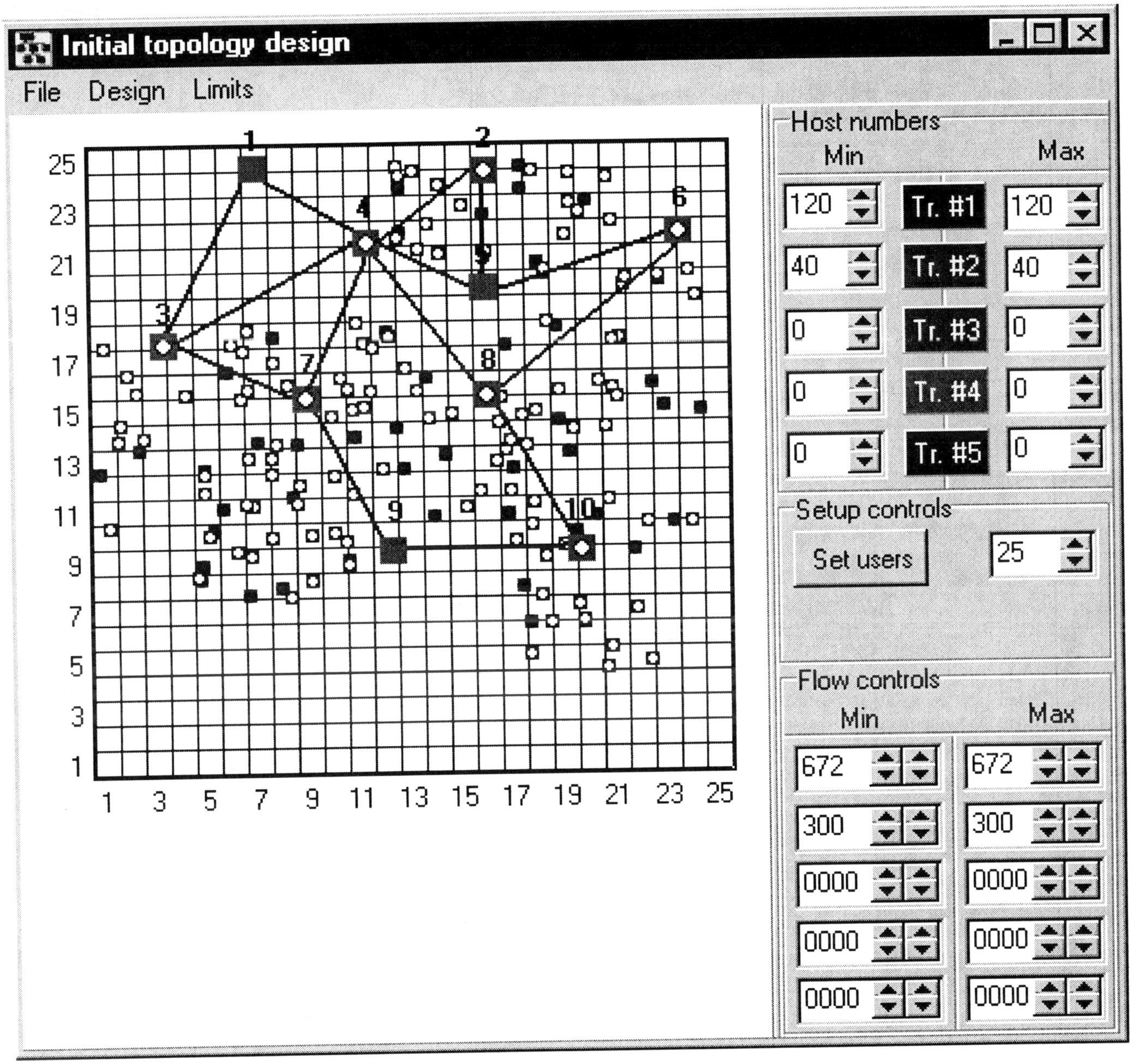

■ Switching network node

◘ User/network switching node

▫ Aggregated voice traffic source

▪ 300 Kbps peak-rate traffic

Figure 2. Topology from [3].

Table 1. Switching capacities.

Switch number	Capacities for result topology	Estimated capacities for topology from [3]
1	500	600
2	990	1560
3	766	980
4	2400	1100
5	2100	820
6	2800	740
7	900	2800
8	1100	2620
9	-	1100
10	-	2380

Table 2. Network topology information for sample networks.

	Our topology	Topology from [3]
No. of switches	8	10
No. of net. nodes	1	3
No. of links	12	14

Kbps voice channels with connection probability 0.7 and t_2 is a traffic with peak bit rate 300 Kbps and burst period 100 ms. We bound link capacity to 155 Mbps and switching capacity to sufficiently big number. In Fig.1 we show the topology constructed by proposed method comparing it to the example from [3].

Table 1 illustrates switching capacities necessary for stable network operation that were obtained by our method. In column 2 we present result values obtained by topology layout design. For adequate comparison, we use the same users distribution on the plane for the topology from [3] and our method is used for capacity estimation only. These values are presented in column 3. Table 2 summarizes the amount of network equipment used in the samples.

8. Conclusion

The correct definition of switching equipment and network layout is a first stage of network design and resource allocation problem. The proposed approach resolves the problem of switching equipment selection together with the optimal topology design. In addition, it is possible to make optimal routing precalculation with respect to congestion and performance degradation avoidance. Besides, the algorithm has the following advantages: 1) By taking into account properties of the smoothing operators that are used in construction of the potential functions $P_i(x)$ $i = 1, 2, 3, 5$ and $P_4(x, y)$ we obtain essential improvement of problem solution quality with growth of corporate users number; therefore, this approach does not meet difficulties of the scaling problem. This follows immediately from a more precise representation of the discrete formulation by the continuous one. 2) The proposed method allows to resolve network problems with non-planar graphs (by using $P_4(x, y)$) for transit links. Hence, it is possible to construct hybrid networks (with wireless links as transit ones), though any local link in the "planar" layer also can be wireless. 3) Our approach allows to take into account the resources of the already functioning network and its resources could be used for the projected network.

References

[1] A.Gersht and R.Weihmayer. Joint optimization of data network design and facility selection. *IEEE Journal on selected areas in communications*, 8(9):1667–1681, December 1990.

[2] A.Kershenbaum, P.Kermani, and G.Grover. Mentor: An algorithm for mesh network topological optimization and routing. *IEEE Transactions on Communications*, 39(4):503–513, April 1991.

[3] D.Medhi. Models for network design, servicing and monitoring of atm networks based on the virtual path concept. *Computer Networks and ISDN Systems*, 29:373–386, 1997.

[4] D.Mitra, J.A.Morrison, and K.G.Ramakrishnan. Atm network design and optimization: A multirate loss network framework. *IEEE/ACM Transactions on Networking*, 10:994–1003, 1996.

[5] I-F.Tsai and R-H.Jan. Internetting connectionless data networks with a wide area public atm network. *Computer Networks and ISDN Systems*, 29:797–810, 1997.

[6] J.A.Fingerhut, S.Suri, and J.S.Turner. Designing minimum cost nonblocking communication networks. *Technical Reports, Washington University*, 6:1–20, 1996.

[7] L.J.Leblanc and S.Narasimhan. Topological expansion of metropolitan area networks. *Computer Networks and ISDN Systems*, 26:1235–1248, 1994.

[8] S.Zhang, G.L.Bilbro, and S.E.Elmaghraby. Atm network topological design: Heuristic and lower bound. *Technical Reports, North Carolina State University*.

[9] V.A.Kaminsky. On steiner's point and finite steiner's set of continuous compacts in finite-dimensional space. *Problems of Mathematics and Mechanics, Proceedings*, 173:134–137, 1979.

An Automated Resource Management Tool for Policy-Driven QoS Control within Integrated Services Intranets[1]

Ranga Ramanujan, Atiq Ahamad, and Ken Thurber
Architecture Technology Corporation, P.O. Box 24344, Minneapolis, MN 55424

Abstract

This paper presents the design of the Automated Resource Management Tool (ARMT), a software-based network management tool that automates the potentially complex manual task of global resource management in a mission-oriented, Intranet environment. It allows the network operator to specify high-level policies defining the network quality of service (QoS) that must be offered to the different applications sharing the IP network, under each operating mode of the network. The tool automatically handles resource conflicts in accordance with the high-level QoS policies defined by the network operator. It also monitors the network to detect events that may lead to deviations from the specified service policy and automatically implements proactive actions to ensure that the network delivers the required QoS. ARMT implements an innovative policy-driven QoS control technique which ensures that multimedia Intranet applications will have an adaptive environment that permits them to coexist with other mission applications. The paper presents our experience with the implementation of a rapid prototype of the ARMT in a laboratory testbed environment.

1. Introduction

The IP network fabric in a mission-oriented, Intranet environment may have to carry traffic from a wide variety of applications ranging from real-time, mission-critical applications to stream-oriented multimedia applications and non real-time messaging applications such as electronic mail. These applications impose diverse quality of service (QoS) requirements on the network in terms of the throughput, latency, and reliability that must be provided to the data packets generated by the applications. Furthermore, applications may have defined priorities that rank them based on how critical they are to meeting the overall mission of the organization. For instance, applications may be broadly classified as mission critical, non-mission critical, administrative, and support. Under each category, there may be further rankings of applications. The mission-oriented network must, therefore, be able to recognize and accommodate these priorities in handling application traffic.

IP networks in such mission-oriented Intranets must satisfy two key requirements:

1. **Flexible QoS Support:** The network must support different quality of service (QoS) classes to meet the diverse requirements of the applications. These applications need IP networks that can support quality of service (QoS) commitments with regard to bandwidth, packet delay, and loss.
2. **Dynamic Resource Allocation:** The network must support priority-driven, dynamic allocation and reconfiguration of shared network resources among competing applications. This would ensure that no application is denied its requested QoS because of contention for network resources from lower priority applications.

The network services supported by the traditional IP architecture fall far short of meeting either of these two requirements. Traditional IP offers a single class of service, i.e., *best-effort* service, which is an unreliable,

[1] This material is based upon work supported by Space and Naval Warfare Systems Command (SPAWAR) under contract number N00039-97-C-0006. Any opinions, findings, and conclusions or recommendations expressed in this paper are those of the authors and do not necessarily reflect the views of SPAWAR.

0-8186-8810-6/98 $10.00 © 1998 IEEE

connectionless network-layer service. Packets using this service are subject to loss, reordering, duplication, and unpredictable queuing delays. For mission-critical applications, the best-effort delivery model of IP may be inadequate even under modest network loads.

Recent efforts of the Internet Engineering Task Force (IETF) have produced extensions to the existing IP standards to facilitate the implementation of what is called an *integrated services IP* [1]. Integrated Services IP addresses the first of the two requirements for mission-oriented networks (i.e., flexible QoS support) by defining enhanced service classes that, if supported by routers, can provide a data flow with certain QoS commitments. In contrast, best-effort traffic entering a router will receive no such service commitments and will have to contend with whatever resources are available. To date, the IETF has defined two QoS classes, i.e., *guaranteed service* and *controlled load* service [3,4].

The level of QoS provided by these enhanced services can be specified on a per-flow basis by the end applications using the Resource Reservation Protocol (RSVP) [2]. Routers process RSVP messages carrying QoS requests from the applications to determine the amount of resources (e.g., bandwidth, buffer space) that must be reserved along with the packet scheduling behavior that must be installed in the routers to provide the desired end-to-end QoS commitment for the data flow. Each router must apply local admission control to requests to ensure that they are accepted only if sufficient local resources are available. In making this check, admission control must consider information supplied by end applications regarding the traffic envelope (e.g., peak data rate, maximum burst size, maximum datagram size). Once an appropriate reservation has been installed in each router along the path, the data flow can expect to receive an end-to-end QoS commitment as long as no path changes or router failures occur during the lifetime of the flow, and as long as the data flow conforms to the traffic envelope supplied with the reservation request.

Although Integrated Services IP implements the enhanced QoS classes needed by mission-critical applications, its inability to support priority-based, dynamic allocation of network resources seriously inhibits its use in mission-oriented Intranets. The admission control algorithms implemented by routers supporting integrated services IP treat all RSVP resource reservation requests in an egalitarian fashion. This has major implications for Intranets built on integrated services IP. Such networks may be shared by a multitude of applications with different priority categories, such as, mission-critical, non mission-critical, and support. In this environment, an RSVP resource reservation request from a mission-critical application may be denied by the admission control function of a router because the needed resources are held by a low-priority application. The mission-critical application can only acquire these resources after they are relinquished voluntarily by the low-priority application. This situation is unacceptable for mission-oriented networks.

Such resource conflicts may be handled manually by the network operator who has to first analyze the data provided by the network monitoring function to diagnose the cause of the conflict. The operator then may issue manual commands to shut down the low-priority application and thereby allow the re-allocation of the released resources to the mission-critical application. In the case described above, the resource conflict was caused by the arrival of a priority demand into the network. Other scenarios that could generate resource conflicts are the failure of network elements, the overloading of multi-access, shared media links such as Ethernet, and a change in the operational mode of the system.

Manual resolution of resource conflicts has a number of drawbacks. First, the delays introduced by the human network operator to diagnose and resolve resource conflicts may be unacceptable. Second, the human operator could easily be overwhelmed by a flood of resource conflicts. Under such situations, the actions taken by the operator in responding to a crisis might be sub-optimal or even erroneous. Third, manual intervention adds significantly to the cost of operating the network. Thus, what is needed is an automated approach for dynamically adapting the allocation of network resources to applications to prevent unacceptable resource conflicts.

Recently, some proposals for incorporating policy-based admission control under RSVP have been submitted for consideration to the IETF. One candidate is the Common Open Policy Service (COPS) [9], that proposes a client-server paradigm for implementing mechanisms for policy-driven resource reservations under RSVP. Under this approach, a server in a routing domain maintains all information relating to QoS policy for the domain. The policy clients are RSVP routers that must exercise policy-based admission control over RSVP usage. COPS defines the basic model of interaction between the policy server and its clients. There is considerable synergy between the ARMT approach described in this paper and the COPS proposal. ARMT provides additional advantages over the current proposal for COPS. First, it is more scalable than the current COPS proposal. This is because unlike COPS, the router does not have to communicate with the policy server for each RSVP reservation request. The ARMT resource control mechanisms are triggered only when incipient resource exhaustion is detected. Second, ARMT accommodates adaptive applications whereas the current COPS proposal lacks support for this capability.

The research effort presented here designed and demonstrated the feasibility of a software-based Automated Resource Management Tool (ARMT), that implements an innovative technique for dynamic resource allocation in a mission oriented, integrated services Intranet environment. ARMT allows the network operator to specify high-level policies defining the network QoS that must be offered to the different applications sharing the IP network under each operating mode of the network. This tool automatically handles resource conflicts in real time in accordance with the high-level QoS policies defined by the network operator. It also monitors the network to detect events that may lead to deviations from the specified policy and automatically implements proactive actions to ensure that the network delivers the required QoS.

ARMT employs a novel policy-driven QoS control technique to ensure that multimedia applications will have an adaptive environment that permits them to coexist with other mission applications. To implement this capability, the tool exploits the inherent adaptiveness of video applications and dynamically adjusts the QoS operating points of these applications in response to changes in available network resources. This allows video applications to provide acceptable service even when dramatic changes in network loading occur.

The rest of this paper is organized as follows. Section 2 describes the architecture of the innovative Automated Resource Management Tool (ARMT). Section 3 describes the rapid prototype of ARMT that was implemented by this research effort. Section 4 summarizes the work and presents conclusions.

2. Automated Resource Management Tool (ARMT)

The Automated Resource Management Tool (ARMT) is targeted for use on enterprise-wide IP networks (or Intranets) where all the routers, probes, and end nodes within the network are within the same administrative control domain and can be accessed by the network management function for the Intranet. Such Intranets may be local area networks or they may be composed of several geographically distributed local-area subnetworks interconnected by dedicated wide-area links (e.g., leased lines).

ARMT relies on routers within the Intranet to support RSVP and one or more of the enhanced QoS service classes defined by the IETF (e.g., guaranteed service, controlled-load service). All applications requiring enhanced QoS, such as multimedia applications and timing-sensitive, real-time, mission-critical applications must use RSVP to reserve the network resources for supporting the required QoS.

Applications requiring enhanced QoS from the network are classified into two categories: *adaptive* applications and *non-adaptive* applications. Adaptive applications are those that are capable of adapting their delivered services to the QoS that is currently supported by the network. Such applications have multiple operating points with successively increasing network QoS requirements and corresponding increases in the services delivered to application users. These applications can operate as long as the QoS delivered by the network is sufficient to accommodate any one of the operating points of the application. Non-adaptive applications, on the other hand, deliver their services to their users in an all-or-nothing fashion. They have a single operating point with an associated QoS requirement and will only operate if this QoS requirement is met by the network.

Layered video is a good example of a class of adaptive applications. Layered video is encoded as a multi-layered stream. It consists of a base layer that contains a video signal of acceptable quality and one or more enhancement layers that successively enhance the quality of the base layer video. Each enhancement layer places successively increasing QoS requirements on the network in terms of bandwidth. For instance, a video with three layers may require 500 Kbps of network bandwidth for the base layer (layer 1) delivering minimum quality video, 900 Kbps for layers 1 and 2 delivering medium quality video, and 1.5 Mbps for all three layers delivering full quality video.

By controlling the operating points of adaptive applications, as described later, ARMT provides an adaptive environment for multimedia applications that allows these applications to operate even when network loading changes dramatically. There are two ways in which information about the operating points of adaptive applications may be conveyed to ARMT. First, the network operator may specify this information during system configuration. Second, the application may provide this information to ARMT by registering itself with the tool each time it starts executing on the network.

As noted earlier, ARMT permits policy-based control of the QoS delivered by the integrated services IP network to the competing applications sharing the network. Network operations policies enforced by ARMT are defined by the network operator in terms of *network operating modes* and *priorities for data flows*. The operator may define several network operating modes where each mode is associated with a set of allowable data flows and priorities for these data flows. Examples of operating modes for a mission-oriented network are normal mode, reduced mode, and emergency mode.

Priorities for data flows can be defined in a hierarchical fashion. For instance, flows may be categorized by the operator into three priority classes: mission critical, mission essential, and support. Within each category, flows may be further assigned relative priorities. Data flows in the network can be identified by specifying one or more of the following parameters: source IP address of the data flow, destination IP address of the data flow, source UDP/TCP port of the data flow, and the destination UDP/TCP port of the data flow.

2.1 ARMT Software Structure

The software for the adaptive network management tool consists of three major functions that are distributed over the network. They are the *QoS Manager*, the *Application Controller*, and the *Network Monitoring Agent*. Figure 3 shows the software structure of the tool.

Network Monitoring Agents are standard SNMP agents responsible for monitoring the resource usage on specific network elements. Two examples of network monitoring agents are *Router Agents* and *RMON Agents*. Router agents reside on network routers and implement the Integrated Services MIB and the RSVP MIB [5,6] being defined by the IETF. A router agent maintains information on the flows over each outgoing link of the router and the resources reserved for the flows passing through the router (i.e., bandwidth, etc.). RMON agents implement the SNMP RMON2 MIB. Each shared media segment of the network (i.e., Ethernet segment, token ring segment) is monitored by an RMON agent. An RMON agent on a segment can measure such parameters as the utilization of the segment, and the top N flows on the segment in terms of utilization.

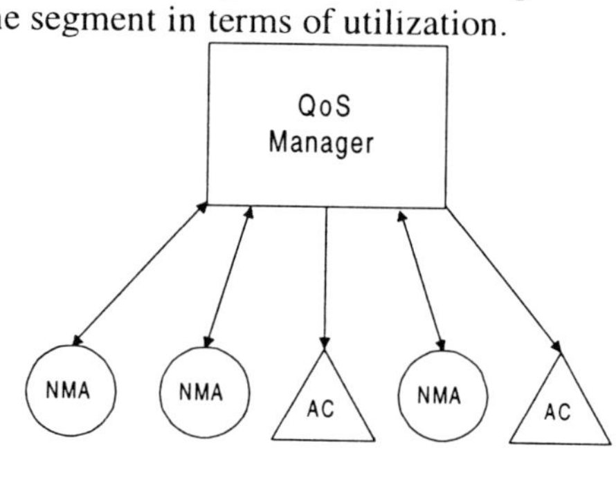

NMA: Network Monitoring Agent
AC: Application Controller

Figure 3: Structure of the Adaptive Resource Management Tool (ARMT)

The *Application Controller* software resides on each end node (or host) of the network. Its primary function is to assist the QoS Manager in reclaiming network resources from an application executing on its host, when needed.

The *QoS Manager* resides on the network management station of the Intranet. It implements the policy-based, dynamic resource allocation mechanism that uses the inputs from the Network Management Agents to generate commands for the Application Controllers, if and when necessary, to ensure network operation in accordance with the operator specified QoS policy. The QoS Manager may be replicated on different machines to protect against failures of the network management station. The graphical user interface for the network operator to specify the QoS policy for the network may either be collocated with the QoS Manager on the network management station or may reside on a remote site. The ARMT's user interface allows the operator to specify such parameters as modes of operation of the network and the relative priorities of the different applications on the Intranet, for each network-operating mode.

2.2 ARMT Operation

ARMT initiates automatic control actions to resolve resource conflicts. In doing so, it reallocates network resources and reconfigures applications. Resource conflicts may be triggered by one or more of the following events in the network : 1) arrival of priority demands; 2) failures of network elements such as routers or links; 3) incipient overload of multi-access, shared media network links; and 4) operator command to change the operational mode of the network. The following paragraphs describe how ARMT handles first two events. Reference [10] presents details on ARMT's handling of the other two events.

Handling of Priority Demands: Resources needed by a newly arriving high priority application may be held by lower priority applications. When ARMT detects this condition, it performs appropriate reconfiguration of the lower priority applications and forces them to free up the resources needed to admit the high priority application. This reconfiguration of the lower priority applications may be achieved by one or both of the following two means: 1) aborting lower priority applications; and 2) decreasing the QoS operating points of lower priority applications.

The following example illustrates the handling of priority demands by ARMT. Consider the network shown in Figure 4 where client station C2 starts running a lower priority application that receives a 3 layered video stream from the video server over the 1.5 Mbits/s T1 link connecting routers R2 and R3. The 3 QoS operating points for the layered video are 0.8 Mbits/s for full quality video containing all three layers, 0.6 Mbits/s for medium quality video containing 2 layers, and 0.4 Mbits/s for low quality video with just the base layer. Some time later, station C1 starts a high priority application that requires streaming of full quality video from the video server at 1 Mbits/s.

Figure 4 shows the sequence of events from the time that the low priority application is admitted to the network leading up to the time that priority demand from C1 is handled by ARMT. These events are described below:

1. C2 requests a video from the video server.
2. The video server sends a RSVP path message to C2 containing the 3 operating points for the layered video.
3. C2 reserves 0.8 Mbits/s over the path between it and the video server.
4. The video server sends a message describing the 3 operating points of the video, along with the source and destination addresses of the video stream, to the QoS manager residing on the network management station. The QoS Manager stores this application information in its QoS Policy database. The video server starts streaming the video to C2.
5. At some later time, C1 requests a video from the video server.
6. The video server sends C1 a path message containing the operating points of the requested video stream. (Assume that full quality video needed by C1 requires 1 Mbits/s).
7. C1 send an RSVP Reservation message to the network. Router R2's admission control algorithm detects that C1's request cannot be admitted.
8. R2 denies C1's reservation and generates an SNMP Trap addressed to the QoS Manager on the network management station. The SNMP Trap message carries information about the parameters of the rejected reservation request.

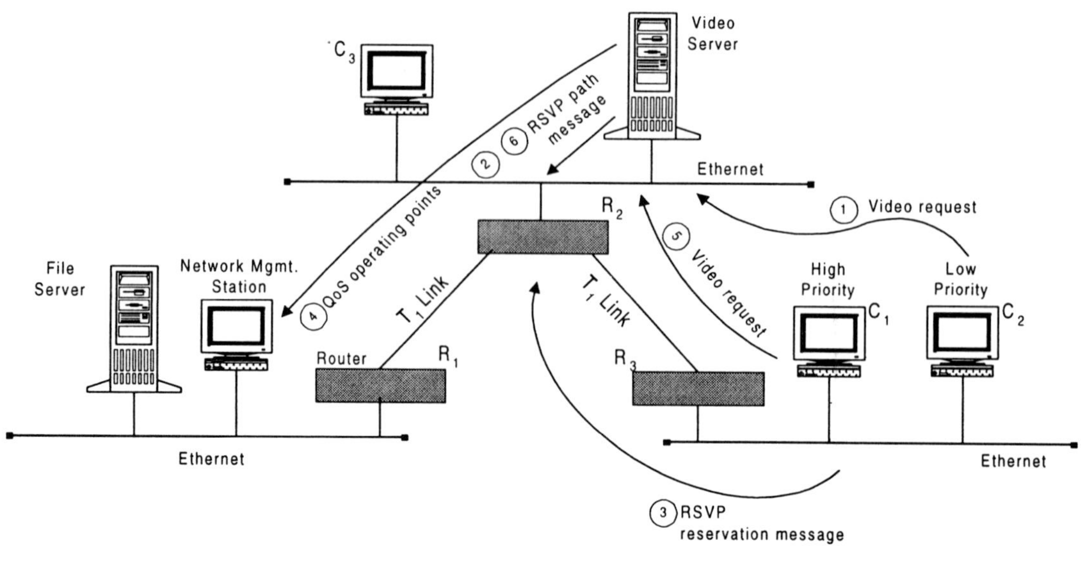

Figure 4(a)

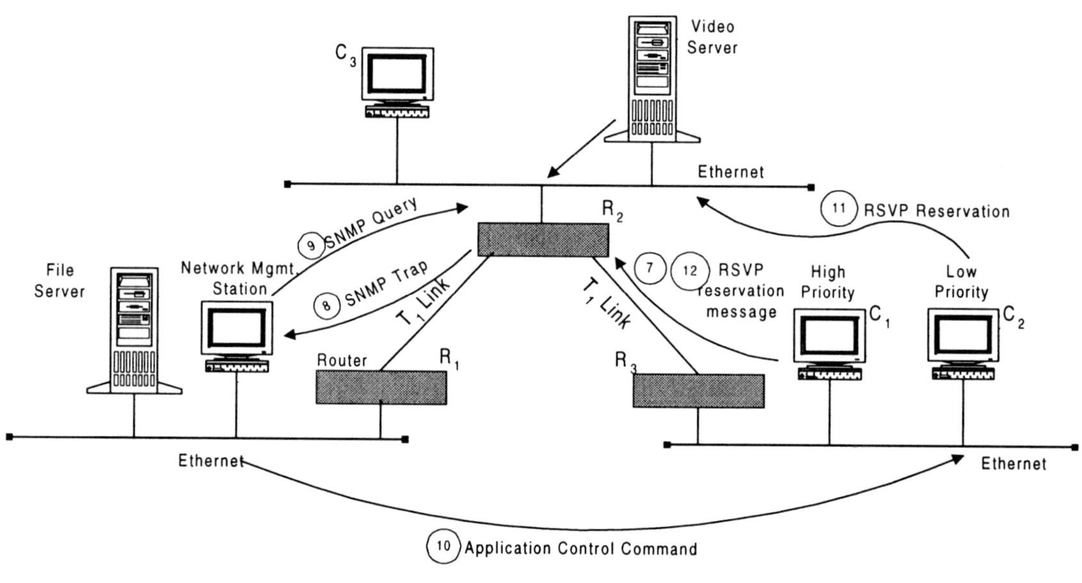

Figure 4(b)

Figure 4: Handling of demand priority by ARMT

9. The QoS Manager sends an SNMP query to the router agent on R2 to get information on the existing bandwidth reservations on the T1 link between R2 and R3. Examining its QoS Policy Database it determines that the rejected reservation has a higher priority that the existing reservation (that was made by C2). It also determines that enough bandwidth for the high priority flow can be accommodated by shutting down layers 2 and 3 of the low priority video stream destined for C2.
10. It sends a command to the application controller on C2 directing it to shut down layers 2 and 3 of the video received by C2.
11. When the application on C2 receives the command from the QoS Manager, it sends

RSVP Teardown messages to the network to shut down data flows associated with layers 2 and 3 of the 3-layered video. The available bandwidth on the link R2R3 is now 1.1 Mbits/s.

12. A preset interval after its last reservation request was rejected, C1 tries again. This time the reservation succeeds and the video session is established.

Handling of Network Failures: Figure 5 illustrates how the adaptive network management tool handles network overload induced by failures of network elements. In the figure, C1 has a high priority application that receives streaming video at 1.2 Mbits/s from the video server over the 1.5 Mbits/s T1 link between R1 and R2. A low priority distributed application running over the stations C2 and C3 has reserved 0.5 Mbits/s of bandwidth over the T1 link between R2 and R3. Now, suppose the T1 link between R1 and R2 fails (step 1). The network routing algorithm will detect the link failure and route all packets from the video server to C1 over the secondary path between the video server and C1, i.e., through routers R2, R3, and R1. Consequently, the next periodic RSVP Path message sent by the video server to C1 will traverse this route and set up a flow state for the video flow at the routers (step 2).

After this, periodic RSVP Reservation messages sent by C1, will also traverse these routers, but in the reverse direction (step 3). Clearly, the first such RSVP Reservation message from C1 over this secondary path will be rejected by the admission control mechanism at R2. This will generate an SNMP Trap directed at the QoS Manager residing on the network management station (step 4). The QoS Manager will query the router agent at R2 to determine existing reservations on the T1 link between R2 and R3 (step 5). Detecting the low priority reservation for the session between C2 and C3, it usurps this bandwidth for the high priority video stream between C1 and the Video Server. To accomplish this, it commands the Application Controllers at C2 and C3 to shut down the data flows for the low priority application (step 6). The Application Controllers send RSVP Teardown messages to the network to release the resources reserved by the low priority application. This frees up enough bandwidth on the link R2-R3 for the high priority application.

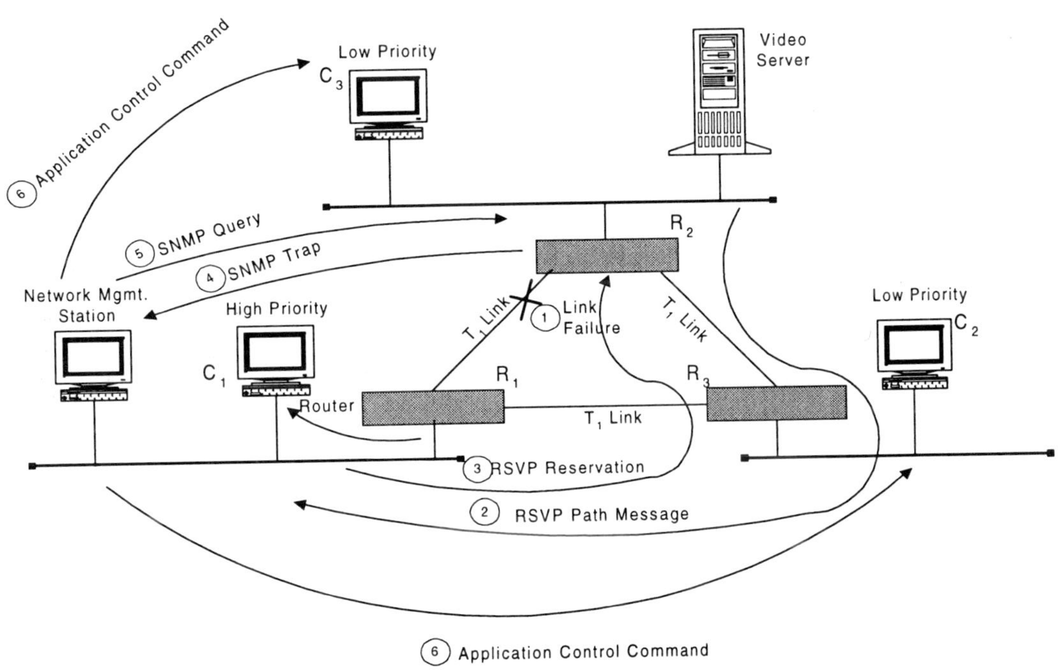

Figure 5: Handling of Network Failures by ARMT

3. Rapid Prototype of ARMT

To establish the feasibility of the design of ARMT, we implemented a rapid prototype and concept demonstration of the tool in a laboratory testbed environment. We successfully demonstrated the capabilities of this rudimentary prototype with actual video applications developed by us under another research effort [7,8].

3.1 Laboratory Testbed

Figure 6 shows the configuration of the laboratory testbed that was employed to implement the concept demonstration of ARMT. As shown in the figure, the network testbed consisted of two Ethernet segments connected together by a PC based Ethernet brouter (Triticom's BrouteIT!). A HP/UX workstation connected to one of the Ethernet segments hosted a video server application. The video server maintained compressed video information that could be played back on demand by video client stations connected to the second Ethernet segment. Each video maintained at the server was encoded using a layered format consisting of a base layer video (layer 1) of acceptable quality, and two enhancement layers (layer 2 and layer 3) that successively enhance the quality of the base layer video signal. The video server used a video streaming protocol to stream layered video data from the disk to the clients over the network. The testbed had three Linux machines running the video player application that served as the video clients for the demonstration. The video player application decoded and played back the layered video received over the network. Thus, up to three video clips could be played back from the server concurrently in this testbed. A traffic generator connected to one of the Ethernet segments of the network was used to inject synthetic traffic into the network to simulate various loading scenarios on the Ethernet.

3.2 Demonstration Scenarios

For demonstration purposes, the server was loaded with four different video clips encoded with three layers each. Table 1 describes the characteristics of the four clips in terms of the network bandwidth required to support the three operating QoS levels for each of these clips. For the demonstration, we used client station based priorities for the video session. Thus video playback sessions at client stations 1,2 and 3 were assigned priorities high, medium, and low respectively.

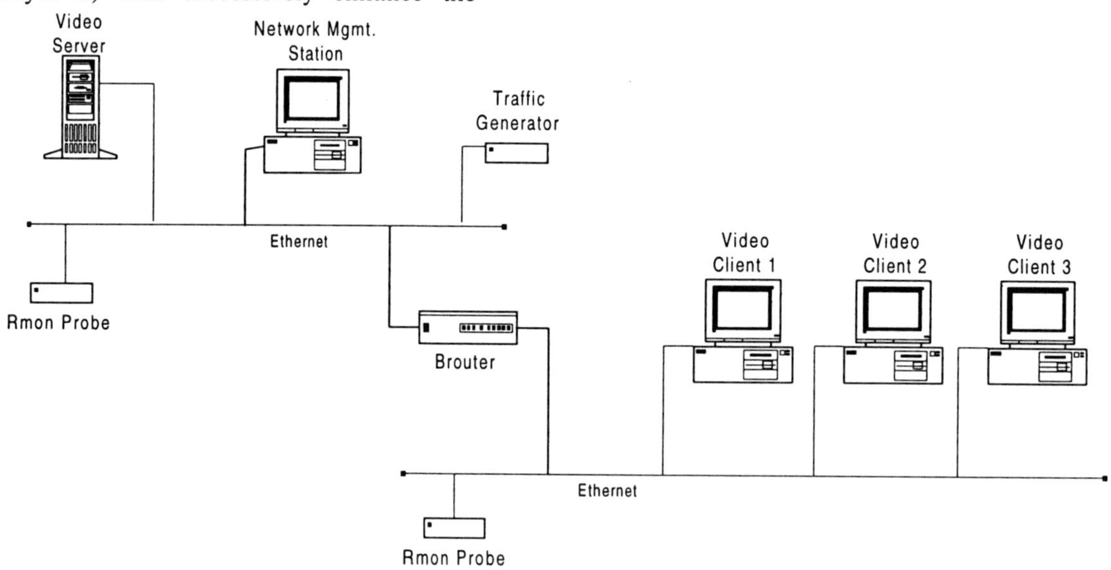

Figure 6 : Testbed for Concept Demonstration of Adaptive Network Management Tool

Clip	Description	Bandwidth Needed (KB/s) 3 layers	2 layers	1 layer
Bosnia 1	UAV surveillance video from Bosnia	68	35	23
Bosnia 2	UAV surveillance video from Bosnia	62	32	21
Venus	Simulated view of the surface of Venus from an orbiting craft	68	32	20
Promo	Promotional video clip	103	49	32

Table 1: Characteristics of Layered Video Used in the Demonstration

Our experience with the network testbed of Figure 6 indicated that the throughput of the brouter between the two Ethernet segments was the bottleneck for video traffic going across the network. When the traffic going across the brouter exceeded 500 Kbytes/s, the packet drop rate at the brouter increases dramatically and severely impacted the quality of the video at the clients. We used this observation of the network behavior to define a simple QoS control policy for the testbed network. ARMT was to ensure that the total traffic across the Ethernet segment never exceed 500 Kbytes/s. The tool had to apply this policy to perform adaptive control of the network under two situations: 1) during the admission of a new application, when the QoS manager must potentially adjust the QoS operating points of already executing applications to accommodate a new application (i.e., handling of priority demands); and 2) during the execution of admitted applications, when adjustments to the QoS operating points of these applications may need to be made in response to changes in network load (i.e., handling of network overload). We performed a number of experiments to demonstrate the capabilities of the ARMT prototype to handle priority demands and network overload. These experiments are described below.

Demonstration of Policy-Based Admission Control (Handling of Priority Demands): To demonstrate the ability of ARMT to handle priority demands, we performed the following steps:

1. We streamed synthetic traffic through the brouter at a rate of 400 Kbytes/s using the traffic generator. This left about 100 Kbytes/s of spare bandwidth across the brouter for video traffic.
2. We requested playback of Bosnia 2 from Client 2 (medium priority). We observed that the request for Bosnia 2 was granted and that the video was admitted to the network at full quality (i.e., 3 layers). The total traffic through the brouter was now 462 Kbytes/s.
3. We requested playback of Bosnia 1 from Client 1 (high priority). We demonstrated how the QoS Manager admitted Client 1 at full quality after adjusting the on-going playback of Bosnia 2 to 2 layers. The effective rate of the traffic through the brouter was now 500 Kbytes/s.
4. We requested playback of Promo from Client 3 (low priority). We observed that the QoS Manager rejected this request, as expected. This was because the traffic through the brouter was already at 500 Kbytes/s. Admission of the low priority video session would have increased this traffic beyond this threshold.
5. We stopped playback of Bosnia 2 at Client 2. The traffic through the brouter now dropped to 468 Kbytes/s.
6. We request playback of Promo at Client 3 (medium priority). We saw that Promo was admitted at low quality (1 layer). The traffic through the brouter increased to 500 Kbytes/s.
7. We requested playback of Venus at Client 2 (medium priority). We observed that the QoS Manager forced the exit of Promo being played at Client 3 (low priority) to admit Venus at 2 layers. The traffic through the brouter was now 500 Kbytes/s.

Demonstration of Dynamic QoS Control (Handling of Network Overload): To demonstrate the ability of the adaptive network management tool to handle network overload, we performed the following steps:

1. We streamed synthetic traffic through the brouter at a rate of 250 Kbytes/s using the traffic generator. This left about 250 Kbytes/s of spare bandwidth across the brouter for video traffic.
2. We requested playback of Bosnia 1, Bosnia 2, and Promo on Client 1 (high priority), Client 2 (medium priority), and Client 3 (low priority), respectively. We observed

that all three video sessions were admitted and the traffic through the brouter increased to about 480 Kbytes/s.

3. We increased the rate of the synthetic traffic to about 300 Kbytes/s. We observed that the QoS Manager reduced the playback quality of Promo to 2 layers and that the resulting video traffic through the brouter was maintained at around 500 Kbytes/s.
4. We decreased the rate of the synthetic traffic to that in Step 1, i.e., 250 Kbytes/s. We observed that the QoS manager detected the availability of additional bandwidth for the video traffic and increased the quality of Promo to 3 layers.
5. We increased the rate of the synthetic traffic to 400 Kbytes/s. We saw that the QoS Manager forced the exit of Promo and adjusted the playback quality of Bosnia 2 to 2 layers.

Even for this ad hoc implementation of the rapid prototype of ARMT, the maximum latency of the automatic control actions taken by the tool was about 5 seconds.

4. Conclusions

This paper presented the design of the Automated Resource Management Tool (ARMT), a software-based network management tool that automates the potentially complex manual task of global resource management in a mission-oriented, Intranet environment. It allows the network operator to specify high-level policies defining the network QoS that must be offered to the different applications sharing the IP network, under each operating mode of the network. The tool automatically handles resource conflicts in accordance with the high-level QoS policies defined by the network operator. It also monitors the network to detect events that may lead to deviations from the specified service policy and automatically implements proactive actions to ensure that the network delivers the required QoS. ARMT has the potential to significantly reduce operator errors and enable cost-effective management of integrated services Intranets.

To establish the feasibility of ARMT, we implemented a rapid prototype and concept demonstration of the tool in a laboratory local area network environment. The rapid prototype was used to control four concurrent video playback applications, each of which streamed a layered video stream over the network. Artificial network overload scenarios were induced using a traffic generator. The network management tool successfully adapted the quality of the delivered video in accordance with a pre-defined policy to ensure optimal quality of the delivered video under each network overload scenario. The maximum latency of the automatic control actions taken by the tool was about 5 seconds, a feat that is impossible to match by human control actions.

6. References

[1] R.Braden, D.Clark, and S.Shenker, "Integrated Services in the Internet Architecture: An Overview," Internet RFC, July 1994.

[2] R.Braden, et al, "Resource Reservation Protocol (RSVP) - Version 1 Functional Specification," Internet RFC, August 1996.

[3] S.Shenker, C. Partridge, and R. Guerin, "Specification of Guaranteed Quality of Service," Internet Draft, August 1996.

[4] J Wroclaski, "Specification of the Controlled-Load Network Element Service," Internet Draft, August 1996.

[5] F. Baker, and J. Krawczyk, "Integrated Services Management Information Base," Internet Draft (work in progress), June 1997.

[6] F. Baker, J. Krawczyk, and A. Sastry, "RSVP MIB," Internet Draft RFC (work in progress), July 1997.

[7] R.S. Ramanujan, et al, "Media Transport Service for Video Retrieval Applications on ATM Networks," Proceeding of the 20th IEEE Local Computer Networks Conference, Oct. 1995.

[8] R.S. Ramanujan, J. Newhouse, M. Kaddoura, A. Ahamad, R. Chartier, and K. Thurber, "Adaptive Streaming of MPEG Video over IP Networks," to appear in the Proceeding of the 22nd IEEE Conference on Local Computer Networks (LCN'97), November 1997.

[9] J. Boyle, R. Cohen, D. Durham, S. Herzog, R. Raman, and A. Sastry, The COPS (Common Open Policy Service) Protocol, Internet Draft (work in progress), Mar. 12, 1998.

[10] R. Ramanujan, and A. Ahamad, "Development of Performance and Traffic Adaptive Management Tool for High Performance Communications Networks," Technical Report F97-004-01, Architecture Technology Corporation, Aug. 1997.

Fairness and Delay/Loss Study of an End-to-End Bandwidth Regulation Scheme

Matthias Frank, Peter Martini
University of Bonn, Institute of Computer Science IV
Römerstraße 164, D-53117 Bonn, Germany
Tel.: +49-228-734550, Fax:+49-228-734571
E-mail: {matthew, martini}@cs.uni-bonn.de

Abstract

*The variety and heterogeneity of different approaches for Quality of Service (QoS) support on different protocol layers result in the need of a solution with end-to-end overview and regulation of data flows in a network. In [6] we proposed the concept of ROBIN (**R**egulation **Of B**andwidth in **I**ntra-**N**etworks) to regulate the sending bandwidth of data flows in heterogeneous campus networks by determining bottlenecks and possible rate limitations with a global knowledge of the network state based on the end-to-end operation of the mechanism. This paper presents latest results of a simulation-based performance analysis studying the throughput fairness of an enhanced version of ROBIN and evaluating the impact of the bandwidth regulation on delays and packet losses in the network.*

1. Introduction

As discussed in [10], the heterogeneity of users, applications and their requirements result in the need for a new service model and a new paradigm for congestion control and avoidance in networks with best-effort service. The desire for distinction of different service types with different properties or quality of service (QoS) becomes clear even in the context of traditional best-effort networks. Also the Internet Draft "Internet Protocol Quality of Service Problem Statement" [2] lists a number of essential requirements for effective support of QoS in the Internet Protocol suite. There are quite a few approaches designed by researchers and developers of networking hardware and software to address these aspects: They intend to integrate new ideas and new functionalities in particular for the Internet Protocol family to support some service distinction and provide quality of service properties in IP networks. The suggestions reach from new networking technologies and specific strategies in medium access to improvements, design or redesign of upper layer communication protocols. But the efficient provision of QoS in a heterogeneous network requires a close cooperation or matching of concepts. Given the variety of existing or proposed approaches addressing several protocol layers, this is a very crucial point.

At the end of 1997 a new working group (Differentiated Services for the Internet -- Diff-Serv) of the Internet Engineering Task Force (IETF) split from the Integrated Services (Int-Serv) working group. The differentiated services intend to introduce a service discrimination in the Internet without the need of per-flow state and signaling at each hop (cf. [11]) and without requiring admission control for flows using this service. Several proposals for service categorization and frameworks for deployment of these services are under discussion (e.g. [9] or [12]). However, there is no information on practical experiences available yet and it is not yet clear if the concept will work efficiently in campus or intra-networks limited to a single domain.

In [1] the authors give some recommendations on active queue management and scheduling algorithms for congestion avoidance of best-effort traffic in the Internet. However, we are still far from reaching consensus on how to address congestion caused by unresponsive or not sufficiently responsive flows (not adapting to indications of congestion like TCP does). [4] also addresses these problems and emphasizes the negative impact of non-controlled best-effort traffic on the Internet in terms of "extreme unfairness ... to the potential for congestion collapse". The authors suggest advanced router support for end-to-end congestion control.

To improve the QoS provision in best-effort networks and to better cope with the congestion problem caused by unresponsive flows we proposed the concept of ROBIN (**R**egulation **Of B**andwidth in **I**ntra-**N**etworks) for a regulation of the sending bandwidth in campus networks. In contrast to approaches like [1] or [4] suggesting to use mechanisms within the network, ROBIN adds some functionality to the sending source hosts. With its end-to-end operation on the transport layer ROBIN is

0-8186-8810-6/98 $10.00 © 1998 IEEE

working independently from lower layer protocols and does not necessarily require feedback from the network elements or protocols. The bandwidth regulation is based on a global knowledge of the network state and flow activities. Basic ideas of the ROBIN concept are as follows:

1. In a campus network that does not support any QoS functionalities at network or lower layer protocols, ROBIN is able to considerably improve this situation by providing a relative QoS based on the different requirements of different applications.
2. ROBIN is able to control the sending bandwidth of flows unresponsive to congestion and thus is able to improve the fairness of network bandwidth distribution between all active flows.
3. As an option, ROBIN is able to make use of or co-operate with different QoS approaches on layers 2 and 3 with a mutual benefit and increase of effectiveness.

This paper presents a part of our continuation of work on ROBIN. The basic concept and very first measurements on a prototype implementation were presented in [6]. In the meantime, further information on the project around ROBIN have been published in [7]. The experiments and measurements with the prototype implementation are accompanied by a detailed performance analysis by simulation addressing important aspects such as network configurations not available for prototype implementation. A detailed description of the simulation model for ROBIN studies and first simulation results may be found in [8]. This paper presents latest results from our simulation studies on the fairness of ROBIN bandwidth regulation and the impact of the regulation on the performance in terms of network delay and packet loss.

The paper is organized as follows: Section 2 briefly summarizes the basic ideas of ROBIN and discusses some new aspects in more detail. Section 3 presents the performance results of new simulation studies on fairness, delay and loss properties with ROBIN operation. Finally, section 4 concludes the paper and gives an outline on future work related to ROBIN.

2. Regulation of bandwidth in intra-networks (ROBIN)

ROBIN is a mechanism for the **R**egulation **O**f **B**andwidth in **I**ntra-**N**etworks. This section describes the basic concept and improvements since or presentation in [6].

2.1. The ROBIN concept

ROBIN operates between transport and network layer protocols as an extension of the protocol stack of each host, cf. Figure 1. ROBIN regulates the bandwidth by a rate control unit at the source of individual data flows. Due to the end-to-end operation of ROBIN, no active co-operation of network protocols and inter-mediate network nodes is required. Thus, no changes to these components are required to use ROBIN. Each instance of ROBIN has knowledge about the complete network topology, the capacity of network elements and the individual bandwidth requirements of "own" flows, i.e. flows leaving the station where the instance is active. This local information is distributed to the peer ROBIN instances frequently. Thus, all ROBIN instances approximately have the same knowledge of the complete network state and the active data flows. In case of overload of particular elements in the network, ROBIN is able to determine the bottlenecks and to allocate the bottleneck bandwidth in an appropriate way by regulating the sending bandwidth of the competing flows. All existing local data flows of transport protocols like UDP, TCP and special purpose protocols are included in the calculation. Of course, the overhead for state exchange and additional calculation limits the area of ROBIN regulation to a campus or intra-network like a typical autonomous system e.g. at a university.

ROBIN offers two types of service: A negotiated bandwidth service (with ROBIN class 0) and a non-negotiated service with the principle of relative QoS (with several application classes, e.g. classes 1 – 4 as proposed in [6]). For class 0, ROBIN supports the negotiation of a certain transmission bandwidth during connection set-up. Applications that are able to specify their bandwidth demand in advance (with parameters similar to RSVP set-up), may reserve bandwidth from ROBIN. If the connection is accepted then these flows are provided with guaranteed bandwidth. The remaining bandwidth of the network (in particular parts of it being a bottleneck) is shared according to the principle of relative

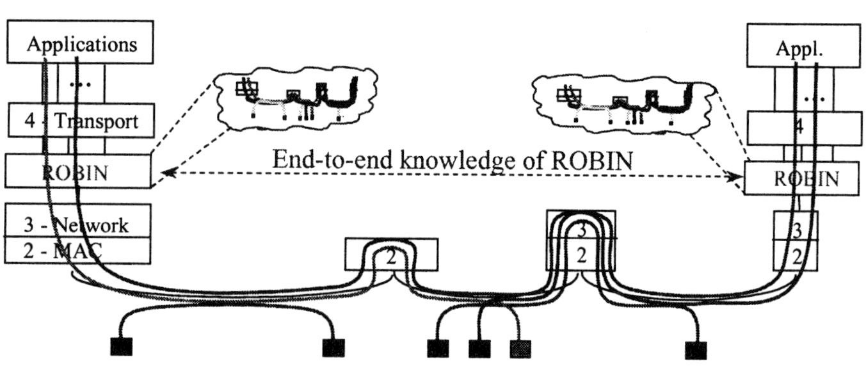

Figure 1: The end-to-end principle of ROBIN

QoS: Different applications are classified according to their requirements in terms of minimum bandwidth (e.g. for video) or relative priorities (e.g. video may have a higher priority than file transfer). The available network bandwidth for each class is equally shared by all active communication flows of this class (e.g. all active video connections). However, the reserved share of the total bandwidth may differ from class to class. The definition of classes, mapping of applications to classes and the allocation of bandwidth to each class in all network components is specified in advance by the system administrator. As an example, in [6] we proposed to have 4 classes for the non-negotiated service with an allocation of bandwidth of 50%, 30%, 15% and 5% for classes 1..4 and an appropriate mapping of applications to classes (e.g. video/audio flows in class 1, ftp in class 2, etc.).

The main advantage of sharing the bandwidth with the principle of relative QoS is that this approach satisfies the bandwidth needs better than a best-effort network service without additional knowledge about flow requirements. As an example, the unfairness problem of TCP is well-known and several enhancements have been proposed (cf. the proposal of [13] and related work cited there). With the calculation of the sending bandwidth of individual flows and a regulation at the source hosts, ROBIN achieves a nearly optimum utilization of the bandwidth available in the network for all active data flows across this network. However, it has to be noted, that a guarantee is only given for the bandwidth allocation of class 0 flows. No guarantee is given in terms of absolute quantities for delay or losses. The non-negotiated service is still a best-effort service without any guarantees for bandwidth, delay or losses of individual flows. Nevertheless, our studies in section 3 point out the gain on overall fairness for throughput of flows and the reduction of delay and losses in the network with ROBIN operation.

Each ROBIN instance consists of the following components: The **Packet Entrance Unit (PEU)** handles incoming data segments and maps these to data flows identified by source and destination IP addresses, port numbers and/or transport protocol identifiers. The data segments are directed to an individual **Rate Throttle (RT)**, which exists for each active flow. A new RT is generated by the PEU for each new flow; a RT is deleted after a certain inactivity timeout. Each RT measures the throughput of data sent for the corresponding flow. If a regulation of the sending bandwidth is activated for a flow, the RT controls the bandwidth of the flow (cf. subsection 2.3).

The **Rate Calculation Unit (RCU)** is the most important component of each ROBIN instance: It maintains a data structure representing the topology of the network, the bandwidth capacity of all network elements operating in the network, and the classification of application flows and per class bandwidth reservation for realizing the relative QoS. Each RCU knows the details (application class, presently consumed bandwidth, bottleneck location) of the flows leaving the host where it resides. It distributes this information to all peer RCUs in frequent intervals of time by a multicast or broadcast state message. By this, all RCUs have almost the same global knowledge of the number and properties of all active flows in the network and are able to determine bottlenecks and to limit the bandwidth of flows involved to avoid congestion.

A more detailed description of the ROBIN concept has been given in [6]. The following subsections discuss modifications and enhancements of the concept since the version described in [6].

2.2. The rate calculation algorithm (RCA)

The algorithm to determine the bottlenecks in the network and to calculate the sending rates has been enhanced to reduce the overhead of the algorithm working on the network graph and to improve the fairness of re-distribution of unused bandwidth.

Figure 2 shows the internal graph representing the network topology and information on active flows. The algorithm to calculate the sending rate for each flow works in two phases on the network graph: In the first phase, the algorithm follows all routes of own flows from the source to the destination within the internal network graph. For each network element with an overload caused

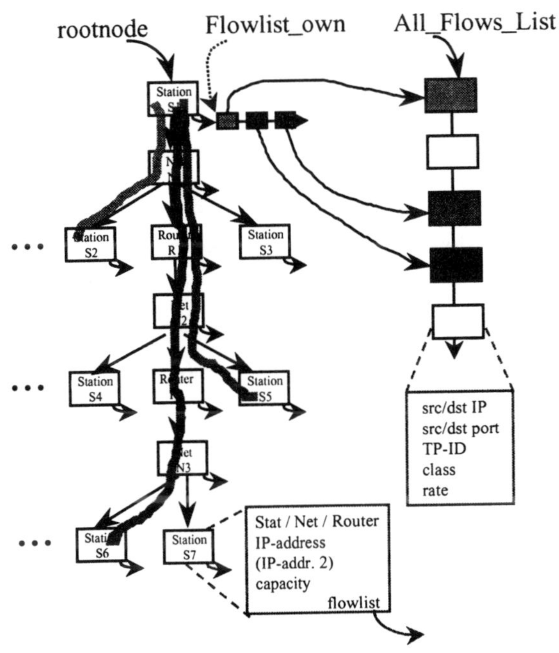

Figure 2: Internal data structure of network

by own and foreign flows passing through, the bandwidth shares of all flows are calculated according to the principle of relative QoS from the pool of bandwidth not used by negotiated service (class 0). The distribution of remaining bandwidth for relative QoS also considers unused bandwidth of empty classes, which is immediately distributed to classes with active flows. In the same step, the bottleneck of each flow is determined when following the routes of the flows and the sending rate is adapted to the bottleneck bandwidth.

After this phase, there may be a situation in single nodes with several flows where some of these flows have their bottleneck at this specific node and other flows having their bottleneck at a different node. Thus, the latter do not use their calculated share completely and bandwidth is left unused. Additionally, it may happen that some flows do not need as much bandwidth as available according to the relative QoS principle. In both cases, the unused bandwidth should be re-used by other flows in these nodes.

Phase 2 tries to re-use possibly unused bandwidth in all bottleneck nodes of own flows. Unused bandwidth of particular flows is firstly distributed to throttled flows of the same class and secondly to flows of other classes (with an order of reuse or priority from classes 1,2, ... down). With all flows belonging to the same class, the ROBIN regulation very well meets the requirements of MaxMin Fairness (cf. [14]), which will be demonstrated in subsection 3.2.

The calculation of the sending bandwidth by the RCA is dominated by the number of own flows leaving the ROBIN instance and the depth of the internal network graph (in terms of nodes in the graph along flow routes) instead of the total number of nodes or active flows in the network. Nevertheless, the scalability of the approach is a critical issue for the performance of ROBIN. The basic version of the ROBIN concept is based on the assumption that each ROBIN instance distributes its information about own flows frequently to all other ROBIN instances, which collect the data and have the knowledge of the complete network present all the time. Although ROBIN usage is limited to a local area, the overhead for distribution of state information and the RCA calculations based on the complete knowledge may already limit the scalability to the order of typical intra-networks.

To improve the scalability of the ROBIN approach, we follow different solutions which may be combined. Up to now, the state exchange and re-calculation of sending bandwidth was done after fixed time intervals causing additional network load and processing overhead in all hosts. To ease this situation, a dynamic determination of points in time for distribution of state information and for re-calculation reduces the overhead. A compromise between "as little as possible" and "as much as necessary" has to be found: Only after relevant changes in the system (such as additional flows, flows leaving, change of parameters within pre-defined tolerance), rates will be re-calculated and a state packet will be sent.

An additional approach would be a hierarchy according to the principle "divide and conquer": The total network is divided into several ROBIN-islands with only local knowledge about island-internal topology and internal flows. The state information is exchanged on two levels: Firstly, within an island for all internal flows, secondly between islands only regarding the flows between islands, where one island does not know all details of other islands. This approach reduces overhead for state exchange and complexity of calculations and additionally allows for a connection of several remote ROBIN islands (e.g. two company network sites connected by a fast direct link).

2.3. The rate throttle (RT)

In [6] we reported on some problems with the RT throughput measurements and rate limitation which caused some inaccuracy and unfairness in the bandwidth calculation of the RCA, in particular for the re-distribution of unused bandwidth. The introduction of fair queuing mechanisms to the RTs in each ROBIN instance solved this problem. In particular we adopted some new ideas coming from [16] where an efficient way of realizing fair queuing by a so called Deficit Round Robin (DRR) has been proposed.

The DRR approach is a simple modification of the traditional round-robin service to avoid the scheduling unfairness with different packet lengths without having high effort for inserting packets into sorted queues. The queues of active flows are served in traditional round-robin manner, but instead of serving one packet per flow for each round a certain quantum of bytes is assigned to each queue. If a packet could not be sent due to a longer packet length, the quantum is added to a deficit counter and the packet is served in one of the next rounds when the deficit counter is larger than the packet length.

Figure 3 depicts the principle of DRR as modified for the use with ROBIN's rate throttles. Each RT has its own buffer for the corresponding flow. An incoming packet is enqueued to the corresponding queue. In case of buffer overflow, packets are discarded. The byte quantum or deficit counter increment for each round is determined as a function of the adapted sending rate for a flow and the time elapsed since the last counter increase. When a packet has been sent, the counter is decremented accordingly. The buffer size is determined as a function of the adapted sending rate to achieve a maximum queuing delay (e.g. 50 ms), which may be selected individually for different application classes of ROBIN.

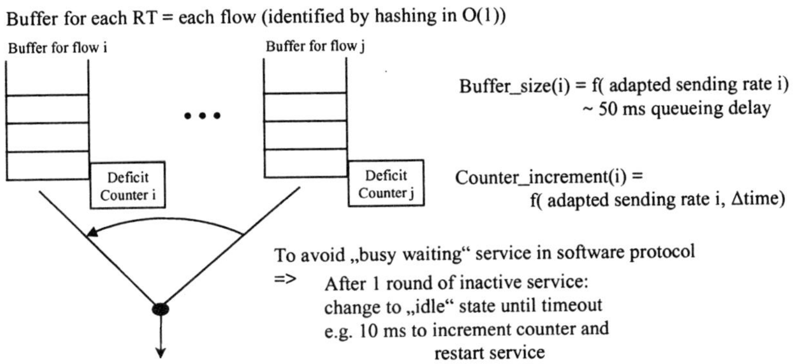

Figure 3: Rate throttles in (modified) deficit round robin mode (DRR)

The DRR proposal is designed for implementation in a router, where the router software including DRR is exclusively using the router CPU. For an implementation in a software protocol working within the operating system on a host (and thus sharing the CPU with application processes), some modifications have to be done to avoid a "busy waiting" service with DRR when only a small quantum of few bytes is added in each round without serving a packet at all. Thus, after one complete round without sending a packet, the service is interrupted until a certain timeout (e.g. 10 ms) to increment the counters and restart the service. The use of one global timer has the advantage of avoiding individual rate timers for each RT which require high precision for high sending rates. We also studied other variations of RT modes (as variations of fair queuing from [3], or rate/burst control as from XTP). However, the DRR approach adopted for ROBIN turned out to be the most promising one.

The actions of the rate throttle to regulate the bandwidth by delaying or in the worst case even discarding packets may interfere with mechanisms of transport protocols. These will be studied in detail to avoid a reduction of the efficiency of these protocols. Nevertheless, this interference may be used for a passive cooperation of ROBIN with transport mechanisms: e.g. TCP's congestion control is sensitive to round-trip delay and packet loss and may adapt its sending bandwidth to the available bandwidth coming from ROBIN regulation.

3. ROBIN performance results

The ROBIN system is designed, specified and implemented as a prototype. The implementation aims at verifying the functionality of ROBIN in a local network environment (cf. [7]). Obviously, performance measurements in a prototype suffer from significant limitations. Therefore, a performance analysis with modeling and simulation of the ROBIN system is carried out. This simulation study evaluates the impact of certain parameters on the ROBIN functionality and analyzes the ROBIN performance in larger scenarios than possible with the prototype implementation. Moreover, these studies investigate bounds on the scalability of the ROBIN approach and give hints for further improvements of the concept (cf. [8]). This section presents latest simulation results from our performance study.

The modeling and program implementation for the simulation study is done with our proprietary simulation tool OOSIM (Object-Oriented SIMulation Library), a library to support discrete, asynchronous, event-driven simulation. Figure 4 shows the simulation model of ROBIN and the information flow between simulation modules of OOSIM (transport and network/MAC protocols and load generator). The receiving part of ROBIN receives the state exchange packets and updates the state information in the RCU's data structures. Additionally, the receiving part of ROBIN monitors the performance of individual flows in terms of throughput, delay and packet loss. The load generator, transport and network modules are predefined simulation objects of OOSIM which can be configured in various ways (load: CBR flows, VBR flows, ... ; transport: TCP, UDP, ... ; network/MAC: Ethernet 10/100 Mbit/s, FDDI, ATM, ...).

For our studies in this paper, we use the load generator with constant bitrate flows with fixed packet size of 1300 bytes with generation rates and numbers of flows as specified below. The interval for exchange of ROBIN state messages between RCUs is set to one second and the calculation of the RCA takes place directly before sending out a state message (thus also once per second). In the following subsection we describe the results of two separate studies of ROBIN performance.

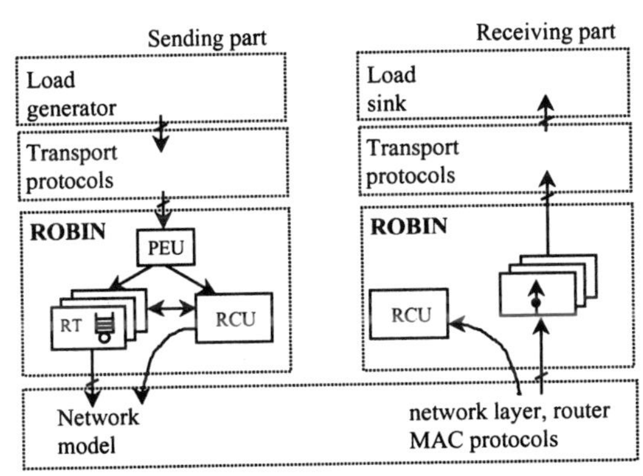

Figure 4: The simulation model of ROBIN bandwidth regulation

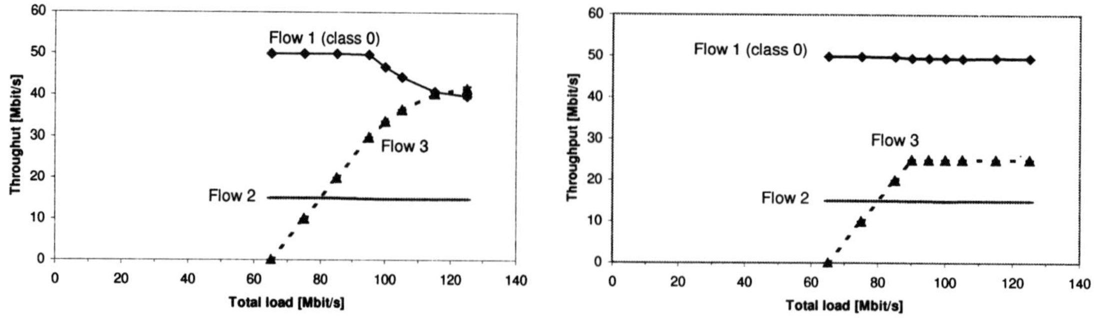

Figure 5: Throughput vs. total load, without ROBIN (left), with ROBIN (right)

3.1. Delay/loss study

The primary goal of ROBIN is to regulate the sending bandwidth at the sources of data flows according to the principle of relative QoS. Thus, all studies of ROBIN performance have to verify that the sending bandwidth calculated by ROBIN and the actual throughput of data flows achieve the desired values. The focus of the following experiment is to show the bandwidth regulation of ROBIN and at the same time evaluate the implications on delays and packet losses with and without ROBIN operation.

The scenario is defined as follows: A local FastEthernet network is shared by several workstations within the same MAC collision domain. Thus, there is a single bottleneck existing for ROBIN bandwidth calculation. Three flows have to share the network: Flow 1 generates a load of 50 Mbit/s and is handled by ROBIN in application class 0 (negotiated service). Flow 2 generates a load of 15 Mbit/s within ROBIN application class 1 (non-negotiated service). The load of flow 3 (also in class 1) is varied for each simulation run from 0 to 60 Mbit/s. Thus, the total load of the shared medium network is varied from 65 Mbit/s (moderate network load) to 125 Mbit/s (overload in the network). With UDP as the transport protocol, none of the flows is responsive to indications of network congestion.

Without ROBIN there is no distinction of application classes, i.e. all flows are treated equally with a best-effort service. For ROBIN operation, the capacity of the Ethernet network segment is selected as 90 Mbit/s which is the target value of ROBIN's bandwidth distribution in this single bottleneck scenario. Thus, flow 1 in class 0 is expected to receive the best service with a negotiated bandwidth of 50 Mbit/s and flows 2 and 3 (both in class 1) have to share the remaining bandwidth of 40 Mbit/s. But flow 2 does not completely use its share of 20 Mbit/s. Therefore, the share of flow 3 according to the principle of relative QoS with ROBIN is expected to be 25 Mbit/s after receiving the unused bandwidth of flow 2.

Figure 5 shows the throughput of the three flows as measured on the receiving host of each flow versus the total generated load. Each value of the plots is an average of 6 simulation batches (of 10 s each) with 90% confidence levels (which are almost invisible in the graphs). For a total load of up to 90 Mbit/s there is no difference between the figures without and with ROBIN. For a higher load, the throughput of flow 1 decreases whereas the throughput of flow 3 still increases. At a total load of 115 Mbit/s the plots of flow 1 and 3 cross because both flows are generating the same load of 50 Mbit/s each. Flow 2 with the lighter generated load of 15 Mbit/s is only slightly influenced in terms of throughput by the overload situation. With ROBIN operation, flow 1 (priority class 0) and flow 2, which does not completely use its share, are not influenced at all. Even with a higher generated load, flow 3 is restricted by ROBIN's bandwidth regulation and its throughput is limited to 25 Mbit/s.

Figure 6 presents the plots of packet delay versus total generated load. The delay measured here is the time difference between generation of a packet in the load generator and the successful reception of the packet in the load sink (lost packets are not considered). Thus, these delays consist of queuing times in RT buffer and MAC sending buffer including Ethernet backoff and the propagation delay on the medium. Without ROBIN, the delays of all flows are rising with increasing total load. The delay of flow 2 is considerably smaller than the other flows due to the lighter generated load of this flow. With ROBIN, flow 1 of class 0 is protected by ROBIN resulting in small delays. In contrast to this, flow 3 which is exceeding its throughput share of 25 Mbit/s and therefore is restricted by ROBIN, has high delays which are mainly caused by the selected RT buffer delay of 50 ms. Interestingly, with higher load flow 2 has a slightly higher delay than without ROBIN regulation. This is caused by the fact that the sending rate of this flow is limited by ROBIN to its initial share of 20 Mbit/s although its generated load is only 15 Mbit/s. Although the flow is not using its allocated share completely, a

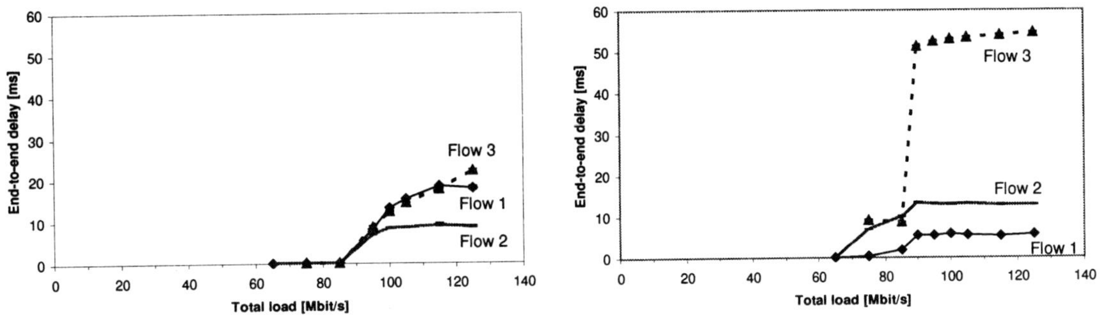

Figure 6: End-to-end delay vs. total load, without ROBIN (left), with ROBIN (right)

regulation of such flows is activated for safety reasons for stability of the overall regulation when the bandwidth demand of the flow is higher than 66% of its bandwidth share. When the Deficit Round Robin service in the rate throttle has been interrupted until the timeout of 10 ms to avoid "busy waiting" (as described in subsection 2.2), some packets have to wait in the RT buffer causing the additional delay.

Total load [%]	Packet losses [%] Without ROBIN			Packet losses [%] With ROBIN		
	Flow 1	Flow 2	Flow 3	Flow 1	Flow 2	Flow 3
65	0,20	0,01	-	0,20	0,01	-
75	0,15	0,01	0,01	0,21	0,01	0,01
85	0,17	0,01	0,01	0,40	0,13	0,01
90	0,38	0,65	0,36	0,89	0,89	0,15
95	0,60	1,41	0,59	0,88	0,83	16,79
105	11,42	1,87	8,87	0,94	0,88	37,57
125	20,38	1,92	30,77	0,96	0,85	58,39

Table 1: Packet loss vs. total load, without and with ROBIN

The percentage of packets lost due to buffer overflow at the sender are presented for each flow in Table 1. Packets are either lost due to RT buffer overflow or MAC sending buffer overflow or are discarded because of unsuccessful transmission attempts after several Ethernet backoff cycles. At heavy load and overload, both flow 1 and 3 encounter heavy packet loss. Even for flow 2 which only generates 15Mbit/s, packet loss rises to more than 1%. With ROBIN, both flow 1 (negotiated bandwidth) and flow 2 (light load) enjoy preferential treatment. In both cases packet loss is below 1%. Note that the Ethernet is still loaded with 90% in case of bandwidth regulation with ROBIN.

The performance study in this subsection clearly showed that ROBIN achieves its primary goal of regulating the sending bandwidth of flows according to the principle of relative QoS. A flow of the negotiated service class 0 is well protected in terms of throughput. So are flows which do not exceed their bandwidth share of relative QoS. However, no absolute guarantee of delays or loss rates is granted by ROBIN. The appropriate selection of the operating point of the network has an important impact on delays and losses with ROBIN regulation. The same experiment carried out with ROBIN using only 80 Mbit/s for the FastEthernet segment lead to a considerable decrease of delay and loss for the protected flows. With a FDDI network with deterministic medium access and no collisions on the medium, even a ROBIN capacity of 90 Mbit/s lead to lower delays compared to the Ethernet study and no packet losses were observed for protected flows.

3.2. Fairness study

The main goal of the study presented in this section is to evaluate the fairness of ROBIN bandwidth calculation in a scenario with several networks and several flows with different bottleneck locations, which leads to a complex scenario of ROBIN rate calculation (with re-use of unutilized bandwidth shares). Again we study delays and losses. The so called "Generic Fairness Configuration 2" (GFC-2) as first defined in [14] is a well-known network configuration which is frequently used for testing the fairness of flow or congestion control schemes in respect to MaxMin fairness. The GFC-2 scenario was originally designed for fairness experiments in ATM networks with flow and congestion control mechanisms of the available bitrate (ABR) service. In our studies of ROBIN operation we focus on campus environments with integration of shared medium networks rather than homogeneously using ATM. Therefore, we adapt the GFC-2 scenario from [14] in the following way: In the original GFC-2, seven ATM switches are connected by 6 links in a single row. The outgoing ATM links connecting two switches were the bottlenecks that had to be shared by several virtual circuits (VCs). The source and destination hosts of VCs were directly connected to a switch and the VCs were traversing at least one link (at least two switches).

For our study, we replace a link (which is a potential bottleneck in GFC-2) by a shared medium FDDI network. The FDDI networks are connected by routers forwarding frames at line rate. Packets with destination in a different network received by the router are directly copied to the MAC sending buffer in the other network. In case of buffer overflow, packets are discarded. Each data flow is traversing at least one subnetwork (similar to the VC routes of GFC-2). Figure 7 shows the modified GFC-2 scenario with 6 connected FDDI subnetworks and the identification of sources and destinations of flows.

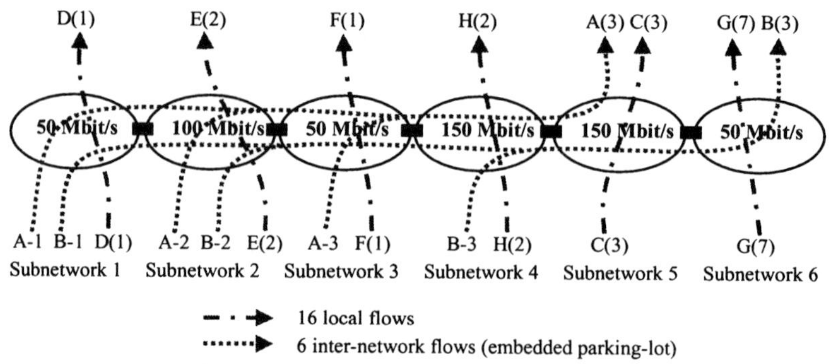

Figure 7: The GFC-2 scenario of our fairness study

To stay as close as possible to the original GFC-2, the networks use nominal data rates that differ from the typical value of 100 Mbit/s for FDDI. The values indicated in Figure 7 are the capacities selected for ROBIN's calculation to allow for a direct comparison of ROBIN results to GFC-2 expected results and equal 90% of the nominal data rate of these networks (e.g. the nominal data rate is 55 Mbit/s in subnetwork 1, 110 Mbit/s in subnetwork 2, etc.). Thus, the target utilization of each network for ROBIN is 90% of the nominal data rate.

The flow identification C(x) denotes that x separate flows are going to the same destination host C along the route as depicted by the arrows in the figure (for routes C, D, ..., H). The six flows A(3) and B(3) have their sources in different subnetworks. The corresponding senders of these flows are marked as A-1, A-2, A-3 and B-1, B-2, B-3. These flows are inter-network flows to destinations A(3) and B(3) with a so called "embedded parking lot" (which means that flows are starting in different subnetworks, and are joining the same path to a common destination subnetwork with having a different number of network hops and different round-trip times). To achieve fairness between such flows in particular when they have to share the same bottleneck on their common path (flows A(x) in subnetwork 3 and flows B(x) in subnetwork 6) is a well-known problem for an end-to-end mechanism (like TCP's flow and congestion control without enhancements in the protocol itself and/or network routers, cf. [13]).

The following figures present the results on throughput, delays and packet loss with ROBIN bandwidth regulation and a comparison to the case without ROBIN. The load generator is now configured as a saturated sender, i.e. each flow tries to send as much as possible in the sending network. All flows are treated by ROBIN within the same application class (class 1 with relative QoS). Therefore, flows sharing the same bottleneck are expected to receive the same bandwidth shares (as required for MaxMin fairness).

Figure 8 presents separate graphs of throughput for the inter-network flows (A-1 ... B-3) for different studies with UDP and TCP flows. The plots show the throughput determined from the data arriving at the receiving hosts averaged over 6 batches of a simulation run. The 90% confidence levels of the averages are omitted because these are far below 1% of the average value.

Without ROBIN regulation, the throughput of most of the flows is much smaller than the expected MaxMin fair value. The inter-network flows starting in different subnetworks (embedded parking lot) suffer from considerable difference in their throughput although they have to share the same bottleneck. This well-known unfairness of TCP is addressed by several proposed enhancements (e.g. [5] or [13] with explicit feedback to TCP, which requires modification of TCP).

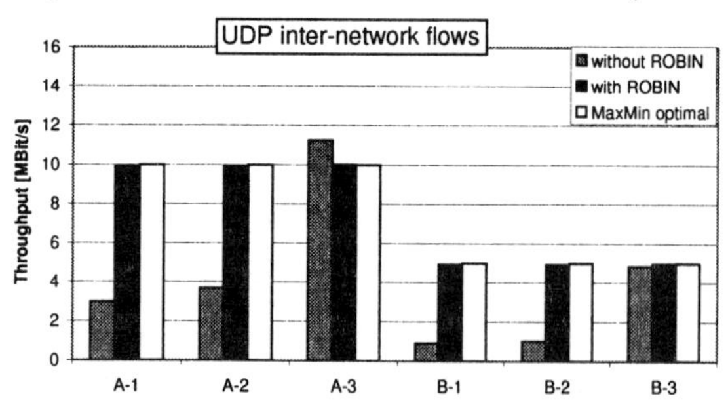

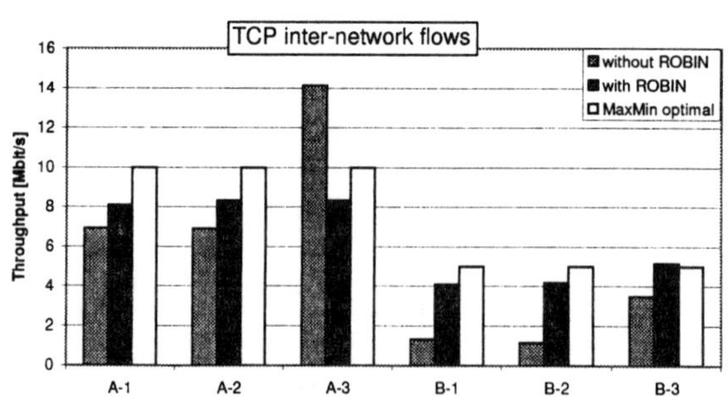

Figure 8: Throughput of flows in GFC-2 scenario

With a bandwidth regulation by ROBIN on the sending hosts, the figures clearly show that the receiver throughput for the UDP flows is exactly matching the expected values according to MaxMin fairness. The throughput in our study with TCP flows does not exactly meet the expected MaxMin optimal values. However, the results with ROBIN operation considerably improve the fairness between these flows sharing the same bottleneck. It was expected that the rate regulation within ROBIN's rate throttle causes an interference with the congestion control mechanisms of TCP, preventing the achievement of optimal throughput values. The correlation of these mechanisms will be studied in detail. Nevertheless, we are optimistic to cope with these correlation problems by adopting ideas from queue management strategies as RED (cf. [1], [4]) or using new proposals for TCP support with per-flow queuing as described in [15].

Separate figures for the local flows are omitted due to space limitations. However, again the bandwidth regulation of ROBIN both for UDP and TCP considerably improves the fairness of achieved throughput according to the MaxMin criterion.

Figure 9 shows the average network delay of packets for UDP inter-network flows, which are unresponsive to congestion indication. To focus on the network performance without and with ROBIN operation, the delays depicted here are the time difference between packets entering the MAC layer on the sender and leaving the MAC layer on the receiver (thus are dominated by queuing delay in the MAC sending buffer in the source hosts and the network routers).

Without ROBIN operation, the delays of all flows are rather high. The impact of the embedded parking lot for flows A(x) and B(x) becomes clearly visible with considerably decreasing delay with a lower number of network hops for the flows to pass through (A-3 and B-3 are lowest).

With ROBIN regulation of the sending bandwidth at the sources, the network delays for all flows are reduced to a small fraction of the values without ROBIN operation. The inter-network flows have a delay of less than 10 ms, the local flows have less than 3 ms delay.

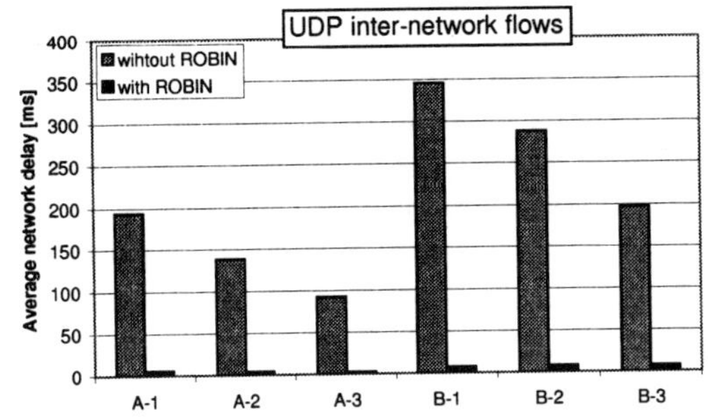

Figure 9: Network delay of flows in GFC-2 scenario (UDP flows)

However, it has to be noted that all flows start at saturated senders and have to be regulated at the sending host. Thus, an additional delay within the RT buffer for each flow is added to the network delay of packets. Nevertheless, with ROBIN bandwidth regulation keeping the network utilization to a predefined level (like 90% for our study) flows of negotiated service (class 0) or flows that do not exceed their fair share according to relative QoS would achieve considerably improved performance in terms of very small delays even on longer routes under the same circumstances.

Figure 10 presents the average packet loss in the MAC sending buffers of the routers due to buffer overflow (note the different scales for UDP and TCP). With ROBIN bandwidth regulation at the source hosts, packet losses within the network are prevented completely both for the studies with UDP and TCP. Without ROBIN and UDP flows, the loss rates in the routers are considerably high. The amount of losses per time depends on the amount of data (or flows) running through the router competing with other sending hosts in the subnetwork and the difference of available bandwidth in each of two connected networks. E.g. the amount of data flowing from subnetwork 3 to 4 is smaller than the available bandwidth for the router competing with 3 sending hosts (B-3 and H(1-2)) in subnetwork 4. Thus, there are no losses in this router at all, neither with nor without ROBIN operation. With TCP and no regulation of

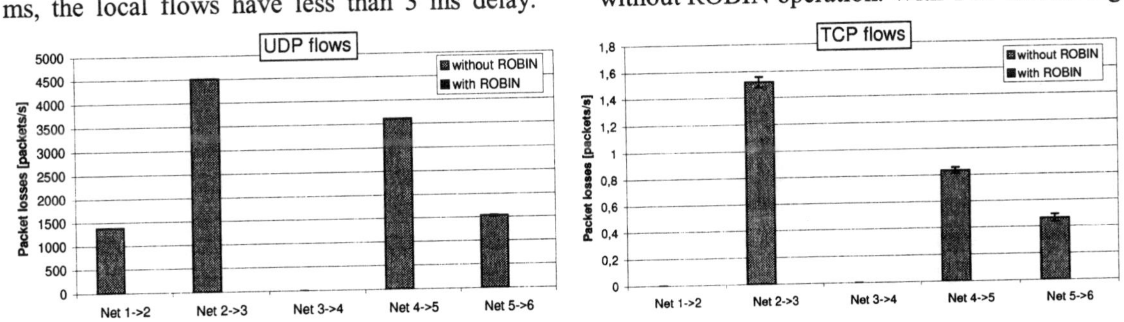

Figure 10: Packet losses in subnetworks in GFC-2 scenario

ROBIN, the packet loss rates are rather small due to the flow and congestion control of TCP, but nevertheless a buffer overflow in the router frequently occurs.

However, the complete prevention of losses in the routers with ROBIN operation underlines the statements given above for the network delay: Flows that have to be protected by ROBIN (class 0 or flows with smaller demand than their fair share) enjoy considerably improved performance also in terms of losses in the network.

To summarize the performance study in this subsection, ROBIN almost achieves the MaxMin fairness and with the regulation of sending bandwidth with an end-to-end overview small delays are achieved and losses in the routers are prevented completely. Although ROBIN still provides a best-effort service without absolute guarantees for delays and losses, the performance is improved considerably and the network is made more predictable with the sender regulation of ROBIN.

4. Conclusions and further work

In this paper we presented latest performance results of ROBIN, a mechanism for end-to-end based regulation of bandwidth in local or campus area networks by controlling the sending rate of application data flows with respect to a relative quality of service principle. Our simulation study had a focus on fairness of the bandwidth distribution between competing flows while also looking at delays and losses in the network. The benefits of the ROBIN approach have been highlighted by a comparison of results with and without ROBIN operation. In contrast to approaches using mechanisms in the network, ROBIN indirectly meets the recommendations of [1] by adding some functionality to the sending source hosts. ROBIN establishes its principle of bandwidth scheduling on an end-to-end basis with a per-flow regulation at the sending hosts. All flows of all transport protocols (also those of unresponsive flows) are considered by ROBIN. The benefits of ROBIN coping with unresponsive flows became clear from the results presented here: The performance is significantly improved in approximately providing MaxMin optimal fairness with low delays and prevention of losses in the network.

The next step of our studies will cover the analysis of bounds on the scalability of the end-to-end ROBIN approach. The overhead for state exchange and rate calculation based on the end-to-end knowledge will be studied in different scenarios. As already addressed in subsection 2.2, enhancements of the concept to increase the scalability such as dynamic points in time for state exchange and recalculation or a hierarchical ROBIN with reduction of global knowledge will be specified and evaluated.

5. References

[1] B. Braden, D. Clark, J. Crowcroft et al. Recommendations on Queue Management and Congestion Avoidance in the Internet. RFC 2309, April 1998

[2] S. Bradner. Internet Protocol Quality of Service Problem Statement. Internet Draft <draft-bradner-qos-problem-00.txt>, IETF, September 1997

[3] J. Bennett, H. Zhang. WF2Q: Worst-case Fair Weighted Fair Queueing. Proceedings of IEEE INFOCOM '96, San Francisco, March 1996

[4] S. Floyd, K. Fall. Router Mechanisms to Support End-to-End Congestion Control. Technical Report LBNL Network Research Group, February 1997

[5] W. Feng, D. Kandlur, D. Saha, K.G. Shin. Understanding TCP Dynamics in an Integrated Services Internet. 7th International Workshop on Network and Operating Systems Support for Digital Audio and Video, NOSSDAV 97, May 1997

[6] M. Frank, P. Martini. Practical Experiences with a Transport Layer Extension for End-to-End Bandwidth Regulation. 22nd Annual Conference on Computer Networks, LCN '97, Minneapolis, November 1997

[7] M. Frank, P. Martini. Prototype Implementation and Simulation Study of an End-to-End Bandwidth Regulation Scheme. 3rd European Conference on Networks & Optical Communications, NOC'98, Manchester, June 1998

[8] M. Frank, P. Martini. Performance Analysis of an End-to-End Bandwidth Regulation Scheme. Sixth International Symposium of Modeling, Analysis and Simulation of Computer and Telecommunication Systems, MASCOTS '98, Montreal, July 1998

[9] S. Kalyanaraman. D. Harrison, S. Arora, K. Wanglee, G. Guarriello. A one-bit feedback enhanced differentiated services architecture. Internet Draft <draft-shivkuma-ecn-diffserv-01.txt>, IETF, March 1998

[10] C. Lefelhocz, B. Lyles, S. Shenker, L. Zhang. Congestion Control for Best-Effort Service: Why We Need a New Paradigm. IEEE Network, January/February 1996

[11] Editors: K. Nichols, S. Blake. Differentiated Services Operational Model and Definitions. Internet Draft <draft-nichols-dsopdef-00.txt>, IETF, February 1998

[12] K. Nichols, V. Jacobson, L. Zhang. A Two-bit Differentiated Services Architecture for the Internet. Internet Draft <draft-nichols-diff-svc-arch-00.pdf>, IETF, November 1997

[13] ATM-Forum, R. Satyavolu, K. Duvedi, S. Kalyanaraman. Explicit rate control of TCP applications. ATM Forum Document 98-0152R1, February 1998

[14] ATM Forum, R.J. Simcoe. Test Configurations for Fairness and Other Tests. ATM Forum Document 94-0557, July 1994

[15] B. Suter, T.V. Lakshman, D. Stiliadis, A.K. Choudhury. Design Considerations for Supporting TCP with Per-flow Queueing. Proceedings of IEEE INFOCOM '98, San Francisco, April 1998

[16] M. Shreedhar, G. Varghese. Efficient Fair Queuing using Deficit Round Robin. IEEE/ACM Transactions on Networking, Vol. 4, No. 3, June 1996

Paper Session 5
Track A: Hardware

Session Chair: Kenneth J. Christensen
University of South Florida

Optical Logic Circuits: A New Approach to the Control of Fiber Optic LANs

Georgios I. Papadimitriou, Amalia N. Miliou and Andreas S. Pomportsis

Department of Informatics,
Aristotle University of Thessaloniki, Box 888,
54006 Thessaloniki, Greece.

Abstract

The centralized filtering of the transmitted packets has been the base of a family of high-performance protocols for WDM Star Networks [19],[20]. Protocols of this family have been proved to achieve a significantly higher performance than the well-known contention-oriented or round-robin protocols. However, the need for electronic control of the filtering mechanism as well as the use of slowly tunable acoustooptic filters have been limiting factors in their performance. Furthermore, since the network hub of WDM Star Networks represents a single point of failure, the extensive use of electronic circuits at this point reduces the reliability of the system. In this paper, an all-optical centralized protocol is introduced. According to this protocol, the passing of the transmitted packets to the star coupler is controlled by means of optical logic circuits, without the need of optical to electronic translation or electronic processing of the network feedback information. In this way, the processing time is drastically reduced, while the need for acoustooptic filters is eliminated. Therefore, a significant performance improvement is achieved. Furthermore, due to the all-optical nature of the network hub, the reliability of the system is improved. The performance of the proposed protocol is studied via extensive analytical and simulation results which indicate that a WDM Star network operating under this protocol achieves a high throughput-delay performance under any load conditions.

1. Introduction

The introduction of broadband services and multimedia applications has led to a dramatical increase in the bandwidth demands of the emerging new generation of fiber optic LANs and MANs.

Due to the limited speed of the stations' electronic circuits, single channel optical networks - such as FDDI, DQDB, Fasnet, Expressnet, etc - were not proved capable of supporting Gigabit data rates. The Wavelength Division Multiplexing (WDM) technique [1],[2] solves this problem by dividing the available optical bandwidth into multiple channels of lower bandwidth which can be easily supported by the stations' electronic circuits. Both, multiplexing and demultiplexing of the multiple channels, are performed in the optical domain without the need of optical to electronic translation and vice versa. In this way, the WDM technique allows the implementation of all-optical networks which are capable of providing Gigabit data rates by using present-day optical and electronic technology.

Broadcast-and-Select Star networks (figure 1) - which are a special category of WDM networks - use a Passive Star Coupler in order to broadcast all inputs to all outputs. There are four possible configurations of the Broadcast-and-Select Star architectural form: a) Fixed optical transmitters and fixed optical receivers [1], [4], b) tunable optical transmitters and tunable optical receivers [1],[12]-[16], c) fixed optical transmitters and tunable optical receivers [1],[3],[5],[9]-[11],[18], and d) tunable optical transmitters and fixed optical receivers [1],[6],[7],[17],[19],[20]. The latter configuration is considered in this paper.

The centralized filtering of the transmitted packets has been the base of a family of high-performance protocols for WDM Broadcast-and-Select Star Networks [19],[20]. Protocols of this family have been proved to achieve a significantly higher performance than the well-known contention-oriented or round-robin protocols. However, the need for electronic control of the filtering mechanism as well as the use of slowly tunable acoustooptic filters have been limiting factors in their performance. Furthermore, since the network hub of WDM Star Networks represents a single point of failure, the extensive use of electronic circuits at this point reduces the reliability of the system.

In this paper, an all-optical centralized protocol is introduced. According to this protocol, the passing of the transmitted packets to the star coupler is controlled by means of optical logic circuits, without the need of optical to electronic translation or electronic processing of the network feedback information. In this way, the processing time is

0-8186-8810-6/98 $10.00 © 1998 IEEE

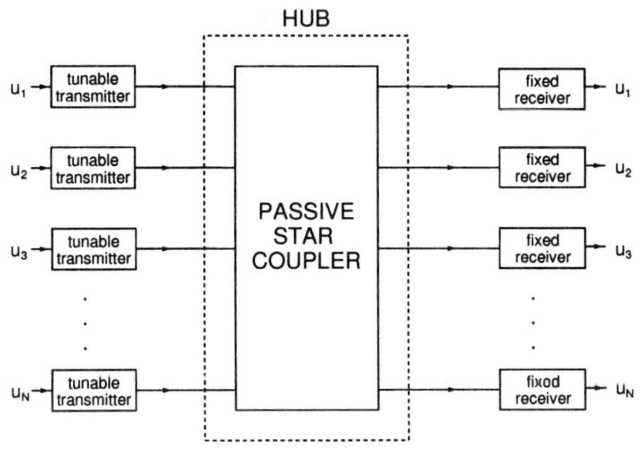

Figure 1: A WDM Broadcast-and-Select Star Network using tunable lasers and fixed optical filters.

drastically reduced, while the need for acoustooptic filters is eliminated. Therefore, a significant performance improvement is achieved. Furthermore, due to the all-optical nature of the network hub, the reliability of the system is improved. The performance of the proposed protocol is studied via extensive analytical and simulation results which indicate that a WDM Star network operating under this protocol achieves a high throughput-delay performance under any load conditions.

The paper is organized as follows: The proposed Optically Controlled Optical Network (OCON) is presented in Section 2, while the Optical Logic Circuit which is the core element for the implementation of OCON is extensively discussed in Section 3. The performance analysis of the proposed protocol in Section 4, is followed by the presentation of simulation results in Section 5. Finally, concluding remarks are given in Section 6.

2. The Optically Controlled Optical Network

The OCON network can be divided into two basic modules which are described below: The Broadcast-and-Select Module and the Packet Filtering Module. The reader can consult figure 2 in order to study an example of the OCON network for four stations and three wavelengths.

2.1. The Broadcast-and-Select Module

The Broadcast-and-Select module is based on the network architecture which is presented in [6] and [7].

The set of nodes is defined as $U = \{u_1, \ldots, u_N\}$, where N is the number of nodes. The set of wavelengths is defined as $\Lambda = \{\lambda_1, \ldots, \lambda_W\}$, where W is the number of wavelengths.

Each transmitter is provided with a tunable laser which can be tuned to each one of the W wavelengths. Optical fibers are used to connect the outputs of the lasers to the network hub. There, the optical signal is fed to a Passive Star Coupler after passing through a packet filtering mechanism, which will be described in Section 2.2.

Each output port of the star coupler is connected to the corresponding receiver, by means of an optical fiber. Each receiver is provided with a set of R fixed optical filters with each of them passing a different wavelength. Therefore, each receiver is capable of concurrently receiving up to R packets which are transmitted on different wavelengths. R is usually very small ($1 \leq R \leq 3$), since a large number of receivers per station would lead to an increase of the network complexity.

2.2. The Packet Filtering Module

The Packet Filtering Module filters the packets arriving at the network hub in such a way, that at most one packet per wavelength is allowed to pass to the star coupler. Its role is similar to a MAC layer firewall, except that it is used for collision avoidance reasons rather than for security ones. It can be separated into three stages.

The first stage consists of an array of N WDM Demultiplexers which separate the different wavelengths of the incoming signals. Since during a time slot each node can transmit at only one wavelength, it follows that at most one of the W output ports of each Demultiplexer contains an optical signal.

The second stage consists of an array of W Optical Logic Circuits (OLCs) with each wavelength being controlled by a separate OLC. The outputs of the demultiplexers which contain wavelength λ_i (for $i = 1, \ldots, W$) are connected to the corresponding OLC which controls this wavelength. Only one of the optical signals which enter the OLC is allowed to exit. All the other signals are blocked. Since, only one packet per wavelength is allowed to pass to the star coupler, collisions are avoided. The design and implementation of the OLC are discussed in Section 3.

The third stage consists of N WDM Multiplexers which recombine the optical signals in order to be fed to the N input ports of the Passive Star Coupler.

2.3. The Operation of the OCON protocol

The time axis is slotted. At the beginning of each time slot, each ready station randomly selects a packet from the waiting queue, chooses at random one of the R wavelengths which the destination node of the packet is capable of receiving and then, it tunes its laser to this wavelength

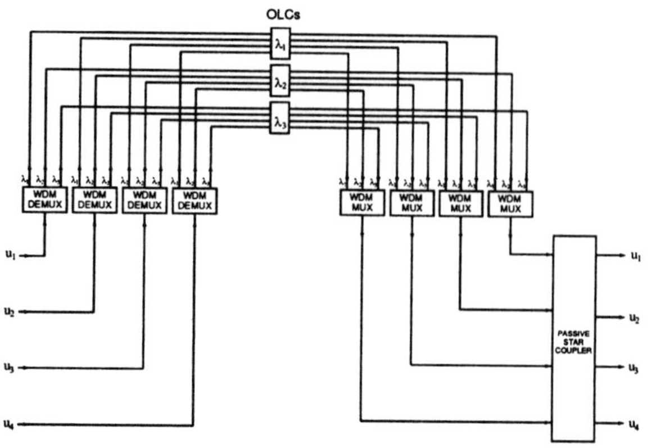

Figure 2: The hub of the Optically Controlled Optical Network.

and transmits the packet. The transmitter can ascertain the result of its transmission by using one of the methods which are reported in [8]. The round-trip propagation delay is assumed to be negligible. Therefore, the feedback information is immediately available. If the transmitted packet is not blocked by the Packet Filtering Module, then the transmitting node deletes the packet from the waiting queue. Otherwise, the packet remains in the queue.

3. The Optical Logic Circuit

The key element of the OCON architecture is the Optical Logic Circuit (OLC). It is an optical device with N input and N output ports which allows only one of the incoming signals to pass to the corresponding output port.

The basic operations of the OLC are the following:

a) Senses the input ports in order to find out which of them contain incoming signals.

b) Selects one of the incoming signals.

c) Allows the selected signal to pass to the corresponding output port, while all the other signals are blocked.

d) The selection of the passing signal must be implemented fairly. None of the input ports must be favored among the others.

e) The device must be all-optical, without any O/E translation of the incoming signals.

First, the logical structure of the OLC device is described at logic gate level and its operation is analyzed. Then, the implementation of the device by means of Directional Couplers is presented. The reader can consult figure 4 in order to study an OLC device with four input and four output ports.

3.1. The OLC Logical Structure

The OLC logical structure can be divided into two basic modules:

1. The packet blocking module
2. The control module

The packet blocking module consists of N AND-NOT gates H_k $(k = 1, \ldots, N)$ which act as taps which allow or block the passing of the incoming packets. It has N input ports I_k, N output ports O_k and N control ports C_k (the "NOT" input ports of the AND-NOT gates), for $k = 1, \ldots, N$. Since, $O_k = \overline{C_k}\, I_k$ it follows that, if a control port C_k is set to 0, then the signal of input port I_k is allowed to pass to the corresponding output port O_k. Otherwise, if control port C_k is set to 1, then the signal of input port I_k is blocked. Since only one of the output ports (say O_p) may contain an optical signal, it follows that C_k $(k = 1, \ldots, N)$ must be defined in such a way that $\overline{C_p}\, I_p = 1$, while $\overline{C_m}\, I_m = 0$, for all $m \neq p$.

The control module controls the operation of the packet blocking module by driving the control ports of the latter. Its role is to sense the incoming signals I_k $(k = 1, \ldots, N)$ and to define C_k's in such a way that only one output port $O_p = \overline{C_p}\, I_p$ is equal to 1, while all the other output ports are set to 0.

In order to simplify the description of the control module we first consider a simplified version of the OLC (figure 3) which satisfies the requirement of leaving only one of the incoming signals to pass, but takes no care about the fairness of the system. After the simplified version is discussed, then the final version of the OLC is presented as an extension of the simplified version.

The core of the control module is an array of N serially connected OR gates (figure 3). Each OR gate G_k evaluates C_k by taking as inputs I_{k-1} and C_{k-1}, for $k = 2, \ldots, N$. In the simplified version, C_1 is always set to 0. Since, $C_k = C_{k-1} + I_{k-1} = I_1 + I_2 + \ldots + I_{k-1}$ (for $k = 2, \ldots, N$) it follows that: $O_k = \overline{C_k}\, I_k = \overline{I_1 + I_2 + \ldots + I_{k-1}} I_k = \overline{I_1}\, \overline{I_2} \ldots \overline{I_{k-1}} I_k$. In other words, $O_k = 1$ only when $I_k = 1$ and $I_m = 0$ for all $m < k$. Therefore, only one of the incoming signals is allowed to pass to the corresponding output port. All the other signals are blocked.

However, this scheme has a serious disadvantage. Since the serial search for an active input port I_p always begins from the same port (I_1), the scheme is not fair. In order to overcome this limitation, the OR gates are cyclically connected, while an AND-NOT gate $F_k (k = 1, \ldots, N)$ is placed between each pair of consecutive OR gates (figure 4). The laser diode which controls the AND-NOT gates transmits a light pulse every N time slots, while each pulse is delayed for a time slot before reaching the next gate, by means of a delay line. In this way, only one AND-NOT gate $F(t)$ is disabled at each time slot t. Furthermore,

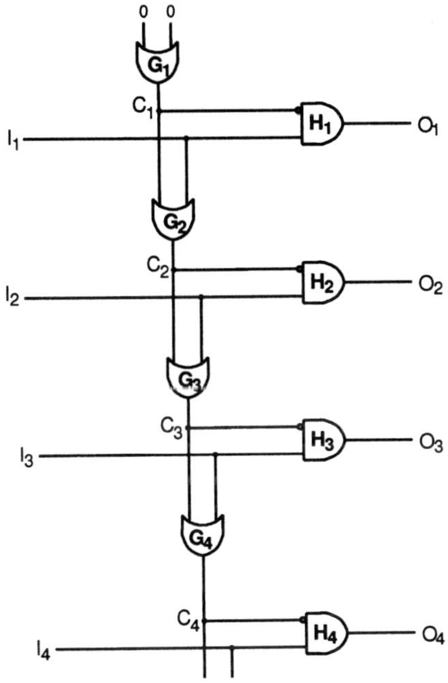

Figure 3: A simplified version of the Optical Logic Circuit.

the disabled gate is cyclically shifted at each time slot. Thus, if $F(t) = F_m$, then $F(t+1) = F_{(m \bmod N)+1}$. If $F(t) = F_m$, then the serial search for an active input port begins from port I_m. Since, F_m is cyclically shifted at each time slot, no input port is favored among the others. Therefore, the resulting scheme is fair.

3.2. Directional-Coupler-Based Implementation

The all-optical approach has met with considerable difficulties, above all due to the high power consumption involved in optical-optical interaction [22]. An intermediate step to the all-optical network would be electrically controlled optical switches, gates etc. operating at high speed.

The system that is described in this paper could be considered all-optical in the sense that information is in optical form except at the point where electronic signal is used to control the switch.

The well developed technology of $LiNbO_3$ directional coupler was chosen, in this work, as a logic device for the nanosecond switching speeds, the low crosstalk and the low insertion loss. Furthermore the $LiNbO_3$ directional coupler is the simplest device that can provide the logic functions needed for the circuit described above. The glass fiber loop was used as a delay-line [23].

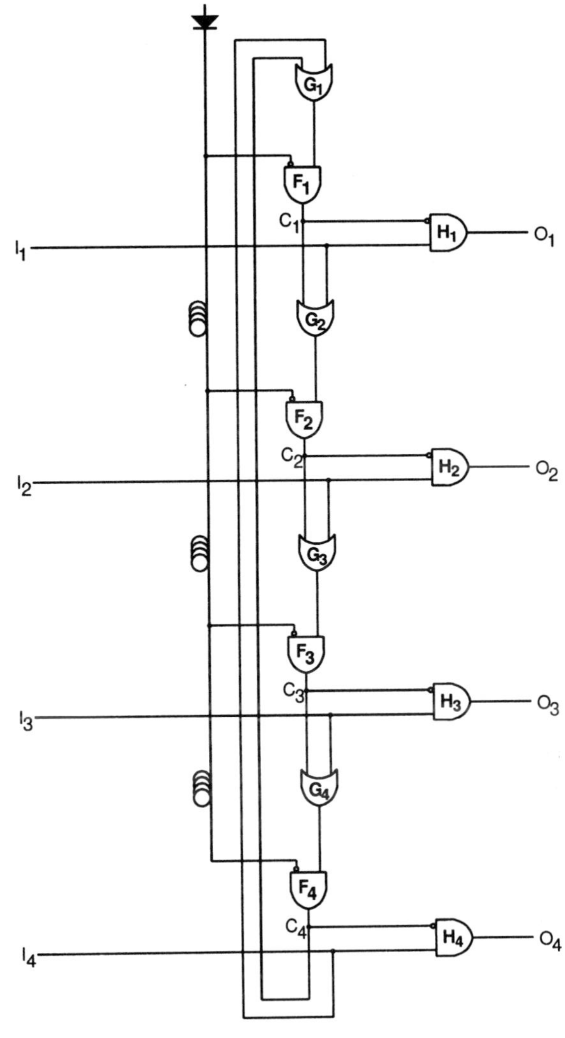

Figure 4: The Optical Logic Circuit.

The switch shown in figure 5 has two optical inputs, A and B, and two optical outputs, D and E. There is also an electronic control input C. The switch requires also a static bias voltage 5V to minimize crosstalk. In the absence of an externally applied voltage at terminal C, light entering input A will emerge at E. Likewise, light entering at B will emerge at D. This is referred to as cross state. Application of the correct voltage at terminal C will cause light entering at A to emerge at D and light entering at B to emerge at E. This is referred to as bar state. The switching voltage applied at C is 5V. The switching depends on electrode configuration and geometry.

From the point of view of the OLC logical structure the $LiNbO_3$ directional coupler can demonstrate the AND-NOT logic function (figure 6) that is utilized in the circuit. The OR logic function is passively implemented by means

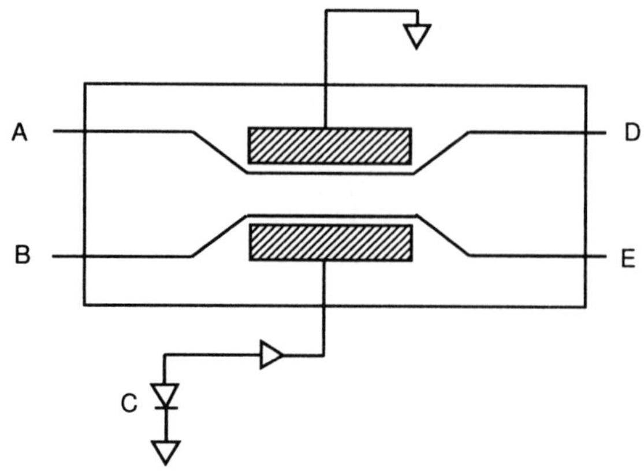

Figure 5: A $LiNbO_3$ directional coupler.

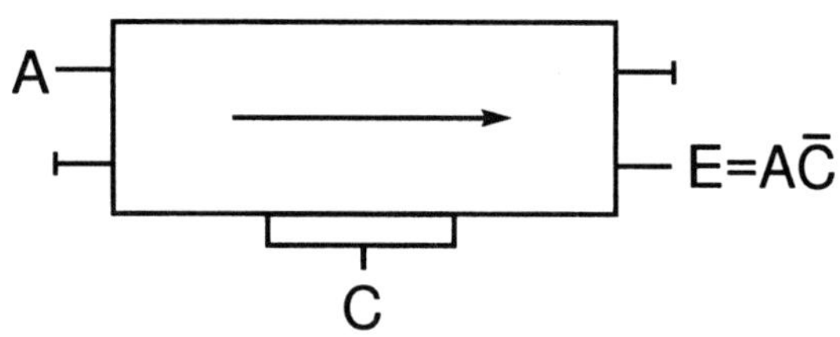

Figure 6: A directional-coupler-based implementation of the AND-NOT gate.

of a combiner (figure 7).

The signal source is a 1310 nm laser diode and the pulse power is adjusted to 1mW. Important parameters that affect the number of stages in the circuit and also the optical power required, are the insertion loss and the crosstalk. The insertion loss was estimated 5 dB and the crosstalk to <20dB. Therefore, there is a need for some means of amplitude restoration along the way of the signal in the circuit described above.

The switching speed of the directional coupler was 0.3 ns which was considerably faster than the switching speed of the drive electronics of the device (1 ns) [24]. The AT&T $LiNbO_3$ switches used were polarization-dependent, thus the inputs require in-line polarization controllers [25].

There are two important issues which must be taken into account in the implementation of OCON.

a) The inputs of the control module must be stable during the slot duration. Thus, an input must be in the "1" state when there is an incoming packet in the corresponding input port, while being in the "0" state when there is no incoming packet. Since, an incoming packet is a sequence of "0" and

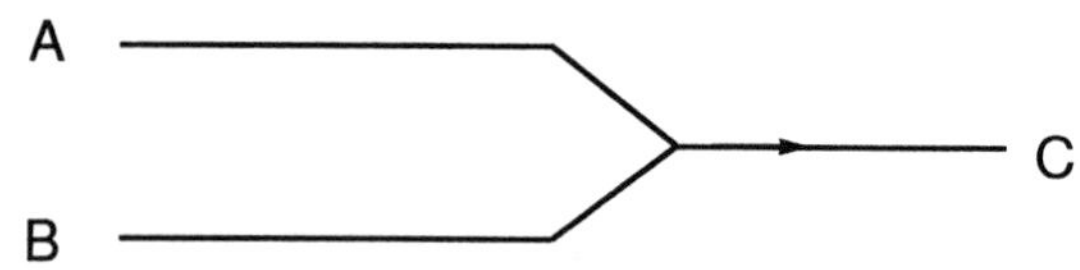

Figure 7: A passive OR gate.

"1" bits, there are two ways to keep the input of the control module stable: i) To use Phase Modulation (BPSK) [21] at the transmitters, so that the intensity of the incoming light signal is stable during each slot. ii) To use Amplitude Modulation [21] at the transmitters and make a proper selection of the light intensity levels which correspond to "0" and "1", so that even when a "0" bit enters the control module, the light intensity is high enough to be considered as "1" by the control module.

b) At the beginning of each time slot the output of the OLC is unstable for a time interval t_u, equal to the propagation delay of the loop $G_1, F_1, G_2, F_2, \ldots, G_N, F_N, G_1$ (figure 4). Therefore, each packet must have a "dummy" preamble of duration t_u. In practice, t_u consists of the delay which is introduced by the logic gates. This delay is in the nanosecond range [23]. Thus, it is three orders of magnitude smaller than the packet duration. So, the introduction of the "dummy" preamble does not affect the performance of the network.

3.3. A Future Perspective: Bistable-Optical-Device-Based Implementation

There is a great deal of interest in developing and using bistable optical devices for implementing optical logic gates. However, even though the use of these devices is very attractive mainly due to the fact that could provide an all-optical network and thus very high speed and reliability, the technology is not yet mature enough. The bistable devices considered in the literature are either having high power consumption or problems with temperature stability. A future perspective for the proposed OLC is its implementation by means of bistable optical devices as soon as they are available.

4. Analysis

In this section we present an analysis of the OCON's performance. The presented analysis approximates the mean throughput and the mean packet delay of a network operating under the OCON protocol. We use an analytical model similar to the one presented in [6]. Let Q be the

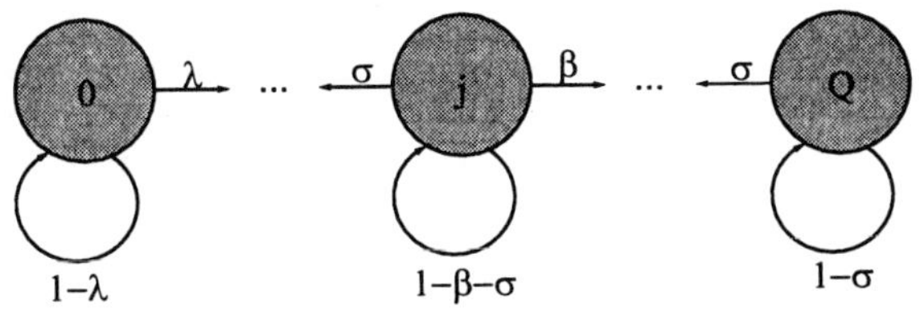

Figure 8: Markov chain for the OCON protocol.

size of the waiting queues, while P denotes the transition probability matrix for a node of the network. Assume that at the beginning of each time slot each node generates a new packet with probability λ (if the offered load is G packets per wavelength per slot, then $\lambda = \frac{W}{N}G$).

P_{jk} represents the transition probability from j packets in the queue of node i at the beginning of a slot to k packets in the queue at the beginning of the next slot (after the new packet arrivals). To calculate the elements of the matrix P we use S, the probability of a successful transmission by this node. Denote,

$$\beta = \lambda(1 - S) \quad ; \quad \sigma = S(1 - \lambda)$$

β and σ are the "birth" and "death" probabilities at state j, i.e., the probabilities that the state increases by 1 or decreases by 1, respectively (except for state 0 for which the birth probability is λ).

The transition probabilities for a node (see figure 8), are then given by

$$P_{jk} = \begin{cases} 1-\lambda & j = k = 0 \\ \lambda & j = 0, k = 1 \\ \sigma & 0 < j \le Q,\ k = j-1 \\ 1-\beta-\sigma & 0 < j < Q,\ k = j \\ \beta & 0 < j < Q,\ k = j+1 \\ 1-\sigma & j = k = Q \\ 0 & \text{otherwise} \end{cases} \tag{1}$$

Let Π denote the steady-state probability vector of the above Markov chain, where Π_j denotes the steady-state probability that a node has j packets in its waiting queue at the beginning of a slot (after the new packet arrivals). By solving the set of equations,

$$\Pi P = \Pi \quad ; \quad \sum_{j=0}^{Q} \Pi_j = 1 \tag{2}$$

we obtain

$$\Pi_j = \frac{\lambda}{\beta}\left(\frac{\beta}{\sigma}\right)^j \Pi_0 \quad ; \quad 0 < j \le Q \tag{3}$$

and,

$$\Pi_0 = \left[1 + \frac{\lambda}{\sigma}\frac{\left(\frac{\beta}{\sigma}\right)^Q - 1}{\frac{\beta}{\sigma} - 1}\right]^{-1} \tag{4}$$

Since the successful transmission of a node depends on the occupancy of all the other nodes, S is a function of the steady state probability Π_0. Assuming that $\lambda > 0$ and $S > 0$ the Markov chain for each node is ergodic, hence having a unique steady state distribution. We are therefore, assured of converging to the correct values.

It remains to calculate S, the probability that a node (say u_i) successfully transmits, given this node is busy.

$$\begin{aligned} S &= \sum_{m=0}^{N-1}\Big(Pr\{m \text{ other nodes are also busy}\} \\ &\qquad \times Pr\{u_i\text{'s packet is allowed to pass}\}\Big) \\ &= \sum_{m=0}^{N-1}\left(\binom{N-1}{m}(1-\Pi_0)^m(\Pi_0)^{N-m-1}\right. \\ &\qquad \left.\times \sum_{k=0}^{m}\frac{1}{k+1}\binom{m}{k}\left(\frac{1}{W}\right)^k\left(1-\frac{1}{W}\right)^{m-k}\right) \end{aligned} \tag{5}$$

Once the Π_j's are obtained, the throughput of a node can be calculated as follows: Given a node is busy, the probability of a successful transmission is S, hence,

$$T = (1 - \Pi_0)S \tag{6}$$

The total system throughput H (in packets per wavelength per slot) is given by

$$H = \frac{N}{W}T \tag{7}$$

The average queue length L can be obtained using

$$L = \sum_{j=0}^{Q} j\Pi_j = 1 \tag{8}$$

and the average delay of a packet D can be found by using the Little's Theorem

N_1	Throughput		Delay	
Load	Analysis	Simulation	Analysis	Simulation
0.2	0.2000	0.2000	1.13	1.13
0.4	0.4000	0.4000	1.36	1.39
0.6	0.6000	0.6000	1.94	2.07
0.8	0.7831	0.7725	4.03	4.27
1.0	0.8552	0.8403	7.43	7.07

N_2	Throughput		Delay	
Load	Analysis	Simulation	Analysis	Simulation
0.2	0.2000	0.2000	1.12	1.13
0.4	0.4000	0.4000	1.35	1.37
0.6	0.6000	0.5998	1.89	1.98
0.8	0.7851	0.7819	3.87	4.07
1.0	0.8612	0.8550	7.28	7.26

Table 1: Analytical and simulation results of the OCON protocol when applied to networks N_1 and N_2.

$$D = \frac{L}{T} \tag{9}$$

It must be noted that in any case the analytical results are very close the simulation ones. Both analytical and simulation results for two different networks N_1 and N_2 which operate under the OCON protocol are presented in Table 1. The specifications of networks N_1 and N_2 are given in the next section.

5. Simulation Results

In the following, the proposed OCON protocol is compared to two other collision-free protocols: RTDMA [6],[7] and HARP [20]. A critical parameter of the HARP protocol is the tuning time T of the acoustooptic filters. Simulation results are presented for T=0 and T=0.2 slots.

The protocols which are under comparison were simulated to be applied to six different networks $(N_1, N_2, N_3$ and $N_4)$. The number of stations N, the number of data wavelengths W, the queue length Q and the number of receivers R of each simulated network, were taken to be as follows:

a) Network $N_1 : N = 40, W = 20, Q = 5, R = 2$.

b) Network $N_2 : N = 20, W = 10, Q = 5, R = 2$.

c) Network $N_3 : N = 20, W = 5, Q = 5, R = 2$.

d) Network $N_4 : N = 60, W = 20, Q = 10, R = 3$.

We have used the following two broadly used performance metrics in order to compare the two protocols:

1) The delay versus throughput characteristic.

2) The throughput versus offered load characteristic.

The delay versus throughput characteristics of the compared protocols when they are applied to networks N_1, N_2, N_3 and N_4 are appeared at figures 9, 11, 13 and 15 correspondingly. The throughput versus offered load characteristics of the compared protocols when they are applied to networks N_1, N_2, N_3 and N_4 are appeared at figures 10, 12, 14 and 16, correspondingly. Each characteristic was constructed by using 21 points, with each point corresponding to a different value of the offered load. The load values were taken to be from 0.005 to 1.00 packets per wavelength per slot.

The following results can be obtained from the above graphs:

1) Under low load conditions, OCON achieves an optimum packet delay, equal to one slot. Under these conditions, each newly arriving packet is transmitted immediately. Since it is probably the only packet in its wavelength, it is not blocked by the corresponding OLC. So, the packet delay is equal to the packet transmission time. On the other hand, the HARP protocol achieves a delay of about two slots: one slot to set a reservation and one slot to successfully transmit the packet. Finally, the RTDMA, due to its round-robin nature, suffers from a high delay, since each station has to wait for about $\frac{N}{R}$ slots before transmitting a newly arriving packet.

2) Under high load conditions, OCON and HARP achieve a high throughput, with OCON achieving a significantly higher throughput than HARP. When the ratio $\frac{N}{W}$ becomes high, the throughput of OCON tends to unity since, at any time slot, there is not any wavelength having no transmissions. On the other hand, RTDMA achieves a significantly lower throughput than OCON and HARP, since it suffers from a large number of idle slots. At a time slot t, a station operating under the RTDMA protocol is allowed to transmit on at most one wavelength. If its waiting queue does not contain packets which can be transmitted on this wavelength the station remains idle and the slot is wasted.

3) When the tuning time of the acoustooptic filters becomes high, an additional overhead is introduced in the operation of the HARP protocol. Under these conditions, the performance of HARP is significantly degraded, making the superiority of OCON even higher.

From the above discussion, as well as from the presented simulation results it becomes clear, that, under any load conditions, OCON achieves a significantly higher throughput and a lower delay than protocols RTDMA and HARP.

6. Conclusion

This paper has presented a new protocol for WDM Star

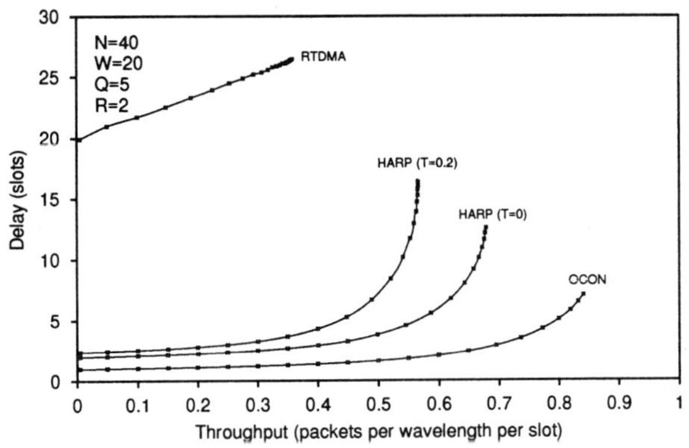

Figure 9: The Delay vs Throughput characteristics of OCON, HARP and RTDMA when applied to network N_1.

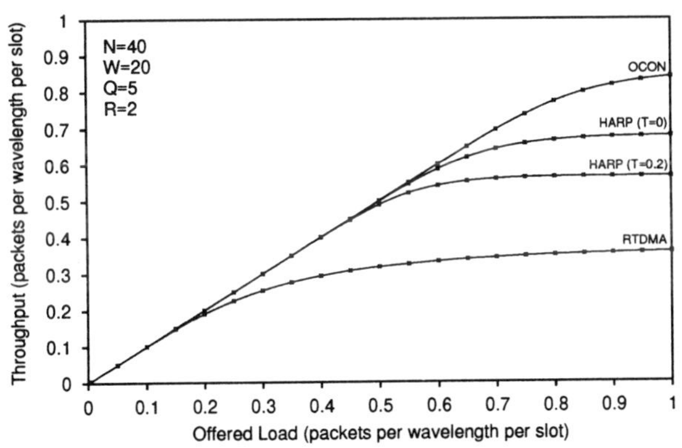

Figure 10: The Throughput vs Load characteristics of OCON, HARP and RTDMA when applied to network N_1.

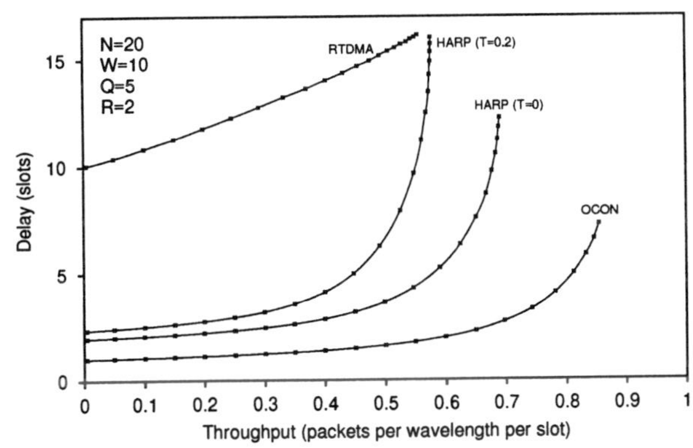

Figure 11: The Delay vs Throughput characteristics of OCON, HARP and RTDMA when applied to network N_2.

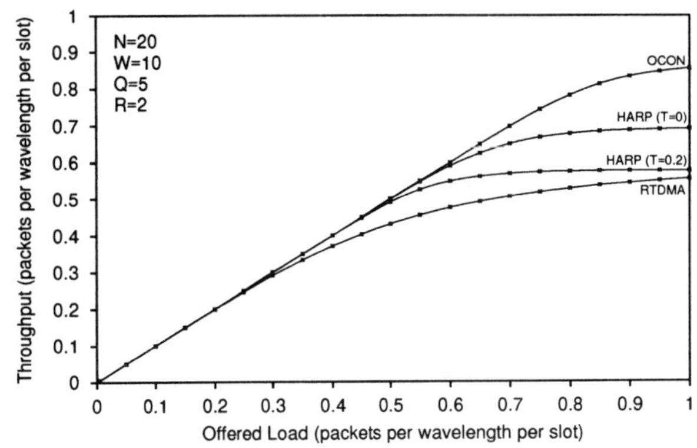

Figure 12: The Throughput vs Load characteristics of OCON, HARP and RTDMA when applied to network N_2.

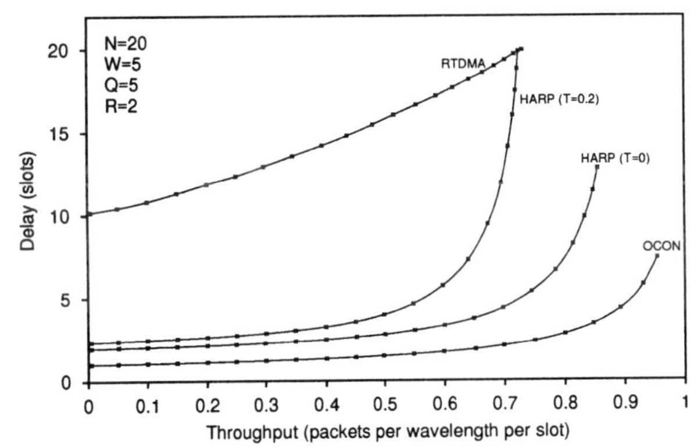

Figure 13: The Delay vs Throughput characteristics of OCON, HARP and RTDMA when applied to network N_3.

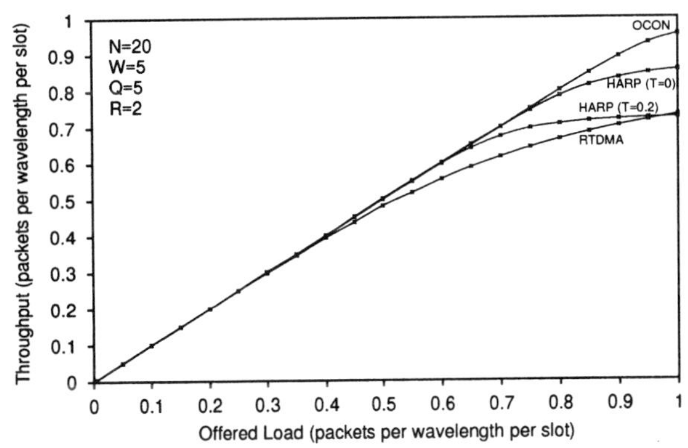

Figure 14: The Throughput vs Load characteristics of OCON, HARP and RTDMA when applied to network N_3.

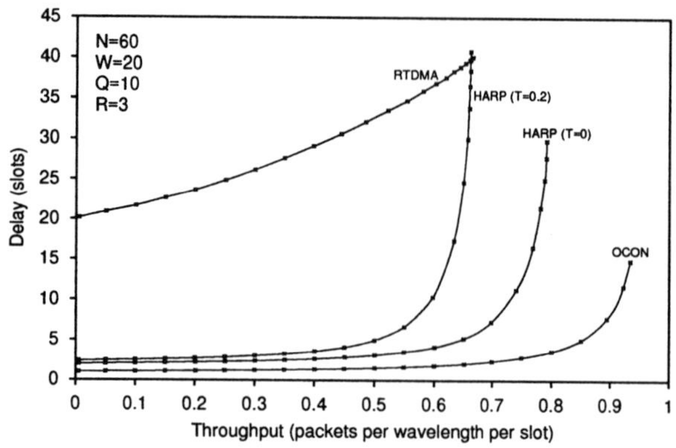

Figure 15: The Delay vs Throughput characteristics of OCON, HARP and RTDMA when applied to network N_4.

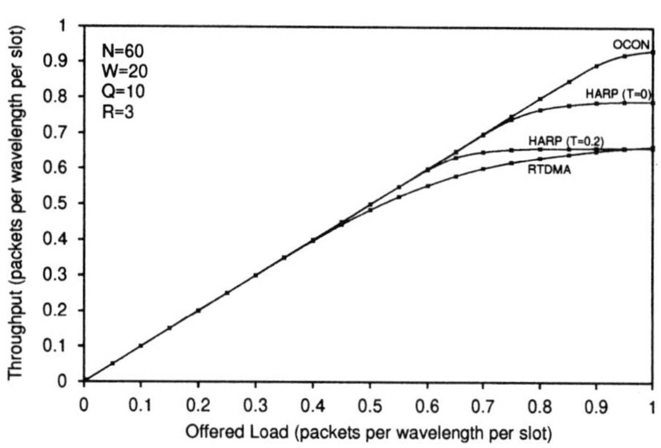

Figure 16: The Throughput vs Load characteristics of OCON, HARP and RTDMA when applied to network N_4.

Networks. According the proposed OCON protocol, the network hub is embellished with an all-optical packet filtering mechanism which controls the passing of the transmitted packets to the Star Coupler. In this way, collisions are prevented so that the network is capable of achieving a high performance under any load conditions.

The main advantages of the proposed OCON protocol are summarized below:

a) The network feedback information is processed in its original form without the need of O/E translation. The use of Optical Logic Circuits instead of a combination of electronic control circuits and acoustooptic filters leads to a significant decrease of the processing time, while the tuning time of the acoustooptic filters is eliminated. Therefore, OCON achieves a high throughput-delay performance under any load conditions.

b) Since the network hub represents a single point of failure, the use of optical control circuits at this point instead of electronic ones leads to a significant increase of the system's reliability.

On the other hand, the extensive use of optical devices leads to a significant increase of the implementation cost. However, the cost increase is limited by the fact that all the optical devices are placed at the same site and consequently, they can be arrayed in a common device. The idea of using optical logic circuits in order to control the operation of optical networks can be the base of a new generation of high performance protocols for fiber optic LANs. We are currently working on this direction.

References

[1] C.A.Brackett, "Dense Wavelength Division Multiplexing Network: Principles and Applications", IEEE Journal on Selected Areas in Communications, vol.8, no.6, pp.948-964, August 1990.

[2] P.S.Henry, "Very High Capacity Lightwave Networks", IEEE ICC 1988, pp.1206-1209.

[3] M.-S.Chen, N.R.Dono and R.Ramaswami, "A Media Access Protocol for Packet Switched Wavelength Division Multiaccess Metropolitan Network", IEEE Journal on Selected Areas in Communications, vol.8, no.6, pp.1048-1057, August 1990.

[4] M.S.Goodman, H.Kobrinski, M.P.Vecchi, R.M.Bulley and J.L.Gimlett, "The LAMBDANET Multiwavelength Network: Architecture, Applications and Demonstrations", IEEE Journal on Selected Areas in Communications, vol.8, no.6, pp.995-1004, August 1990.

[5] N.R.Dono, P.E.Green, K.Liu, R.Ramaswami and F.F.-K.Tong, "A Wavelength Division Multiple Access Network for Computer Communication", IEEE Journal on Selected Areas in Communications, vol.8, no.6, pp.983-994, August 1990.

[6] A.Ganz and Z.Koren, "WDM Passive Star - Protocols and Performance Analysis", IEEE INFOCOM'91, 7-11 April 1991, Bal Harbour, Florida, U.S.A., pp.991-1000.

[7] A. Ganz, "End-to-End Protocols for WDM Star Networks", Protocols for High-Speed Networks, edited by H.Rudin and R.Williamson, North-Holland, Amsterdam, 1989, pp.219-235.

[8] K.M.Sivalingam, K.Bogineni and P.W.Dowd, "Pre-allocation media access control protocols for mul-

tiple access WDM photonic networks", ACM SIGCOMM'92, Baltimore, U.S.A, 17-20 August 1992.

[9] P.E.Green, L.A.Coldren, K.M.Johnson, J.G.Lewis, C.M.Miller, J.F.Morrison, R.Olshansky, R.Ramaswami and E.H.Smith Jr., "All-Optical Packet-Switched Metropolitan Area Network Proposal", IEEE Journal of Lightwave Technology, vol.11, no.5/6, pp.754-763, May/June 1993.

[10] F.J. Janniello, R.Ramaswami and D.G.Steinberg, "A Prototype Circuit-Switched Multi-Wavelength Optical Metropolitan Area Network", Journal of Lightwave Technology, vol.11, no.5/6, pp.777-782, May/June 1993.

[11] L.G.Kazovsky and P.T.Poggiolini, "STARNET: A Multi-gigabit-per-second Optical LAN Utilizing a Passive WDM Star", Journal of Lightwave Technology, vol.11, no.5/6, pp.1009-1027, May/June 1993.

[12] B.Mukherjee, "WDM-Based Local Lightwave Networks, Part I: Single-Hop Systems", IEEE Network, vol.6, no.3, pp.12-27, May 1992.

[13] G.N.M.Sudhakar, N.Georganas and M.Kavehrad, "Slotted-Aloha and Reservation- Aloha Protocols for Very High Speed Optical Fiber Local Area Networks Using Passive Star Topology", Journal of Lightwave Technology, vol.9, no.10, pp.1411-1422, October 1991.

[14] F.Jia and B.Mukherjee, "The Receiver Collision Avoidance (RCA) Protocol For A Single-Hop WDM Lightwave Network", Journal of Lightwave Technology, vol.11, no.5/6, pp.1053-1065, May/June 1993.

[15] C.-S.Li and M.-S.Chen and F.F.-K.Tong, "POPSMAC: A Medium Access Protocol for Packet Switched Passive Optical Networks using WDMA", Journal of Lightwave Technology, vol.11, no.5/6, pp.1066-1077, May/June 1993.

[16] J.H.Laarhuis and A.M.J.Koonen, "An Efficient Medium Access Control Strategy for High-Speed WDM Multiaccess Networks", Journal of Lightwave Technology, vol.11, no.5/6, pp.1077-1087, May/June 1993.

[17] G.I.Papadimitriou and D.G.Maritsas, "Self-Adaptive Random Access Protocols for WDM Passive Star Networks", IEE Proceedings - Computers and Digital Techniques, vol.142, no.4, pp.306-312, July 1995.

[18] G.I.Papadimitriou and D.G.Maritsas, "Learning Automata-Based Receiver Conflict Avoidance Algorithms for WDM Broadcast-and-Select Star Networks", IEEE/ACM Transactions on Networking, vol.4., no.3, pp.407-412, June 1996.

[19] G.I.Papadimitriou and D.G.Maritsas, "WDM Passive Star Networks: A Learning Automata Based Architecture", Computer Communications, vol.19, no.6-7, pp.580-589, June 1996.

[20] G.I.Papadimitriou and D.G.Maritsas, "WDM Star Networks: Hybrid Random Access and Reservation Protocols with High Throughput and Low Delay", Computer Networks and ISDN Systems, vol.28, no.6, pp.773-787, April 1996.

[21] P.E.Green, "Fiber Optic Networks", Prentice Hall, 1993.

[22] J.Yumoto, S.Fukushima and K.Kubodera, "Observation of optical bistability in $CdS_xSe_{(1-x)}$-doped glasses with 25-psec switching time", Optics Letters, vol.12, no.10, pp.832-834, October 1987.

[23] H.F.Jordan, V.P.Heuring and R.Feuerstein, "Optoelectronic Time-of-Flight Design and the Demonstration of an All-Optical, Stored Program, Digital Computer", Proceedings of the IEEE, vol.82, no.11, pp.1678-1688, November 1994.

[24] F.T.Stone, J.E.Watson, D.T.Moser and W.J.Minford, "Performance and yield of pilot-line quantities of lithium niobate switches", SPIE, vol.1177, pp.322-325, Integrated Optics and Optoelectronics, 1989.

[25] B.G.Koehler and J.E.Bowers, "In-line single-mode fiber polarization controllers at 1.55, 1.30 and 0.63 μm", Applied Optics, vol.24, no.3, pp.349-353, February 1985.

Comparison of the Gigabit Ethernet Full-Duplex Repeater, CSMA/CD, and 1000/100-Mbps Switched Ethernet

Kenneth J. Christensen
Computer Science and Eng
University of South Florida
Tampa, FL 33620
Email: *christen@csee.usf.edu*

Mart Molle
Computer Science
University of California, Riverside
Riverside, CA 92521
Email: *mart@cs.ucr.edu*

Sifang Li
Computer Science and Eng
University of South Florida
Tampa, FL 33620
Email: *li@csee.usf.edu*

Abstract

Recently, the Full-Duplex Repeater (FDR) has been proposed as an alternative to half-duplex operation using CSMA/CD for controlling shared access to Gigabit Ethernet. In this paper, the basic FDR architecture is described and two extensions for traffic control are introduced. Using simulation methods, the performance of the Gigabit FDR is studied under different topologies and population sizes for a range of offered load. It is shown that the FDR provides a dramatic performance improvement over CSMA/CD (using both BEB and BLAM arbitration) at high load. The Gigabit FDR is also compared with switched Ethernet in the context of medical image retrieval. It is shown that for medical image retrieval, the performance of the Gigabit FDR is much better than 100/100 or 1000/100-Mbps switched Ethernet, and equivalent to 1000/1000-Mbps switched Ethernet for low levels of non-image background traffic.

1. Introduction

Ethernet with a 1-Gbps data rate was standardized by the IEEE 802.3 working group in June 1998 (see [8]). The Gigabit Ethernet standard supports both full-duplex operation with IEEE 802.3x PAUSE flow control (see [7]), and half-duplex operation using Carrier Sense Multiple Access / Collision Detection (CSMA/CD). In order to support 100-meter link lengths, CSMA/CD has been modified to include carrier extension and frame bursting. Under carrier extension, the minimum duration of a successful packet transmission was effectively increased from 64 bytes to 512 bytes by requiring the transmitter to append extended carrier symbols to the end of a small packet until the minimum length is met (see [6]). To improve the efficiency of carrier extension, frame bursting was added to the Gigabit Ethernet standard (see [12]). In frame bursting, a transmitting host can concatenate additional packets into the same burst of carrier until a burst length timer expires. Frame bursting allows shared Gigabit Ethernet using CSMA/CD to attain surprisingly high throughput, although the delays tend to grow more quickly with network load than in 100-Mbps Ethernet (see [12]).

An alternative approach to providing shared access to a Gigabit Ethernet channel is the Full-Duplex Repeater (FDR), as proposed in [4]. The FDR is a packet-forwarding device that broadcasts incoming packets to all ports, similar to a conventional half-duplex repeater. However, each host is connected to a port on the FDR using a full-duplex link, similar to a conventional packet switch (see [11]). Thus, the FDR represents a middle-point between shared-bandwidth, distributed arbitration (i.e., CSMA/CD) and parallel-bandwidth, centralized arbitration (i.e., switched Ethernet). The FDR implements shared-bandwidth with centralized arbitration, allowing multiple attached hosts to share 1-Gbps of bandwidth without any collisions. For the first time, in this paper the performance of 1-Gbps shared-bandwidth Ethernet using an FDR is evaluated and compared directly with the performance of switched Ethernet. Performance of the two methods is studied for transferring large image files within a workgroup of less than 130 hosts.

The remainder of this paper is organized as follows. Section 2 describes the Gigabit FDR as proposed to the IEEE 802.3 working group, along with the IEEE 802.3x PAUSE flow control. Section 2 also proposes several additions to the base Gigabit FDR architecture and briefly describes Ethernet switch architectures. In Section 3 the class of "Gigabit applications" is discussed and an empirical traffic model for medical image transfers is described. Section 4 describes a simple throughput model, the simulation model, and performance evaluation experiments. The results from the simulation study are presented in Section 5 followed by a summary.

0-8186-8810-6/98 $10.00 © 1998 IEEE

2. The FDR and Ethernet Switching

A traditional 10BASE-T or 100BASE-T Ethernet repeater is used to forward bits from any port to all other ports. The repeater does not contain any Media Access Control (MAC) function or packet buffering. Transmission arbitration is done in the hosts via the distributed, half-duplex CSMA/CD and Binary Exponential Backoff (BEB) algorithms. In a Gigabit FDR, shown in Figure 1, full-duplex MAC function, packet buffering, and centralized transmission arbitration is added to the repeater. Connection between host and repeater is via a full-duplex link. All hosts share access to a common 1-Gbps bus in the repeater. An arbitration, or scheduling, scheme such as round robin or weighted fair queueing (see [5]) is used to select the next packet to be forwarded from the repeater input buffers. A selected packet is then forwarded to all output ports with MAC-layer filtering of packets occurring at the receiving hosts. In the case of multiple transmitting hosts, IEEE 802.3x PAUSE flow control is used to throttle the sending hosts to a maximum 1-Gbps transmission rate.

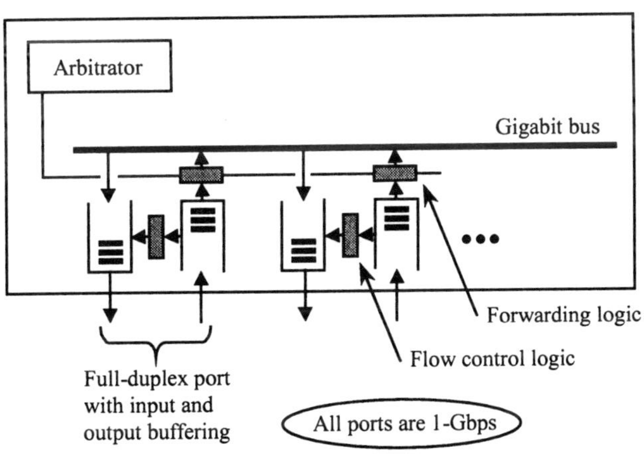

Figure 1 - Gigabit Full-Duplex Repeater (FDR)

The IEEE 802.3x task force has standardized Ethernet packet-based flow control via a specially defined PAUSE MAC frame (see [7]). The PAUSE MAC frame contains a field specifying a pause time, expressed as a multiple of a 512-bit quantum, that a receiving host MAC should withhold transmission of packets. A host Ethernet MAC receiving a PAUSE MAC frame completes any current packet transmission and then begins its forced idle pause time. If an already "pausing" host receives a PAUSE MAC frame, the host will replace its current pause time with the received pause value, possibly increasing or decreasing the forced idle time, or ending it if a pause time of zero is received. PAUSE flow control is used by the FDR to prevent overflow of the input buffers. Each input buffer has a low and high threshold defined. An arriving or departing packet that causes a threshold to be crossed can initiate a PAUSE MAC frame to be sent on the output link of the port. It is assumed that PAUSE MAC frames are priority queued, that is a PAUSE MAC frame is always the next packet sent after any current packet transmission. Figure 2 shows an algorithm for sending PAUSE MAC frames where `In_port[i]` is the input buffer for port `i` and a global variable `Over_flag` is initialized to `FALSE`. It can be seen that PAUSE flow control is used essentially as an XON/XOFF protocol to turn on and off host packet transmission.

```
if ((In_port[i] == over high threshold) &&
    (Over_flag == FALSE)) {
  send PAUSE packet with large pause value;
  Over_flag = TRUE;
}
if ((In_port[i] == under low threshold) &&
    (Over_flag == TRUE)) {
  send PAUSE packet with zero pause value;
  Over_flag = FALSE;
}
```

Figure 2 - Algorithm for sending PAUSE MAC frame

Within the Gigabit FDR, backpressure from an output to an input queue is needed to prevent multiple forwarding hosts from overflowing an output buffer. This internal backpressure is implemented via an extended poll time. A threshold is defined in the output buffer of each port and if exceeded the next poll time is extended by a time equal to the number of bits the threshold is exceeded divided by the port link data rate. This extended poll time allows the output buffer to drain below the threshold. Figure 3 shows the round robin polling algorithm with extended poll time. In the algorithm, `Num_ports` in the number of ports in the Gigabit FDR, `In_port[i]` is the input buffer for port `i`, and `Out_port[i]` is the output buffer for port `i`. If the internal backpressure causes an input buffer to fill beyond its high threshold, PAUSE flow control extends the backpressure to the sending host.

```
i = 0;
while(TRUE) {
  if ((In_port[i] has packet(s) queued) {
    remove and release a packet on the bus;
    wait for transmission on bus to complete;
  }
  Over = 0;
  for (j = 0; j < Num_ports; j++) {
    Over = bits Out_port[j] is over threshold;
    if (Over > 0)
      wait for Over bit times;
  }
  i = (i + 1) % Num_ports;
}
```

Figure 3 - Round robin polling with backpressure

2.1 Port bursting and packet spacing extensions

In this paper, two additions to the base FDR architecture are introduced: port bursting and packet spacing. Port bursting can be used at high offered loads to insure fairness for small packet traffic and to provide a per port bandwidth allocation scheme. Packet spacing can control the peak transmission rate of a host onto the Gigabit network.

The base FDR with round robin polling is fair by packet transmission count, but not necessarily by bytes transmitted. That is, if one port has small packets queued and another port large packets, then the port with large packets will receive a greater portion of the shared bandwidth when offered load is high. To minimize this unfairness and provide a provision for allocating bandwidth between ports, a port (or packet) bursting capability is proposed similar to timed token holding in FDDI and frame bursting in Gigabit CSMA/CD. In port bursting, a port may continue releasing packets from its input buffer on to the bus until a byte counter (`Byte_count` initialized to `BURST_SIZE`) that counts bytes transmitted is decremented to zero or the input buffer is empty. Ports with larger `BURST_SIZE` will be able to transmit more data than ports with smaller `BURST_SIZE` on their respective round robin polling cycle. Figure 4 shows the port burst capability added to the round robin polling algorithm of Figure 3 (the extended poll time of Figure 3 is omitted).

```
i = 0;
while(TRUE) {
  if (In_port[i] has packet(s) queued) {
    Byte_count = BURST_SIZE;
    while((Byte_count > 0) &&
          (In_port[i] has packet(s) queued)) {
      remove and release a packet on the bus;
      wait for transmission on bus to complete;
      decrement Byte_count by packet size;
    }
    i = (i + 1) % Num_ports;
  }
}
```

Figure 4 - Round robin polling with port burst counter

Using packet spacing, the peak bandwidth usage of a port can be limited to a predetermined value. Figure 5 shows the modified round robin algorithm whereby a port is only allowed to forward packets if a calculated `Packet_gap_time[i]` has expired. `Packet_gap_time[i]` is computed as the last packet transmission time divided by the percentage of total bandwidth the port has been allocated, subtracted by the last packet transmission time. For example, for 50% allocated bandwidth the `Packet_gap_time[i]` is exactly equal to the last packet transmission time. In the case of a time greater than `Packet_gap_time[i]` before a port with packet(s) queued is subsequently polled, the next port time-out period, timed by `Port_timer[i]`, is appropriately reduced (as shown in Figure 5). Thus, the mean port time-out period will be equal to, or greater than, the computed mean `Packet_gap_time[i]`. `Port_timer[i]` is initialized to zero. Implementation of this packet spacing requires that high-resolution timers be implemented in all ports of the Gigabit FDR.

```
i = 0;
while(TRUE) {
  if ((In_port[i] has packet(s) queued) &&
      (Port_timer > 0)) {
    remove and release a packet on the bus;
    wait for transmission on bus to complete;
    compute Packet_gap_time[i];
    set Port_timer[i] to Packet_gap_time[i];
    subtract from Port_timer[i] the time since
      last packet release by In_port[i];
    start Port_timer[i] if greater than zero;
  }
  i = (i + 1) % Num_ports;
}
```

Figure 5 - Round robin polling with packet spacing

2.2 Brief overview of switched Ethernet

Packet switching of Ethernet packets is implemented via "switched Ethernet" at 10, 100, and 1000-Mbps. Switched Ethernet is an implementation of IEEE 802.1D transparent bridging where packets are filtered based on MAC address. Thus, an Ethernet switch must contain address tables, address learning, and other functions needed to support the IEEE 802.1D standard. Figure 6 shows a simplified view of a 1000/100-Mbs Ethernet switch. In such a switch, a non-blocking switch fabric (e.g., a cross-bar or high-speed bus) is used to forward packets between ports. For full-throughput operation, the bandwidth of the switch fabric must equal the total bandwidth of all connected ports. PAUSE flow control is still needed in the case of multiple hosts (input ports) simultaneously forwarding packets to a single output port and thus causing potential buffer overflows. Due to the need for MAC function, high-speed packet buffering, high speed interconnect, and address table memory and learning function, the cost of a switch is higher than that of a repeater. By providing mixed-speed switches based on expected traffic patterns, the cost can be lowered. For example, one higher-speed port can be designated for a frequently accessed server connection and multiple lower-speed ports for client connections.

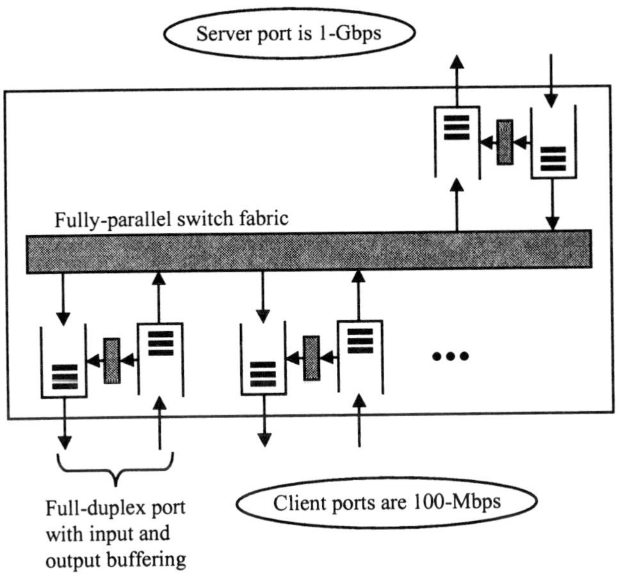

Figure 6 - 1000/100-Mbps Ethernet switch architecture

3. Model for Medical Image Transfers

Gigabit network capacity can be utilized by several classes of applications including backbones for multiple lower-speed LANs, and first-level (or workgroup) configurations for server farming, data warehousing, high-speed back-up systems, three dimensional imaging, direct transfer of print-copy from desktop to printer, and various image-rich applications including medical imaging. Developing traffic models for these types of applications is currently an area of research.

3.1 Model for medical imaging and background traffic

For this paper, we consider a medical imaging system such as Picture Archiving and Communication Systems (PACS) (see [14]) as a representative and interesting Gigabit application. A large PACS can contain more than 150 diagnostic workstations (client hosts) and the average image size can be in the range of tens or hundreds of Megabytes. A study of image sizes of a PACS at Hammersmith hospital in the United Kingdom is shown in Table 1 (from [14]) with a mean exam size of approximately 13.5 Mbytes. Doctors prefer to view images at a diagnostic workstation within 2 seconds of an image request (see [1]). In our studies we use 2 seconds as a performance bound for "satisfactory" image transfer time performance. It is expected that both the image resolution and depth will likely increase to provide better quality diagnosis (see [14]). With 3-D imaging, the network bandwidth requirements will become much larger. For example, in [3] the Zoomable Brain Database is shown to require from 720 to 11520-Mbps bandwidth to view 3-D brain images.

Modality	Image size	Exams / yr
X-radiography	13.5 Mbytes	73.5 %
Computed tomography	18.8	5.6
Ultrasound	12.8	11.0
Fluoroscopy	7.4	3.2
Angiography	10.0	1.7
Magnetic resonance	7.5	1.1
Nuclear medicine	0.2	3.8

Table 1 - Image statistics from a PACS (from [14])

In a centralized PACS system, all medical images are stored in one high performance image server. Diagnostic workstations throughout the hospital request images from the server. In addition to the image traffic, background traffic from client-to-client interaction and other applications will also be present. For the image transfer time component of this study, two traffic models were developed:

- **Image traffic model** - The image traffic model generates large-packet (1500 byte Ethernet packet size) traffic bursts with a burst size corresponding to an empirical distribution of image sizes based on Table 1. We assume that an image server can transmit image packets at a full 1 Gigabit data rate.
- **Background traffic model** - The background traffic model generates Poisson background traffic with packet sizes corresponding to the "IEEE workstation mix" distribution (from [6]). The mean packet size of the IEEE workstation mix is 616 bytes.

Figure 7 shows the network configuration of N hosts, one image server and $N-1$ clients. The flow of image requests is from client-to-server and images then flow from server-to-client. The number of hosts is the same as the number of ports in the Gigabit FDR or Ethernet switch. For the image traffic model, client hosts independently request images from the server with a given request rate. We assume that:

1. A client will not request a new image before it finishes receiving the previously requested image.
2. The image server serves the clients' requests concurrently if multiple unsatisfied requests exist.
3. The image server is dedicated for image requests and no background traffic goes to or comes from the server.

The second assumption is significant when a 1000/100 switch is used, since the resulting overlapping of packets destined for the multiple clients allows the higher bandwidth of the server link to be fully utilized.

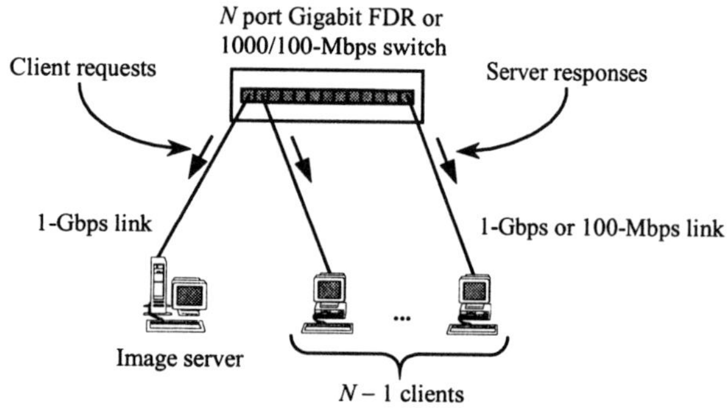

Figure 7 - Configuration for medical image retrieval

4. Performance Evaluation Experiments

Simulation models of a Gigabit FDR and an Ethernet switch were constructed using the process-oriented, station-centric method described in [2]. The CSIM18 function library (see [15]) was used to implement the models. The additions to the base FDR architecture (described in Section 2.1 of this paper) were included in the Gigabit FDR model. Settable parameters in the Gigabit FDR and switch implementations include:

- Sizes (specified in bytes) of input and output buffers for each port
- Thresholds (specified in bytes) for PAUSE flow control and internal backpressure (FDR only)
- Poll time (FDR only)
- Propagation delay from host to and through the repeater or switch
- Link speed
- Burst size and maximum bandwidth for the port bursting and packet spacing additions

Settable parameters in the host implementation include:

- Size (specified in packets) of packet queue
- Link speed

Independent to each host, a traffic source process (a model of an application) "feeds" the host packet queue with Ethernet packets. If a host queue reaches capacity, then the traffic source is blocked.

4.1 A simple throughput model for the Gigabit FDR

Using a fluid-flow approximation, we can estimate the mean image transfer time for a shared-bandwidth network configuration with a single image server and a given background traffic load. The image transfer time is,

$$T_{image} = \frac{S_{image}}{R - L_{background}}, \quad (1)$$

where T_{image} is the image transfer time in seconds for an image of S_{image} bits in size, R bits per second shared bandwidth, and $L_{background}$ bits per second background traffic load (where $0 \le L_{background} \le R$). We will compare the equation (1) model against simulation results for medical image transfer times. Offered load is expressed as a percentage of the available bandwidth (e.g., a background traffic offered load of 10% is $L_{background}$ = 100-Mbps).

4.2 Design of the experiments

Two sets of experiments are defined. The first set of experiments studies the throughput and packet delay behavior of the Gigabit FDR and CSMA/CD given simple Poisson offered traffic. The second set of experiments compares the Gigabit FDR with 100/100, 1000/100, and 1000/1000-Mbps switched Ethernet for simulated medical imaging traffic. Gigabit FDR's are available commercially (in mid-1998) in 12-ports only (see [13]). However, we study more than 12-ports to evaluate scaling of the Gigabit FDR architecture to larger host population sizes. For all experiments, packet size is measured as the number of bytes from the start of the MAC destination address field through the end of the Frame Check Sequence (FCS) field. Offered load and port throughput is measured on these fields only. The standard Ethernet 8-byte preamble and 12-byte interpacket gap are overhead. Gigabit FDR bus throughput is measured as the utilization of the shared bus.

For the first set of experiments, the primary measures of interest are the *throughput*, and *packet delay* mean and standard deviation. Packet delay is defined as the time of packet entry into a sending host packet queue to the packet received at its destination host. The Gigabit FDR contains 16 Kbytes of input buffering and 16 Kbytes of output buffering per port. The low and high thresholds for PAUSE flow control are 5 Kbytes and 10 Kbytes. For output port backpressure, the threshold is set at 8 Kbytes. Polling time is 16 nanoseconds per port. Unless otherwise stated, the end-to-end propagation time is 2000 bit times. The host packet queue is of size 100. For the CSMA/CD comparisons (experiment #1 only), the same propagation delay and host parameters are assumed. Both BEB and BLAM (see [10]) arbitration are used. A CSMA/CD burst size (see [12]) of 8-Kbytes is assumed. The first set of experiments consists of:

- **Experiment #1** - general Gigabit FDR performance and comparison with CSMA/CD. Increasing offered load with 12 and 96 port configurations. Offered load is IEEE workstation mix. Destination addresses are uniformly randomly chosen for each packet.

- **Experiment #2** - non-symmetrical topology delay fairness. Same as experiment #1 (for 12 ports only) except one link has host-to-repeater propagation delay of 10 bit times, the remaining hosts have 1000 bit times.
- **Experiment #3** - small packet fairness and port bursting. Same as experiment #1 (for 12 ports only) except offered load is 64-byte packets from one host and 1500-byte packets from all remaining hosts. The port burst counter of Section 2.1 is evaluated for improving small packet fairness.
- **Experiment #4** - bandwidth management with combined port bursting and packet spacing. Same as experiment #1 (for 12 ports only) except port 1 has a maximum bandwidth of 41.66-Mbps (1-Gbps divided by 24, or 50% offered load shared by all ports) set by packet spacing. In addition, all ports have a `BURST_SIZE` of 1500 bytes except port 2 has a `BURST_SIZE` of 3000 bytes. Port bursting is evaluated for increasing the bandwidth share for a port and packet spacing as a means of limiting the bandwidth of a port.

For the second set of experiments, the primary measure of interest is the *mean image transfer time* defined as the total time from client image request to the last packet of a requested image be received by the client. For all experiments, the Gigabit FDR contains 12 Kbytes of input buffering and 4 Kbytes of output buffering per port. The low and high thresholds for PAUSE flow control are 4 Kbytes and 8 Kbytes. For output port back pressure, the threshold is set at 3 Kbytes. Polling time is 16 nanoseconds per port. Unless otherwise stated, the end-to-end propagation time is 250 bit times. The Ethernet switch models are configured with the same buffer sizes as the Gigabit FDR. There is no poll time in the Ethernet switch, immediate forwarding of a received packet is assumed if the destination output port has sufficient space for the packet. The transfer time of the packet within the Ethernet switch is assumed to be the same as the port speed (i.e., either 1-Gbps or 100-Mbps). The second set of experiments consists of:

- **Experiment #5** - increasing port count. Comparative evaluation of Gigabit FDR, 100/100, and 1000/100-Mbps Ethernet switching. Increasing port count of 12, 24, 48, 64, 80, 96, 112, and 128. Each client requests one new image with an exponentially distributed mean of 204 seconds (following the download of the previous image) and generates 4-Mbps of background traffic. The mean image request rate is based on the observation in [9] that medical doctors spend a mean of 204 seconds per image study.
- **Experiment #6** - increasing background traffic for a fixed port count of 12. Comparative evaluation of Gigabit FDR and 1000/1000-Mbps Ethernet switching. The background traffic offered load is increased as, 10%, 20%, ..., 80% of the Gigabit bandwidth. The image requests arrive as in experiment #5.

5. Performance Evaluation Results

5.1 Gigabit FDR and CSMA/CD comparison

Experiment #1 evaluates the general performance of the Gigabit FDR in terms of the mean and standard deviation of packet delay as a function of throughput for a range of offered loads and populations sizes, and compares the results with CSMA/CD. This simulation experiment was run for 1.1 million packets for all offered loads and the first 100-thousand packet completions were discarded as a "warm-up" period. Confidence intervals, measured with the CSIM18 built-in batch means method, are within 1% accuracy (for 95% confidence interval) in all cases except for a few of the very high offered load measurements. Figure 8 shows packet delay as a function of throughput for a 12 port configuration. In this case, the FDR offers a very significant performance improvement over CSMA/CD, although CSMA/CD with BLAM is somewhat better than with BEB. However, one must keep in mind that a one-millisecond delay is almost a hundred times larger than the transmission time for a maximum length packet on a Gigabit network. Thus, in reality CSMA/CD only provides good delay performance below 30% load, whereas the FDR provides good performance all the way up to 90% load. Figure 9 shows throughput as a function of offered load for the same experiment. In this case, the FDR throughput matches the offered load until complete saturation (100% offered load). BLAM offers some throughput improvement over BEB, but the FDR provides much better performance than either one.

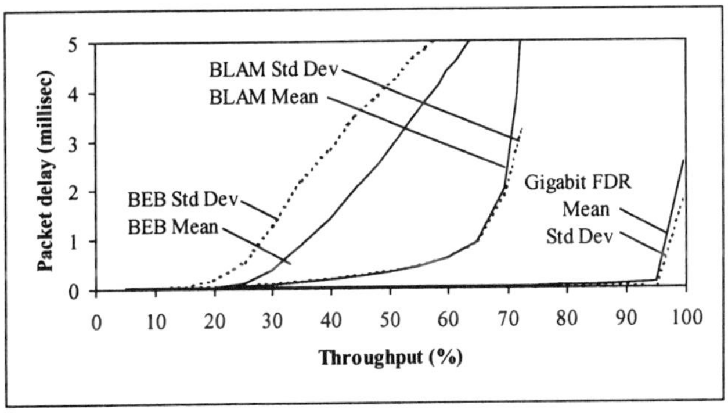

Figure 8 - Gigabit FDR and CSMA/CD packet delay

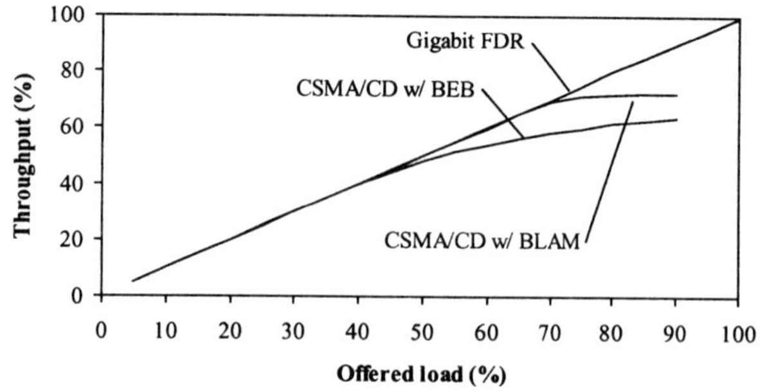

Figure 9 - Gigabit FDR and CSMA/CD throughput

Figure 10 shows the analogous delay performance for a 96 port configuration. Increasing the total number of hosts had no effect on the Gigabit FDR throughput. In fact, no packet losses were recorded in any of the simulation trials. Similarly, the delays are also quite similar to the 12 port configuration until the network approaches saturation, at which point the delays are significantly higher than for the 12 port configuration. This is expected because of Little's Law: since we have eight times as many hosts, the total number of waiting packets will be much higher when all hosts are saturated. The results for CSMA/CD show more of a change compared to the 12 port configuration. In this case, CSMA/CD using both BEB and BLAM only provide good delay performance up to an offered load of about 20%. Moreover, BLAM provides significantly worse mean delay (but better standard deviation of delay) than BEB. This performance degradation of BLAM is caused by the large slot time, which adds significant overhead to the BLAM arbitration mechanism in large population systems.

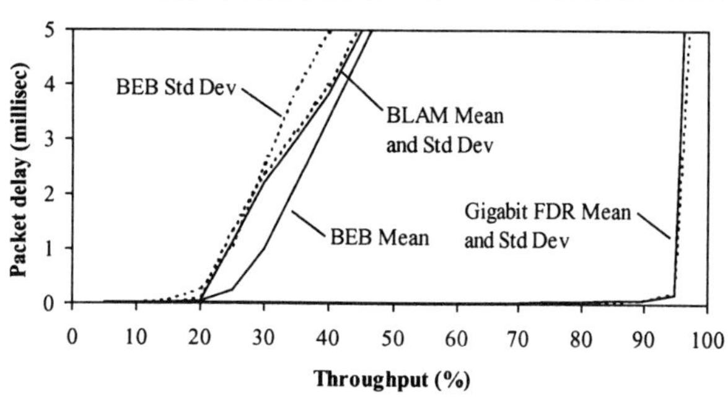

Figure 10 - Gigabit FDR and CSMA/CD packet delay

5.2 Results for a non-symmetrical topology

Experiment #2 evaluates the general performance of the Gigabit FDR given a non-symmetrical physical topology. Figure 11 shows the throughput in Mbps, measured at port 1 and average of ports 2 through 12 (the series are directly on top of each other!). This experiment shows that the Gigabit FDR does not favor "near" or "far" hosts.

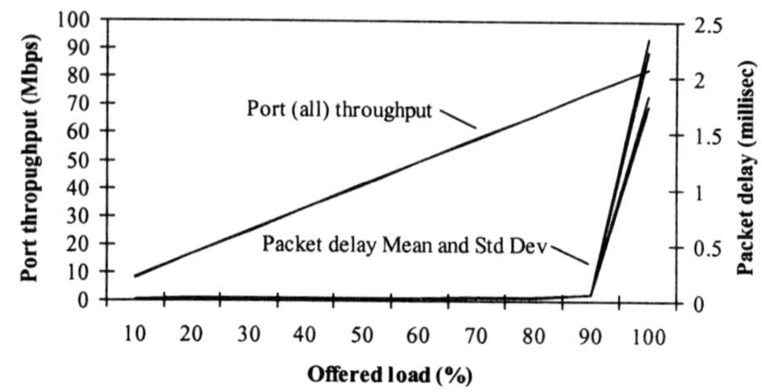

Figure 11 - Port throughput and packet delay results

5.3 Results for small packet throughput fairness

Experiment #3 evaluates the throughput performance of the Gigabit FDR given offered load consisting of small packets from one port and large packets from the remaining ports. This simulation experiment was run identically to experiment #1. Figure 12 shows the throughput at port 1 and average of ports 2 to 12 for two cases, 1) without burst counter enabled, and 2) with burst counter enabled and `BURST_SIZE` of 1500 bytes. It can be seen that without the burst counter at high offered loads ("Infin" is fully saturated queueing), the port with small packets is starved. With the addition of the port burst counter, all ports receive a fair share of the bandwidth.

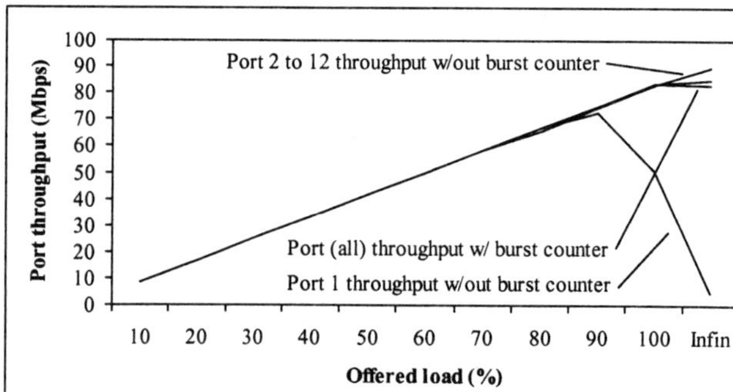

Figure 12 - Port throughput results

5.4 Results for simple bandwidth management

Experiment #4 demonstrates simple bandwidth management in a Gigabit FDR using the port bursting and packet spacing additions of Section 2.1. Figure 13 shows the experiment #4 results for port throughput for port 1 (with packet spacing for 41.66-Mbps maximum bandwidth), port 2 (with BURST_SIZE double that of all other ports), and the remaining ports. It can be seen that up to 50% offered load all ports have the same throughput, above 50%, port 1 is throttled to its designated bandwidth, and then at saturation port 2 has twice the throughput of ports 3 through 12.

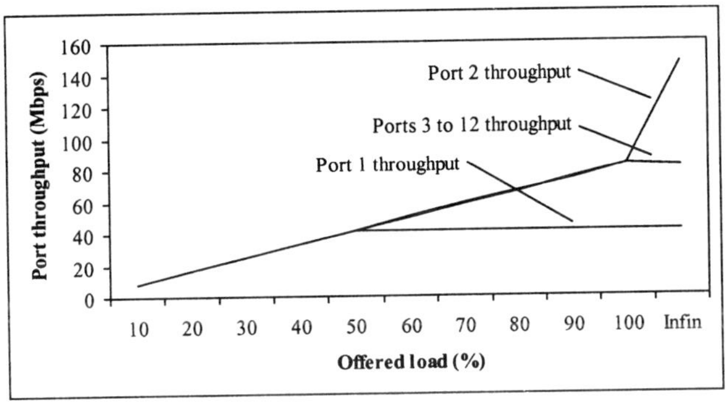

Figure 13 - Port throughput results

5.5 Results for medical image retrieval

Figure 14 shows the mean image transfer time results for experiment #5. It can be seen that both the Gigabit FDR and 1000/100-Mbps Ethernet switch are within the performance bound for up to, at least, 128 hosts. The 100/100-Mbps Ethernet switch does not achieve acceptable performance for greater than about 80 hosts.

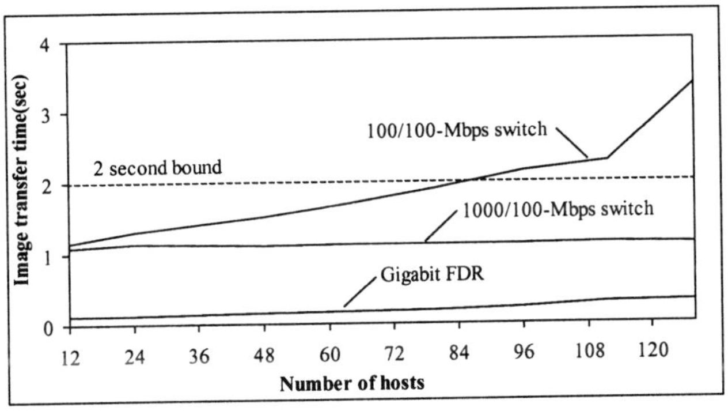

Figure 14 - Number of hosts and image transfer time

The histogram of image transfer times was plotted for each of the network configurations for a population of 80 hosts. For the Gigabit FDR and 1000/100-Mbps switched Ethernet, all image transfer times were less than 2 seconds even for a population of 128 hosts. However, for the 100/100-Mbps switched Ethernet approximately 34% of the image transfer times were greater than 2 seconds for 80 hosts. This is shown in Figure 15.

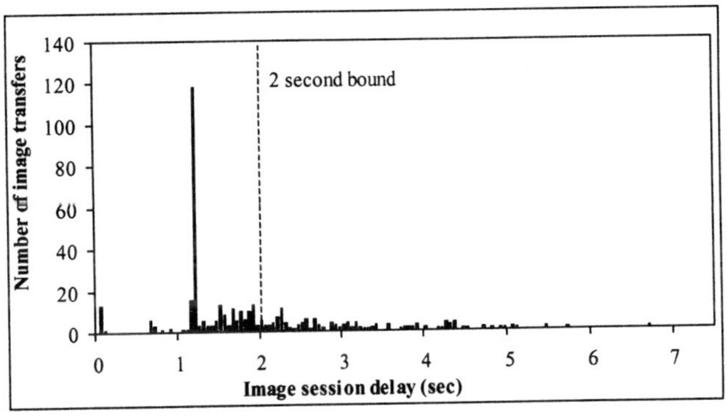

Figure 15 - Image transfer times for 80 hosts

Figure 16 shows the mean image transfer time results for experiment #6 illustrating the impact of background traffic on image transfer time. For the 1000/1000-Mbps Ethernet switch the background traffic utilizes the parallel bandwidth of the switch and does affect image transfer time. In a Gigabit FDR, however, the background traffic shares the same bandwidth as the image traffic and image transfer times are affected. The "ideal Gigabit FDR" is based on equation (1). Due to overheads the actual performance is slightly worse than the ideal case.

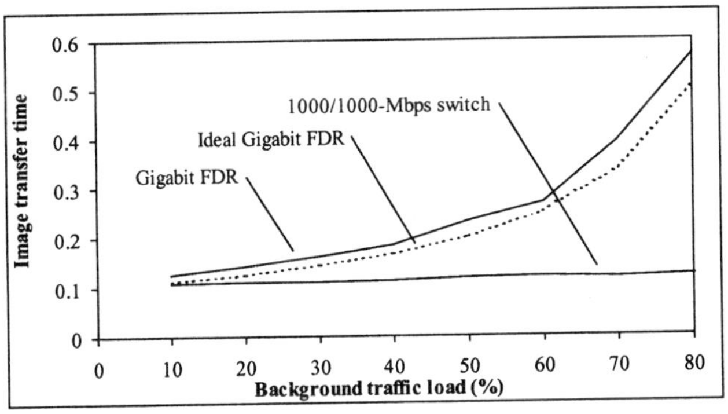

Figure 16 - Background traffic and image transfer time

6. Summary

The Gigabit FDR has been shown to be an efficient and fair architecture for sharing 1-Gbps bandwidth, which offers significantly better performance than CSMA/CD. The Gigabit FDR can offer full-throughput performance and is stable across a range of offered loads and host populations (port counts). The improvement in both throughput and packet delay for the Gigabit FDR, compared to CSMA/CD operation, is remarkable.

The FDR architecture fairly allocates bandwidth for small and large population networks and is not affected by "near" and "far" hosts. To improve small packet fairness at high offered loads, a port burst counter was introduced. The port burst counter and a packet spacing capability can be used to manage bandwidth in a Gigabit FDR. Port bursting allows long-term bandwidth allocations per port, and packet-spacing allows instantaneous transmission rates to be set. A likely and representative application for Gigabit Ethernet is medical PACS systems. A comparison of Gigabit FDR and 100/100, 1000/100, and 1000/1000-Mbps switched Ethernet demonstrated the suitability of Gigabit FDR for this type of application. Future work will focus on improving scheduling disciplines for Gigabit Ethernet for better bandwidth management and Quality of Service support

Acknowledgements

The authors would like to thank Boaz Yeger, of the University of California, Riverside, for his assistance in the execution of the CSMA/CD simulation experiments.

References

[1] W. Chimiak, "The Radiology Environment," *IEEE Journal on Selected Areas in Communications*, Vol. 10, No. 7, pp. 1133 - 1144, September 1992.

[2] K. Christensen, M. Molle, and B. Yeger, "The Design of a Station-Centric Network Model for Evaluating Changes to the IEEE 802.3 Ethernet Standard," under review for *Simulation*.

[3] M. Claypool, J. Riedl, J. Carlis, G. Wilcox, R. Elde, E. Retzel, A. Georgopoulos, J. Pardo, K. Ugurbil, B. Miller and C. Honda, "Network Requirement for 3-D Flying in a Zoomable Brain Database," *IEEE Journal on Selected Areas in Communications*, Vol. 13, No. 5, pp. 816 - 827, June 1995.

[4] B. Daines, "Gigabit Buffered Distributor Proposal," *IEEE 802.3z Plenary Meeting*, Vancouver, Canada, November 1996. URL: *http://grouper.ieee.org/groups/802/3/z/public/presentations/nov1996/BDbufdis.pdf.*

[5] A. Demers, S. Keshav, and S. Shenker, "Analysis and Simulation of a Fair Queueing Algorithm," *Computer Communication Review*, Vol. 19, No. 4, pp. 1 - 12, September 1989.

[6] H. Frazier, Jr., "Review and Update of Carrier Extension Proposal," *IEEE 802.3z Plenary Meeting*, Vancouver, Canada, November 1996. URL: *http://grouper.ieee.org/groups/802/3/z/public/presentations/nov1996/HFcarext.pdf.*

[7] IEEE P802.3x (Specification for 802.3x Full Duplex Operation), P802.3x/D3.1, *Institute of Electrical and Electronic Engineers*, New York, December 16, 1996.

[8] IEEE P802.3z (Specification for 802.3z Gigabit Operation), P802.3z/D5, *Institute of Electrical and Electronic Engineers*, New York, June 29, 1998.

[9] H. Kalyoncu and B. Sankur, "Design and Performance Evaluation of Picture Archival and Communication Systems," *Simulation,* Vol. 64, No. 2, pp. 77 - 90, February 1995.

[10] M. Molle, "A New Binary Logarithmic Arbitration Method for Ethernet," *Technical Report CSRI-298*, Computer Systems Research Institute, University of Toronto, 1994.

[11] M. Molle and G. Watson, "100Base-T / IEEE 802.12 / Packet Switching," *IEEE Communications Magazine*, Vol. 34, No. 8, pp. 64 - 73, August 1996.

[12] M. Molle, M. Kalkunte, and J. Kadambi, "Scaling CSMA/CD to 1 Gb/s with Frame Bursting," *Proceedings of the 22nd IEEE Conference on Local Computer Networks*, pp. 211 - 219, November, 1997.

[13] Packet Engines, Inc. FDR(tm) Gigabit Ethernet Hub, 1998. URL: *http://www.packetengines.com/f_productsandsolutions.htm.*

[14] R. Reynolds, "Digital Radiology and PACS: Pictorial Archiving and Communication Systems," Grainger and Allison's Diagnostic Radiology : A Textbook of Medical Imaging, Churchill Livingstone, New York, 1997.

[15] H. Schwetman, "Introduction to Process-Oriented Simulation and CSIM," *Proceedings of the 1990 Winter Simulation Conference*, pp. 154 - 157, December 1990.

Design and Implementation of OTCA MAC protocol for High-Speed Point-to-Point Ring Network

Yeshik Shin, Jin-su Ahn, Hyung-rok Lee, and Deog-Kyoon Jeong

School of Electrical Engineering, Seoul National University
San 56-1, Shinlim-Dong, Kwanak-Gu, Seoul, Korea, 151-742
{shinys, jsahn, hrlee, dkjeong}@griffin.snu.ac.kr
TEL: +822-880-7437, FAX: +822-872-6125

Abstract: *In this paper, we describe the design and implementation of OTCA (Ownership-Tagged Cell Allocation) MAC protocol for a unidirectional slotted ring network with a distributed fair medium access. A point-to-point (p2p) interconnection network in a ring topology with a high-speed serial link and the sharing of network bandwidth among multiple communicating nodes offers a very promising low cost solution in the growing gigabit communication system, where it is a challenge to run high quality real-time multimedia. Some services have explicit timing requirements. The OTCA MAC protocol provides the deterministic network behavior guaranteeing the worst latency bound and the minimum bandwidth availability. On a 1.063Gpbs p2p ring network comprising 4 nodes, the OTCA MAC protocol ensures a bandwidth of 265Mbps for synchronous data, 232Mbps for asynchronous data (thus a total of 497Mbps for a node), and the worst medium access latency is bounded with 17.46 us.*

1. Introduction

The performance of a network system is highly dependent on the underlying physical link layer, especially on the medium access control. Most popular architecture is, due to its simplicity, a bus, thus, not permitting concurrent transmission on a passive shared transmission medium. Ethernet and token bus belong to this category.

Buses have an inherently imperfect transmission characteristic because they have intermittent taps where the various devices connect to, which form stubs that cause reflections leading to signal distortions due to ringing. The only way to overcome this ill effect is to allow the signal enough time to settle - limiting achievable bandwidth. For this reason, high bandwidth buses can not support a large number of network connections or only limited bandwidth is allowed for a large number of network connections. Besides being limited by the medium itself, the fundamental limitations are mostly related to the one-at-a-time nature of shared access: when one user talks, everyone listens.

As an enhancement, the shared medium can be partitioned into small disjoint segments and signal transmission rate in such small segments can be improved [1]. Collision cannot occur in disjoint point-to-point (p2p) link segments. In this way, by allowing concurrent transmission over the multiple segments, the aggregate throughput of the networked system can be increased far beyond its single link capacity.

Similar in principle to a CSMA/CD (Carrier Sense Multiple Access/Collision Detection) bus [1], the p2p interconnection network uses an arbitration method in a distributed manner. In the former case, when the transmission medium - here the bus - is in use, a node does not transmit. After the detection of the idle state in transmission medium, every possible node tries to transmit a message. If a collision is detected, when two or more nodes access the media simultaneously, all nodes involved go to the back-off state, and tries again after random time delay. However, the MAC protocol mentioned above may cause arbitrarily long waiting time for successful transmission due to unresolved contention. To overcome this kind of access control limited by the broadcasting bus-style transmission line, the p2p interconnection network limits signal propagation only to the right adjacent node, and repeats such peer to peer connections in a chain. Thus, very high-speed signaling is possible and each node checks the incoming packet status and resolves medium access control in a distributed manner [2].

In this paper, we describe the design and implementation of OTCA (Ownership-Tagged Cell Allocation) MAC protocol for a unidirectional slotted ring network with a distributed fair medium access. Among various network topologies, a ring has almost the same complexity as a bus and linear topology. The ring topology allows a wide range of communication services, from a small scale clustering of I/O devices in a desktop area to a large scale networking of computer machines in a distributed computing area [3]-[5]. In a smart automobile, for example, the CPU node might reside in the trunk, the display near the steering wheel, and the

0-8186-8810-6/98 $10.00 © 1998 IEEE

various field devices, like sensors and actuators in scattered areas. A single compact optical ring interconnection network along the frame of a car can be a good candidate to integrate entire flow of information.

The contribution of this paper is as follows: 1) With the design and implementation of a new MAC protocol, we show the feasibility of a new network protocol that is well-suited for the next generation multimedia environment. 2) By placing cell ownership field in a cell header, we make it relatively easy to manage fair bandwidth sharing in a unidirectional ring network guaranteeing the worst latency bound and the minimum bandwidth availability.

The rest of the paper is organized as follows. In the next section, the RingLink network architecture is introduced as a background of the OTCA MAC protocol foundation. Following this, in section 3, we present several key points of the OTCA protocol. In section 4, we describe the design and implementation of OTCA MAC protocol. In section 5, we show analysis of network throughput and the guaranteed network parameters. A summary and concluding remarks are in section 6.

2. Background: RingLink Architecture

In this section, the overall architecture of the RingLink is introduced, which is an experimental foundation of the high-speed MAC protocol, and several key points of the debating aspects in the selection of particular choices are explained. The design goal of the OTCA MAC protocol is to provide a low-latency, high-bandwidth communication mechanism whose performance is competitive with or better than existing network systems. Therefore, background knowledge of the RingLink architecture helps to understand the OTCA MAC protocol.

2.1 Ring Adaptor

Figure 1 depicts the overall architecture of a p2p ring interconnection network. The way it looks in illustrations often differs from its real life appearance. Generally, a p2p ring interconnection network does not need an additional switching box, for the network is built by stringing cables from one processing node to another chaining those nodes together in a ring. Thus, only a NIC (Network Interface Card) for a host interface needs to be developed, not in parallel with a switcher development.

The architecture of the RingLink adaptor, which is entry point to the ring network, is shown in Figure 2. Each node accesses the ring network via an adaptor specially designed for this experiment. The cabling of unidirectional link may be coaxial or optic. We used optical cables attached to a PHY chip [6] allowing

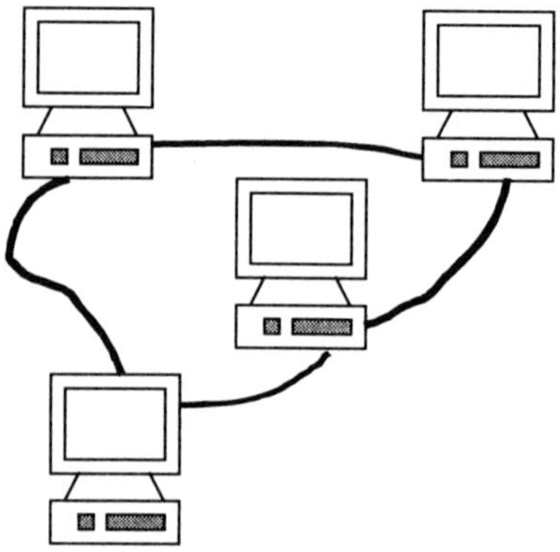

Figure 1. Point-to-point (p2p) ring network.

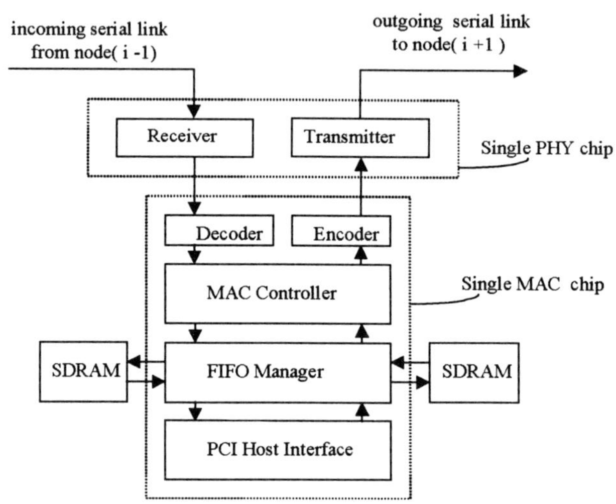

Figure 2. Overall architecture of RingLink adaptor.

1.063Gbps signaling speed. The PHY chip is called SERDES (SERializer and DESerializer) doing a parallel to serial conversion and vice versa in the transmitter and receiver block, respectively. The line code used in RingLink is based on ABI (Alternate Bit Inversion) coding [7], which does transition minimization for low power, low EMI operation in electrically driving a transmission line.

The single MAC chip comprises a 8B/10B line coder, a MAC controller implementing the OTCA MAC protocol, a FIFO manager controlling external SDRAM (Synchronous Dynamic Random Access Memory) components, and a PCI host interface that allows user level network access eliminating kernel crossing overhead. This ring adaptor forms three-way communication paths consisting of an incoming serial link, an outgoing serial link, and a parallel bus to a host.

The PCI host interface includes two DMA engines, one for data sending and the other for data receiving. As

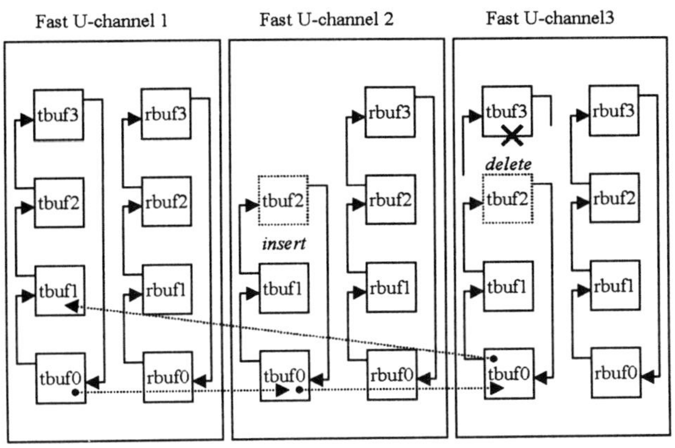

Figure 3. Fast U-channel ring buffer

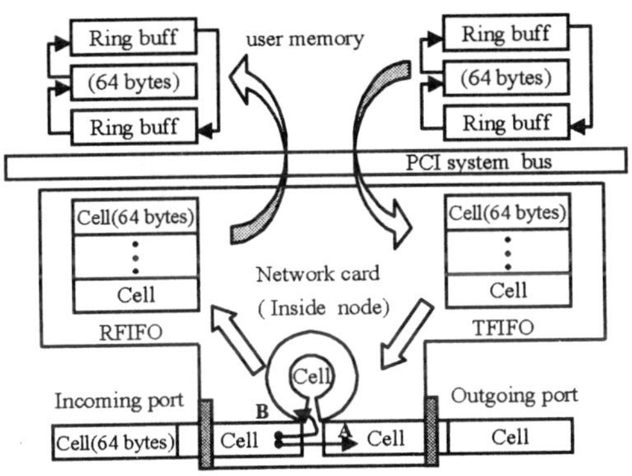

Figure 4. Cell movement in RingLink network.

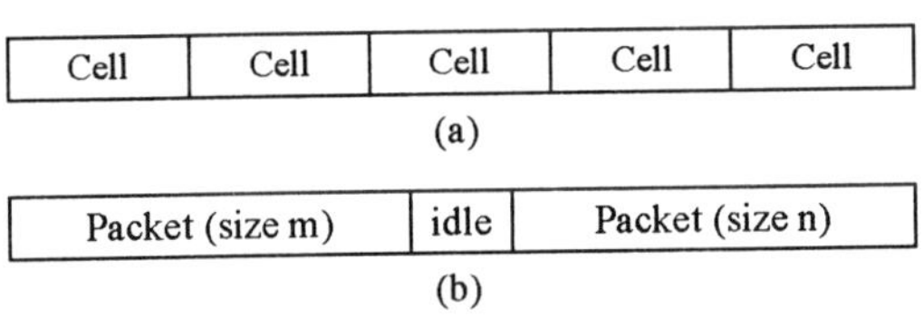

Figure 5. Ring length extension: (a) cell insertion. (b) buffer insertion.

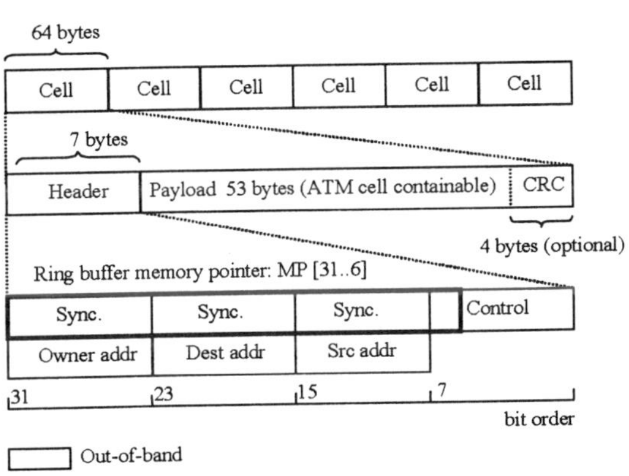

Figure 6. RingLink 64 byte cell format.

shown in Figure 3, the hardware-based sender in adaptor polls three Fast U-channels (user interface) and one K-channel (kernel interface) in a round-robin order. K-channel has the same structure to Fast U-channels. If the ring buffer (locked-down memory) in a channel is not empty, the sender fetches the data into the transmitter FIFO through TDMA and, then, the data is sent to an outgoing serial link. If the channel is empty, the sender continues to poll the next channel. In spite of context switches by OS, the sender in the adaptor keeps packet atomicity among multiple channels. On the other hand, the hardware-based receiver does the reverse operation of the sender. If an outstanding cell in the receiver FIFO is addressed to one of the current active channels, the receiver in adaptor demultiplexes the data into the corresponding channel. Otherwise, it sends the data into K-channel, and there, the data is demultiplexed into the corresponding upper layer by a device driver. The size of the ring buffers in Fast U-channels and K-channel is fixed as 64 bytes.

Figure 4 depicts cell movement in RingLink network. The device driver performs the segmentation and reassembly for normal applications using K-channel interfacing TCP/IP layer. But, in specific applications using Fast U-channels, a user directly manages the ring buffer in a linked list avoiding unnecessary copying overhead. The length of the ring buffer chain is flexible in user memory. If the application needs more memory, such as a video link, the chain of the linked list may be longer.

RingLink adaptor transfers a 33MHz, 32bit parallel PCI transaction in 64 byte message containers. In the slotted ring, a fixed-size cell, or slot, is used as a message container. In our work, the size of the ring buffer in user memory and that of cell in the adaptor are equivalent. One slot time of 64 bytes is about 0.485us.

The slots that are formed from built-in intrinsic physical ring delay (the propagation time over the transmission lines + the processing time in interim nodes) are called static slots. Ring length control logic in the MAC controller enforces full usage of ring rotation time by register insertion technique, which adds a delay to the short slot time to align the head of incoming slot to the tail of outgoing slot. We call it a static ring mode (SSRM) where only static cells are allowed.

In addition to static slots, as shown in Figure 5, RingLink allows ring length extension, which enables immediate cell allocation instead of waiting the medium access opportunity. The cells generated by this on-demand cell insertion technique are called dynamic slots. In Figure 5, if the incoming cell is switched to path **B** from path **A**, the node is extending ring length. Otherwise, to **A** path from path **B**, then, the node is recovering the extended ring length. It is similar to the conventional buffer insertion technique, however, the buffer size is restricted to be a fixed size. Generally, the term of packet is used for variable sized message container. An arbitrary sized packet and non-deterministic packet gap make the packet processing difficult in a node. We call it a dynamic slotted ring mode (DSRM) where the ring length varies with dynamic cell insertion in a node. DSRAM is enforced under a controlled manner on top of SSRM.

2.2 Owner Addressed Cell Format

As shown in Figure 6, the cell size of RingLink is 64 bytes long, which can encapsulate an ATM cell. The cell structure is equivalent to the ring buffer structure except some parts that are converted in movement. 7 bytes are used for synchronization (3 bytes), control of cell processing (1 byte), and addresses of an owner node (1 byte), a destination node (1 byte), and a source node (1 byte). Therefore, the overhead of a cell header in the RingLink is about 11%. The tail 4 bytes are used optionally for 32-bit CRC (Cyclic Redundancy Check), which is controlled by a bit in the control field.

The synchronization field is used for cell delineation and the 8-bit control field is used as follows:

- *CTL.b7*: Validation of the owner address field
- *CTL.b6*: Validation of the destination address field
- *CTL.b5*: Ring mode
- *CTL.b4*: Traffic class
- *CTL.b3*: CRC option
- *CTL.b2*: Receiver buffer overrun query
- *CTL.b1*: Cell loss priority
- *CTL.b0*: Binary semaphore

If *CTL.b5* is on, the message is allocated using a dynamic cell. If *CTL.b4* is marked, the message belongs to a synchronous traffic (otherwise, to an asynchronous traffic). *CTL.b2* enforces the first destination node (not subsequent destination nodes of cell-reuse) to give the confirmation (of correct delivery without buffer overrun in the receiver) to the owner node by toggling this bit. If the cell loss priority bit is high, a node having more urgent message can override the passing cell. The last bit is used as a binary semaphore to solve producer-consumer problem in the ring buffer usage indicating whether the ring buffer is full or empty.

Each address field is 8 bit wide. In RingLink system, 128 nodes can be addressed individually excluding special addressing such as multicast and broadcast. The addresses of nodes are assigned in a *monotonously increasing* order until they fold back to the starting address at the end. The controller must be able to determine whether the owner node of a cell is a predecessor node or a successor of the destination node of the current cell to send. When the ring network is initialized, the server node elected as a coordinator gives a unique ring address. Ring buffer

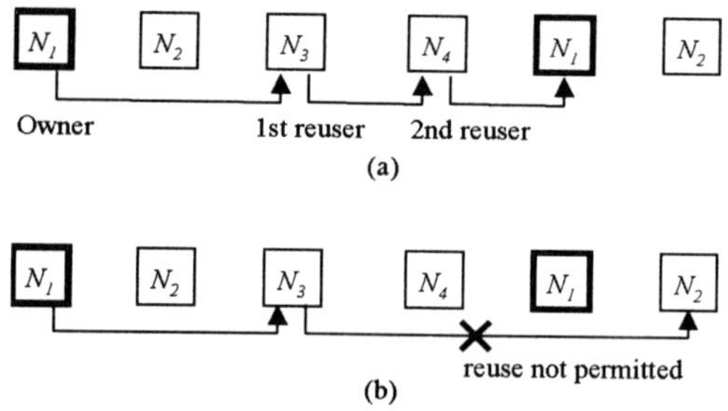

Figure 7. Fairness constraint in cell-reuse: (a) permissible reuse. (b) Reuse failure.

memory pointer, MP[31:6], which is 26 bit wide indicating the next 64 byte ring buffer in the linked list, is replaced with three synchronization characters and the two address validation bits.

3. Fairness Guaranteed Cell-Reuse

Under the ring architecture described in section 2, we present how the OTCA MAC protocol provides fairness in a bandwidth-limited shared medium and, then, we show the built-in traffic classification of the OTCA MAC protocol.

3.1 Fairness Constraint in Cell-Reuse

In some time critical applications, echo packets are of little use and may present an unnecessary overhead. Some traffic sources, such as video or audio, may need not confirming, nor any retransmission on bad delivery.

In conventional networks such as token ring and FDDI network, the packet returns to a source node being empty after it arrives at the destination. It wastes available network bandwidth. In recent networks [4]-[5], for a higher network throughput, a node attempts to reuse a cell at destinations. However, due to the cell-reuse at destination, it is prone to cause unfair bandwidth utilization among nodes. Under such circumstances, the utilization priorities are easily subject to the geometric ring position [8], [9]. Unfair access mechanism may even cause a deadlock, not to mention reduced network throughput and unbounded network delay.

To address this problem, RingLink system realizes a preventive fairness control by tagging the owner address in every cell. The ownership of a cell is similar to the token in a token ring network, however, in RingLink, every cell embeds the token function in the ownership field. The ownership of a static cell is handed over to the next node. In this way, the ownership of a cell walks around in the ring network. Meanwhile, that of a dynamic cell is parked to the owner node that generated the dynamic cell. The fairness constraint in RingLink is that the destination node must be reached before or at the owner node.

Figure 7 depicts the fairness constraint in cell-reuse by showing two examples. In Figure 7-(a), during a ring revolution from an owner node, a cell is used 3 times successfully until the cell comes back to the owner node, N_1. However, in Figure 7-(b), N_3 addressed N_2, which is beyond the N_1, thus the reuse attempt is failed. In that case, N_3 should relinquish the cell to the next node, N_4.

3.2 Built-in Traffic Classification

In the OTCA MAC protocol, the cell-reuse constraint for the fairness control guarantees that a cell returns to the owner node for availability in time. Thus, the bandwidth allocated with cell ownership is adequate for synchronous traffic guaranteeing regularity in medium access latency. The synchronous traffic sources can be video and audio, which have a constant inter-arrival time and deadline constraints [10]-[11]. On the other hand, the cell-reuse opportunity varies depending on the relative distance in a ring between the owner node and destination nodes. Thus, the network bandwidth obtained by cell-reuse is proper for asynchronous traffic with a soft timing constraint.

In RingLink system, the network bandwidth is classified in three categories. When a message is going to be contained in a cell, *CTL.b5* and *CTL.b4* in the cell header are used to classify the traffic into following classes:

- Isochronous traffic when *CTL.b5=1* and *CTL.b4=1*
- Synchronous traffic when *CTL.b5=0* and *CTL.b4=1*
- Asynchronous traffic when *CTL.b4=0*

We distinguish the synchronous bandwidth obtained in DSRM from that in SSRM. The former is mostly used for isochronous traffic.

The transmitter FIFO is partitioned into three different kinds of buffers. Above three traffics are loaded into the corresponding buffer, i.e., an isochronous traffic to the isochronous buffer, a synchronous traffic to the synchronous buffer, and an asynchronous traffic to the asynchronous buffer. Similarly to the transmitter FIFO, the receiver FIFO is composed of three classes of storage.

A higher priory asynchronous traffic (*CTL.b1=0*) can override a passing lower priority traffic (*CTL.b1=1*), thus, the lower priority traffic can be lost from the ring if the network load is heavy. A video application is expected to use this bit. As the network situation becomes better, the quality of video becomes better without cell loss in a receiver, while a sender transmits the video stream with *CTL.b1* off. However, the minimum quality is guaranteed by keeping the cell loss priority low.

4. Implementation of OTCA MAC Protocol

4.1. MAC Rules in SSRM

In SSRM, eventually, the ownership of a particular cell circulates over all nodes in a ring. Consequently, the global fairness is achieved, distributing the equal medium access opportunity to all nodes on the ring. The medium access rule in SSRM is as follows:

Table 1. Global Fair Cell Allocation Algorithm in SSRM

```
If (CTL.b7=1) /* Owner address is not valid)*/
  If (CTL.b6=0) /* Destination address is not valid */
        CTL.b7 ← 1;
        OA ← LNA; /* Take the ownership */
        Sync. message → outgoing cell;
  elsif (DA=LNA) /* Destination address = local node address */
        CTL.b7 ← 1;
        OA ← LNA ;
        Incoming message → Sync. buffer ;
  else
        CTL.b7 ← 0; /* Invalidate the ownership */
        CTL.b6 ← 0; /* Make the cell empty */
        /* ERROR in normal ring operation */
elsif ( OA=LNA) /*Owner address = local node address */
  If (CTL.b6=0) /* Destination address is not valid */
        CTL.b7 ← 0; /* Ownership hand-over */
  elsif (DA=LNA) /* Destination address = local node address*/
        CTL.b7 ← 0;
        Incoming message → Async. buffer;
  else
        CTL.b7 ← 0; /* Invalidate the ownership */
        CTL.b6 ← 0; /* Make the cell empty */
        /* ERROR in normal ring operation * /}
else{ /* Owner address = remote node address */
  If (CTL.6=0) /* Destination address is not valid */
        Async. message → outgoing cell;
  elsif(DA=LNA) /* Destination address = local node address */
        If CTL.b4 = 1
            Incoming message → Sync. buffer;
        else
            Incoming message → Async. buffer;
        Async. Message → outgoing cell;
  else
        If CTL.b1=1
        Async. Message → outgoing cell;
```

In the ring initialization period, when a node is started, it sends a static cell (with *CTL.b7=0, CTL.b6=0,* and *CTL.b5=0*) to the next node continuously until the ring is stabilized. If the ring is stabilized, a node takes the ownership of the cell making the ownership field valid as shown in Table 1. If the ring operates normally, the ownership field of a static cell is kept valid except the time when the ownership is transferred to the next node along the ring in a round-robin manner.

4.2. MAC Rules in DSRM

In DSRM, a node generates an empty dynamic cell (with *CTL.b7=1, CTL.b6=0, CTL.b5=1,* and *OA=LNA*). If a node has a message to send, then, the target node address is written on *DA* field and *CTL.b6* becomes valid. In DSRM, the ownership is not handed over, but each node keeps the ownership. This eliminates the waste time taken to hand-over the cell ownership in SSRM. The medium access rule in the DSRM is as follows:

Table 2. Local Fair Cell Allocation Algorithm in DSRM

```
If (CTL.b7='0') /* Owner address is not valid */
        CTL(b7) ← '0'; /* Invalidate the ownership */
        CTL(b6) ← '0'; /* Make the cell empty */
        /* ERROR in normal ring operation */}
elseif (OA=LNA) /*Owner address = local node address */
  If (CTL.b6='0') /* Destination address is not valid */
        Isochr. message → outgoing cell;
  elseif (DA=LNA) /* Destination address = local node address */
        Incoming message → Aync. buffer;
        Isochr. message → outgoing cell;
  else
        CTL.b7 ← '0'; /* Invalidate the ownership */
        CTL.b6 ← '0'; /* Make the cell empty */
          /* ERROR in normal ring operation */}
else{
  If (CTL.b6='0') /* Destination address is not valid */
        Async. message → outgoing cell;
  elseif(DA=LNA) /* Destination address = local node address */
        If CTL.b4 = '1'
           Incoming message → Sync. buffer;
        else
           Incoming message → Async. buffer;
        Async. message → outgoing cell;
  else
        If CTL.b1=1
        Async. Message → outgoing cell;
```

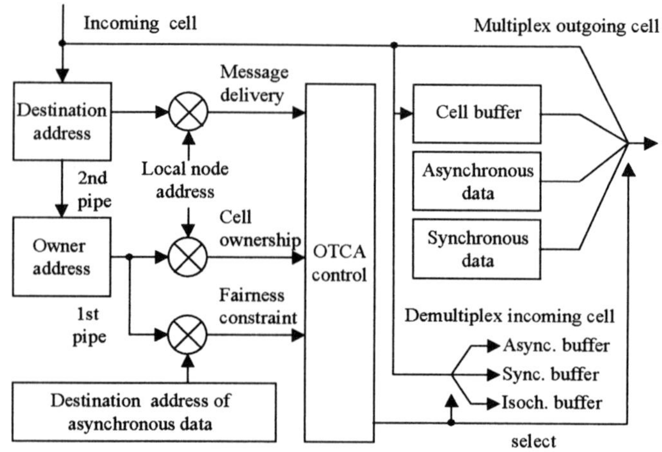

Figure 8. Overall block diagram of OTCA protocol.

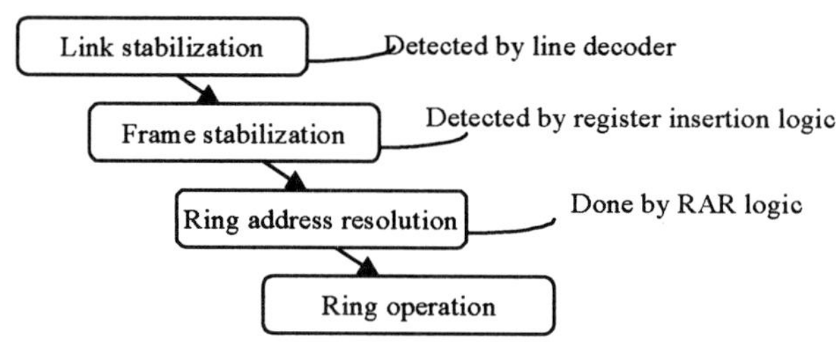

Figure 9. Ring initialization procedure.

4.3 Core of OTCA MAC protocol engine

Figure 8 depicts the block diagram of the OTCA core. The cell is processed in a pipeline manner. By comparing the owner address with the local address and the destination address with the local address, a node recognizes the cell ownership and message delivery, respectively. The destination address of asynchronous data is compared with the owner address of the cell to validate the fairness constraint. The comparison results are used in the OTCA controller to select the proper cell to the outgoing port and to demultiplex the incoming cell to the corresponding buffer.

4.4. Ring Address Resolution

Figure 9 depicts the ring initialization procedure in RingLink. After a power-on, ring management FSM (Finite State Machine) in the MAC controller checks the stabilization of the line, cell train format, and ring address. The line status is reported from the line decoder logic. If invalid code set (which cannot be appeared in the normal line status) comes at unacceptable level, the link cannot be used. Also, if the head of incoming cell cannot be relayed to the tail of outgoing cell in spite of register insertion, the link is malfunctioning.

After the ring is stabilized without a line and frame error, a node enters RAR (Ring Address Resolution) step. The ring elects a single coordinator, or ring server, that is the process with the largest IP number assigned to node statically. The IP is unique in the ring. A node uses the dynamic cell, which revolves along the ring checking if the IP of the node is the largest number. If other node has larger IP, the node marks a specific bit on the dynamic cell. If the cell comes to the owner node unmarked, the node becomes the coordinator node. The node address of the coordinator is zero, and the subsequent nodes are assigned with a number increased by one from the previous node.

5. Guaranteed Network Parameter

Network scheduling requires the interconnect to have guaranteed worst case latency, guaranteed worst case bandwidth, and the ability to insure that tasks running in the background using excess bandwidth do not interfere with those that are currently scheduled to receive the available bandwidth. How well the interconnect adapts to scheduled environment determines how much of the available bandwidth can be scheduled and guarantees that all scheduled tasks will be completed in time [12].

5.1 Latency Bound

In SSRM, if a cell arrives at an owner node, the owner node hands over the ownership of the cell to the next adjacent node for fair sharing of the network bandwidth. If the next owner node has no message to send, it relinquishes the cell usage to the next node. However, the cell ownership is still kept to the node, thus the revolution time of the cell ownership is deterministic in SSRM. Ignoring jittering caused by cell-insertion in a node, the inter-arrival time between successive ownership of a particular cell is bounded as follows:

$$M\cdot\tau+N\cdot M\cdot\tau \le T_s(o) \le M\cdot\tau+N\cdot M\cdot\tau+K_s\cdot\tau \qquad (5.1)$$

where M is the number of static cells, τ is slot time, N is the number of nodes, and K_s is the number of cell-insertions during the ownership walk time. K_s is ranged 0 to N^2.

On the other hand, in DSRM, the inter-arrival time of the ownership of a particular cell is as follows:

$$M\cdot\tau \le T_d(o) \le M\cdot\tau+K_d\cdot\tau \qquad (5.2)$$

where K_d is the number of cell insertions during the cell revolution time in the ring, which is ranged 0 to N-1.

Figure 10 shows the probability of mean time between ownership (MTBO) of a particular cell under an assumption that a node performs the dynamic cell-

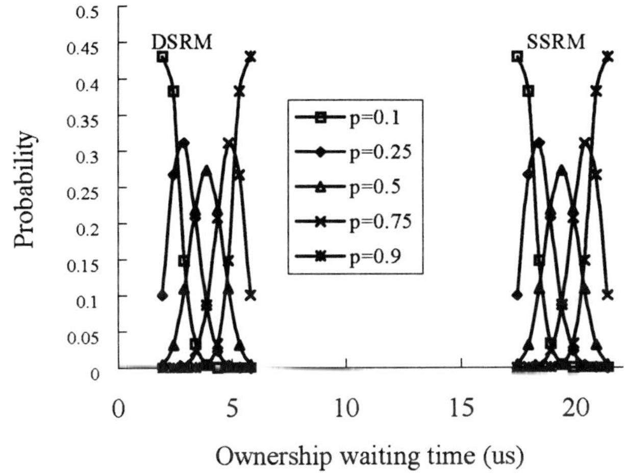

Figure 10. MTBO in the two ring modes.

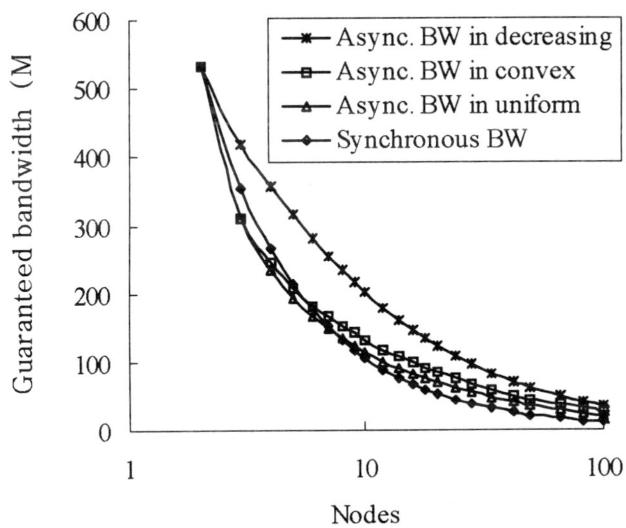

Figure 11. Worst-case bandwidth availability.

insertion with the probability p. If the number of node is 8 and the number of static cells is 4, then, MTBO in SSRM ranges 17.46 us to 48.5 us from (5.1) and 1.94 us to 5.34 us from (5.2). In the figure, we assumed that each node has a capability of the cell-insertion on-demand. Thus, 8 cells can be critically instantiated, leading to the worst case jittering. If the N is 4 and M is 4, then we can estimate that the worst ownership waiting time in SSRM is 17.46 us.

When compared to back-off time in gigabit Ethernet, which ranges from 4.1us (512 byte slot time) to 4194.3 us (binary truncated after 10 trials), the latency bound of the OTCA protocol is smaller and deterministic.

5.2 Bandwidth Availability

Figure 11 depicts the worst case bandwidth availability in the ring. The line speed of the ring is 1.063Gpbs. We assumed that the network load is 1, i.e., all nodes have a message to send always. As the number of node, or *N*, is increased, the guaranteed synchronous bandwidth per node is decreased by inverse scale of *N*. Under three destination address models, we analyzed the expected bandwidth for asynchronous data gained by cell-reuse. In the one side linearly decreasing model, the probability to select a node in short distance is higher. The uniform distribution is the simplest case where each node tries to communicate with the other with equal probability. A more realistic distribution might be a two-sided linearly decreasing distribution, or concave model, where the nodes with frequent bi-directional communication are closely connected.

The synchronous bandwidth allocated to a node under the worst case network load is 265Mbps, 132Mbps, and 66Mbps, for 4, 8, and 16 nodes, respectively. Under the uniform destination distribution model, the asynchronous bandwidth is 232Mbps (358Mbps under decreasing model and 245Mbps under concave model), 134Mbps (235Mpbs under decreasing model and 151Mbps under concave model), and 81Mbps (145Mbps under decreasing and 98Mbps under concave model), for 4, 8, and 16 nodes, respectively.

In the OTCA MAC protocol, the bandwidth for asynchronous data becomes larger than that for synchronous data as *N* is increased. However, the bandwidth availability for a node under the worst case is *C/N*, where *C* is link capacity. A node can estimate the available bandwidth from the ring revolution time reporting this information to the upper layers, and these parameters about the bandwidth allocation from the MAC layer play an active part in system setting and adjusting the rate control parameter values. The two end nodes can control the rate control parameters of the current traffic source. Being similar to the round trip delay used in the TCP/IP protocol [13], where a node can tell the degree of network congestion from the delayed response time, it is a natural way to negotiate the traffic parameter between the network and the user.

6. Concluding Remarks

In this paper, we have shown the design and implementation the OTCA MAC protocol for high-speed p2p ring network. The RingLink system implementing the OTCA MAC protocol prevents starvation of lower-priority traffic while satisfying the needs of higher-priority traffic, and gives flexibility to accommodate built-in traffic classification providing three classes of the network usage - isochronous, synchronous, and asynchronous. Unlike Ethernet, which relies on random probability, RingLink guarantees a bounded medium access latency and minimum bandwidth availability. We expect that the OTCA protocol is well-suited for real-time multimedia environment, where real-time scheduling requires the interconnect to have a guaranteed worst case latency, a guaranteed worst case bandwidth, and the ability to insure that tasks running in the background do not interfere with those that are currently scheduled.

7. Acknowledgment

We thank Dr. David D. Lee who motivated us into this work.

References

[1] Howard W. Johnson, "Fast Ethernet", Prentice Hall.

[2] David B. Gustavson, "The Scaleable Coherent Interface and Related Standards Projects", *IEEE Micro*, Feb 1992.

[3] RamLink, "High Bandwidth Memory Interface Based on SCI Signalling Technology", May 1993.

[4] Israel Cidon, Yoram Ofek, "MetaRing-A Full-Duplex Ring with Fairness and Spatial Reuse", *IEEE transactions on communications*, Vol.41, NO.1, pp. 110-120, Jan. 1993.

[5] Andrew Hopper, Roger M. Needham, "The Cambridge Fast Ring Networking System", *IEEE transactions on communications*, Vol.37, NO.10, pp. 1214-1223, Oct. 1988.

[6] IBM, 1063 Mb/s Optical Link Module – Technical Data Sheet.

[7] Yeshik Shin, *et al*, "Transition-controlled digital encoding and signal transmission system", U.S. patent pending

[8] Steven L. Scotte, et al., "Performance of the SCI Ring", *Proceedings of the 19th Annual International Symposium on Computer Architecture*, pp. 403-414, May 1992.

[9] Dan Picker, et al, "An Extension to the SCI Flow Control Protocol for Increased Network Efficiency", *IEEE/ACM Transactions on Networking*, VOL. 4, NO. 1, Feb. 1996.

[10] B. Chen, et al, "Optimal synchronous capacity allocation for hard read-time communications with the timed token protocol", *Proceedings of the Real-Time Systems Symposium*, pp. 198-207, Dec. 1992.

[11] S. Mukherjee, et al, "A Bandwidth Allocation Scheme for Time Constrained Message Transmission on a Slotted Ring LAN", *Proceedings of IEEE Real-Time Systems Symposium*, 1993.

[12] Sally Floyd, et al., "Link-sharing and Resource Management Models for Packet Networks", *IEEE/ACM Transactions on Networking*, Vol. 3, No. 4, Aug. 1995.

[13] Stephen A. Thomas, "Ipng and the TCP/IP Protocols", *Wiley Computer Publishing, John Wiley & Sons, Inc.*

Data and Buffer Management in ATM Systems

S.Varada, Y.Yang, and D. Evans
TranSwitch Corporation
3 Enterprise Dr.
Shelton, CT 06484.
{varada, yang, dave}@txc.com

Abstract

The paper discusses the handling of data traffic, at an end-user host or access concentrator performing network adaptation functions, in a high speed Asynchronous Transfer Mode (ATM) network environment. The challenges of handling data traffic in high speed networks are the processing power and space requirements. The hardware implementation of the required protocol processing, through a high gate density Application Specific Integrated Circuit (ASIC), provides much of the processing power; however, the space requirements for data handling are still demanding. From the reasons of cost and space, on a network adapter card, often such ASICs rely upon the host for data buffers in the host memory in addition to control and configuration. Such a reliance places demand on the host memory and requires a data and buffer management mechanism that provides a framework for optimization of the memory utilization and data packet latency.

The design and implementation details of one such data and buffer management mechanism, the Scatter and Gather mechanism, are discussed in the paper. The mechanism implementation encompasses both host and ASIC (or, device) domains. The host domain implementation is carried out in the Network Driver Interface Specifications (NDIS) framework [1] and is given emphasis in the paper. Critical performance parameters in the proposed mechanism are identified and modelled. The mechanism had been tested to perform satisfactorily with a high performance programmable Segmentation and Reassembly (SAR) device [2] with multitude of features.

1.0 Scatter and Gather mechanism

ATM networks [3] offer user traffic the kind of services which are only inherent to them. High speed interconnectivity, service integration, quality of service (QoS) guarantees, and bandwidth on demand are a few of those services. Because of the high-speed nature of ATM networks, the protocol processing functionality is typically implemented in hardware (figure 1). The variable length higher layer Protocol Data Units (PDUs) or User Payloads are supported, over ATM, through their mapping to the Service Data Unit (SDU) of the AAL Convergence Sub-layer. The mapping process requires data buffers to facilitate protocol processing. From the reasons of cost and space, on a network adapter card, ASICs rely upon the host for buffers in the host memory. As a result, utilizing the buffer space efficiently without affecting packet latency becomes a concern for the system designer. The Scatter and Gather mechanism addresses this concern.

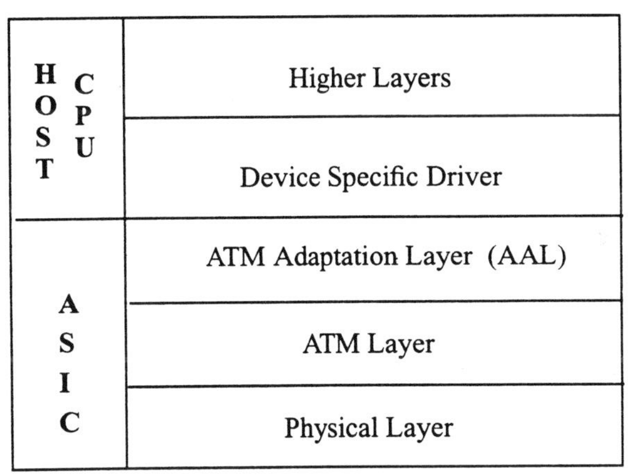

Figure 1. Protocol Layer Model

The mechanism performs the distribution (Scatter) and collection (Gather) of data to be transmitted to or received from network into and from one or more buffers (figure 2). The buffers are of optimally chosen size. The ability to scatter higher layer data into multiple buffers, at one end, and gather at the other end, among two interacting entities, gives a system designer the control over utilization of the finite buffer resources. In the absence of the above

0-8186-8810-6/98 $10.00 © 1998 IEEE

feature, it is difficult to effectively utilize the buffer space, as the buffer size should then be so chosen to support largest PDU size possible, when handling variable length data. The effect of poor buffer space utilization is the buffer over-runs, under certain traffic conditions, which would lead to overall degradation in the QoS offered to traffic.

The buffers (referred as mapping, shared, or host buffers) are allocated in the host memory during system initialization. They are described by their size and location in the memory. The size and number are, typically, configuration parameters providing tuning flexibility to achieve optimum latency and buffer space utilization through trade-offs.

The mechanism uses buffers, on demand, during the Scatter process and recycles after the Gather process is completed. A host based buffer management entity manages FREE buffers, to provide them to the scatter process, and INUSE buffers, to recycle them when the Gather process is completed.

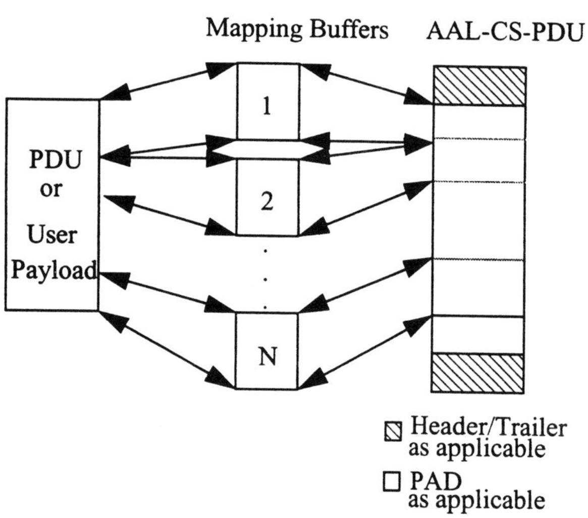

Figure 2. Two-way Scatter/Gather Mechanism

Either the host CPU (when transmitting data to network) or the ASIC (when receiving data from network) performs the scattering process while the other performs the Gathering process (figure 3). The ASIC combines the scatter and ATM cell re-assembly processes together. That is, the reassembly of the ATM cells received from the network is performed in host buffers by ASIC. To aid in the cell re-assembly process, the host creates and assigns ASIC a pool of FREE buffers (the receive FREE buffers pool) during system initialization. Once assigned, ASIC uses this pool in cell re-assembly process, however, depends on the host for buffer recycling. That is, used buffers are recycled back to the FREE pool when host gathers PDUs.

The host, for its own use, creates and maintains a pool of FREE buffers (the transmit FREE buffers pool) in delivering data to ASIC for network transmission. Buffers which are in use are tracked through per virtual circuit (VC) based linked lists. When buffers used are no longer needed by ASIC they are deposited back to the transmit FREE buffers pool.

2.0 Implementation Requirements

The implementation requirements for the Scatter/Gather mechanism are presented here. The primary components required are the Device-to-Host interface, Host Buffers, Buffer Management Entity, and host resident Transmit/Receive data modules.

2.1 Device-Host Interface

As the mechanism cover both the ASIC and host domains, definition of the interface between them is needed. The interface is based on the request and indicate message model.The host makes service requests, and the ASIC indicates acknowledgments, receives, error events, and other asynchronous events. The required set of messages for realizing the mechanism is given below:

- Add buffer to receive FREE pool (Host to device request)
- TxmtSegment (Host to device request)
- TxmtEndSegment (Host to device request)
- TxmtSegment ACK (Device to host indicate)
- RxdPduSegment (Device to host indicate)
- RxdPduEndSegment (Device to host indicate)
- RxdPduWithError (Device to host indicate)

To exchange messages, a mail box facility is needed. The mail box facility is a host memory resident entity accessed both by host CPU and Direct Memory Access (DMA) capable ASIC. To facilitate read and write accesses to mail box by host and ASIC, the ASIC need to incorporate a hardware assist function. The physical interface between the host CPU and ASIC is the Peripheral Component Interconnect (PCI) bus [4,5].

2.2 Host Buffers

The memory space for buffers shall be allocated during system initialization as part of the device specific driver software. The amount of space to be allocated is proportional to the buffer size and the number of buffers required, considering the simplest case of homogeneous buffers (i.e., buffers with same size). The allocated memory shall be shared between the DMA capable ASIC and host CPU to avoid interruptions to host CPU when data transfer is needed by ASIC. The buffers are to be described by buffer descriptors and linked up to form lists of two FREE buffer pools for transmit and receive operations.

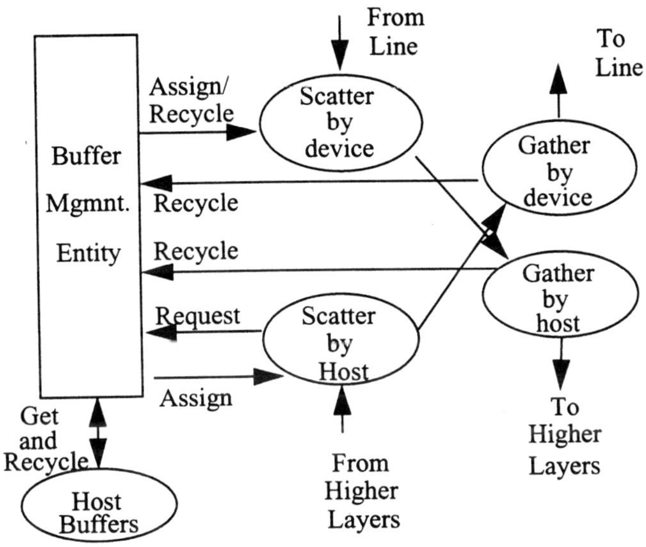

Figure 3. Buffer Management and Data Flow

2.3 Buffer Management Entity

The Buffer Management Entity is host resident. Its functions are to assign buffers to ASIC and host, and recycle used buffers. The management entity shall assign, during initialization, ASIC with the receive FREE buffers pool for its exclusive use in reassembly process. The recycling of receive buffers is performed in the host after PDU-gathering is performed.

The transmit buffers are assigned on demand to the host's transmit data module. A list of INUSE buffers is to be maintained on a per VC basis for them to be recycled back to the FREE buffers pool when ASIC's transmit acknowledgment is received at the host.

The above functionality requires three concurrent processes. One to handle transmit FREE buffer pool access requests and assign receive FREE buffer pool to ASIC, and others to handle buffer recycle requests by the transmit and receive data modules, respectively.

2.4 Transmit Data Module

The functions of this module are to (1) receive higher layer send requests, (2) accept or reject the request based on FREE buffers availability, (3) transfer PDU contents into available FREE buffers, if the requested is accepted (4) place send request messages with buffer context to ASIC for data transmission, and (5) initiate buffer recycling when acknowledgments are received from ASIC.

The above functionality requires two concurrent processes: one to handle the higher layer send requests, and the other to handle ASIC acknowledgments. These processes interact with higher layers (through NDIS), buffer management entity, and ASIC (figure 4). The handshaking between Transmit Data Module and NDIS is as per NDIS framework. The process that handles send requests employ the buffered I/O approach in transferring PDU to ASIC. Alternatively, one may choose to employ the direct I/O, if feasible and performance is an issue.

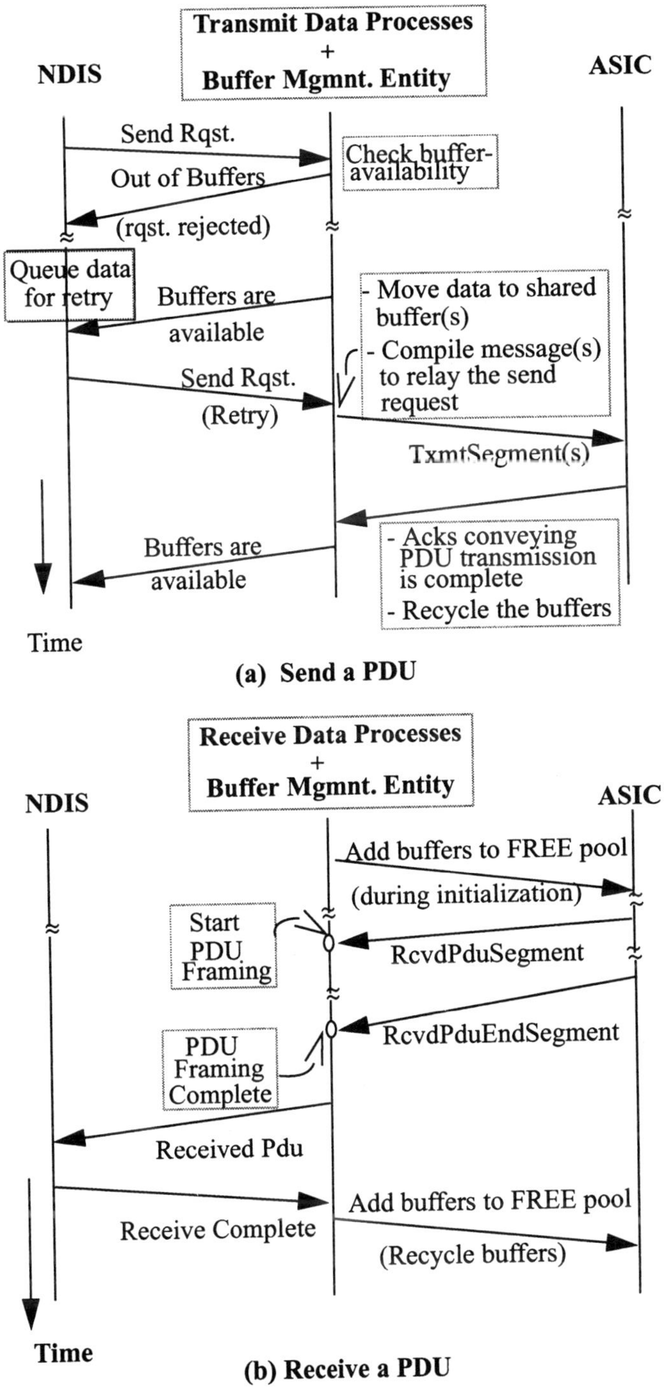

Figure 4. Send and Receive PDUs

2.5 Receive Data Module

The functions of this host resident module are to (1) receive ASIC PDU segment indications, (2) frame the received segments in to a PDU, (3) indicate to higher layers if a complete PDU is framed, and (4) recycle used buffers back to ASIC's FREE pool.

The above functionality doesn't require concurrent processes due to the sequential nature of execution. The interactions of this module with the higher layers (through NDIS), buffer management entity, and ASIC are represented in the figure 4. The handshaking between the Receive Data Module and NDIS is as per NDIS framework. The data handling shall be based on buffered I/O approach.

3.0 Implementation Methodology

The methodology for implementing the Host Buffers, Buffer Management Entity, Scatter and Gather mechanisms in the host domain is presented below.

3.1 Host Buffers

The buffers are portions of shared memory. The shared memory allocation is performed through the following NDIS library call at system initialization.

```
VOID
  NdisAllocateSharedMemory(
    IN NDIS_HANDLE NdisAdapterHandle,
    IN ULONG Length,
    IN BOOLEAN Cached,
    OUT PVOID *VirtualAddress,
    OUT PNDIS_PHYSICAL_ADDRESS PhysicalAddress
    );
```

The result of a successful call is non-NULL pointers as virtual and physical addresses. The returned physical address will be supplied to ASIC for referencing and accessing buffers while the host uses the virtual address. An unsuccessful call, typically, is a result of lack of shared memory in the system. The call shall be made, supplying buffer size as length, as many times as the number of buffers required. After each successful call, the size and location of the allocated memory segment shall, then, be stored in an instance of data structure of type LIST_ELEMENT.

```
typedef struct {
   struct BufferDescriptor{
        ULONG Length,
        PVOID *VirtualAddress,
        PNDIS_PHYSICAL_ADDRESS PhysicalAddress
   };
        PLIST_ENTRY ListEntry;
}LIST_ELEMENT;
```

Each such list element shall be attached to a created linked list to form a FREE buffer pool. To create and perform operations on singly linked list, the NDIS framework provides the following library functions.

```
// Initialize the list head
  VOID
   NdisInitializeListHead(
     IN PLIST_ENTRY ListHead
     );

// Insert List Element at the Tail
PLIST_ENTRY
   NdisInterlockedInsertTailList(
     IN PLIST_ENTRY ListHead,
     IN PLIST_ENTRY ListEntry,
     IN PNDIS_SPIN_LOCK SpinLock
     );
// Remove a List Element from the head of list
PLIST_ENTRY
   NdisInterlockedRemoveHeadList(
     IN PLIST_ENTRY ListHead,
     IN PNDIS_SPIN_LOCK SpinLock
     );
```

The NDIS library calls have provision, the spinlock, to make the list multiprocessor safe in Symmetric Multiprocessor (SMP) Environment. Using the above facilities one shall be able to create separate transmit and receive FREE buffer pools which the Buffer Management Entity can manage.

3.2 Buffer Management Entity

During the system startup, after buffer pools are created, the Buffer Management Entity shall assign ASIC the created receive FREE buffers pool for use in common part CS-PDU (CPCS-PDU) reassembly process. Once assigned, the ASIC manages buffers; however, it depends on the Buffer Management Entity to recycle used buffers. The buffer assignment and recycling can be performed through the device service interface.

To assign buffers for transmit operation, the management entity works in conjunction with the Transmit Data Module. Buffers are assigned only when requested by the Transmit Data Module. The request shall only arrive, if the transmit data module has verified that the list is not empty using the list status monitor that it maintains.

To help in recycling, a list of INUSE buffers shall be maintained on a per VC basis. The singly linked list can be created with the aforementioned NDIS library calls. Every time a buffer is used, the list element corresponding to the buffer descriptor shall be put into the list at the tail. When ASIC acknowledgments are received, the buffer descriptors (or, the list elements) from the head of the list only shall be removed. This simple recycle mechanism is a virtue of sequence integrity maintenance in ATM. That is, whichever PDU or its segments sent first are transmitted and acknowledged first. The removed buffer descriptors are, then, deposited (attached at the tail or head of list) back into the transmit FREE buffers pool.

3.3 Transmit Data Module

The acceptance, upon reception, of a higher layer send request is based on the availability of buffer space. There are two approaches to doing this.

(1) Send All or None
(2) Best-effort delivery

3.3.1 Send all or none Approach. In this approach, send request acceptance and initiation of PDU Scatter, if needed, can only be performed if there is sufficient buffer space for the entire PDU. The steps involved are as follows.

1. Get PDU size and location in non-shared system space
2. Compute the number of shared buffers required (using buffer and PDU sizes)
3. Perform buffer(s) availability verification
   If the verification result implies buffer availability, proceed to step 4; Otherwise, reject the request. In such a case, the PDU transmission would have to re-attempted later. The reattempt can be triggered by buffer available indication to NDIS by the Transmit Data module when buffers are recycled. Until then, the send NDIS function queues up the data making the whole process transparent to higher layers.
4. Get a buffer from the buffer management entity
5. Move data into shared buffer, and decrement the BufferCount counter
6. Generate the TxmtSegment (or, TxmtEndSegment for the last or single segment) message to ASIC for segmentation and transmission
7. Repeat steps 4 through 6 until complete PDU is given for transmission

Repeat steps 1 through 7 for every higher layer send request. The buffer availability verification (step 3) requires the BufferCount to keep track of the number of buffers in transmit FREE buffers pool. The counter shall be initialized to the number of buffers allocated during system initialization. It is decremented every time buffers are used, by the number of buffers used, and incremented every time buffers are recycled, by the number of buffers recycled. The current count is the criterion for accepting a higher layer send request. That is, if the Buffer Count is greater than or equal to the buffers required, the send request is accepted.

3.3.2 Best-effort Delivery Approach. In this approach, send request acceptance and initiation of PDU-scatter can be performed, if at least one buffer is available. Then, the process will be continued as and when buffers are available (or, recycled), thus, making the approach event driven (figure 5).

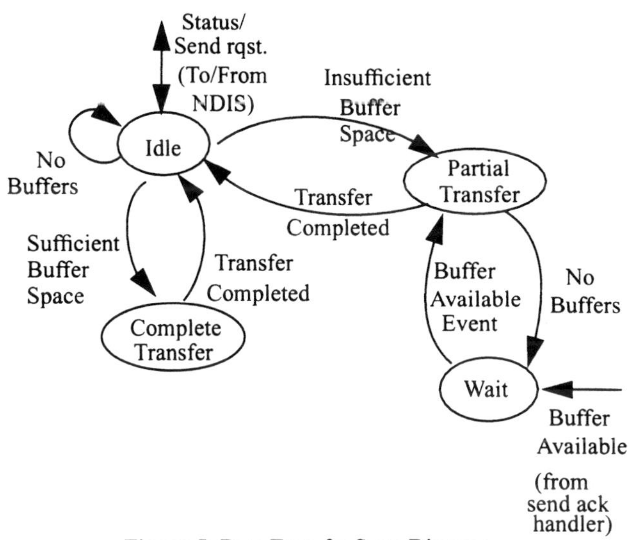

Figure 5. Data Transfer State Diagram

The steps involved in the approach are listed below:

1. Get PDU size and location in non-shared system space
2. Get a buffer from the buffer management entity
   If no buffer is available, wait until a buffer available event is available
3. Move user data into a shared buffer
4. Generate the TxmtSegment (or, TxmtEndSegment for the last or single segment) message to ASIC for segmentation and transmission
5. Repeat steps 2 through 4 until complete PDU is given for transmission

Much to our surprise the Best-effort delivery approach didn't perform better (in handling high PDU rate) over the Send All or None approach. The reason for low performance is that the Best-effort delivery approach required an efficient event signalling mechanism to signal the buffer recycling event. It couldn't be created efficiently in NDIS4.0 framework.

Implementation of either of the approaches requires a handler (the send handler). To handle ASIC acknowledgments, buffer recycle and indication of buffer availability status to either NDIS, in Send all or none approach, or send handler, in Best effort delivery approach, another handler (the send ack handler) is required.

3.4 Receive Data Module

The receive data flow from the ASIC to host is represented in the figure 6. The interface shown between the ASIC and Receive Data Module is abstract. The actual interface involves an interrupt processing module. The upper edge handlers of the module are part of the implementation of host and device service interface. These handlers assist PduFramer in framing a PDU that is received from line and scattered over one or more buffers by ASIC. The PduExtractor extracts and indicates the framed PDU to higher layers (through NDIS). The following sections identify the data structures required and division of functionality among the components.

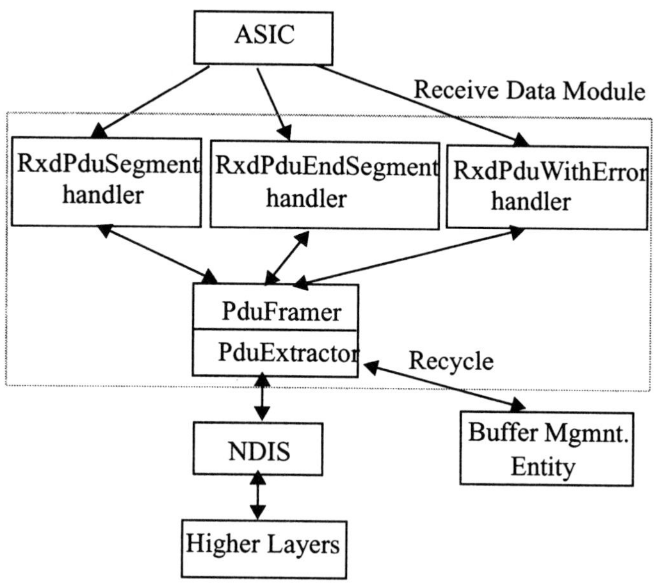

Figure 6. Receive Data Flow

3.4.1 Data structures. A table with entries of receive connection management data structures is required. The number of entries in the table is proportional to the number of receive connections supported in the system. The storage space for the table shall be allocated during the system initialization. An entry in the table is dynamically assigned, by the host, to a receive VC when established and unassigned when closed. An assigned entry is identified by a unique and simple connection ID (VcID) which the host shall make known to ASIC. The connection ID is of local significance, and the host requires it to be supplied by ASIC when indicating receives or other asynchronous events identifying a connection. The host uses it as an index to the table for accessing connection management data structures for purposes such as managing received PDU segments.

The framing of segments into a PDU requires a PDU_Framer_ Table (figure 7). The table entries are pointers to packet descriptors. The number of entries in the table is proportional to the maximum number of receive VCs supported in the system. The storage space for the table shall be allocated during the system initialization.

A packet descriptor describes a PDU mapped by one or more buffer descriptors (figure 6). It is allocated at the beginning of a PDU reception at the host and de-allocated at the completion of PDU assembly. Alternatively, one can allocate a packet descriptor just once, at the initialization of service, and re-initialize and reuse it for every next PDU reception to reduce allocation and de-allocation overhead. So, at any time, there can be only one packet descriptor for a VC.

The buffer descriptors are required to map portions of PDU scattered over one or more buffers. A buffer descriptor shall be allocated and mapped to an indicated PDU segment of a VC. It is then attached to the packet descriptor, belonging to the same VC, at the tail of the buffer descriptors list to preserve sequence integrity.

The allocation of the packet and buffer descriptors require allocation of respective pools during system initialization. The NDIS provides a framework for creating instances of pools, packet and buffer data structures along with facilities for recycling them.

```
// Create a packet descriptor pool
VOID
  NdisAllocatePacketPool(
     OUT PNDIS_STATUS Status,
     OUT PNDIS_HANDLE PoolHandle,
     IN UINT NumberOfDescriptors,
     IN UINT ProtocolReservedLength
     );

// Allocate a packet descriptor from packet descriptor pool
VOID
  NdisAllocatePacket(
     OUT PNDIS_STATUS Status,
     OUT PNDIS_PACKET *Packet,
     IN NDIS_HANDLE PoolHandle
     );

// Recycle Packet Descriptor to packet descriptor pool
VOID
  NdisFreePacket(
     IN PNDIS_PACKET Packet
     );

// Create Buffer Descriptor pool
VOID
  NdisAllocateBufferPool(
     OUT PNDIS_STATUS Status,
     OUT PNDIS_HANDLE PoolHandle,
     IN UINT NumberOfDescriptors
     );
```

```
// Allocate a Buffer Descriptor from Buffer Descriptor pool
VOID
  NdisAllocateBuffer(
    OUT PNDIS_STATUS Status,
    OUT PNDIS_BUFFER *Buffer,
    IN NDIS_HANDLE PoolHandle,
    IN PVOID VirtualAddress,
    IN UINT Length
    );

// Recycle Buffer Descriptor to buffer descriptor pool
VOID
  NdisFreeBuffer(
    IN PNDIS_BUFFER Buffer
    );
```

The result of a successful allocation call is either non-NULL pointers or returned success status. All data structures (including tables) are host memory resident. The framing process along with the data structures involved are shown in the figure 6. When a complete PDU is indicated to host, the framing process stops for that VC, and PDU extraction process is initiated.

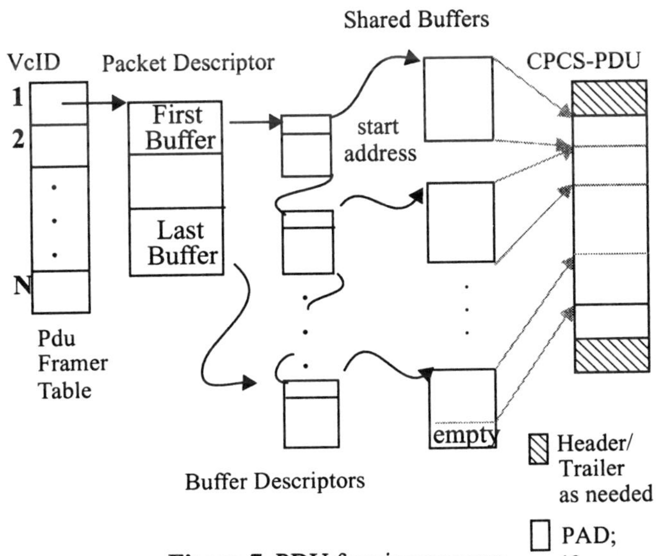

Figure 7. PDU framing process

The extraction process involves dynamic allocation of non-paged and non-shared system memory, based on the received PDU size. The NDIS framework provides a mechanism to calculate the size of PDU mapped by shared buffers. Once the memory is successfully allocated, packet and buffer descriptors are allocated to describe the allocated memory. The information content from shared buffers is moved to allocated memory one buffer at a time. The allocation of non-shared memory and transfer of contents is necessary to tackle the asynchronous nature of reads at higher layers. The shared buffers are then recycled, with the aid of Buffer Management Entity, to the ASIC's pool for reuse. The packet and buffer data structures describing buffers are recycled to respective pools using NDIS library calls. The extracted PDU is then indicated to interested higher layers. On return of control, the memory is then de-allocated. The above mechanism allows for simultaneous reception and framing of PDUs belonging to several VCs and facilitates efficient replenishment of shared buffers to ASIC receive pool.

The implementation requires the following non-concurrent handlers, as further interrupts to host CPU are disabled when the interrupt due to current receive indication is being processed. The handlers are RcvdPduSegment, RcvdPduEndSegment, RcvdPdu-WithError, PduFramer, and PduExtractor. Receive indication message could either be RcvdPduSegment, RcvdPduEndSegment, or RcvdPduWithError and processed by the associated handler. The functionality of these handlers are given below.

3.4.2 Handling Receive Indications. The handling of receive indications is triggered by the interrupt handler after determining the receive related interrupt. The message handlers does message specific processing along with processing common to all of them. The steps involved are given below with message specific processing identified in italics:

1. Get the connection ID from the ASIC's message
2. Use connection ID to index into the table of VC connection management data structures
3. Store the following in VC connection management data structure
   - Connection ID
   - Buffer context
   - Information length in the shared buffer
   - Segment Index
   - Segment type (to help PduFramer frame PDUs)
     - *RxdPduSegment handler sets it to either Beginning or Continuation of PDU*
     - RxdPduEndSegment handler sets it to either End or Single Segment PDU
   - Error indication
     - *RxdPduWithError handler uses it to indicate CS-PDU Length and CRC Errors*
4. Make a call to PDU Framer handler supplying connection management data structure
5. On return from PduFramer, set Segment Index to
   - *0 in RxdPduEndSegment and RxdPduWithError handler*
   - *next-value (current-value+1) in RxdPduSegment handler*

3.4.3 Handling PDU Framing. The steps involved in handling PDU framing are as follows. In the procedure outlined, erroneous and non-erroneous PDUs are treated alike. However, one may so choose to drop the erroneous PDUs.

1. Get the connection ID from VC connection management data structure
2. Get the Segment Type
3. Do the processing specific to Segment Type

```
if(Segment Type is Single Segment)
{
  - Allocate packet and buffer descriptors
  - Map the buffer with PDU segment by the buffer descriptor
  - Attach buffer descriptor to the packet descriptor
  - Make a call to PDU extraction handler supplying
    the packet descriptor
  - On return from PduExtractor,
    set Pdu_Framer_Table[connection ID] to NULL
  - return to RxdPduEndSegment or RxdPduWithError handler
}
else if(Segment Type is Beginning Segment)
{
  - Allocate packet and Buffer Descriptor
  - Map the buffer with PDU segment by buffer descriptor
  - Attach buffer descriptor to packet descriptor
  - Store packet descriptor pointer at
    Pdu_Framer_Table[connection ID]
  - return to RxdPduSegment handler
}
else if(Segment Type is Continuing Segment)
{
  - Allocate buffer descriptor and map the buffer with
    PDU segment
  - Get the associated packet descriptor pointer
    from Pdu_Framer_Table[connection ID]
  - Attach buffer descriptor to packet descriptor
  - return to RxdPduSegment handler
}
else if (Segment Type is End Segment)
{
  - Allocate buffer descriptor and map the buffer with
    PDU segment
  - Get associated packet descriptor pointer
    from Pdu_Framer_Table[connection ID]
  - Attach buffer descriptor to packet descriptor
  - Make a call to Pdu Extraction handler supplying
    pointer to packet descriptor
  - On return from PduExtractor,
    set Pdu_Framer_Table[connection ID] to NULL
  - return to RxdPduEndSegment or RxdPduWithError handler
}
endif
```

3.4.4 Handling PDU Extraction. The steps involved in extracting a PDU are given below:

1. Get payload data size and pointer to first buffer descriptor
2. Allocate, dynamically, memory
3. Allocate packet and buffer descriptors
4. Map the memory by buffer descriptor, and attach buffer descriptor to the packet descriptor
5. Move data from buffers to allocated memory pointed by payload pointer
6. Recycle buffer and packet/buffer descriptors
7. Indicate received PDU to NDIS
8. on return from NDIS de-allocate system memory
9. return to PduFramer handler

If resource allocation fail at any step either in PDU Framer or Extractor, do the following:

1. Release any prior allocated resources (i.e., memory and packet/buffer descriptors).
2. Abort the framing process.
3. Recycle buffers back to ASIC pool. The PDU currently being framed is lost.
4. Maintain the discarded PDU count, if needed.

The steps involved in retrieving a PDU (step 5) from one or more buffers are given below:

1. Get pointer to first_buffer descriptor
   Current_Buffer <-- First buffer descriptor in chain
2. If Current_Buffer pointer is not NULL, query current buffer descriptor for
   - Virtual address of mapped buffer
   - Shared buffer size
3. Move data from buffer to allocated memory pointed by the payload pointer
4. Increment the payload pointer by the number of bytes copied
5. Get pointer to next buffer descriptor in chain
   Next_Buffer <-- Next buffer descriptor in chain
6. Assign Current_Buffer <-- Next_Buffer
7. Repeat steps 2 through 6 until all of the PDU is moved

4.0 Performance Metric

The performance metrics of interest to a system designer are the *receive buffer recycle rate* and *number of host buffers allocated.* At high data rate traffic conditions, e.g., small sized PDUs with shorter inter-arrival times, buffers are consumed at a faster rate. If buffer recycling can't be performed at a high rate, it is difficult to keep up with the arriving data traffic. The effect of it is increased PDU latency and, ultimately, data loss if ASIC starts discarding received cells due to lack of reassembly space. A low probability scenario that quantifies the issue is as follows. Consider the scenario of a single cell length PDU with cell arrivals in every other cell slot on the link. The Peak Cell Rate, or the PDU rate in our case, in such a situation corresponds to half the link capacity, with the corresponding buffering requirement approximately at 185, 000 buffers/sec. for an OC-3 interface.

Therefore, in a typical finite buffer scenario, the buffers have to be recycled at an arbitrary rate that prevents latencies and loss. Given the number of buffers allocated (N) and average buffer consumption rate (C buffers/sec), one can arrive at the estimate of required average buffer recycle rate (R buffers/sec). Conversely, given the average buffer recycle and consumption rates, one can estimate the number of buffers required to sustain the arriving data traffic. We will present the time-domain relations among the aforementioned parameters in the typical case of 'C' greater than 'R' in the following section.

4.1 System Model

The Figure 8 models the system in hand. In the model, the server reassembles several PDUs, in the host provided buffers, at a time from the interleaved cell stream received from the line. The host is indicated, with a receive, when a buffer is filled with either a complete PDU (case of buffer size greater than the PDU size) or a portion of it (case of buffer size smaller than the PDU size). The host recycles a buffer, back to the free buffer pool for the device's use, after its contents are extracted. The buffers are recycled in the order they are given to host.

Characterizing the server, it is busy, if PDUs are being reassembled, and idle, if all the buffers are occupied. The average buffer recycle rate is, typically, slower than the average service rate of the server, and, therefore, it controls the PDU service rate.

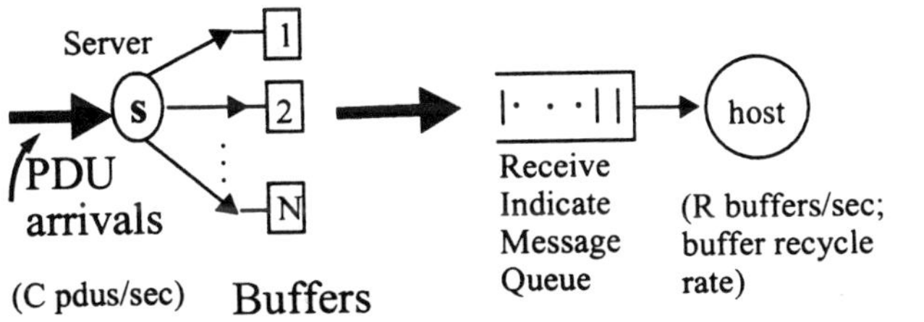

Figure 8. System Model

Using the above model, the time-domain expressions for the parameters of interest are formulated. In arriving at the expressions the following cases were considered:

+ a PDU is small enough to be assembled in one buffer (of a given size).
+ all active virtual circuits exhibit the same traffic characteristics

The formulations, thus, are as follows. The number of buffers to be allocated, to sustain the packet arrivals for 't' seconds given the buffer recycle and consumption rates, can be computed from the following relation.

$$N \geq (C - R) \bullet t;\ (C > R)$$

The required buffer recycle rate, to sustain the packet arrivals for 't' seconds given the number of buffers allocated and the buffer consumption rate, can be computed from the following relation.

$$R \geq (C - \frac{N}{t});\ (C > R)$$

5.0 Conclusions

The hardware implementation of ATM protocol processing, for data traffic handling, meets the requirements of processing power. Meeting the space requirements, however, is still challenging. The challenge can be met with the provision of buffer space in the host and an efficient buffer management mechanism to manage it. The Scatter and Gather mechanism meets the requirements of such a management mechanism. The performance of the Scatter and Gather mechanism depends on the two critical parameters; the *number of buffers allocated* and *receive buffer recycle rate*. These parameters are modeled to facilitate the design of system that meets the needs of a specific application.

6.0 References

[1] Microsoft Corporation, Windows NT DDK, ver. 4.0, http://www. microsoft.com, 1997.
[2] TranSwitch Corporation, Segmentation and Reassembly device with embedded RISC, http://www.transwitch.com, 1997.
[3] Martin De Prycker, Asynchronous Transfer Mode: Solution for Broadband ISDN, Ellis Horwood Limited, 1995.
[4] T. Shanley and D. Anderson, PCI System Architecture, Ed.3, Addison Wesley, 1995.
[5] PCISIG, PCI Local Bus Specifications, Rev. 2.1, 1995.

Track B: Real-Time

Session Chair: Gary Kessler
Hill Associates

New Protocols for Hard Real-time Communication in the Switched LAN Environment

Samphel Norden G. Manimaran
C. Siva Ram Murthy*
Department of Computer Science and Engineering
Indian Institute of Technology, Madras 600 036, INDIA

Abstract

The problem of real-time communication over a multiple access network has been well studied in the recent past. But, there has been no prior work addressing real-time communication over a Switched Local Area Network (SLAN), where several LAN segments are connected through a switch. In this paper, we propose real-time protocols for the SLAN. The proposed protocols are based on CSMA/CD with deterministic collision resolution and belong to the dynamic planning based category, where an admission test is performed for guaranteeing message transmission. This test is based on the worst case channel access time that can elapse before a particular node can transmit its message. We also compute the worst case buffer requirement at the switch. We study the effectiveness of the proposed protocols through extensive simulation studies.

Keywords: *Real-time protocols, Multiple access network, Switched LAN, Collision resolution, Planning based protocols, Admission test.*

1. Introduction

In a distributed real-time system, timely execution of tasks and delivery of messages across the communication network within their associated deadlines are of prime importance. These time-constrained messages are the basis for applications that operate in a real-time environment. Applications are either of the hard real-time category, where message loss is not tolerated, or of the soft real-time category, where some amount of message loss is allowed (as in multimedia applications).

*Author for correspondence. Email:murthy@iitm.ernet.in

Every message in a real-time system is characterized by its service time requirement and its deadline [9]. In such a system, the scheduling mechanism should not only ensure guarantees on message delivery, but should also be adaptive to the dynamic nature of message traffic. An adaptive protocol should be able to dynamically prioritize messages, based on the degree of criticality of the messages.

The most common scheme for communication in a local area network (LAN) is the multiple access network [4]. In this type of network, nodes transmit messages via a shared channel (bus). Only one message can be successfully transmitted over the channel at any time. A collision occurs if the transmission of two or more messages overlap in time. Based on how collisions are handled the multiple access protocols can be broadly divided into three categories : (i) Inference avoiding protocols such as the CSMA based protocols [3] that do not take the past history of the channel into account, (ii) Inference seeking protocols [1] which make inferences based on collision history, (iii) and Deterministic or Collision-free protocols such as Time Division Multiple Access (TDMA) which seek to avoid collisions.

Numerous real-time LAN communication protocols have been devised to transmit messages in distributed real-time environments. The Virtual Time CSMA (VTCSMA) [12] uses a probabilistic approach to collision resolution. In another proposal [6], the rate monotonic algorithm with an appropriate priority arbitration scheme is used in the LAN for real-time communication. The Deterministic Collision

0-8186-8810-6/98 $10.00 © 1998 IEEE

Resolution Protocol (CSMA/CD-DCR) [5] was proposed with an approach to resolve collision in a deterministic way by arbitrating between the nodes of the LAN in some implicit order. We had extended this protocol to a new protocol called Modified Deterministic Collision Resolution-Preorder (MDCR-P) [8] to support multiple packet[1] messages. We had also proposed the laxity[2] based deterministic collision resolution protocol (LDCR-G) [8] with guarantees, and the Modified DCR (MDCR-G) protocol [8] with guarantees, which belong to the dynamic planning based category and ensure predictability of message transmission using admission tests.

Due to the proliferation of real-time multimedia applications such as video-conferencing and video-on-demand, the need for bandwidth has tremendously increased. The real-time LAN is unable to cope with the current demand for bandwidth. A solution to this problem is the Switched LAN (SLAN) [10]. In a SLAN, nodes are connected through a local bus to form a *LAN segment*. Several LAN segments are interconnected by a switch. This approach offers greater bandwidth by reducing the number of nodes sharing a channel, resulting in less contention for that channel. However, solving the problem of inadequate bandwidth is not sufficient. Since these applications are of real-time nature, there is a need to develop protocols for guaranteeing message transmission before the associated deadlines in a SLAN. We propose the Extended LDCR (ELDCR) and the Extended MDCR (EMDCR) protocols for supporting real-time communication in the SLAN.

The rest of this paper is organised as follows. Section 2 provides an overview of the SLAN and prior work in this area. We then introduce the motivation and present the features of the proposed protocols in Section 3. In Section 4, we describe our simulation model and analyze the simulation results. Finally, in Section 5, we make some concluding remarks.

2. Overview of Switched LAN

As mentioned earlier, the switch or remote bridge is an electronic device that connects the different LAN segments, and does the job of forwarding the packets from a node in one LAN segment to a node in another segment. By dedicating links between the switch and different nodes, we can reduce the channel contention as well as the load on a particular link, and consequently offer more bandwidth for applications that utilize that link. Further every node is able to choose a link to the switch depending on its bandwidth requirements. Figure 1 depicts the typical SLAN topology.

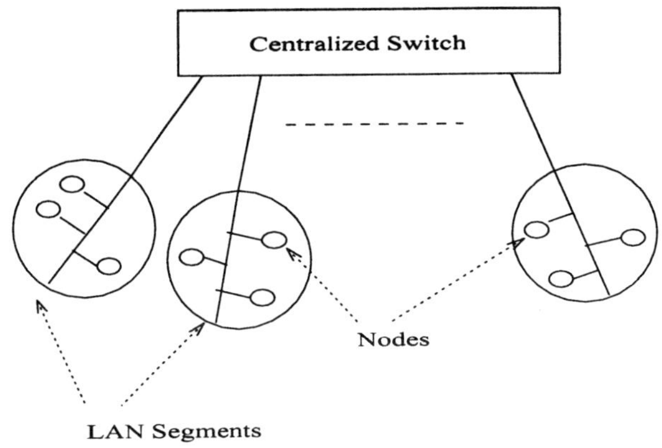

Figure 1. SLAN Topology

2.1. Switch Architecture and Design

The architecture of the switch can be centralized, distributed, or hybrid. In a centralized architecture (see Figure 2), there is a single main CPU (MCPU) which handles all packets coming from every LAN segment (MAC port) as shown. The distributed architecture requires a processor (MCPU) with buffer space for every MAC port, and the processors are interconnected using a cross-bar switch. Each MAC port has DMA capability to read/write the main memory of the MCPU. The MCPU does the forwarding of the packet. The tasks performed by the MCPU in real-time are: buffer management, bridging, and execution of the IEEE 802.1d spanning tree protocol.

To understand the working of SLAN, let us trace the flow of a packet that arrives at the switch from a LAN segment destined to the same/another LAN segment (see Figure 3). The MAC module stores the received packet into an allocated space in the buffer memory. The packet is then processed by the switching module by referring to the filtering database. Processing involves examining the header of the packet to decide whether the packet is to be filtered (discarded) or is to be forwarded. If the destination MAC is connected to the same port on which the packet arrived, then the

[1] Packet is a basic unit of data.

[2] Laxity is the maximum amount of time that a message can be delayed before transmission.

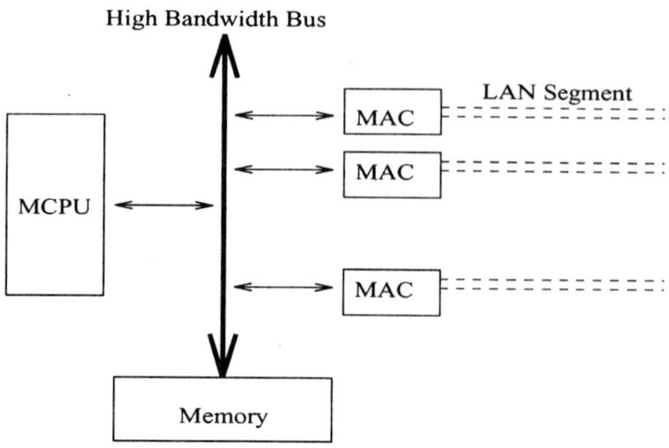

Figure 2. Centralized Switch Architecture

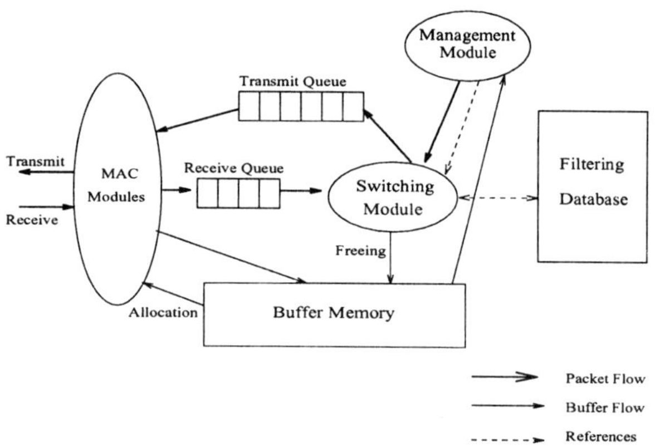

Figure 3. Internal Working of a Switch

packet is discarded. If not, the filtering database, which is a simplified routing table, will contain information about the port number for the destination MAC. The packet will then be placed in the transmit queue and subsequently forwarded by the MAC module to the destination LAN segment after which the buffer space is deallocated.

2.2. Existing SLAN Protocols

The most popular protocol in the SLAN environment is the CSMA/CD based Ethernet [7]. However, it suffers from some critical limitations that render it unsuitable for real-time traffic. They are :

- Absence of guaranteed channel access to any node due to the probabilistic nature of collision resolution in CSMA/CD. This by far, is the most serious limitation, especially with respect to hard real-time traffic where the consequences of missing the message deadlines can be catastrophic, when predictability of message transmission cannot be ensured.

- Lack of control over the share of throughput between the nodes connected in the network. This may lead to priority inversion, when we have multiple prioritized classes of traffic.

When we consider the 100Base-T (IEEE 802.3u) "fast Ethernet" protocol [11], the problems of using CSMA/CD are again introduced. The 802.12 demand priority protocol [11] has a round-robin scheduling policy, which may ensure fairness at the expense of priority inversion, making it unsuitable for heterogeneous real-time traffic. The presence of just two priority levels highlights this problem. Also once a node accesses the channel, it can transmit a single frame only. This restriction limits its use to fixed length packets. This problem is worsened when different nodes generate frames of different lengths. The 802.12 protocol would be unfair to nodes generating shorter frames, which could be critical in the context of real-time applications. Another problem with the 802.12 standard is that since it does not reserve network resources according to the dynamic node requirements, it cannot be used in an environment where the real-time traffic load of the network fluctuates due to the admission/rejection of new real-time messages.

To the best of our knowledge, there has been no prior work to support hard real-time communication in a SLAN. In this paper, we propose new dynamic planning based protocols for guaranteeing transmission of time-constrained messages in the SLAN.

3. New Planning Based SLAN Protocols

From the above discussion, it can be observed that there is a need to develop protocols that can guarantee message transmission, as well as allocate bandwidth in an equitable manner. Predictability in message transmission is achieved by bounding the worst case channel access delay experienced by a newly arrived message. In a dynamic planning based protocol, when a message arrives at a node, the message scheduler at the node dynamically determines the feasibility of scheduling this message without jeopardizing the guarantees made for the previously admitted messages.

The LDCR-G [8] and MDCR-G [8] are dynamic planning based real-time LAN protocols that satisfy the above requirements. The protocols use notifiers for disseminating message information in a distributed environment.

We extend these protocols to propose the Extended LDCR (ELDCR) and Extended MDCR (EMDCR) for hard real-time communication in the SLAN.

In this section, we first introduce the LDCR-G and MDCR-G LAN protocols and their admission policy, which is extended in our proposed SLAN protocols. We then present the new planning based real-time protocols for implementation in the SLAN environment. The new protocols guarantee message transmission using a new admission test. We prove the correctness of the admission test proposed and derive a finite bound for the buffer requirements at the centralized switch as well as at a node in the SLAN environment.

3.1. LDCR-G : A Real-time LAN Protocol

The LDCR-G protocol admits a message based on the worst case channel access delay experienced by the message, and ensures successful transmission of all the admitted messages. The semantics of the protocol is as follows: *messages are admitted based on an estimate of worst case message service time, and their transmission is guaranteed if their service times do not exceed this estimate.*

The protocol uses the notion of *message deferment*, by which we mean that a message with higher laxity is deferred to allow messages with lower laxities to be transmitted, thus preventing the potential priority inversion, where laxity is used as a measure of priority. In LDCR-G, the nodes of the LAN are mapped to the vertices of a Collision Resolution (CR) tree. The CR tree is a binary tree which is traversed whenever collision in message transmission occurs and access arbitration must take place between nodes. The traversal of the CR tree is in pre order, i.e. when a collision occurs, the next three slots are reserved for the root, the left subtree, and the right subtree,respectively. Each node maintains a queue of messages sorted on the increasing order of laxity. The queues are modelled as *delta lists* [2] in the actual implementation, as this approach involves minimal overhead when updating the laxities of messages. The working of the protocol is as follows:

1. Contention Mode : Idle channel

(a) Each node examines the message at the head of its queue. If the laxity of the message is negative, the message is dropped.

(b) Otherwise, it attempts to transmit notifier for the message. The notifier is a broadcast message containing the service time (C_i), and deadline (D_i).

(c) If the notifier transmission is successful, the message is transmitted.

(d) If a collision occurs during notifier transmission, all nodes enter into CR mode by traversing the CR tree in pre order.

2. CR Mode : Pre order tree traversal

(a) When a node n_i gets its turn in the CR mode, it transmits its notifier. Thus every other node is informed of the message requirements of node n_i.

(b) If the laxity of a message (first message at queue of n_i) is less than a threshold (but non-negative), then the message is transmitted, else the message is deferred and pre order traversal continues. If two or more messages have the laxity less than or equal to the threshold value, the preference is given to message with shorter service time. This minimizes the time that the channel is blocked, thereby improving the chances of successful transmission for subsequent messages.

(c) Even after the CR tree is completely traversed, if some deferred messages are still to be transmitted, the protocol enters into the LLF mode.

3. LLF Mode : To transmit deferred messages

(a) In the LLF mode, all the deferred messages are transmitted, based on the laxity order of messages among nodes. This phase is required to enable those messages, that arrived in the current *epoch*[3], to be transmitted before the next epoch. By doing this, the overhead incurred due to collision between messages of two different epochs is eliminated.

(b) If all the messages are either transmitted or dropped, the next epoch begins.

3.2. MDCR-G : A Real-time LAN Protocol

This protocol is based on the MDCR protocol proposed in [8]. The semantics of the admission policy are similar to that of the LDCR-G protocol whereby a message once admitted is guaranteed to be transmitted. The working of the MDCR protocol is summarised below for ease of understanding :

1. The node i senses the channel, and attempts to transmit the notifier (C_i, D_i) of a message.

[3] The time elapsed from the time of collision detection to the time of completion of CR and LLF modes, that includes the time for transmission of messages at nodes.

2. If no collision occurs and the message notifier is transmitted successfully, the node i begins transmission of the message provided $C_i \leq D_i$, else message is dropped. During transmission, no other node tries to transmit over the channel.

3. If notifier transmission fails, all nodes enter the CR mode.

4. In the CR mode, the CR tree is traversed in pre-order where the current node transmits a notifier for its message (if any), and then actually transmits the message if $C_i \leq D_i$, else the message is dropped.

3.3. Admission Test

We now present the admission test which ensures predictability of message transmission in the LAN. We subsequently extend this test to ensure predictability in the SLAN. The key aspect of this test is that *it computes the worst case channel access delay incurred before a newly arrived message can be transmitted.* If this delay called WCT allows the message to still be transmitted before its deadline, then the message is admitted into the system, otherwise the message is dropped. For achieving this predictability in message transmission, we have derived an equation for computing the WCT taken by a node to access the channel before it begins transmission of the newly arrived message. We use this value to perform the admission test that is crucial to ensure predictability of message transmission. The manner of computation of WCT is given below :

We first define the important terms used in the test :
Queue : Each node maintains a queue of messages in the order of arrival, which are to be transmitted in subsequent epochs. M_{est} : worst case service time estimate, N : number of nodes, $Rank$: position of message in the queue, Pos_tree : position of node in the tree, N_col : maximum number of collisions in the tree traversal, $Time\_for\_Not$: time for notifier transmission, t : current time;
(a) First we compute the time slots used for transmission of all messages, which are to be transmitted in epochs, prior to the epoch in which the new message is to be transmitted. The number of such epochs is captured by the rank term, k. This time is
$T_{prior} = (M_{est} + Time\_for\_Not) * (N * (k - 1))$.
(b) Next we compute the time elapsed due to transmission of messages, at nodes above the current node in the pre order traversal of the CR tree. This time is
$T_{current} = (M_{est} + Time\_for\_Not) * (Pos\_tree - 1)$.
(c) Lastly, we add the overhead due to collision. This time is $T_{oh} = N\_col * k$. Combining these times, we get :

$$WCT_j^k = T_{prior} + T_{current} + T_{oh}$$

The admission test (AT) for message at node j having rank k at the arrival time t of the message is given as:

$$WCT_j^k + C_j^k \leq D_j^k - t$$

There is a tradeoff between performance and the strictness of the admission test. A larger value for M_{est}, implies a more pessimistic estimate of WCT, which results in lower performance. Thus, the value of M_{est} should be carefully chosen depending on the application requirements. The validity of the test AT has already been shown in [8].

3.4. System Model for the SLAN

We now present the system model for the SLAN, along with a few observations.

- The maximum number of nodes possible on any segment is known to all nodes.

- Centralized switch architecture is assumed. The choice of centralized architecture is due to the prohibitive overhead in distributed architectures. Since in a distributed approach, every processor has its own associated filtering database (FDB), the destination of the inter segment messages cannot be resolved in a single lookup of the FDB as in the centralized scheme.

- The number of segments connected by the switch is known to all nodes in each segment.

- Every pair of nodes has atmost one switch between them, i.e. a message needs to be transmitted through atmost two hops. This is not the limitation of the protocol. This assumption has been made to simplify the explanation of worst case computation time.

3.5. ELDCR and EMDCR : SLAN Protocols

The ELDCR and EMDCR protocols for real-time communication in the SLAN are based on the LDCR-G and the MDCR-G protocols respectively. We had earlier proposed an admission test AT, which we will now extend to support guaranteed message transmission over the SLAN. Apart from the admission policy, the working of the ELDCR and EMDCR are the same as in the LDCR-G and MDCR-G protocols.

The key idea of the SLAN admission test is that *it assumes worst case channel access time* (WCT) *at the source LAN segment, switch, and the destination LAN segment.* Thus, the WCT computation must incorporate two aspects which are characteristic of the SLAN architecture:

- The inter segment message should access the channel at the source LAN segment, in order to reach the switch.
- The message buffered at the switch must access the channel at the destination LAN segment to reach the destination node.

The manner of computation of the WCT and the admission test is given in the following section.

3.6. New Admission Test for the SLAN

We now present the core of our real-time SLAN protocols, namely, the admission test that ensures predictability of message transmission. We also prove that if a message passes the admission test proposed, it is guaranteed to be transmitted before its deadline. The admission test is the basis for the dynamic planning based nature of our protocol, whereby once a message is admitted, guarantees given to previous messages will not be violated, similar to the semantics of the LDCR-G and MDCR-G protocols. The admission test is split into two phases :

Phase 1 : We perform the first phase of the admission test (AT_1) within the LAN segment for both inter segment and intra segment messages :

$$WCT_{segment} + C_i \leq D_i - t$$

Phase 2 : The second phase (AT_2) intended for inter segment messages is as follows :

$$WCT_{max} + C_i \leq D_i - t$$

The term WCT as before, represents the worst case channel access time. For the phase AT_1, the motivation is as given earlier, and has to be performed for all messages irrespective of whether they are inter segment or intra segment messages. This is because in both the situations, the node has to access the channel and transmit the message upto the centralised switch from where the message is forwarded or discarded depending on whether the destination is in a different segment or in the same LAN segment, respectively.

For the second phase AT_2 intended for inter segment messages, WCT_{max} is computed as follows. We recreate the Worst Case Collision Resolution (WCCR) tree for the largest (worst case) LAN segment, at the sending node. The WCCR tree is actually the CR tree for the largest LAN segment, augmented with $(n - 1)$ virtual nodes for an SLAN with n segments. We assign the $(n - 1)$ virtual nodes to all LAN segments other than the worst case LAN segment. Inter segment messages from a node in a particular LAN segment will always arrive at the assigned virtual node. In Figure 4, for a 3-segment SLAN (LAN_1, LAN_2, LAN_3) with LAN_2 being the worst case LAN segment, we show the WCCR tree.

The concept of a virtual node is to abstract the switch and the source node into a single node that is virtually attached to the CR tree of the worst case LAN segment. This allows us to model inter segment and intra segment message transmission in the same way. If the worst case segment is the destination segment, then successful message transmission is achieved when the virtual node accesses the channel on the destination LAN segment. Therefore, we have logically reduced the two hops necessary for inter segment message transmission into a single hop by using the virtual node abstraction. This further helps simplify the computation of the worst case channel access delay.

Two schemes for assigning the virtual nodes to the LAN segments can be adopted in order to compute the WCT. The worst case time, WCT_{wccr} for the WCCR tree is computed by the source node, by assuming that the LAN segment to which it belongs, is assigned the last virtual node in the WCCR. By doing this, the source node can accurately compute the largest (upper bound) amount of time that it has to wait before its message can access the channel. Alternately, LAN segments could be assigned unique positions in the WCCR tree. It is also possible to give higher priority to the virtual nodes, by positioning them at the beginning of the pre order traversal of the CR tree. This can be justified since we are adding a relatively small number of virtual nodes, as generally, there will be fewer LAN segments compared to the number of nodes within a segment. Even though the slots assigned to the virtual nodes may be idle most of the time, they do not waste much bandwidth. This allows higher priority to inter segment traffic over intra segment traffic.

The worst case time WCT_{wccr}, is added to the worst case time $WCT_{segment}$ from the phase AT_1 to generate the WCT_{max} value, used in phase AT_2.

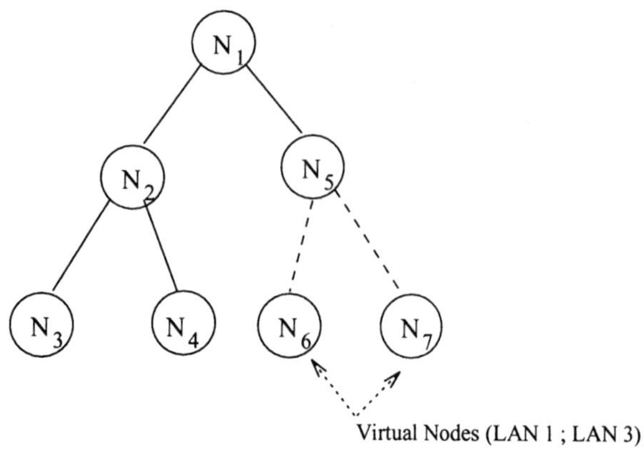

Figure 4. WCCR Tree for LAN_2

Thus the equation for WCT_{max} is :

$$WCT_{max} = WCT_{wccr} + WCT_{segment}$$

3.7. Proof of Correctness

To prove the correctness of the message admission phase AT_2, we need to highlight the following issues involved in computing the worst case channel access delay accurately, in spite of a lack of knowledge on the global state of the system.

1. For a message at some node in a LAN segment, there is no *a priori* knowledge of the destination, i.e., the destination LAN segment of the message is not known to the source.

2. Another problem that arises is when several nodes in different LAN segments simultaneously try to send messages to a node (of some LAN segment). There is no knowledge of the order in which these simultaneous messages will be serviced by the centralized switch.

We make the following claim of correctness for AT_2.

Claim : If a message passes AT_2, and its service time is less than or equal to the worst case service time estimate M_{est}, then the protocol guarantees the successful transmission of the message.

Proof : There are two cases :

case (i) : Source and destination nodes of a message belong to the same LAN segment.

If AT_1 holds, guarantees for intra segment LAN traffic are not violated as explained in [8].

case (ii) : Source and destination nodes of a message belong to different LAN segments and the phase AT_2 is applied. The two problems that contribute to the lack of global knowledge are handled as follows :

(a) In case (ii), the worst case situation occurs when the destination of the messages is a node in the LAN segment with the largest number of nodes (worst case LAN segment). The WCCR tree is the tree representing the worst case LAN segment. This tackles the first problem, since we compute WCT using the WCCR tree.

(b) The worst case delay a message can encounter at the switch would be atmost the channel access time for a virtual node (LAN segment) that is assigned the last position in the WCCR tree. This worst case scenario is assumed while computing WCT in admission phase AT_2. Hence, the order in which the messages are serviced by the switch does not violate the guarantees.

Thus, our claim of guaranteed message transmission holds as we use the upper bound on channel access delay for admitting messages.

3.8. Buffer Capacity at the Switch

We will now focus on the issue of the capacity of the buffer that is maintained at the centralized switch. Since in reality, the size of the buffer in any commercial switch is finite, we need to show that the number of messages buffered at any time cannot exceed a finite worst case upper bound, which we define as Buf_{max} for our discussion.

We define the upper bound on the buffer capacity at any instant as :

$$Buf_{max} = \Sigma_{i=1}^{n}(N_i * \lceil (WCT_{max}/t_i^{epoch})\rceil)$$

where n is the number of LAN segments, N_i is the number of nodes in segment i, t_i^{epoch} is the time for an epoch in segment i where an epoch is the time taken for message transmission in collision resolution and least laxity first modes of operation in the admission test for the ELDCR protocol, and WCT_{max} is the worst case channel access delay as explained in the ELDCR protocol.

The time for an epoch in segment i is :

$$t_i^{epoch} = (M_{est} + Time\_for\_Not) * N_i + N\_col$$

where M_{est} is the estimated service time used in computation of WCT, $Time\_for\_Not$ is the overhead for notifier transmission, N_i is the number of nodes in segment i, and N_col is the number of collisions in one round of collision resolution.

Claim : The worst case bound for the buffer size at the centralized switch is Buf_{max}.

Proof : The result is proved by adopting the worst case scenario as in the derivation for the admission phase AT_2. Consider a message m_{new}, that has been admitted at a LAN segment. The worst case channel access delay used in the admission test is WCT_{max} for m_{new}. We need to compute the number of messages that can arrive at the switch before m_{new} can be transmitted.

There may be several messages that have been admitted already and will access the channel within the time interval $[t, t + WCT_{max}]$, where t is the time at which m_{new} was admitted. These messages will be buffered at the centralized switch. To find the maximum number of such messages, we estimate the maximum number of epochs t_i^{epoch}, that will elapse for the segment i within the interval $[t, t + WCT_{max}]$. In the epoch t_i^{epoch}, the worst case would occur when all the N_i nodes transmit their messages. Therefore, the maximum number of messages that can arrive at the switch from a LAN segment is upper bounded by $(N_i * \lceil (WCT_{max}/t_i^{epoch}) \rceil)$. Then, the summation of the above expression over all the LAN segments gives the worst case bound on the buffer size at the switch, Buf_{max}. Note that in practice, Buf_{max} will never be reached as all the messages stored in the buffer will access the channel within the interval of WCT_{max}. Hence the actual buffer capacity will be less than Buf_{max}.

4. Simulation Studies

To study the effectiveness of the proposed protocols, we have conducted extensive simulation studies. For each simulation run, 60,000 messages were generated for the SLAN. The simulation experiments were performed at 95% confidence levels. The simulation parameters and the performance metrics used are given below.

Simulation Parameters

N : Number (No.) of nodes on the network.

$N_{segment}$: No. of segments connected to the switch.

M : Average message length (or service time) in slots. Message arrival follows a Poisson distribution on a per node basis. A message is characterized by the service time - C_i slots, deadline - D_i slots, and whether it is an inter segment or intra segment message.

M_{est} : Estimate of worst case service time which is used in computation of WCT for the admission tests.

α : Laxity parameter which decides the deadline of messages, directly proportional to deadline. The deadline is uniformly chosen in the interval $(C_i, \alpha * C_i)$.

Performance Metrics

Success Ratio (SR) : This is defined as the ratio of the total number of messages transmitted successfully to the total number of messages that arrived in the system.

Effective Channel Utilization (ECU) : This is the ratio of the time slots used for successful transmission to the time slots that elapse until all messages are transmitted or dropped.

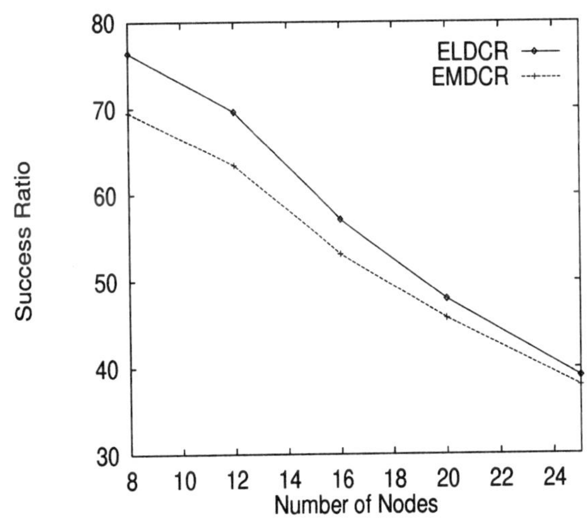

Fig.5a Effect of N on SR

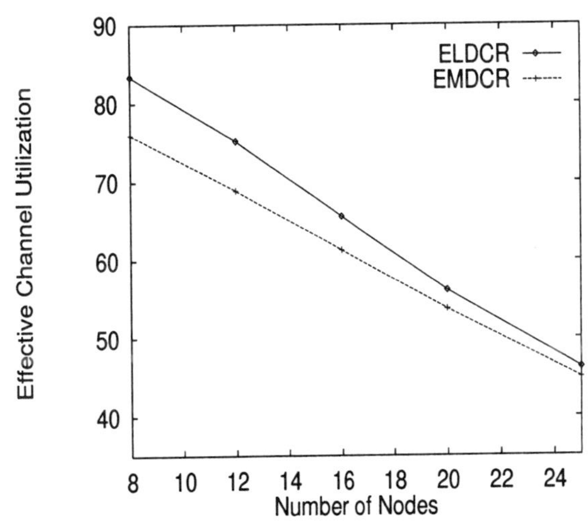

Fig.5b Effect of N on ECU

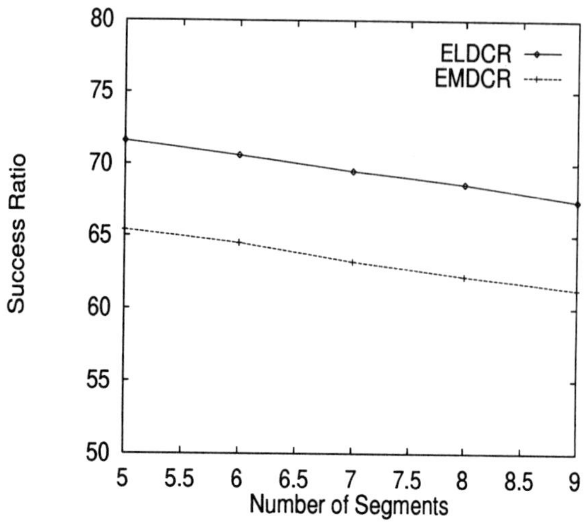

Fig.6a Effect of N_{seg} on SR

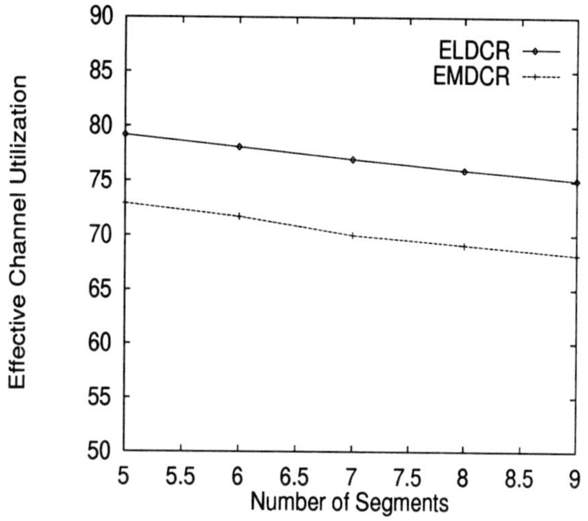

Fig.6b Effect of N_{seg} on ECU

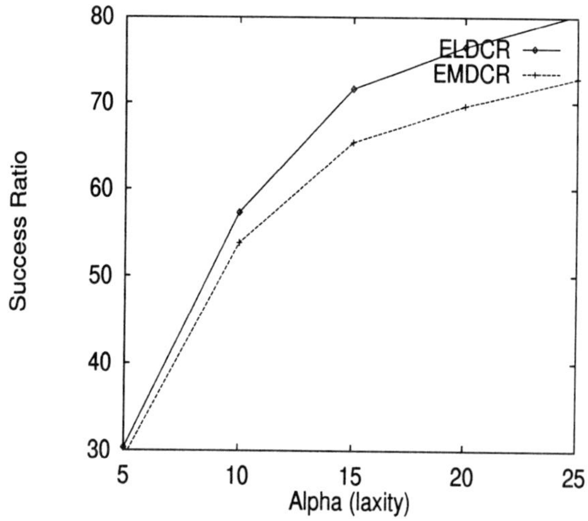

Fig.7a Effect of α on SR

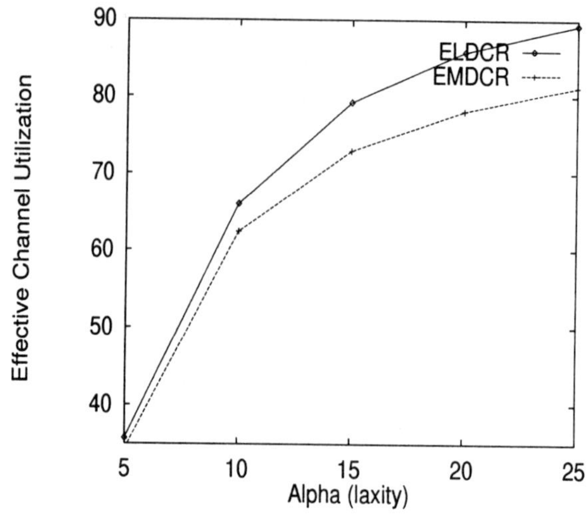

Fig.7b Effect of α on ECU

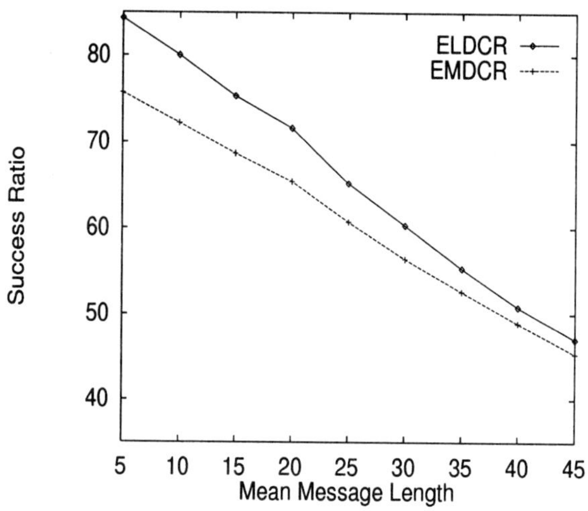

Fig.8a Effect of M_{est} on SR

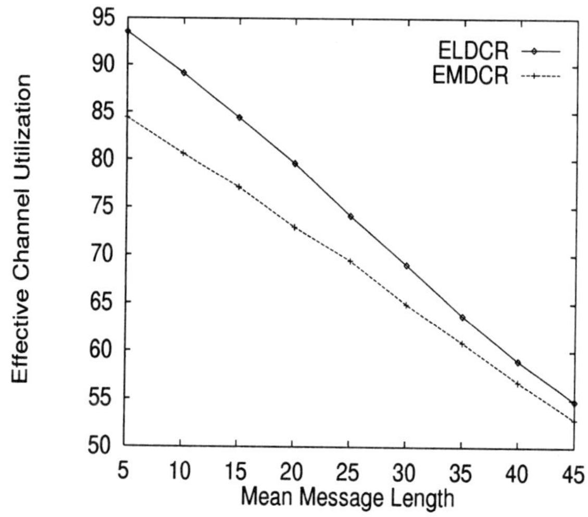

Fig.8b Effect of M_{est} on ECU

Effect of No. of Nodes / No. of Segments

With an increase in the number of nodes as well as the number of segments, more traffic is generated, and as a consequence the contention for the channel increases leading to more messages missing their deadlines (Figs. 5-6a). This increase in traffic is due to message arrivals following a Poisson distribution on a per node basis. This contributes to a fall in channel utilization (Figs. 5-6b), as less number of messages utilize the channel for successful transmission. ELDCR shows much better performance, in both the metrics due to its dynamic prioritization approach.

Effect of α (Laxity Parameter)

As expected, both SR and ECU increase (Fig. 7a-b) with increasing α as the deadlines of the messages also increase. This allows more number of messages to be successfully transmitted.

Effect of Worst Case Service Time Estimate

The SR and ECU decrease with increasing values of the worst case message length (service time) estimate, as WCT computed in the admission tests increases resulting in lower SR and ECU (Fig. 8a-b). This reflects the inherent tradeoff between the strictness of the admission test (using large M_{est}) versus the performance. At small values of M_{est}, the protocol is essentially performing like a best effort protocol, where we cannot guarantee that an admitted message will be transmitted as the criteria for the correctness of the admission test AT_2 may become invalid.

5. Conclusions

In this paper, we have addressed the problem of real-time communication over a Switched LAN, which is emerging as a strong candidate for supporting bandwidth-rich applications. The ELDCR and EMDCR protocols proposed are among the first for hard real-time communication on the SLAN and belong to the dynamic planning based category in which our admission test ensures predictability of message transmission. We have derived an expression to show that the buffer capacity at the centralized switch is finite. The effectiveness of the proposed protocols have been studied through simulation over a wide range of parameters and different performance metrics. Our simulation results reveal that the ELDCR is superior to the EMDCR protocol for both the performance metrics - success ratio and effective channel utilization.

References

[1] J. Capetanakis. Tree algorithm for packet broadcast channels. *IEEE Trans. on Communications*, 27(10):1476–1484, January 1979.

[2] D. Comer and D. Stevens. *Internetworking with TCP/IP-Volume II.* Prentice-Hall International Inc., Englewood Cliffs, NJ, U.S.A., 1994.

[3] L. Kleinrock. Packet switching in radio channels : Part 1 - carrier sense multiple access modes and their throughput-delay characteristics. *IEEE Trans. on Communications*, 23(12):1400–1416, December 1975.

[4] J. Kurose, M. Schwartz, and Y. Yemini. Multiple-access protocols and time-constrained communication. *ACM Computing Surveys*, 16(1):43–70, March 1984.

[5] G. Le Lann and N. Rivierre. Real-time communications over broadcast networks : The csma-dcr and the dod-csma-cd protocols. *Technical Report, Institut National De Recherche En Informatique Et En Automatique, France*, March 1993.

[6] N. Malcolm and W. Zhao. Hard real-time communication in multiple-access networks. *Real-time Systems*, 8:35–77, 1995.

[7] R. Metcalfe and D. R.Boggs. Ethernet distributed packet switching for local computer networks. *Communications of the ACM*, 19(7):395–403, 1976.

[8] S. Norden, S. Balaji, G. Manimaran, and C. Siva Ram Murthy. Deterministic best effort and planning based protocols for real-time communication in multiple-access networks. *Proc. of the 6th IEEE International Workshop on Parallel and Distributed Real-time Systems*, March 1998.

[9] J. Stankovic and K. Ramamritham. *Hard Real-time Systems.* Computer Society Press of IEEE, 1730, Massachussets Avenue,Washington D.C., 1993.

[10] D. Venkatesulu and T. Gonsalves. Efficient fault-tolerant reliable broadcast in an extended lan. *To appear in Computer Communications.*

[11] G. Watson and M. Molle. 100 base-t/ieee 802.12/packet switching. *IEEE Communications magazine*, August 1996.

[12] W. Zhao and K. Ramamritham. Virtual time csma protocols for hard real-time communication. *IEEE Trans. on Software Engineering*, 13(8):938–52, August 1987.

Hierarchical Architecture for Real Time Causal Delivery

A. Abouaissa & A. Benslimane

LaRIS - l'Institut Polytechnique de Sévenans Belfort FRANCE
Email : Abdelhafid.Abouaissa@utbm.fr, Abder.Benslimane@utbm.fr

Abstract

The evolution of communication technology makes possible distributed real-time multimedia applications. Unlike traditional data traffic, real-time multimedia traffic requires that temporal relationships among media units must be maintained, and needs that all sites impose a consistent causal order to receive the same media at a given time. Yet delay jitter, the absence of global clock, and the crash failure may disrupt these temporal relationships. This paper proposes a new hierarchical architecture of k-local groups, where k represents the number of local groups composing the group communication system. This architecture ensures real-time causal ordering, and guarantees a automatic reconfiguration, in presence of a crash failure, by insuring at least a partial real-time communication between active local groups, while keeping the amount of control information within a reasonable size.

Keyword : *causal ordering, real-time, distributed multimedia systems, delta-causality, group communication system.*

1. INTRODUCTION

Recently, the progress of high-speed networks based on optic fibres allows to integrate different types of media units in distributed real-time multimedia applications, such as video-conference, tele-teaching. These systems require that the temporal relationships between media units must be maintained in order to guarantee a continuous data transfer.

As a multimedia application is made up of a set of media units types, all members belonging to the group communication system must playback the same media units in the same order as their sent. Asynchronous transfer-mode (ATM) technology is widely accepted platform for future integrated services networks. Due to the nature of asynchronous transmission, the temporal relationships among media units tend to be disrupted that the playback discontinuity will be perceptible to humans. The asynchrony of communication mediums can be qualified as one of the major source of the non-determinism in distributed systems, which in turn is a major cause of problems when implementing distributed applications.

Causal ordering [18] reduces much of the communication medium asynchrony. This abstraction guarantees that whenever a message is delivered to a site, then all causally prior messages have been already delivered to it. However, the causal ordering can not ensure real-time data traffic that is governed by the need for low delivery-time in real-time multicast mechanism.

Several protocols [7, 18, 21, 22] have been presented to implement causal ordering of messages. These protocols use the concept of the logical clocks and time stamps [13]. Logical clocks are a good tool to capture causal ordering messages at a logical level, but they increment only when an event happens, such as the transmission or reception of a message. So, they have little correlation to physical time. Real-time systems require the notion of physical time because of the constraints imposed by the deadline on the data, for example real-time multimedia data traffic requires that temporal relationships among media units must be maintained during the communication. Therefore, logical clocks are not appropriate for real-time systems. As there is no physical global clock in a distributed systems, it is necessary to synchronize local clocks in order to guarantee these temporal relationships. In other hand, multimedia data has a limit lifetime after which it can not be used. Thus, data is only useful during a certain interval of time. Consequently, the dependency on previous messages applies to it only for a limited time. This time constraints is referred to as Δ *-causality* [2, 24], and is defined formally in the next section.

In multimedia applications, the process playing the role of the sender collects media units and sends them to the receiver, to be played back. A simple way to connect processes in one application is to build a

0-8186-8810-6/98 $10.00 © 1998 IEEE

virtual connection between each sender and receiver pair. These virtual connections form a complete graph, which allows a fast and a direct communication between two processes. However, complete graph may cause a waste of buffers, that the price of running multimedia applications will become too high to be feasible, because receivers must buffer media separately [26].

In this paper we propose a new topological structure for the group communication system. This architecture solves the local clocks synchronization problem by according to a time reference, which is used by each process as its own clock value. This model supports real-time causal ordering in presence of a crash failure, by ensuring at least a partial communication between processes in group communication system.

Our solution is based on a hierarchical structure of k-local groups, where k represents the number of local groups that compose the system. Within each local group, there is only one single server that plays the role of the local root of that group. The set of local servers forms a virtual group, where one of them will play even the role of the Master server for that group system, and consequently the global root of this hierarchical architecture.

Unlike direct connections (complete graph) where the buffer size increases with total number of connections, with the variation of propagation delay, and with the delay jitter of the connection, the proposed architecture allows to reduce theses constraints, since the communication presented in this model is a reliable point-to-point one. That will reduce the amount of control information and the total buffer size.

Consequently, this hierarchical structure allows members of the group to exchange messages containing data with real-time constraints in causal order, even allows to synchronize easily local clocks.

Several protocols have been presented for reducing the amount of control information [18, 19]. These approaches do not describe the topological structure within the local group. Both these protocols do not address issue of real-time delivery that supports fault-tolerance.

This paper is structured as follows: The section 2 presents the formal definitions of causal order and Δ-causality. The proposed model of group communication system is presented in section 3, it is based on hierarchical structure in k-local groups. The section 4 provides the correctness of the proposed protocol. Finally, concluding remarks are given in section 5.

2. CAUSAL ORDERING ABSTRACTION

2.1. *CAUSAL ORDERING*

Concepts of group and causality are of major importance in the design of distributed systems. When, mixing both concepts, we can define causal multicast delivery in overlapping groups. These concepts insure that messages sent before other messages should be received in that order. As there is no global clock in distributed systems, the information added to the messages must include the acknowledge of other messages in the system that were sent before it. The added information is called the interval of the dependency of that message, it allows to the receiver site to have some information about causal delivery rule, without it, the receiver can not respect the causal delivery of messages. Thanks these informations, a message will not be delivered until all the messages that it depends upon have been delivered.

Consider the events of type *send* and *del* (as delivery event) produced by all the processes in groups. These events are structured by the following partial order relation [16] :

i. for any produced event e, e → e.
ii. for two events e_1 and e_2 produced by the same process such that : e_1 → e_2, where ($e_1 \neq e_2$), then it is not the case that e_2 → e_1.
iii. if there exists event e_1, e_2, and e_3 such that e_1 → e_2 and e_2 → e_3, then e_1 → e_3.
iv. if there exists an event e that is $send_p(m)$ or $del_p(m)$ and an event e' that is $send_p(m')$ or $del_p(m')$, then e→e' or e' → e.
v. if there exists an event e that is $send_p(m)$ and an event e' that is $del_q(m)$, where $p \neq q$ then e→e'.

Such a relation characterizes any distributed computation based on multicast within groups executed in an asynchronous environment. To be a causal order, this relation has to satisfy the following definition :

Let g_x and g_y be two local groups belonging to the group communication system G.

Definition 1 : *A distributed computation respects causal order if any two messages m and m' that have produced respectively by two processes $P_i \in g_x, P_j \in g_y$, where $P_i \neq P_j$, then for any process P_k :if $send_i(m)$→$send_j(m')$ have the same destination process P_k then, we must have $del_k(m)$→$del_k(m')$.*

Such causal order is not sufficient in real-time multimedia traffic, because it has not take into account that the message can be discarded if it arrives at its destination after the expiration of its deadline. Therefore, the dependency condition of message delivery is applied only in a bound time interval [2, 25].

2.2. Δ *-CAUSALITY ORDER*

The communication model of Δ *-causality* is mainly used in multimedia application [10, 25] such as teleconference, video-conference, where all participants require to exchange audio/video information in real-time over network. To preserve the real-time interaction and a high QoS of such applications, the audio/video information have a maximum transmission delays, since it can not degrade the QoS [8, 11, 23].

Definition 2 : *A distributed computation respects* Δ *-causality ordering if :*

i. All messages that arrive within Δ *are delivered during their validity time* Δ *, all the others are never delivered (they are lost or discarded);*

ii. All delivery events respect causal order (definition 1).

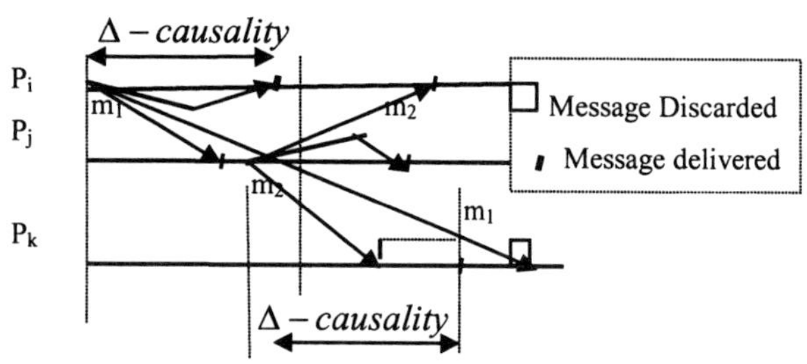

Figure 2.1. Δ *-causally ordered communications*

An implementation of Δ *-causality* ordering consists of an underlying system, where three types of events are associated with each message : «send», «delivery», and «arrival» (only send and delivery events are visible to processes). Due to delivery constraints imposed by Δ *-causality* ordering, when a message arrives within its deadline, and it have not been delivered, it can be delayed until its delivery condition becomes true (figure 2.1). Thus, the core of this new abstraction consists then in defining the delivery condition DC(m) that is associated with each message. In such a way these messages are delivered as soon as possible.

Once all processes have synchronized their local clocks, each one of them has a variable called *current_time* that is continuously updated by the local clock. Basing in the delivery condition presented in [2], each process manages the following two variables : $sent_i$: array [1..n,1..n] of time and del_i : array [1..n] of time, where n is the number of processes composing the group communication system.

The matrix $sent_i$[x,y] represents the knowledge of process P_i about sending time of the last message sent by P_x to P_y. The matrix del_i[j] represents the sending time of the last message sent by P_j to P_i and delivered to P_i.

Each message m piggybacks the following control information :

ST_m is a copy of the matrix *«sent»* of the sending process at m's sending time ;

$send\_time_m$ is the time at which m has been sent (occurrence of the associated send event)

A message m is discarded if it misses its deadline that is ($send\_time_m + \Delta > current\_time$).

By definition, all messages arriving at their destination within their deadline must be delivered as soon as possible. More formally, the delivery condition DC(m) of message m sent to P_i is expressed as :

$$\forall x : (ST_m[x,i] \leq del_i[x]) \vee (ST_m[x,i] < current\_time - \Delta) \quad (1)$$

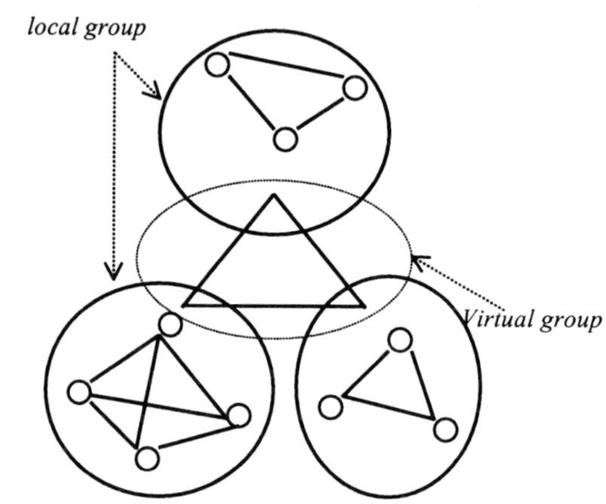

Figure 3.1 : A well connected k-local groups

In a large group sizes, the dimension of the matrix piggybacked on messages is $O(n^2)$ [17,18]. This complexity can be reduced to O(n) if we consider broadcast communication among processes. Either, if we consider that within a local group the communication channels are reliable, so we can reduce this complexity to O(n).

Since each non-loss message arrives at all processes via their local servers, we replace the sent array in the condition (1) with the vector VT, in particular in each process, each row of the sent array will have the same value. Thus we define a Vector VT_i[j] : array [1..n] of time. Where VT_i[j] represents the knowledge of the process p_i about the sending time of the last message broadcast by p_j, hence now ST_m is a copy of the vector VT of the sending process at his sending time.

3. GROUP MULTICAST

3.1. GROUP CONCEPT

We consider a group communication system G, as a complete graph composing of n processes P_1, .., P_n that communicate by exchanging messages through FIFO channels, and the communication channels are bounded. There is neither common shared memory

nor global clock. The communication is made without degradation and without duplication or loss of messages. In other words the underlying network is reliable and asynchronous.
Cooperation between processes is structured with the group concept. Each process has a distinguish identity. The information of identity will be used for synchronizing local clocks in the system.
The group communication system is built upon an hierarchical architecture of k-local groups, where k represents the number of groups in the system G. Each group is defined as a set of processes, that forms a tree structure where the root is a member of that group, and is called the local server. We assume that the group communication system can detect process failures, and report them to the local server. Processes belonging to different local groups can exchange their messages only via their local servers. For that a virtual group is created as a collection of local serves in order to ensure the communication between all groups in the system.

Definition 1. A group g_x is defined as a set of «m» processes $\{P_1, .., P_m\}$ which possess distinct identities.

Definition 2. A group communication system G is a set of k-local groups noted : $G = \bigcup_{i=1}^{k} g_i$.

Definition 3. We define a virtual group as a collection of local servers P_s,(where $P_s \in (g_i \cap g_v)$ which each one of them is member of a local group g_i: $g_v = \bigcup_{i=1}^{k} P_s$

Definition 4. g_x and g_v (represent respectively a local and a virtual group) are called overlapped groups if there exists a process P_s (that plays the role of local server), that belongs to both groups : $g_x \cap g_v = \{P_s\}$.

3.2. DISTRIBUTED ELECTION ALGORITHM

The network of processes is divided into local groups, such that each process is a member of only one local group, as illustrated in figure 3.1.
Only one process is chosen in group by a distributed election as local server, in order to ensure real-time causal delivery. All local servers are also members of another group called virtual group (figure 3.1), and one of them is selected as the Master server to be the global root of the group system.
In order to ensure real-time data traffic, we synchronize users' local clocks. This synchronization allows us to compensate for local clock drift. We assume that each local group has a local server, when each one receives a message from other groups, it broadcasts it to all processes of its group as soon as possible. Our scheme synchronizes the clocks of all users in the groups according to a time reference [9]. Thus, the value of time reference is the value of master server clock selected by distributed election algorithm. This value is used by all processes in the distributed system as their own local clock value. Note that each process adds a synchronization delay to the VMT value in order to have the same clock value, at a given time, with its Master server.
We suppose that the network is a complete graph, there is neither process nor link failure during the distributed election, and the communication channels are reliable, and bounded. However in the case of a failure detection, all processes in this local group ignore the existence of the failure process, and if it joins the group after the local server election, it will be added at the end of the LIST by all members of this local group. Our algorithm is divided in two phases :

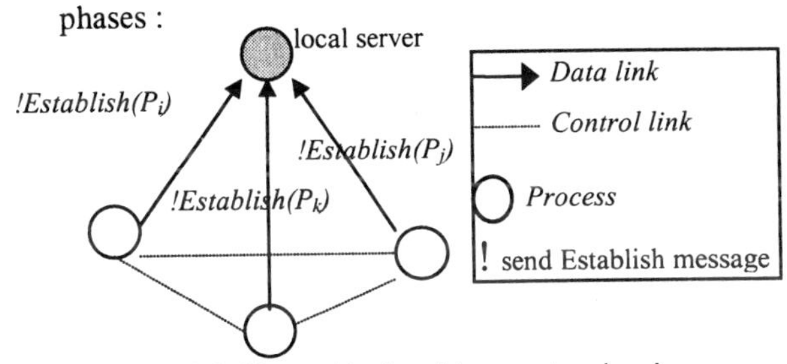

Figure 3.2. Hierarchical architecture in a local group

- In the first one, each process in its local group generates its own identity value and broadcasts a «Init(P_i, Id_i)» message to all members of its local group, where Id_i is the identity value of P_i. Each one sorts these values, in its own list «$LIST_i$», in an ascending order. The order of the processes in every LIST represents their priority to become the next local server of that group. The process generating the lowest identity Id_i is then selected as a local server. Once the local server has been elected, all other process send each one a «Establish(P_i)» message to their local server. In response, the server multicasts a «Ok(P_s, $LIST_s$)» message to acknowledge the connection and to build its hierarchical group model (figure 3.2, 3.3).
- In the second phase, when the local servers in each local group have been selected, they create a virtual group, where they can exchange and broadcast their messages. So, each one of them multicasts a «Req_id(P_s, Id_s, g_x)» message where g_x indicates the local group identifier in which that server belong to. Like in the first phase, each local server sorts the received identity values in ascending order. The server generating the lowest value is selected as Master server of that group communication system. Once the Master server

has been elected, all other local servers in virtual group send a «Connect(P_s,g_x)» message to establish the connection, as illustrated in figure 3.4. In response, they receive an ACK(P_{master}, $LIST_{master}$,VMT) message, where VMT represents the virtual master time value, of the master server P_{master}, that will be used by all server for synchronizing their local clocks. Therefore, all processes in groups takes the VMT value via their local server as their own local clock. Thus, all participants in groups has the same time value at a given time.

For maintaining this synchronization the Master server broadcasts periodically its VMT to inform all participants in the group communication system of the current time taking by itself. By this manner, we solve the local clock drift problem.

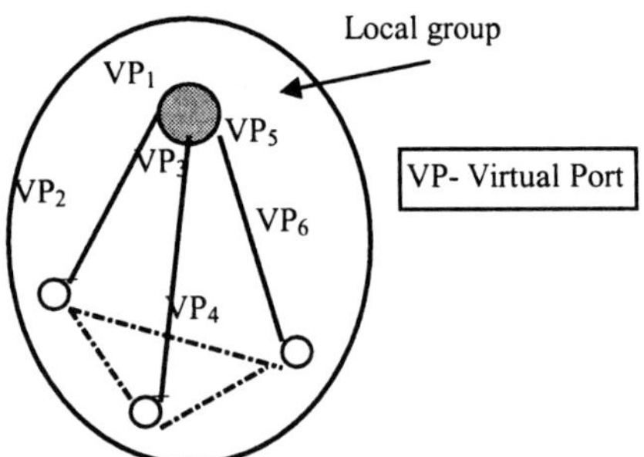

Figure 3.3. VP-procedure in a local group

3.3. VP- PROCEDURE

By Applying the Depth-First algorithm, the local server visits each process in its LIST and assigns a VP number at its incoming port (figure 3.3, and 3.4). The main role of the VP numbers is to maintain the hierarchical structure in life in case of a process or a server failure. The objective is to obtain disjoint sub-tree for the connect processes to ensure continuos communication among them. For assuring its successor, the local server closes every process failure by deleting its VP numbers from its LIST.

Termination procedure is guaranteed since eventually all the processes in the group are labelled. Correctness follows since each VP of each process is labelled exactly once, and the number VP is incremented by one to create a unique VP identifier in the local group.

A new process x can join the comunication architecture by first connecting to their immediate neighbor process i. Since the the election algorithm is distributed, each process has a full knowledge of the grouping information such as the list of of the local server. Thus each process can give the addresse of the local server to the new process x. The new porcess, after getting addresses from their immediate neighbors makes connections with the local servers and negociates the QoS to insure real-time traffic (like maximum and-to-end delays). Once the QoS are negotiated the new process is qualified to join the local group, and it is added to the end of the LIST by all processes. In the extreme case, if the new process is not qualified for any local group, then the process x becomes a local server and communicates directly through virtual group with other local servers.

```
Do
        Let Ps be the local server (root) of the group
        starting from Ps ;
        let DF be the Depth-First order ;

        let VP the virtual port number ;

        traverse of the group hierarchical structure

        For each unlabelled input Pi visited by DF
                Do
                        VP = VP +1 ;
                        Assign VP to Pi ;
                        Mark Pi as labelled in LISTs.
                EndDo
EndDo.
```

If a process wants to leave the group, it informs the local server and breaks the connections, it is removed from the list by all other processes via their local server. However, if a local server wants to leave the communication, then it informs all local group members. As each member of that local group has the same LIST contents, each one of them establishes a connection with the local server's successor.

After the connections are established, processes can get messages through the old local server, or the new local server. The new local server informs the processes that it can start to receive their messages at a time stamp T, this time is the prefetch time of the old local server. In other hand, all local group members synchronize their local clocks by adding the new synchronization delay value to the VMT value.

Having a virtual hierarchical structure, the links of the network are divided into two types :

(i) data links are a part of the hierarchical structure, their role is to transfer multimedia traffic to their destinations ;

(ii) control links are all the rest, their role is to inform the other processes in groups in the case of a process or a link failure by transporting control information like the Master server's LIST content, or to update VMT value.

3.4. DELTA-PROCEDURE

Once the virtual group has elected the Master Server, a mechanism must be provided to compute the Δ - value. This value is the global communication delay in the group system that will represent the lifetime of media unit, after which that media unit can not be useful for the playing back.

We denote by d_{min} the minimum communication delay between the Master Server and the nearest process belonging to its local group, and d_{max} the maximum communication delay between the Master and the farthest site in the group system G. These variables represent the transit time, the time spent in their local servers, the collection delay and the delivery delay between the Master and the nearest respectively the farthest site. If τ_{master} is the arrival time of messages to the Master Server. Then the earliest and the latest time at which message from the Master is available to be played back by a site i is bounded by :

$$Q_{min} = \tau_{master} + 2.d_{min}.$$

$$Q_{max} = \tau_{master} + 2.d_{max}.$$

Thus, the lifetime Δ of multimedia data is bounded by : $Q_{min} \le \Delta \le Q_{max}$

Local clock drift :

Once all local clocks have been synchronized, we must keep this synchronization among the communication exchange to insure the real-time relationships. If that constraint is relaxed, the clocks are no more than ε time units out of synchronization with each other. To solve that local clock drift without changing to the algorithm, it is suitable to update only the definition of Δ . For that, the selected Master Server sends periodically its VMT value to all members in the group system, in order to keep clocks synchronized within 5-10 milliseconds [9, 14].

If $\varepsilon = H_{new}-H_{old}$, Where $H_{new} = VMT + \tau_i$ is the time value of a local clock according to the Master clock (VMT) and τ_i is the synchronization delay of the local clock, is non-zero, then Δ is defined to be the time data in a message with the maximum clock drift : $\Delta_{new} = \Delta_{old} + \varepsilon$

This change does not have an influence upon the functionality and the validity of the protocol, because Δ defines only the lifetime of a message.

3.5. PROTOCOL BEHAVIOUR IN A FAILURE DETECTION

Note that if a non-server member of the group fails, then the local server of that group discards it by closing the VP that connects it to that process. In the same time, the server updates its $LIST_s$ by removing the identity value of the failure process. All members of the group will be informed by receiving the contents of $LIST_s$, from the successor of the local server, via control links. The main of this mechanism is to guarantee efficiently the local server successor.

However, a failure of a local server is problematic since it is a member at least of two groups (local and virtual groups), and it is the single way by which all processes in groups can communicate together. When a local server fails, the local group it belongs to is reconfigured as soon as possible. The new one is the successor of the failed server in $LIST_i$. As all members of the group has the same $LIST_i$, then the selected server will be the same process at each participant level.

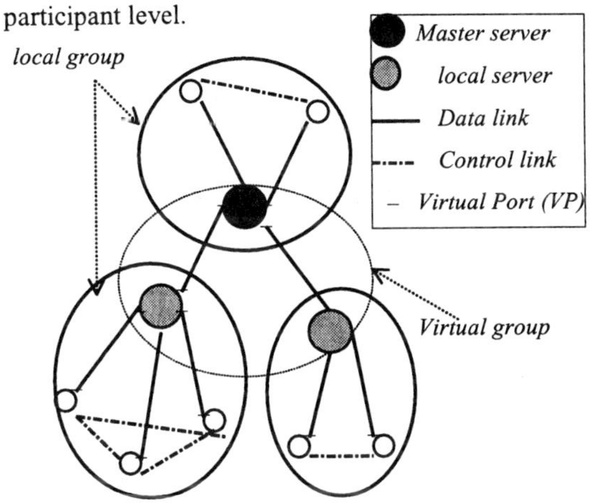

Figure 3.4. Hierarchical architecture in k-groups

Thus, once the new server is selected, all members of group establish a connection for building their hierarchical structure. In other hand, when the Master server detects a failure server, it closes immediately the corresponding VP to that server in order to ensure at least a partial real-time communication between non failure members of the virtual group. By this way we obtain two sub-tree and we can preserve the real-time causal delivery of messages. Thus, the presented protocol ensures the real-time causal delivery in the group system communication.

4. CORRECTENESS

In this section, before proving the liveness and safety properties of the presented protocol, we demonstrate that each local group composing the communication system is represented by only one local server. These servers are known and are reached by all members of the group belonging to. In other hand, we prove that the group communication system has only one single Master server and all k-groups can reach it.

4.1. CORRECTNESS OF THE HIERARCHICAL MODEL

Lemma 1 : *Every local group g_x is represented by one and only one local server, and all locally members know it.*

Proof :

Let g_x a local group belonging to the group communication system G.

In the first phase of distributed election, each process P_i of g_x receives (n_x-1) Init(P_i, Id_i) messages, where n_x is the number of processes belonging to the local group g_x and Id_i is the identity value of process P_i. Every process in the groups records these messages in its own list $LIST_i$ in ascending order. As the communication is reliable and bounded, all Init messages will be received by all participants at a given time. It means that all processes are known by all members of the group g_x, and they have the same LIST contents. Therefore, all processes will select the same process which has the lowest identity value as their local server. Then, once it has been selected, Every P_i of g_x establishes a connection with its local server, for building the hierarchical structure for g_x, and each one of them receives an OK message from the local server as an acknowledgement message. Consequently, all members of the group know that there is only one local server in the group. Thus, in each local group belonging to the group communication system, there exists only one local server.

Lemma 2 : *In the virtual group, which is a collection of the local servers, there is one and only one Master server.*

Proof :

In lemma 1 we proved that every local group g_x belonging to the group communication system, is represented by only one local server and it is known by all its members in that group.

The virtual group g_v is composed of k-local servers. In the second phase of distributed election, each local server receives 'k-1' Req_id messages from all participants in that g_v, where k is the number of local groups in the communication system. As in the first phase, all messages are recorded in $LIST_s$ of each local server. At a given time, all server will select the same local server, which has the lowest identity, as Master one. Therefore, all local servers in the virtual group know the Master server and each one of them sends a Connect message for establishing a connection with it. Therefore, all local servers can reach the Master server.

Theorem 1 : *The group communication system is represented by one and only one Master server.*

Proof : lemma 1 and lemma 2.

Now, we prove that the hierarchical structure of k-groups guarantees Δ*-causality* ordering and each received message will be eventually delivered in its deadline.

4.2. LIVENESS

We prove that in spite of the presence of failure, the presented architecture is able to deliver messages by respecting theirs deadlines.

Lemma 3 : *For a local group, all sent messages will be received, and delivered by respecting the Delivery Condition .*

Proof :

When a process sends a message to their participants in the local group. This message is timestamped by ST_m and broadcasted to the members via its local server. Since the hierarchical structure in the local group uses a reliable point-to-point communication, and the same connecting channel to reach the destination via the local server (lemma1), all messages must be received and delivered when their delivery conditions become true. However, if a sent message is not received by a destination or is received after that its condition delivery becomes true, then this message is discarded. But, this case is never happen, because the Δ value is computed for ensuring efficiently the delivery of messages in their lifetime, mainly in the local group. In other hand, the communication is reliable, and if a message is not received in its lifetime validity, we can assume that the process sending this message has used another communication channel than the specified one in the presented topological structure(control link). However, the proposed architecture is a hierarchical one, not a complete graph, where each process can reach the destination by choosing a link among several direct connections to reach the destination. Therefore, all processes send their messages to the server via the same and the specified point-to-point data link to be multicasted. Thus, the presented protocol ensures the delivery condition for each received message in the local group.

Lemma 4 : *For the virtual group, that is composed with local servers and Master server, the protocol guarantees that all sent message will be received and delivered by respecting the Delivery Condition.*

Proof :

When the local server receives the message from a process to forward it among the virtual group. This message is broadcasted to the other local groups via the Master server. As the topological structure in the virtual group is defined as a tree one, then each server can reach its Master server via the same specified data link that is used for sending multimedia data (lemma2). Each group receives the message in its deadline and can delivers it if its delivery condition becomes true. However, if a sent message is not received by a local group or is received after that its condition delivery becomes true, then this message is discarded. This case is never happen, because the communication in the virtual group is reliable point-to-point one, and if a message is not received before its deadline, it means that the local server sending this message has used another communication channel than the specified one in the presented topological structure. In the case of a complete graph, each local server can reach other server by using one link among the available direct connections, not always the same communication link, and the message can probably be received by the destination after its lifetime (because the communication delay is not the same at each communication link level). But, in the proposed hierarchical structure, all local servers send their messages to the Master via the same and the specified point-to-point data link, and the communication delay is known in the virtual group. Therefore, this architecture guarantees the delivery condition for each received message in the virtual group.

Theorem 2 : *Every sent message, and is received by a not crash process before its deadline is delivered to all its recipients by respecting the Delivery Condition DC(m).*

Proof :

Let g_x and g_y two local groups, and g_v the virtual group. We can distinguish two cases :

- $g_x = g_y$, in this case we are in the same local group, so we can use Lemma 3;
- $g_x \neq g_y$ by applying lemma 4. In both cases we obtain that the topological structure is a hierarchical one, and guarantees the delivery of the received messages in their lifetime.

4.2. SAFETY

We prove that the hierarchical architecture guarantees the real-time causal delivery.

Lemma 5 : *In a local group, the protocol respects the real-time causal delivery.*

Proof :

Let $P_i, P_j \in g_x$ be two processes belonging to a local server g_x. We assume that $send_i(m) \rightarrow send_i(m')$, and we want prove that both messages are delivered before their deadlines to the process P_j: $del_j(m) \rightarrow del_j(m')$.

When P_i sends $send_i(m) \rightarrow send_i(m')$ using the point-to-point data link, it timestamps the messages by $ST_m[i,j]$ respectively $ST_{m'}[i,j]$. It means that the message m is causally delivered before m' by all participants in the group. Thus, in the local server $ST_m[i,j] < ST_{m'}[i,j]$ indicating that m' will be multicasted after the message m. Consequently, the receiver will deliver the message m before m' following the Condition Delivery. However, if P_j receives m' before m, and its delivery condition becomes true, the receiver considers that the message m is lost, and delivers m'. The message m will be discarded if P_j receives it after delivering m'. If that is happened, it means that the process P_i has sent the message m' by another link (using direct connection, where the communication delay in very low) than the specified data one in the architecture. This communication type is available only in a complete graph case, where the sender and receiver pair can exchange their messages via a direct connection. But, this is never happen in the present architecture, because all messages travel through the same local server (lemma 1), and that server respects the causal delivery rule. Therefore, the hierarchical structure ensures the real-time causal delivery in a local group. Thus if an event $send_i(m) \rightarrow send_i(m')$ is produced then the result is $del_j(m) \rightarrow del_j(m')$.

Theorem 3 : *The presented architecture respects real-time causal delivery.*

Proof :

Let $P_i \in g_x$ and $P_j \in g_y$ be two processes. We assume that $send_i(m) \rightarrow send_j(m')$, and we want prove by way of contradiction that if both messages are delivered before their deadlines to an other process $P_k \in g_z$ so the destination process will deliver the message m' before m: $del_k(m') \rightarrow del_k(m)$.

Two cases are possible :

- $g_x = g_y$, this cannot happen because the local server receives message m before m' : $ST_m[i,k] < ST_{m'}[i,k]$ (i=j) (lemma 5). Thus, we have $del_k(m) \rightarrow del_k(m')$;
- if $g_x \neq g_y$ we have the following relation :

$send_i(m) \rightarrow send_j(m')$, it means that message m is causally delivered at the local server P_{g_y} of g_y group, by the time it forwards m' to the other groups via the master server P_{master} (figure 3.4). Thus, in the master server we have, $ST_m[i,k] < ST_{m'}[j,k]$ indicating that m' follows causally m (lemma 4).

Let P_{g_z} be the server group of g_z where $P_{g_z} \in (g_z \cap g_v)$. Since, at the master server level m' has a timestamp value that follows m, meaning that in virtual group g_v the message m will be delivered after m'. Therefore, P_{g_z} must deliver m before it delivers m' $del_k(m) \rightarrow del_k(m')$. If is not the case, it means that the message m' is sent from P_{g_y} to P_{g_z} via another link than the specified one in the proposed topological structure. However, this is never happen because the presented structure is an hierarchical one, and there is only one path to reach the destination in the virtual group via the Master server (lemma2). Therefore, all sent messages must travel through the Master server, which forwards them by respecting the causal relationships to be received and delivered before their lifetime expirations. Thus every process $P_k \in g_z$ will delivers the message m before m' : $del_k(m) \rightarrow del_k(m')$.

5. CONCLUSION

In this paper we have presented the hierarchical architecture composed of k-local groups that supports fault-tolerant real-time causal ordering. This architecture can tolerate crash failure, while keeping the amount of control information small.

The choice of Virtual Port allow us to reduce the time of system reconfiguration and to ensure at least a partial real-time communication in the local group or between local groups, while the hierarchical architecture allow us to minimise the amount of exchanging messages for synchronizing easily the local clocks, and reduce the amount of control messages for maintaining the temporal relationships in order to reduce the local clocks drift.

The proposed structure can support efficiently causal ordering in real-time multimedia applications by updating only the delta value to solve the loos of synchronization clocks without changing the algorithm, even in the case of the Master server failure. Thus, the real-time multimedia traffic of each participant must be received by all recipients in communication system before its deadline, to be delivered and played back in the same time.

Since our scheme can tolerate process and link failures, it may be possible to apply it in a mobile computing environment. This may require some work on the definition of the QoS to support a Wireless multimedia application from one cell to another, in other to guarantee a real-time delivery of each message. This is left for future research.

REFERENCES

[1] F. Adelstein, M. Singhal, 'Real-Time Causal message ordering in multimedia sysytems', In Proceeding of the 15th IEEE International conf. On Distributed Computing Systems pp : 36-43, 1995

[2] L. Amanton, M. Naïmi, 'Total and causal Ordering in Distributed Computing' Journal of Computing and Information, Vol. 2, N° 1, pp. 308-321, 1996.

[3] R. Baldoni, A. Mostefaoui and M. Raynal, 'Causal Delivery of messages With Real-Time Data in Unreliable Network', Real-Time Systems vol.10, No.3, pp : 1-18, 1996.

[4] R. Baldoni, A. Friedman and R.V. Renesse,'The Hierarchical Daisy Architecture for Causal Delivery', September 1996, Email : baldoni@dis.uniroma1.it

[5] R. Baldoni, R. Prakash, M. Raynal and M. Singhal,'Broadcast With Time and Causality Constraints for Multimedia Applications' Research Rapport No.2976 september 1996.

[6] K. Birman and T. Joseph, 'Reliable Communication in Presence of Failure', ACM Trans. on Computer Systems 5(1) :47-76, February 1987.

[7] K. Birman, and T. Joseph,'Exploiting Virtual Synchrony in Presence of Failure' In Proc. of the 11th ACM Symp. On Operating Systems Principales, pp :123-138, December 19987.

[8] K. Birman, A. Schiper, and P. Stephenson,'Lightweight Causal and Atomic Group Multicast', ACM Trans. on Computer Systems, 9(3) :272-314, August 1991.

[9] D. Ferrari,'Clients requirements for Real-Time Communication Services' IEEE Comm. Magazine, pp : 65-72, 1994.

[10] R. Gusella, S. Zatti,'The Accuracy of the Clock Synchronization Achieved by TEMPO in Berkley UNIX 4-3 BSD', IEEE Trans. on Software Engineering, 15(7) :847-853, july 1989.

[11] S. Greonenberg, and D. Marwood,' Real-Time Groupware as a Distributed Systems : Concurrency Control and its Effect on the Interface', In Proc. of ACM Conf. on Cooperative Support for Cooperative Work, ACM press pp : 207-217, 1994.

[12] T. Houdoin, D. Bonjour,'ATM and AAL Layer Issues Concerning Multimedia Applications', Annual of Telelcommunication, 49(5) :230-240, 1994.

[13] L. Lamport,'Time, Clocks, and the Ordering of Events in a Distributed Systems', Communication of the ACM, vol. 21, No. 7, pp : 558-565, July 1978.

[14] F. Matter,'Virtual Time and Global States of Distributed Systems', Proc. of the International Workshop on Parallel and Distributed Algoritms pp :215-226, Amsterdam 1989.

[15] D. Mills,'Internet Time Synchronization : The Network Time Protocol', IEEE Trans. on Comm. 39(10) :1482-1493, October 1991.

[16] L. Moser, Y. Amir et al., 'Extended Virtual Synchrony', Proc. The 14th Int. Conf. on Distributed Computing System. Poznan Poland 1994, pp : 56-65.

[17] S. Mullender,'Distributed Systems', ADDISON-WESLEY 1995.

[18] R. Prakash, M. Raynal, and A. Singhal,'An Efficient Causal Ordering Algorithm for mobile Computing Environnement', Proc. of the 16th IEEE Int. Conf. on Distributed Computing Systems, Hong-Kong, june 1996.

[19] M. Raynal, A Schiper, and S. Toueg,'The Causal Ordering Abstraction and a Simple Way to

Implement it', Information Processing Letters, 339-343, 1991.

[20] R. Rodrigues and P. Verissimo,'Causal Separators and Topological Timestamping in Large scale systems' Proc. of the 15th International Conference on Distributed Systems May 1995

[21] R. V. Renesse, K. Birman, and S. Maffeis,'Horus : A flexible Group communication Systems', Communication of the ACM, 39(4) :76-83, April 1996.

[22] A. Schiper, J. Eggli, and A. Sandoz,'A new Algorithm to Implement Causal Ordering', Proc. Of the Int. Workshop on Distributed Algorithms, 1989, in Lecture Note Computer Science 392, Spring-Verlagn New York, pp : 219-232.

[23] R. Schwarz and F. Mattern,'Detecting Causal Relations in Distributed Computing : in Search of the Holy Grail', Distributed Computing, 7(3) :149-174, 1994.

[24] I. Wakeman'Packetized video : options fo Interaction between the User, the Network and the Codec', The Computer Jounal, 36(1) :55-66,1993

[25] R. Yavatkar'MPC : a Protocol for Coordination and Temporal Synchronization in Multimedia Collaborative Applications', Proc. of the 12th IEEE Inter. Conf. on Distributed Computing Systems, IEEE press, 606-613.

[26] R. Yavatkar, and K. Lakshman,'Communication Support for Distributed Collaborative Applications', Multimedia Systems, 2 :74-88.

[27] W. Yen and I.F. Akyildiz, 'The hierarchical architecture for buffer managing in integrated services networks', Multimedia Systems vol. 4, N°. 3, pp :131-139. 1996.

Cell Loss Ratio and Multiplexing Gain of an ATM Multiplexer for VBR Voice Sources

Seong-Ho Jeong and John A. Copeland
Georgia Institute of Technology
Atlanta, Georgia 30332
sjeong@ee.gatech.edu

Abstract

Asynchronous Transfer Mode (ATM) is designed to support various traffic classes. It is necessary to select a proper traffic class to support a specific application. Voice traffic in its inherent nature is time-sensitive and variable. Therefore, it is natural to consider voice as real-time VBR traffic. Human speech has a voice activity factor of about 42% on an average, which makes it possible to multiplex a lot of voice sources together. The study of cell loss is of great importance to the design of an ATM multiplexer whose input consists of voice sources. With a maximum delay allowed in the network, it is the behavior of cell loss, rather than the variation of network delay, that determines the quality of reconstructed voice at receivers. This paper analyzes the cell loss performance and multiplexing gain of an ATM multiplexer loaded with VBR voice sources, where multiple voice streams, utilizing compression and silence detection, are multiplexed into a fixed bandwidth circuit such as T1 or T3 ATM trunk. This paper shows that the cell loss ratio and multiplexing gain depend on the voice activity factor, the mean talkspurt length, the mean silence period, the link capacity, the compression ratio, and the buffer size of the ATM multiplexer.

1. Introduction

Asynchronous Transfer Mode (ATM) supports a number of different traffic classes, including Constant Bit Rate (CBR), Available Bit Rate (ABR), and Variable Bit Rate (VBR). Applications wishing to use a particular class must determine the set of traffic parameters which characterize the connection. In this paper, we consider one particular application: VBR Voice. With this application, many voice sources are multiplexed together into a fixed bandwidth circuit such as T1 or T3. Each voice connection utilizes silence suppression and compression via codecs such as PCM [17], ADPCM[18], or LD-CELP [19].

Due to the silence suppression, the multiplexed voice stream has a variable rate, and therefore VBR (in particular, real-time VBR) is the appropriate choice for a service class. To guarantee high-quality voice in any VBR connection, the user must request the required quality of service quality (QoS) using a set of QoS parameters such as cell transfer delay (CTD), cell loss ratio (CLR), and cell delay variation (CDV). In particular, the CLR is of great importance to the design of an ATM multiplexer whose input consists of voice sources. When a maximum delay is allowed in the network, it is the behavior of cell loss, rather than variation of network delay, that determines the quality of reconstructed voice at receivers. In fact, a given limit for the cell loss ratio determines the maximum number of voice sources which can be supported in an ATM network.

Performance evaluation results for general packet voice multiplexing systems were already presented extensively in the previous literature. In this paper, we analyze specifically the loss performance/multiplexing gain of an ATM multiplexer loaded with VBR voice sources, where multiple voice streams, utilizing compression and silence detection, are multiplexed into a fixed bandwidth circuit such as T1 or T3 ATM trunk. The loss performance is examined by using simulation to measure cell loss ratio.

This paper shows that the cell loss ratio depends on the voice activity factor, the mean speech length, the mean silence period, the total link capacity, and the buffer size of the ATM multiplexer. Some of previous work presented a sensitivity analysis when multiple ATM switches are connected between source and destination. In this paper, we focus on an ATM multiplexer and cell loss

0-8186-8810-6/98 $10.00 © 1998 IEEE

performance of the multiplexer. Simulation results using OPNET are shown to present how these factors affect the loss performance. We also investigate the number of VBR voice sources which can be supported in the ATM multiplexer, for a given cell loss ratio. In addition, we examine the necessity of voice cell buffering and show that it is possible to design an ATM multiplexer without buffering only at the expense of supporting a fewer number of calls.

The rest of the paper is organized as follows. Section 2 describes the effect of cell loss in further detail, followed by our model description in Section 3. Section 4 presents simulation results varying several key factors mentioned above which affect the cell loss performance. Finally, we summarize the results in Section 5.

2. Effect of Cell Loss Ratio

Cell loss ratio (CLR) is defined as the number of lost cells divided by the total number of cells transmitted by users. Severe cell loss can occur under peak loads and congestion in the network. In general, data cells are not time-sensitive, and lost data cells can be appropriately recovered through retransmission. However, lost voice cells cannot be adequately recovered in this manner. Lost voice cells can be a severe problem, depending on the type of packet network that is being used. Fortunately, ATM networks can provide better cell loss performance compared to IP networks because current IP networks do not guarantee quality of voice and usually exhibit a higher incidence of lost voice packets. However, it is desirable to keep the CLR to an acceptable level in ATM networks.

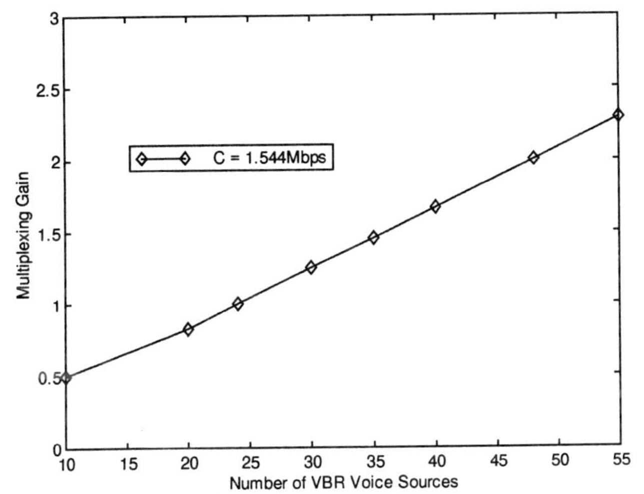

Figure 1. Multiplexing Gain vs. Number of Voice Sources

Acceptable CLR depends on the characteristics of the application and network conditions. An increase in the acceptable CLR allows the network to drop more cells and still support acceptable voice. Acceptable CLR is closely related to the multiplexing gain which is defined here as the ratio of the number of VBR voice sources to the number of CBR voice channels that could be supported. The maximum cell loss ratio requirement determines the maximum number of voice sources which can be supported in an ATM multiplexer. A higher acceptable CLR value clearly increases the multiplexing gain for network. Figure 1 illustrates the multiplexing gain versus VBR voice sources when the link capacity is 1.544 Mbps assuming that the voice activity factor is 0.42 and the data rate of each voice source is 64 kbps (PCM). Given a cell loss ratio, the number of voice sources carried over T1 ATM trunk can be obtained by mathematical analysis or simulation. Then, we can find the corresponding multiplexing gain.

The CLR as a number in itself does not capture the voice quality requirement. Voice quality also depends on the cell loss distribution. For instance, losing 10 cells in sequence will cause more degradation in voice quality than losing 10 cells spaced over a longer time interval. In any case, to guarantee high quality voice, it is desirable to keep the CLR to a minimum.

3. Model Description

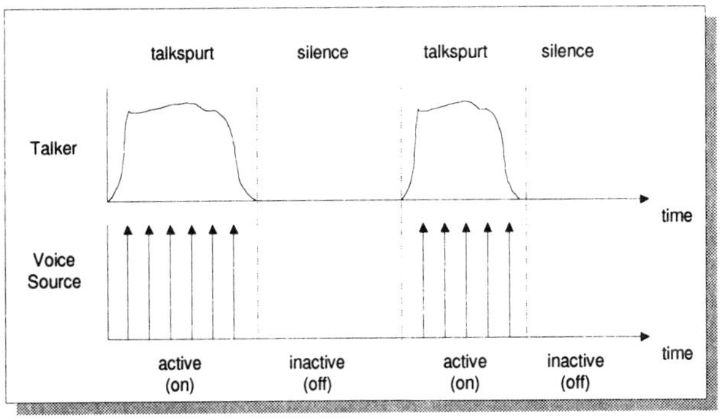

Figure 2. Voice Source Behavior

Typical behavior of a voice source for ATM multiplexer, which generates cells from a voice signal, is illustrated in Figure 2. A voice source is active when the talker is actually speaking. During active periods, the voice source generates cells at regular intervals as depicted in Figure 2 by vertical arrows. The voice source is inactive and generates no cells during periods in which the speaker is silent. In normal conversation, the duration of active periods fits an exponential distribution reasonably well while the duration of inactive periods is not approximated as well by an exponential distribution. Nonetheless, to facilitate analysis, the lengths of both active and inactive periods are assumed to be exponentially distributed for the calculations done in this paper. The quality of resulting model has been found to be quite good if the number of voice sources is more than 25 and less suitable if the number of voice sources is less than about 10 [7].

Figure 3 shows the system being modeled where there are N independent voice sources. Our model for the source is based on the assumption of the two-state, on-off model for each voice user. The on period corresponds to the active period and the off period corresponds to the inactive period. When "on", each source sends cells at a rate of P ATM cells per second, which depends on the voice source rate. Both the on and off periods are exponentially distributed for each voice source. The cells generated by active users are fed into the common queue or buffer where it is served at a rate of C where C is the channel capacity.

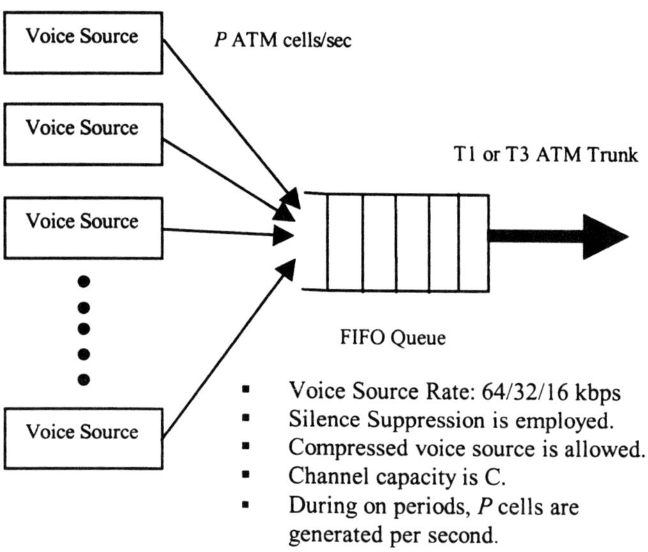

Figure 3. An ATM Multiplexer Loaded with VBR Voice Sources

Assume that the transition rate from on to off is α, and the transition rate from off to on is λ. The aggregation of N such users into a single connection can then be modeled by the $N+1$ state birth-death process as depicted in Figure 4 [6]. Each state represents the number of active voice sources. Each active source delivers one cell from the queue when it is nonempty at a rate of C. For simplicity, we consider only first-in-first-out (FIFO) for the service discipline of the multiplexer. It is also assumed that per-VC (virtual circuit) queueing is used in the ATM multiplexer.

Suppose there are n active voice sources and the maximum number of voice sources which can be supported in the multiplexer is m. Then, there are three possible conditions. First, If n is less than m, the arrival rate of cells to the common queue is less than the average service rate. In this case, the queue length decreases if the queue is nonempty. If the queue is empty, then it remains empty. Cell loss does not occur in the first case. Second, if n is equal to m, the cell arrival rate and service rates are equal so that the rate of change of the queue length is zero. Thus, no cell loss occurs. Third, if n is greater than m, the average arrival rate of cells to the queue exceeds the service rate. In this case, the length of queue increases and cell loss occurs after the queue is full. In order to show the loss performance more accurately, we performed simulation experiments using OPNET. The following section presents the simulation results in detail.

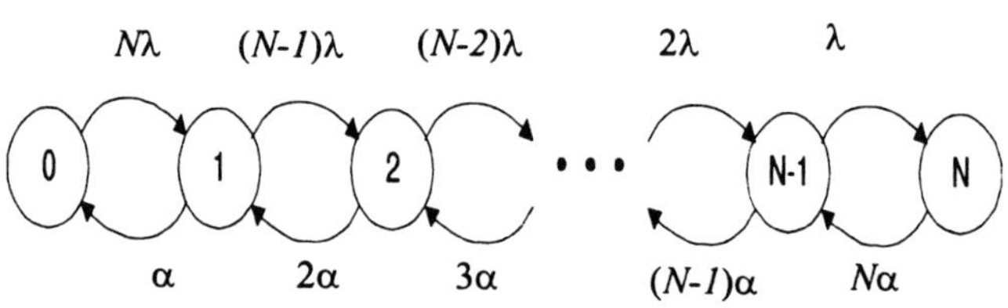

Figure 4. Birth-Death Process for Modeling N Voice Sources

4. Simulation Results

In this section, we discuss the cell loss performance in a finite-buffered ATM multiplexer loaded with N voice sources by presenting simulation results under several factors. Here, the loss performance is evaluated by measuring the CLR. As mentioned before, CLR can be obtained by measuring the total number of lost cells in the ATM multiplexer to the total number of transmitted cells by voice sources.

CLR depends on the voice activity factor, the mean talkspurt (on) length, the mean silence (off) length, the total link capacity, the compression ratio, and the buffer size of the ATM multiplexer. In the following sections, we present the impact of these factors on the CLR performance of an ATM multiplexer in detail. In the simulation experiments, it is assumed that the voice packetization period is 6 ms and the voice cells are generated at regular intervals during the talkspurt period. It is also assumed that all voice sources are homogeneous, and therefore each voice source has the same distribution characteristics. Specifically, the lengths of both active and inactive periods of each voice source are assumed to be exponentially distributed. We selected 352 ms for the default mean length of the active period and 650 ms for default mean length of the inactive period, which are commonly accepted values [13]. The default voice source rate is 64 kbps, and the voice sources are multiplexed over a T1-rate (1.544 Mbps) link. In addition, the default buffer size is 2 assuming per-VC queueing.

4.1 CLR vs. Voice Activity Factor

Let us denote the duration of the average talkspurt period by τ and the duration of the average silence period by s. Then, since the mean talkspurt length and the mean silence length are assumed to follow an exponential distribution, the voice activity factor v, over very long periods, will be approximately equal to $\tau/(\tau + s)$.

Figure 5 shows the impact of voice activity factor, where the number of voice sources ranges from 10 to 90, and the link capacity is 1.544 Mbps. The voice activity varies from 0.35 to 0.50. An increase in the voice activity factor indicates either an increase in the mean talkspurt length or a decrease in the mean silence length. As shown in the figure, as the voice activity factor increases, the cell loss ratio increases. Therefore, given a maximum cell loss ratio, the maximum number of voice sources decreases as the voice activity increases. In other words, increase in the voice activity factor causes a lower multiplexing gain.

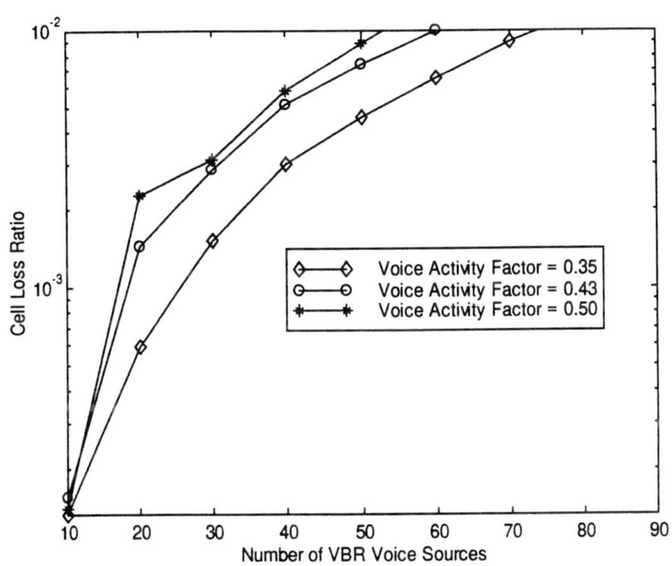

Figure 5. CLR vs. Voice Activity Factor

4.2 CLR vs. Mean Talkspurt/Silence Length

The mean talkspurt length and the mean silence length also affect the CLR, for the same voice activity factor. Theoretically, multiplying the mean talkspurt length and the mean silence length by a constant which is larger than 1 should not change the cell loss ratio over a large time-interval because the voice activity factor is constant. However, in reality, the increase in the talkspurt length increases the burstiness in voice activity as shown in Figure 6, which is difficult for a network with small queues to handle. This increase in burstiness results in an increase in cell loss. For a given activity factor, the cell loss increases with an increase in the mean talkspurt length, and hence there is a decrease in the multiplexing gain achieved. The increased burstiness may not be easily captured in a simple mathematical analysis.

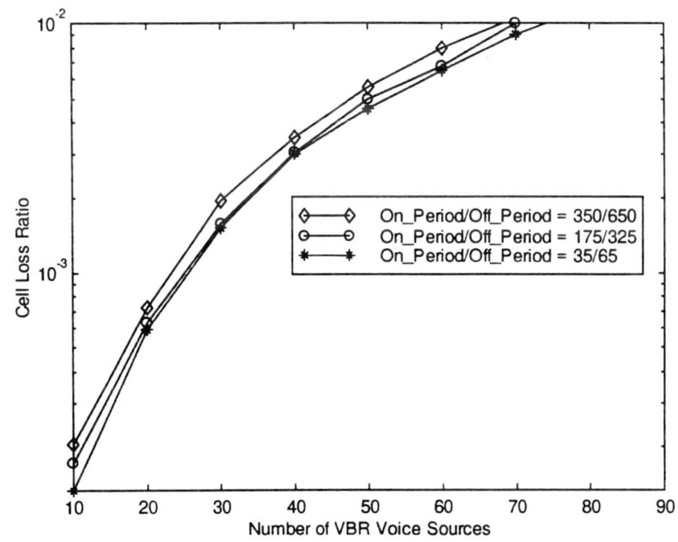

Figure 6. CLR vs. Mean talkspurt Length/Mean Silence length

4.3 CLR vs. Link Capacity

Total link capacity is closely related to cell loss ratio and multiplexing gain. In the simulation, we considered voice sources with rate R = 64 kbps and activity factor v = 0.35. The link capacity varies from 0.772 Mbps to 3.088 Mbps. Increasing the overall link capacity definitely increases the network's capability to handle more fluctuations in the voice sources. Therefore, cell loss ratio decreases as the link capacity increases as shown in Figure 7. Accordingly, the multiplexing gain increases with an increase in the total link capacity.

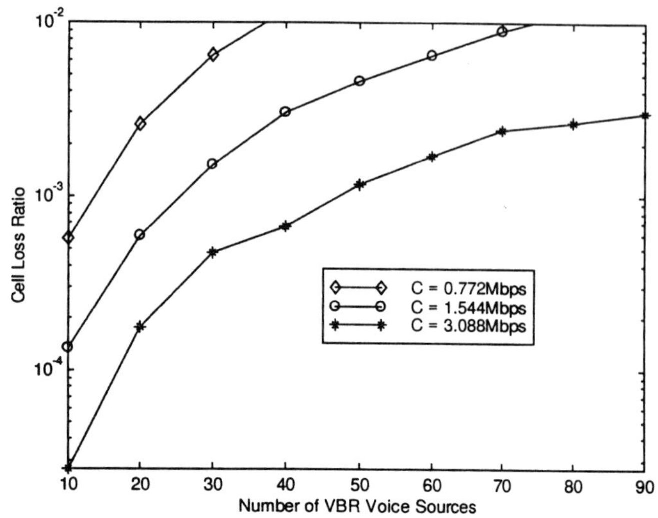

Figure 7. CLR vs. Link Capacity

4.4 CLR vs. Compression Ratio

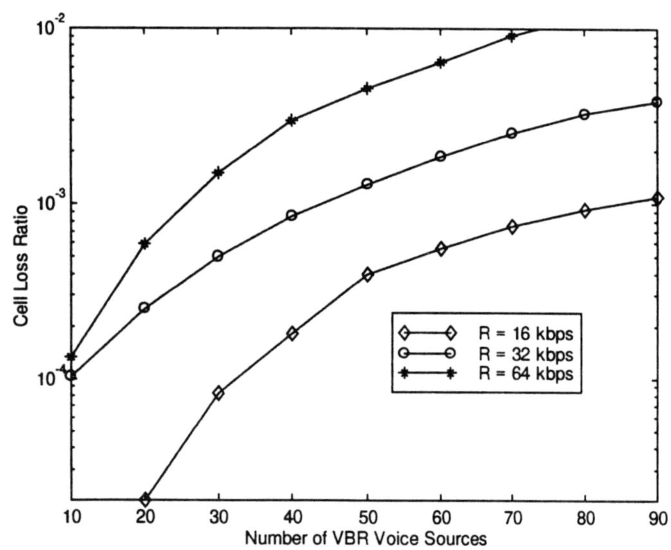

Figure 8. CLR vs. Compression Ratio

To obtain the effect of compression ratio, we used voice sources whose data rates are 64 kbps (uncompressed), 32kbps, and 16 kbps. As shown in Figure 8, compression ratio greatly affects cell loss ratio. Given a cell loss ratio, the number of 32 kbps voice sources carried over T1 ATM trunk is less than the number of 16 kbps voice sources. In other words, as compression ratio increases, cell loss ratio decreases. Accordingly, multiplexing gain increases as the compression ratio increases. This is because compressed voice greatly reduces the bandwidth required to support a single voice channel.

However, all voice compression schemes are basically lossy, and therefore higher compression ratio means more degradation in the voice quality. This degradation occurs even without any cell loss. With cell loss, compressed voice will suffer more degradation than uncompressed 64 kbps plain PCM. There is more correlation between subsequent cells with increased compression. In addition, the compression schemes increase the coding and the packetization delay. The compression scheme chosen for a given network will depend on the coding delay and the acceptable end-to-end delay.

4.5 CLR vs. Buffer Size

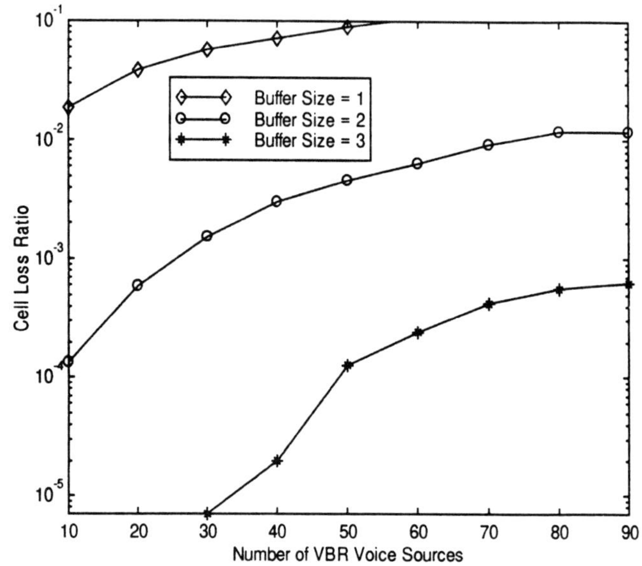

Figure 9. CLR vs. Buffer Size

It is possible to design an ATM multiplexer without buffering, only at the expense of supporting a fewer number of calls. In other words, multiplexers loaded with small number of voice users can be designed with no buffering. The advantage of no buffering is that the voice protocols can be greatly simplified, especially for congestion and destination cell playout schemes. However, in most cases, it is desired to support as many voice users as possible, and therefore buffering is necessary. Voice cell buffering helps to reduce voice cell discard. Increased buffer size reduces cell blocking ratio in the ATM multiplexer, which results in improving cell loss performance. However, once a voice buffer of an ATM multiplexer is full, it remains full for a certain period, during which many voice cells are possibly blocked, resulting in consecutive clipping in voice. Also buffers in network nodes increases cell delay variation, which necessitates a larger buffer at the receiver to compensate for the delay variation.

Figure 9 shows the effect of buffer size. Again, it is assumed that per-VC queueing is used, and the buffer size varies from 1 to 3. As shown in the figure, larger buffer size decreases the cell loss ratio, and multiplexing gain increases accordingly. However, the buffer size must be properly chosen since increasing buffer size may increase the delay and delay variation of voice cells, which may degrade the quality of voice services.

5. Concluding Remarks

This paper presented the cell loss performance and multiplexing gain of an ATM multiplexer loaded with VBR voice sources using simulation. In the simulation model, multiple VBR voice streams are multiplexed into a fixed bandwidth circuit. Study of cell loss is of great importance to the design of an ATM multiplexer whose input consists of voice sources. We showed that how the loss performance and multiplexing gain depend on the voice activity factor, the mean talk-spurt length, the mean silence period, the total link capacity, compression ratio, and the buffer size of the ATM multiplexer. The increase in the voice activity factor and on period increases the cell loss ratio, which results in the decrease in the multiplexing gain. The increase in the compression ratio, the buffer size, and the link capacity decreases the cell loss ratio, and the multiplexing gain increases accordingly. However, the buffer size should be controlled properly because the delay and delay variation of voice cells may be excessive. In addition, the compression scheme which is basically lossy should be carefully chosen so that the quality of voice services is not degraded and the acceptable CLR does not decrease by a large amount.

References

[1] K. Sriram, S. McKinney, "Voice Packetization and Compression in Broadband ATM Network," IEEE JSAC, Vol. 9, No.3, pp. 294-304, April 1991.

[2] J. Iyer, R. Jain, and S. Dixit, "Performance of VBR Voice over ATM: Effect of Scheduling and Drop Policies," ATM Forum 97-0608, July 1997.

[3] S.H. Kang and D. K. Sung, "Real-Time Cell Loss Estimation for ATM Multiplexers with Heterogeneous ON/OFF Sources," ICC'97, 1997.

[4] J. Feng, K-T. Lo, and H. Mehrpour, "Simulation Analysis on Statistical Multiplexing of MPEG Video Sources," ICC'97, 1997.

[5] S-Q. Li, "A New Performance Measurement for Voice Transmission in Burst and Packet Switching," IEEE Trnas. on Communications, Vol. COM-35, No. 10, October 1987.

[6] J. N. Daigle, "Models for Analysis of Packet Voice Communications Systems," IEEE JSAC, Vol. SAC-4, No. 6, September 1986.

[7] C.J. Weinstein, "Fractional Speech Loss and Talker activity model for TASI and for Packet-Switched Speech," IEEE Transactions on Communications, Vol. COM-26, pp. 253-1257, September 1978.

[8] J. Cosmas, G. Petit, R. Lehnert, C. Blondia, K. Kontovassilis, O. Casals, T. Theimer, "A Review of Voice, Data and Video Traffic Models for ATM," European Transactions on Telecommunication and Related Technologies, Vol.5, No.2, pp. 139-153, March-April 1994.

[9] J. Iyer, R. Jain, and S. Muhail, "Factors Affecting the Multiplexing Gain for VBR Voice," ATM Forum 97-808, Sept. 1997.

[10] T. Okuda, H. Akimura, M. Sakai, "A Simplified Performance Evaluation for Packetized Voice Systems," The Transactions of the IEICE, Vol.E73, No.6, pp.936-941, June 1990.

[11] K. Zhang, F. Yegenoglu, "Impact of multiplexing and buffering on VBR voice performance," ATM Forum 97-1021, Dec. 1997

[12] D. Anick, D. Mitra, and M. Sondhi, "Stochastic Theory of a Data-Handling System with Multiple Sources," The Bell System Technical Journal, Vol. 61, No.8, October 1982.

[13] P. T. Brady, "A Model for Generating ON_OFF Speech Patterns in Two Way Conversations," Bell System Tech. Journal, Vol. 48, pp. 2445-2472, September 1969.

[14] K. Knodo and M. Ohno, "Packet Speech Transmission on ATM Networks Using a VBR Embedded ADPCM Scheme," IEEE Trans. Communications, Vol. 42, No. 2-4, pp.243-47, 1994.

[15] F. Faris et al., "Basic Voice Call Transport over ATM with Optional Silence Removal and Voice Compression," ATM Forum Contribution 95-1643, December 1995.

[16] ITU-T Recommendation I.363, "B-ISDN ATM Adaptation Layer (AAL) Specification," 1993.

[17] ITU-T Recommendation G.711, "Pulse Code Modulation (PCM) of Voice Frequencies."

[18] ITU-T Recommendation G.726, "40, 32, 24, 16 kb/s Adaptive Differential Pulse Code Modulation (ADPCM)."

[19] ITU-T Recommendation G.728, "Coding of Speech at 16 kb/s Using Low Delay Code Excited Linear Prediction (LDCELP)."

Providing Rate Guarantees to TCP over the ATM GFR Service*

Rohit Goyal, Raj Jain, Sonia Fahmy, Bobby Vandalore
Department of Computer Information Science
The Ohio State University
2015 Neil Avenue, DL 395
Columbus, OH 43210
E-mail: goyal@cis.ohio-state.edu
Phone: 614-688-4482, Fax: 614-292-2911

Abstract

The ATM Guaranteed Frame Rate (GFR) service is intended for best effort traffic that can benefit from minimum throughput guarantees. Edge devices connecting LANs to an ATM network can use GFR to transport multiple TCP/IP connections over a single GFR VC. These devices would typically multiplex VCs into a single FIFO queue. It has been shown that in general, FIFO queuing is not sufficient to provide rate guarantees, and per-VC queuing with scheduling is needed. We show that under conditions of low buffer allocation, it is possible to control TCP rates with FIFO queuing and buffer management. We present analysis and simulation results on controlling TCP rates by buffer management. We present a buffer management policy that provides loose rate guarantees to SACK TCP sources when the total buffer allocation is low. We study the performance of this buffer management scheme by simulation.

1 Introduction: The Guaranteed Frame Rate Service

Guaranteed Frame Rate (GFR) has been recently proposed in the ATM Forum as an enhancement to the UBR service category. Guaranteed Frame Rate will provide a minimum rate guarantee to VCs at the frame level. The GFR service also allows for the fair usage of any extra network bandwidth. GFR requires minimum signaling and connection management functions, and depends on the network's ability to provide a minimum rate to each VC. GFR is likely to be used by applications that can neither specify the traffic parameters needed for a VBR VC, nor have cability for ABR (for rate based feedback control). Current internetworking applications fall into this category, and are not designed to run over QoS based networks. These applications could benefit from a minimum rate guarantee by the network, along with an opportunity to fairly use any additional bandwidth left over from higher priority connections. In the case of LANs connected by ATM backbones, network elements outside the ATM network could also benefit from GFR guarantees. For example, IP routers separated by an ATM network could use GFR VCs to exchange control messages. Figure 1 illustrates such a case where the ATM cloud connects several LANs and routers. ATM end systems may also establish GFR VCs for connections that can benefit from a minimum throughput guarantee.

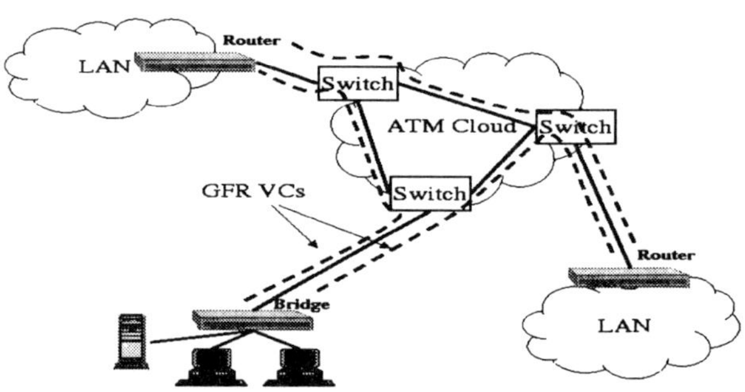

Figure 1: Use of GFR in ATM connected LANs

The original GFR proposals [11, 12] give the basic definition of the GFR service. GFR provides a minimum rate guarantee to the **frames** of a VC. The guarantee requires the specification of a maximum frame size (MFS) of the VC. If the user sends packets (or frames) smaller than the maximum frame size, at a rate less than the minimum cell rate (MCR), then all the packets are expected to be delivered by the network with minimum loss. If the user sends packets at a rate higher than the MCR, it should still receive at least the minimum rate. The minimum rate is guaranteed to the untagged frames of the connection. In addition, a con-

*This research was partially sponsored by the NASA Lewis Research Center under Grant Number NAS3-97198

0-8186-8810-6/98 $10.00 © 1998 IEEE

nection sending in excess of the minimum rate should receive a fair share of any unused network capacity. The exact specification of the fair share has been left unspecified by the ATM Forum. Although the GFR specification is not yet finalized, the above discussion captures the essence of the service.

There are three basic design options that can be used by the *network* to provide the per-VC minimum rate guarantees for GFR – tagging, buffer management, and queueing:

1. **Tagging:** *Network based tagging* (or policing) can be used as a means of marking non-conforming packets before they enter the network. This form of tagging is usually performed when the connection enters the network. Figure 2 shows the role of network based tagging in providing a minimum rate service in a network. Network based tagging on a per-VC level requires some per-VC state information to be maintained by the network and increases the complexity of the network element. Tagging can isolate conforming and non-conforming traffic of each VC so that other rate enforcing mechanisms can use this information to schedule the conforming traffic in preference to non-conforming traffic. In a more general sense, policing can be used to discard non-conforming packets, thus allowing only conforming packets to enter the network.

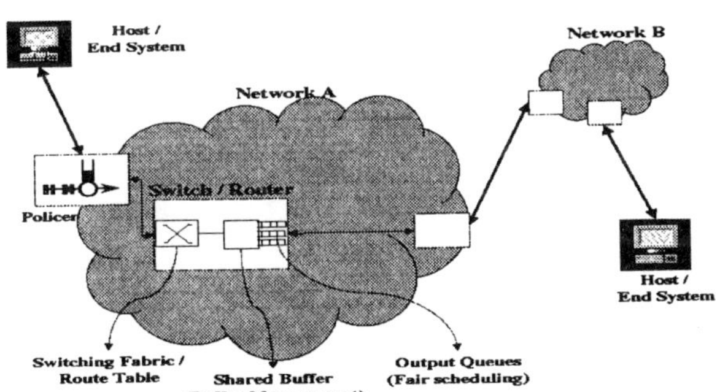

Figure 2: Network Architecture with tagging, buffer management and scheduling

2. **Buffer management:** Buffer management is typically performed by a network element (like a switch or a router) to control the number of packets entering its buffers. In a shared buffer environment, where multiple VCs share common buffer space, per-VC buffer management can control the buffer occupancies of individual VCs. Per-VC buffer management uses per-VC accounting to keep track of the buffer occupancies of each VC. Figure 2 shows the role of buffer management in the connection path. Examples of per-VC buffer management schemes are Selective Drop and Fair Buffer Allocation [9]. Per-VC accounting introduces overhead, but without per-VC accounting it is difficult to control the buffer occupancies of individual VCs (unless non-conforming packets are dropped at the entrance to the network by the policer). Note that per-VC buffer management uses a single FIFO queue for all the VCs. This is different from per-VC queuing and scheduling discussed below.

3. **Scheduling:** Figure 2 illustrates the position of scheduling in providing rate guarantees. While tagging and buffer management control the entry of packets into a network element, queuing strategies determine how packets are scheduled onto the next hop. FIFO queuing cannot isolate packets from various VCs at the egress of the queue. As a result, in a FIFO queue, packets are scheduled in the order in which they enter the buffer. Per-VC queuing, on the other hand, maintains a separate queue for each VC in the buffer. A scheduling mechanism can select between the queues at each scheduling time. However, scheduling adds the cost of per-VC queuing and the service discipline. For a simple service like GFR, this additional cost may be undesirable.

Several proposals have been made [3, 4, 8] to provide rate guarantees to TCP sources with FIFO queuing in the network. The bursty nature of TCP traffic makes it difficult to provide per-VC rate guarantees using FIFO queuing. Per-VC scheduling was recommended to provide rate guarantees to TCP connections. However, all these studies were performed at high target network utilization, i.e., most of the network buffers were allocated to the GFR VCs. We show that rate guarantees are achievable with a FIFO buffer for low buffer allocation.

All the previous studies have examined TCP traffic with a single TCP per VC. Per-VC buffer management for such cases reduces to per-TCP buffer management. However, routers that would use GFR VCs, would multiplex many TCP connections over a single VC. For VCs with several aggregated TCPs, per-VC control is unaware of each TCP in the VC. Moreover, aggregate TCP traffic characteristics and control requirements may be different from those of single TCP streams.

In this paper, we study two main issues:

- Providing minimum rate guarantees to TCP like adaptive traffic with FIFO buffer *for low rate allocations.*
- Buffer management of VCs with aggregate TCP flows.

Section 2 discusses the behavior of TCP traffic with controlled windows. This provides insight into controlling TCP rates by controlling TCP windows. Section 3 describes the effect of buffer occupancy and thresholds on TCP throughput. Section 4 presents a simple threshold-based buffer management policy to provide TCP throughputs in proportion to buffer thresholds for low rate allocations. This scheme assumes that each GFR VC may carry multiple TCP connections. We then present simulation results with TCP traffic over LANs interconnected by an ATM network. *In our simulation and analysis, we use SACK TCP [10] as the TCP model.*

2 TCP Behavior with Controlled Windows

TCP uses a window based mechanism for flow control. The amount of data sent by a TCP connection in one round trip is determined by the window size of the TCP connection. The window size is the minimum of the sender's congestion window (CWND) and the receiver's window (RCVWND). As a result, TCP rate can be controlled by controlling the window size of the TCP connection.

However, a window limit is not enforceable by the network to control the TCP rate. TCP sources respond to packet loss by reducing the source congestion window by one-half, and then increasing it by one segment size every round trip. As a result, the average TCP window can be controlled by packet discard at specific CWND values.

Figure 3 shows how the source TCP congestion window varies when a single segment is lost at a particular value of the congestion window. The figure is the CWND plot of the simulation of the configuration shown in Figure 4 with a single SACK TCP source (N=1). The figure shows four different values of the window at which a packet is lost. The round trip latency (RTT) for the connection is 30 ms. The window scale factor is used to allow the TCP window to increase beyond the 64K limit.

For window based flow control, the throughput (in Mbps) can be calculated from the average congestion window (in Bytes) and the round trip time (in seconds) as:

$$\text{Throughput (Mbps)} = \frac{8 \times 10^{-6} \times \text{CWND}_{\text{avg}}}{\text{Round Trip Time)}} \qquad (1)$$

Where CWND_{avg} is the average congestion window in bytes, and Round Trip Time is in seconds. The factor 8×10^{-6} converts the throughput from bytes per sec to Megabits per sec. The average TCP CWND during the linear increase phase can be calculated as

$$\text{CWND}_{\text{avg}} = \frac{\Sigma_{i=1}^{T} \text{CWND}_{\text{max}}/2 + \text{MSS} \times i}{\text{T}} \qquad (2)$$

where T is the number of round trip times for the congestion window to increase from $\text{CWND}_{\text{max}}/2$ to CWND_{max}. Note that this equation assumes that during the linear increase phase, the TCP window increases by one segment every round trip time. However, when the TCP delayed acknowledgment option is set, TCP might only send an ACK for every two segments. In this case, the window would increase by 1 segment every 2 RTTs.

From Figure 3, the average congestion windows in the linear phases of the four experiments are approximately 91232 bytes, 181952 bytes, 363392 bytes and over 600000 bytes. As a result, the average calculated throughputs from equation 1 are 24.32 Mbps, 48.5 Mbps, 96.9 Mbps, and 125.6 Mbps (126 Mbps is the maximum possible TCP throughput for a 155.52 Mbps link with 1024 byte TCP segments). The respective throughputs obtained from the simulations of the four cases are 23.64 Mbps, 47.53 Mbps, 93.77 Mbps and 25.5 Mbps. The throughput values calculated from the average congestion windows are close to those obtained by simulation. This shows that controlling the TCP window so as to maintain a desired average window size enables the network to control the average TCP throughput.

3 TCP Window Control using Buffer Management

In the previous section, an artificial simulation was presented where the network controlled the TCP rate by dropping a packet every time the TCP window reached a particular value. In practice, the ATM network knows neither the size of the TCP window, nor the round trip time of the connection. A switch can use per-VC accounting of the TCP packets in its buffer to estimate the bandwidth used by the connection.

In a FIFO buffer, the output rate of a connection is determined by the number of packets of the connection in the buffer. Let μ_i and x_i be the output rate and the buffer occupancy respectively of VC_i. Let μ and x be the total output rate and the buffer occupancy of the FIFO buffer respectively. Then, by the FIFO principle, in steady state,

$$\mu_i = \frac{x_i}{x}\mu$$

$$\text{or} \quad \frac{x_i/x}{\mu_i/\mu} = 1$$

If the buffer occupancy of every active VC is maintained at a desired threshold, then the output rate of each VC can also be controlled. In other words, if a VC always has x_i cells in the buffer with a total occupancy of x cells, its average output rate will be at least $\mu x_i/x$.

Adaptive flows like TCP respond to segment loss by reducing their congestion window. A single packet loss is sufficient to reduce the TCP congestion window by one-half. Consider a drop policy that drops a single

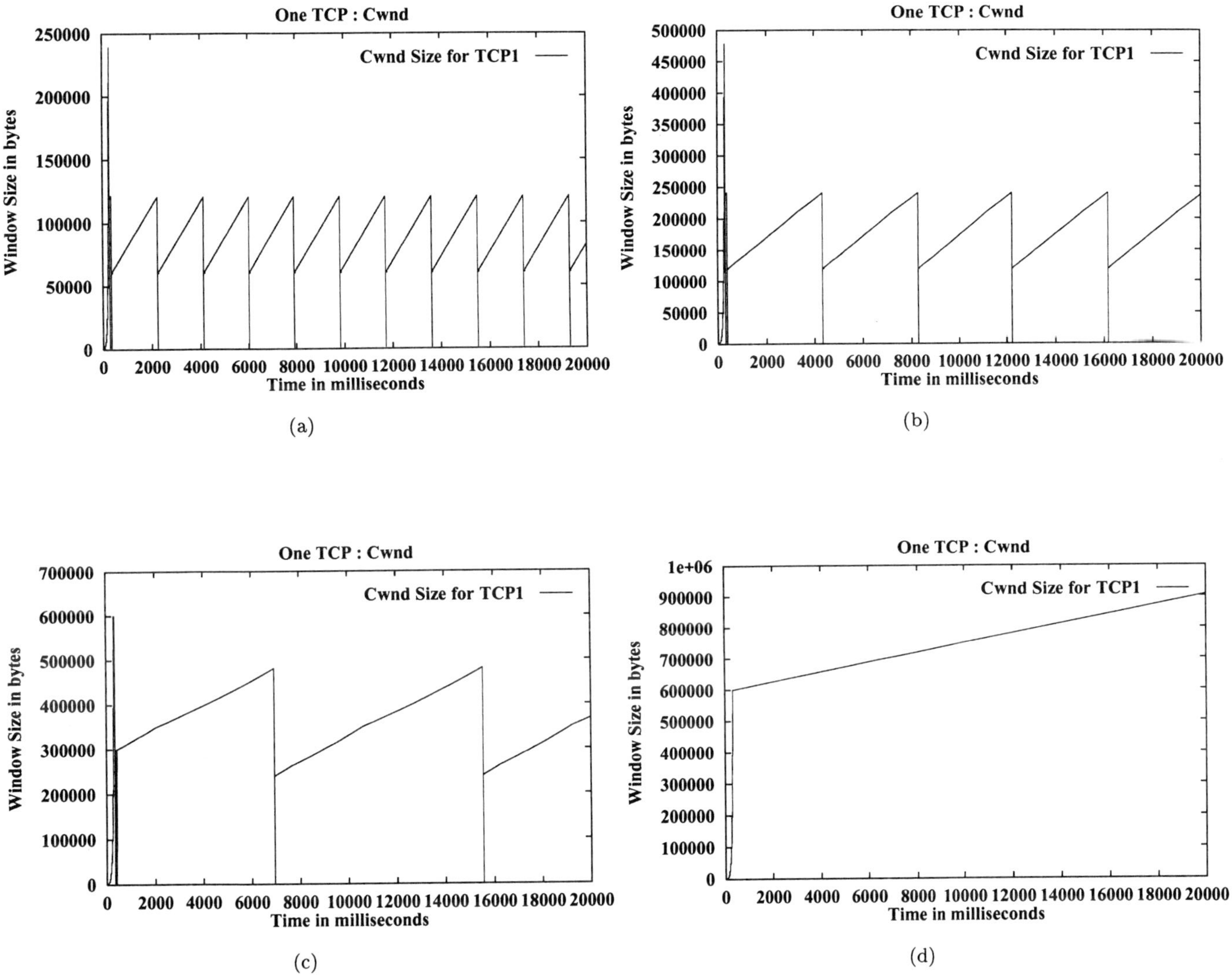

Figure 3: Single TCP Congestion Window Control. Drop thresholds (bytes) = 125000, 250000, 500000, None

TCP packet from a connection every time the connection's buffer occupancy crosses a given threshold. The drop threshold for a connection determines the maximum size to which the congestion window is allowed to grow. Because of TCP's adaptive nature, the buffer occupancy reduces after about 1 RTT. The drop policy drops a single packet when the TCP's buffer occupancy crosses the threshold, and then allows the buffer occupancy to grow by accepting the remainder of the TCP window. On detecting a loss, TCP reduces its congestion window by 1 segment and remains idle for about one-half RTT, during which the buffer occupancy decreases below the threshold. Then the TCP window increases linearly (and so does the buffer occupancy), and a packet is again dropped when the buffer occupancy crosses the threshold. In this way, TCP windows can be controlled quite accurately to within one round trip time. As a result, the TCP's throughput can also be controlled by controlling the TCP's buffer occupancy.

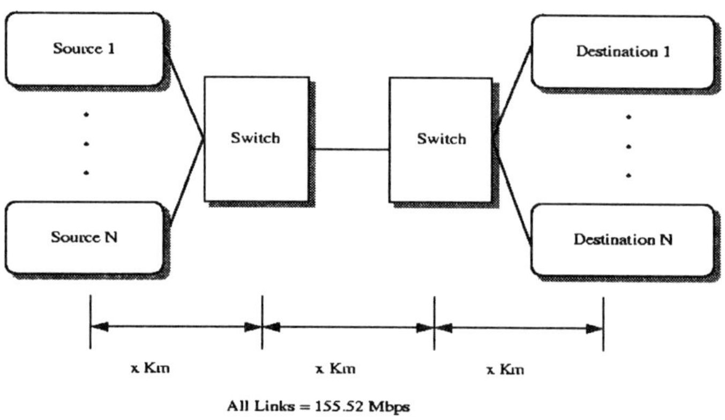

Figure 4: N source configuration

Table 1: Fifteen TCP buffer thresholds

Experiment #	1	2	3	4
TCP number	Threshold per TCP (cells) (r_i)			
1-3	305	458	611	764
4-6	611	917	1223	1528
7-9	917	1375	1834	2293
10-12	1223	1834	2446	3057
13-15	1528	2293	3057	3822
Tot. Thr (r)	13752	20631	27513	34392

Using this drop policy, we performed simulations of the TCP configuration in Figure 4 with fifteen TCP sources divided into 5 groups of 3 each. Each TCP source was a separate UBR VC. Five different buffer thresholds (r_i) were selected, and each of three TCP's in a group had the same buffer threshold. Table 1 lists the buffer thresholds for the VC's in the FIFO buffer of the switches. We performed experiments with

Table 3: Fifteen TCP buffer:throughput ratio

Experiment #	1	2	3	4
TCP number	Ratio (μ_i/μ_i^e)			
1-3	1.00	1.03	1.02	1.08
4-6	0.98	1.01	1.03	1.04
7-9	0.98	1.00	1.00	1.02
10-12	0.98	0.99	0.98	0.88
13-15	1.02	0.98	0.97	1.01

4 different sets of thresholds as shown by the threshold columns. The last row in the table shows the total buffer allocated ($r = \Sigma r_i$) to all the TCP connections for each simulation experiment. The total buffer size was large (48000 cells) so that there was enough space for the buffers to increase after the single packet drop. For a buffer size of 48000 cells, the total target buffer utilizations were 29%, 43%, 57%, 71% in the 4 columns of table 1 respectively. The selected buffer thresholds determine the MCR achieved by each connection. For each connection, the ratios of the thresholds to the total buffer allocation should be proportional to the ratios of the achieved per-VC throughputs to the total achieved throughput. In other words, if μ_i, μ, r_i and r represent the per-VC achieved throughputs, total throughput, per-VC buffer allocations, and total buffer allocation respectively, then we should have

$$\mu_i/\mu = r_i/r$$

or the expected per-VC throughput is

$$\mu_i^e = \mu \times r_i/r$$

Table 2 shows the average throughput obtained per TCP in each group for each of the four simulations. The TCP throughputs were averaged over each group to reduce the effects of randomness. The last row of the table shows the total throughput obtained in each simulation. Based on the TCP segment size (1024 bytes) and the ATM overhead, it is clear that the TCPs were able to use almost the entire available link capacity (approximately 126 Mbps at the TCP layer).

The proportion of the buffer usable by each TCP (r_i/r) before the single packet drop should determine the proportion of the throughput achieved by the TCP. Table 3 shows the ratios (μ_i/μ_i^e) for each simulation. All ratios are close to 1. This indicates that the TCP throughputs are indeed proportional to the buffer allocations. The variations (not shown in the table) from the mean TCP throughputs increased as the total buffer thresholds increased (from left to right across the table). This is because the TCPs suffered a higher packet loss due to the reduced room to grow beyond the threshold. Thus, high buffer utilization produced more variation in achieved rate (last column of Table 3), whereas in low utilization cases, the resulting

Table 2: Fifteen TCP throughputs

Experiment #	1	2	3	4	
TCP number	Achieved throughput per TCP (Mbps) (μ_i)				Expected Throughput
					($\mu_i^e = \mu \times r_i / \Sigma r_i$)
1-3	2.78	2.83	2.95	3.06	2.8
4-6	5.45	5.52	5.75	5.74	5.6
7-9	8.21	8.22	8.48	8.68	8.4
10-12	10.95	10.89	10.98	9.69	11.2
13-15	14.34	13.51	13.51	13.93	14.0
Tot. throughput (μ)	125.21	122.97	125.04	123.35	126.0

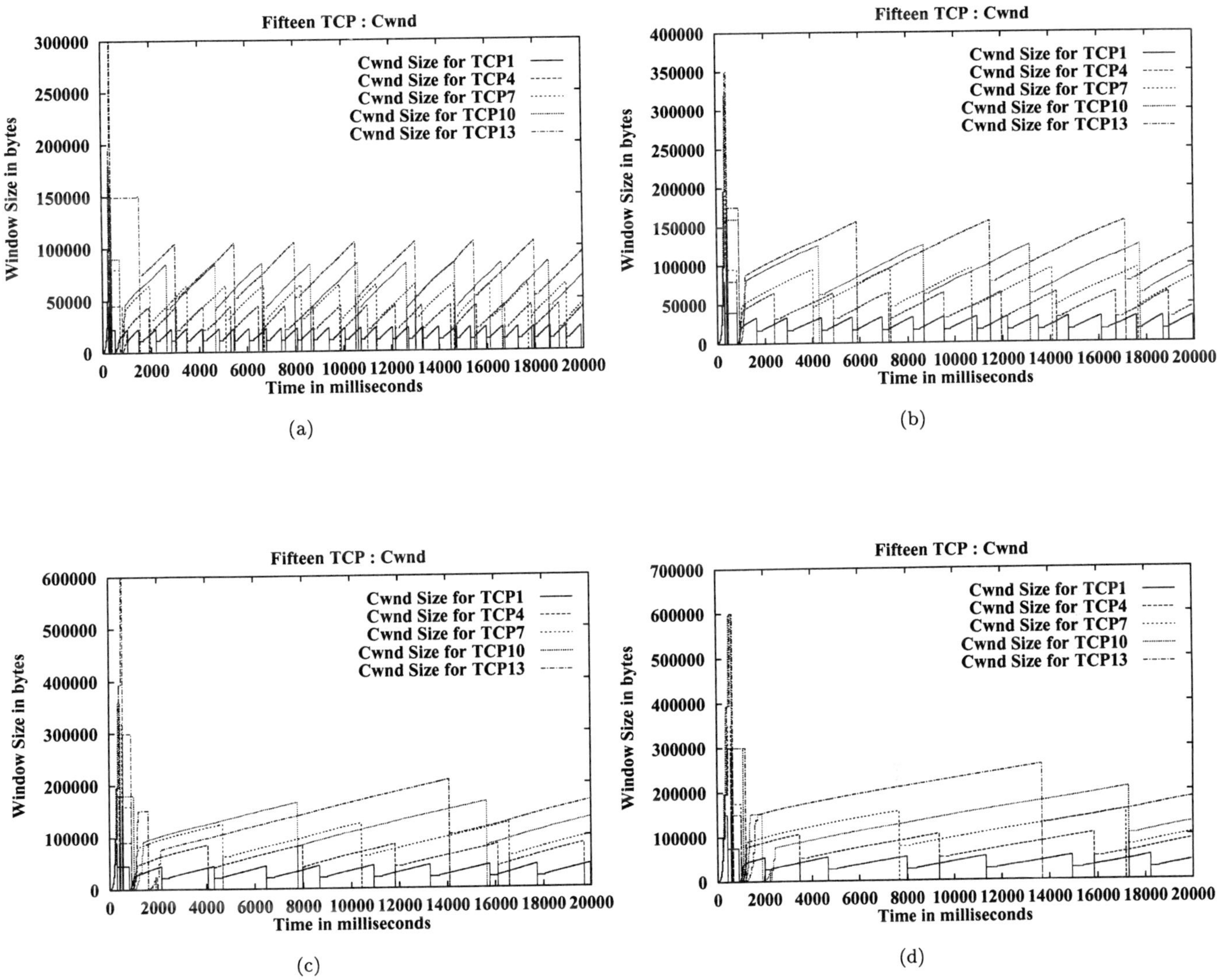

Figure 5: 15 TCP rate control by packet drop

throughputs were in proportion to the buffer allocations.

Figure 5 shows the congestion windows of one TCP from each group for each of the four simulations. The graphs illustrate that the behaviors of the TCP congestion windows are very regular in these cases. The average throughput achieved by each TCP can be calculated from the graphs using equations 1 and 2. An intersting observation is that for each simulation, the slopes of the graphs during the linear increase are approximately the same for each TCP, i.e., for a given simulation, the rate of increase of CWND is the same for all TCPs regardless of their drop thresholds. We know that TCP windows increase by 1 segment every round trip time. Thus, we can conclude that for a given simulation, TCPs sharing the FIFO buffer experience similar queuing delays regardless of the individual per-connection thresholds at which their packets are dropped. This is because, if all TCP's buffer occupancies are close to their respective thresholds (r_i), then when a packet arrives at the buffer, it is queued behind cells from $\Sigma(r_i)$ packets, regardless of the connection to which it belongs. Consequently, each TCP experiences the same average queuing delay.

However, as the total buffer threshold increases (from experiment (a) to (d)), the round trip time for each TCP increases because of the larger total queue size. The larger threshold also results in a larger congestion window at which a packet is dropped. A larger congestion window means that TCP can send more segments in one round trip time. But, the round trip time also increases proportionally to the increase in CWND (due to the increasing queuing delay of the 15 TCPs bottlenecked at the first switch). As a result, the average throughput achieved by a single TCP remains almost the same (see table 2) across the simulations. The formal proof of these conclusions will be presented in an extended version of this paper.

The following list summarizes the observations from the graphs:

1. TCP throughput can be controlled by controlling its congestion window, which in turn, can be controlled by setting buffer thresholds to drop packets. This statement clearly assumes that in cases where the offered load is low, and a queue is never built up, then the TCP is allowed to use as much capacity as it can.

2. With a FIFO buffer, the average throughput achieved by a connection is proportional to the fraction of the buffer occupancy of the connection's cells.

3. As long as the fraction of buffer occupancy of a TCP can be controlled, its relative throughput is independent of the total number of packets in the buffer, and depends primarily on the fraction of packets of that TCP in the buffer.

4. At a very high buffer utilization, packets may be dropped due to buffer unavailability. This results in larger variations in TCP throughputs. At very high thresholds, the queuing delay also increases significantly, and may cause the TCP sources to timeout.

5. At very low buffer thresholds (high loss rates), TCP sources become unstable and tend to timeout. Also, very low buffer occupancies result in low network utilization. Since TCP can maintain a flow of 1 CWND worth of packets each round trip time, a total buffer occupancy of 1 bandwidth-delay product should provide good utilization [13].

4 Buffer Management for GFR

In this section, we further develop the drop policy to design a buffer management scheme for the GFR service category. The goal of the scheme is to soft rate guarantees to SACK-TCP like adaptive traffic over ATM connections. The policy assumes that multiple TCP connections are multiplexed on a single VC. In this section we present the preliminary design and simulation results of the buffer management scheme. A parameter study and sensitivity analysis will be presented in a future study. Simulation results of heterogeneous TCP and non-TCP environments will be presented in a future study. *We assume a model in which TCPs may be merged into a single VC, in which case, the cells of different frames within a VC are not interleaved.* This allows the network to drop frames without having to identify the source that generated the frame.

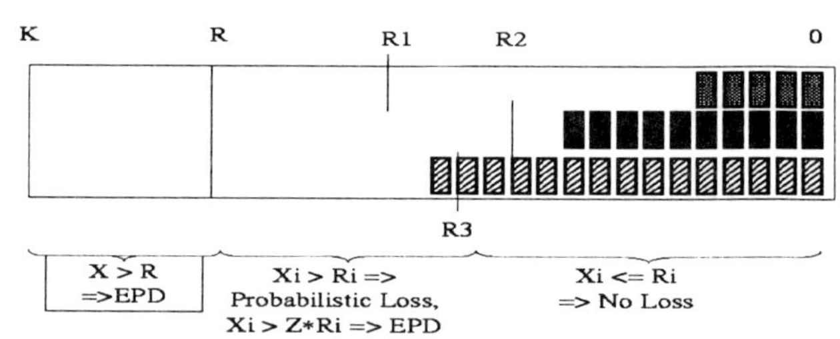

Figure 6: Drop behavior of Buffer Management scheme

Figure 6 illustrates a FIFO buffer for the GFR service category. The following attributes are defined:

- K: Buffer size in cells.
- R: Congestion threshold in cells ($0 \leq R \leq K$). EPD is performed when buffer occupancy is greater than R.

- R_i: Threshold for VC_i. (for example R_i = function of $(\frac{MCR_i}{\text{Total UBR capacity}})$
- X: Number of cells in the buffer.
- X_i: Number of cells of VC_i in the buffer.
- Z: Scaling parameter for R_i ($Z > 1$).
- W_i: Weight of VC_i for probability calculation.
- u: Uniform(0,1) random number.

When the first cell of a frame arrives at the buffer, if the number of cells (X_i) of VC_i in the buffer is less than its threshold (R_i) and if the total buffer occupancy X is less than R, then the cell and frame is accepted into the buffer. If X_i is greater than R_i, and if the total buffer occupancy (X) is greater than the buffer threshold (R), or if X_i is greater than $Z \times R_i$, then the cell and frame are dropped (EPD). Thus Z specifies a maximum per-VC buffer occupancy during congestion periods. Under low or mild load conditions, $R \times Z$ should be large enough to buffer a burst of cells without having to perform EPD. If the X_i is greater than R_i, and X is less than R, then the cell/frame are dropped in a probabilistic manner. The probability of frame drop depends on how much X_i is above R_i, as well as the weight (W_i) of the connection. As X_i increases beyond R_i, the probability of drop increases. Also, the drop probability should be higher for connections with a higher threshold. This is because, TCP flows with higher windows (due to higher thresholds) are more robust to packet loss than TCP flows with lower windows. Moreover, in the case of merged TCPs over a single VC, VCs with a high threshold are likely to carry more active TCP flows than those with a low threshold. As a result, a higher drop probability is more likely to hit more TCP sources and improve the fairness within a VC. W_i is used to scale the drop probability according to desired level of control.

The frame is dropped with a probability

$$P\{drop\} = W_i \times \frac{X_i - R_i}{Z \times Ri - Ri}$$

In addition, if X_i is greater than R_i, then all tagged frames may also be dropped. Tagging support is not yet tested for this drop policy.

The resulting algorithm works as follows. When the first cell of a frame arrives:

```
IF ((Xi < Ri AND X < R)) THEN

        ACCEPT CELL AND REMAINING
CELLS IN FRAME

ELSE IF  ((X < R) AND (Xi < Z*Ri)  AND
          (Cell NOT Tagged)  AND
          (u > Wi*(Xi - Ri)/(Ri(Z-1))))

     THEN ACCEPT CELL AND REMAINING
     CELLS IN FRAME

     ELSE DROP CELL AND REMAINING
     CELLS IN FRAME

ENDIF
```

If the bufer occupancy exceeds the total buffer size, then, the cell must be dropped. In this case partial packet discard is performed.

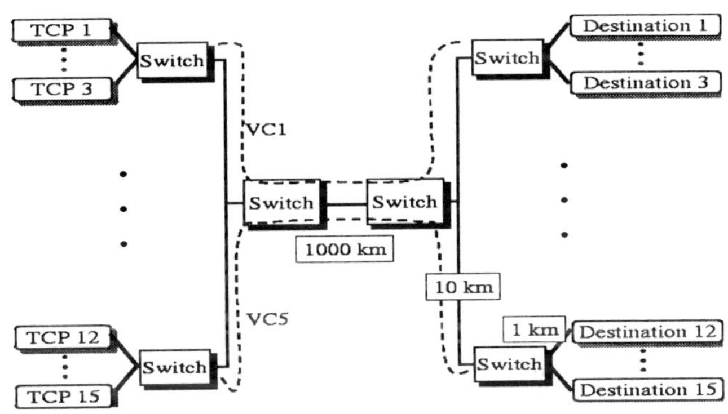

Figure 7: N source VC merge configuration

Figure 7 illustrates the 15 TCP configuration in which groups of three TCPs are merged into 1 single VC. Each local switch (edge device separating the LAN from the backbone ATM network) merges the 3 TCPs into a single GFR VC over the backbone link. The backbone link has 5 VCs going through it, each with 3 TCPs. The local switches ensure that the cells of frames within a single VC are not interleaved. The backbone switches implement the buffer allocation policy described above. The local switches are not congested in this configuration.

We simulated the 15 merged TCP configuration with 3 different buffer threshold sets. The parameter Z was set to 1.5, therefore, EPD was performed for each VC when its buffer occupancy was $1.5 \times R$. Table 4 shows the thresholds used for each VC at the first bottleneck switch.

Table 5 shows the ratio $(\mu_i/\mu)/(r_i/\Sigma r_i)$ for each VC for the configuration in Figure 7 and the corresponding thresholds. In all cases, the achieved link utilization was almost 100%. The table shows that TCP throughputs obtained were in proportion to the buffers allocated (since most of the ratios in table 5 are close to 1). The highest variation (not shown in the table) was seen in the last column because of the high threshold values.

In our simulations, the maximum observed queue sizes in cells in the first backbone switch (the main bot-

Table 4: Buffer Management Thresholds

VC number	Threshold (cells)		
1	152	305	611
2	305	611	1223
3	458	917	1834
4	611	1223	2446
5	764	1528	3057
Total	2290	4584	9171

Table 5: Simulation results

VC number	Ratio $(\mu_i/\mu)/(r_i/r)$		
1	1.04	1.01	1.16
2	1.05	1.02	1.06
3	0.97	0.99	1.05
4	0.93	1.00	1.13
5	1.03	0.99	0.80

tleneck) were 3185, 5980 and 11992 respectively. The total allocated buffer thresholds were 2230, 4584 and 9171 cells for the experiments. At higher buffer allocations, the drop policy cannot provide tight bounds on throughput.

5 Summary and Future Work

In this paper, we have used FIFO buffers to control SACK TCP rates by buffer management. An optimal set of thresholds should be selected that is high enough to provide sufficient network utilization, and is low enough to allow stable operation. The achieved TCP throughputs are in proportion to the fraction of the average buffer occupied by the VC.

More work remains to be done to further modify the buffer management scheme to work with a variety of configurations. In particular, we have only studied the performance of this scheme with SACK TCP. Its performance with heterogeneous TCPs is a topic of further study. We have not studied the effect of non adaptive traffic (like UDP) on the drop policy. It appears that for non adaptive traffic, the thresholds must be set lower than those for adaptive traffic (for the same MCR), and the dropping should be more strict when the buffer occupancy crosses the threshold. In this paper we have not studied the effect of network based tagging in the context of GFR. In the strict sense, GFR only provides a low CLR guarantee to the CLP=0 cell stream i.e., the cells that were not tagged by the source and passed the GCRA conformance test. However, when source (this could be a non-ATM network element like a router) based tagging is not performed, it is not clear if the CLP0 stream has any significance over the CLP1 stream. Moreover, network tagging is an option that must be signaled during connection establishment.

References

[1] ATM Forum, "ATM Traffic Management Specification Version 4.0," April 1996, ftp://ftp.atmforum.com/pub/approved-specs/af-tm-0056.000.ps

[2] Debashis Basak, Surya Pappu, "TCP over GFR Implementation with Different Service Disciplines: A Simulation Study"

[3] Debashis Basak, Surya Pappu, "GFR Implementation Alternatives with Fair Buffer Allocation Schemes," ATM Forum 97-0528.

[4] Olivier Bonaventure, "A simulation study of TCP with the proposed GFR service category," DAGSTUHL Seminar 9725, High Performance Networks for Multimedia Applications, June 1997, Germany

[5] John B. Kenney, "Satisfying UBR+ Requirements via a New VBR Conformance Definition," ATM FORUM 97-0185.

[6] John B. Kenney, "Open Issues on GFR Frame Discard and Frame Tagging," ATM FORUM 97-0385.

[7] Juha Heinanen, and Kalevi Kilkki, "A fair buffer allocation scheme," Unpublished Manuscript.

[8] R. Goyal, R. Jain et.al, "Simulation Experiments with Guaranteed Frame Rate for TCP/IP Traffic," ATM Forum 97-0607.

[9] R. Goyal, R. Jain, S. Kalyanaraman, S. Fahmy and Seong-Cheol Kim, "UBR+: Improving Performance of TCP over ATM-UBR Service," Proc. ICC'97, June 1997.

[10] R. Goyal, R. Jain et.al., "Selective Acknowledgements and UBR+ Drop Policies to Improve TCP/UBR Performance over Terrestrial and Satellite Networks," To appear, Proc. IC3N'97, September 1997. [1]

[11] Roch Guerin, and Juha Heinanen, "UBR+ Service Category Definition," ATM FORUM 96-1598, December 1996.

[12] Roch Guerin, and Juha Heinanen, "UBR+ Enhancements," ATM FORUM 97-0015, February 1997.

[13] Sastri Kota, Rohit Goyal, Raj Jain, "Satellite-ATM Network Architectural Considerations and TCP/IP Performance," Proc. of the 3rd Ka-Band Utilization Conference, Italy, 1997.

[1] All our papers and ATM Forum contributions are available from http://www.cis.ohio-state.edu/~jain

Author Index

Notes

Notes

Notes

IEEE COMPUTER SOCIETY

Press Activities Board

IEEE Computer Society Publications

The world-renowned Computer Society publishes, promotes, and distributes a wide variety of authoritative computer science and engineering texts. These books are available in two formats: 100 percent original material by authors preeminent in their field who focus on relevant topics and cutting-edge research, and reprint collections consisting of carefully selected groups of previously published papers with accompanying original introductory and explanatory text.

Submission of proposals: For guidelines and information on Computer Society books, send e-mail to cs.books@computer.org or write to the Project Editor, IEEE Computer Society, P.O. Box 3014, 10662 Los Vaqueros Circle, Los Alamitos, CA 90720-1314. Telephone +1 714-821-8380. FAX +1 714-761-1784.

IEEE Computer Society Proceedings

The Computer Society also produces and actively promotes the proceedings of more than 130 acclaimed international conferences each year in multimedia formats that include hard and softcover books, CD-ROMs, videos, and on-line publications.

For information on Computer Society proceedings, send e-mail to cs.books@computer.org or write to Proceedings, IEEE Computer Society, P.O. Box 3014, 10662 Los Vaqueros Circle, Los Alamitos, CA 90720-1314. Telephone +1 714-821-8380. FAX +1 714-761-1784.

Additional information regarding the Computer Society, conferences and proceedings, CD-ROMs, videos, and books can also be accessed from our web site at http://computer.org/cspress

4/16/98